The Papers of
George Washington

The Papers of George Washington

W. W. Abbot, *Editor*

Dorothy Twohig, *Associate Editor*

Philander D. Chase and Beverly H. Runge

Revolutionary War Series

1

June–September 1775

Philander D. Chase, Editor

UNIVERSITY PRESS OF VIRGINIA

CHARLOTTESVILLE

This edition has been prepared by the staff of
The Papers of George Washington
sponsored by
The Mount Vernon Ladies' Association of the Union
and the University of Virginia
with the support of
the National Endowment for the Humanities.

THE UNIVERSITY PRESS OF VIRGINIA

First published 1985

3 5 7 9 8 6 4 2

Library of Congress Cataloging in Publication Data

Washington, George, 1732–1799.
The papers of George Washington.

"Sponsored by the Mount Vernon Ladies' Association of the Union and the University of Virginia with the support of the National Endowment for the Humanities."
Includes bibliography and indexes.
Contents: [A] Colonial series. 1. 1748–August 1755— 2. August 1755–April 1756 — [B] Revolutionary War series. 1. June–September 1775/Philander D. Chase, editor.
1. Virginia—History—Colonial period, ca. 1600–1775. 2. United States —History—French and Indian War, 1755–1763. 3. Washington, George, 1732–1799. 4. Presidents—United States—Correspondence. 5. United States—History—Revolution, 1775–1783—Campaigns. 6. United States—Politics and government—1789–1797. I. Abbot, W. W. (William Wright), 1922– . II. Twohig, Dorothy. III. Chase, Philander D. IV. Mount Vernon Ladies' Association of the Union. V. University of Virginia. VI. Title.
E312.72 1983. 973.4'1'0924 81-16307
ISBN 0-8139-1040-4 (V.1)

Printed in the United States of America

Contents

Preface xvii
Editorial Apparatus xxiii
Symbols Designating Documents xxiv
Repository Symbols and Abbreviations xxiv
Short Title List xxv

1775

Address to the Continental Congress, 16 June 1
To Martha Washington, 18 June 3
Commission from the Continental Congress, 19 June 6
From John Adams, 19 or 20 June 8
To Burwell Bassett, 19 June 12
To John Parke Custis, 19 June 15
To the Officers of Five Virginia Independent Companies, 20 June 16
To John Augustine Washington, 20 June 19
Instructions from the Continental Congress, 22 June 21
From Brigadier General Horatio Gates, 22 June 23
From the Massachusetts Delegates, 22 June 25
To Martha Washington, 23 June 27
From Valentine Crawford, 24 June 28
To the Continental Congress, 25 June 32
To John Hancock, 25 June 34
Instructions to Major General Philip Schuyler, 25 June 36
Address from the New York Provincial Congress, 26 June 40
Address to the New York Provincial Congress, 26 June 41
From John Hancock, 28 June 42
From the Delaware Delegates, 29 June 44
From Richard Henry Lee, 29 June 44
From Major General Philip Schuyler, 1 July 47
From Henry Ward, 1 July 49
General Orders, 3 July 49
Address from the Massachusetts Provincial Congress, 3 July 52
General Orders, 4 July 54
From George Clinton, 4 July 58
Address to the Massachusetts Provincial Congress, c.4 July 59

From James Warren and Joseph Hawley, 4 July 61
General Orders, 5 July 62
From John Hancock, 5 July 64
From Joseph Hawley, 5 July 65
From the Massachusetts Provincial Congress, 5 July 66
General Orders, 6 July 67
From John Fenton, 6 July 68
From the Massachusetts Committee of Safety, 6 July 68
From Daniel Murray, 6 July 69
From the Pennsylvania Delegates, 6 July 70
General Orders, 7 July 71
General Orders, 8 July 75
From the Fairfax Independent Company, 8 July 77
General Orders, 9 July 78
Council of War, 9 July 79
General Orders, 10 July 82
To John Hancock, 10–11 July 83
I. Notes for Letter 84
II. Letter Sent 85
From John Hancock, 10 July 97
To Richard Henry Lee, 10 July 98
From Alexander Scammell, c.10 July 100
To Major General Philip Schuyler, 10–11 July 101
From Brigadier General John Thomas, 10 July 103
To James Warren, 10 July 103
General Orders, 11 July 106
General Orders, 12 July 107
From Nicholas Cooke, 12 July 108
From Edmund Pendleton, 12 July 109
From the Virginia Delegates, 12 July 110
General Orders, 13 July 111
From Jonathan Trumbull, Sr., 13 July 112
From Jonathan Trumbull, Sr., 13 July 113
General Orders, 14 July 114
To John Hancock, 14 July 115
General Orders, 15 July 118
From Major General Philip Schuyler, 15 July 120
General Orders, 16 July 122
General Orders, 17 July 123
From Patrick Henry, 17 July 124
From Jonathan Trumbull, Sr., 17 July 124
From Hunking Wentworth, 17 July 126
General Orders, 18 July 127

To Nicholas Cooke, 18 July 128
From Major General Philip Schuyler, 18 July 129
To Jonathan Trumbull, Sr., 18 July 131
To Jonathan Trumbull, Sr., 18 July 132
General Orders, 19 July 132
From John Hancock, 19 July 132
General Orders, 20 July 133
To Samuel Washington, 20 July 134
General Orders, 21 July 136
To John Hancock, 21 July 136
To John Hancock, 21 July 143
To John Hancock, 21 July 144
From Benjamin Harrison, 21–24 July 145
From Brigadier General William Heath, 21 July 151
To Jonathan Trumbull, Sr., 21 July 152
General Orders, 22 July 153
From Captain Joshua Davis, 22 July 156
From Captain Richard Dodge, 22 July 157
General Orders, 23 July 158
To Brigadier General John Thomas, 23 July 159
To James Warren, 23 July 162
General Orders, 24 July 163
From John Hancock, 24 July 164
General Orders, 25 July 169
From John Dickinson, 25 July 169
From Captain Richard Dodge, 25 July 170
To George William Fairfax, 25 July 170
From Brigadier General John Thomas, 25 July 171
General Orders, 26 July 172
From Colonel Donald Campbell, 26 July 173
To Nicholas Cooke, 26 July 175
To George William Fairfax, 26 July 176
From the Virginia Delegates, 26 July 177
General Orders, 27 July 177
From Captain Joshua Davis, 27 July 179
To John Hancock, 27 July 180
To Major General Philip Schuyler, 27 July 181
To John Augustine Washington, 27 July 183
General Orders, 28 July 185
From Lieutenant Colonel Loammi Baldwin, 28 July 185
To Major General Philip Schuyler, 28 July 188
General Orders, 29 July 190
From Lieutenant Colonel Loammi Baldwin, 29 July 192

To James Warren, 29 July 193
General Orders, 30 July 194
To James Warren, 30 July 195
General Orders, 31 July 197
From Lieutenant Colonel Loammi Baldwin, 31 July 198
From Nicholas Cooke, 31 July 199
From Colonel Timothy Danielson, 31 July 200
From Colonel Timothy Danielson, 31 July 201
From Patrick Henry, 31 July 201
From Major General Philip Schuyler, 31 July–2 August 202
From Jonathan Trumbull, Sr., 31 July 203
From the Massachusetts General Court, July or August 205
General Orders, 1 August 205
From Richard Henry Lee, 1 August 209
From the Massachusetts Committee of Supplies, 1 August 211
General Orders, 2 August 212
From Lieutenant Colonel Loammi Baldwin, 2 August 213
From the Massachusetts Committee of Supplies, 2 August 213
From Brigadier General John Sullivan, 2 August 214
General Orders, 3 August 215
Council of War, 3 August 215
From Lieutenant Colonel Loammi Baldwin, 3 August 216
From the New York Provincial Congress, 3 August 217
From James Warren, 3 August 218
General Orders, 4 August 218
From Lieutenant Colonel Loammi Baldwin, 4 August 219
To Nicholas Cooke, 4 August 221
To John Hancock, 4–5 August 223
To a Committee of the Massachusetts Council, 4 August 240
To Lewis Morris, 4 August 240
To the New Hampshire Committee of Safety, 4 August 242
To William Trent, 4 August 242
To Jonathan Trumbull, Sr., 4 August 244
General Orders, 5 August 245
From Jacob Duché, 5 August 246
To James Otis, Sr., 5 August 247
From James Warren, 5 August 249
General Orders, 6 August 249
From Lieutenant Colonel Loammi Baldwin, 6 August 250
From Jonathan Boucher, 6 August 252
From Major General Philip Schuyler, 6 August 255

To James Warren, 6 August 259
General Orders, 7 August 260
From the Norwich Committee of Correspondence, 7 August 262
To James Otis, Sr., 7 August 264
To Joseph Palmer, 7 August 265
From Jonathan Trumbull, Sr., 7 August 267
General Orders, 8 August 268
From Lieutenant Colonel Loammi Baldwin, 8 August 270
From Nicholas Cooke, 8 August 271
To the New York Provincial Congress, 8 August 274
From James Otis, Sr., 8 August 275
From Jonathan Trumbull, Sr., 8 August 276
General Orders, 9 August 277
Instructions to John Goddard, c.9 August 280
To Jonathan Trumbull, Sr., 9 August 280
General Orders, 10 August 281
From the Officers of Colonel Samuel Gerrish's Regiment, 10 August 282
To Peter Van Brugh Livingston, 10 August 283
From the Marblehead Committee of Safety, 10 August 284
From Captain Levi Spaulding's Company, 10 August 285
From Major General Artemas Ward, 10 August 286
From Lieutenant Colonel Jonathan Ward, c.10 August 286
General Orders, 11 August 287
From Lieutenant Colonel Loammi Baldwin, 11 August 287
From Nicholas Cooke, 11 August 288
To Lieutenant General Thomas Gage, 11 August 289
From a Committee of the Massachusetts Council, 11 August 291
From Jonathan Trumbull, Sr., 11 August 293
General Orders, 12 August 295
To John Brown, 12 August 295
From Lieutenant Desambrager, 12 August 296
To the Massachusetts General Court, 12 August 296
From Jonathan Trumbull, Sr., 12 August 299
General Orders, 13 August 300
From Lieutenant Colonel Loammi Baldwin, 13 August 300
From Lieutenant General Thomas Gage, 13 August 301
From the Massachusetts General Court, 13 August 303
General Orders, 14 August 303
To Nicholas Cooke, 14 August 304
To Major General Philip Schuyler, 14 August 305

To Jonathan Trumbull, Sr., 14 August 307
General Orders, 15 August 309
From Lieutenant Colonel Loammi Baldwin, 15 August 311
From Major Christopher French, 15 August 311
General Orders, 16 August 312
From Lieutenant Colonel Loammi Baldwin, 16 August 312
From Andrew Hamilton, 16 August 314
To James Otis, Sr., 16 August 316
General Orders, 17 August 317
From Lieutenant Colonel Loammi Baldwin, 17 August 318
From the Pennsylvania Committee of Safety, 17 August 318
From Major General Artemas Ward, 17 August 321
General Orders, 18 August 321
From Lieutenant Colonel Loammi Baldwin, 18 August 322
From the Massachusetts General Court, 18 August 323
General Orders, 19 August 325
From Captain Richard Dodge, 19 August 325
To Lieutenant General Thomas Gage, 19 August 326
From Major General Artemas Ward, 19 August 328
General Orders, 20 August 329
From Captain Richard Dodge, c.20 August 330
To Major General Philip Schuyler, 20 August 331
To Lund Washington, 20 August 334
General Orders, 21 August 340
From Captain Richard Dodge, 21 August 342
From Peter Van Brugh Livingston, 21 August 342
From Jonathan Trumbull, Sr., 21 August 344
General Orders, 22 August 346
From Lieutenant Colonel James Babcock, 22 August 348
From Captain Richard Dodge, 22 August 348
From Major General William Howe, 22 August 349
To Joseph Palmer, 22 August 349
From Lieutenant John Parke, 22 August 351
From Captain John Randall, 22 August 352
General Orders, 23 August 352
To Major General William Howe, 23 August 352
From Major General Charles Lee, 23 August 353
To Jonathan Trumbull, Sr., 23 August 353
From William Tudor, 23 August 354
To James Warren, 23 August 356
General Orders, 24 August 356
From the Gloucester Committee of Safety, 24 August 359
From Lieutenant Colonel Jonathan Ward, 24 August 360

General Orders, 25 August 360
To George Clinton, 25 August 361
From Captain Richard Dodge, 25 August 362
From Major General Artemas Ward, 25 August 362
From Major General Artemas Ward, 25 August 363
To Anthony White, 25 August 365
General Orders, 26 August 366
From Captain Richard Dodge, 26 August 366
General Orders, 27 August 367
From Major General Philip Schuyler, 27 August 367
General Orders, 28 August 370
General Orders, 29 August 371
To Richard Henry Lee, 29 August 372
To the Massachusetts Council, 29 August 376
From Brigadier General David Wooster, 29 August 377
General Orders, 30 August 379
From Burwell Bassett, 30 August 379
From Nicholas Cooke, 30 August 382
To the Delaware Delegates, 30 August 384
To John Dickinson, 30 August 385
To Peter Van Brugh Livingston, 30 August 385
General Orders, 31 August 387
To Clark & Nightingale, 31 August 387
To Nicholas Cooke, 31 August 388
From Captain Richard Dodge, 31 August 388
To Major Christopher French, 31 August 389
To John Hancock, 31 August 390
From Major General Philip Schuyler, 31 August 393
General Orders, 1 September 395
From Lieutenant Colonel Loammi Baldwin, 1 September 396
General Orders, 2 September 397
From Captain Abiathar Angel, 2 September 398
Instructions to Captain Nicholson Broughton, 2 September 398
From Clark & Nightingale, 2 September 401
From Nicholas Cooke, 2 September 402
From the Pennsylvania Committee of Safety, 2 September 403
Instructions to Nathaniel Tracy, 2 September 404
To Jonathan Trumbull, Sr., 2 September 405
To Brigadier General David Wooster, 2 September 407
General Orders, 3 September 408
Instructions to Reuben Colburn, 3 September 409

From Major Christopher French, 3 September 410
General Orders, 4 September 412
From Penuel Cheney, 4 September 412
To the Massachusetts Council, 4 September 413
To Brigadier General John Sullivan, 4 September 413
General Orders, 5 September 414
From Jonathan Trumbull, Sr., 5 September 416
General Orders, 6 September 418
Address to the Inhabitants of Bermuda, 6 September 419
To Nicholas Cooke, 6 September 420
From Lieutenant David Perry, c.6 September 422
From Peyton Randolph, 6 September 422
From Jonathan Trumbull, Sr., 6 September 424
From Joseph Trumbull, 6 September 425
General Orders, 7 September 426
From Ensign Levi Bowen, 7 September 427
From Captain Nicholson Broughton, 7 September 428
From the Gloucester Committee of Safety, 7 September 429
To John Hancock, 7 September 430
From Major General Artemas Ward, 7 September 431
General Orders, 8 September 431
Circular to the General Officers, 8 September 432
From Robert Carter Nicholas, 8 September 434
From Elisha Phelps, 8 September 436
To Major General Philip Schuyler, 8 September 436
To Jonathan Trumbull, Sr., 8 September 437
General Orders, 9 September 438
From Lieutenant Colonel Loammi Baldwin, 9 September 439
From Lieutenant Colonel Loammi Baldwin, 9 September 439
From Captain Nicholson Broughton, 9 September 440
From Nicholas Cooke, 9 September 441
From the New York Committee of Safety, 9 September 442
From John McKesson, 9 September 444
To Jonathan Trumbull, Sr., 9 September 444
General Orders, 10 September 445
From Brigadier General Nathanael Greene, 10 September 445
To James Warren, 10 September 446
To John Augustine Washington, 10 September 447
General Orders, 11 September 448
Council of War, 11 September 450
From Captain Gideon Foster, 11 September 451
From Major William Raymond Lee, 11 September 452

General Orders, 12 September 452
From Lieutenant Colonel Loammi Baldwin, 12 September 452
From Perez Morton, 12 September 453
General Orders, 13 September 454
General Orders, 14 September 455
To Colonel Benedict Arnold, 14 September 455
Instructions to Colonel Benedict Arnold, 14 September 457
From Captain John Baker, 14 September 460
Address to the Inhabitants of Canada, c.14 September 461
From Nicholas Cooke, 14 September 463
General Orders, 15 September 465
From Lieutenant Colonel Loammi Baldwin, 15 September 466
From John Collins, 15 September 466
From Nicholas Cooke, 15 September 467
From Jonathan Trumbull, Sr., 15 September 468

Index 473

Illustrations

Washington's map of the Boston area 186
John Trumbull's "Plan of Lines at Roxbury" 234
John Trumbull's "General Sketch of the Lines at Charlestown, Prospect Hill & Roxbury" 236

Preface

This is the first volume of the second chronological series in *The Papers of George Washington*. When finished, the second series, containing Washington's Revolutionary War papers, will number many more printed volumes than any other series in this comprehensive edition of Washington's papers. Of the more than 100,000 documents that form the corpus of Washington's documentary legacy, well over one half come from the years 1775 to 1783. The papers from the Revolutionary years present the editor with peculiar problems. The difficulties arise not from the number of documents but from the sort of documents so many of them are.

Washington as commander in chief of the Continental army for over eight years was constantly generating and accumulating documents at his headquarters. Given the nature of his role in the birthing of the nation, it was inevitable that his correspondence during the Revolution should be both extensive and varied. He corresponded regularly, of course, with officers of the Continental army and units of the militia serving with the army. Less often, he wrote letters to and received letters from French and British officers, his allies and his enemies on the field of battle. Throughout the war there was a steady flow of letters back and forth between Washington and the president of the Continental Congress, members of Congress, its committees, and its boards. His position also made it necessary for him often to correspond with public officials outside of Congress, with state governors in particular but also with state legislatures, with committees of safety, state conventions, and councils, and even with representatives of foreign governments. When private citizens wrote Washington to praise him, to seek his help, to offer him advice, or to complain of an injustice, their letters had to be answered. Through it all, Washington managed to carry on a private correspondence with friends, family, and business associates, including a regular exchange with Lund Washington of reports and letters of instruction about the management of the plantation at Mount Vernon.

The commander in chief from the start recognized that he must have at his headquarters men of judgment and experience, who were competent penmen, to relieve him of some of the drudgery of letter writing and to help him carry out the other duties of his command. Beginning with Joseph Reed and Thomas Mifflin, and followed by such men as Robert Hanson Harrison, Tench Tilghman, Alexander Hamilton, Richard Kidder Meade, John Laurens, Jonathan Trumbull, Jr., and Richard Varick, the secretaries and aides-de-camp whom

Washington recruited were, with rare exceptions, able and effective. Washington and his first secretary, Joseph Reed, worked out general procedures for dealing with the voluminous correspondence of the commander in chief. It became Washington's practice to begin by giving his secretary, or sometimes an aide, oral instructions about what should go into a letter that was to be written. The secretary or an aide then prepared a draft of the letter based on Washington's instructions. Washington himself, or more often the secretary or an aide, would review the draft and make appropriate changes and necessary corrections. The secretary or aide then had to make a clean copy of the corrected draft for Washington's signature so that the letter could be dispatched to the addressee. In every instance, the process by which one of Washington's letters was prepared has to be deduced from the letter itself, and the letters themselves reveal that the process varied considerably from letter to letter and from time to time. For instance, Washington on occasion acted as his own clerk, drafting official letters himself and docketing incoming ones. It was also his custom, it seems, to write personal letters himself, retaining a copy only when the letter included references to business matters.

After the first few months of the war the secretary began simply to keep the corrected draft of a letter for the record rather than enter it into a letter book. The secretary also attended to the incoming correspondence. He docketed letters and other documents as they were received and saw to it that they were filed. It should be noted that Reed and his successors often conveyed instructions or information from the commander in chief in letters written over their own signatures. Such staff letters most often related to matters of army routine.

The way General Washington conducted his official correspondence through secretaries and aides sometimes causes the editor of his papers problems of one sort or another, but these are far less serious than those arising from the vast accumulation of other kinds of documents relating to the routine functioning of the Continental army. Washington directed the daily operation of the army principally through his general orders, augmented by proclamations and instructions to individuals. He also convened councils of war, for which careful records were kept of the questions posed, the decisions reached, and any written opinions submitted by participating officers. This was not the end of it, though. The administration of the army and the conduct of the war produced thousands of miscellaneous documents that ended up in the commander in chief files: troop returns, reports, rosters, inventories, lists, estimates, vouchers, warrants, invoices, bills, receipts, payrolls, ledger accounts, commissions, oaths of allegiance, passes, leaves of absence, discharges, and the like. Confronted with this daunting miscellany of papers, the editor of what purports to be a comprehensive edition of George Washington's papers must ask which of these many documents should be printed in full, which calendared, which only accounted for, and which ignored altogether.

As the war progressed and the mound of papers grew, Washington became more and more concerned about the management and preservation of his papers. On 4 April 1781 he wrote the president of Congress:

> The business that has given constant exercise to the Pen of my Secretary; and not only frequently, but always, to those of my Aides de Camp, has rendered it impracticable for the former to register the Copies of my Letters, Instructions &ca in Books; by which means valuable documents which may be of equal public utility and private satisfaction remain in loose Sheets; and in the rough manner in which they wer[e] first drawn.
>
> This is not only attended with present inconvenience but has a tendency to expose them to damage & loss.
>
> Unless a set of Writers are employed for the sole purpose of recording them it will not be in my power to accomplish this necessary Work—and equally impracticable perhaps to preserve from injury & loss such valuable papers—but to engage these without the sanction of Congress I have not thought myself at liberty.
>
> The business now, must be performed in some quiet retreat and yet not so far from Camp but that I may, without much inconvenience have recourse to the Papers. It must be done under the Inspection of a Man of character in whom entire confidence can be placed—and who is capable of arranging the papers, and methodizing the register—Such an one, with as many clerks as can be employed to advantage I will endeavor to engage with the permission of Congress (DNA:PCC, item 152).

Congress was quick to agree to what Washington proposed, and on 25 May he appointed Lt. Col. Richard Varick to supervise the sorting and copying of his papers that had been accumulating from the time he took command of the Continental army in 1775. He directed Varick to sort the papers into six designated classes and to arrange the papers in each class by date. Varick gathered a team of copyists at Poughkeepsie and supervised them as they transcribed GW's outgoing correspondence and the minutes of his councils of war in bound volumes according to GW's scheme. When completed in forty-four volumes at the end of 1783, the transcripts also included general orders and those letters of Washington's private correspondence for which he retained copies. The great mass of incoming papers was not transcribed and remained unclassified and unsorted.

The trunks of papers that Washington transported to Mount Vernon were filled with (1) the Varick transcripts of his outgoing letters and orders from 1775 to 1783, (2) most of the letter books and drafts of letters and orders from which Varick's clerks made their copies, and (3) the incoming letters and other documents that had accumulated through the years at Washington's headquarters. These documents from the Revolution were the largest part of the public papers at Mount Vernon which Washington looked on until his death "as a Species of Public property, sacred in my hands." These, too, with some losses, are among the papers that the United States acquired in the nineteenth century when it bought George Washington's papers from his heirs; and the papers that were bought now make up, with some additions, that part of the great collection of Washington's papers in the Library of Congress devoted to the period of the American Revolution. The editors of *The Papers of George Washington* have added to Washington's own collection of his Revolutionary papers copies of thousands of additional documents. Among the items that have been located are receiver's copies of many letters from Washington, for some of which there was no retained copy; letter-book copies and drafts of letters written to Washington, the originals of which were in some instances not kept by Washington or have been lost; and many miscellaneous military reports and other such documents directed to Washington or his headquarters but not found in the papers he sent to Mount Vernon in 1784.

Washington's papers augmented in this way must include a fair proportion of the documents that came into or went out of George Washington's headquarters between 1775 and 1783, but just as certainly a fair proportion of the headquarters papers have not been, and in many cases cannot be, identified or, if identified, tracked down. Fortunately the task immediately at hand is not to collect and print every surviving document relating to the Continental army. Rather, it is to identify and print those surviving documents written by and to George Washington between 1775 and 1783 that deal directly with Washington as commander in chief of the Continental army or simply as a man. Specifically, these include the letters that Washington wrote or that went out under his name; his addresses, proclamations, general orders, and special instructions; the minutes of his councils of war; and letters written to Washington by others. Such things as recommendations for appointment or promotion and petitions requesting discharges, passes, leaves, or pardons ordinarily are not printed. Certain other documents dealing with routine matters or which are repetitive are calendared. When found, enclosures in letters are either printed or, more often, are identified and described in footnotes. Opinions submitted to Washington by general officers are calendared or treated in notes. Letters written by officers on Washington's staff often are alluded to in footnotes but are not consistently identified.

And the construction of Washington's military and personal accounts for publication must be deferred.

This first volume of the Revolutionary War series of the *Papers* covers the period from Washington's appointment on 16 June 1775 as commander in chief of the Continental army to 15 Sept. 1775 after he had taken charge of the siege of British-occupied Boston. A number of documents that in later volumes would have been omitted have in the first volume been calendared, and others that would have been calendared have been printed in full. During these early months of the war Washington himself was deeply involved in the details of army administration. What later became only matters of routine outside Washington's immediate concern or even notice were at first often directly related to his policy for shaping the Continental officer corps, to his notions about army organization and discipline generally, or to his approach to the relations of the military to civilian authority.

Editorial Apparatus

Transcription of the documents in the volumes of *The Papers of George Washington* has remained as close to a literal reproduction of the manuscript as possible. Punctuation, capitalization, paragraphing, and spelling of all words are retained as they appear in the original document. Dashes used as punctuation have been retained except when a period and a dash appear together at the end of a sentence. The appropriate marks of punctuation have always been added at the end of a paragraph. Errors in spelling of proper names and geographic locations have been corrected in brackets or in annotation only if the spelling in the text makes the word incomprehensible. When a tilde is used in the manuscript to indicate a double letter, the letter has been silently doubled. Washington and some of his correspondents occasionally used a tilde above an incorrectly spelled word to indicate an error in orthography. When this device is used the editors have silently corrected the word. In cases where a tilde has been inserted above an abbreviation or contraction, usually in letter-book copies, the word has been expanded. Otherwise, contractions and abbreviations have been retained as written and a period has been inserted after an abbreviation. When an apostrophe has been used in contractions it is retained. Superscripts have been lowered and if the word is an abbreviation a period has been added. If the meaning of an abbreviation or contraction is not obvious, it has been expanded in square brackets "H[is] M[ajest]y." Editorial insertions or corrections in the text also appear in square brackets. Angle brackets ⟨ ⟩ are used to indicate illegible or mutilated material. A space left blank in a mänuscript by the writer is indicated by a square-bracketed gap in the text [ ]. Deletions from manuscripts are not indicated. If a deletion contains substantive material, it appears in a footnote. If the intended location of marginal notations is clear from the text, they are inserted without comment; otherwise they are recorded in the footnotes. The ampersand has been retained and the thorn transcribed as "th." The symbol for per ( ) is used when it appears in the manuscript. The dateline has been placed at the head of a document regardless of where it occurred in the manuscript. In the Revolutionary series, the titles of the documents include current military ranks of persons on duty with the contending armies or mobilized militia units.

Symbols Designating Documents

AD	Autograph Document
ADS	Autograph Document Signed
ADf	Autograph Draft
ADfS	Autograph Draft Signed
AL	Autograph Letter
ALS	Autograph Letter Signed
D	Document
DS	Document Signed
Df	Draft
DfS	Draft Signed
L	Letter
LS	Letter Signed
LB	Letter Book Copy
[S]	Used with other symbols to indicate that the signature on the document has been cropped or clipped.

Repository Symbols and Abbreviations

CLjJC	James S. Copley Library, La Jolla, Calif.
CSmH	Henry E. Huntington Library, San Marino, Calif.
Ct	Connecticut State Library, Hartford
CtHi	Connecticut Historical Society, Hartford
CtY	Yale University, New Haven, Conn.
DLC	Library of Congress
DLC:GW	George Washington Papers, Library of Congress
DNA	National Archives
DNA:PCC	Papers of the Continental Congress, National Archives
DTP	Tudor Place, Carostead Foundation, Washington, D.C.
MAnP	Phillips Academy, Andover, Mass.
M-Ar	Massachusetts Archives Division, Boston
MH	Harvard University, Cambridge, Mass.
MHi	Massachusetts Historical Society, Boston
MiU-C	William L. Clements Library, University of Michigan, Ann Arbor
MoSW	Washington University, St. Louis
MWA	American Antiquarian Society, Worcester, Mass.
N	New York State Library, Albany
Nh	New Hampshire State Library, Concord

Nh-Ar	New Hampshire Division of Records Management and Archives, Concord
NHi	New-York Historical Society, New York
NjMoNP	Washington Headquarters Library, Morristown, N.J.
NjP	Princeton University, Princeton, N.J.
NN	New York Public Library, New York
NNebgGW	Washington Headquarters, Jonathan Hasbrouck House, Newburgh, N.Y.
NNPM	Pierpont Morgan Library, New York
NNS	New York Society Library, New York
PHi	Historical Society of Pennsylvania, Philadelphia
PPAmP	American Philosophical Society, Philadelphia
P.R.O.	Public Record Office, London
PWCD	David Library of the American Revolution, Washington Crossing, Pa.
RG	Record Group (designating the location of documents in the National Archives)
RHi	Rhode Island Historical Society, Providence
RPJCB	John Carter Brown Library, Providence
Vi	Virginia State Library, Richmond
ViHi	Virginia Historical Society, Richmond
ViMtV	Mount Vernon Ladies' Association of the Union
ViU	University of Virginia, Charlottesville

Short Title List

Bartlett, *R.I. Records.* John Russell Bartlett, ed. *Records of the Colony of Rhode Island and Providence Plantations in New England.* 10 vols. Providence, 1856–65.

"Bixby Diary." "Diary of Samuel Bixby." *Proceedings of the Massachusetts Historical Society*, 1st ser., 14 (1875–76), 285–298.

Bouton, *N.H. Provincial Papers.* Nathaniel Bouton, ed. *Provincial Papers: Documents and Records Relating to the Province of New-Hampshire, from 1764 to 1776.* 7 vols. Concord and Nashua, 1867–73.

Butterfield, *Adams Diary and Autobiography.* L. H. Butterfield et al., eds. *Diary and Autobiography of John Adams.* 4 vols. Cambridge, Mass., 1961.

Butterfield, *Adams Family Correspondence.* L. H. Butterfield et al., eds. *Adams Family Correspondence.* 4 vols. to date. Cambridge, Mass., 1963—.

Clark, *Naval Documents.* William Bell Clark et al., eds. *Naval Docu-*

ments of the American Revolution. 8 vols. to date. Washington, D.C., 1964—.

Davies, *Documents of the American Revolution*. K. G. Davies, ed. *Documents of the American Revolution, 1770–1783 (Colonial Office Series)*. 21 vols. Shannon, Ireland, 1972–81.

Diaries. Donald Jackson and Dorothy Twohig, eds. *The Diaries of George Washington*. 6 vols. Charlottesville, 1976–79.

Fitzpatrick, *Writings*. John C. Fitzpatrick, ed. *The Writings of George Washington from the Original Manuscript Sources, 1745–1799*. 39 vols. Washington, D.C., 1931–44.

Force, *American Archives*. Peter Force, ed. *American Archives*. 9 vols. Washington, D.C., 1837–53.

Gregory and Dunnings, "Gates Papers." James Gregory and Thomas Dunnings, eds. "The Horatio Gates Papers, 1726–1828." Glen Rock, N.J., 1978. Microfilm.

Hening. William Walter Hening, ed. *The Statutes at Large; Being a Collection of All the Laws of Virginia from the First Session of the Legislature, in the Year 1619*. 13 vols. 1819–23. Reprint. Charlottesville, 1969.

Hinman, *Historical Collection*. Royal R. Hinman, comp., *A Historical Collection, from Official Records, Files &c., of the Part Sustained by Connecticut, during the War of the Revolution*. Hartford, 1842.

JCC. Worthington C. Ford et al., eds. *Journals of the Continental Congress*. 34 vols. Washington, D.C., 1904–37.

Jones, "Cooke Correspondence." Matt B. Jones, ed. "Revolutionary Correspondence of Governor Nicholas Cooke, 1775–1781." *Proceedings of the American Antiquarian Society*, new ser., 36 (1926), 231–353.

Jones, *History of N.Y.* Thomas Jones. *History of New York during the Revolutionary War . . . .* Ed. Edward F. DeLancey. 2 vols. New York, 1879.

Ledger B. Manuscript Ledger in George Washington Papers, Library of Congress.

"Lunt's Book." "Paul Lunt's Book." *Proceedings of the Massachusetts Historical Society*, 1st ser., 12 (1871–1873), 192–207.

"Mass. Council Journal," July 1775–Feb. 1776 sess. "Records of the Great & General Court or Assembly for the Colony of the Massachusetts Bay in New England Begun and Held at Watertown in the County of Middlesex, on Wednesday the Twenty sixth Day of July 1775." Microfilm Collection of Early State Records.

Mass. Hist. Soc., *Proceedings*. *Proceedings of the Massachusetts Historical Society*. Boston, 1859—.

Mass. House of Rep. Journal, July-Nov. 1775 sess. *A Journal of the Honorable House of Representatives of the Colony of the Massachusetts-Bay in New-England.* Watertown, Mass., 1775. Microfilm Collection of Early State Records.

Mass. Prov. Congress Journals. William Lincoln, ed. *The Journals of Each Provincial Congress of Massachusetts in 1774 and 1775, and of the Committee of Safety.* Boston, 1838. Microfilm Collection of Early State Records.

Microfilm Collection of Early State Records. Microfilm Collection of Early State Records prepared by the Library of Congress in association with the University of North Carolina.

N.Y. Prov. Congress Journals. *Journals of the Provincial Congress, Provincial Convention, Committee of Safety, and Council of Safety of the State of New-York, 1775–1776–1777.* 2 vols. Albany, 1842. Microfilm Collection of Early State Records.

Pa. Archives. Samuel Hazard et al., eds. *Pennsylvania Archives.* 9 ser., 138 vols. Philadelphia and Harrisburg, 1852–1949.

Pa. Col. Records. *Colonial Records of Pennsylvania, 1683–1800.* 16 vols. Philadelphia, 1852–53.

Sabine, *Smith's Historical Memoirs.* William H. W. Sabine, ed. *Historical Memoirs from 16 March 1763 to 9 July 1776 of William Smith, Historian of the Province of New York . . . .* 2 vols. New York, 1956–58.

Sizer, *Trumbull Autobiography.* Theodore Sizer, ed. *The Autobiography of Colonel John Trumbull.* 1953. Reprint. New York, 1970.

Smith, *Letters of Delegates.* Paul H. Smith et al., eds. *Letters of Delegates to Congress, 1774–1789.* 10 vols. to date. Washington, D.C., 1976—.

Sparks, *Writings.* Jared Sparks, ed. *The Writings of George Washington: Being His Correspondence, Addresses, Messages, and Other Papers, Official and Private, Selected and Published from the Original Manuscripts.* 12 vols. Boston, 1833–37.

"Stevens Journal." "The Revolutionary Journal of James Stevens of Andover, Mass." *The Essex Institute Historical Collections,* 48 (1912), 41–71.

Taylor, *Papers of John Adams.* Robert J. Taylor et al., eds. *Papers of John Adams.* 6 vols. to date. Cambridge, Mass., 1977—.

Van Schreeven, *Revolutionary Virginia.* William J. Van Schreeven, Robert L. Scribner, and Brent Tarter, eds. *Revolutionary Virginia: The Road to Independence.* 7 vols. Charlottesville, 1973–83.

Wilson, *Heath's Memoirs.* Rufus R. Wilson, ed. *Heath's Memoirs of the American War.* 1798. Reprint. New York, 1904.

The Papers of George Washington
Revolutionary War Series
Volume 1
June–September 1775

Address to the Continental Congress

[Philadelphia, 16 June 1775]

The President[1] informed Colo. Washington that the Congress had yesterday, Unanimously made choice of him to be General & Commander in Chief of the American Forces, and requested he would accept of that Appointment;[2] whereupon Colo. Washington, standing in his place, Spake as follows.

"Mr President, Tho' I am truly sensible of the high Honour done me in this Appointment, yet I feel great distress, from a consciousness[3] that my abilities & Military experience may not be equal to the extensive & important Trust: However, as the Congress desire i⟨t⟩ I will enter upon the momentous duty, & exert every power I Possess In their service & for the Support of the glorious Cause: I beg they will accept my most cordial thanks for this distinguished testimony of their Approbation.

"But lest some unlucky event should happen unfavourable to my reputation, I beg it may be rememberd by every Gentn in the room, that I this day declare with the utmost sincerity, I do not think my self equal to the Command I ⟨am⟩ honoured with.[4]

"As to pay, Sir, I beg leave to Assure the Congress that as no pecuniary consideration could have tempted me to have accepted this Arduous emploiment at the expence of my domestk ease & happi⟨ness⟩[5] I do not wish to make any proffit from it: I will keep an exact Account of my expences; those I doubt not they will discharge & that is all I desire."[6]

D, in Edmund Pendleton's writing, DNA:PCC, item 152; copy, DNA:PCC, item 169. The presence of the introductory paragraph indicates that GW did not deliver his address from the Pendleton document. However, the insertion of a phrase in GW's writing (see note 5 below) suggests that he subsequently reviewed the document and corrected it to read as he thought it should.

1. John Hancock (1737–1793) of Massachusetts was elected president of the Second Continental Congress on 24 May 1775 in place of Peyton Randolph, who, as speaker of the Virginia House of Burgesses, felt obligated to return to Virginia to attend the June session of the Burgesses. Hancock served as president of Congress until 29 Oct. 1777.

2. The only known account of Congress's debate on GW's appointment as commander in chief is given by John Adams in his autobiography. Speaking to the committee of the whole sometime before 15 June, Adams moved that Congress adopt the army outside Boston and appoint a general to command it. He then added "that though this was not the proper time to nominate a

General, yet as I had reason to believe this was a point of the greatest difficulty, I had no hesitation to declare that I had but one Gentleman in my Mind for that important command, and that was a Gentleman from Virginia who was among Us and very well known to all of Us, a Gentleman whose Skill and Experience as an Officer, whose independent fortune, great Talents and excellent universal Character, would command the Approbation of all America, and unite the cordial Exertions of all the Colonies better than any other Person in the Union. Mr. Washington, who happened to sit near the Door, as soon as he heard me allude to him, from his Usual Modesty darted into the Library Room. . . . The Subject came under debate and several Gentlemen declared themselves against the Appointment of Mr. Washington, not on Account of any personal Objection against him: but because the Army was all from New England, had a General of their own [Artemas Ward], appeared to be satisfied with him and had proved themselves able to imprison the British Army in Boston, which was all they expected or desired at that time. Mr. [Edmund] Pendleton of Virginia [and] Mr. [Roger] Sherman of Connecticutt were very explicit in declaring this Opinion, Mr. [Thomas] Cushing and several others more faintly expressed their Opposition and their fears of discontent in the Army and in New England. Mr. [Robert Treat] Paine expressed a great Opinion of General Ward and a strong friendship for him, having been his Classmate at [Harvard] Colledge, or at least his contemporary: but gave no Opinion upon the question. The Subject was postponed to a future day. In the mean time, pains were taken out of doors to obtain a Unanimity, and the Voices were generally so clearly in favour of Washington that the dissentient Members were persuaded to withdraw their Opposition, and Mr. Washington was nominated, I believe by Mr. Thomas Johnson of Maryland, unanimously elected, and the Army adopted" (L. H. Butterfield et al., eds., *Diary and Autobiography of John Adams*, 4 vols. [Cambridge, Mass., 1961], 3:322–23). GW was unanimously chosen general by ballot on 15 June (*JCC*, 2:91).

3. The word "doubt" is struck from the main line, and the word "consciousness" is inserted above it in Pendleton's writing.

4. Many years later Dr. Benjamin Rush of Philadelphia wrote that shortly after GW was appointed commander in chief of the Continental forces, "I saw Patrick Henry at his lodgings, who told me that General Washington had been with him, and informed him that he was unequal to the station in which his country had placed him, and then added with tears in his eyes 'Remember, Mr. Henry, what I now tell you: From the day I enter upon the command of the American armies, I date my fall, and the ruin of my reputation'" (George W. Corner, ed., *The Autobiography of Benjamin Rush* [Princeton, 1948], 113).

5. The phrase "at the expence of my domestk ease & happi⟨ness⟩" appears above the line in GW's writing.

6. Immediately before selecting GW as commander in chief on 15 June, Congress resolved that the general who commanded the Continental forces have "five hundred dollars, per month, . . . for his pay and expences" (*JCC*, 2:91). GW's refusal of any salary generally pleased the delegates. "There is Something charming to me, in the Conduct of Washington," John Adams

wrote to Elbridge Gerry on 18 June. "A Gentleman, of one of the first Fortunes, upon the Continent, leaving his delicious Retirement, his Family and Friends, Sacrificing his Ease, and hazarding all in the Cause of his Country. His Views are noble and disinterested. He declared when he accepted the mighty Trust, that he would lay before Us, an exact account of his Expences, and not accept a shilling for Pay" (MoSW). Eliphalet Dyer of Connecticut was equally impressed with GW's character, but he expressed some concern about the cost of the general's anticipated expenses. "He is Clever, & if any thing too modest," Dyer observed in a letter of 17 June to Joseph Trumbull. "He seems discret & Virtuous, no harum Starum ranting Swearing fellow but Sober, steady, & Calm. His modesty will Induce him I dare say to take & order every step with the best advice possible to be obtained in the Army. His allowance for Wages [for his staff] expences & every thing is we think very high, not less than £ 150 lawll per month, but it was urged that the largeness of his family, Aide Camps, Secretary Servts &c, beside a Constant table for more or less of his officers, daily expresses, dispatches &c Must be very expensive" (Paul H. Smith et al., eds., *Letters of Delegates to Congress, 1774–1789* [Washington, D.C., 1976—], 1:499–500). GW's expense account for the war, covering the period June 1775 to 1 July 1783, is in DNA: RG 56, General Records—Treasury Department; a duplicate original is in DLC:GW.

Letter not found: to Brigadier General Horatio Gates, 17 June 1775. On 22 June Gates wrote to GW: "Last night I was Honourd by the receipt of your Obliging Letter of 17th Instant."

To Martha Washington

My Dearest, Philadelphia June 18th 1775.

I am now set down to write to you on a subject which fills me with inexpressable concern—and this concern is greatly aggravated and Increased when I reflect on the uneasiness I know it will give you—It has been determined in Congress, that the whole Army raised for the defence of the American Cause shall be put under my care, and that it is necessary for me to proceed immediately to Boston to take upon me the Command of it. You may beleive me my dear Patcy, when I assure you, in the most solemn manner, that, so far from seeking this appointment I have used every endeavour in my power to avoid it, not only from my unwillingness to part with you and the Family, but from a consciousness of its being a trust too great for my Capacity and that I should enjoy more real happiness and felicity in one month with you, at home, than I have the most distant prospect of reaping abroad, if my stay was to be Seven times Seven years. But, as it has been a kind of destiny that has thrown me upon this Service, I shall hope that my undertaking of it, is designd to answer some good purpose—You might, and I suppose did perceive, from the Tenor of my letters, that I was apprehensive I could not avoid this appointment, as I did not even pretend ⟨t⟩o intimate when I should return[1]—that was the case—it was utterly out of my power to refuse this appointment without exposing my Character to such censures as would have reflected dishonour upon myself, and given pain to my friends—this I am sure could not, and ought not to be pleasing to you, & must have lessend me considerably in my own esteem.[2] I shall rely therefore, confidently, on that Providence which has heretofore preservd, & been bountiful to me, not doubting but that I shall return safe to you in the fall—I shall feel no pain from the Toil, or the danger of the Campaign—My unhappiness will flow, from the uneasiness I know you will feel at being left alone—I therefore beg of you to summon your whole fortitude & Resolution, and pass your time as agreeably as possible—nothing will give me so much sincere satisfaction as to hear this, and to hear it from your own Pen.

If it should be your desire to remove into Alexandria (as you once mentioned upon an occasion of this sort) I am quite pleased that you should put it in practice, & Lund Washington may be directed, by you, to build a Kitchen and other Houses there proper for your reception[3]—if on the other hand you should rather Incline to spend good part of your time among your Friends below, I wish you to do so[4]—In short, my earnest, & ardent desire is, that you would pursue any Plan that is most likely to produce content, and a tolerable degree of Tranquility as it must add greatly to my uneasy feelings to hear that you are dissatisfied, and complaining at what I really could not avoid.

As Life is always uncertain, and common prudence dictates to every Man the necessity of settling his temporal Concerns whilst it is in his power—and whilst the Mind is calm and undisturbed, I have, since I came to this place (for I had not time to do it before I left home) got Colo. Pendleton to Draft a Will for me by the directions which I gave him, which Will I now Inclose[5]—The Provision made for you, in cas⟨e⟩ of my death, will, I hope, be agreeable; I have Included the Money for which I sold my own Land (to Doctr Mercer) in the Sum given you, as also all other Debts.[6] What I owe myself is very trifling—Cary's Debt excepted, and that would not have been much if the Bank stock had been applied without such difficulties as he made in the Transference.[7]

I shall add nothing more at present as I have several Letters to write, but to desire you will remember me to Milly[8] & all Friends, and to assure you that I am with most unfeigned regard, My dear Patcy Yr Affecte

Go: Washington

P.S. Since writing the above I have receivd your Letter of the 15th and have got two suits of what I was told wa⟨s⟩ the prettiest Muslin. I wish it may please you—it cost 50/. a suit that is 20/. a yard.[9]

ALS, DTP. Martha Washington destroyed nearly all of GW's letters to her shortly before her death in 1802. The letter of this date and the one of 23 June 1775 printed below were found by Martha Parke Custis Peter, one of Martha Washington's granddaughters, in a drawer of a small desk that she inherited from Mrs. Washington. See Armistead Peter, *Tudor Place* (Washington, D.C., 1969), 44–45.

1. No previous letters from GW to Martha Washington have been found.

2. GW expressed remarkably similar thoughts to his mother nearly twenty years earlier regarding the soon-to-be-proffered command of the Virginia Regiment. See GW to Mary Ball Washington, 14 Aug. 1755.

3. Between 1769 and 1771 GW engaged workmen to build a small town house on a half-acre lot that he owned at the corner of Pitt and Cameron streets in Alexandria. Lacking a kitchen and some of the other outbuildings conducive to prolonged residence, the house was used by GW during the early 1770s only for occasional overnight stays in town. Lund Washington (1737–1796), a distant cousin of GW, lived at Mount Vernon and served GW as business manager from 1765 to 1785. Mrs. Washington did not ask Lund to make any additions to the Alexandria property, nor did she move to town despite the fears that some Alexandria citizens and others had for her safety at Mount Vernon. Soon after Mrs. Washington realized that GW would not be able to return home in the fall, she set out to join him at his camp in Cambridge (GW to Lund Washington, 20 Aug. 1775; Lund Washington to GW, 5, 29 Oct. 1775).

4. Martha Washington's mother, two brothers, and two sisters all lived near the Pamunkey River in the lower Virginia tidewater. During late October and early November 1775, she visited at the home of her sister Anna Maria Dandridge Bassett in New Kent County (GW to Burwell Bassett, 19 June 1775; Lund Washington to GW, 22 Oct., 5 Nov. 1775).

5. No copy of this will has been found. Edmund Pendleton (1721–1803) of Caroline County, Va., whom GW had previously engaged as a lawyer for the

Custis estate as well as for some of his own affairs, was one of his fellow delegates in both the First and Second Continental Congresses. Pendleton left Congress on 22 July and declined to return because of poor health. He became president of the Virginia committee of safety in August and was elected president of the Virginia conventions that sat the following December and May. When the house of delegates first met in October 1776, Pendleton was chosen its speaker. A fall from a horse in the winter of 1777 crippled him for life and greatly restricted his subsequent political activities. Pendleton, nevertheless, became presiding judge of the Virginia court of chancery in 1778 and the next year assumed the same position on the state court of appeals.

6. In the spring of 1774 GW sold his boyhood home, Ferry Farm, located on the Rappahannock River across from Fredericksburg, to Dr. Hugh Mercer (c.1725–1777) of that town for £2,000 Virginia currency. Mercer agreed to pay the sum in five annual installments but proved unable to make the first payment due this year (Hugh Mercer to GW, 6 April 1774; Fielding Lewis to GW, 14 Nov. 1775). After Mercer's death in January 1777 from wounds suffered at the Battle of Princeton, one of his executors apparently discharged the debt (GW to Lund Washington, 18 Dec. 1778, 17 Aug. 1779).

7. In June 1774 GW directed Robert Cary & Co. of London to sell the Bank of England stock in the estate of his deceased stepdaughter Martha Parke Custis and to apply the proceeds to the debt that he owed the firm for goods imported from England (GW to Robert Cary & Co., 10 Nov. 1773, 1 June 1774). The legal documents that GW and Mrs. Washington submitted for that purpose were unacceptable to the bank directors, however. In the spring of 1775, shortly before he set out to attend the Continental Congress, GW learned that they would have to execute a new set of documents. He failed to attend to the matter before departing Virginia, and so he was unable to get it done until sometime after the end of the war (GW to Lund Washington, 10 May 1776; GW to Wakelin Welch, 30 Oct. 1783, 27 July 1784, July 1786; Ledger B, 26, 234).

8. Amelia Posey, daughter of GW's former neighbor Capt. John Posey and a girlhood friend of Martha Parke Custis, apparently lived at Mount Vernon throughout most of the war years.

9. Martha Washington's letter has not been found. GW recorded the £5 in cash that he spent for Mrs. Washington's two suits under the date 20 June 1775 in his cash memorandum book for 3 May 1775 to 22 Dec. 1784 (DLC:GW).

Commission from the Continental Congress

[Philadelphia, 19 June 1775]

In Congress

The delegates of the United Colonies of New-hampshire, Massachusetts bay, Rhode-island, Connecticut, New-York, New-

Jersey, Pennsylvania, New Castle Kent & Sussex on Delaware, Maryland, Virginia, North Carolina & South Carolina[1]

To George Washington Esquire

We reposing especial trust and confidence in your patriotism, conduct and fidelity[2] Do by these presents constitute and appoint you to be General and Commander in chief of the army of the United Colonies and of all the forces raised[3] or to be raised by them and of all others who shall voluntarily offer their service and join the said army for the defence of American Liberty and for repelling every hostile invasion thereof And you are hereby vested with full power and authority to act as you shall think for the good and Welfare of the service.

And we do hereby strictly charge and require all officers and soldiers under your command to be obedient to your orders & diligent in the exercise of their several dut⟨ies.⟩ And we do also enjoin and require you to be careful in executing the great trust reposed in you, by causing strict discipline and order to be observed in th⟨e⟩ army and that the soldiers are duly exercised an⟨d⟩ provided with all convenient necessaries.

And you are to regulate your conduct in every respect by the rules and discipline of war (as herewith given you) and punctually to observe and foll⟨ow⟩ such orders and directions from time to time as you shall receive from this or a future Congress of the said United Colonies or a committee of Congress for that purpose appointed.[4]

This Commission to continue inforce until revoked by this or a future Congress.

By order of the Congress
John Hancock President

Dated Philadelphia June 19th 1775.
Attest Chas Thomson secy[5]

DS, DLC:GW; copy, DNA:PCC, item 1. The text of the commission in DLC:GW is in the writing of Timothy Matlack, clerk to the secretary of Congress, Charles Thomson. It is signed by Hancock and Thomson. The PCC copy is in the rough journal of the Continental Congress in Thomson's writing. It is dated 17 June 1775, the day that Congress approved the commission. Significant variations in this copy are noted below. The journal version was printed in *Dunlap's Pennsylvania Packet, or, the General Advertiser* (Philadelphia), 11 Dec. 1775.

GW's commission was drafted by a committee of three delegates, Richard Henry Lee, Edward Rutledge, and John Adams, who were appointed for that purpose on 16 June immediately after GW's speech accepting the command of the Continental forces. They reported to Congress the next day, at which time the commission, "being read by paragraphs and debated, was agreed to." Congress then ordered it to "be fairly transcribed, to be signed by the president, and attested by the secretary, and delivered to the General" (*JCC*, 2:93, 96–97). On 18 June, Hancock wrote to Joseph Warren: "The Congress have Appointed George Washington Esqr. General & Commander in Chief of the Continental Army, his Commission is made out, & I shall Sign it tomorrow" (Smith, *Letters of Delegates*, 1:507–8). When Hancock signed the commission, he apparently changed the date by writing "19" over the "17" written by Matlack.

1. The copy in the rough journal of the Continental Congress reads "The Counties of Newcastle, Kent & Sussex on Delaware." The words "in congress assembled" appear after "South Carolina."

2. In the rough journal this phrase reads "your patriotism, valour, conduct & fidelity."

3. The rough journal reads "now raised."

4. The articles of war were adopted by Congress on 30 June, a week after GW left Philadelphia, and on 5 July Hancock forwarded them to Cambridge. See Richard Henry Lee to GW, 29 June 1775, n.3, and Hancock to GW, 5 July 1775. GW received a set of instructions from Congress on 22 June, which he carried with him. See that document printed below.

5. Charles Thomson (1729–1824) of Philadelphia was elected secretary of the First Continental Congress on 5 Sept. 1774 and the Second Continental Congress on 10 May 1775. He held the latter position until Congress ceased to exist in 1789. Thomson officially notified GW of his election as president in April 1789.

From John Adams

Dear Sir Phyladelphia June [19 or 20] 1775

In Complyance with your Request, I have considered of what you proposed, and am obliged to give you my Sentiments, very briefly, and in great Haste.

In general, Sir, there will be three Committees, either of a Congress, or of an House of Representatives, which are and will be composed of our best Men, Such, whose Judgment and Integrity may be most relyed on. I mean the Committee on the State of the Province, the Committee of Safety, and the Committee of Supplies.[1]

But least this should be too general, I beg leave to mention particularly James Warren Esqr. of Plymouth, Joseph Hawley Esqr. of Northampton, John Winthrop Esqr. L.L.D. of Cambridge, Dr Warren, Dr Church, Coll Palmer of Braintree, Elbridge Gerry Esqr. of Marblehead. Mr Bowdoin, Mr Sever, Mr Dexter, lately of the Council will be found to be very worthy Men, as well as Mr Pitts who I am Sorry to hear is in ill Health.[2]

The Recommendations, of these Gentlemen, may be rely'd on. Our President was pleased to recommend to you, Mr William Bant for one of your Aid du Camps. I must confess, I know not where to find a Gentleman, of more Merit, and better qualified for Such a Place.[3]

Mr Paine was pleased to mention to you Mr William Tudor a young Gentleman of the Law, for a Secretary to the General. and all the rest of my Brothers, you may remember, very chearfully concurr'd with him. His Abilities and Virtues are such as must recommend him to every Man who loves Modesty, Ingenuity, or Fidelity: but as I find an Interest has been made in behalf of Mr Trumbull of Connecticut, I must Submit the Decision to your further Inquiries, after you shall arrive at Cambridge. Mr Trumbulls Merit is Such that I dare not Say a Word against his Pretensions. I only beg Leave to Say, that Mr Tudor is an Exile from a good Employment and fair Prospects in the Town of Boston, driven by that very Tyranny against which We are all contending.[4] There is another Gentleman of liberal Education and real Genius, as well as great Activity, who I find is a Major in the Army; his Name is Jonathan Williams Austin. I mention him, sir, not for the Sake of recommending him to any particular Favour, as to give the General an opportunity of observing a youth of great abilities, and of reclaiming him from certain Follies, which have hitherto, in other Departments of Life obscurd him.[5]

There is another Gentleman, whom I presume to be in the Army either as a Captain, or in Some higher Station, whose Name is William Smith: as this young Gentleman is my Brother in Law, I dont recommend him for any other Place, than that in which the Voice of his Country has placed him. But the Countenance of the General, as far as his Conduct shall deserve it, which in an Army is of great Importance, will be gratefully acknowledged as a particular obligation by his Brother.[6]

With great Sincerity, I wish you, an agreable Journey, and a Successfull, a glorious Campaign: and am with great Esteem, sir, your most obedient Servant

John Adams

ALS, MHi: Adams Papers. The fact that this letter remains undated in the Adams Papers suggests that it was not sent to GW. Adams apparently laid it aside in order to join in the similar letter which the Massachusetts delegates sent to GW on 22 June. This joint letter, printed below, is also in Adams's writing. Its first two paragraphs and closing paragraph are nearly identical to the corresponding ones in Adams's private letter. The third paragraphs of the two letters, where various Massachusetts leaders are named, differ significantly only in that nine additional names appear in the delegates' letter. Adams's recommendations of Bant, Tudor, Austin, and Smith in his private letter are omitted in the delegates' letter. He may have orally recommended these young gentlemen.

In the dateline Adams left a short space between "June" and "1775." Charles Francis Adams says that this letter "was written probably on the 19th or 20th" (Charles Francis Adams, ed., *The Works of John Adams*, 10 vols. [Boston, 1850–56], 9:359, n.1). That it was written no later than 20 June is indicated by Adams's letters of 20 June to William Tudor and James Warren in which he tells each man that he has mentioned his name to GW (Robert J. Taylor et al., eds., *Papers of John Adams* [Cambridge, Mass., 1977—], 3:33, 34–37).

1. With the collapse of royal authority in Massachusetts outside of Boston during the fall of 1774, an extralegal provincial congress was convened to replace the General Court. In the spring of 1775 the provincial congress asked the Continental Congress for advice about how the colony should be governed in the future. The Continental Congress recommended on 9 June that the offices of governor and lieutenant governor be considered vacant and that the General Court be reestablished in accordance with the colony's charter. The provincial congress readily accepted this advice and on 20 June called for the election of a house of representatives. The new house met for the first time on 19 July. Two days later it elected a new council, and on 28 July it authorized the council to act as governor of the colony. The committees of safety and of supplies continued under the reestablished General Court, but the committee on the state of the province ceased to exist after May 1775.

2. Dr. Joseph Warren (1741–1775), a prominent physician and political figure in Boston, became president of the Massachusetts provincial congress on 23 April 1775. He was killed at the Battle of Bunker Hill on 17 June, but news of his death apparently did not reach Philadelphia until ten days later (Richard Henry Lee to GW, 29 June 1775). James Warren (1726–1808) succeeded Joseph Warren as president of the provincial congress, and on 19 July he was elected speaker of the new house of representatives. Eight days later he was appointed Continental paymaster general. Joseph Warren, Benjamin Church (1734–c.1778), and Joseph Palmer (1716–1788) were members of the committee of safety; Elbridge Gerry (1744–1814) served on the commit-

tee of supplies; and James Warren and Joseph Hawley (1723–1788) had been on the committee on the state of the province. Dr. Church was appointed director and chief physician of the Continental army hospital on 27 July 1775, but he was soon discovered to be carrying on a traitorous correspondence with the British. See Council of War, 3–4 Oct. 1775. Of the four former councillors named here, three were elected to the reestablished Massachusetts council on 21 July 1775: James Bowdoin (1726–1790) and James Pitts (d. 1776) both of Boston and William Sever (Seaver; 1729–1809) of Kingston. Pitts did not serve because of his bad health. Among the others elected to the new council were Joseph Palmer and Harvard College's distinguished professor of mathematics and natural philosophy, John Winthrop (1714–1779). Winthrop received an honorary LL.D. degree from the University of Edinburgh in 1771 and another from Harvard in 1773. Samuel Dexter (1726–1810) of Dedham served on the old council from 1768 to 1774, but he retired from public life in July 1775 and moved to Connecticut.

3. Congress resolved on 16 June to allow GW three aides-de-camp with monthly salaries of $33 each (*JCC*, 2:94). William Bant (d. 1779) was a Boston merchant who had been associated in business with John Hancock since 1767. When Hancock was elected president of the Massachusetts provincial congress in October 1774, Bant became his business manager, and he continued to act in that capacity during Hancock's tenure as president of the Continental Congress. Bant was not appointed an aide-de-camp to GW or to any other position in the Continental army.

4. The position of secretary to the commander in chief was coveted both for its prestige and its remuneration. The salary set by Congress when it authorized a secretary for the general on 16 June was $66 a month (*JCC*, 2:94). In addition, the secretary, as a member of the general's military family, lived on the general's expense account. Joseph Trumbull (1737–1778), a son of Gov. Jonathan Trumbull, Sr., of Connecticut, was recommended for the position by Silas Deane, one of the Connecticut delegates to Congress, immediately after GW accepted command of the army. Deane was encouraged by GW's response. "He told Me," Deane wrote Joseph Trumbull on 18 June, "he was wholly disengaged, & should pursue one rule of Conduct invariably—To prefer so farr as in his power only those equall to the Post to be filled—That if You were desirous of it, and my recommendation was agreeable elsewhere (Viz) to the province he will be in [Massachusetts], it would suit him" (Smith, *Letters of Delegates*, 1:506–7). The other Connecticut delegates, Eliphalet Dyer and Roger Sherman, joined Deane in pushing Trumbull's candidacy, and on 20 June Dyer informed Trumbull: "I . . . procured all the Gentn. of the Massachusett Bay to Confirm our recommendation all which believe will Succeed for your Appointment unless the Massachusett Gent. behind the Curtain have made Interest for some Other person which I ought not to Suspect" (ibid., 1:521–22). Adams's letter to GW reveals, however, that Dyer had reason to be suspicious. William Tudor (1750–1819) of Boston, a former law clerk to Adams, was recommended to GW for secretary by one of Adams's "Brothers" in the Massachusetts delegation, Robert Treat Paine (1731–1814).

On 20 July Adams wrote Tudor that he also had recommended him as secretary and that the other Massachusetts delegates "very chearfully and unanimously concurr'd with me in the warmest Terms. A great Interest is making however for Mr. Jos. Trumbull and for others. What the General will do I know not" (Taylor, *Papers of John Adams*, 3:33). GW decided the matter before his arrival at Cambridge by choosing Joseph Reed of Philadelphia as his secretary, but he did not neglect Trumbull and Tudor. On 10 July GW recommended to Congress that Trumbull, who had been commissary general of the Connecticut forces since April, be made Continental commissary general, and Congress appointed him on 19 July. See GW to Hancock, 10–11 July 1775, Document II. Letter Sent, n.12, and General Orders, 31 July 1775, n.1. On 14 July Tudor was offered the position of Continental judge advocate general, which he eagerly accepted. See GW to Hancock, 21 July 1775 (first letter), n.8, and General Orders, 30 July 1775, n.1.

5. Jonathan Williams Austin (1751–1779), a Chelmsford youth who had clerked in Adams's law office with William Tudor, was a major in Col. Paul Dudley Sargent's Massachusetts regiment outside Boston. As a student at Harvard College in 1768, Austin instigated a rebellion of his fellow students against the tutors and their regulations, and only after several prominent men intervened on his behalf were the college authorities persuaded to let Austin continue his studies and graduate the following year. Austin was not promoted in the Continental army despite steady support from Adams. On 5 Nov. 1776 he disgraced himself by burning the courthouse and about sixteen dwellings at White Plains, N.Y., contrary to general orders. At his court-martial he tried to excuse himself on the grounds of drunkenness, but he was found guilty and was dishonorably discharged from the service.

6. William Smith, Jr. (1746–1787), of Lincoln, Abigail Adams's only brother, commanded a company of minutemen at the Battle of Concord on 19 April 1775 and served the remainder of the year as a captain in Col. John Nixon's Massachusetts regiment stationed outside Boston. His only subsequent military activity occurred in 1777 when he served briefly as a captain of marines aboard a privateer that was captured by the British. Dull-witted and undependable, Smith failed to satisfy his family's high expectations for him as a scholar and businessman.

To Burwell Bassett

Dear Sir, Philadelphia, June 19th 1775.

I am now Imbarkd on a tempestuous Ocean from whence, perhaps, no friendly harbour is to be found. I have been called upon by the unanimous Voice of the Colonies to the Command of the Continental Army—It is an honour I by no means aspired to—It is an honour I wished to avoid, as well from an unwillingness to quit the peaceful enjoyment of my Family as from a thorough conviction of my own Incapacity & want of experience in the conduct of so momentous a concern—but the partiallity of the Congress added to some political motives, left me without a choice—May God grant therefore that my acceptance of it may be attended with some good to the common cause & without Injury (from want of knowledge) to my own reputation—I can answer but for three things, a firm belief of the justice of our Cause—close attention in the prosecution of it—and the strictest Integrety—If these cannot supply the places of Ability & Experience, the cause will suffer, & more than probable my character along with it, as reputation derives it principal support from success—but it will be rememberd I hope that no desire, or insinuation of mine, placed me in this situation. I shall not be deprivd therefore of a comfort in the worst event if I retain a consciousness of having acted to the best of my judgment.

I am at liberty to tell you that the Congress in Committee (which will, I daresay, be agreed to when reported) have consented to a Continental Currency, and have ordered two Million of Dollars to be struck for payment of the Troops, and other expences arising from our defence—as also that 15,000 Men are voted as a Continental Army, which will I daresay be augmented as more Troops are Imbark'd & Imbarking for America than was expected at the time of passing that Vote.[1] As to other Articles of Intelligence I must refer you to the Gazettes as the Printers pick up every thing that is stirring in that way. The other Officers in the higher departments are not yet fixed—therefore I cannot give you their names.[2] I set out to morrow for Boston where I shall always be glad to hear from you;[3] my best wishes attend Mrs Bassett—Mrs Dandridge[4] & all our Relations and friends—In great haste, as I have many Letters to write and other business to do I remain with the sincerest regard Dr Sir Yr Most Obedt & Affecte Hble Servt

Go: Washington

P.S. I must Intreat you & Mrs Bassett, if possible, to visit at Mt Vernon as also my Wife's other friends—I could wish you to take her down, as I have no expectations of returning till Winter & feel great uneasiness at her lonesome Situation[5]—I have sent my Chariot & Horses back.[6]

ALS, ViMtV.

Burwell Bassett (1734–1793) was married to Martha Washington's sister, Anna Maria Dandridge Bassett (1739–1777). The Bassetts lived at Eltham in New Kent County, Va., where GW and Mrs. Washington visited often during the 1760s and early 1770s, usually in conjunction with their trips to Williamsburg, some twenty miles southeast of Eltham. Burwell Bassett represented his county in the Virginia House of Burgesses from 1762 to 1775 and in the first four Virginia conventions between 1774 and 1776.

1. During this period the Continental Congress met on most days as a committee of the whole. No official records were kept of those meetings, but the letters of some of the delegates indicate that it was probably 14 June when the committee of the whole approved a Continental army of 15,000 men (10,000 in Massachusetts and 5,000 in New York) and the following day when it voted to issue up to two million dollars in bills of credit for the defense of America (Virginia Delegate to Unknown, 14 June 1775, Edmund Pendleton to Joseph Chew, 15 June 1775, in Smith, *Letters of Delegates,* 1:486–87, 488–91). The currency resolution was reported to the floor of Congress on 22 June and was formally approved with little or no change (*JCC,* 2:103; Instructions from the Continental Congress, 22 June 1775). The other resolution, however, did not reach the floor. Reports of the arrival of British reinforcements at Boston and the difficulty of determining the exact size of the enemy's force apparently persuaded the delegates to empower GW to set the Continental army's strength at an appropriate level not exceeding double that of the enemy. See the second instruction in Instructions from the Continental Congress, 22 June 1775. The injunction to keep the proceedings of Congress secret was specifically lifted with regard to its decisions on the army, the currency, and GW's appointment as commander in chief so that the delegates could write home about these important matters. This news was not supposed to appear in the newspapers, however.

2. Congress today finished the task of choosing the major generals but did not select the brigadier generals until 22 June. See GW to Officers of the Five Virginia Independent Companies, 20 June 1775, n.4.

3. GW did not depart for the American camp at Cambridge until 23 June.

4. Frances Jones Dandridge (1710–1785), Martha Washington's mother, lived at Chestnut Grove in New Kent County, Va., about six miles west of Eltham.

5. The Bassetts went to Mount Vernon in late August, and on 17 Oct. Mrs. Washington set out for a visit to Eltham (Burwell Bassett to GW, 30 Aug. 1775; Lund Washington to GW, 22 Oct. 1775).

6. The chariot and horses apparently left Philadelphia for Mount Vernon on the morning of 16 June, for GW paid to have his horses kept in the city only through 15 June (Cash Memorandum for 3 May 1775 to 22 Dec. 1784, DLC:GW). During the next few days, he purchased five new horses costing £239 in Pennsylvania currency and a light phaeton for £55 Pennsylvania currency. These items were the first ones that he charged to the Continental Congress in his expense account (DNA: RG 56, General Records—Treasury Department).

To John Parke Custis

Dear Jack, Philadelphia June 19th 1775.

I have been called upon by the unanimous voice of the Colonies to take the command of the Continental Army—It is an honour I neither sought after, or was by any means fond of accepting, from a consciousness of my own inexperience, and inability to discharge the duties of so important a Trust. However, as the partiallity of the Congress have placed me in this distinguished point of view, I can make them no other return but what will flow from close attention, and an upright Intention. for the rest I can say nothing—my great concern upon this occasion, is the thoughts of leaving your Mother under the uneasiness which I know this affair will throw her into; I therefore hope, expect, & indeed have no doubt, of your using every means in your power to keep up her Spirits, by doing every thing in your power, to promote her quiet—I have I must confess very uneasy feelings on her acct, but as it has been a kind of unavoidable necessity which has led me into this appointment, I shall more readily hope, that success will attend it, & crown our Meetings with happiness.

At any time, I hope it is unnecessary for me to say, that I am always pleased with yours & Nelly's abidance at Mount Vernon, much less upon this occasion, when I think it absolutely necessary for the peace & satisfaction of your Mother; a consideration which I have no doubt will have due weight with you both, & require no arguments to inforce.[1]

As the publick Gazettes will convey every article of Intelligence that I could communicate in this Letter, I shall not repeat them, but with love to Nelly, & sincere regard for yourself I remain Yr Most Affecte

Go: Washington

P.S. Since writing the foregoing I have receiv'd your Letter of the 15th Instt—I am obliged to you for the Intelligence therein containd—and am glad you directed about the Tobacco, for I had really forgot it. You must now take upon yourself the entire management of your own Estate, it will no longer be in my power to assist you, nor is there any occasion for it as you have never discover'd a disposition to put it to a bad use.[2]

The Congress, for I am at liberty to say as much, are about to strike two Million of Dollars as a Continental Currency, for the support of the War as Great Britain seems determined to force us into, and there will be at least 15,000 rais'd as a Continental Army[3]—as I am exceedingly hurried I can add no more at present than that I am. &ca

G.W——n

ALS, ViHi.

John Parke Custis (1754–1781), called Jack or Jacky by his relatives and friends, was Martha Washington's son by her first marriage and the principal heir to the large Custis estate. GW became Jack's guardian and the administrator of the Custis estate shortly after he married Martha Washington in January 1759.

1. John Parke Custis married Eleanor (Nelly) Calvert (1754–1811) in February 1774. For two or three years after their marriage, the young couple apparently lived alternately at Mount Vernon and Mount Airy, the home of Nelly's parents in Prince Georges County, Maryland.

2. John Parke Custis's letter of 15 June 1775 has not been found. The tobacco mentioned was probably grown on the Custis lands on the Pamunkey and York rivers and on the Eastern Shore of Virginia. Arrangements had to be made each year for shipping the Custis crop to England to be sold. Jack, who did not reach the age of 21 until November of this year, apparently did assume immediate responsibility for running his plantations, but final settlement of GW's guardianship accounts and the transfer of Jack's bonds was not made until the following year (GW to George Mason, 10 May 1776; GW to Lund Washington, 10 May 1776). Jack proved to be a poor businessman. By the time of his death at the age of 27, the value of the Custis estate was much diminished and its affairs were in great disorder.

3. For a discussion of these resolutions, see GW to Burwell Bassett, 19 June 1775, n.1.

To the Officers of Five Virginia Independent Companies

Gentlemen Philadelphia June 20. 1775

I am now about to bid adieu to the Companies under your respective commands, at least for a while—I have launched into a wide & extensive field, too boundless for my abilities, & far, very far beyond my experience—I am called by the unanimous voice of the Colonies to the command of the Continental army: an honour I did not aspire to—an honor I was sollicitous to avoid upon full conviction of my inadequacy to the importance of the service; the partiallity of the Congress however, assisted by a political motive, rendered my reasons unavailing & I shall, to morrow, set out for the camp near Boston[1]—I have only to beg of you therefore (before I go—especially as you did me the honor to place your Companies under my directions, and know not how soon you may be called upon in Virginia)[2] for an exertion of your military skill, by no means to relax in the discipline of your Respective companies.

I am at liberty to inform you Gentlemen, That the Congress in a Committee, (which will, I dare say be agreed to when reported) have consented to a Continental currency—Ordered Two millions of Dollars to be struck & Voted 15,000 men; Which number I am Inclined to think will be augmented, as more Troops have embarked & are embarking for America, than were expected at the time of passing that Vote.[3]

The Arrangement of Officers in the higher departments of the army is not yet fixed, ultimately, but I beleive they will stand thus; Genl Ward, Genl Lee, Genl Putnam, & Genl Scyler—Major Genls—The Brigadier Genls are not yet proposed—Major Gates Adjutant Genl[4]—For other articles of Intelligence, the Gazettes will furnish you with them more precisely than I can, as the printers let no news pass by them—The Chief end of my writing to you at this time being, to Recommend a diligent attention to the disciplining of your Companies, & Seeing that they are well provided with ammunition—I shall not Enlarge as I am very much hurried with one thing and another in consequence of my appointment—I shall only add therefore that I am with sincere regard & esteem Gentlemen Your Most Obedt & Hble servant

Go: Washington

P.S. you will, I am persuaded, excuse my addressing a joint Letter to you, as I had it not in my power to write seperate ones, & could not think of departing without affording you this Testimonial of my regard. Yrs

Copy, in Robert Hanson Harrison's writing, Vi. The cover is addressed "To The Independant Companies of Fairfax—Prince William—Fauquier—Spotsylvania & Richmond." Robert Hanson Harrison, who later became GW's secretary, was a subaltern in the Fairfax Independent Company. GW's original letter apparently was delivered to the Fairfax officers, who had copies made and sent to the other four companies (Officers of the Fairfax Independent Company to GW, 8 July 1775). The first paragraph of GW's letter was printed in the supplement to Alexander Purdie's *Virginia Gazette* (Williamsburg), 14 July 1775.

Independent companies of gentlemen volunteers were organized in many Virginia counties during the latter part of 1774 and in early 1775. By choosing GW as field commander, these five independent companies provided for the possibility of acting together if they were called out. They never took the field, although it seemed for a while in late April that they might march to Williamsburg to resist Governor Dunmore's seizure of the colony's principal powder supply. Rumors also circulated of a march to Boston. The independent companies were superseded in August 1775, when the third Virginia convention established a new and more comprehensive military system to defend the colony. See Burwell Bassett to GW, 30 Aug. 1775. The Richmond Independent Company was organized in the Northern Neck county of that name, not in the town of Richmond.

1. GW left Philadelphia on 23 June.

2. In the version of this paragraph that appears in Purdie's *Virginia Gazette*, 14 July 1775, the parentheses are better placed: one before the word "especially" and the other after the word "skill."

3. For a discussion of these resolutions, see GW to Burwell Bassett, 19 June 1775, n.1.

4. On 17 June Congress made Artemas Ward (1727–1800) of Massachusetts first major general and Charles Lee (1731–1782), a British half-pay officer, second major general. Two days later Philip Schuyler (1733–1804) of New York became the third major general and Israel Putnam (1718–1790) of Connecticut, the fourth one. The eight brigadier generals for the Continental line were not chosen until 22 June. Horatio Gates (c.1728–1806), a retired British army major living in Virginia, was appointed adjutant general with the rank of brigadier general on 17 June. As a member of GW's staff, Gates was not included among the line brigadiers (*JCC*, 2:97, 103). Although Ward's military skill was questioned even by some of his fellow New Englanders, it was thought necessary to appoint him second in command to GW because he had commanded the army outside Boston since the beginning of the siege and was well liked by most of the New England troops. The fact that Lee was not a native American raised dark suspicions about him in the minds of some delegates, but his considerable military experience in Europe and GW's strong desire to be assisted by him induced Congress to make the appointment. Lee, who was in Philadelphia at this time, delayed accepting his commission until Congress on 19 June passed a resolution promising to indemnify him for any loss of his English property resulting from his service in the Continental army (*JCC*, 2:98–99). Schuyler was "appointed Majr Genll in [New] York department to Sweeten, Add to, & keep up the spirit in that Province," Connecticut delegate Eliphalet Dyer wrote to Joseph Trumbull on 20 June (Smith, *Letters of Delegates*, 1:521–22). The appointment of Putnam, however, did not please everyone in Connecticut, where two other officers outranked him in that

colony's establishment. See GW to Hancock, 10–11 July 1775, Document II. Letter Sent, n.20, and Jonathan Trumbull, Sr., to GW, 13 July 1775 (second letter).

To John Augustine Washington

Dear Brother, Philadelphia June 20th 1775.

I am now to bid adieu to you, & to every kind of domestick ease, for a while. I am Imbarked on a wide Ocean, boundless in its prospect & from whence, perhaps, no safe harbour is to be found[.] I have been called upon by the unanimous Voice of the Colonies to take the Command of the Continental Army—an honour I neither sought after, nor desired, as I am thoroughly convinced; that it requires greater Abilities, and much more experience, than I am Master of, to conduct a business so extensive in its nature, and arduous in the execution, but the partiallity of the Congress, joind to a political motive, really left me without a Choice; and I am now Commissioned a Generl & Commander in Chief of all the Forces now raisd, or to be raisd, for the defence of the United Colonies—That I may discharg[e] the Trust to the Satisfaction of my Imployers, is my first wish—that I shall aim to do it, there remains as little doubt of—how far I may succeed is another point—but this I am sure of, that in the worse event, I shall have the consolation of knowing (if I act to the best of my judgment) that the blame ought to lodge upon the appointers, not the appointed, as it was by no means a thing of my own seeking, or proceeding from any hint of my friends.

I am at liberty to inform you, that the Congress, in a Committee (which will I dare say be agreed to when reported) have converted to a Continental Currency—have ordered two Million of Dollars to be struck for payment of the Troops &ca and have voted 15,000 Men as a Continental Army—which number will be augmented, as the strength of the British Troops will be greater than was expected at the time of passing that vote.[1] Genl Ward—Genl Lee—Genl Schuyler—and Genl Putnam—are appointed Major Genls under me—the Brigadier Genls are not yet appointed. Majr Gates Adjutant Genl—I expect to set out to morrow for Boston[2] & hope to be joind there in a little time by Ten Companies of Rifle men from this Provence, Maryland, & Virginia[3]—for other Articles of Intelligence, I shall refer you to the Papers, as the Printers are diligent in collecting every thing that is stirring.

I shall hope that my Friends will visit, & endeavour to keep up the Spirits of my Wife as much as they can, as my departure will, I know, be a cutting stroke upon her; and on this acct alone, I have many very disagreeable Sensations—I hope you & my Sister,[4] (although the distance is great) will find as much leisure this Summer, as to spend a little time at Mt Vernon[.] My sincere regards attend you both as also the little ones and I am Dr Sir Yr most Affecte Brother

Go: Washington

ALS, DLC:GW.

GW's brother John Augustine Washington (1736–1787) lived at Bushfield in Westmoreland County, Virginia. At this time he was a member of the Westmoreland County committee of safety and apparently an officer in the Westmoreland independent company. He represented his county at the third Virginia convention during the summer of 1775 and at the fourth Virginia convention the following winter.

1. For a discussion of these resolutions, see GW to Burwell Bassett, 19 June 1775, n.1.

2. GW left Philadelphia on 23 June.

3. On 14 June Congress authorized the raising of six companies of riflemen in Pennsylvania, two in Maryland, and two in Virginia. Two additional Pennsylvania rifle companies were approved on 22 June. Each company was to consist of 4 officers, 4 sergeants, 4 corporals, a drummer or trumpeter, and 68 privates (*JCC*, 2:89, 104). "These are said," John Adams wrote to Elbridge Gerry on 18 June 1775, "to be all exquisite marksmen, and by means of the excellence of their firelocks, as well as their skill in the use of them, to send sure destruction to great distances" (Taylor, *Papers of John Adams*, 3:25–27). The riflemen, who were to be employed as light infantry, were directed to join the army besieging Boston as soon as possible. The first rifle companies arrived in late July and the remainder in August (GW to Schuyler, 28 July 1775).

4. GW is referring to his sister-in-law, John Augustine Washington's wife, Hannah Bushrod Washington.

Instructions from the Continental Congress

Philadelphia June 22d 1775

In Congress

This Congress having appointed you to be General & Commander in chief of the army of the United Colonies and of all the forces raised or to be raised by them and of all others who shall voluntarily offer their service and join the said army for the defence of American liberty and for repelling every hostile invasion thereof,[1] you are to repair with all expedition to the colony of Massachusetts-bay and take charge of the army of the United Colonies.

For your better direction

First, You are to make a return to us, as soon as possible of all forces, which you shall have under your command, together with their military stores and provisions; and also as exact an account as you can obtain of the forces, which compose the British army in America.

Secondly, You are not to disband any of the men you find raised until further direction from this Congress; and if you shall think their numbers not adequate to the purpose of security, you may recruit them to a number you shall think sufficient not exceeding double that of the enemy.

Thirdly, In all cases of vacancy occasioned by death or a removal of a Colonel or other inferior officer, you are by Brevet or Warrant under your seal to appoint another person to fill up such vacancy, until it shall be otherwise ordered by the provincial Convention or Assembly of the colony, from whence the troops, in which such vacancy happen, shall direct otherwise.[2]

Fourthly, You are to victual at the continental expence all such volunteers as have joined, or shall join the united army.

Fifthly, You shall take every method in your power, consistent with prudence, to destroy or make prisoners of all persons, who now are, or who hereafter shall appear in arms against the good people of the United Colonies.

Sixthly, And whereas all particulars cannot be foreseen, nor positive instructions for such emergencies so beforehand given, but that many things must be left to your prudent and discreet management, as occurrences may arise upon the place or from time to time fall out; You are, therefore, upon all such accidents or any occasion, that may happen, to use your best circumspection and (advising with your council of war) to order and dispose of the said army under your command, as may be most advantageous for the obtaining the end, for which these forces have been raised, making it your special care, in discharge of the great trust committed unto you that the liberties of America receive no detriment.

By Order of Congress,
John Hancock President

In addition to yr Instructions it is Resolved by Congress, That the troops including the volunteers be furnished with camp Equipage & blankets if necessary at the continental expence.

That the Officers now in the army receive their commissions from the Genl & commander in chief.

That a Sum not exceeding two Millions of Spanish milled dollars be emitted by the Congress in bills of Credit for the defence of America.[3]

Chas Thomson Secy
By Order of Congress
John Hancock President

DS, CSmH; copy, DNA:PCC, item 1; copy, DNA:PCC, item 3; LB, NN: Schuyler Papers; LB, NHi: George and Martha Washington Papers. The document in the Huntington Library is apparently the one that GW received, because it is endorsed in his writing. The text is in Charles Thomson's writing, except for the words "Philadelphia June 22d 1775" and "By Order of Congress" (appearing twice), which are in John Hancock's writing. Each man signed his own name.

The instructions were drafted by the committee appointed on 16 June to draw up GW's commission: Richard Henry Lee, Edward Rutledge, and John Adams. On 20 June the committee reported the instructions to Congress, which promptly approved them. The next day "Mr. [Patrick] Henry informed the Congress, that the general had put into his hand sundry queries, to which he desired the Congress would give an answer." GW's queries were referred to a committee composed of Silas Deane, Patrick Henry, John Rutledge, Samuel Adams, and Richard Henry Lee, who reported to Congress on 22 June. In apparent response to their report, Congress that same day passed six resolutions concerning the army. Among them were the three resolutions which appear at the bottom of GW's instructions (*JCC*, 2:101–4).

1. This wording was taken from GW's commission of 19 June 1775.

2. Although Congress appointed all general officers for the Continental army, the field and company grade officers for the regiments and other units

were usually appointed by the legislative body of the colony in which they were raised. For an example of GW's use of his brevetting power, see the draft of Christopher Greene's brevet commission as a lieutenant colonel dated 12 Sept. 1775 in DLC:GW.

3. For a discussion of this resolution, see GW to Burwell Bassett, 19 June 1775, n.1.

From Brigadier General Horatio Gates

Dear General Travellers-Rest 22th June 1775

Last night I was Honourd by the receipt of your Obliging Letter of 17th Instant,[1] I shall Obey your Commands with all possible Expedition, & hope to be in philadelphia Thursday next, & wish earnestly to find you there.[2] I must take the Liberty to entreat it of you, not to leave the Congress, until you are provided not only with all the Powers, but all the Means, their Power can bestow, if it is indispensibly necessary you should leave philadelphia before I get there, I hope to find with Colonel Harrison,[3] your possitive, & particular Commands, in regard to any business you may leave unsettled behind you—the request for the Riffle Men was well received in this province, and in Maryland, Major Stevenson Commands one of the Companys from hence, & I believe Cap. Morgan the other. both excellent for the Service, Col. Creasup told me on Monday morning that his Son, had Eighty Riffle Men ready to March, those go for one of the Companys from Maryland.[4] Immediately upon the Arrival of your Express, I dispatch'd your packets to your Brother, & Col: Stephen. if their Answers don't come in half an hour, I will bring them with me.[5]

My Gratefull Thanks are most Respectfully due to the Congress, for the very Handsome manner in which they conferred their Commission.

I will not intrude more upon that Time, which is now so precious to you, only to assure you I will not lose a moment in paying you my personal attendance, with the greatest respect for your Charactor, & the sincerest attachment to your person, I am Dear General Your most Faithfull, & Obedient Humble Servant,

Horatio Gates

ALS, DLC:GW.

Horatio Gates (c.1728–1806), the newly appointed adjutant general of the Continental army, had known GW since the ill-fated Braddock expedition in 1755. An Englishman by birth, Gates entered the British army at an early age and served in America as a captain throughout most of the French and Indian War. In 1762 he was promoted to major, but during the postwar period he was frustrated in his attempts to gain further advancement. He sold his commission in 1769, and in 1772 he moved his family from England to America. The following year he bought a plantation in the lower Shenandoah Valley of Virginia. His home, Traveller's Rest, stands near present-day Kearneysville, West Virginia. Gates visited at Mount Vernon 2–3 May 1775, just before GW left to attend the Continental Congress (*Diaries*, 3:325). Gates served as GW's adjutant general until May 1776, when he was promoted to the rank of major general and was given a field command. He commanded the American forces in the Saratoga victory of 1777 but suffered a humiliating defeat at Camden, S.C., in 1780.

1. Letter not found.

2. Gates apparently did arrive in Philadelphia on Thursday, 29 June. See Hancock to GW, 28 June 1775, and Richard Henry Lee to GW, 29 June 1775, source note. Gates joined GW at Cambridge by 9 July.

3. Benjamin Harrison (c.1726–1791) of Charles City County, Va., was a delegate to the Continental Congress.

4. Hugh Stephenson (d. 1776) of Berkeley County, Va. (now W.Va.), the county in which Gates lived, raised one of the two Virginia rifle companies authorized by Congress. The other company was raised in neighboring Frederick County, Va., by Daniel Morgan (c.1735–1802), the hard-driving frontiersman who later distinguished himself at Quebec and Saratoga and in 1780 became a brigadier general in the Continental army. The two Maryland rifle companies were raised in Frederick County, Md., by Michael Cresap (1742–1775), youngest son of Thomas Cresap (c.1694–1790) of Oldtown, Md., and Thomas Price (1732–1795) of the town of Frederick. The officers for these companies were selected by their respective county committees of safety. GW had long been a friend of the Stephenson family and knew well both Cresaps, with whom he was currently disputing claims to western lands. See GW to Michael Cresap, 26 Sept. 1773, and GW to Thomas Cresap, 7 Feb. 1775. GW may have met Daniel Morgan as early as 1755 when Morgan served as a wagoner on the Braddock expedition or the following year when he was a member of John Ashby's ranger company.

All four rifle companies were quickly raised. "Volunteers presented themselves from every direction," one of Stephenson's men remembered some years later; "none were received but young men of Character, and of sufficient property to Clothe themselves completely, find their own arms, and accoutrements, that is, an approved Rifle, handsome shot pouch, and powderhorn, blanket, knapsack, with such decent clothing as should be prescribed, but which was at first ordered to be only a Hunting shirt and pantaloons, fringed on every edge, and in various ways" (Danske Dandridge, *Historic Shepherdstown* [Charlottesville, 1910], 79). More riflemen were recruited than were authorized by Congress. Morgan raised 96 officers and men, Stephenson 95, and Price 85. The final strength of Cresap's company is not known. Difficulty in obtaining good rifles delayed the departure of the companies for several weeks. Morgan marched first, crossing the Potomac with his men on 15 July, and by a series of forced marches, he reached the American camp at Cambridge on 6 August. Stephenson's and Price's companies followed close behind Morgan. Stephenson arrived at Cambridge on 11 Aug., and Price about the same date. Cresap's company was at Watertown, Mass., on 20 Aug. and apparently reached Cambridge soon afterwards.

5. Gates must have meant to say that if the answers did come within half an hour, he would bring them with him. GW's brother Samuel Washington (1734–1781) and Adam Stephen (c.1718–1791), who had been GW's second in command in the Virginia Regiment during the French and Indian War, both lived in Berkeley County within a few miles of Traveller's Rest. On this day Samuel Washington wrote to Gates from his house, Harewood: "Your favr I Recd last night after I was in Bed. I now inclose you two letters wch shall be much Obliged to you to take Charge of. would have waited on you my self, but am by Appointmt to meet some People on business this Evening[.] as my Brother has been Prevail'd on to take the Command of the Continental Army I am happy in your being with him in the Capacity you & he mentions. as your Greater Experience will Assist him in the Arduous business. God Grant you may both Return safe to yr families. Crowned with Laurels" (James Gregory and Thomas Dunnings, eds., "The Horatio Gates Papers, 1726–1828" [Glen Rock, N.J., 1978, Microfilm]). No correspondence between GW and his brother Samuel or between GW and Adam Stephen has been found for this period.

Adam Stephen represented Berkeley County at the second Virginia convention in the spring of 1775 and was chairman of the Berkeley County committee of safety and commander of the county's militia. Appointed a colonel in the Continental army in February 1776, Stephen was promoted to brigadier general in September 1776 and major general in February 1777, but he was dismissed from the service in November 1777 for bad behavior. Samuel Washington, troubled by poor health and financial difficulties, played no role in the political or military affairs of the Revolution outside of Berkeley County.

From the Massachusetts Delegates

Sir Phyladelphia June 22. 1775

In Complyance with your Request We have considered of what you proposed to us, and are obliged to give you our Sentiments, very briefly, and in great Haste.

In general, Sir, there will be three Committees, either of a Congress, or of an House of Representatives, which are and will be composed of our best Men; Such, whose Judgment and

Integrity, may be most rely'd on; the Committee on the State of the Province, the Committee of Safety, and the Committee of Supplies.

But least this Should be too general, We beg leave to mention particularly Messrs Bowdoin, Sever, Dexter, Greenleaf, Darby, Pitts, Otis of the late Council—Hon. John Winthrop Esq. L.L.D. Joseph Hawley Esqr. of Northampton, James Warren Esqr. of Plymouth Coll Palmer of Braintree, Coll Orne and Elbridge Gerry Esqr. of Marblehead, Dr Warren, Dr Church Mr John Pitts all of Boston, Dr Langdon President of Harvard Colledge, and Dr Chauncey and Dr Cooper of Boston. Coll Forster of Brookfield.[1]

The Advice and Recommendations of these Gentlemen, and of Some others whom they may introduce to your Acquaintance may be depended on.

With great Sincerity, We wish you, an agreable Journey and a glorious Campaign; and are with much Esteem and Respect, Sir, your most obedient Servants.

Samuel Adams John Hancock
John Adams Thomas Cushing
Robt Treat Paine

LS, in John Adams's writing, DLC:GW. John Hancock addressed the cover, and each delegate signed his name to the letter. See John Adams to GW, 19 or 20 June 1775, source note, for a comparison of that letter and this one.

Three of the Massachusetts delegates were Bostonians: John Hancock, Samuel Adams (1722–1803), and Thomas Cushing (1725–1788). John Adams lived in Braintree and Robert Treat Paine in Taunton. Samuel Adams wrote to James Warren on this date: "Our patriotick General Washington will deliver this Letter to you. The Massachusetts Delegates have joyntly given to him a List of the Names of certain Gentlemen in whom he may place the greatest Confidence. Among these you are one. We have assurd him that he may rely upon such others as you may recommend to him" (Harry Alonzo Cushing, ed., *The Writings of Samuel Adams*, 4 vols. [New York and London, 1904–8], 3:219). Adams wrote a similar letter to Elbridge Gerry on this date (ibid., 218–19), and on 21 June Thomas Cushing wrote a letter to James Bowdoin introducing GW (Smith, *Letters of Delegates*, 1:530).

1. All but nine of the names listed here appear in John Adams's letter to GW of 19 or 20 June 1775 and are identified there. Former councillors Benjamin Greenleaf (1732–1799) of Newburyport and James Otis, Sr. (1702–1778), of Barnstable were elected to the reestablished Massachusetts council on 21 July 1775. Otis, father of the famous political pamphleteer James Otis, Jr. (1725–1783), served for a time as president of the new council. Richard

Derby, Jr. (1712–1783), of Salem was elected to the old council in May 1774, but he did not become a member of the new one until May 1776. Both of the two militia colonels, Azor Orne (1731–1796) and Jedediah Foster (1726–1779), were elected councillors on 21 July 1775. Orne declined to sit on the council, but he served as a member of the committee of safety. John Pitts (1737–1815), son of former councillor James Pitts, was on the committee of supplies and had served on the committee on the state of the province before it ceased to exist at the end of May 1775. Samuel Langdon (1723–1797), Charles Chauncy (1705–1787), and Samuel Cooper (1725–1783) were Congregational clergymen with honorary doctorates from Scottish universities, the first two from Aberdeen, and Cooper from Edinburgh. Langdon was pastor of a church in Portsmouth, N.H., until October 1774, when he became president of Harvard College. He served as chaplain to the American troops at Cambridge from 29 April to 30 Oct. 1775. Chauncy, pastor of the First Church of Boston from 1727 to 1787, left Boston in May 1775 and lived with his wife at Medfield during the British occupation of the city. Cooper, pastor at Boston's Brattle Street Church from 1746 to 1783, fled Boston with his wife on 8 April 1775 after learning that the British authorities intended to arrest him for his outspoken opposition to the royal government. He stayed for a time at Weston and then moved to Waltham before returning to Boston when the British evacuated the city in March 1776.

To Martha Washington

My dearest, Phila. June 23d 1775.

As I am within a few Minutes of leaving this City, I could not think of departing from it without dropping you a line; especially as I do not know whether it may be in my power to write again till I get to the Camp at Boston—I go fully trusting in that Providence, which has been more bountiful to me than I deserve, & in full confidence of a happy meeting with you sometime in the Fall—I have not time to add more, as I am surrounded with Company to take leave of me—I retain an unalterable affection for you, which neither time or distance can change, my best love to Jack & Nelly, & regard for the rest of the Family concludes me with the utmost truth & sincerety Yr entire

Go: Washington

ALS, ViMtV.

GW set out for the American camp at Cambridge early this morning. With him went major generals Charles Lee and Philip Schuyler and two young Philadelphians: Maj. Thomas Mifflin, whom GW had chosen as an aide-de-camp, and Lt. Col. Joseph Reed, who was to become GW's secretary. "The Three Generals were all mounted, on Horse back," John Adams wrote on this date to his wife Abigail. "All the Delegates from the Massachusetts with their Servants, and Carriages attended. Many others of the Delegates, from the Congress—a large Troop of Light Horse, in their Uniforms. Many Officers of Militia besides in theirs. Musick playing &c. &c." (L. H. Butterfield et al., eds., *Adams Family Correspondence* [Cambridge, Mass., 1963—], 1:226–27). The delegates and the Philadelphia militia officers accompanied GW's party only a few miles out of the city and then turned back. The Philadelphia Light Horse, commanded by Capt. Abraham Markoe, continued on with GW to New York.

From Valentine Crawford

Dear Sir Jacobs Creek [Pa.] June 24th 1775

I [am] verey Sorrey to Enform you I Recved a Letter from Mr Cleaveland of the 7th of June wherein he Seems to be in a good dale of destress[.] five of the Sarvents has Run a way and plagued him a good dale[.] the[y] got to the Indens towns Butt by the Esesten [assistance] of one Mr duncan a trador he has got them again and he has Sent three of them up By a Man he had hired with a Letter to My Brother willim or My Selfe to Sell them for you but the man Sold them him Selfe Som where about wheeling on his way up and Never brought them to us for £20 pen. Currency and give one years Credit which wase verey Low and he did Not Recve one Shilling which wase Contraray to Cleavelands orders to him as he wase to Rais Som Cash by the Sails for to purches provesins and I think it would be advisable if the Men they are Sold tow is Nott good to take them from them and Sell them again but the Man Shant be Stopt for want of Money for I will furnish him and will Esest Mr Simson in geting Started as quick as posable with his Canew and previsons[.] Mr Cleaveland Left Som Corn att Mr Simsons when he went down and I will get him Som Flower to Load his Canew[.] Mr Cleaveland Sank a Canew a going down and Lost five or Six Caske of Corn and Severell other things and James Mccarmick and Charls Morgen found a bag of ⟨Clo⟩ths and Severell other things a few day after as ⟨they⟩ wase a going [down] the River deliverd them to Mr Cleaveland again as the[y] New they belong to His Company By Som papers they found in the Bundle[.] Cleaveland dose Not Mention of geting Eney but the three Sarvent he Sent to be Sold but Mr duncan told Me yesterday att fort don More that he had got the hole five that Run a way[.][1] docter Crakes Manager has had very Bad Luck for in the Canew that wase Sunk he Los⟨t⟩ all his papers and wase Much att a Loss to find his Land or att Least to find the Corner trees but I have Sent him all the plats and Instructions I had from the docter[.] Least a Letter I have wrote to him Should Miscarey you Can Enform him I hope to be down in Fairfax as Soon as Ever I Reap My harvest and will Setle all My acoumpt with you.[2]

we had Chose Cometees out here and are a Raiseng Independent Company and Regu[l]a⟨te⟩ Maters the best we Can but an unhappy Confusio⟨n⟩ hapend the other day[.] the pencelvanans Came to fort pitt and tuck Major Coneley a bout Mid Night with the Sheriff and a bout 20 men and Cared him as far ⟨as⟩ Legenier the verey Night Before we wase to have the [meeting] with the Indens and Severell of the pencelvania tradors by the Indens Story wase Indevering to put Ill in the Minds of the Indens But on Majr Coneley being taken the people of Shirtee Came in in a Companey and Sceised three of the pencla. Magestrats who where Concernd in taking of Coneley—George Willson Joseph Speer and dedreck Smith and Snt them in an old Leakey Boat down to Fort fincastle under a gard Butt our Court had Now hand in this Butt it wase done by a Mob or Sett of Coneleys frends that Lives on Shirtees Creek.

But there wase all the Members of our Cometee wrote a verey Sperited Litter to the Gentlmen of pen. Cometee to demand Coneley Back and all Signd it and Sent it with an axpress on the Recpt of which they amedently Sent Majr Coneley Back and things Seemes to be a Little Modreited and I bleve the Indens wonts Nothing but peace but it Seemd to Elarm verey Much to here our grate Man wase Stole and Indeed it Elarmed us all verey Much as Majr Coneley wase the Man that had done and transacted all the besness with them before Now other parson wase So able to Setle besness with them as him[3] So I hope you will Escuse the Lenth of My Letter and I am dr Sir your Most Hble Savet

Vale: Crawford

N.B. pleas to give my Complements to Mr Lund Washington and tell him his people is well and in a verey good wey to Make a good Crop of Corn.[4]

V.C.

ALS, DLC:GW.

Valentine Crawford (d. 1777) lived on Jacobs Creek in western Pennsylvania, several miles north of Stewart's Crossing on the Youghiogheny River (now the site of Connellsville, Pa.), where his brother William Crawford (1732–1782) had settled. Both men were deeply involved in GW's efforts to acquire large holdings of land west of the Allegheny Mountains. During the late 1760s and early 1770s, William Crawford surveyed a number of tracts for GW, including one on the Youghiogheny, one near Chartiers Creek, and several along the Kanawha and Ohio rivers. To preserve his titles to those Kanawha and Ohio lands, GW engaged Valentine Crawford in the spring of 1774 to take a party of workers down the Ohio and seat his tracts by building houses and cultivating fields as required by Virginia law (3 Hening 312–13). That expedition was canceled before it started because of the outbreak of Dunmore's War.

1. On 10 Jan. 1775 GW hired James Cleveland of Loudoun County, Va., to do what Valentine Crawford had been prevented from doing the previous year: lead an expedition down the Ohio to improve his Ohio and Kanawha lands. Cleveland reached GW's tract near the mouth of the Kanawha in late April, but his work went slowly. He described his difficulties, in particular the problem of the runaway indentured servants, to GW in letters of 12 and 21 May and 7 June 1775. The five runaways who tried to escape to the Shawnee town on the Muskingum River were caught, but one man ran off again before he could be brought back to Cleveland's camp. Cleveland did not think it worth the time to try to recapture him. Of the four servants who were returned, Cleveland considered three to be poor workers, and apparently they were the ones sold. The Indian trader who assisted Cleveland in recovering the runaways was David Duncan of Shippensburg, Pennsylvania. During the latter part of the Revolution, Duncan moved his home to western Pennsylvania and served as deputy quartermaster general at Fort Pitt. Fort Pitt was called Fort Dunmore by Virginians during 1774 and 1775 in honor of their royal governor, John Murray, fourth earl of Dunmore. Gilbert Simpson, Jr., with whom Cleveland left three barrels of corn, was GW's manager at Washington's Bottom, the tract of land that GW owned on the Youghiogheny River at the site of present-day Perryopolis, Pennsylvania. For Cleveland's account of the canoe that sank on the way down the Ohio, see Cleveland to GW, 12 May 1775. James McCormick (died c.1789) of Berkeley County, Va. (now W.Va.), served as a soldier under GW during the Fort Necessity campaign in 1754. Charles Morgan became GW's rent collector in western Pennsylvania in 1794.

2. Dr. James Craik (1730–1814) of Port Tobacco, Md., a close friend of GW, was granted several thousand acres of land on the Ohio and Kanawha rivers for his service as a surgeon during the Fort Necessity campaign. He was

appointed one of the Continental army's chief hospital physicians in October 1780 and became chief physician and surgeon of the army in March 1781.

3. Jurisdiction over the area around the Forks of the Ohio had long been contested between Virginia and Pennsylvania, and by 1775 the two colonies had established rival local governments in the region. Virginia included the disputed territory within the boundaries of its District of West Augusta, and in February 1775 a court for West Augusta was convened at Pittsburgh. Pennsylvania considered the area to be part of its Westmoreland County, whose court sat at Hannastown, about thirty miles east of Pittsburgh. Dr. John Connolly (c.1743–1813), a physician and land speculator, was Governor Dunmore's chief representative at Pittsburgh despite the fact that Connolly was a native Pennsylvanian. Appointed commandant of militia at Pittsburgh by Dunmore, Connolly took possession of the abandoned Fort Pitt in January 1774, renamed it Fort Dunmore, and summoned the local inhabitants to form a militia under his command. His actions greatly angered Pennsylvania's adherents in the area, and there ensued a series of arrests and counterarrests by Virginia and Pennsylvania officials, of which the ones mentioned in this letter were only the latest. On 22 June 1775 the sheriff of Westmoreland County, John Carnaghan, arrived at Pittsburgh with a force of men, including Westmoreland justice George Wilson (d. 1777) of Georges Creek, and freed James Cavet and Robert Hanna, two Westmoreland justices whom Connolly had held under arrest since February. At the same time Carnaghan arrested Connolly and took him to the house of Arthur St. Clair, a Westmoreland justice and future Continental general, who lived at Fort Ligonier, about forty-five miles east of Pittsburgh. In reprisal for Carnaghan's actions, a group of Connolly's supporters from Chartiers Creek southwest of Pittsburgh, led by Capt. George Gibson, seized George Wilson and two other Westmoreland justices, Joseph Spear and Devereaux Smith, both Indian traders residing at Pittsburgh. Those three prisoners were sent to Fort Fincastle at Wheeling, which a Virginia force commanded by William Crawford had built the year before.

The problems caused by these arrests were settled by the committees of safety for the two rival governments, both of which were chosen on 16 May 1775. The West Augusta committee included not only Virginia justices, such as William Crawford, but also two of the Pennsylvania justices who were seized in June, George Wilson and Devereaux Smith. John Connolly was not a member of the West Augusta committee, however. Because of his close ties to Governor Dunmore, he became a staunch Loyalist, and he was attempting at this time to organize support for the royal government on the western frontier. The West Augusta committee was particularly fearful that Connolly would use his considerable skills as an Indian negotiator to persuade the Indians living north of the Ohio to ally themselves with the king against his rebelling subjects, but they also found themselves in the embarrassing position of having to depend on Connolly to conduct a previously scheduled peace council with those Indians. At the conclusion of Dunmore's War in October 1774, Governor Dunmore promised the defeated Indians that their hostages would be returned and a final peace made at Pittsburgh the next spring. Connolly was preparing to negotiate this peace under the watchful eyes of the members of the West Augusta committee when he was suddenly carried off by the Pennsylvanians, leaving the assembled chiefs puzzled and the committee members frustrated in their desire to placate the Indians. To remedy the unfortunate turn of events, the West Augusta committee not only persuaded the Westmoreland committee to return Connolly but also secured the release of the three Pennsylvania justices, whose seizure it condemned as illegal. Connolly conferred with the Indian chiefs at Pittsburgh on 29 June, and between 3 and 6 July he concluded a peace that satisfied the West Augusta committee, even though the Shawnee were absent. During the next several months Connolly vigorously pursued a scheme for raising a Loyalist force west of the Alleghenies. In November 1775 American authorities arrested Connolly and eventually imprisoned him at Philadelphia. See William Cowley to GW, 12 Oct. 1775, and Lund Washington to GW, 3 Dec. 1775. The border dispute between Virginia and Pennsylvania was not settled until 1780.

4. William Crawford procured a tract of land near the Youghiogheny River for Lund Washington sometime before the fall of 1770 (*Diaries*, 2:290, 323).

To the Continental Congress

Gentlemen New York June [25] 1775

The Rain on Friday Afternoon & Saturday—the Advice of several Gentlemen of the Jerseys & this City, by no Means to cross Hudsons River at the Lower Ferry, and some other Circumstances, too trivial to mention,[1] prevented my Arrival at this Place untill the Afternoon of this Day.[2]

In the Morning, after giving General Schuyler such Orders as, from the Result of my Enquiry into Matters here, appear necessary, I shall set out on my Journey to the Camp at Boston; and shall proceed with all the Dispatch in my Power.[3] Powder is so essential an Article that I cannot help again repeating the Necessity of a Supply—The Camp at Boston, from the best Account I can get from thence, is but very poorly supplied—At this place they have scarce any—How they are provided in General Worster's Camp I have not been able yet to learn.[4]

Governor Tryon is arriv'd and General Schuyler directed to advise you of the Line of Conduct he moves in—I fear it will not be very favorable to the American Cause.[5] I have only to add that I am with great Respect & Regard Gentlemen, Your most Obedt & Oblid hble Serv.

L, in Thomas Mifflin's writing, DNA:PCC, item 152; LB, DLC:GW; copy, DNA:PCC, item 169; copy, NjMoNP; Varick transcript, DLC:GW. The cover of the letter is addressed in GW's writing. All copies of this letter are dated 24

June 1775. GW did not reach New York City until the afternoon of 25 June, however (see note 2). His letter of this day to John Hancock was also incorrectly dated.

1. The letter-book copy reads "& some other Occurrencies too trivial to mention (which happened on the Ro⟨ad⟩)."

2. GW's traveling party reached New Brunswick, N.J., on 24 June. From there Philip Schuyler wrote to Peter Van Brugh Livingston, president of the New York provincial congress, then sitting in New York City: "General Washington . . . proposes to be at Newark by nine to-morrow morning. The situation of the men of war at New-York, (we are informed,) is such as may make it necessary that some precaution should be taken in crossing Hudson's river; and he would take it as a favour if some gentlemen of your body would meet him to-morrow, at Newark, as the advice you may then give him, will determine whether he will continue his proposed route, or not" (*Journals of the Provincial Congress, Provincial Convention, Committee of Safety and Council of Safety of the State of New-York, 1775–1776–1777*, 2 vols. [Albany, 1842], 2:10–11, Microfilm Collection of Early State Records). Shortly after nine o'clock on the morning of 25 June, the provincial congress ordered Thomas Smith, Sloss Hobart, Gouverneur Morris, and Richard Montgomery to meet GW at Newark. The advice they gave him was sound. The lower Hudson River ferry, running between Paulus Hook (now Jersey City) and a wharf at the foot of Cortlandt Street in New York, was within a mile of the Battery, off which lay the British warship *Asia*, ready to protect the king's friends in the city with its sixty-four guns. GW crossed this afternoon on the upper ferry from Hoboken to Col. Leonard Lispenard's country estate some two miles north of the city (near the foot of present-day Laight Street), where he landed about four o'clock in the afternoon. Nine companies of uniformed New York militiamen and a host of local Patriot leaders greeted GW and his companions on the beach. According to Loyalist Thomas Jones of New York, they were then conducted "amidst the repeated shouts and huzzas of the seditious and rebellious multitude" to Lispenard's house, "where they dined, and towards evening were escorted to town, attended and conducted in the same tumultuous and ridiculous manner" (Thomas Jones, *History of New York during the Revolutionary War . . .*, ed. by Edward F. DeLancey, 2 vols. [New York, 1879], 1:55). A newspaper reported that the escorting throng included "a greater Number of the principal Inhabitants of this City, than ever appeared here on any Occasion before" (*New-York Gazette: and Weekly Mercury*, 26 June 1775), and a Moravian pastor noted in his diary that "at one Church the Minister was obliged to give over; for the People went out, when the General came, who was received with much ado" (Shewkirk's diary in Isaac Newton Phelps Stokes, *The Iconography of Manhattan Island*, 6 vols. [New York, 1915–28], 4:894). The procession ended on Broadway at Robert Hull's tavern, where GW probably lodged for the night.

3. GW's instructions to Philip Schuyler, dated 25 June 1775, are printed below. GW left New York City for Cambridge sometime after two-thirty in the afternoon on 26 June.

4. David Wooster (1711–1777), who was appointed a major general of the

Connecticut forces in April 1775 and a Continental brigadier general on 22 June, marched about this time from his camp at Greenwich, Conn., with approximately eighteen hundred Connecticut soldiers to assist in the defense of New York City. GW encountered Wooster and his men at New Rochelle, N.Y., on 27 June. Wooster camped on the outskirts of New York City the next day and remained near the city or on Long Island throughout the summer. Despite his previous service on the Louisburg expedition of 1745 and as a Connecticut colonel during the French and Indian War, the garrulous Wooster proved to be a slack and undependable commander in the Revolution. For the scarcity of gunpowder, see GW to Hancock, this date, n.2.

5. William Tryon (1729–1788), royal governor of New York since 1771, went to England in the spring of 1774 to consult with the ministry. By chance he returned to New York on the same day that GW arrived there. News that Tryon was expected to land at the city about one o'clock in the afternoon put the members of the New York provincial congress in a quandary. They were prepared to fight in defense of American rights and wished to assure GW of their support. Most, however, were not yet ready to break all ties with the mother country, nor had they any desire to offend an energetic and resourceful governor who remained personally popular in the colony. They decided to send two companies of militia to meet generals Washington, Schuyler, and Lee, while ordering the other companies to stand "ready to receive either the Generals or Governor Tryon, which ever shall first arrive, and to wait on both as well as circumstances will allow" (*N.Y. Prov. Congress Journals*, 1:54). As it happened, Tryon did not land until about eight o'clock in the evening. He was welcomed by most of the city's leading citizens, including many who had greeted GW only a few hours earlier. "What a farce! What cursed hypocrisy!" remarked Thomas Jones (Jones, *History of N.Y.*, 1:57). William Smith of New York viewed events a bit differently: "Mr Tryon was only attended by a Crowd who received him at the Ferry Stairs & escorted him to Mr [Hugh] Wallace's. . . . He appeared grave this Evening & said Little. . . . There was much Shouting in the Procession—A Proof that the Populace esteem the Man, tho' they at this Instant hate his Commission & would certainly have insulted any other in that Station" (William H. Sabine, ed., *Historical Memoirs from 16 March 1763 to 9 July 1776 of William Smith, Historian of the Province of New York . . .*, 2 vols. [New York, 1956–58], 1:228d).

To John Hancock

Sir New York Sunday [25] June 1775 5 OClock P.M.

Upon my Arrival here this Afternoon I was informd that an Express was in Town from the provincial Camp in massachusets Bay; and having seen among other papers in his possession a Letter directed to you as president of the Congress I have taken the Liberty to open it.

I was induced to take that Liberty by several Gentlemen of New York who were anxious to know the particulars of the Affair of the 17th Inst. and agreeable to the Orders of many Members of the Congress who judgd it necessary that I should avail myself of the best Information in the Cour[s]e of my Journey.[1]

You will find Sir by that Letter a great want of Powder in the provincial Army; which I sincerely hope the Congress will supply as speedily & as effectually as in their Power.[2]

One thousand pounds in Wt were sent to the Camp at Cambridge three days ago from this City; which has left this Place almost destitute of that necessary Article; there being at this Time from the best Information not more than four Bbs. of powder in the City of N. York.[3]

I propose to sett off for the provincial Camp to Morrow and will use all possible Dispatch to join the Forces there.[4]

Please to make my Compliments to the Gentlemen of the Congress & beleve to be Sir Your Obliged humle Obdt

Go: Washington

LS, in Thomas Mifflin's writing, DNA:PCC, item 152; copy, DNA:PCC, item 169; copy, NjMoNP. All copies of this letter are dated 24 June. For the correct date and GW's arrival in New York City, see GW to the Continental Congress, this date, source note and n. 2. Sunday fell on 25 June, not 24 June, in 1775.

1. GW opened the letter of 20 June 1775 from the Massachusetts provincial congress to the Continental Congress, containing a general account of the Battle of Bunker Hill. A sketchy report of the battle reached Philadelphia on 22 June, the day before GW left that city. Other accounts soon followed, but apparently none to date were so authoritative or complete as this one (Richard Henry Lee to GW, 29 June 1775). "We think it our indispensable duty to inform you," wrote the members of the Massachusetts provincial congress, "that reenforcements from Ireland, both of horse and foot, being arrived, the number unknown, and having good intelligence that general Gage was about to take possession of the advantageous posts in Charlestown, and on Dorchester point, the committee of safety advised, that our troops should prepossess them, if possible; accordingly, on Friday evening, the 16th instant, this was effected by about twelve hundred men." There follows a detailed account of the battle on the following day. The letter then continues: "The number of killed and missing on our side is not known; but supposed by some to be about sixty or seventy, and by some, considerably above that number. Our most worthy friend and president, Doct. [Joseph] Warren, lately elected a major general, is among them. This loss we feel most sensibly. . . . Three colonels, and perhaps one hundred men are wounded. The loss of the enemy is doubtless great. By an anonymous letter from Boston, we are told, that they

exult much in having gained the ground, though their killed and wounded amount to about one thousand; but this account exceeds every other estimation. The number they had engaged is supposed to be between three and four thousand. If any error has been made on our side, it was in taking a post so much exposed" (William Lincoln, ed., *The Journals of Each Provincial Congress of Massachusetts in 1774 and 1775, and of the Committee of Safety* [Boston, 1838], 365–66, Microfilm Collection of Early State Records). For American casualties, see GW to Hancock, 10–11 July 1775, Document II. Letter Sent, n.29, and for British casualties, see GW to Hancock, 14 July, n.3; 21 July 1775 (third letter), n.3.

2. The members of the Massachusetts provincial congress said: "As soon as an estimate can be made of public and private stocks of gunpowder in this colony, it shall be transmitted without delay; which, we are well assured, will be very small, and by no means adequate to the exigencies of our case. We apprehend, that the scantiness of our stock of that article cannot fail to induce your honors still to give your utmost attention to ways and means of procuring full supplies of it. We feel ourselves infinitely obliged to you for your past care in this respect" (*Mass. Prov. Congress Journals*, 365–66). In response to an earlier Massachusetts plea for gunpowder, the Continental Congress on 10 June resolved that the New England colonies should "immediately furnish the American army before Boston with as much powder out of their town, and other publick stocks as they can possibly spare." All colonies were directed to collect saltpeter and sulfur for manufacturing gunpowder (*JCC*, 2:85–86). The shortage of gunpowder, nevertheless, remained a persistent problem during the siege of Boston.

3. On 20 June the New York provincial congress, learning that about thirteen hundred pounds of gunpowder could be bought in New York City, authorized the purchase of the entire supply and directed that 1,000 pounds be sent to the army near Boston and 300 pounds to Ticonderoga (*N.Y. Prov. Congress Journals*, 1:47). "Bbs." is apparently an abbreviation for barrels.

4. GW's determination to pursue his journey to Cambridge without undue delay undoubtedly was reinforced by the last paragraph of the letter from the Massachusetts provincial congress to the Continental Congress: "We beg leave humbly to suggest, that, if a commander in chief over the army of the United Colonies should be appointed, it must be plain to your honors, that no part of this continent can so much require his immediate presence and exertions, as this colony" (*Mass. Prov. Congress Journals*, 365–66). GW left New York City on the afternoon of 26 June.

Instructions to Major General Philip Schuyler

Sir New York 25 June 1775.

You are to take upon you the Command of all the Forces destined for the New York Department; and see that the Orders of the Continental Congress are carried into Execution with as much precision and Exactness as possible.

For your better Government therein you are herewith furnished with a Copy of the Instructions given to me by that Honorable Body.[1]

Such parts thereof as fall within the Line of your Duty, you will please to pay particular Attention to.

Delay no Time in occupying the several posts recommended by the provincial Congress of this Colony, and putting them in a fit posture to answer the End designed—neither delay any Time in securing the Stores which are or ought to have been removed from this City by Order of the Continental Congress.[2]

Keep a watchful Eye upon Governor Tryon; and if you find him attempting directly or indirectly any Measures inimical to the common Cause use every Means in your power to frustrate his Designs—It is not in my power at this Time, to point out the Mode, by which this End is to be accomplished; but if forceable Measures are adjudged necessary respecting the person of the Governor, I should have no Difficulty in ordering of it, if the Continental Congress were not sitting: but as this is the Case and seizing of Governors quite a new Thing and of exceeding great Importance, I must refer you to that Body for Direction, in Case his Excellency the Governor should make any *Move* towards encreasing the Strength of the Tory party or in arming them against the Cause we are embarked in.[3]

In like Manner watch the Movements of the Indian agent (Colonel Guy Johnson) and prevent as far as you can the Effect of his Influence to our Pr⟨ej⟩udice with the Indians[4]—Obtain the best Information you can of the Temper and Disposition of these people; and also of the Canadians, that a proper Line may be mark'd out to conciliate their good Opinions and facilitate any future Operation.

The posts on Lake Champlain &c. you will please to have properly supplied with provision and ammunition, and this I am persuaded you will aim at doing upon the best Terms, to prevent our good and just Cause from sinking under a heavy Load of Expence.[5]

You will be pleased also to make regular Returns once a Month to me and to the Continental Congress (and oftner as Occurrences may require) of the Forces under your Command—Of your provisions, Stores &c. and give me the earliest Advises of every piece of Intelligence, which you shall judge of Importance to be speedily known.

Your own good Sense must govern in all Matters not particularly pointed out, as I do not wish to circumscribe you within too narrow Limits. I remain with great Regard Sir Your most obedt Servt

Go. Washington

LB, in John Lansing's writing, NN: Schuyler Papers; LB, in Richard Varick's writing, NHi: George and Martha Washington Papers; LB, DLC:GW; Varick transcript, DLC:GW. Both Lansing and Varick were secretaries for Schuyler.

Philip John Schuyler (1733–1804), known almost universally as Philip Schuyler, first met GW in Philadelphia on 15 May 1775 when he arrived to attend the Second Continental Congress as one of New York's delegates. During the following weeks, the two men served together on several committees concerned with military matters, and in that short time they apparently came to know and like one another. Both were wealthy and wellborn landowners, tall in stature and rather austere in manner. They shared interests in surveying, canals, gristmills, land speculation, and, most importantly, military affairs. Like GW, Schuyler gained valuable experience as a colonial officer in the French and Indian War. Serving on the New York frontier, he learned much about supplying and transporting large forces in wilderness areas, and that knowledge served him well during the Revolution. Schuyler commanded the New York department until August 1777, when, following the fall of Ticonderoga to the advancing British, he was relieved of his command. Schuyler resigned his commission in April 1779. He served as a delegate to the Continental Congress in 1777, 1779, and 1780. In 1780 he also assisted GW in reorganizing the army's staff departments and developing a scheme of cooperation with the French forces.

1. GW's instructions of 22 June 1775 from the Continental Congress are printed above.

2. Among the defensive measures that the Continental Congress recommended to the inhabitants of New York on 15 May 1775 was the removal of military stores from New York City (*JCC*, 2:52). In a letter of the next day to the city's committee of one hundred, the New York delegates cautioned that military stores belonging to the crown were not intended to be included (Smith, *Letters of Delegates*, 1:353), and on 8 June the New York provincial congress forbade the removal of stores from the royal depot at Turtle Bay (*N.Y. Prov. Congress Journals*, 1:35). A band of radical patriots nevertheless raided the Turtle Bay depot on 20 July and sent the stores to the Continental army. The posts to which GW refers were apparently two that the New York provincial congress was thinking of building in the Hudson highlands. Drawing on a report of a committee on which both Schuyler and GW served, the Continental

Congress recommended on 25 May that the highlands be fortified in order to prevent hostile warships from going up the Hudson and that a post be built at King's Bridge at the northern tip of Manhattan Island to protect New York City's land communication with the rest of the colony (*JCC*, 2:52, 57, 59–60). A committee of the New York provincial congress on 13 July presented a plan for erecting posts on opposite sides of the Hudson near West Point, but another committee on 7 July rejected the King's Bridge site as being too vulnerable to attack and insufficient in itself to safeguard the city's land communication against a superior enemy force (*N.Y. Prov. Congress Journals*, 1:31, 40–41). The highlands posts were not finally approved by the provincial congress until 18 August. See Schuyler to GW, 1 July 1775, n.6.

3. When Isaac Sears of New York revealed to Schuyler on 3 July a plan to seize Tryon that night and send him to Hartford, Schuyler denounced it "as rash and unjustifiable, and what the Congress would not countenance." Sears, a radical Whig who had recently returned to New York from a visit to the Continental Congress, responded that "many of the Delegates had mentioned it to him as a proper Measure, and [he] did not yield till Schuyler informed him, that he had written orders from General Washington on the Subject" (Smith, *Historical Memoirs*, 1:232). Many Patriots feared that Tryon, a colonel in the British army, was preparing some military action, but the governor remained quiet throughout the summer and early fall. After the Continental Congress recommended on 6 Oct. that the revolutionary authorities in each colony arrest anyone "whose going at large may, in their opinion, endanger the safety of the colony, or the liberties of America," Tryon moved to the safety of a British ship in New York Harbor (*JCC*, 3:280). Later in the war he commanded troops in raids on the Connecticut coast and the Hudson River.

4. Guy Johnson (c.1740–1788) succeeded his father-in-law, Sir William Johnson, as superintendent of Indian affairs in the northern department after the latter's death in July 1774. GW undoubtedly had heard the reports circulating in Philadelphia that Guy Johnson was urging the northern Indians to take up the hatchet against the rebelling colonists. The reports were true. At his house, Guy Park, on the Mohawk River near Amsterdam, N.Y., Johnson was acting on secret orders from Gen. Thomas Gage to do all in his power to attach the Indians to the royal cause. Threatened with retaliation from local revolutionary committees, Johnson marched west at the end of May with a mixed force of whites and Indians to Lake Ontario. There he "assembled 1458 Indians and adjusted matters with them in such a manner that they agreed to defend the communication [on the lake] and assist His Majesty's troops in their operations." At the beginning of July, Johnson moved to Montreal, where on 17 July he "convened a second body of the northern confederates to the amount of 1700 and upwards who entered into the same engagements" (Guy Johnson to the Earl of Dartmouth, 12 Oct. 1775, in K. G. Davies, ed., *Documents of the American Revolution, 1770–1783*, 21 vols. [Shannon and Dublin, 1972–81], 11:142–44). Johnson did not resign his superintendency until 1782.

5. New England forces commanded by Ethan Allen and Benedict Arnold seized the fort at Ticonderoga on 10 May 1775, and two days later the small British garrison at Crown Point surrendered to some of the New Englanders. Upon learning of the fall of Ticonderoga, the Continental Congress on 18 May cautiously ordered that the fort be abandoned and all cannon and stores moved to the south end of Lake George. The order provoked protests in New England and northern New York, and on 31 May Congress directed the governor of Connecticut to reinforce both Ticonderoga and Crown Point and instructed the New York provincial congress to supply the two posts "with provisions and other necessary stores, and to take effectual care that a sufficient number of Batteaus be immediately provided for the lakes" (*JCC*, 2:55–56, 73–74).

Address from the New York Provincial Congress

May it please Your Excellency [New York] June 26th 1775.

At a Time when the most loyal of his Majesties Subjects, from a Regard to the Laws and Constitution by which he sits on the Throne, feel themselves reduced to the unhappy Necessity of taking up Arms to defend their dearest Rights and Priviledges; While we deplore the Calamities of this divided Empire, We rejoice in the Appointment of a Gentleman from whose Abilities and Virtue we are taught to expect both Security and Peace.

Confiding in you Sir, and in the worthy Generals immediately under Your Command, We have the most flattering Hopes of Success in the glorious Struggle for American Liberty; And the fullest Assurances that whenever this important Contest shall be decided, by that fondest Wish of each American Soul, an Accomodation with our Mother Country; You will chearfully resign the important Deposit committed into Your Hands, and reassume the Character of our worthiest Citizen.

By order.

P. V. B. Livingston President[1]

DS, DLC:GW; Df, N: New York Provincial Congress, Revolutionary Papers.

On the morning of 26 June the New York provincial congress approved this address and appointed Gouverneur Morris and Isaac Low to inquire of GW when the members should wait on him with it. Morris and Low promptly brought word that GW would receive them at 2:30 P.M. A copy of the address was then ordered to be engrossed. After transacting some other business, the provincial congress recessed until 5:00 P.M. and went to meet GW. Upon reconvening, it ordered the address and GW's reply, which is printed below, to be published (*N.Y. Prov. Congress Journals*, 1:55–56). Both documents appear in the *New-York Journal; or the General Advertiser*, 29 June 1775; *Rivington's New-York Gazette; or the Connecticut, Hudson's River, New-Jersey, and Quebec Weekly Advertiser*, 29 June 1775; and the *New-York Gazette; and the Weekly Mercury*, 3 July 1775.

1. Peter Van Brugh Livingston (1710–1792), a wealthy New Yorker who had profited greatly from military contracts during the colonial wars, was elected president of the New York provincial congress on its opening day, 23 May 1775, and on 8 July he became its treasurer. He held both positions until 28 Aug. 1775 when he withdrew from all public affairs because of poor health.

Address to the New York Provincial Congress

⟨Gentlemen⟩ [New York] June 26.[1] 1775.

At ⟨the same time that with you I deplore⟩ the unhappy Necessity of suc⟨h an Appointment, as that⟩ with which I am now honoured, ⟨I cannot but feel sentiments⟩ of the highest Gratitude for this af⟨fecting Instance of⟩ Distinction & Regard.

May your warmest w⟨ish[2] be realized in⟩ the Success of America at this importa⟨nt and interesting⟩ Period; & be assured that, every Exertion ⟨of my worthy Colleagues⟩ & myself, will be equally extended to ⟨the re establishment⟩ of Peace & Harmony between the Mother ⟨Country and the⟩[3] Colonies. As to the fatal, but necessary Opera⟨tions of War.⟩[4] When we assumed the Soldier, we did not ⟨lay aside the⟩ Citizen, & we shall most sincerely rejoice ⟨with you in⟩ that happy Hour, when the Establishment ⟨of American⟩ L⟨iber⟩ty on the most firm, & solid Foundat⟨ions, shall enable us⟩ to return to our private Stations in ⟨the bosom of a⟩ free, peaceful, & happy Country.

Go: ⟨Washington.⟩

LS, in Joseph Reed's writing, N: New York Provincial Congress, Revolutionary Papers; Varick transcript, DLC:GW. The LS was badly damaged in the New York State Library fire of 1911. Missing portions of the text are supplied within angle brackets from the Varick transcript.

President Peter Van Brugh Livingston informed the New York provincial congress, when it reconvened at 5:00 P.M. today, "that to prevent mistakes he had obtained a copy of the answer of General Washington to the address of this Congress." It was read, filed, and ordered to be published with the provincial congress's address (*N.Y. Prov. Congress Journals*, 1:56). For the appearance of both documents in the New York newspapers, see Address from the New York Provincial Congress, this date, source note.

Soon after replying to the provincial congress, GW left New York City "attended by the several New-York Military Companies, and likewise by a Troop of Gentlemen of the Philadelphia Light Horse, commanded by Capt. Markoe, and a Number of the Inhabitants of this City" (*New-York Gazette: and Weekly Mercury*, 3 July 1775). GW lodged this night at King's Bridge at the northern end of Manhattan Island. Philip Schuyler remained with him until ten o'clock the next morning when the two men parted company at New Rochelle, Schuyler returning to New York City to begin his new duties there. The Philadelphia Light Horse also returned to New York City that day and left for Philadelphia on 29 June. Charles Lee, Thomas Mifflin, and Joseph Reed continued with GW to Cambridge.

1. Joseph Reed wrote "25," but the date was corrected by someone, possibly GW, writing a "6" over the "5" in heavy ink.

2. The Varick transcript reads "every wish." Printed copies of the document in the *N.Y. Prov. Congress Journals*, 1:56 and 2:1, and the three New York newspapers cited above read "warmest wishes."

3. The wording in the *N.Y. Prov. Congress Journals*, 1:56 and 2:1, and the New York newspapers is "mother country and these."

4. Whether the phrase "As to the fatal, but necessary operations of War" was intended to be part of the preceding sentence or the following one is not clear. In the Varick transcript and the *N.Y. Prov. Congress Journals*, 1:56, the phrase is attached to the preceding sentence with a comma after "Colonies" and a period after "War." In ibid., 2:1, and *Rivington's New-York Gazette*, 29 June 1775, "Colonies" is followed by a period, and "War" by a comma, making the phrase part of the following sentence. The *New-York Gazette: and the Weekly Mercury*, 3 July 1775, also shows the phrase as part of the following sentence with a colon and dash after "Colonies" and a comma after "War." The *New-York Journal; or the General Advertiser*, 29 June 1775, is vague on this point, having a colon and a dash after "Colonies" and a very long dash after "War."

From John Hancock

Sir Philadelphia June 28th 1775

By Direction of the Congress I now Transmitt you severall Resolutions pass'd yesterday, by which you will Observe they have Directed Major General Schuyler to Examine into the State of the Posts at Ticonderoga & Crown Point, and of the Troops Station'd there, as also to Enquire into the Disposition of the Canadians and Indians. You will likewise find they have Directed him to Take or Destroy all Vessells, Boats or Floating Batteries prepar'd by Governor Carlton on or near the Waters of the Lakes, and to Take possession of St Johns & Montreal if he finds it practicable, & not Disagreeable to the Canadians—The Alteration of the Sentiments of Congress since your Departure relative to making an Impression into Canada was

Occasion'd by a Letter they Receiv'd from the Committee of Albany, a Copy of which you have Inclos'd, they gave their Directions upon these important matters directly to Major General Schuyler, as he would be near the Posts abovemention'd, and as their being Sent to you would Occasion such Delay as might prove Detrimental to the Service.[1]

I Send you the Remainder of the Commissions Sign'd, should you have Occasion for more, please to Acquaint me, & they shall be immediately Transmitted you.

Brigr Genl Gates not yet Arriv'd in the City, I Expect him to morrow, and shall Deliver him his Commission, and promote his Joining you as soon as possible—Inclos'd is a Letter from him.[2] With my best wishes for every personal Happiness, and Success in all your undertakings, I have the Honor to be, Sir Your most Obedt Hume servt

John Hancock President

ALS, DLC:GW; ADf, sold by John F. Fleming, *Some Fundamental Documents in the Early History of the United States*, New York, 1974, pp. 8–10.

1. On 1 June, the day after Congress resolved to garrison Ticonderoga and Crown Point, it forbade military action "by any colony, or body of colonists, against or into Canada" (*JCC*, 2:75). The matter, nevertheless, continued to be discussed in the ensuing weeks. "Whether We Should march into Canada with an Army Sufficient to break the Power of Governor Carlton, to overawe the Indians, and to protect the French has been a great Question," John Adams wrote to James Warren on 7 June. "It Seems to be the general Conclusion that it is best to go, if We can be assured that the Canadians will be pleased with it, and join" (Taylor, *Papers of John Adams*, 3:17–18). The issue was settled by the four resolutions of 27 June. Schuyler was directed to seize not only St. Jean and Montreal, if he could and the French Canadians did not object, but also to take "any other parts of the country, and pursue any other measures in Canada, which may have a tendency to promote the peace and security of these Colonies" (*JCC*, 2:109–10). The letter dated 21 June from the Albany committee of safety which prompted the change asserted that the Caughnawaga Indians "had taken up the Hatchet" on behalf of the king and "that Governor Carelton was giving them presents daily." The committee also reported that Carleton was "building Floating Batteries and Boats" at St. Jean, but that his preparations had been hampered by the refusal of English merchants at Montreal "to take up arms against the *yankees*" (DNA:PCC, item 67). On this date Hancock sent a copy of the Albany committee's letter and Congress's resolutions of 27 June to Schuyler at New York (Smith, *Letters of Delegates*, 1:554). The copies of those documents that Hancock enclosed in his letter to GW are in DLC:GW.

Guy Carleton (1724–1808), a career soldier with the rank of major general in the British army, was appointed governor of Quebec on 10 Jan. 1775 and served until 1778. At this time he had four to five hundred regulars defending the strategically important town of St. Jean, 15 miles east of Montreal, and two armed sloops under construction there for use on the Richelieu River and Lake Champlain. His attempt to call out the militia on 9 June was defied by both the English merchants and the French inhabitants. Carleton served as British commander in chief in America from May 1782 to November 1783 and was again governor of Quebec between 1786 and 1796. He was created Baron Dorchester in 1786.

2. The enclosed letter may have been that of 22 June 1775 from Horatio Gates to GW.

From the Delaware Delegates

Philadelphia, 29 June 1775. Recommend the bearer John Parke,[1] who "is an Ensign in the 2d Battalion of the Militia here, and is desirous of serving his country as a Volunteer under you. He has frequently drawn his *pen* and is now resolved to draw his *sword* in support of the American cause."

LS, in Thomas McKean's writing, DLC:GW. The letter is signed by Caesar Rodney (1728–1784) and Thomas McKean (1734–1817). The third member of the Delaware delegation, George Read (1733–1798), was temporarily absent from the Continental Congress on this date.

1. John Parke (1754–1789) of Kent County, Del., was a former law clerk of Thomas McKean. He was appointed assistant quartermaster general of the Continental army on 16 Aug. 1775 and served in that position with the rank of major until 29 June 1776, when he became lieutenant colonel of a regiment of artificers. He subsequently served in Col. John Patton's Additional Continental Regiment and resigned from the army in October 1778. In 1786 Parke dedicated a volume of poetry to GW.

From Richard Henry Lee

Dear Sir, Philadelphia 29th June 1775

Nothing material has occurred since you left this place, except the imperfect accounts we have of the Charlestown battle, which upon the whole seems to have nothing unfavorable to our great cause, but the loss of Dr Warren—To an infant Country, it is loss indeed, to be deprived of wise, virtuous, and brave Citizens. I hope however, still to hear, that our Enemies have lost Characters very useful to them. We received the account of this engagement late on Saturday evening last, and a few of us immediately applied to, and prevailed with the Committee of this City, to dispatch 90 odd quarter Casks of powder to the Camp, which I hope will arrive safe and in good time.[1]

We are this day informed in Congress that the six Nations and Canada Indians are firmly disposed to observe a strict nieutrality, and I think we shall endeavor to cultivate their friendship.[2] The Congress has been engaged these two days about the mutiny and military regulations, and at last we shall adopt those of Massachusetts with very few alterations.[3] You will see that we have again taken up the business of entering Canada, and have left the propriety of it to Gener. Schuyler. If it can be done, in a manner agreeable to the Canadians, it will certainly shut the door against dangerous tampering with the Indians on all our Western frontiers.[4] Nothing has yet been done about a Military Hospital, and I suppose we shall wait for your return of the state of the Army—Dr Shippen says that three young Gentlemen here, perfectly compitent, will be ready when called on, to se[r]ve in the capacity of Surgeons.[5] I have only to assure you, that it will always make me happy to hear from you, and that I am, with great regard, dear Sir, Your Affect. and obedient servant

Richard Henry Lee

ALS, DLC:GW. The cover includes the notation "favored by General Gates."

Richard Henry Lee (1732–1794) of Westmoreland County, Va., was first elected to the Virginia House of Burgesses in 1758, the same year that GW first became a burgess, and the two men subsequently served together not only in that body but also in the first two Virginia conventions and both Continental Congresses. A son of one of Virginia's oldest and proudest families, Lee bitterly resented Parliament's encroachments on colonial rights. During the Stamp Act crisis, he emerged as a leading defender of those rights and began a lifelong political alliance with Patrick Henry, whose stirring oratory he complemented with his own considerable oratorical skills. In the Continental Congress Lee became deeply involved with the problems of confederation and diplomacy. Poor health caused him to give up his seat in 1779, but he later regained political prominence as an Antifederalist.

1. Although the Continental Congress received a brief report about the Battle of Bunker Hill on 22 June, it did not learn of Dr. Joseph Warren's death on the battlefield until 11:00 P.M. on Saturday, 24 June, at which time, John Adams said, "an hundred Gentlemen flocked to our Lodgings to hear the News. At one O Clock Mr. H[ancock] Mr. [Samuel] A[dams] and myself, went out to enquire after the Committee of this City, in order to beg some Powder. We found Some of them, and these with great Politeness, and Sympathy for

their brave Brethren in the Mass. agreed, to go that night and send forward about Ninety Quarter Casks, and before Morning it was in Motion" (Adams to James Warren, 27 June 1775, in Taylor, *Papers of John Adams*, 3:49–51).

2. This favorable intelligence apparently was contained in several letters and speeches from the chiefs of the Stockbridge Indians that were read in Congress on this date (*JCC*, 2:110–11). The delegates, nevertheless, had reason to apprehend that the northern tribes might not be steadfast in their neutrality, for other reports indicated that royal officials were already meeting with some success in their efforts to turn the Indians in New York and Canada against the Patriots. See GW to Schuyler, 25 June 1775, n.4, and Hancock to GW, 28 June 1775, n.1. With those other reports in mind, Congress resolved on 1 July that if any Indians were induced "to commit actual hostilities against these colonies, or to enter into an offensive Alliance with the British troops," the colonies should retaliate by making alliances "with such Indian Nations as will enter into the same, to oppose such British troops and their Indian Allies" (ibid., 2:123). For the American efforts to persuade the northern Indians to remain neutral, see in particular GW to Schuyler, 20 Aug. 1775, and Schuyler to GW, 27 Aug. 1775.

3. GW was appointed on 14 June to the committee that was charged with drafting "Rules and regulations for the government of the army," and he apparently attended at least one meeting of that committee before leaving Congress. Those rules and regulations, or articles of war as they are usually called, were finally approved by Congress on 30 June (*JCC*, 2:90, 111–23; *Diaries*, 3:336). For the articles of war adopted by the Massachusetts provincial congress on 5 April 1775 for the use of that colony's troops, see *Mass. Prov. Congress Journals*, 120–29. The Continental articles of war include an additional sixteen articles relating to furloughs, musters and returns, sutlers, pardons, the personal effects of deceased officers and enlisted men, and the signing of the articles by all members of the army. The Continental articles also define more specifically the punishments imposed by court-martials than do the Massachusetts articles.

4. For Congress's instructions to Schuyler regarding Canada, see Hancock to GW, 28 June 1775, n.1.

5. On 19 July Congress appointed a committee "to report the method of establishing an hospital," and eight days later it approved the creation of "an hospital for an army, consisting of 20,000 men" (*JCC*, 2:191, 209–11). William Shippen, Jr. (1736–1808), professor of anatomy in the medical school of the College of Philadelphia, was Richard Henry Lee's brother-in-law. GW visited Shippen's house on several occasions while attending the First and Second Continental Congresses (*Diaries*, 3:274–75, 284, 329–30). Shippen was appointed in July 1776 to be chief physician for the militia units from Pennsylvania, Delaware, and Maryland that were formed into a flying camp, and November 1776 he assumed responsibility for the Continental army's sick and wounded west of the Hudson River. He became director general of all Continental army hospitals in April 1777. The three young surgeons may be those who were at Cambridge in early August. See GW to Committee of the Massachusetts Council, 4 Aug. 1775.

From Major General Philip Schuyler

Sir [New York] Saturday July 1st 1775.

I do myself the Honor to advise your Excellency that the Connecticut Troops, that arrived in this Colony under the Command of Brigadier Wooster are encamped within two Miles of this Town. I have not yet had a Return of their Numbers[.] as soon as my Order for that Purpose is complied with I shall transmit it.[1]

Inclose You Sir a Copy of the Resolutions of the Hono: the Continental Congress of the 27th ult. I shall prepare with all possible Dispatch to carry into Execution their Views and propose leaving this for Albany in my way to Ticonderoga on Monday next.[2]

Eight Transports with Troops, that have been at Sandy Hook since Thursday last are to sail from thence to Day. Reports prevail that the Men on Board have muntinied, that they refused to go to Boston, of this however I have not been able to get any Certainty. Hand Bills have been introduced amongst them to encourage them to quit on the first favorable Opportunity a Service which must render them odious to all honest Men.[3]

Governor Tryon's Conduct has hitherto been unexceptionable and from the Information I have been able to procure, some of which I put great Confidence in, I have reason to beleive that the Line he has chalked out for himself is such as we would wish he should hold.[4]

I beleive the Commissions for this Department were already forwarded to You before my Letter (In Obedience to Your Order) to the Congress on that Subject arrived. If they are to be sent back, I beg of You to Order them to be directed to the President of the Provincial Convention here.[5]

No Preparation has as yet been made to occupy a Post in the Highlands. by what I can learn the Provincial Convention have Doubts about the Propriety (which they have or mean to state to Congress) arising from the Want of Ammunition, to maintain the Post after it shall be compleated.[6]

A Ship from London in five Weeks advises that the Remonstrance sent by the Assembly of this Colony to the House of Commons has been rejected by them as containing Sentiments derogatory to the Rights of Parliament: This Manoevre has already had Salutary Effects. many whose Sentiments are friendly to America, but who differed as to the Mode of procuring Redress, now publickly declare that they will no longer sit idle Spectators of their Country's Wrongs.[7]

That Success and Happiness equal to the Merit & Virtue of my General may crown all his Operations is the Wish of every honest American by none more sincerely than me. I am Your Excellency's Most Obedt & Most Humb. Servt

Ph: Schuyler

LS, DLC:GW; LB, NN: Schuyler Papers.

1. Schuyler informed the Continental Congress on 28 June that Wooster's force "arrived to within two miles of this town about 8 this Morning and got Sheltered in Barns and outhouses, as soon as the weather (which is at present Wet And Stormy) will permitt, I propose to Encamp them on the south side of Sand hill which is nearly two miles from hence" (DNA:PCC, item 153).

2. For a discussion of these resolutions regarding Canada, see Hancock to GW, 28 June 1775, n.1. The copy of the resolutions that was enclosed in Schuyler's letter to GW is in DLC:GW. The next Monday was 3 July.

3. Between 24 and 27 June seven British transport ships carrying reinforcements arrived off Sandy Hook, N.J., from Cork, Ireland, and anchored there to take on fresh water. They were joined on 27 June by another transport loaded with some troops from the New York garrison. Two more transports, apparently from Cork, reached Sandy Hook on 30 June, and that same day all ten transports sailed for Boston under escort of a British warship.

4. "Governor Tryon I have reason to believe will not create any trouble in his Government," Schuyler wrote to Congress on 28 June. "It is said that he laments (and is sincere) that the unhappy Controversy has been carryed so far and that he wishes a happy termination of It on principle⟨s⟩ friendly to both" (DNA:PCC, item 153). Schuyler lodged directly across Broadway from the house in which William Tryon was staying. According to Loyalist historian Thomas Jones, Schuyler attempted to call on the governor to congratulate him on his return to the colony, but Tryon refused to see him because he came in his uniform and presented himself as "*General* Schuyler," a rank that the governor would not recognize (Jones, *History of N.Y.*, 1:58).

5. In his letter of 28 June to Congress, Schuyler wrote: "General Washington before we parted desired me to Inform Your Honors that he thought It most advisable that the Commissions for the Officers in the New York department should be directly sent to me to be filled up" (DNA:PCC, item 153). GW could spare no blank commissions from those that Hancock forwarded to him, and Congress did not send any to Schuyler until September (GW to Schuyler, 10–11 July; New York Provincial Congress to GW, 3 Aug.; GW to Peter Van Brugh Livingston, 10 Aug.; Livingston to GW, 21 Aug. 1775).

6. For a discussion of the two posts that were proposed for the West Point area in the Hudson highlands, see Instructions to Schuyler, 25 June 1775, n.2. On 18 Aug. the New York provincial congress ordered those posts to "be

immediately erected" and appointed commissioners to oversee their construction (*N.Y. Prov. Congress Journals*, 1:110).

7. On 25 Mar. 1775 the New York general assembly sent addresses to the king, the House of Lords, and the House of Commons protesting the infringement of colonial rights but reaffirming its loyalty and expressing hopes for reconciliation. Edmund Burke, a member of Parliament and agent for New York, read the remonstrance to the House of Commons, the boldest of the three addresses, to that body on 15 May 1775. "He then moved for Leave to bring it up to the Table, and the Question being put by the Speaker, that this Remonstrance be now brought up, Lord North paved the Way for getting rid of the main Question by moving an Amendment; that the Words 'which is derogatory to the Supreme Authority of the British Parliament.' be added. Upon which a short Debate ensued, the House divided, for the Amendment 186. against it 67. of course the main Question was lost" (*Town and Country Magazine*, May 1775, DNA:PCC, item 75).

From Henry Ward

Providence, 1 July 1775. Transmits by order of the Rhode Island general assembly "the inclosed Vote, putting the Rhode Island Army under your Command."

ALS, DLC:GW.

Henry Ward (1732–1797) served as provincial secretary of Rhode Island from 1761 to 1797. This letter apparently was sent under cover of one from Ward to Brig. Gen. Nathanael Greene, commander of the Rhode Island forces. Greene received his letter on 4 July and probably forwarded GW's letter to him that same day. The transfer of the Rhode Island command to GW, Greene wrote to Deputy Gov. Nicholas Cooke on 4 July, "is perfectly agreeable and I shall conduct myself accordingly" (Richard K. Showman et al., eds., *The Papers of General Nathanael Greene* [Chapel Hill, 1976—], 1:94–96). The copy of the Rhode Island general assembly's resolution of 28 June that was enclosed in Ward's letter to GW is in DLC:GW.

General Orders

Head Quarters, Cambridge, July 3rd 1775

Parole, Lookout. Counter Sign, Sharp.

The Colonels or commanding Officers of each Regt are ordered forthwith, to make two Returns of the Number of men in their respective Regiments; distinguishing such as are sick, wounded or absent on furlough: And also the quantity of ammunition each Regimt now has.

It appearing by the Report of Henry Woods,[1] the Officer of the main guard, that one William Alfred is confin'd for taking two horses, belonging to some Persons in Connecticut; but that he has made Satisfaction to the injured parties, who request that they may not be longer detain'd as witnesses: It is ordered that he be discharged, and after receiving a severe reprimand, be turned out of camp.

After Orders. 4 oClock. P:M:

It is order'd that Col. Glovers Regiment be ready this evening, with all their Accoutrements, to march at a minutes warning to support General Falsam of the New Hampshire forces, in case his Lines should be attack'd.

It is also order'd, that Col. Prescott's Regiment equip themselves, march this evening and take Possession of the Woods leading to Leechmores point, and in case of an Attack, then[2] Col. Glover's Regiment to march immediately to their support.[3]

Varick transcript, DLC:GW; copy, in Joseph Reed's writing, MWA. The Reed copy includes only the after orders and is addressed to "Mr Henshaw Adjutt General."

GW and Charles Lee reached Cambridge about midday on Sunday 2 July. "The greatest civility and attention was paid to the Generals on their arrival at the camp," wrote an anonymous correspondent on 3 July (*Pennsylvania Gazette* [Philadelphia], 12 July 1775). On the morning of 2 July the troops in Cambridge assembled on the parade ground to receive GW and Lee but were dismissed before the generals arrived because of the onset of a rainstorm that lasted until dark. The next day Lt. Paul Lunt, who was posted in Cambridge with Col. Moses Little's Massachusetts regiment, wrote in his journal: "Turned out early in the morning, got in readiness to be reviewed by the general. New orders given out by General Washington" ("Paul Lunt's Book" in Mass. Hist. Soc., *Proceedings*, 1st ser., 12 [1871–73], 194). Lt. Joseph Hodgkins, also of Little's regiment, wrote to his wife at 8:00 A.M. on 3 July: "I have nothing Remarkebel to rite Except that geaneral Washington & Leas got into Cambridge yesterday and to Day thay are to take a vew of ye Army & that will be atended with a grate deal of grandor there is at this time one & twenty Drummers & as many feffors a Beting and Playing Round the Prayde" (Herbert T. Wade and Robert A. Lively, *This Glorious Cause: The Adventures of Two Company Officers in Washington's Army* [Princeton, 1958], 171). Private James Stevens noted in his journal entry for 3 July that "nothing hapeng extrorderly we preaded thre times" ("The Revolutionary Journal of James Stevens of Andover, Mass.," in Essex Inst., *Hist. Collections*, 48 [1912], 50).

Upon arriving at Cambridge, GW and Charles Lee took up residence at the house of the president of Harvard College, Samuel Langdon, located on Harvard Square. The Massachusetts provincial congress, in its deliberations of 26

June, agreed to give the two generals the use of the entire house, except for one room that was reserved for Langdon. On 6 July the provincial congress instructed the Massachusetts committee of safety to inquire of GW and Lee if there was any other house at Cambridge that would be more agreeable to them, and within the next two days GW decided to move into the elegant mansion belonging to John Vassal, a wealthy Tory who earlier in the year had gone to Boston for refuge (*Mass. Prov. Congress Journals*, 398–99, 460, 593). Vassal's house, which stands about a half a mile west of Harvard College, was cleaned for GW by 15 July and was probably occupied by him about that time. It remained GW's headquarters until the following spring. Charles Lee established himself at Medford, 4 miles north of Cambridge, sometime before 26 July.

1. Henry Woods (Wood) was a major in Col. William Prescott's Massachusetts regiment.

2. The Reed copy reads "Attack there."

3. In the weeks following the Battle of Bunker Hill, the American army outside of Boston was frequently alarmed by rumors of another British attack. South of the city, Roxbury and Dorchester Heights were the most likely places for an assault, while to the north, Prospect Hill, Winter Hill, and Lechmere's Point all lay within easy striking distance of the British lines on Bunker Hill. Winter Hill, the position occupied by Maj. Gen. Nathaniel Folsom (1726–1790) and his New Hampshire troops, was particularly vulnerable to attack, because it was flanked on the north by the Mystic River, up which the British might move the three floating batteries that they had anchored near the mouth of that river (GW to Hancock, 10–11 July 1775). The lines on Winter Hill, furthermore, were at this time deficient in both men and heavy artillery, a state of affairs about which Gen. Folsom wrote to his colony's committee of safety on 1 July 1775: "Wednesday last [28 June] the whole of the New Hampshire Troops fit for Duty were order'd to their alarum Posts, when I found that we were not able to line our Breastwork more than two deep, our Lines being necessarily extensive on account of the situation of our Camp; Therefore desire that the two remaining Companies now station'd at Portsmouth [N.H.] and Hampton [N.H.] may be sent, if you can possibly spare them; There being not one quarter part of the Troops in ours as in the other lines at Cambridge, Roxbury and on Prospect Hill. In a few days the Breastwork will be compleated, by which time, the Cannon I wrote for, I hope, will arrive: So that we may be prepared to give the ministerial Troops a proper Reception, should they attempt to force our Lines" (Nathaniel Bouton, ed., *Provincial Papers: Documents and Records Relating to the Province of New-Hampshire, from 1764 to 1776*, 7 vols. [Concord and Nashua, 1867–73], 7:557). Lechmere's Point, located about two miles east of Cambridge by land and about a half a mile southwest of Bunker Hill by water, was an obvious landing place for any British force sent to attack Cambridge, despite the fact that the marsh behind the point flooded during high tides making it in effect an island (GW to Hancock, 11 Nov. 1775). A false report that British regulars were landing at Lechmere's Point alarmed the Cambridge camp on 23 June ("Stevens Journal," 49), and

on 4 July, in response to another alarm, an American working party was sent to entrench Lechmere's Point ("Lunt's Book," 194). Col. John Glover (1732–1797) and Col. William Prescott (1726–1795) commanded Massachusetts regiments stationed at Cambridge.

Address from the Massachusetts Provincial Congress

[Watertown, Mass., 3 July 1775]

May it please your Excellency

The Congress of the Massachusetts Colony impress'd with every Sentiment of Gratitude, and Respect, beg leave to congratulate you on your safe arrival; and to wish you all imaginable Happiness and Success in the execution of the important duties of your elevated Station. While we applaud that attention to the public good, manifested in your appointment, We equally admire that disinterested Virtue and distinguish'd Patriotism, which alone could call you from those Enjoyments of domestic Life which a sublime, & manly Taste, joined with a most affluent Fortune can afford: to hazard your Life, and to endure the fatigues of War, in the Defence of the Rights of Mankind, and for the good of your Country.

The laudable Zeal for the common Cause of America, and Compassion for the Distresses of this Colony, exhibited by the great dispatch made in your Journey hither, fully justifies the universal safisfaction we have, with pleasure, observed on this occassion; and are promising presages that the great Expectations formed from your personal Character, and military Abilities are well founded.

We wish you may have found such Regularity, and Discipline already establish'd in the Army, as may be agreeable to your Expectation. The Hurry with which it was necessarily collected, and the many disadvantages, arising from a suspension of Government, under which we have raised, and endeavour'd to regulate the Forces of this Colony have render'd it a work of Time. And tho' in a great measure effected, the completion of so difficult, and at the same time so necessary a Task, is reserved to your Excellency; and we doubt not will be properly consider'd, and attended to.

We would not presume to prescribe to your Excellency, but supposing you would choose to be informed of the general Character of the Soldiers, who compose this Army beg leave to represent, that the greatest part of them have not before seen Service. And altho' naturally brave and of good understanding, yet for want of Experience in military Life, have but little knowledge of divers things most essential to the preservation of Health and even of Life.

The Youth in the Army are not possess'd of the absolute Necessity of Cleanliness in their Dress, and Lodging, continual Excercise, and strict Temperance to preserve them from Diseases frequently prevailing in Camps; especially among those who, from their Childhood, have been us'd to a laborious Life.

We beg Leave to assure you, that this Congress will, at *all times*, be ready to attend to such Requisitions as you may have Occassion to make to us; and to contribute all the Aid in our power, to the Cause of America, and your Happiness, and Ease, in the Discharge of the Duties of your exalted Office.

We most fervently implore Almighty God, that the Blessings of Divine Providence may rest on you: That your Head may be cover'd in the day of Battle; That every necessary Assistance may be afforded; and that you may be long continued in Life and Health a Blessing to Mankind.

D, CSmH; Df, M-Ar: Revolution Letters. The document at the Huntington Library is endorsed in GW's writing, indicating that it was the copy he received.

On 29 June the Massachusetts provincial congress, sitting at Watertown, appointed James Warren, Joseph Hawley, William Whiting, Daniel Hopkins, and Jonathan Greenleaf as "a committee to prepare an address to Generals Washington and Lee, to be presented to them on their arrival here." The committee prepared two addresses, one to each general, apparently completing its work by 1 July when Joseph Hawley, Samuel Dexter, and John Pickering, Jr., were ordered "to draw up a resolve to be prefixed to the addresses" (*Mass. Prov. Congress Journals*, 418, 437). The following resolution, dated 3 July 1775, appears before the address to GW in the document at the Huntington Library: "Resolved, That the Hon. the President [James Warren] Honble Major [Joseph] Hawley, Mr [John] Pickering [Jr.], Colo. [Ezra] Richmond, Doctr [John] Taylor, Mr [George] Partridge & Mr [Samuel] Phillips be a committee of this Congress to present the following address to his Excellency Genl Washington." This resolution does not appear in the draft or in the journal of the provincial congress. It is not known either when or where the committee presented the address to GW.

General Orders

Head Quarters, Cambridge, July 4th 1775.

Parole. Abington. Countersign, Bedford.

Exact returns to be made by the proper Officers of all the Provisions⟨,⟩ Ordnance, Ordnance stores, Powder, Lead, working Tools of all kinds, Tents, Camp Kettles, and all other Stores under their respective care, belonging to the Armies at Roxbury and Cambridge. The commanding Officer of each Regiment to make a return of the number of blankets wanted to compleat every Man with one at least.

The Hon: Artemus Ward, Charles Lee, Philip Schuyler, and Israel Putnam Esquires, are appointed Major Generals of the American Army[1] and due Obedience is to be paid them as such. The Continental Congress not having compleated the appointments of the oth⟨er⟩ officers in said army, nor had sufficient time to prepare and forward the⟨ir⟩ Commissions; every Officer is to continue to do duty in the Rank and ⟨Sta⟩tion he at present holds untill further orders.[2]

Thomas Mifflin Esqr. is appointed by the Gen⟨eral⟩ one of his Aid-de-Camps. Joseph Reed Esqr. is in like manner appoin⟨ted⟩ Secretary to the General, and they are in future to be consider'd and regarded as such.[3]

The Continental Congress having now taken all the Troops of the several Colonies, which have been raised, or which may be hereafter raised, for the support and defence of the Liberties of America; into their Pay and Service: They are now the Troops of the United Provinces of North America; and it is hoped that all Distinctions of Colonies will be laid aside; so that one and the same spirit may animate the whole, and the only Contest be, who shall render, on this great and trying occasion, the most essential service to the great and common cause in which we are all engaged.

It is required and expected that exact discipline be observed, and due Subordination prevail thro' the whole Army, as a Failure in these most essential points must necessarily produce extreme Hazard, Disorder and Confusion; and end in shameful disappointment and disgrace.

The General most earnestly requires, and expects, a due observance of those articles of war, established for the Government of the army, which forbid profane cursing, swearing & drunkeness; And in like manner requires & expects, of all Officers, and Soldiers, not engaged on actual duty, a punctual attendance on divine service, to implore the blessings of heaven upon the means used for our safety and defence.[4]

All Officers are required and expected to pay diligent Attention, to keep their Men neat and clean—to visit them often at their quarters, and inculcate upon them the necessity of cleanliness, as essential to their health and service. They are particularly to see, that they have Straw to lay on, if to be had, and to make it known if they are destitute of this article. They are also to take care that Necessarys be provided in the Camps and frequently filled up to prevent their being offensive and unhealthy. Proper Notice will be taken of such Officers and Men, as distinguish themselves by their attention to these necessary duties.[5]

The commanding Officer of each Regiment is to take particular care that not more than two Men of a Company be absent on furlough at the same time, unless in very extraordinary cases.

Col. Gardner is to be buried to morrow at 3, OClock, P: M. with the military Honors due to so brave and gallant an Officer, who fought, bled and died in the Cause of his country and mankind. His own Regiment, except the company at Malden, to attend on this mournful occasion. The places of those Companies in the Lines on Prospect Hill, to be supplied by Col. Glovers regiment 'till the funeral is over.[6]

No Person is to be allowed to go to Fresh-water pond a fishing or on any other occasion as there may be danger of introducing the small pox into the army.[7]

It is strictly required and commanded that there be no firing of Cannon or small Arms from any of the Lines, or elsewhere, except in case of necessary, immediate defence, or special order given for that purpose.[8]

All Prisoners taken, Deserters coming in, Persons coming out of Boston, who can give any Intelligence; any Captures of any kind from the Enemy, are to be immediately reported and brought up to Head Quarters in Cambridge.[9] Capt. Griffin is appointed Aid-de-Camp to General Lee and to be regarded as such.[10]

The Guard for the security of the stores at Watertown, is to be increased to thirty men immediately.

A serjeant and six men to be set as a Guard to the Hospital, and are to apply to Doctor Rand.[11]

Complaint having been made against John White Quarter Master of Col. Nixon's Regmt for misdemeanors in drawing out Provisions for more Men than the Regiment consisted of;[12] A Court Martial consisting of one Captain and four Subalterns is ordered to be held on said White,[13] who are to enquire, determine and report.

After Orders. 10 OClock

The General desires that some Carpenters be immediately set to work at Brattle's Stables, to fix up Stalls for eight Horses, and more if the Room will admit, with suitable racks, mangers &c.[14]

Varick transcript, DLC:GW; copy, in Joseph Reed's writing, MWA; copy, in Thomas Mifflin's writing, DNA: RG 93, Orderly Books, 1775–83. The Reed copy omits the after orders. In the Mifflin copy the after orders are followed by a copy of Reed's signature, "J. Reed Secry," and the address, "To Mr Henshaw Adjt Genl," both in Mifflin's writing.

1. The words "by the Honr. Continental Congress" appear here in the Reed copy.

2. Although Congress appointed eight brigadier generals on 22 June, GW decided to delay announcing those appointments when he learned shortly after his arrival in Cambridge that some of the New England officers, unhappy at not being given higher rank or precedence, might refuse their commissions. See James Warren and Joseph Hawley to GW, 4 July 1775, n.1, and GW to Hancock, 10–11 July 1775, Document II. Letter Sent, n.20.

3. Thomas Mifflin (1744–1800) and Joseph Reed (1741–1785), handsome and articulate young Philadelphians already prominent in the business and political circles of their city and colony, became well known to GW during the First and Second Continental Congresses when he dined at their homes on several occasions (*Diaries*, 3:277, 284, 286, 328–29). Mifflin, a well-educated Quaker merchant who served in both Continental Congresses, was one of the youngest and most radical of the delegates and quickly distinguished himself as "a sprightly and spirited Speaker" (Butterfield, *Adams Diary and Autobiography*, 2:150). On 27 May 1775 Mifflin was named with GW and several other delegates to a committee charged with finding ways to supply the colonies with ammunition and military stores (*JCC*, 2:67). Reed, a more moderate advocate of the American cause than Mifflin, had a growing legal practice in Philadelphia and was an active land speculator. Through the family of his English-born wife, he became acquainted with Lord Dartmouth, secretary of state for the American colonies, and from December 1773 to February 1775, he corresponded regularly with Dartmouth, explaining and defending colo-

nial opinions and actions. Reed served with Mifflin on the Philadelphia committee of correspondence, and in January 1775 he was elected president of the second Pennsylvania provincial congress. Following the battles of Lexington and Concord, both Reed and Mifflin joined Philadelphia's military associators: Reed as a lieutenant colonel and Mifflin as a major. Although neither man had any other military experience, GW chose them for his staff because he needed efficient managers in his headquarters more than he needed expert soldiers. He wished to have about him intelligent confidants to whom he could delegate a wide variety of tasks.

Mifflin accepted a position as aide-de-camp before GW left Philadelphia. Reed, however, was reluctant to abandon his family and business to become GW's secretary, and he at first agreed only to accompany GW part of the way to Cambridge. It was apparently at New York that Reed finally accepted GW's offer. Reed explained to Elias Boudinot on 13 Aug. that GW "expressed himself to me in such Terms that I thought myself bound by every Tye of Duty and Honour to comply with his Request to help him through the Sea of Difficulties" (John F. Roche, *Joseph Reed, A Moderate in the American Revolution* [New York, 1957], 65–66). Reed acted as GW's secretary until 30 Oct. 1775, when he took a prolonged leave of absence to go home to Philadelphia. He returned to the army the following June as adjutant general with the rank of colonel. In January 1777 Reed resigned from the army, but he served as a volunteer aide to GW during the ensuing campaign. Reed was a member of the Continental Congress in 1778, and from 1778 to 1781 he was president of the Pennsylanvia executive council. Mifflin became quartermaster general of the Continental army on 14 Aug. 1775. He was promoted to colonel on 22 Dec. 1775, to brigadier general on 16 May 1776, and to major general on 19 Feb. 1777. Accused of negligence and corruption in executing his duties as quartermaster general, Mifflin resigned from the army in February 1779. He served again in the Continental Congress from 1782 to 1784, and while president of that body, he accepted GW's resignation at the end of the war.

4. These matters are covered by articles 1, 2, and 19 of the Massachusetts articles of war, which correspond to articles 2, 3, and 20 of the Continental articles of war. For a discussion of the articles of war, see Richard Henry Lee to GW, 29 June 1775, n.3. Artemas Ward, GW's predecessor as commander of the American army, issued general orders on 14 June 1775 requiring attendance at daily prayers and Sunday services, and on 30 June he prohibited "all prophane Cursing & Swearing, all indecent Language and Behavior" in camp (Ward's orderly book, MHi: Ward Papers).

5. General Ward had earlier attempted to enforce a similar order by threatening to punish those who did not obey it. "The commanding Officer of each Regiment, Detachmt or Company," Ward ordered on 1 June 1775, shall "daily visit his Soldiers whether in Barracks or Tents & oblige them to keep themselves clean—The Officers who do not strictly adhere to this order are to be reported at Head Quarters and the Soldiers that disobey the Officers Orders, in this Respect are to be confind, at the main Guard till they shall receive some punishment adequate to a crime so heinous" (ibid.).

6. Thomas Gardner (1723–1775) of Cambridge was mortally wounded at

the Battle of Bunker Hill on 17 June while leading reinforcements into the American lines. He died on the night of 3 July.

7. A smallpox hospital had been established for the army near Fresh Pond, which lies about a mile and a half west of the Cambridge common. On 19 June 1775 General Ward directed that a sentry be posted constantly at the gate to the smallpox hospital with orders "to permit no person to go in or out except the Doctor & such as the Doctor shall permit to pass." On 2 July Ward ordered each company in the army to be inspected daily for smallpox symptoms. Any man suspected of having the disease was to be removed at once (ibid.).

8. Unauthorized firing of small arms remained a problem for some time. See General Orders, 26 July and 4 Aug. 1775.

9. More detailed instructions regarding the disposition of British deserters are given in General Orders, 27 July 1775.

10. Samuel Griffin (1746–1810), formerly of Virginia and more recently a resident of Philadelphia, accompanied GW and Charles Lee from that city to Cambridge. He served as an aide-de-camp to Lee until late the next winter, when he resigned to go into business. On 19 July 1776 Congress appointed him adjutant general of the flying camp with the rank of colonel, and he returned to the army. In December 1776 GW offered Griffin an opportunity to raise and command a regiment, but Griffin declined to do so and apparently moved soon afterwards to Williamsburg. He was appointed to the Virginia board of war in June 1777 and was elected mayor of Williamsburg in December of that year.

11. Dr. Isaac Rand (c.1718–1790) of Charlestown, Mass., was commissioned by the Massachusetts provincial congress on 28 June 1775 to be surgeon and physician to the smallpox hospital near Cambridge, and on 7 July he became surgeon of the hospital at Roxbury.

12. The words "& for abusive Behaviour" are added here in the Reed copy.

13. In the Reed copy the words "at 9 oClock To Morrow morning" are inserted here. John White of Massachusetts continued to serve as a regimental quartermaster until 30 July 1777, when he became a brigade quartermaster. Col. John Nixon (1727–1815) commanded one of the Massachusetts regiments.

14. William Brattle (1706–1776), a prominent Cambridge Loyalist, fled to Boston for safety in September 1774, leaving his large estate, which was located a short distance west of town, in the care of his widowed daughter. Among the horses that were to be stabled at Brattle's place were some that had been taken from the enemy this morning and given to GW for his use (General Orders, 5 July 1775, source note).

From George Clinton

4 July 1775. Recommends the bearer, "Mr. White, the Son of Anthony White Esq'r of New Jersey. . . . Inspired with Love for our much injured Country he now vissits your Camp to offer his Service as a Vollenteer in the Army under your Command."[1]

Hugh Hastings and J. A. Holden, eds., *Public Papers of George Clinton,* 10 vols. (1899–1914; reprint, New York, 1973), 1:208–9. This letter may be incorrectly dated. GW in his letter of 25 Aug. 1775 to Clinton writes "Mr White presented me with your favour of the 27th Ulto."

George Clinton (1739–1812) of Ulster County, N.Y., took his seat with the New York delegation in the Second Continental Congress on 15 May 1775. He was in New York, however, from late June until late July, when he returned to Philadelphia. In December 1775 Clinton was appointed a brigadier general in the New York militia, and in March 1777 he became a Continental brigadier general. A lawyer whose previous military experience was limited to brief service as a subaltern during the French and Indian War, Clinton did not greatly distinguish himself as a general in the Revolution, but as governor of New York from 1777 to 1795 and 1801 to 1804, he proved to be an able politician and administrator.

1. Anthony Walton White (1750–1803), son of Anthony White of New Brunswick, N.J., stayed at Cambridge until late October, when, failing to obtain appointment as an aide-de-camp to GW, he returned home to seek a place in the Continental forces being raised by New Jersey. White was appointed lieutenant colonel of the 3d New Jersey Battalion in February 1776, but lost that position during the ensuing year because of conduct unbecoming an officer. With GW's assistance White became lieutenant colonel of the 4th Continental Light Dragoons during 1777, and in January 1780 GW sent him to the South to take command of the 1st Continental Light Dragoons. White was not promoted to colonel despite several appeals to Congress. He fought in the South until 1782. For GW's later criticism of White's military abilities, see GW to Timothy Pickering, 9 Sept. 1798.

Address to the Massachusetts Provincial Congress

Gentlemen [Cambridge, c.4 July 1775]

Your kind Congratulations on my Appointment, & Arrival demand my warmest Acknowledgements, and will ever be retained in grateful Remembrance.

In exchanging the Enjoyments of domestic Life for the Duties of my present honourable, but arduous Station, I only emulate the Virtue & publick Spirit of the whole Province of Massachusetts Bay, which with a Firmness, & Patriotism without Example in modern History, has sacrificed all the Comforts of social & political Life, in Support of the Rights of Mankind, & the Welfare of our common Country. My highest Ambition is to be the happy Instrument of vindicating those Rights, & to see this devoted Province again restored to Peace, Liberty & Safety.

The short Space of Time which has elapsed since my Arrival does not permit me to decide upon the State of the Army—The Course of human Affairs forbids an Expectation, that Troops formd under such Circumstances, should at once possess the Order, Regularity & Discipline of Veterans—Whatever Deficiencies there may be, will I doubt not, soon be made up by the Activity & Zeal of the Officers, and the Docility & Obedience of the Men. These Quali⟨ties,⟩ united with their native Bravery, & Spirit will afford a happy Presage of Success, & put a final Period to those Distresses which now overwhelm this once happy Country.

I most sincerely thank you, Gentlemen, for your Declarations of Readiness at all Times to assist me in the Discharge of the Duties of my Statio⟨n.⟩ they are so complicated, & extended that I shall Need the Assistance of every good Man, & Lover of his Country; I therefore repose the utmost Confidence in your [Aids][1]—In Return for your affectionate Wishes to my-self permit me to say, that I earnestly implore that Divine Being in whose Hands are all human Events, to make[2] you & your Constituents, as distinguished in private, & publick Happiness, as you have been by ministeria⟨l⟩ Oppression, by private & publick Distress.

D, in Joseph Reed's writing, M-Ar: Revolution Letters. There is no dateline on the manuscript in the Massachusetts Archives, but in Jared Sparks, ed., *The Writings of George Washington: Being His Correspondence, Addresses, Messages, and Other Papers, Official and Private, Selected and Published from the Original Manuscripts*, 12 vols. (Boston, 1833–37), 3:14–15, this address is dated 4 July 1775. It could not have been written earlier than 3 July, the date of the address from the Massachusetts provincial congress to which it is a reply, nor is it likely that it was written later than 5 July because it appears in the *New-England Chronicle: or, the Essex Gazette* (Cambridge, Mass.) of 6 July 1775.

1. The word "Aids" is taken from the text printed in the *New-England Chronicle*. The manuscript in the Massachusetts Archives originally read "in yours." The "s" in "yours" was subsequently struck out, and the word "Support," written by either Joseph Reed or Thomas Mifflin, was inserted above the line. "Support," however, is also struck out, and no substitute appears in the manuscript.

2. The word "implore," apparently written by Charles Lee, is inserted above the line in place of the original wording "hope & wish." Lee also apparently inserted the word "to" before "make" in place of the original word "will."

From James Warren and Joseph Hawley

Sir Watertown [Mass.] July 4: 1775

As Pomroy is now Absent and at the distance of an hundred miles from the Army, if it can be Consistent with your Excellencys Trust & the Service to retain his Commission untill you shall recieve Advice from the Continental Congress and we shall be Able to prevail with Heath to make a Concession Honourable to himself, and Advantageous to the publick. We humbly Concieve the way would be open to do Justice to Thomas.[1] We have the Honour to be Your Excellencys Most Obedient Humbe Servts

Jas Warren
Joseph Hawley

LS, in James Warren's writing, DLC:GW.

James Warren (1726–1808) was president of the Massachusetts provincial congress, and Joseph Hawley (1723–1788) was vice president. Both men were radical Patriots who had long been active in the political affairs of the colony and their respective localities. Warren, a merchant and gentleman farmer from Plymouth, represented his town in various legislative bodies from 1766 to 1778 and served on many local revolutionary committees. He was elected president of the provincial congress on 19 June 1775 and became speaker of the new house of representatives on 19 July 1775. His close friends John and Samuel Adams tried without success to have him appointed a Continental brigadier general, but on 27 July 1775 Warren was made Continental paymaster general, which office he held until the following April. Warren also served on the navy board for the eastern department from 1776 to 1781 and was a major general in the Massachusetts militia from 1776 to 1777. Hawley, a lawyer from Northampton, was one of the leading political figures in western Massachusetts, and like Warren, he represented his town in the colony's assemblies for many years. Hawley served as a chaplain at the siege of Louisburg in 1745, and as major of Hampshire County during the French and Indian War, he was involved in raising and supplying troops. In 1774 Hawley was elected to the First Continental Congress, but he declined to attend, probably because of poor health. A mental breakdown in the fall of 1776 forced him to retire permanently from all public affairs.

1. The arrangement of the eight brigadier generals appointed by the Continental Congress on 22 June occasioned great consternation in Massachusetts. John Thomas (1724–1776) of Kingston, a much-respected officer who had commanded a provincial regiment during the French and Indian War, was designated the sixth brigadier, while William Heath (1737–1814) of Roxbury, an inexperienced soldier whom Thomas outranked in the Massachusetts service, was named the fourth brigadier (*JCC*, 2 : 103). Both Thomas and Heath were appointed generals in the Massachusetts army by the colony's

provincial congress on 8 Dec. 1774 (*Mass. Prov. Congress Journals*, 65), but when the siege of Boston began in April 1775, Thomas quickly emerged as a leading figure in the American army, taking command of the camp at Roxbury. "His Merits in the military way have surprised us all," James Warren wrote of Thomas in a letter to John Adams on 27 June. "I cant describe to you the Odds between the two Camps. While one [Cambridge] has been Spiritless, sluggish, Confused, and dirty . . . The other [Roxbury] has been Spirited, Active regular, and clean. He has Appeared with the dignity and Abilities of a General" (Taylor, *Papers of John Adams*, 3:51–53). Thomas was commissioned a lieutenant general by the provincial congress on 19 May (Mass. Hist. Soc., *Proceedings*, 2d ser., 18 [1903–4], 423), and Heath was appointed to the lesser provincial rank of major general on 21 June (*Mass. Prov. Congress Journals*, 363, 367). Unacquainted with any of the New England generals before his arrival at Cambridge, GW was cautious in forming his opinions of them, but he soon agreed that Thomas deserved better treatment than he had received from the Continental Congress. "The General," James Warren informed John Adams in a letter of 7 July 1775, "was very Sorry and somewhat Embarrassed with the Neglect of Thomas" (Taylor, *Papers of John Adams*, 3:68–70). See also GW to John Hancock, 10–11 July 1775.

Fortunately, a solution to the problem seemed to be at hand. Seth Pomeroy (1706–1777) of Northampton, a veteran of two colonial wars whom the Continental Congress appointed first brigadier general, was expected to decline his commission because of his advanced age. If he did, Thomas could be put in his place. Heath promptly agreed to this change, and GW delayed his reorganization of the army until Pomeroy made known his decision. No word, however, was forthcoming from Pomeroy, who had gone home to Northampton after the Battle of Bunker Hill. Unable to wait any longer, GW announced the new arrangement for the army on 22 July, and Thomas indicated that he would quit the army rather than accept a position below Heath. GW wrote to Thomas on 23 July, urging him to remain until a verdict on his commission arrived from the Continental Congress. The delegates in Philadelphia, in fact, resolved on 19 July to appoint Thomas first brigadier general "in the room of Gen [Seth] Pomeroy, who never acted under the Commission sent to him" (*JCC*, 2:191). Thomas's new commission reached Cambridge by 4 Aug., and he accepted it (Hancock to GW, 24 July 1775; GW to Hancock, 4–5 Aug. 1775).

General Orders

Head Quarters, Cambridge, July 5th 1775

Parole, Bedford. C. Sign, Cambridge.

The Adjutant of each Regiment is required to take special care, that all general orders are communicated, as well to the private men, as to the officers—that there may be no Plea of

Ignorance—they will be deemed answerable for all the consequences which may follow a neglect of this order.

A General Court martial is ordered to sit to morrow at 10 oClock A.M. for the Trial of William Patten charged with "leaving his post on guard." David Wells and Gideon Cole for "sleeping on their posts as centinels"—John Scott for "insulting the Centry and attempting to pass the guard at Boston" and James Foshe[1] for "*theft*"—When the Witnesses are to attend and the parties charged, are to have notice this day that they may be prepared for their trials.[2]

The General most earnestly recommends, & requires of all the Officers, that they be exceeding diligent and strict in preventing all Invasions and Abuse of private property in their quarters, or elsewhere[.] he hopes, and indeed flatters himself, that every private soldier will detest, and abhor such practices, when he considers, that it is for the preservaton of his own Rights, Liberty and Property, and those of his Fellow Countrymen, that he is now called into service: that it is unmanly and sully's the dignity of the great cause, in which we are all engaged, to violate that property, he is called to protect, and especially, that it is most cruel and inconsistant, thus to add to the Distresses of those of their Countrymen, who are suffering under the Iron hand of oppression.

The General again urges, a speedy and exact Return, of the Forces, Stores, Provisions &c.; as desired in the Orders already issued and for the future, these Returns to be made once a week, on saturday Morning regularly. The General is much pleased with the expedition and care which some Officers have already shewn in their obedience to this order.

The Colonel or commanding Officer of each Regiment, is to direct an Officer of each Company, to call over the Rolls of their men, at six oClock every morning, and to make proper Inquiry after the absentees.

Varick transcript, DLC:GW; copy, in Joseph Reed's writing, MWA; copy, in Thomas Mifflin's writing, DNA: RG 93, Orderly Books, 1775–83. The Mifflin copy includes "After Orders" which consist entirely of a letter from Joseph Reed "to the Adjutt General" dated 4 July: "His Excelly the General directs you woud send some careful Person to Reading & bring with him from thence one Ingerfield a Person who came out of Boston yesterday: In the Purpose you can make Use of two of the Horses brought in from the Enemy yesterday & now at Brattles Stables or Pasture." The fact that those horses were captured on the morning of 4 July indicates that Reed's letter should be dated 5 July. See Massachusetts Committee of Safety to GW, 6 July 1775, n.1.

1. The Reed copy gives this name as "James Foster," as does also a memorandum attached to the Mifflin copy. See note 2.

2. The Mifflin copy includes a memorandum on the accused men: "Wm Patton & David Wells belong to Capt. [Samuel] Gridly's Compy Col. [Richard] Gridlys Regimt—Gideon Cole belongs to Captn [John] Chesters Company General [Israel] Puttnams Regimt. John Scott belongs to Captn Money's Company in Col. [ ] Regimt—James Foster belongs to Captn [Joseph] Butler's Company in Col. [John] Nixons Regimt." The first two sentences of this memorandum appear also in the Reed copy.

From John Hancock

Sir Philadelphia July 5th 1775

Since my last to you by Alexander the Express nothing has Taken place in Congress that particularly Respects your Department.

By Direction of the Congress I now Transmitt you by Mr Fessenden our Return Express,[1] the Rules & Articles pass'd by Congress for the Government of the Troops under your Command,[2] I wish them safe to hand. I have not Time to add, but that I am with much Respect, Sir Your most Obedt hum. servt

John Hancock President

Should you have Occasion for a further Supply of Commissions, please to Inform me & they shall be immediately Transmitted you.

ALS, DLC:GW. This letter is docketed in Joseph Reed's writing "Congress Letter July 5th 1775 Recd July 10th—acknowldgd July 11th." See GW to Hancock, 10–11 July 1775.

1. Josiah Fessenden, a courier for the Massachusetts provincial congress, frequently carried dispatches between GW and the Continental Congress during the next several months.

2. For a discussion of the Continental articles of war, see Richard Henry Lee to GW, 29 June 1775, n.3. On 30 June, the same day that the articles were approved by the Continental Congress, a committee of three delegates was appointed to have the articles printed as soon as possible (*JCC*, 2:122–23). They were subsequently printed by William and Thomas Bradford as *Rules and Articles, for the Better Government of the Troops Raised, or to Be Raised, and Kept in Pay by and at the Joint Expence of the Twelve United English Colonies of North-America* (Philadelphia, 30 June 1775).

From Joseph Hawley

Watertown [Mass.], July 5, 1775.

Sir: You were pleased the other day to mention to Colonel *Warren* and me, as your opinion, that it was highly probable *Gage's* Troops would very shortly attack our Army in some part or other. I believe your opinion is not ill-founded; and I am sure your Excellency will be pleased with every intimation that may, in any degree, aid you in the choice of measures tending to success and victory. Therefore, that I may not be tedious, I ask your pardon when I suggest, that although in the *Massachusetts* part of the Army there are divers brave and intrepid officers, yet there are too many, and even several Colonels, whose characters, to say the least, are very equivocal with respect to courage. There is much more cause to fear that the officers will fail in a day of trial, than the privates. I may venture to say, that if the officers will do their duty, there is no fear of the soldiery. I therefore most humbly propose to your consideration the propriety and advantage of your making immediately a most solemn and peremptory declaration to all the officers of the Army, in general orders, or otherwise, as your wisdom shall direct, assuring them that every officer who, in the day of battle, shall fully do his duty, shall not fail of your kindest notices and highest marks of your favour; but, on the other hand, that every officer who, on such a day, shall act the poltron, dishonour his General, and by failing of his duty, betray his Country, shall infallibly meet his deserts, whatever his rank, connexions, or interest may be; and that no intercessions on his behalf will be likely to be of any avail for his pardon.[1]

I know that your Excellency is able to form a declaration of the kind, conceived in such a style, and replete with such determined sentiments and spirit, as cannot fail of begetting a full belief and persuasion in the hearts of such to whom it shall be addressed, that the same will be infallibly executed. I am almost certain the measure will have the happiest tendency. *Sed sapienti verbum sat est.* Pray pardon my prolixity; I never was happy enough to be concise.

I am, with the greatest respect and deference, your Excellency's most obedient humble servant,

Joseph Hawley.

Peter Force, ed., *American Archives*, 9 vols. (Washington, D.C., 1837–53), 4th ser., 2:1589.

1. The General Orders, 7 July 1775, include such a statement couched in words similar to those used by Hawley. Several officers had recently been accused of behaving in a cowardly manner at the Battle of Bunker Hill (GW to Hancock, 21 July 1775 [first letter]).

From the Massachusetts Provincial Congress

In Provincial Congress [Watertown, Mass.] July 5th 1775

This Congress had Ordered the inclosed Resolution to be prepared and sent to Generals Ward & Thomas. but By the agreable event of your Excellency's appointment to the Chief command of the American Army and arrival at Camp, the propriety of that Step ceases. we mean not to dictate to your excellency but presume that To Secure the health of the Army and relief for the sick, will naturally engage your Attention.[1] Every thing in the power of this Congress to enable you to discharge with ease the duties of your Exalted and important station will be by us attended to with the greatest alacrity—If the inclosed Resolution has that tendency we attain the end intended by transmitting to you the same. and are with respect yr Excellencys most humble Servants

Df, M-Ar: Revolution Letters.

1. On 1 July the provincial congress instructed three members, Dr. John Taylor, Joseph Fox, and Daniel Bragdon, "to bring in a resolve, directing how the sick and wounded shall be removed to the hospitals." The committee's report, submitted later that same day, was accepted without change, and a copy was ordered to be sent to Artemas Ward at Cambridge and John Thomas at Roxbury. On 4 July the provincial congress appointed another committee, consisting of John Pickering, Jr., George Partridge, and Ichabod Goodwin, to prepare a letter to GW "informing him of the provision this Congress has made for the sick and wounded of the army." That committee reported the next day, when the letter printed here was approved (*Mass. Prov. Congress Journals*, 436–37, 445, 455–56). The text of the 1 July resolution which was enclosed with this letter appears with minor changes in wording as the last paragraph of General Orders, 7 July 1775.

General Orders

Head Quarters, Cambridge, July 6th 1775.
Parole, Cumberland. C. sign, Derby.

A General Court Martial is ordered to sit to morrow at 10 oClock A:M: for the Trial of John Semsy,[1] John Batcheler, and William Crostin all of Col. Gridley's Regiment, charged with "Desertion and Theft." At the same time, they are to hear and determine, the Case of Edward Dunley[2] a Stroller, accused of "Theft"—Notice to be given to the Prisoners to day.

Captain Leonard of Col. Woodbridges Regiment and the remainder of his Company, are ordered to join the Guard at Water town.[3]

The Cloathing provided by the Massachusetts Committee of Supplies, for those Men of their Government, who lost their Cloaths in the late Action on Bunkers-hill, to be distributed to the most needy and necessitous Men of each Regimt & an Account to be kept thereof by the commanding Officer of each regiment.[4]

Varick transcript, DLC:GW; copy, in Joseph Reed's writing, MWA; copy, in Thomas Mifflin's writing, DNA: RG 93, Orderly Books, 1775–83.

1. The name of this soldier is given as "John Seymour" in the Reed copy and as "John Semore" in the Mifflin copy.

2. In the Reed copy the name "Edward" is struck out, and the name "Thomas" is inserted above it.

3. Capt. Noadiah Leonard (1737–1790) served in Col. Benjamin Ruggles Woodbridge's Massachusetts regiment until the end of 1775. For the guard at Watertown, see General Orders, 4 July 1775.

4. On 19 June, two days after the Battle of Bunker Hill, Artemas Ward's secretary Joseph Ward informed the Massachusetts provincial congress "that, in the late action, many of the soldiers lost their blankets and clothes; they are now in a very suffering condition on that account, and must, in order to fit them for duty, be immediately supplied, especially with blankets; and many that were not in the action are destitute of blankets." The provincial congress responded on the same day by ordering the committee of supplies to furnish clothes and blankets to "those destitute soldiers . . . who shall produce from the colonel of the regiment they belong to, certificates of their having lost such clothes and blankets in the late engagement." The order was extended on 3 July to include noncommissioned officers as well as private soldiers (*Mass. Prov. Congress Journals*, 355, n.1, 358, 444).

From John Fenton

Medford [Mass.] 6 July 1775. "Tho' I am quite a Stranger to your Excellency, yet the peculiarity of my Situation induces me to request that you will indulge me so far as to take me under your protection at Head Quarters." He wishes to explain his reasons in person.

ALS, NjMoNP; Sprague transcript, DLC:GW.

John Fenton (d. 1785), an active and outspoken New Hampshire Loyalist, was seized by a Patriot mob in Portsmouth, N.H., on 13 June 1775. The colony's provincial congress declared on 29 June "that Colo John Fenton is not a friend to this country" and two days later sent him to the headquarters of the New Hampshire forces at Medford, Mass. (Bouton, *N.H. Provincial Papers*, 7:543–44). An Irishman, Fenton served as a captain in the British army during the French and Indian War. He married an American, and when his regiment was reduced at the end of the war, he left the army and settled in Massachusetts. In 1771 Fenton moved to New Hampshire, where he had been given a large grant of land. By allying himself closely with the colony's royal governor, John Wentworth, he soon became a prominent political figure, holding among other offices a colonelcy in the New Hampshire militia and the clerkship of Grafton County. GW responded to Fenton's plea for protection from his New Hampshire enemies by sending him to Hartford as a prisoner on parole. On 19 Sept. the Continental Congress directed GW to release Fenton "on his giving his parole of honour to proceed to New York, and from thence to Great Britain or Ireland, and not to take up arms against the good people of this Continent" (*JCC*, 2:255). See also Hancock to GW, 26 Sept. 1775. Fenton sailed to England soon afterwards and never returned to America.

From the Massachusetts Committee of Safety

[Watertown, Mass., 6 July 1775]

May it please your Excellency:—The bearer, Capt. Brown, is the officer who took the horses that came off from Bunker's hill; you'll please to direct said horses being delivered to his care.[1]

Mass. Prov. Congress Journals, 589.

1. A party of men, commanded by a Captain Brown of Salem, Mass., took four horses from the enemy on or near Charlestown Neck on the morning of 4 July. That same day GW, "having occasion to visit the Lines with his Aid De Camps," asked the Massachusetts committee of safety for use of the captured horses, and Benjamin Church, chairman of the committee, promptly ordered all four to be sent to him. "His Excellency," Church wrote in his order, "will return them to the Captors or pay for them if they are willing to part with

them" (Church to ——, 4 July 1775, M-Ar: Revolution Letters). Captain Brown and his men soon laid claim to the horses, and the dispute about whose property they were was referred by the committee of safety to the provincial congress, which resolved on 13 July that the "horses be delivered into the hands of Capt. Brown . . . until the further order of this Congress, or some future house of representatives of this colony" (*Mass. Prov. Congress Journals*, 496). GW's displeasure with the handling of this affair is evident in the letter that Joseph Reed wrote about 16 July to the Massachusetts committee of supplies: "By the General's Direction two of the Horses which came from the Enemy some time ago, are herewith sent you, One of them Capt. Brown sent to his Father contrary to the General's Inclinations & without his Knowledge—The General is clearly of Opinion that the Idea of their being the Property of the Captors is to be wholly discouraged, as dangerous to the Service; by exposing the Soldiers to the Temptation of leaving their Posts in Quest of Plunder—The remaining Horse is in General Putnam's particular Service, but holds himself accountable to the Publick—In the Direction of them, you will doubtless do it, so as not to encourage the Notion which has been taken up & too much prevails thro' the Camp, that by such Means they become private Property" (M-Ar: Revolution Letters).

From Daniel Murray

6 July 1775. States "that he has received the repeated Commands of his Father, now a resident in Boston, to assist his Sister & two Brothers now at Waltham; in procuring them a pass into the town of Boston." He requests GW to grant such a pass.

ALS, M-Ar: Revolution Letters.

Daniel Murray (1751–1832) of Rutland, Mass., and his family were zealous Loyalists. During the summer of 1774, Murray left his legal practice in Brookfield, Mass., to take over the family estate at Rutland from his father, Col. John Murray (d. 1794), who fled to Boston in order to escape the wrath of a Patriot mob that wished to force him to resign from the mandamus council instituted by one of the Intolerable Acts. Two of Murray's younger brothers, John Murray (b. 1758) and Robert Murray (b. 1760), and one of his sisters were now trying to join their father in Boston. GW instructed Joseph Reed to send Murray's letter to the Massachusetts committee of safety. In a covering letter dated 6:00 P.M., 6 July 1775, Reed explained to the committee: "As the General is wholly unacquainted with the Circumstances of the Case & the Propriety of granting or refusing the Request; he refers himself to your Advice & would be glad of your Opinion on the Subject as early as convenient" (M-Ar: Revolution Letters). The committee of safety promptly forwarded both Reed's and Murray's letters to the provincial congress, which on 7 July rejected Murray's request as part of a general policy, in effect since 24 June, of denying entry into Boston (*Mass. Prov. Congress Journals*, 387, 463, n.1, 465). The three Murray children eventually did get into the town and accompanied their father to Halifax in the spring of 1776 when Boston was evacuated by the British army. In early 1777 Daniel Murray abandoned the family property at Rutland to move inside British lines. In June 1777 he became captain of a company of Loyalist volunteers, and in Feb. 1781 he was appointed a major in the King's American Dragoons.

From the Pennsylvania Delegates

Sir Philadelphia 6th July 1775

We inclose a Resolution of our Assembly authorising us to recommend proper Officers for the Battalion of Rifflemen to be raised in this Province, and a Letter from the Committee of York County, where a Company of an hundred Men has been raised.[1]

We therefore beg Leave to recommend Mr Michael Dowdle for Captain; Mr Henry Miller for first Lieutenant; Mr John Dill for second Lieutenant; and Mr John Matson for third Lieutenant of that Company.[2] We are, with the greatest Esteem, Sir Your most obedient Servants

John Dickinson
Geo: Ross
Cha. Humphreys
James Wilson

LS, in James Wilson's writing, NN. Each delegate signed his own name.

John Dickinson (1732–1808) of Philadelphia, George Ross (1730–1779) of Lancaster, and Charles Humphreys (1712–1786) of Haverford served in both the First and Second Continental Congresses. James Wilson (1742–1798) of Carlisle was elected to the Second Continental Congress on 6 May 1775.

1. Having authorized the raising of six companies of Pennsylvania riflemen on 14 June, Congress on 22 June approved two more Pennsylvania rifle companies and instructed the colony's assembly to recommend officers for all eight companies (*JCC*, 2:89–90, 104). The Pennsylvania assembly took up the matter on 24 June and resolved that the colony's delegates to the Continental Congress should serve as a committee to make the recommendations. A copy of the assembly's resolution is in DLC:GW. The Pennsylvania delegates relied on suggestions from the committees of correspondence in the counties where the riflemen were raised. The York County committee informed the delegates on 1 July that its company was ready to march and recommended the four officers named here. "They are men whose courage we have the highest opinion of," wrote the committee. "We hope no alteration will be made in the officers. The Capt. has behaved very well on this occasion,

and has done all in his power by advancing money &c. to forward the important common cause. Mr Miller is known to some of you gentlemen; the other officers are men of worth and property. They have all wives and families and are entitled to the warmest thanks of their country" (Sprague transcript, DLC:GW). The York County company departed for Cambridge on 1 July and arrived on 25 July.

2. Michael Doudel (Doudle, Dowdle) resigned his commission because of poor health on 13 Aug. 1775 and was replaced as captain of the York County rifle company by Henry Miller (1751–1824). Miller became a lieutenant colonel in the 2d Pennsylvania Regiment before he left the army in December 1778. The name of the third lieutenant in the York rifle company is given as James Matson in "Roll of Captain Michael Doudel's Company," *Pa. Archives*, 2d ser., 10:20–23.

General Orders

Head Quarters, Cambridge, July 7th 1775

Parole, Dorchester. C. Sign Exeter.

It is with inexpressible Concern that the General upon his first Arrival in the army, should find an Officer sentenced by a General Court Martial to be cashier'd for Cowardice—A Crime of all others, the most infamous in a Soldier, the most injurious to an Army, and the last to be forgiven; inasmuch as it may, and often does happen, that the Cowardice of a single Officer may prove the Distruction of the whole Army: The General therefore (tho' with great Concern, and more especially, as the Transaction happened before he had the Command of the Troops) thinks himself obliged for the good of the service, to approve the Judgment of the Court Martial with respect to Capt. John Callender, who is hereby sentenced to be cashiered. Capt. John Callender is accordingly cashiered and dismissd from all farther service in the Continental Army as an Officer.[1]

The General having made all due inquiries, and maturely consider'd this matter is led to the above determination not only from the particular Guilt of Capt. Callenders, but the fatal Consequences of such Conduct to the army and to the cause of america.

He now therefore most earnestly exhorts Officers of all Ranks to shew an Example of Bravery and Courage to their men; assuring them that such as do their duty in the day of Battle, as brave and good Officers, shall be honor'd with every mark of distinction and regard; their names and merits made known to the General Congress and all America: while on the other hand, he positively declares that every Officer, be his rank what it may, who shall betray his Country, dishonour the Army and his General, by basely keeping back and shrinking from his duty in any engagement; shall be held up as an infamous Coward and punish'd as such, with the utmost martial severity; and no Connections, Interest or Intercessions in his behalf will avail to prevent the strict execution of justice.[2]

Capt. Scotts and Capt. Styles's Company's from New Hampshire, are to be incorporated, or added to Col. Serjants Regiment, agreeable to the application made for that purpose.[3] No Officer or Soldier, posted in the Lines for the defence of them, on Prospect Hill, or Winter Hill, or elsewhere, are upon any account to sleep out of their encampment or leave it at night. The Troops from New Hampshire are particularly requir'd to attend to this Order, from their particular Circumstances of situation.

No Soldier, belonging to these Post's, or elsewhere, to be suffered to straggle at a distance from their respective parade, on any pretence; without leave from his Officers: As an unguarded Hour, may prove fatal to the whole army, and to the noble Cause in which we are engaged. The Importance of which, to every man of common understanding, must inspire every good Officer and Soldier, with the noblest Ardour and strictest attention, least he should prove the fatal Instrument of our ruin.

The Adjutant General[4] is required, to make a return as quick as possible, of the Troops in Cambridge, their number, and the duty they do.

Complaints having been made with respect to the Bread, as being sour and unwholesome; the Quarter Master General[5] is hereby directed to enquire into the matter and report upon it: At the same time to inform the Bakers that if any Complaints are made; and they shall be found just, they will be most severely punished.

The Guards on the Roads leading to Bunker's Hill, are ordered not to suffer any person to pass them, unless an Officer is sent down from the Lines to order it, or they will be severely punished.

The General has great Reason; and is highly displeased, with the Negligence and Inattention of those Officers, who have placed as Centries, at the out-posts, Men with whose Characters they are not acquainted. He therefore orders, that for the future, no Man shall be appointed to those important stations, who is not a Native of this Country, or has a Wife, or Family in it, to whom he is known to be attached. This Order is to be consider'd as a standing one and the Officers are to pay obedience to it at their peril.

A Complaint of the most extraordinary kind, having been made to the General, that Soldiers inlisted in one Regiment, have been seduced to reinlist into others, by Agents employed for that purpose under the specious promises of money, or leave of absence from the army, a procedure so subversive of all order, discipline, and of the very Existance of the army, cannot be forgiven—the strictest Orders are therefore given against such practices, and the General most earnestly declares, that if any Agent or Soldier, shall hereafter be found so offending, he will punish them with the utmost severity.[6]

A General Court Martial having sat upon William Pattin and reported, that no Evidence appeared against him, to support the Charge; the General defers his decision upon the Report, untill farther consideration. In the mean time, the Adjutant General is ordered to wait on Col. Ward,[7] by whom the Prisoner was confin'd and learn from him upon whose complaint, and what Witnesses, there are to support it.

A regimental Court Martial is ordered to sit to morrow 10 oClock, on Samuel Bartlett of the Company late Capt. Callenders, and Col. Gridley's Regiment, confin'd for "abusive behaviour."

A General Court Martial to sit to morrow, 10 oClock A:M: for the Trial of Thomas Daniely, charged with "stealing"; each of the above Prisoners to have Notice to day, and the Witnesses in like manner order'd to attend.

In order that all the sick and wounded in the Army may be provided for, and taken Care of in the best way and manner possible: It is order'd, that when any Officer or Soldier is so ill, either by a Wound, or otherwise, that the Surgeon of the Regt to which he belongs, finds he cannot be properly taken care of in such Regt such surgeon shall send him to the Camp Hospital to which they belong, with a Certificate of the Man's Name, the

Company[8] to which he belongs, and in that case the Surgeon of the Hospital shall receive said sick and wounded; and in case such Hospital shall be too full, in that case the surgeons of said Hospital shall send such of his patients, as may be removed with safety, to the Hospital at Water-town, with the like Certificate as above, on which the Surgeon of Water-town Hospital, is to receive, and take care of him.[9]

Varick transcript, DLC:GW; copy, in Joseph Reed's writing, MWA.

1. John Callender (d. 1797), a captain in Col. Richard Gridley's Massachusetts artillery regiment, was tried by a court-martial on 27 June 1775 for cowardice and disobedience of orders during the Battle of Bunker Hill. His chief accuser was Maj. Gen. Israel Putnam, who told a committee of the Massachusetts provincial congress "that in the late action, as he was riding up *Bunker's Hill*, he met an officer of the Train drawing his cannon down in great haste; he ordered the officer to stop and go back; he replied, he had no cartridges; the General dismounted and examined his boxes, and found a considerable number of cartridges, upon which he ordered him back; he refused, until the General threatened him with immediate death, upon which he returned up the hill again, but soon deserted his post and left the cannon." Some excuse for Callender's actions was provided by an unnamed "officer of rank," who testified "that he absolutely knew that some of the cartridges and balls were too large for the cannon, and that it was necessary to break the cartridges before they could be of use." In addition, Callender as a Massachusetts officer apparently did not feel bound to obey Putnam, who at that time was a general only in the Connecticut service. Putnam was supported in the essentials of his account by several officers, and he threatened to quit the army if Callender was not severely punished. "The defeat of that day," Putnam declared, "was owing to the ill-behaviour of those that conducted the artillery. . . . the reenforcements ordered up the hill could not be prevailed upon to go; the plea was, the Artillery was gone, and they stood no chance for their lives in such circumstances, declaring they had no officers to lead them" (Force, *American Archives*, 4th ser., 2:1438). Callender soon reentered the army as a volunteer artillery cadet, and at the Battle of Long Island in August 1776, he redeemed his reputation. Taking command of his unit's guns after his superiors were killed, Callender continued to fire, despite being wounded, until he was taken prisoner. He was exchanged in 1777 and served in the Continental artillery as a captain-lieutenant until 1784.

2. This paragraph is based on the suggestions that Joseph Hawley made to GW in his letter of 5 July 1775.

3. Col. Paul Dudley Sargent (1745–1828) of Salem commanded a regiment of Massachusetts infantry until the end of 1776. Capt. William Scott (1742–1796) of Peterborough, N.H., transferred to the 1st New Hampshire Regiment in the fall of 1776 and was wounded at the Battle of Saratoga the following year. He retired with the rank of major in January 1781. Capt.

Jeremiah Stiles (c.1744–1800) of Keene, N.H., commanded a company at the Battle of Bunker Hill.

4. Col. William Henshaw, adjutant general of the Massachusetts forces, acted as GW's adjutant general until Horatio Gates assumed that office on 9 July.

5. The quartermaster general at this time was apparently Joseph Pearse Palmer (1750–1797) who had held that position in the Massachusetts service since 1 May 1775. A Continental quartermaster general was not named until Thomas Mifflin was appointed to the office on 14 August.

6. Disputes over conflicting enlistments are referred to the brigade commanders in General Orders, 25 July 1775.

7. Jonathan Ward of Southborough became lieutenant colonel of Maj. Gen. Artemas Ward's Massachusetts regiment in June 1775 after a dispute over the position with William Henshaw was resolved by the provincial congress. When GW decided in September that generals could not have regiments (see GW to Hancock, 4–5 Aug. and 21 Sept. 1775), Jonathan Ward assumed the colonelcy of General Ward's regiment and served as a regimental commander until the end of 1776, at which time he left the army.

8. The Reed copy reads "The Company & Regiment."

9. This paragraph is a copy of the resolution that the Massachusetts provincial congress passed on 1 July 1775 with minor wording changes. See Massachusetts Provincial Congress to GW, 5 July 1775, n.1.

General Orders

Head Quarters, Cambridge, July 8th 1775.

Parole, Essex. Counter-sign, Falkland.

Ordered that the main guard on no Account whatever, be without a Drum, which is to beat to Arms on any Alarm and be followed by all the drums in the Camp; On which every Officer and Soldier is immediately to repair to the Alarm post.

The Commanding Officer of each Regiment or Corps in Cambridge as soon as the Men are paraded after an Alarm, to send an Officer to Head Quarters for orders.

The commanding Officers at Roxbury, Prospect hill Winter-hill and Sewalls point to send Expresses in case of Alarm to Head Quarters with an account of the Situation and the movements of the enemy—If they are not each provided with a Horse for that purpose; the Adjutant General to apply to the Committee of supplies.[1]

Col. Gridley of the Artillery,[2] or the next in Command, to give in a Return of his men, stores, and Ammunition, agreeable to the Order of the 4th Instant, and to distinguish the Posts to which his Regiment is assigned in Case of alarm: The same order as to a Return of the Men, Ammunition and Blankets is given to the Commanding Officers of the Regiments late Col. Gar[d]ner's Col. Glovers, & Col. Gerrishes, who have omitted complying with the above Orders hitherto.[3]

The Commanding Officers at Winter-hill, Prospect-hill and Roxbury are to make particular enquiry into the Ammunition of the Men in those Lines, and if there is any Deficiency immediately to report it to the General at Head quarters.

A General Court Martial is order'd to set on monday next 10, oClock A:M: for the Trial of Lieut. Brigham charged with, "rescuing a Prisoner when in lawful custody."[4]

Varick transcript, DLC:GW; copy, in Joseph Reed's writing, MWA.

1. Sewall's Point, located on the south side of the Charles River about two miles downstream from Cambridge, was the site of an American redoubt which some called Brookline fort. For the horses that were provided for this and the other posts, see Council of War, 9 July 1775, and GW to James Warren, 10 July 1775, n.3.

2. Richard Gridley (1710–1796) was appointed chief engineer of the Massachusetts forces by the provincial congress on 26 April 1775, and about the same time he was asked to organize a train of artillery. Gridley was a natural choice for both jobs, having studied military engineering under a British officer as a young man and having commanded provincial artillery during the Crown Point expedition of 1755 and at Quebec in 1759. On 23 June 1775 the provincial congress gave Gridley a commisssion as chief engineer and colonel of the Massachusetts artillery with the rank of major general, and on 20 Sept. the Continental Congress commissioned him colonel of the Continental artillery. So great were the antagonisms that he engendered in the artillery corps, however, that Congress was forced to remove him from his command on 17 November. Gridley continued to serve as chief engineer in the army until some time in 1776, and he was engineer general for the eastern department from 1777 to 1780.

3. Joseph Reed wrote to Col. Samuel Gerrish on 7 July 1775: "I am directed by his Excelly the General to beg you wou'd without delay see that a Return is made of your Regiment, agreeable to Orders issued the 4th Instant—The Express [to the Continental Congress] has been detain'd some time thro' this Inattention The Forces raised in Connecticut, New Hampshire & Rhode Island having sent in their Returns very complete" (MH: Loammi Baldwin Papers). GW was anxious to forward a full report on the strength of the army to the Continental Congress in accordance with Congress's instructions of 22 June, but delays in obtaining the returns from the Massachusetts regiments named here obliged him to wait until 10 July. See GW to Hancock, 10–11 July 1775, Document II. Letter Sent, n.10, and GW to Richard Henry

Lee, 10 July 1775, n.2. Samuel Gerrish (c.1729–1795) of Newbury, Mass., was cashiered on 19 Aug. 1775 for conduct unbecoming an officer (General Orders, that date).

4. At the end of this paragraph, the Reed copy includes the sentence: "The Prisoner to have Notice to Day." Near the bottom of the page appears the memorandum: "Leut. Brigham belongs to Capt. Woods Company Genl Wards Regimt." Timothy Brigham was actually first lieutenant of Capt. Samuel Hood's company in Maj. Gen. Artemas Ward's Massachusetts regiment.

From the Fairfax Independent Company

May it please your Excellency. Alexandria July 8. 1775

Your favor of the 20 Ulo notifying your Intended departure for the Camp, we Received; and after transmitting copies to the different officers, to whom it was directed,[1] we laid it before a full meeting of your Company this day—At the same time that they deplore the unfortunate occasion, that calls you, their patron, friend & worthy citizen from them, & your more tender connections, they beg your acceptance of their most hearty congratulations upon your appointment to the supreme military command of the American confederated forces.

Firmly convinced Sir, of your zealous attachment to the rights of your Country & those of mankind, and of your earnest desire that harmony & Good will should again take place between us & our parent state, we well know that your every exertion will be invariably employed, to preserve the one & effect the other.

Your kind recommendation, that a strict attention be had, to disciplining the Company, shall be complied with, & every possible method used for procuring arms & ammunition.

We are to inform you Sir, by desire of the Company, that if at any ⟨ti⟩me you shall judge it expedient for them to join the Troops at Cambridge, or to march elsewhere, they will cheerfully do it.

As the success of our arms, during the unhappy contest for our liberties, will ever afford us the highest satisfaction, and as reports heretofore have been various & unauthentic, we Intreat your Excellency, should there be any future Engagement & your leisure permit, to favour us with an Account. Let our concerns for the cause we are Imbarked in, claim your excuse for this freedom.

We now Recommend you to the favor of him, by whom Kings Reign & Princes decree justice, and wishing all your councils & operations to be directed by his gracious providence to an happy and lasting union between us & Great Britain We are with great regard for selves & the Company Your Excellency's most Obedt & Humble servants

James Hendricks
Geo. Gilpin
Rob. H. Harrison

LS, in Robert Hanson Harrison's writing, DLC:GW. Each officer signed his own name.

James Hendricks of Alexandria was captain of the Fairfax Independent Company. He became major of the 6th Virginia Regiment in February 1776, lieutenant colonel of that regiment the following August, and colonel of the 1st Virginia Regiment in September 1777. Hendricks resigned his commission in March 1778. George Gilpin (1740–1813) and Robert Hanson Harrison (1745–1790) were lieutenants in the Fairfax Independent Company. Both men were natives of Maryland who moved to Alexandria in the late 1760s. Gilpin, a wheat merchant and flour inspector, served as major of the Fairfax County militia from 1777 to 1778 and apparently became colonel of the militia before the end of the war. In the 1780s he was closely associated with GW as one of the directors of the Potomac Company. Harrison, a lawyer whose services GW used on several occasions before the Revolution, served as clerk of the Fairfax County committee of safety from 1774 to 1775. He was appointed one of GW's aides-de-camp on 6 Nov. 1775, and on 16 May 1776 he became GW's military secretary. He held the latter position until March 1781, when he resigned to become chief justice of the Maryland general court.

1. GW's letter of 20 June 1775 was addressed to the officers of the independent companies in the five Virginia counties of Fairfax, Prince William, Fauquier, Spotsylvania, and Richmond.

Letter not found: to Lund Washington, 8 July 1775. In a letter of 15 Oct. 1775 to GW, Lund Washington referred to GW's letter of "July 8th."

General Orders

Head Quarters, Cambridge, July 9th 1775.

Parole, Effingham. C. Sign, Watertown.

The Continental Congress having been pleased to appoint Horatio Gates Esqr. Brigadier General, and Adjutant General of the Army; he is to be obeyed as such; and all Orders transmitted through him from the Commander in Chief, whether written, or verbal, are to be punctually, and immediately obey'd.[1]

All soldiers, more than two a Company, who are at present absent on Furlough, and all Officers, non Commissioned Officers, and Soldiers, who have not join'd their respective Corps, to be ordered forthwith to Camp. The Commanding Officers of Corps to be answerable to the General, for an immediate obedience to this order.[2]

The General (or in his absence) The Commanding Officer at Roxbury,[3] to send a report every day in writing, sealed up, to the Commander in Chief at Head Quarters, in Cambridge, of all the material Occurrences of the preceeding day; mentioning particularly, all Arrivals of Ships and Vessels in the bay; and what changes and alterations are made, in the Stations of the Men of war, Transport's, and floating batteries &c.

Varick transcript, DLC:GW.

1. Horatio Gates was appointed adjutant general by the Continental Congress on 17 June (*JCC*, 2:97).

2. GW included a similar directive in General Orders, 4 July 1775.

3. Brig. Gen. John Thomas was the commanding officer at Roxbury at this time.

Council of War

[Cambridge, 9 July 1775]

At a Council of War held at Head Quarters Cambridge July 9th 1775.

Present His Excelly General Washington

M. Generals	Ward	B. Genls	Thomas
	Lee		Heath
	Putman		Greene[1]
			Gates.

The General laid before the Council a Letter from Mr Warren President of the Congress of Massachusetts Bay inclosing a Letter from Mr Gerry of Marblhead dated July 8th.[2]

1. A Question was proposed & considered viz. What is the Numbr of the Enemy in & near Boston, including the Troops formerly & lately arrived, & there expected, the Tories who may take Arms, such Sailors as may be spared from the Fleet &

the Negroes—Upon which it was agreed, that from the best Intelligence the Force on the Side of the Enemy now amounts to about Eleven thousand, five hundred Men.[3]

2d A Question was proposed, & considerd whether it is expedient to keep & defend the Posts at present occupied, or to retire farther back into the Country: Upon which it was *unanimously* determd that the publick Service requires the Defence of the present Posts.[4]

3. A Question was proposed what Number of Troops may be necessary for the present Service in & near Boston to defend the Posts now occupied against the Force supposed to be employed against us. Upon which it was agreed that the Army for the above Purpose ought to consist of at least 22,000 Men.

4. As by the Returns now made the Number of effective Men is far short of the above Estimate a Question was made in what Manner the Deficiency shall be supplied[5] And it was agreed that the same ought to be done by sending an Officer from each Company of the Forces raised in Massachusetts Bay to recruit the Regiments to which they respectively belong, to the Establishment fixed by the provincial Congress; The Colonies of Rhode Island & Connecticut being already engaged in recruiting;[6] And that in the mean Time his Excelly the General do apply to the provincial Congress of this Province for their Assistance in procuring a temporary Reinforcement; subject to the same military Rules as the Army now raised; Inasmuch as the present Extent of Lines & the great Probability of an early Attack render such Reinforcement indispensably necessary.[7]

5. As the Events of War are uncertain & a Want of a proper Rendezvous might in Case of any Misfortune occasion a Dissolution of the whole Army, it was proposed to appoint a proper Place for this Purpose in Case our present Situation should not be tenable.

Nemine Contradicente. N.C. Agreed that the Welch Mountains near Cambridge & in the Rear of the Roxbury Lines is a suitable Place.[8]

6. A Question was proposed whether it is expedient to take Possession of Dorchester Point or to oppose the Enemy if they should attempt to possess it.

Unanimously Agreed in the Negative as to both.[9]

7. N.B. That 10 Horses with Bridles & Saddles be provided in order to carry Intelligence from the Out Posts & Camps.[10]

8. That a Beacon be erected on Blue Hill.[11]

D, in Joseph Reed's writing, DLC:GW; copy, in Joseph Reed's writing, DNA: PCC, item 152; copy, DNA: RG 93, Miscellaneous Numbered Records ("Manuscript File"), 1775–84; Varick transcript, DLC:GW. The copy in PCC, which was enclosed in GW's letter to Hancock of 10–11 July 1775, does not include decisions number seven and eight. The copy in RG 93 omits decision number eight. An extract containing only decisions number three and four was enclosed in GW's letter to James Warren of 10 July 1775 (*Mass. Prov. Congress Journals*, 482–83, n.1).

1. Nathanael Greene (1742–1786), commander of the Rhode Island forces, was one of the eight brigadier generals appointed by the Continental Congress on 22 June. He became a major general in August 1776 and rendered invaluable service to the American cause as Continental quartermaster general from 1778 to 1780 and as commander of the Southern army from 1780 to 1783.

2. Neither letter has been found.

3. Transport ships carrying four regiments of reinforcements from Ireland arrived at Boston at various times between 22 June and 19 July 1775, bringing the strength of the British regular forces in the town to about six thousand men fit for duty and about fourteen hundred sick or wounded. See also Schuyler to GW, 1 July 1775, n.3.

4. GW expressed his personal views on this question in his letter to Richard Henry Lee of 10 July 1775.

5. The returns showed that the American army outside Boston consisted of about sixteen thousand men, of whom about fourteen thousand were fit for duty. See GW to Richard Henry Lee, 10 July 1775.

6. GW instructed the Massachusetts colonels to send out recruiting officers in General Orders, 10 July 1775. The authorized strength of each Massachusetts regiment was 590 men. Nathanael Greene wrote to Deputy Gov. Nicholas Cooke of Rhode Island on 9 July: "A General Council of War was held to Day at Cambridge, at the close of which his Excellency General Washington, directed me to acquaint you, that he thinks it necessary that the recruits be forwarded as Soon as possible, and What Tents are made or can be got made be forwarded as Soon as may be, The Captains or one of the Subbalterns come forward with the recruits of each Company. I am informed by his Excellency that the expense is to be a Continental expence, this you may be assured off—And as every Government will receive pay for the number of Troops they send I hope the People will enlist chearfully" (Matt B. Jones, ed., "Revolutionary Correspondence of Governor Nicholas Cooke, 1775–1781," in Amer. Antiquarian Soc., *Proceedings*, new ser., 36 [1926], 255).

7. GW wrote to James Warren about these reinforcements on 10 July 1775. See especially note 2.

8. In his first version of this paragraph, Reed wrote that the Welch Moun-

tains lay "about 5 Miles from Cambridge," but in a second version written at the end of the draft, he changed the wording to "near Cambridge." The Welch Mountains were probably the hills at Newton, Massachusetts.

9. Reed also rewrote this paragraph at the end of the draft. In his first version the two questions involved were rendered as separate items, numbered six and seven.

10. GW requested these horses from the Massachusetts provincial congress in his letter to James Warren of 10 July 1775.

11. The Great Blue Hill, located a short distance south of Milton, has an elevation of 635 feet, providing a view of the entire Boston area.

General Orders

Head Quarters, Cambridge, July 10th 1775

Parole Frederick. Counter-sign. Gloucester.

The General Court Martial of which Col. William Prescott was president, having tried William Pattin of Col. Gridley's regiment, and found him guilty of "threatening and abusing a number of persons, when prisoner in the Quarter Guard:" The Court sentence the prisoner to ride the wooden Horse, fifteen minutes.[1] The General approves the sentence, and orders it to be put in execution at the head of the regiment.

David Wells soldier in Col. Gridley's Regimt tried by the abovementioned General Court Martial for "sleeping upon his post when sentry," is acquitted by the court.

No non Commission'd Officer, or soldier, but such as are guilty of capital Offences; to be confin'd in the Main Guard; All those guilty of crimes triable by a Regimental Court Martial, to be sent to the Quarter Guards of their respective Corps, to be tried by regimental Court martial.[2] The General Court Martial, whereof Col. William Prescott is president, to set again this day at the usual hour:[3] All Evidences and Persons concerned to attend the court. Whenever a General Court Martial is ordered, it is expected that the Evidences and persons by whom the prisoners are confin'd, *do* punctually attend to support the accusation, as they will answer the contrary at their peril.[4]

The Colonels of the Massachusetts regiments, to order one subaltern from each Company in their respective Corps, forthwith upon the recruiting service; proper Instructions will be given by the Adjutant General to the Officers ordered upon that service.[5] They will therefore call at Head Quarters as soon as possible to receive their Instructions. The General recommends it to the Colonels to send active and vigilant Officers upon this service, and those who are most in esteem with people in the District they are sent to recruit in.

Varick transcript, DLC:GW.

1. The wooden horse consisted of a sharp ridged rail supported by four tall legs. The prisoner was seated on the rail with his hands tied behind his back and weights attached to his feet for the time prescribed. The use of this painful and potentially injurious punishment was not specifically prohibited by the Massachusetts articles of war but the Continental articles of war did not include it among the authorized punishments (*JCC*, 2:119).

2. Both the Continental and Massachusetts articles of war provided that "the commissioned officers of every regiment may, by the appointment of their Colonel or commanding officer, hold regimental courts-martial for the enquiring into such disputes or criminal matters as may come before them, and for the inflicting corporal punishment, for small offences" (*JCC*, 2:117; also in *Mass. Prov. Congress Journals*, 126–27). Regimental court-martials were specifically authorized to handle cases involving the sale or waste of military equipment and stores, absences without leave from camp or parade, drunkenness, and abuse of people bringing provisions into the camp. More serious crimes, such as mutiny, desertion, dueling, plundering, sleeping on guard duty, giving false alarms, and treasonous correspondence, were reserved for general court-martials.

3. General court-martials held during the previous week met at 10:00 A.M. Both the Continental and Massachusetts articles of war prohibited "any proceedings or trials [to] be carried on, excepting between the hours of eight in the morning, and three in the afternoon, except in cases which require an immediate example" (*JCC*, 2:117; also in *Mass. Prov. Congress Journals*, 126).

4. Court-martials were permitted by the Continental and Massachusetts articles of war to punish at their discretion anyone "called to give evidence, . . . who shall refuse to give evidence" (*JCC*, 2:120; also in *Mass. Prov. Congress Journals*, 129).

5. Horatio Gates's recruiting instructions, dated 10 July 1775, were printed as a broadside (Gregory and Dunning, "Gates Papers").

To John Hancock

[Cambridge, 10–11 July 1775]

In preparation for the writing of this letter, GW composed a list of topics which he wished to be covered in it. Those undated notes, which are printed here, apparently were then used by Joseph Reed to make a rough draft of the letter. Reed's draft has not been found, but a draft written by him was reported to be in the possession of James

Wilkinson in the early nineteenth century.[1] The finished letter that was sent to Hancock, also printed here, is in Reed's writing and is signed by GW. Although all of the manuscript copies of the finished letter are dated 10 July, internal evidence indicates that its last paragraph and postscript were written on 11 July (see Document II. Letter Sent, notes 28 and 31). Furthermore, the letter-book copy of that document has the notation: "Sent by Alexander who set out the 11th July about 5 oClock P.M. inclosing Proceeds. of Council of War July 9. 1775." Not all of the topics listed in GW's notes were discussed in the finished letter (see Document I. Notes for Letter, notes 2 and 4), and some new topics were introduced.

1. James Wilkinson, *Memoirs of My Own Times*, 3 vols. (Philadelphia, 1816), 1:855.

I. Notes for Letter

The time of my arrival.

The Situation of the Troops—Works—& things in genl—Enemy on Bunkers Hill.

The almost impossibility of giving up the present Incampment in the Face of the Enemy, & after so much work has been bestowd notwithstanding our Situation from the devidedness of it, & length of our lines &ca is by no means desirable.

The exceeding difficulty of getting returns of the Forces &ca is the reason why I could not write sooner—to this may be added the necessity of bestowing a good deal of time & attention to the defence of our lines wch are within gunshot of the Enemy.

Want of Tents a great disadvantage as the men are much dispers'd in Quarters, & unavoidably so, which is an essential reason for continuing in the Quarters at Cambridge & Roxbury.

Express gratitude for the readiness wch the Congress & difft Committees[1] have shewn to make every thing as convenient & as agreeable as possible, but point out the Inconvenence of depending ⟨up⟩on a number of Men & different chann⟨el⟩s through which these supplies are to be furnishd and the necessity of appointg a Com[missar]y Genl for these purposes—recomd Mr Trumbell for this Office.

The necessity also of a Quarter Master Genl—Comy of Musters—&ca—Also the want of Money for these difft branches of business. The want of Laws for the Governmt of the army[2]—

and the want of Cloathing which I do not find is likely to be had here.

Comply with Instruction's in giving answr and acknowledge the rect of Mr Hancocks Letter & answer it.[3]

A great want of Engineers—and our distress on that acct as well as for the want of Powder which must be kept for small arms.

The great dissatisfaction at the appointment of Genl Officers—Genl Spencer will not continue because Genl Putnam is appointed over. Genl Thomas much esteemd & earnestly desired to remain, the Provincial Congress requesting that Genl Pomroy (who was when I came here, & now is abst) might not have his Comn given—Spencer gone home without leave.

Tents to be sent from Phila.

More riffle Men.[4]

Engen.

provision Return.[5]

AD, RPJCB.

1. GW is referring to the Massachusetts provincial congress and the various committees appointed by that body, such as the committee of safety and the committee of supplies.

2. This matter was omitted from the letter sent to Hancock because Hancock's letter of 5 July 1775, which reached Cambridge on 10 July, informed GW of the approval of the Continental articles of war.

3. See Instructions from the Continental Congress, 22 June 1775, and Hancock to GW, 28 June 1775.

4. Riflemen are not mentioned in the letter sent to Hancock.

5. These two words are in Joseph Reed's writing.

II. Letter Sent

Sir Camp at Cambridge July 10[–11] 1775

I arrived safe at this Place on the 3d Instt, after a Journey attended with a good deal of Fatigue, & retarded by necessary Attentions to the successive Civilities which accompanied me in my whole Rout[1]—Upon my Arrival, I immediately visited the several Posts occupied by our Troops, & as soon as the Weather permitted, reconnoitred those of the Enemy.[2] I found the latter strongly entrench'd on Bunker's Hill about a Mile from Charlestown, & advanced about half a Mile from the Place of the late

Action, with their Centries extended about 150 Yards on this Side of the narrowest Part of the Neck leading from this Place to Charlestown; 3 floating Batteries lay in Mystick River near their Camp; & one 20 Gun Ship below the Ferry Place between Boston & Charlestown. They have also a Battery on Copse Hill on the Boston Side which much annoyed our Troops in the late Attack.[3] Upon the Neck,[4] they are also deeply entrenched & strongly fortified. Their advanced Guards till last Saturday Morning occupied Brown's Houses about a Mile from Roxbury Meeting House, & 20 Roods from their Lines: But at that Time, a Party from General Thomas's Camp surprized the Guard, drove them in & burnt the Houses.[5] The Bulk of their Army commanded by General Howe lays on Bunkers Hill, & the Remainder on Roxbury Neck, except the Light Horse, & a few Men in the Town of Boston—On our Side we have thrown up Intrenchments on Winter & Prospect Hills, the Enemies Camp in full View at the Distance of little more than a Mile. Such intermediate Points as would admit a Landing, I have since my Arrival taken Care to strengthen down to Sewal's Farm, where a strong Entrenchment has been thrown up.[6] At Roxbury General Thomas has thrown up a strong Work on the Hill, about 200 Yards above the Meeting House, which with the Brokenness of the Ground & great Numbers of Rocks has made that Pass very secure—The Troops raised in New Hampshire, with a Regiment from Rhode Island occupy Winter Hill. A Part of those from Connecticut under General Puttnam are on Prospect Hill: The Troops in this Town are entirely of the Massachusetts: The Remainder of the Rhode Island Men, are at Sewalls Farm: Two Regiments of Connecticut & 9 of the Massachusetts are at Roxbury. The Residue of the Army to the Number of about 700 are posted in several small Towns along the Coast to prevent the Depredations of the Enemy: Upon the whole, I think myself authorized to say that considering the great Extent of Line, & the Nature of the Ground we are as well secured as could be expected in so short a Time, & under the Disadvantages we labour. These consist in a Want of Engineers to construct proper Works & direct the Men, a Want of Tools, & a sufficient Number of Men to man the Works in Case of an Attack: You will observe by the Proceedings of the Council of War, which I have the Honour to inclose, that it is our unanimous

Opinion to hold and defend these Works as long as possible.[7] The Discouragement it would give the Men, & its contrary Effects on the ministerial Troops, thus to abandon our Incampment in their Face, form'd with so much Labour,[8] added to the certain Destruction of a considerable & valuable Extent of Country, and our Uncertainty of finding a Place in all Respects so capable of making a Stand, are leading Reasons for this Determination; at the same Time we are very sensible of the Difficulties which attend the Defence of Lines of so great Extent, and the Dangers which may ensue from such a Division of the Army.

My earnest Wishes to comply with the Instructions of the Congress in making an early and complete Return of the State of the Army,[9] has led into an involuntary Delay of addressing you, which has given me much Concern. Having given Orders for this Purpose immediately on my Arrival, & unapprized of the imperfect Obedience which had been paid to those of the like Nature from General Ward, I was led from Day to Day to expect they would come in, & therefore detained the Messenger.[10] They are not now so complete as I could wish but much Allowance is to be made for Inexperience in Forms, & a Liberty which had been taken (not given) on this Subject—These Reasons I flatter myself will no longer exist, & of Consequence more Regularity & Exactness in future prevail. This with a necessary Attention to the Lines, the Movements of the ministerial Troops, & our immediate Security, must be my Apology, which I beg you lay before the Congress with the utmost Duty & Respect.

We labour under great Disadvantages for Want of Tents, for tho. they have been help'd out by a Collection of now useless Sails from the Sea Port Towns, the Number is far short of our Necessities. The Colleges & Houses of this Town are necessarily occupied by the Troops which affords another Reason for keeping our present Situation: But I most sincerely wish the whole Army was properly provided to take the Field, as I am well assured, that besides greater Expedition & Activity in Case of Alarm it would highly conduce to Health & Discipline. As Materials are not to be had here I would beg Leave to recommend the procuring a farther Supply from Philadelphia as soon as possible.[11]

I should be extremely deficient in Gratitude, as well as Justice, if I did not take the first Oppy to acknowledge the Readiness & Attention which the provincial Congress & different Committees have shewn to make every Thing as convenient & agreeable as possible: but there is a vital & inherent Principle of Delay incompatible with military Service in transacting Business thro. such numerous & different Channels. I esteem it therefore my Duty to represent the Inconvenience which must unavoidably ensue from a Dependance on a Number of Persons for Supplies, & submit it to the Consideration of the Congress whether the publick Service will not be best promoted by appointing a Commissary General for these Purposes—We have a striking Instance of the Preference of such a Mode in the Establishment of Connecticut, as their Troops are extremely well provided under the Direction of Mr [ ] Trumbull & he has at different Times assisted others with various Articles—Should my Sentimts happily coincide with those of your Honours in this Subject, I beg Leave to recommend Mr Trumbull as a very proper Person for this Department. In the Arrangement of Troops collected under such Circumstances, & upon the Spur of immediate Necessity several Appointments are omitted, which appear to be indispensably necessary for the good Government of the Army, & particularly a Quartermaster General, A Commissary of Musters & a Commissary of Artillery. These I must earnestly recommend to the Notice & Provision of the Congress.[12]

I find myself already much embarassed for Want of a military Chest—these Embarassments will increase every Day: I must therefore request that Money may be forwarded as soon as possible. The Want of this most necessary Article, will I fear produce great Inconveniencies if not prevented by an early Attention. I find the Army in general, & the Troops raised in Massachusetts in particular, very deficient in necessary Cloathing. Upon Inquiry there appears no Probability of obtaining any Supplies in this Quarter. And on the best Consideration of this Matter I am able to form, I am of Opinion that a Number of hunting Shirts not less than 10,000 would in a great Degree remove this Difficulty in the cheapest & quickest Manner.[13] I know nothing in a speculative View more trivial, yet if put in Practice would have a happier Tendency to unite the Men, &

abolish those Provincial Distinctions which lead to Jealousy & Dissatisfaction. In a former Part of this Letter I mentioned the Want of Engineers; I can hardly express the Disappointment I have experienced on this Subject: The Skill of those we have, being very imperfect & confined to the mere manual Exercise of Cannon. Whereas—the War in which we are engaged requires a Knowledge comprehending the Duties of the Field and Fortification: If any Persons thus qualified are to be found in the Southern Colonies, it would be of great publick Service to forward them with all Expedition[14]—Upon the Article of Ammunition I must re-echo the former Complaints on this Subject: We are so exceedingly destitute, that our Artillery will be of little Use without a Supply both large & seasonable: What we have must be reserved for the small Arms, & that managed with the utmost Frugality.[15]

I am sorry to observe that the Appointments of the General Officers in the Province of Massachusetts Bay[16]—have by no Means corresponded with the Judgment & Wishes of either the civil or Military. The great Dissatisfaction expressed on this Subject & the apparent Danger of throwing the Army into the utmost Disorder, together with the strong Represen⟨ta⟩tions of the Provincial Congress, have induced me to retain the Commissions in my Hands untill the Pleasure of the Congress should be farther known (except General Puttnams which was given the Day I came into Camp & before I was apprized of these Uneasinesses).[17] In such a Step I must beg the Congress will do me the Justice I beleive,[18] that I have been actuated solely by a Regard to the publick Good: I have not, nor could have any private Attachments; every Gentleman in Appointment, was an entire Stranger to me but from Character. I must therefore rely upon the Candour[19] of the Congress for their favourable Construction of my Conduct in this Particular. General Spencer was so much disgusted at the Preference given to Gen. Puttnam, that he left the Army without visiting me, or making known his Intentions in any Respect.[20] General Pomroy had also retired before my Arrival occasioned (as is said) by some Disappointment from the Provincial Congress. General Thomas is much esteemed & earnestly desired to continue in the Service: and as far as my Opportunities have enabled me to judge I must join in the general Opinion that he is an able good Officer & his Resignation would be a publick Loss. The postponing him to Pomroy & Heath whom he has commanded would make his Continuance very difficult, & probably operate on his Mind, as the like Circumstance has done on that of Spencer.[21]

The State of the Army you will find ascertained with tolerable Precision in the Returns which accompany this Letter.[22] Upon finding the Number of Men to fall so far short of the Establishment, & below all Expectation I immediately called a Council of the general Officers whose Opinion as to the Mode of filling up the Regiments; & providing for the present Exigency, I have the Honour of inclosing, together with the best Judgment we are able to form of the ministerial Troops.[23] From the Number of Boys, Deserters, & Negroes which have been listed in the Troops of this Province, I entertain some Doubts whether the Number required can be raised here; and all the General Officers agree that no Dependance can be put on the Militia for a Continuance in Camp, or Regularity and Discipline during the short Time they may stay.[24] This unhappy & devoted Province has been so long in a State of Anarchy, & the Yoke of ministerial Oppression has been laid so heavily on it that great Allowances are to be made for Troops raised under such Circumstances. The Deficiency of Numbers, Discipline & Stores can only lead to this Conclusion, that their Spirit has exceeded their Strength. But at the same Time I would humbly submit to the Consideration of the Congress, the Propriety of making some farther Provision of Men from the other Colonies. If these Regiments should be completed to their Establishment, the Dismission of those unfit for Duty on Account of their Age & Character would occasion a considerable Reduction, and at all Events they have been inlisted upon such Terms, that they may be disbanded when other Troops arrive: But should my Apprehensions be realized, & the Regiments here not filled up, the publick Cause would suffer by an absolute Dependance upon so doubtful an Event, unless some Provision is made against such a Disappointment.[25]

It requires no military Skill to judge of the Difficulty of introducing proper Discipline & Subordination into an Army while we have the Enemy in View, & are in daily Expectation of an Attack, but it is of so much Importance that every Effort will be made which Time & Circumstance will admit. In the mean Time I have a sincere Pleasure in observing that there are Materials for a good Army, a great Number of able-bodied Men, active zealous in the Cause & of unquestionable Courage.

I am now Sir, to acknowledge the Receipt of your Favour of the 28th Instt,[26] inclosing the Resolutions of the Congress of the 27th ult. & a Copy of a Letter from the Committee of Albany, to all which I shall pay due Attention.

General Gates & Sullivan[27] have both arrived in good Health—My best Abilities are at all Times devoted to the Service of my Country, but I feel the Weight, Importance & Vanity of my present Duties too sensibly, not to wish a more immediate & frequent Communication with the Congress. I fear it may often happen in the Course of our present Operations, that I shall need that Assistance & Direction from them, which Time & Distance will not allow me to receive.

Since writing the above, I have also to acknow. your Favour of the 4th Instt by Fessenden, and the Receipt of the Commissions & Articles of War.[28] The Former are yet 800 short of the Number required, this Deficiency you will please to supply as soon as you conveniently can. Among the other Returns, I have also sent one of our killed, wounded & missing in the late Action, but have been able to procure no certain Account of the Loss of the ministerial Troops my best Intelligence fixes it at about 500 killed & 6 or 700 wounded but it is no more than Conjecture, the utmost Pains being taken on their Side to conceal it.[29] I have the Honour to be with the most respectful Regard, Sir Your Obed: Hbble Servt

Go: Washington

P.S. Having ordered the commanding Officer[30] to give me the earliest Intelligence of every Motion of the Enemy by Land or Water discoverable from the Heighths of his Camp: I this instt as I was closing my Letter received the inclosed from the Brigade Major: The Design of this Manuevre I know not, perhaps it may be to make a Descent some where along the Coast—it may be for New York, or it may be practised as a Deception on Us.[31] I thought it not improper however to mention the Matter to you. I have done the same to the commanding Officer at New

York,[32] & I shall let it be known to the Committee of Safety here—so that Intelligence may be communicated as they shall think best along the Sea Coast of this Government.

G. W——n

LS, in Joseph Reed's writing, DNA:PCC, item 152; LB, DLC:GW; copy, DNA:PCC, item 169; Varick transcript, DLC:GW. The LS is endorsed "Read before Congress 19 July." For the Continental Congress's resolutions in response to this letter, see *JCC*, 2:190–92.

1. GW reached Cambridge on 2 July. See General Orders, 3 July 1775, source note. For the ceremonies in GW's honor at New York on 25 and 26 June, see GW to the Continental Congress, 25 June 1775, n.2, and Address to the New York Provincial Congress, 26 June 1775, source note. At New Haven, where GW spent the night of 28 June, he was escorted on his way out of town early the next morning "by great Numbers of the Inhabitants" and three military companies, including one composed of Yale students (*Connecticut Journal, and the New-Haven Post-Boy*, 5 July 1775). On 29 June GW lodged at Wethersfield, Conn., and the next day he was greeted at Springfield, Mass., by Dr. Benjamin Church and Moses Gill, who were sent by the Massachusetts provincial congress to receive him and Charles Lee "with every mark of respect" and "to provide proper escorts for them" (*Mass. Prov. Congress Journals*, 398). On 1 July a number of gentlemen from Springfield accompanied the generals to Brookfield, Mass., and another group of gentlemen conducted them to Marlborough, Massachusetts. A troop of horsemen from Marlborough provided an escort on 2 July for the last leg of the journey to Cambridge.

2. On the afternoon of 2 July, GW and Charles Lee "Road out to the line of forts at Prospect Hill," but a steady downpour of rain that lasted all afternoon apparently prevented them from seeing much of the opposing British lines on Bunker Hill. The weather cleared the next day, when the generals inspected troops and fortifications as far south as Brookline fort at Sewall's Point. On the morning of 5 July, they viewed the lines and forts at Roxbury (Noah Chapin, Jr.'s diary in Samuel Francis Batchelder, *Bits of Cambridge History* [Cambridge, Mass., 1930], 262–63).

3. Copp's Hill, located in the north end of Boston, overlooked the Charlestown ferry landing. The Royal Navy constructed a battery there in April 1775, and during the Battle of Bunker Hill its heavy guns supported the British assault on the American lines.

4. The letter-book copy in DLC:GW reads "Upon Roxbury Neck." Also called Boston Neck, this narrow natural bridge lying north of the town of Roxbury provided the only access to Boston by land before 1786.

5. The Americans wished to destroy the advanced British position at Brown's house because it gave the enemy a good view of the activities in the provincial camp at Roxbury. Attempts were made to burn the house and its outbuildings on 24 and 25 June, but both failed ("Diary of Samuel Bixby" in Mass. Hist. Soc., *Proceedings*, 1st ser., 14 [1875–76], 288; Rufus R. Wilson, ed., *Heath's Memoirs of the American War* [1798; reprint, New York, 1904], 31). The

successful attack was made about two-thirty in the morning on Saturday, 8 July, by a force of 200 volunteers led by majors Benjamin Tupper and John Crane. "They detached 6 men about 10 o'clock in the evening [of 7 July], with orders to cross on a marsh up to the rear of the guard house, and there to watch an opportunity to fire it; the remainder of the volunteers secreted themselves in the marsh on each side the Neck: about 200 yards from the house; two pieces of brass artillery were drawn softly on the marsh within 300 yards (and upon a signal from the advanced party of 6 men) two rounds of cannon shot were fired through the guardhouse: Immediately the regulars, who formed a guard of 45, or 50 men, quitted the house, and were then fired on by the musketry, who drove them with precipitation into their lines; the 6 men posted near the house, set fire to it, and burnt it to the ground; after this they burnt another house nearer the enemy without losing a man, they took two muskets, and accoutrements, a halbert, &c. all which were bloody, and shewed evident marks of loss on the part of the regulars" (extract of a letter from the camp at Cambridge, 9 July 1775, in *New-York Journal; or the General Advertiser*, 27 July 1775). Brown's store or shop, the last remaining building in the group around his house, was burned by an American party on the night of 10 July.

6. Samuel Sewall (1745–1811), a Loyalist who fled to Boston in April 1775, owned a large farm at Brookline, a short distance south of Sewall's Point.

7. See decision number two of the Council of War, 9 July 1775. The copy of the council's proceedings which GW enclosed to Hancock (consisting only of decisions one through six) is in DNA:PCC, item 152.

8. The letter-book copy reads "Labour & Expence."

9. See Instructions from the Continental Congress, 22 June 1775.

10. For the delay in receiving the returns, see General Orders, 8 July 1775, n.3. For Artemas Ward's attempts to obtain complete returns from the army, see his general orders for 21, 30 April, 9 May, 14, 21 June, and 1 July 1775 in his orderly book (MHi: Ward Papers). The messenger was Alexander (see editorial note).

11. Cambridge was nearly deserted by its inhabitants, the army having taken over most of the town's houses and the buildings at Harvard College. A variety of temporary structures also housed soldiers in the American camps. "Every tent is a portraiture of ye temper and taste of ye persons that incamp in it," the Rev. William Emerson of Concord, Mass., wrote to his wife on 17 July 1775. "Some are made of boards, some of sailcloth, and some partly of one and partly of the other. Others are made of stone and turf, and others again of Birch and other brush. Some are thrown up in a hurry and look as if they could not help it—mere necessity—others are curiously wrought with doors and windows done with wreaths and withes in the manner of a basket. Some are your proper tents and marquees, and look like ye regular camp of the enemy. These are the Rhode-islanders, who are furnished with tent equipage from among ourselves and every thing in the most exact English taste" (Allen French, *The First Year of the American Revolution* [Boston and New York, 1934], 300). On 19 July Congress applied to the Philadelphia committee of safety for materials to make tents (*JCC*, 2:190).

12. Joseph Trumbull, commissary general of the Connecticut forces, was appointed by Congress on 19 July to "be commissary general of stores and provisions for the army of the United Colonies." That same day the Congress resolved "that the appointment of a quarter master general, Commissary of Musters, and a Commissary of Artillery, be left to General Washington" (*JCC*, 2:190–91). See also Benjamin Harrison to GW, 21–24 July 1775, n.5, and Hancock to GW, 24 July 1775, n.5.

13. Long a favorite garment among American backwoodsmen, the simple, loose-fitting hunting shirt was worn by some ranger units during the French and Indian War, and it was included in the "Indian dress" that GW suggested for use of the Virginia Regiment in 1758 (GW to Henry Bouquet, 3 July 1758). In 1775 the rifle companies raised in Virginia, Maryland, and Pennsylvania adopted the hunting shirt as part of their uniform. Silas Deane, who saw some of the Pennsylvania riflemen in Philadelphia, described their hunting shirts in a letter of 3 June 1775 to his wife Elizabeth: "They take a peice of Ticklenburgh, or Tan Cloth that is stout and put it in a Tann Fatt, untill it has the shade of a dry, or fading Leaf, then they make a kind of Frock of it reaching down below the knee, open before, with a Large Cape, they wrapp it round them tight on a March, & tye it with their Belt in which hangs their Tomahawk" (Smith, *Letters of Delegates*, 1:436–38). The men usually decorated their hunting shirts by fringing them along the edges and adding fringed bands to the arms. The Continental Congress agreed to GW's proposal for outfitting the whole army in hunting shirts and recommended that they be made of tow cloth obtained from Rhode Island and Connecticut. See Hancock to GW, 24 July 1775, n.3. When tow cloth proved to be unavailable in those colonies, the project had to be abandoned (GW to Hancock, 21 Sept. 1775). GW, nevertheless, encouraged the use of hunting shirts for troops without proper uniforms in General Orders, 6 May and 24 July 1776.

14. These remarks offended some of the New England delegates who put great faith in the engineering abililies of Richard Gridley and William Burbeck. See Benjamin Harrison to GW, 21–24 July 1775, n.4. Charles Lee, however, concurred with GW on this point. "We were assured at Philadelphia that the army was stock'd with Engineers," he wrote to Robert Morris on 4 July 1775. "We found not one" (*The Lee Papers*, in N. Y. Hist. Soc., *Collections*, 4 [1871], 188).

15. Congress responded to this plea on 19 July by authorizing Hancock to write to the Philadelphia and New York gunpowder committees or committees of safety, requesting them "to forward to the Camp as much good gunpowder as they can spare" (*JCC*, 2:191).

16. The letter-book copy reads "the Provinces of Massachusetts & Connecticut."

17. See General Orders, 4 July 1775, and James Warren and Joseph Hawley to GW, 4 July 1775.

18. The letter-book copy reads "to believe."

19. The wording in the letter-book copy is "the Candour & Indulgence."

20. In the Connecticut service David Wooster ranked first, having been commissioned a major general by the colony's assembly in April 1775. Under

him were Joseph Spencer (1714–1789), first brigadier general, and Israel Putnam (1718–1790), second brigadier general. Congress, however, ignored the colony's arrangement in appointing general officers for the Continental army. On 19 June Putnam was made a Continental major general, and three days later Wooster and Spencer were appointed Continental brigadier generals (*JCC*, 2:99, 103). It was Putnam's reputation as an indefatigable warrior that won him the favor of the delegates. "He is no adept either at political or religious canting & cozening," Connecticut delegate Silas Deane wrote to his wife Elizabeth on 20 July 1775; "he is no shake hand body, he therefore is totally unfit for every thing, but only fighting" (Smith, *Letters of Delegates*, 1:638–40). "Old Put," as he was familiarly known, served with Robert Rogers's rangers during the French and Indian War. In 1762 he survived a shipwreck on the ill-fated Havana expedition, and during Pontiac's War he commanded Connecticut troops on a march to Detroit. An ardent Patriot, Putnam played a leading role in the early stages of the siege of Boston. His raids of 27 and 28 Mar. 1775 on Noddles and Hog islands in Boston Harbor particularly impressed the delegates in Philadelphia, who received news of those actions shortly before voting on major generals.

Wooster and Spencer, by contrast, possessed more prosaic military records. Neither man had achieved any great distinction despite long service in the colonial wars, nor had either ever shown an aptitude for anything other than routine military duties. Both thought, nevertheless, that they had been snubbed by Congress, and despite pleas from the Connecticut delegates not to cause trouble, they soon made their displeasure known. Wooster, who received his Continental commission from GW at New Rochelle on 27 June, sent the undated commission to Roger Sherman on 7 July with a request "to deliver it to Mr Hancock with my best compliments, and desire him not to return it to me. I have already a commission from the assembly of Connecticut" (Lewis Henry Boutell, *The Life of Roger Sherman* [1896; reprint, Ann Arbor, 1980], 88–89). Wooster remained with his troops, but Joseph Spencer chose to leave the army, evoking a storm of criticism from the delegates in Philadelphia. "Suffice it to say," Deane wrote in his letter of 20 July to his wife, "the Voice here is that he [Spencer] acted a part, inconsistent, with the Character, either of a Soldier, a Patriot, or even of a Common Gentleman to desert his post in an hour of Danger, to sacrifice his Country, which he certainly did as farr as was in his power, and to turn his back sullenly on his General, a General too of such exalted worth, and Character" (Smith, *Letters of Delegates*, 1:638–40). Gov. Jonathan Trumbull of Connecticut and his council were also disturbed by Spencer's action, and at a long conference with Spencer on 13 July, they persuaded him to return to the army and to accept his new commission. Spencer reached the American camp six days later (GW to Hancock, 21 July 1775 [first letter]).

In August 1776 Spencer was promoted to major general, and during the campaign of 1777, he commanded troops in Rhode Island. He resigned from the army in January 1778. Wooster, for his part, never became a Continental major general. After serving in the Canadian campaign of 1775–76, he returned to Connecticut and took command of the state's troops as a Connecticut major general. He was mortally wounded during the British raid on Danbury, Conn., in April 1777.

Israel Putnam commanded the center of the American army throughout the remainder of the siege of Boston and was in charge of Continental forces on Long Island, N.Y., during the battle there in August 1776. He could not cope with the new circumstances of the Revolution, however, and after 1776 he was relegated to ever less important duties. A paralytic stroke in December 1779 put an end to his military service.

21. For a discussion of the controversy about John Thomas's rank, see James Warren and Joseph Hawley to GW, 4 July 1775, n.1. Thomas was appointed first brigadier in place of Seth Pomeroy on 19 July, the day that this letter was read in Congress (*JCC*, 2:191).

22. These returns have not been found, but GW gives some totals based on them in his letters of this date to Richard Henry Lee and James Warren.

23. See decisions number one and four of the Council of War, 9 July 1775.

24. For a discussion of the steps taken by the Massachusetts provincial congress to call out part of the colony's militia as a temporary reinforcement for the Continental army, see GW to James Warren, 10 July 1775, n.2.

25. Congress recommended to the New England colonies on 19 July that they complete their regiments and urged Rhode Island and Connecticut to raise as soon as possible the additional troops that their assemblies had recently approved: 360 men from Rhode Island and 1,400 from Connecticut (*JCC*, 2:191–92; Hancock to GW, 24 July 1775).

26. The letter-book copy reads "28 June," the correct date.

27. John Sullivan (1740–1795), a lawyer from Durham, N.H., who represented his colony in the First and Second Continental Congresses, was appointed a brigadier general in the Continental army on 22 June despite the fact that his previous military experience was limited to a few years of service as a major in the New Hampshire militia. Energetic and ambitious to an extreme, Sullivan with experience became one of GW's more competent generals, but his disputatious nature repeatedly brought him into open conflict with others both inside and outside the army. Soon after his arrival at Cambridge, Sullivan was put in command of a brigade on Winter Hill. He subsequently fought in most of the major northern battles but is best remembered for commanding American forces during the abortive Franco-American operation against Newport in 1778 and for leading a successful expedition against the Iroquois during 1779. Poor health obliged Sullivan to resign from the army in November 1779. He again served in the Continental Congress from 1780 to 1781 and was chief executive of New Hampshire for three terms during the latter 1780s.

28. This is undoubtedly a reference to Hancock's letter of 5 July 1775, which Joseph Reed docketed as being received on 10 July and answered on 11 July. That docket and the fact that the express rider Alexander did not set out for Philadelphia with GW's letter until about five o'clock on the afternoon of 11 July indicate that this paragraph was added to the letter sometime in the morning or afternoon of 11 July.

29. The return of American casualties at the Battle of Bunker Hill, which

was enclosed with this letter, reports 138 men killed, 304 wounded, and 7 missing (DLC:GW). Slightly different totals are given in GW's letters to Samuel Washington, 20 July; to George William Fairfax, 25 July; and to John Augustine Washington, 27 July 1775. For British casualties in the battle, see GW to Hancock, 21 July 1775 (third letter), and GW to Lund Washington, 20 Aug. 1775.

30. The letter-book copy reads "the commanding Officer at Roxbury." For this order, see General Orders, 9 July 1775.

31. This enclosure has not been found, but it probably contained news of the sailing of the small British convoy that weighed anchor in Boston Harbor on 11 July and sailed up the coast of Maine to Nova Scotia in order to obtain hay and wood. The date of the convoy's departure indicates that, like the last paragraph in the main body of the letter, this postscript was probably written sometime on 11 July. John Thomas's brigade major was apparently Samuel Brewer (General Orders, 30 Aug. 1775).

32. See GW to Schuyler, 10–11 July 1775.

From John Hancock

Sir

Philadelphia July 10th 1775

Since my last to you, nothing has Taken place in Congress particularly Respecting your Department.

I by order of Congress forward you the Declaration, & Address to the People of England.[1]

I must beg the favour you will Reserve some birth for me, in such Department as you may Judge most proper, for I am Determin'd to Act under you, if it be to take the firelock & Join the Ranks as a Volunteer. I have the Honor to be with profound Respect, Sir Your most Obedt servt

John Hancock

I hope to be with you soon, as there seems to prevail an Opinion that we may have an adjournmt in a little Time[.][2] We Expect soon to hear from you, all Military matters are suspended till your State arrives.

ALS, DLC:GW.

1. On 8 July Congress approved an address to the inhabitants of Great Britain, which professed a continued desire on the part of the colonists for reconciliation with the mother country (*JCC*, 2:162–70).

2. Congress adjourned for several weeks beginning on 2 August. During the recess, Hancock, who had earlier harbored some hope that he would be offered command of the Continental army, went to Massachusetts, but he did not join the army in any capacity. Both his lack of significant military experi-

ence and his recurring spells of gout argued against such a step, nor did GW know how to employ him. See GW to Hancock, 21 July 1775 (second letter). On 28 Aug. Hancock married Dorothy Quincy, whom he had courted for some years, at Fairfield, Conn., and shortly afterwards he returned to Philadelphia to continue serving as president of Congress.

Letter not found: to Benjamin Harrison, 10 July 1775. On 21 July Harrison wrote to GW: "I received your very acceptable favor of the 10th Instant by express."

To Richard Henry Lee

Dear Sir, Camp at Cambridge July 10th 1775.

I was exceeding glad to receive a Letter from you, as I always shall be whenever it is convenient, though perhaps my hurry, till such time as matters are drawn a little out of the Chaos they appear in at present, will not suffer me to write you such full and satisfactory answers, or give such clear, and precise accts of our Situation & views, as I could wish, or you might expect.

After a journey, a good deal retarded, principally by the desire the different Townships through which I traveld, express'd of shewing respect to the Genl of your armies; I arrivd here on this day week;[1] since which I have been labouring with as much assiduity by fair, and threatning means to obtain returns of our strength in this Camp and Roxbury, & their Dependencies, as a man could do, and never have been able to accomplish the matter till this day—now, I will not answer for the correctness of them, although I have sent several of the Regimental returns back more than once to have mistakes rectified. I do not doubt but the Congress will think me very remiss in not writing to them sooner but you may rely on it yourself, and I beg you to assure them, that it has never been in my power till this day, to comply with their orders. could I have conceivd, that which ought, and in a regular Army would have been done in an hour, would employ eight days, I should have sent an Express off the 2d Morning after I arrivd with a genl acct of things. but expecting in the Morning to receive the Returns in the Evening, and in the Evening surely to find them in the Morning (& at last getting them full of Imperfections) I have been drilled on from day to day, till I am ashamed to look back at the time which has elapsed since my arrival here.[2]

You will perceive by the returns, that, we have but about 16,000. effective men in all this department, whereas by the accts which I receivd from even the first Officers in Command, I had no doubt of finding between 18. and 20,000—out of these there are only 14000 fit for duty—So soon as I was able to get this state of the army, & came to the knowledge of our Weakness, I immediately summond a Council of War, the result of which you will see, as it is Inclosed to the Congress.[3] Between you and me I think we are in an exceeding dangerous Situation, as our Numbers are not much larger than we suppose, from the best accts we are able to get, those of the Enemy to be; theirs situated in such a manner as to be drawn to any point of attack without our having an hours previous notice of it (if the Genl will keep his own Council) whereas we are obliged to be guarded at all points, & know not where, with precission, to look for them—I should not, I think, have made choice of the present Posts in the first Instance altho. I beleive, the Communication between the Town and Country could not have been so well cut off without; but, as much labour has been bestowed in throwing up lines—making redoubts &ca—as Cambridge Roxbury and Watertown must be immediately exposed to the Mercy of the Enemy were we to retreat a little further in the Country—as it would give general dissatisfaction to this Colony—dispirit our own People, and Incourage the Enemy, to remove at this time to another place we have for these reasons resolved in Council to maintain our ground if we can—Our Lines on Winter & Prospect Hills, & those of the Enemy on Bunkers Hill, are in full view of each other, a Mile distant, our advanc'd guard much nearer, & the centries almost near enough to converse—At Roxbury & Boston Neck it is the same between these, we are obliged to guard sevl other Places at which the Enemy may Land. The Enemy have strongly fortified, or will in a few days, their Camp on Bunkers Hill; after which, & their new Landed Troops have got a little refreshd,[4] we shall look for a visit, if they mean, as we are told they do, to come out of their Lines—their great Command of Artillery, & adequate Stores of Powder &ca gives them advantages which we have only to lament the want of—The abuses in this army, I fear, are considerable. and the new modelling of it, in the Face of an Enemy, from whom we every hour expect an attack exceedingly difficult, & dangerous—if things therefore should not turn out as the Congress would wish I hope they will make proper allowances—I can only promise & assure them, that, my whole time is devoted to their Service, & that as far as my judgment goes, they shall have no cause to complain. I need not tell you that this Letter is written in much haste. The fact will sufficiently appear from the face of it; I thought a hasty Letter would please you better than no Letter, & therefore I shall offer no further appology, but assure you that with sincere regard for my fellow Labourers with you. Doctr Shippens Family &ca. I am Dr Sir Yr Most Affecte Servt

G. Washington

ALS, PPAmP: Lee Family Papers.

1. GW reached Cambridge on 2 July. For an account of his journey from Philadelphia, see GW to Hancock, 10–11 July 1775, Document II. Letter Sent, n.1.

2. For GW's attempts to obtain the returns wanted by Congress, see General Orders, 8 July 1775, n.3.

3. See Council of War, 9 July 1775.

4. For a discussion of the British reinforcements from Ireland, see ibid., n.3.

From Alexander Scammell

[c.10 July 1775]

General Folsom[1] begs leave to lay before your Excellency a Memorandum of what is immediately wanted at Winter Hill. Viz. three Teems, 20 Wheelbarrows. two Thousand Tenpenny Nails Four, Inch Augres. A Gouge, and four Chizzles.

Alxdr Scammell Brigde Major.

ALS, MHi: Norcross Papers. At the end of this document GW wrote "The Committee, or Commissary of supplies is desired to furnish the above things immediately if to be got. July 10th 1775. Go: Washington."

Alexander Scammell (1747–1781), a native of Massachusetts who moved to New Hampshire about 1772, was a protégé of John Sullivan, under whom he studied law during the years immediately preceding the Revolution. On 30 June 1775 Scammell was commissioned brigade major for the New Hampshire forces at Winter Hill, and when GW reorganized the Continental army a short time later, he was continued as Sullivan's brigade major (General Orders, 15 Aug. 1775). During the New York campaign of 1776, Scammell served Sullivan as an aide-de-camp, and in December 1776 he was appointed colonel of the 3d New Hampshire Regiment. On 5 Jan. 1778 Congress made him adjutant general of the Continental army, a position that he held for two years. Scammell became commander of the 1st New Hampshire Regiment early in 1781 and was mortally wounded later that year at the siege of Yorktown.

1. Nathaniel Folsom (1726–1790) of Exeter, N.H., was elected to the First Continental Congress in 1774, and in April 1775 the New Hampshire provincial congress gave him the command of all the colony's troops sent to the American army outside Boston. Folsom was commissioned a major general in the New Hampshire service on 30 June, but receiving no Continental rank, he retired from the army before the end of July. He returned to New Hampshire, and on 24 Aug. he was named general officer of the colony's militia. Folsom served in Congress from 1777 to 1778 and from 1779 to 1780 and was a member of the camp committee that conferred with GW in the winter of 1778.

To Major General Philip Schuyler

Sir Cambridge 10th[–11] July 1775

I receivd your Favor of 1st Inst. by Express from New york; but as I am exceedingly hurried in making out my Dispatches for the Hble Congress at Philadelphia it is not in my Power to answer it in so full a Manner as I wish.

Notwithstanding Governor Tryon's plausible Behaviour I recommend it to you to watch him narrowly and as any unlucky Change of Affairs on our part may produce in him a Change of his present *unexceptionable Conduct*; I expect you will on the first Appearance of such Change pursue the Advice given in my last Letter.[1] The like Advice I give you re[s]pectg General Haldiman who is supposd by some to have gone to N. York with a Design to counteract us in that provin⟨ce.⟩[2] The Commissions which have been forwarded to me, are not sufficient to answer the Demand I have for them there being at least 1000 Officers in this Department & not more than 500 Commissions in my Possession. As you are so much nearer to Philada than I am I request you to apply to Congress for as many as you are like to Want.

The disper[s]ing of hand Bills amongst the Troops on their arrival at N. York has my most hearty approbation—& may have a good Effect here.

Our Enemies have attempted Nothing against us since my Arrival here—They are strongly posted on Bunkers Hill and are still busy in throwing up additional Works. We have thrown up several Lines & Redoubts between Mystick River & Dorchester point to prevent their making way into the Country & in a few Days shall be well prepared to receive them in Case a Sortie is attempted.

I sincerely thank you for your Attention to the Directions of the Congress & for your kind Wishes and am with much regard Sir Yr Obedt friend & most Obedt H: Ser.

G. Washington

P.S. I herewith Inclose a report this Minute received from the Camp at Dorchester—The Design of this Manoevre I am at a loss to know; but suppose it may be intended as a diversion to our Forces here. It howevr behooves you to keep a good look out to prevent any surprize your way.[3]

DfS, in Thomas Mifflin's writing, NHi: Joseph Reed Papers; LB, DLC:GW; Varick transcript, DLC:GW. The closing, signature, and postscript of the draft are all in GW's writing. Although the postscript is not dated, it was apparently written on 11 July. See note 3.

1. For GW's earlier instructions regarding William Tryon, see GW to Schuyler, 25 June 1775, n.3.

2. Frederick Haldimand (1718–1791), a Swiss officer who had become a British major general, sailed from Boston for New York on 16 June 1775, but his trip had no military purpose. Recently recalled to England after long years of service in America, he went to New York to board the July packet ship for its voyage home across the Atlantic. Haldimand first joined the British army in 1756 as a lieutenant colonel in the Royal Americans, and after the French and Indian War he remained with the army in America, becoming a major general in 1772. While Gen. Thomas Gage was in England from 1773 to 1774, Haldimand assumed the duties of commander in chief for North America, and when Gage returned, Haldimand became his second in command. In the spring of 1775 it was decided in London to remove Haldimand from that position in order to preclude any possibility of the principal command devolving on a foreign-born officer in the midst of the grave new crisis in America. Haldimand remained in England until June 1778 when he was appointed governor and commander in chief for Canada, positions which he held until November 1784.

3. This enclosure has not been found, but it undoubtedly contained news of the British convoy that set sail in Boston Harbor on 11 July. See GW to Hancock, 10–11 July 1775, Document II. Letter Sent, n.31. The date of the convoy's sailing indicates that GW added this postscript to the letter sometime on 11 July.

From Brigadier General John Thomas

Rexbuy [Roxbury] Camp [Mass.]
Sir July the 10th: 1775

A Maister of a vesel that Came out of Boston Saturday Night in order to Take Charge of a vesel at S[t]oneington in Coniticut Loaded with malases to Purseed to New york as he Saith his aquaintance in the Country Infor[m] that he has bin a Suspected Person & I Think it my Duty to forward him to your Exelency for you[r] Exemi[n]ation[.][1] I am Sir with Respect you[r] mest obeduet Humble Servt

Jno. Thomas

ALS, M-Ar: Revolution Letters.

1. The shipmaster was William Lightly, and the vessel at Stonington, Conn., was the brigantine *Nancy*, which had recently arrived there under the command of Capt. Thomas Davis with a large cargo of molasses belonging to the widow and children of Joshua Winslow, a Boston Loyalist. The ultimate destination of the *Nancy*, the Patriots suspected, was not New York but Boston. On 12 July the Massachusetts provincial congress ordered Lightly to be confined in jail at Concord and approved a letter to Gov. Jonathan Trumbull of Connecticut, urging him to detain both the *Nancy* and her cargo, "or such part of it as belongs to . . . Winslow, for the use of the colonies, rather than to suffer them to fall into the hands of General Gage, where they will be improved to the support of our enemies, and to augment the distress of these colonies" (*Mass. Prov. Congress Journals*, 487–88). Connecticut authorities soon afterwards sent the *Nancy* to Norwich, Conn., and removed her cargo, sails, and rigging for storage (Jonathan Trumbull, Sr., to GW, 17 July 1775). See also Simon Pease to GW, 18 Sept. 1775.

To James Warren

Sir Head Quarters Cambridge July [10] 1775.

After much Difficulty & Delay I have procurd such Returns of the State of the Army as will enable us to form a Judgment of its Strength. It is with great Concern I find it far inadequate to our general Expectations and the Duties which may be requird of it. The Number of Men fit for Duty in the Forces raisd in this Province including all the Out Posts and Artillery does not amount to Nine thousands. The Troops raisd in the other Colonies are more compleat; but yet fall short of their Establishment. So that upon the whole, I cannot estimate the present

Army at more than Fourteen thousands five hundred Men capable of Duty.

I have the Satisfaction to find the Troops both in Camp & Quarters very healthy; so that the Deficiency must arise from the Regiments never having been filled up to the Establishment, and the Number of Men on Furlough. But the former is much most considerable.[1] Under all these Circumstances I yesterday calld a Council of War; and, enclosed, I send you an Extract of our Determinations, so far as they respect the province of Massachusetts Bay.[2]

Your own Prudence will suggest the Necessity of Secrecy on this Subject as we have the utmost Reason to think the Enemy suppose our Numbers much greater than they are: an Error which is not our Interest to remove.

The great Extent of our Lines and the Uncertainty which may be the point of Attack added to the Necessity of immediate Support have induced me to order that Horses ready saddled should be kept at several Posts in Order to bring the most speedy Intelligence of any Movement of the Enemy.

For this Purpose I should be glad that Ten Horses might be provided as soon as possible.[3] I have the Honor to be Sir Your most Obed. & very hbe Servt

Go: Washington

P.S. As I am informed the Congress proposes to rise immediately, I should be glad to know what Committees are left, or upon whom the executive Business devolves.[4]

G: W——n

LS, in Thomas Mifflin's writing, M-Ar: Revolution Letters; LB, DLC:GW; copy, NHi: Joseph Reed Papers; Varick transcript, DLC:GW. The LS was erroneously dated 9 July 1775 by Mifflin. That the date should be 10 July is indicated by GW's statement in the second paragraph: "I yesterday calld a Council of War," a reference to the council of war held on 9 July. The letter-book copy and the copy at the New-York Historical Society, both in Joseph Reed's writing, are correctly dated 10 July, as is the Varick transcript.

1. The letter-book copy and the copy at the New-York Historical Society read "by much the most considerable."

2. The enclosed extract consists of the third and fourth decisions of the Council of War, 9 July 1775, which concern the need for immediate reinforcement of the American army (*Mass. Prov. Congress Journals*, 482–83, n.1). The provincial congress this day referred GW's letter to a committee of three members, Col. Elisha Porter, Dr. John Taylor, and Maj. Eleazer Brooks, who

were "directed to confer with General Washington on the subject of his letter, and particularly inform him of the number of men we had generally estimated in the Massachusetts forces, from the returns of the general officers, from the money paid out of the treasury, for a month's advance pay to the soldiers, and from the provision made for billeting the said forces" (ibid., 482). The next afternoon the provincial congress appointed two committees to deal with the matter of the reinforcements. One, consisting of Elbridge Gerry, Samuel Phillips, Jr., and Colonel Porter, was ordered "to repair immediately to General Washington, and know of him what number of men he would have this Congress raise, for a temporary reinforcement of the army; and to inform the General of the powers vested by this Congress, in the committee of safety, and to confer with the General, at large, on the state of the army, and in particular, with respect to some soldiers of the army who have enlisted twice." The other committee, consisting of James Warren, Col. Joseph Palmer, Dummer or Abel Jewett, Capt. Josiah Stone, and Col. Michael Farley, was instructed "to devise some means of raising speedily a temporary reenforcement of the army, and to bring in an establishment." The committee appointed to confer with GW about the reinforcements reported on the morning of 12 July with a letter from him (ibid., 486, 489). The letter was apparently the one of 12 July which Joseph Reed wrote to James Warren for GW: "Upon a Conference with the other Generals respecting the Militia, it has been concluded that 1000 Men to be stationed in & about Medford will be sufficient for the present Service. His Excelly has also directed me to request of the Congress in his Name that they would urge the Committees in the several Towns to forward & promote the new Levies as much as possible—and that they would exert themselves to send to the Camp such Soldiers as have staid beyond their Furlows, or have left the Service & may be returned to their former Homes" (M-Ar: Revolution Letters). The letter was promptly referred to the committee charged with devising a means of raising reinforcements, and Colonel Porter, Jonathan Glover, and Capt. Timothy Parker were added to that committee. The enlarged committee reported on the afternoon of 12 July, at which time the provincial congress resolved to recommend to various towns that they each immediately raise and send to Cambridge a specified number of "men, provided with a good fire-lock, ammunition, and blanket, each, who shall be detained not longer than one month, at farthest, from the beginning of their march, and shall be honorably paid for their service by the colony, all due regard being had to the present urgency of farming business, and the inconvenience of complying with such a requisition at this juncture." GW, however, decided later this day, on the basis of new intelligence, that the temporary militia reinforcements were not needed, and on the morning of 13 July, the provincial congress canceled all plans for the militia mobilization (*Mass. Prov. Congress Journals*, 491–93; Joseph Reed to James Warren, 9:00 P.M., 12 July 1775, DLC:GW, printed below in GW to Hancock, 14 July 1775, n.1).

3. The provincial congress on this date ordered the committee of supplies to furnish GW immediately "with ten good horses, with saddles and bridles, for the public use" (*Mass. Prov. Congress Journals*, 481). On 18 July Joseph

Reed wrote on behalf of GW to Brig. Gen. John Thomas: "As most of the Horses provided for Intelligence are disposed of you will please to direct some careful Person to call for one reserved to be Stationed on Sewall's Point, a Place at which it is very probable there may be some Occasion for him—As these Horses are kept for very important & necessary Purposes, his Excellency requests particular Care may be taken that they are not misapplied or taken off from the Duty for which they are particularly Appropriated" (owned [1981] by Ronald von Klaussen).

4. The provincial congress adjourned for a week beginning on 13 July 1775. When it reconvened on 19 July, it promptly dissolved itself to clear the way for the first meeting of the new house of representatives later that same day. See John Adams to GW, 19 or 20 June 1775, n.1. The committees of safety and of supplies conducted the business of the colony during the recess of the provincial congress.

General Orders

Head Quarters, Cambridge, July 11th 1775

Parole, Guilford. Counter-Sign, Hartford

The Court Martial of which Col. William Prescott was president is dissolved. A General Court Martial to be assembled at Cambridge, as soon as possible, to try such prisoners as shall be brought before them: All Evidences, and persons concern'd to attend the court.

The General understanding, there is a bad Custom prevailing, of the Non-Commissioned Officers and soldiers absenting themselves from Guard, under pretence of going for Provisions; it is therefore order'd, that all Officers and Soldiers, bring their provision to the Guard they mount, and on no pretence quit their Guard, untill it is regularly dissmissed.[1]

Notwithstanding the orders of the provincial Congress, some persons are so daring as to supply the Soldiers with immoderate Quantities of Rum, and other spiritous Liquors; any Sutler, Tavern-keeper, or licenced Innholder, who shall presume after the date of this order, to sell to any non-commissioned Officer, or Soldier, any spiritous liquor whatsoever, without an Order in writing, from the Captain of the company to which such non-Commissioned Officer and Soldier belongs; he or they so offending, may expect to be severely punished.[2]

Lieut: Col. Ward president of the Court Martial.

Varick transcript, DLC:GW.

1. This order was repeated in General Orders, 24 July 1775, because of a lack of full compliance with it.

2. On 6 July the Massachusetts provincial congress, acting in response to a letter from Maj. Gen. Nathanael Greene, appointed a committee to study the matter of liquor sales to soldiers, and two days later the following resolution was approved: "The Congress having taken into consideration the difficulties and troubles which have [arisen] and daily are arising in our camps, by reason of divers evil-minded persons selling spirituous liquors, . . . therefore, *Resolved*, that if any licensed person shall, after the 15th instant, presume to sell any spirituous liquors to any soldier, without a permit from the captain, or commanding officer of the company he belongs to, specifying the quantity, he shall, for the first offence, forfeit his license, and for the second, suffer such punishment as shall be inflicted on him or her, by a court martial." The next day the committee of safety resolved: "Whereas, a number of soldiers in the American army, are from time to time, observed to be much disguised with spirituous liquors, and should not some effectual measures be taken to put a stop to this disorder, not only the morals and health, but also the lives and liberties of this people will be endangered; therefore, . . . that it be, and it is hereby recommended to his Excellency General Washington, that an order be issued to suppress retailers of spirituous liquors within and near the camps, in such manner as to him may seem meet" (*Mass. Prov. Congress Journals*, 461, 475, 590–91).

General Orders

Head Quarters, Cambridge, July 12th 1775

Parole, Falmouth. C. Sign, Worcester.

The Adjutant General will deliver at orderly time, a certain number of printed returns, to the Adjutant of each regiment; so that no excuse can for the future be admitted, for not making regular and exact Returns when demanded; as it is only filling up the Blanks, with the Numbers proper to be placed in them. The Commander in Chief will not for the future, admit of any palliative for making a false return, and is resolved, to bring any Officer of what Rank soever, to a Court Martial who is found delinquent.

When any Trumpeter, or Flagg of Truce, is sent from Boston, or any Post occupied by the Enemy; they are to be stop'd by the first Sentry they are permitted to approach, who is to call for the Serjeant of the Guard, who will conduct them to the Officer of his guard, and such Trumpeter, or Flagg of Truce, is not to be allowed to stir one step beyond that Guard. The Officer commanding the Guard, will send any Letters or Messages brought from the enemy, immediately to the Commander in Chief, and no other person.

A General Court Martial of the Line to sit at Head Quarters, in Cambridge, to morrow morning at Nine OClock, to try Col. Scammons of the Massachusetts Forces accused of "Backwardness in the execution of his duty, in the late Action upon Bunkers-hill." The Adjutant of Col. Scammons regiment, to warn all Evidences, and persons concern'd to attend the court.[1]

Col. Nixon president of the above Court.

Varick transcript, DLC:GW.

1. James Scammans (c.1740–1804) of Biddeford, District of Maine, marched his regiment about noon on the day of the battle toward Lechmere's Point to prevent a British landing there. Near the point Col. John Whitcomb, then acting as a Massachusetts general, informed Scammans that the enemy was not threatening that place and directed him to march elsewhere. Whitcomb testified at the court-martial that he told Scammans to go to "where he could do the most service," but several of Scammans's officers and men said that Whitcomb ordered Scammans to go to "the hill," which most understood to be a small rise near Prospect Hill, about a mile from Bunker Hill. Scammans, being of that opinion, posted his regiment on the small hill and sent two sergeants to Bunker Hill to inquire if he was needed there. After a short wait at the small hill, Scammans on his own initiative marched his regiment to Bunker Hill, where he found matters in great confusion. Scammans's regiment never got close enough to engage the British, but most witnesses agreed that Scammans himself showed no signs of backwardness and encouraged his men to advance up the hill before finally ordering a retreat in the face of the rapidly deteriorating situation. On 17 July the court-martial acquitted Scammans (*Historical Magazine*, 2d ser., 3 [1868], 400–402; General Orders, 18 July 1775). Scammans resigned from the army at the end of 1775.

From Nicholas Cooke

Sir, Providence July 12th 1775

I beg Leave to congratulate your Excellency upon your being appointed General of the Armies of the United Colonies; which hath given sincere Pleasure to every Friend of America, and will I hope prove glorious to yourself, and be attended with essential Advantages to your Country.

The General Assembly of this Colony have the deepest Sense of the Necessity of a strict Union, and the most vigorous Efforts, of the Colonies to preserve them from unlimited Servitude; and their utmost Exertions in the common Cause may be depended upon.

I also assure your Excellency that I shall give you every possible Assistance in my Power; and that I am with very great Regard, Sir, Your Excellency's most obedient humble Servant

Nichols Cooke

LS, DLC:GW.

Nicholas Cooke (1717–1782), a merchant and distiller in Providence, was elected deputy governor of Rhode Island on 3 May 1775 and almost immediately became acting governor when the colony's general assembly, offended by Gov. Joseph Wanton's Loyalist sympathies, prohibited him from renewing his oath of office. The assembly declared the governorship vacant in November 1775, and Cooke was elected to the office in his own right. He served until May 1778.

Letter not found: from the Massachusetts Committee of Supplies, 12 July 1775. On 12 July Horatio Gates wrote on behalf of GW to the committee of supplies: "His Excellency General Washington has commanded me to acknowledge the receipt of your letter dated this day from Watertown; when the application was made yesterday, to know the Quantity of Tents Boards, & Sails, that could be procured immediately; The General wish'd to Supply Roxbury Camp, with as much as is wanted there; & sufficient to Cover One Thousand Men, & their Officers, in this Districkt."[1]

1. M-Ar: Revolution Letters.

From Edmund Pendleton

Dear General Phila. July 12th 1775.

My freind Mr George Baylor will be the bearer of this, who has caught such a Military Ardor as to travel to the Camp For instruction in that Art, I beg leave to recommend him to your Countenance & Favor, not only on Account of his worthy Father, but from my Opinion of his own Merit. He is a Lieutent in our independant Company & has gained great Applause there by his diligent Attention to the duties of his Office & the bravery he has indicated;[1] Be so obliging as to make my Complts to Genl Lee, Genl Gates, Majr Mifflin & Mr Griffin & intreat their countenance and assistance to him also.

We are hourly in Expectation of hearing From you; We yesterday voted an Additional Co. of Riflemen to go From this Province to gratifie one that was raised & impatient to come to you. we have also consented to employ a German Hussar who is to raise his 50 men & come to the Camp.[2]

We have heard you remain quiet, except some Cannon shot exchanged between Roxbury & Boston. You have my most cordial wishes for success in every undertaking, who have the Honr to be with great esteem Dr sr Yr mo. Obt humble Servt

Edmd Pendleton

ALS, DLC:GW.

1. George Baylor (1752–1784) of Newmarket in Caroline County, Va., became an aide-de-camp to GW on 15 Aug. 1775, and despite a passing fancy for joining the artillery in March 1776, he apparently continued in GW's military family until he was appointed colonel of the 3d Continental Dragoons in January 1777. For GW's comments on Baylor's shortcomings as a penman, see GW to Joseph Reed, 20 Nov. 1775 and 23 Jan. 1776, and GW to Charles Lee, 10 Feb. 1776. On 28 Sept. 1778 Baylor's dragoons were surprised by a British force at Old Tappan, N.J., and Baylor was bayoneted and captured. He was later exchanged, and in Nov. 1782 he assumed command of the 1st Continental Dragoons. Baylor died in Barbados shortly after the war from complications of the wound that he received at Old Tappan. Baylor's father, Col. John Baylor (1705–1772), entertained GW at Newmarket during the French and Indian War and in 1756 led a body of Caroline County militiamen to join GW at Winchester.

2. Congress agreed on 11 July to accept two rifle companies from Lancaster County, Pa., instead of one, because it had learned that in addition to the county's authorized rifle company enlisted under Capt. Matthew Smith, there were "a Number of Men Raised by Mr. James Ross out of which a good Company may be formed" (Pennsylvania Delegates to Lancaster County Committee, 11 July 1775, in Smith, *Letters of Delegates*, 1:621–22). That same day Congress directed the Pennsylvania delegates "to treat with and employ 50 Hussars, who have been in actual service, and send them forward to join the troops before Boston under Genl Washington." The hussar unit was never raised. On 1 Aug. the Pennsylvania delegates were instructed to put an end to the scheme and to discharge any hussars who had enlisted (*JCC*, 2:173, 238).

From the Virginia Delegates

Philadelphia, 12 July 1775. Recommend "the bearer Mr George Baylor, not only on Account of the memory of his worthy Father, wth whom you was acquainted, but For his own merit . . . . His Ardor in the noble cause has drawn him to your school for instruction & emploiment as far as his services may be required."

LS, in Edmund Pendleton's writing, CtY: Pendleton Papers. In addition to Pendleton, the letter was signed by Patrick Henry, Richard Henry Lee, and Benjamin Harrison.

General Orders

Head Quarters, Cambridge, July 13th 1775

Parole, Georgia. Counter Sign, Huntingdon.

As the Army will be forthwith form'd into Brigades:[1] The Adjutant General will at Orderly Time this day, deliver to the Adjutant of each Regiment, a Number of printed Returns, one of which, must be immediately fill'd up, and sign'd by the Commanding Officer of each regiment, and sent as soon as possible, to the Adjutant General; by the Adjutant of each Regiment; on the Back of the Return, it will be necessary to mention; where and in what manner, the regiment is at present posted.

The Commanding Officer at Chelsea, is as soon as possible, after the receipt of this order, to direct all the Cattle, upon pullein point, Shirley point, and the intermediate space between powder horn-hill and the Sea, to be driven off; and it is recommended to the Commissary General, to endeavour to agree with the Owners of the said Cattle, and to purchase them for the use of the Army.[2]

Varick transcript, DLC:GW.

1. For GW's reorganization of the army into divisions and brigades, see General Orders, 22 July 1775.

2. Joseph Reed conveyed this order to the officer commanding at Chelsea in a letter of this date (DLC:GW). Four companies from Col. Samuel Gerrish's regiment were stationed at or near Chelsea to defend the coast. Lt. Col. Loammi Baldwin assumed command at Chelsea by 28 July, but Richard Dodge, captain of one of the four companies, was apparently acting as commander there at this time. On 14 July Dodge sent to GW a return of the livestock "Brought of Poollins Pint & Pint Shirley (viz.) 80 Horn Creuters 883 Sheep" (DLC:GW). Pullen Point (now part of the town of Winthrop) and Point Shirley flank Boston Harbor on the north. Powder Horn Hill is on the north side of Chelsea. The commissary general of the Massachusetts forces was John Pigeon. No Continental commissary general was appointed until 31 July.

From Jonathan Trumbull, Sr.

Sir Lebanon [Conn.] 13th July 1775

Suffer me to join in Congratulating you, on your appointment to be General and Commander in Chief of the Troops raised or to be raised for the Defence of American Liberty.

Men who have tasted of Freedom, and who have felt their personal Rights, are not easily taught to bear with encroachments on either, or brought to submit to oppression. Virtue ought always to be made the Object of Government: Justice is firm and permanent.

His Majesty's Ministers have artfully induced the Parliament to join in their Measures, to prosecute the dangerous and increasing Difference between Great Britain and these Colonies with Rigour and Military Force: whereby the latter are driven to an absolute necessity to defend their Rights and Properties by raising Forces for their Security.

The Honorable Congress have proclaimed a Fast to be Observed by the Inhabitants of all the English Colonies on this Continent, to stand before the Lord in one Day, with public Humiliation; Fasting and Prayer, to deplore our many sins, to offer up our joint supplications to God, for forgiveness, and for His merciful Interposition for us in this Day of unnatural Darkness and Distress.[1]

They have with one united voice appointed you to the high station you possess—The supream Director of all Events hath caused a wonderful Union of Hearts and Counsells to subsist amongst Us.

Now therefore be strong and very courageous, may the God of the Armies of Israel, shower down the blessings of His Divine Providence on You, give you Wisdom and Fortitude, cover your Head in the Day of Battle and Danger, add Success—convince our Enemies of their mistaken measures—and that all their attempts to deprive these Colonies of their inestimable constitutional Rights and Liberties are injurious and Vain. I am, with great Esteem & Regard Sir Your most Obedient humble Servant

Jonth. Trumbull

ALS, DLC:GW; LB, Ct: Trumbull Papers.

Jonathan Trumbull, Sr. (1710–1785), of Lebanon, Conn., the only colonial governor to side with the Patriots, served as Connecticut's chief executive from 1769 to 1784. The religious tone of this letter stems from his preparation for the ministry as a young man. The death of an elder brother kept him from the pulpit because he felt obliged to replace that brother as his father's business associate. Knowledgeable in the ways of commerce and politics as well as theology, Trumbull successfully managed the flow of food, clothing, and munitions to the Continental army from his colony throughout the war. Despite occasional misunderstandings, GW and Trumbull established a close working relationship with one another, and GW came to hold the governor in great esteem. Three of Governor Trumbull's sons also served with distinction in the Revolution. Joseph Trumbull (1738–1778) became the first commissary general of the Continental army on 31 July 1775. Jonathan Trumbull, Jr. (1740–1809), was Continental paymaster general for the northern department from 1775 to 1778, comptroller of the treasury from 1778 to 1779, and GW's military secretary from 1781 to 1783. John Trumbull (1756–1843), an artist, acted as an aide-de-camp to GW between 27 July and 15 Aug. 1775 and later served as a brigade major and as a deputy adjutant general.

1. On 12 June 1775 the Continental Congress recommended 20 July "as a day of public humiliation, fasting and prayer" (*JCC*, 2:87; General Orders, 16 July 1775).

From Jonathan Trumbull, Sr.

Sir Lebanon [Conn.] 13th July 1775

I have to observe to your Excellency, That the Honorable Congress have altered the Arrangement of the Generals appointed by our Assembly, Wish the Order we adopted had been pursued, Fear Generals Wooster and Spencer will think they have reason to complain. They are Gentlemen held in high Estimation, by Our Assembly, and by the Officers and Troops under their Command.

There are reasons to fear that inconvenienies will arise from the Alterations made by the Congress in the Rank and Station of those Generals. At the same time, they have the highest sense of General Putnam's singular Merit, and Services. Is it impracticable to devise some Method to obviate the difficulties that are apprehended.

The Army before Boston is necessarily thrown into two Grand Divisions. General Spencer with a Number of Our Troops hath hitherto been at Roxbury, and General Putnam at Cambridge—That Destination continued and Observed, may prevent uneasy Competition; preserve good order, and promote the public Service.[1] I am, with great Truth and Regard Sir Your Obedient Humble Servant

Jonth. Trumbull

ALS, PHi: Dreer Collection; LB, Ct: Trumbull Papers.

1. For a discussion of the dispute over the precedence of the general officers from Connecticut, see GW to Hancock, 10–11 July 1775, Document II. Letter Sent, n.20.

General Orders

Head Quarters, Cambridge, July 14th 1775

Parole, Hallifax. Counter Sign, Inverness.

As the Health of an Army principally depends upon Cleanliness; it is recommended in the strongest manner, to the Commanding Officer of Corps, Posts and Detachments, to be strictly diligent, in ordering the Necessarys to be filled up once a Week, and new ones dug; the Streets of the encampments and Lines to be swept daily, and all Offal and Carrion, near the camp, to be immediately buried: The Officers commanding in Barracks, or Quarters, to be answerable that they are swept every morning, and all Filth & Dirt removed from about the houses: Next to Cleanliness, nothing is more conducive to a Soldiers health, than dressing his provisions in a decent and proper manner. The Officers commanding Companies, should therefore daily inspect the Camp Kitchens, and see the Men dress their Food in a wholesome way.

The Commanding Officers in those parts of the Lines and Redoubts, where the Pikes are placed, will order the Quarter Masters of Corps, to see the pikes greas'd twice a week; they are to be answerable also that the pikes are kept clean, and always ready and fit for service.

The General observing great remissness, and neglect in the several Guards in and about the Camp, orders the Officers commanding any Guard to turn out his Guard immediately upon the near Approach of The Commander in Chief or any of the Gene⟨ral⟩ Officers, and upon passing the Guard; The Commander in Chief is to be received with *rested Arms*; the Officer to salute, and the Drums to beat a march: The Majors General with *rested Arms*, the Officer to salute and the Drums to beat two Ruffles; The Brigadiers General with *rested Arms*, the Officer to salute and the Drums to beat one Ruffle. There being something awkward, as well as improper, in the General Officers being stopp'd at the out-posts; ask'd for passes by the Sentries, and obliged often to send for the Officer of the Guard (who it sometimes happens is as much unacquainted with the Persons of the Generals, as the private Men) before they can pass in or out: It is recommended to both Officers and Men, to make themselves acquainted with the persons of all the Officers in General Command, and in the mean time to prevent mistakes: The General Officers and their Aids-de-Camp, will be distinguished in the following manner.

The Commander in Chief by a light blue Ribband, wore across his breast, between his Coat and Waistcoat.

The Majors and Brigadiers General, by a Pink Ribband wore in the like manner.

The Aids-de-Camp by a green ribband.[1]

The Court martial of which Col. Ward is Presdt is dissolved.

Daniel Carmiele, soldier in Col. Pattersons Regiment,[2] tried for "Disobedience of orders, for reinlisting and taking advance Money twice over, and for Drunkenness" is found guilty of the several Charges and ordered to be whipt on the bare back, with 39 Lashes, and discharged from the army. The General approves the Sentence and orders it to be executed to morrow Morning, at the head of the Regiment he belongs to.

Varick transcript, DLC:GW.

1. Insignias for field and company officers and noncommissioned officers were designated in General Orders, 23 July 1775. Major generals were given their own distinctive color of ribbon in General Orders, 24 July 1775.

2. Col. John Paterson (1744–1808), a lawyer from Lenox, commanded a Massachusetts regiment at an important redoubt near Prospect Hill. He was promoted to brigadier general in February 1777, and although he saw little action, he served to the end of the war.

To John Hancock

Sir Camp. Cambridge July 14. 1775

Since I did myself the Honour of addressing you the 10th Instt nothing material has happened in the Camp. From some authentick & later Advices of the State of the Ministerial Troops & the great Inconvenience of calling in the Militia in the midst of Harvest, I have been induced for the present to waive it;[1] but in the mean Time recruiting Parties have been sent throughout this Province to fill up the Regiments to the Establishment of the Provincial Congress.[2] At the same Time that I received these Advices, I also obtained a List of the Officers of the Enemy killed and wounded in the late Battle at Charles Town which I take this Opportunity to inclose.[3] The great Scarcity of fresh Provisions in their Army has led me to take every Precaution to prevent a Supply, for this Purpose I have ordered all the Cattle & Sheep to be drove from the low Grounds & Farms within their Reach[4]—A Detachment from General Thomas's Camp on Wednesday Night went over to Long Island & brought from thence 20 Cattle & a Number of Sheep with about 15 Labourers who had been put on by a Mr Ray Thomas to cut the Hay &c. By some Accident they omitted burning the Hay & returned the next Day at Noon to complete it; which they effected amidst the Firing of the Shipping with the Loss of one Man killed & another wounded.[5]

Last Evening also a Party of the Connecticut Men stroll'd down on the Marsh at Roxbury & fired upon a Centry which drew on a heavy Fire from the Enemys Lines & floating Batteries, but attended with no other Effect than the Loss of one killed by a Shot from the Enemy's Lines[6]—In the mean Time we are on both Sides continuing our Works, but there has been no other Movement than what I have noticed above. I shall endeavour to give a regular & particular Account of all Transactions as they occur which you will please to lay before the Hon. Congress. I have the Honour to be Sir, Your most Obed. & very Hbble Servt

Go: Washington

LS, in Joseph Reed's writing, DNA:PCC, item 152; LB, DLC:GW; copy, DNA:PCC, item 169; copy, NjMoNP; Varick transcript, DLC:GW. This letter was read in Congress on 24 July 1775 (*JCC*, 2:203).

1. For a discussion of the steps taken by the Massachusetts provincial congress to call out part of the colony's militia as a temporary reinforcement for the Continental army, see GW to James Warren, 10 July 1775, n.2. At 9:00 P.M. on 12 July 1775, Joseph Reed wrote to James Warren: "By some late intelligence from Boston received this day of the State and Situation of the En-

emy in and about Boston His Excellency the Genl is of opinion that the Reinforcement of the Militia proposed to the Congress, may [be] dispensed with at present, without any Injury to the Public Service; The Time of Harvest, the expected Troops from the Southward and the repeated Calls, which have been made of the like Nature from this Province, are strong Reasons to postpone this Measure if consistent with Safety; and as these Advices are so authentic as to deserve Confidence, the General hopes his determination will be agreeable to the Congress. You will therefore be pleased to Communicate this to them, in order, that the most early Countermand may be given to Orders if already Issued, or prevent them if they have not" (Varick transcript, DLC:GW).

2. For the sending of Massachusetts officers on recruiting service, see General Orders, 10 July 1775.

3. The unsigned enclosure, which is dated "Roxbury July 11th 1775," gives ninety-two as the number of British officers who were killed or wounded at the Battle of Bunker Hill although only ninety names are listed. Some general intelligence from behind the enemy lines is also included in the enclosure: "A Gentleman who got out of Boston Monday July 10th says that the Inhabitants were numberd & amounted to 6573 The Soldiers—women & Children, to 13600—300 Tories are chosen to Patrole the Streets, 49 of a night—Very Sickley from 10 to 30 funerals in a day, & no Bells allow'd to Toll, Master [James] Lovell taken up & put in Goal, which being in consequence of Some Letters found in Doctr [Joseph] Warren's pockets; & Master [John] Leach also, Released out of Goal, 4, Mr [Shrimpton] Hunt saying that he wish'd the Americans might kill them all, was confin'd in Goal—11 dead of the wounded prisoners at Charlestown. Collo. [Moses] Parker dead, he having declard at his last hour, if he got well he would do the same, The Officers saying Damn the Rebells that they wou'd not flinch—A Great number of floating batteries are building & 5 Transports & 3 Sloops are Sail'd for Hay & Wood to the Eastward. This Gentleman also says that the Officers & Soldiers Triumph Very much at the Death of Doctr Warren saying it is Better to them than five hundred men" (DNA:PCC, item 152).

4. For the removal of livestock in the area around Chelsea, see General Orders, 13 and 15 July 1775.

5. Long Island in Boston Harbor was a source of much-needed livestock and hay for the British garrison at Boston. On Tuesday evening, 11 July, Maj. Benjamin Tupper led about four hundred volunteers in a raid on the island to seize the livestock and any Loyalists that they might find. Setting off in whaleboats from Germantown on Hough's Neck a short distance east of Braintree, the raiding party avoided the British warships in the harbor and landed on Long Island about ten o'clock in the evening. In a house and barn on the island, they found fifteen men and two or three women, who had been sent there to mow hay by Nathaniel Ray Thomas (1731–1787), a Loyalist from Marshfield who had fled to Boston after the Battle of Concord. They made prisoners of the mowers and took them to Dorchester in the whaleboats along with the captured livestock. "Our Heroes came of in triumph not being ob-

served by their Enimies," Abigail Adams wrote to John Adams on 16 July 1775. "This spiritted up other[s]. They could not endure the thought that the House and barn should afford them [the enemy] any shelter. They did not distroy them the night before for fear of being discoverd" (Butterfield, *Adams Family Correspondence*, 1 : 245–51). In a daring daylight raid on the morning of 12 July, a second American party, which consisted of 136 men commanded by Lt. Col. John Greaton, set out in ten whaleboats from Moon Island, located between Long Island and Squantum Point, to burn not only the buildings on Long Island but also the approximately seventy tons of hay that was stored there in bundles awaiting shipment to Boston. The American raiders succeeded in crossing the half-mile strait between the two islands and in setting fire to the buildings and hay but not without being detected by British warships. "A number of armed cutters immediately Surrounded the Island, [and] fired upon our Men," Abigail Adams reported to her husband. "They came of with a hot and continued fire upon them, the Bullets flying in every direction and the Men of Wars boats plying them with small arms. Many in this Town [Braintree] who were spectators expected every moment our Men would all be sacrificed, for sometimes they were so near as to be calld to and damnd by their Enimies and orderd to surrender yet they all returnd in safty" (ibid.). See also Richard Cranch to John Adams, 24 July 1775, ibid., 258–60. The one soldier who was killed was hit by enemy fire on Moon Island while covering the retreat of the others.

6. "Last night a party undertook to capture the enemy's sentries, but did not succeed," Samuel Bixby wrote at Roxbury on this date. "The party was discovered, & fired upon, & a smart skirmish took place. We lost one man belonging to the Connecticut forces" ("Bixby Diary," 290). Maj. Gen. William Heath, who was also at Roxbury, noted: "The British fired several cannon, and a Connecticut soldier was killed in the street, near the George tavern. The shot entered his body, drove it some distance, and lodged in him in a remarkable manner" (Wilson, *Heath's Memoirs*, 33).

General Orders

Head Quarters, Cambridge, July 15th 1775

Parole, Virginia. Counter Sign, Maryland

The Commanding Officers of each Regiment to report the Names of such Men in their respective Corps as are most expert in the management of whale boats.[1]

When any Commission'd, or non Commission'd Officer is sent upon any Detachment or Duty of Honor, or Fatigue, or to see the execution of any particular work: He is, so soon as the service is perform'd to make a Report thereof to his commanding officer.

It being found advantageous to the public service, to remove sundry horn'd Cattle and Sheep, from the Ground upon which they were grazing near Chelsea, (to prevent their falling into the Enemy's hands) it is earnestly recommended to the several Commissaries, to purchase such of them, as are fit for slaughter, of the Owners, in Order that they may suffer the least loss possible, from the unavoidable necessity of removing them from the rapacious claws of our enemies.

Col. Gridley, Chief Engineer, is desired to report what Chevaux-de-Frise are made, and what forwardness those are in, that are now making—It is necessary those upon hand be compleated without delay.[2]

Notwithstanding the Orders already given, the General hears with astonishment, that not only Soldiers, but Officers unauthorized, are continually conversing with the Officers and Sentrys of the Enemy[.] any Officer, Non Commissioned Officer or Soldier, or any Person whatsoever, who is detected holding any Conversation, or carrying on any Correspondence with any of the Officers or Sentrys of the advanc'd posts of the enemy, will be immediately brought before a General Court Martial, and punished with the utmost severity. The General is alone to judge of the propriety of any intercourse with the enemy and no one else is to presume to interfere.

The Chief Engineer, Col. Gridley, to order an Engineer, and a Field Officer of Artillery, to go round the Lines and Redoubts, to examine if the Guns are placed properly in the Embrassures; and if the Embrassures are properly made, and properly sloped towards the country. The Engineer and Artillery Officer, to report to the Commander in Chief, as soon as they have obeyed this order.

Varick transcript, DLC:GW.

1. A large number of whaleboats had been acquired by Massachusetts authorities for the use of the colony's forces, and GW intended to employ some of them for routine night patrols of Boston Harbor as well as for occasional raids. See GW to Hancock, 21 July 1775, n.4 (first letter).

2. Chevaux-de-frise were portable obstacles, each consisting of a long wooden beam traversed by wooden spikes five or six feet long. GW planned to use these devices to block the entrances to the various American redoubts and lines in the event of an attack, but he was forced to make other arrangements when it became clear that the chevaux-de-frise would not soon be ready. See General Orders, 18 and 23 July 1775.

From Major General Philip Schuyler

Dear Sir Saratoga [N.Y.] July 15th 1775.

Since I did Myself the Honor to write Your Excellency from New York Nothing very material occurred until Yesterday, when I received the Inclosed Letters, the Accounts contained in that marked Number 1 are truly alarming in the present defenceless State of the Counties of Tryon and Albany, and Especially as the Assistance I can afford them either of Men or Money is next to Nothing, the few Troops at Tionderoga &ca being at too great a Distance and not more than sufficient to guard the Posts they occupy. I should have been at Tionderoga this Day had not the Information from Tryon County arrived, which may make my Presence there absolutely necessary. If it should be confirmed; I therefore propose remaining here untill to Morrow, when I hope to be farther informed;[1] I wish I may be able to proceed to Tionderoga as I am very much wanted there, the Greatest Confusion having taken Place in the Controversy between the Officers claiming the Command in that Quarter, some have taken the Liberty to disband Troops. Others refused to serve unless this or that particular Person Commanded. The Sloop is left without either Captain or Pilot, both of which are dismissed or come away, Much Provision wasted or embezzalled, and on the Seventh instant only one Barrel of Flour at Tionderoga; I shall have an Augean Stable to clean there.[2]

I do Myself the Honor to inclose a Return of the Forces in this Colony. It is doubtless imperfect as I have been under a Necessity of forming it out of Returns which were evidently so, I hope soon to send You a more compleat one.[3]

Be assured my General that I shall use my best Endeavours to establish Order and Disipline in the Troops under my Command. I wish I could add That I had a Prospect of much Success in that Way. It is extreamly difficult to introduce a proper Subordination amongst a People where so little Distinction is kept up.

Our Accounts of the Disposition of the Canadians and Canada Indians continue to be favorable, tho' the Intelligence is not very Authentic. I am your Excellency's Most Obedt & Most Humble Servt

Ph: Schuyler

LS, DLC:GW; LB, NN: Schuyler Papers.

Schuyler owned a large estate at Saratoga, which included a dwelling house, a store, and mills for lumber, flour, and flax. He left New York City on or shortly after 3 July and on 9 July arrived at Albany. He proceeded a few days later to Saratoga on his way north to Ticonderoga.

1. Copies of two letters were enclosed: one of 13 July 1775 from the Tryon County committee of safety to the committees of safety at Albany and Schenectady, signed by Christopher P. Yates, and one of 14 July 1775 from the Albany committee to Schuyler, signed by Abraham Yates, Jr. Both are in DLC:GW. The letter from the Tryon County committee (marked number one) reported that the committee had heard "that Coll [Guy] Johnson was ready with eight or nine hundred Indians to make an invasion of this County that the same Indians were to be under the Command of Joseph Brandt and Walter Butler and that they were to fall on the inhabitants below the little falls in order to divide the people in two parts—and were to march yesterday or the day before. . . . We have sent off a party of people by way of a scout to find out if possible the Rout of the Indians and to give us early intelligence. Our ammunition is so scant that we cannot furnish three hundred men so as to be able to make a stand against so great a number—In these deplorable circumstances we look up to you for Assistance both in men and ammunition to save this Country from slaughter and desolation which we beg you will not be backward to afford us as soon as possible." The Albany committee forwarded copies of this letter to both the New York provincial congress and Schuyler. In its covering letter of 14 July to Schuyler, the Albany committee inquired "whether it will not be advisable to let the Company of Capt. Van Dyck [Cornelius Van Dyke] (which we find you have ordered up to Lake George) March up the Mohawk river towards their Relief—And as that Company has no ammunition (and we have here about three hundred weight) whether you will think it proper to furnish them from the store here And whether you will not think it necessary to send up some of the Remainder to furnish the Inhabitants." Schuyler agreed to all three of these suggestions (Schuyler to Hancock, 15 July 1775, DNA:PCC, item 153). Early on 16 July, however, Schuyler learned that the reports of an impending Indian attack were unfounded. He left Saratoga later that day and arrived at Ticonderoga on 18 July.

2. The command of Ticonderoga and Crown Point was disputed between Col. Benedict Arnold, who commanded a force of Massachusetts volunteers at the posts, and Col. Benjamin Hinman, who arrived in the area with Connecticut reinforcements on 17 June. Arnold refused to yield the command to Hinman, but six days later a committee from the Massachusetts provincial congress appeared with new instructions which put him under Hinman. Arnold angrily resigned his commission on 24 June and disbanded his little force of two to three hundred men. He arrived at Albany on 11 July and at Schuyler's request wrote a report on the conditions at Fort George, Ticonderoga, and Crown Point.

3. The return, dated 15 July 1775 and signed by Schuyler, reports a total of 2,857 officers and men stationed between New York City and Crown Point.

In addition, there are eleven staff officers on the return, and ninety men listed as dead, deserted, discharged, or not joined (DLC:GW).

General Orders

Head Quarters, Cambridge, July 16th 1775.

Parole Carolina. Countersign, Springfield.

The Continental Congress having earnestly recommended, that "Thursday next the 20th Instant, be observed by the Inhabitants of all the english Colonies upon this Continent; as a Day of public Humilation, Fasting and Prayer; that they may with united Hearts & Voice, unfeignedly confess their Sins before God, and supplicate the all wise and merciful disposer of events, to avert the Desolation and Calamities of an unnatural war:"[1] The General orders, that Day to be religiously observed by the Forces under his Command, exactly in manner directed by the proclamation of the Continental Congress: It is therefore strictly enjoin'd on all Officers and Soldiers, (not upon duty) to attend Divine Service, at the accustomed places of worship, as well in the Lines, as the Encampments and Quarters; and it is expected, that all those who go to worship, do take their Arms, Ammunition and Accoutrements, & are prepared for immediate Action if called upon. If in the Judgment of the Officers, the Works should appear to be in such forwardness as the utmost security of the Camp requires, they will command their men to abstain from all Labour upon that solemn day.

It was with much surprise and concern that the General in passing along the New Hampshire Lines Yesterday, observed a most wanton, mischevious, and unprofitable Abuse of property, in the Destruction of many valuable Trees, which were standing along the side of the road, out of the way of our works or guns, he therefore orders, that an effective stop be put to such practices for the future, or severe punishment will fall upon the Transgressors of this order.

William Palfrey Esqr. is appointed Aid-de-Camp to Major General Lee, all Orders whether written, or verbal, coming from General Lee, and delivered by Capt. Palfrey, are to be punctually obeyed.[2]

A particular Return to be deliver'd to the Adjutant General to morrow, at Orderly time, of the Regiment of Artillery; distinguishing how every man and Officer, in that Corps, is at present imployed, and where posted.

Varick transcript, DLC:GW.

1. Congress issued its call for the fast day on 12 June 1775 (*JCC*, 2:87–88).

2. William Palfrey (1741–1780), a Boston merchant and business associate of John Hancock, was one of the group of gentlemen who greeted GW and Charles Lee at Worcester, Mass., on their way to Cambridge. Palfrey was promoted to lieutenant colonel and made an aide-de-camp to GW on 6 March 1776. On 27 April 1776 he was chosen to succeed James Warren as paymaster general, a post he held until his appointment as United States consul to France in November 1780. The ship on which Palfrey sailed to his new assignment was lost at sea the following month.

General Orders

Head Quarters [Cambridge] July 17th 1775

Parole Boston. Counter Sign, Salem.

There is reason to apprehend, that the General orders are not regularly published, to the Non Commissioned Officers, & Soldiers of the army; as pleading Ignorance of Orders, will not for the future be admitted in excuse of any delinquency: It is once more ordered, that the Adjutants of the several Corps, will be exact, in seeing the Orders, read every evening to the Men off duty, of their respective Corps, as they may depend upon answering, before a Court Martial, for any neglect in obeying this order.[1]

The General Court Martial whereof Col. John Nixon is president, to sit again to morrow morning at eight OClock, to try such prisoners, as shall be brought before them; all Evidences, and persons concern'd to attend the court.

There being a great Neglect in sending in the Returns to the Adjutant General, as directed by the General Orders of Friday last[2] (especially from the Regiments posted in, and near Roxbury) The General assures Commanding Officers of Corps, from whom the Returns are expected, that he will not for the future, pass over the slightest Neglect, in sending Returns to Head Quarters, at the Time directed by the General Orders; if there is any remissness in the Adjutants, the Colonels will confine the Transgressors.

After Orders.

Capt. Benjamin Perkins of Col. Little's Regiment, confined by

Col. Doolittle, for assisting and abetting Soldiers to mutiny, in rescuing a prisoner from the Quarter Guard of Col. Doolittles Regiment, is to be tried to morrow morning, by the Court Martial whereof Col. Nixon is President; all Evidences, and Persons concern'd, to attend the court.[3]

Varick transcript, DLC:GW.

1. For GW's previous instructions concerning the communication of orders to all ranks, see General Orders, 5 July 1775.

2. GW is apparently referring to the order that he gave in General Orders, Thursday, 13 July 1775, concerning the printed returns that were to be filled in by the regimental adjutants. See also General Orders, 12 July 1775.

3. Benjamin Perkins (1748–1797) of Newbury served until the end of 1776 as a captain in the Massachusetts regiment commanded by Col. Moses Little (1724–1798) of Newbury. Col. Ephraim Doolittle (d. 1807), a hatter and merchant from Petersham, Mass., resigned his commission in October 1775.

From Patrick Henry

Philadelphia, 17 July 1775. Introduces Benjamin Ellery of Rhode Island, who "wishes to visit your Camp."[1]

ALS, MiU-C: Thomas Gage Papers. The document's location indicates that the British intercepted it before it reached GW.

Patrick Henry (1736–1799) of Hanover County, Va., served with GW in the First Continental Congress and was a member of the Second Continental Congress until early August 1775, at which time he was appointed colonel of the newly authorized 1st Virginia Regiment and commander in chief of the colony's regular forces, positions which he held until February 1776. Henry was governor of Virginia from 1776 to 1779 and 1784 to 1786.

1. Benjamin Ellery (1726–1797), a merchant in Newport, was a son of William Ellery (d. 1764), who served as deputy governor of Rhode Island from 1748 to 1750, and the brother of William Ellery (1727–1820), who was a member of the Continental Congress from 1776 to 1781 and 1782 to 1786.

From Jonathan Trumbull, Sr.

Sir Lebanon [Conn.] 17th July 1775

On the first Instant I met the Honble Assembly of this Colony, to deliberate on the Request & pressing Reasons sent us from the Massachusetts for an imediate Augmentation of Troops from this Colony—our Assembly agreed to augment with two Regiments of 700 Men each, who are now raising to join the Continental Army—It was wished that we could have had the Advice & Direction of the Congress or your Excellency before we took this Step—but thought the present critical Scituation of our affairs would not admit the Delay of obtaining it—Since your Arrival at Camps before Boston, View and Consideration, of their Scituation & Circumstances, shall gladly be advised—& shall attend your Request for the hastening and Marching the Men.[1]

There are 1391 Barrels of Flour come to the Care of Colo. Jedh Huntington at Norwich[2] for the Use of the Army which I have ordered forward—the busy Season with the Farmers renders its speedy Transportation difficult—please to advise of the Need of Hurry, & where it shall be ordered to be delivered.

Our Assembly supplied Majr General Schuyler with £15,000—in Cash—and 40 half Bbs. of another Necessary Article[3]—Accounts from the Northward are favourable—the Brig Nancy, Thomas Daviss Master, which arrived at Stonington with Molasses is removed to Norwich—she hath on Board 18, or 19,000 Galls.—the Comittee of Inspection & Correspondence, I trust, will take proper Care respecting both Vessell & Cargoe.[4]

The Road by my Door being the nearest for Post Riding from Cambridge to Philadelphia, shall be obliged, whenever your Excellency has Occasion to send to that City, if the Rider may be directed this Way & to call on me, for the Convenience of any Dispatches I may have Occasion to forward by him—Fessenden has passed this Way more than once. I am, with great Esteem and Regard Sir Your obedient, and most humble Servant

Jonth. Trumbull

ALS, DLC:GW; LB, Ct: Trumbull Papers; copy, DNA:PCC, item 66; copy, DNA:PCC, item 169.

1. The members of the Massachusetts provincial congress wrote Governor Trumbull on 24 June that in view of the incomplete state of the American army and the arrival of British reinforcements, "we cannot, a moment longer, forbear addressing your honor, and most earnestly suggesting to the immediate consideration of your general assembly, not only the expediency, but indispensable necessity, of an immediate augmentation of the troops from your colony, for the more effectual strengthening of the army. . . . We need not express to your honor, the indispensable necessity of despatch in making reenforcements, nor the propriety and advantage of marching any new levies, which your assembly may order, with all possible speed, without the first raised companies waiting for the completing of others; inasmuch as your colony has here, on the spot, all the proper officers to make the necessary dis-

position for their reception, and as the season of their being of any advantage for the support of our army, may be irrevocably lapsed before their arrival, if the least unnecessary delay should be indulged" (*Mass. Prov. Congress Journals*, 387–89). The two new regiments authorized by the Connecticut general assembly in its special session of 1 July 1775 were commmanded by colonels Charles Webb and Jedediah Huntington (Royal R. Hinman, ed., *A Historical Collection, from Official Records, Files &c., of the Part Sustained by Connecticut, during the War of the Revolution* [Hartford, 1842], 185–86). Huntington joined the American army with part of his men by 9 Aug., but Webb's regiment apparently did not arrive until sometime in September (General Orders, 9 Aug. 1775; Trumbull to GW, 15 Sept. 1775).

2. Jedediah Huntington (1743–1818), a merchant in Norwich and son-in-law of Governor Trumbull, had been active in the Sons of Liberty and had served as an officer in the Connecticut militia since 1769. In April 1775 he was a colonel in the Lexington alarm, and during the next two years he commanded one or another of Connecticut's regiments in the Continental army. He became a Continental brigadier general in May 1777 and served until the end of the war.

3. The Connecticut general assembly resolved on 1 July that Governor Trumbull should immediately send £15,000 in bills of credit to Schuyler and such quantity of ammunition as Trumbull and his council "should judge proper and necessary" (Hinman, *Historical Collection*, 187).

4. For a discussion of the brigantine *Nancy* and her cargo, see John Thomas to GW, 10 July 1775, n.1.

From Hunking Wentworth

Portsmouth, N.H., 17 July 1775. Encloses on behalf of the Portsmouth committee of safety "an authenticated copy of a vote pass'd by them for preventing the admission of our Inhabitants into the Camp, upon speculation, without a recommendation or pass first had and obtained from them, Their Inducement to this measure arises from their Fears that some may be too freely and incautiously admitted who are suspected of a want of that attachment & cordiality to our Cause, that we have a right to expect from those who are indulged with every priviledge in common with us all." He communicates the committee's congratulations to GW on his appointment to command the American army and their wishes for his success.

LS, DLC:GW.

Hunking Wentworth, "an old gentleman of seventy-eight years, . . . and lately extremely impaired by recent epileptic fits," was chosen in October 1774 to be chairman of the Portsmouth, N.H., "committee of Ways and Means," which later became the town's committee of safety (John Wentworth to Earl of Dartmouth, 15 Nov. 1774, in Bouton, *N.H. Provincial Papers*, 7:417–18). A prominent resident of Portsmouth for many years, Hunking Wentworth was an uncle of New Hampshire's last royal governor, John Wentworth (1737–1820).

General Orders

Head Quarters, before Boston, July 18th 1775.

Parole Wilmington. Counter Sign, Chester.

As the Chevaux-de-Frise are not in readiness; The Officers commanding the different Lines and Redoubts are, as speedily as possible, to provide a sufficient number of Gabions, which are to lay empty at the Entrances of their respective posts, in order to be filled up as occasion may require. Gen: Putnam will forthwith order his post to be furnished with a large quantity of Fascines.[1]

The Officers commanding the different Posts, to send an exact Return to Head Quarters, this afternoon, of all the intrenching Tools in their possession: vizt Spades, pick-Axes, wheel-Barrows, Hand Barrows, axes and Crow-Barrs; and to mention the number and quality, of any of these Implements, that are still wanting, to carry on their respective works.

Six Captains, twelve Subalterns, twelve Serjeants and three hundred Rank & file, to parade to morrow morning, immediately after divine service, from the Regiments now station'd in Cambridge, as a working party to assist in raising the New Hampshire lines.

Col. James Scammons of the Massachusetts bay Forces, tried by the General Court Martial of which Col. John Nixon was president, for "Disobedience of orders, and Backwardness in the execution of his duty" The Court after duly examining the Evidence, for and against the prisoner, together with what the prisoner had to say in his defence; are of opinion that Col. Scammons is Not guilty of the Crimes wherewith he was accused, and therefore do acquit the prisoner—Col. Scammons to be immediately released from his arrest.[2]

If after what has happened, the Enemy in Revenge of their late Loss, should dare to attempt forcing our Lines, The Army may be assured, that nothing but their own Indolence and Remissness, can give the least hope of success to so rash an Enterprise: It is therefore strongly recommended to the Commanding Officers of Corps, Guards and Detachments; that they be assiduously alert in parading their Men, at their several posts, half an hour before day break, and remain there, untill the Commanding Officers think proper to dismiss them.

The General hears with Astonishment, the very frequent Applications, that are made to him, as well by Officers as Soldiers for Furloughs: Brave Men, who are engaged in the noble Cause of Liberty; should never think of removing from their Camp, while the Enemy is in sight, and anxious to take every Advantage, any Indiscretion on our side may give them: The General doubts not, but the Commanding Officers of Corps will anticipate his wishes, and discourage those under them, from disgracefully desiring to go home, untill the Campaign is ended.

Varick transcript, DLC:GW.

1. For GW's previous order regarding chevaux-de-frise, see General Orders, 15 July 1775. Gabions were large wicker baskets, cylindrical in form and usually open at both ends, which were filled with earth for use in building a variety of field fortifications. Fascines, long bundles of brushwood tied firmly together, were also used for many military engineering tasks including revetting the interiors of batteries and embrasures and filling ditches when assaulting fortifications. See also General Orders, 23 July 1775.

2. For a discussion of the accusations against Scammans, see General Orders, 12 July 1775, n.1.

To Nicholas Cooke

Sir Cambridge Camp July 18 1775

You will please to accept my Sincere Acknowledgments for your favor delivered me by General Green, on my Appointment to the chief Command of the American Army—The Voluntary Choice of Freemen contending in the great Cause of civil Liberty, & the concurring Approbation of the wise and good, at the same Time that they confer the highest Honour upon the Object of that Choice, demand the utmost Energy & Exertion of my poor Abilities; Such as they are, my Country has & shall at all Times command them. Allow me now Sir, to express my warmest Wishes for your Health & Happiness, and to assure you that I am, with much Respect Sir Your most Obedt Hble Servt

Go: Washington

LS, in Thomas Mifflin's writing, NjP: deCoppet Collection; LB, DLC:GW; Varick transcript, DLC:GW.

Letter not found: from Lewis Morris, 18 July 1775. On 4 Aug. GW wrote to Morris: "I have been favoured with your Letter of the 18th Ulto."

From Major General Philip Schuyler

Dear Sir Tionderoga [N.Y.] July 18th 1775

I do myself the Honor to inform Your Excellency of my Arrival at this Place early this Morning; and, as a Person is just going to Hartford, I sit down to give you the little Information I have procured.

A Canadian, who twelve days ago left St Johns, advises me that General Carlton has about four hundred men at that place; that he has thrown up a strong intrenchment, covered with Chevaux de Frise; picketted the ditch, and secured it with an Abbatis;[1] that he has an advanced post of fifty men, intrenched a league on this side; that there are many Indians in Canada, but believes neither they or the Canadians will join him: the latter he is sure will not unless compelled by force.

You will expect that I should say something about this place and the troops here. Not one earthly thing for offence or defence has been done; *the Commanding officer had no orders: he only came to reinforce the garrison, and he expected the General*:[2] But this, my dear General, as well as what follows in this paragraph I pray may be entre nous for reasons I nee⟨d⟩ not suggest. About ten last night I arrived at the Landing pla⟨ce⟩ the north end of Lake George; a post occupied by a Captain and 100 men. A Centinel on being informed I was in the boat quitted his post to go and awake the guard, consisting of three men, in which he had no success. I walked up and came to another, a serjeant's Guard. Here the centinel challenged, but suffered me to come up to him, the whole guard, like the first, in the soundest sleep. With a penknife only I could have cut off both guards, and then have set fire to the blockhouse, destroyed the stores, and starved the people here. At this post I have pointedly recommended vigilance and Care; as all the stores from Fort George must necessarily be landed there—But I hope to get the better of this inattention. The officers and men are all good looking people, and decent in their deportment, and I really believe will make good soldiers as soon as I can get the better of this non-chalance of theirs. Bravery I believe they are far from wanting. As soon as I am a little settled, I shall do myself the Honor to send you a return of my strength both on land and water.

Inclose your Excellency a Copy of a letter from Col. Johnson, with Copy of an Examination of a person lately from Canada, contradictory of the accounts I gave you in my last from Saratoga. You will perceive that he is gone to Canada.[3] I hope Carlton, if he should be able to procure a body of Indians, will not be in a hurry to pay us a visit. I wish to be a little more decently prepared to receive him—in doing which be assured I shall lose no time.

I have no way of sending you any letters, with a probable hope of their coming to hand, unless by express, or by the circuitous rout of Hartford; by which only I can expect to be favored with a line from you.

Generals Lee and Gates share with you in my warmest wishes. I shall devote the first hour I can call my own to do myself the honor to write them. I am Most sincerely, Your Excellency's Obedient, and Humble Servant,

Ph: Schuyler

Permit me, Sir, thro. you to enquire the health of Colo. Read, Major Mifflin and Mr Griffin.

LS, DLC:GW; LB, NN: Schuyler Papers.

1. An abatis is a defensive obstacle formed by felled trees with sharpened branches facing the enemy.

2. The commanding officer at Ticonderoga was Col. Benjamin Hinman (1720–1810), who arrived in the area on 17 June 1775 with 1,400 Connecticut troops. On 7 July Hinman wrote to Schuyler: "I wait Sr with Impatance for your Arivel as I find myself very unAble to stere in this Stormy Cituation[.] Sumtimes wee have no Flower and a constant crye for Rum and want Melases for bear which was engagd to Our people[.] the falliour of those who provide gives grate Uneasayness to the Men[.] hope for better times on your Arivel" (DNA:PCC, item 153).

3. Col. Guy Johnson's letter, dated at Ontario on 8 July, is addressed to the president of the New York provincial congress, Peter Van Brugh Livingston. "I trust," Johnson wrote in response to insinuations that he was inciting Indians to attack the colonists, "I shall always manifest more humanity than to promote the destruction of the innocent inhabitants of a Colony to which I have been always warmly attached a declaration that must appear perfectly suitable to the character of a man of honour and principle who can on no account neglect those duties that are consistent therewith however they may differ from sentiments now adopted in so many parts of America" (DLC:GW). The enclosed examination contains statements made to the Albany committee of safety on 15 July by Gerrit Roseboom, an Albany resident who left Montreal on 26 June and was at Oswego about 7 July. Roseboom reported that the British authorities in Canada were failing in their attempts to secure the services of either Indians or Canadians. At Oswego he observed Guy Johnson holding a council with several Indian tribes and learned that Johnson intended to go to Oswegatchie [Ogdensburg, N.Y.] to confer with Canadian Indians. The Indians at Oswego told Roseboom that they did not intend to fight against the Americans, but in his opinion, "Considering the Fickleness of their Disposit⟨ion⟩ and probably the Over Persuasion of our Enemies no great Dependance can be made on their Assura⟨nces.⟩" Both enclosures are in DLC:GW.

To Jonathan Trumbull, Sr.

Sir — Cambridge July 18. 1775

Allow me to return you my Sincerest thanks for the kind Wishes & favourable Sentiments exprss'd in yours of the 13th Instant: its the Cause[1] of our Common Country calls us both to an Active & dangerous Duty, I trust that Divine Providence which wisely orders the Affairs of Men will enable us to discharge it with Fidelity & Success—The uncorrupted Choice of a brave & free People has raised you to deserved Eminence; that the Blessing of Health & the still greater Blessing of long continuing to govern *such* a People may be yours is the Sincere Wish of Sir Your Most Obedient very humble Servant

Go. Washington

LB, Ct: Trumbull Papers; LB, DLC:GW; Varick transcript, DLC:GW.

1. The letter-book copy in DLC:GW reads "As the Cause."

To Jonathan Trumbull, Sr.

Sir Cambridge July 18. 1775.

It is with no small Concern that I find the Arrangement of General Officers made by the Honourable Continental Congress has produced Dissatisfaction.[1] As the Army is upon a general Establishment, their Right to controul & supersede a Provincial one must be unquestionable: and in such a Cause I should hope every Post would be deemed honourable which gave a Man Opportunity to serve his Country.

A Representation from the Congress of this Province, with such Remarks as occurr'd to me on this Subject, is now before the Continental Congress. In the mean Time I beg Leave to assure you, that unbyass'd by any private Attachments, I shall studiously endeavour to reconcile their Pretensions to their Duty, & so dispose them as to prevent if possible any Inconvenience to the publick Service from this Competition. I have the Honour to be with much Respect & Esteem Sir, Your most Obedt & very Hbble Servt

Go: Washington

LS, in Joseph Reed's writing, MiU-C: Schoff Collection; LB, Ct: Trumbull Papers; LB, DLC:GW; Varick transcript, DLC:GW. The LS is endorsed "recd 23d p. Fessenden."

1. For a discussion of the dispute over the precedence of the general officers from Connecticut, see GW to Hancock, 10–11 July 1775, Document II. Letter Sent, n.20.

General Orders

Head Quarters Cambridge, July 19th 1775.

Parole Derby. Counter Sign Marblehead.

Varick transcript, DLC:GW.

From John Hancock

Philadelphia, 19 July 1775. Introduces the bearers, "Mr Ogden & Mr Burr of the Jerseys," who "Visit the Camp not as Spectators, but with a View of Joining the Army & being Active during the Campaign.[1] . . . Your Dispatches Reach'd me last Eveng. I shall forward you the Papers immediately. The Results of Congress you shall know as early as possible."[2]

ALS, DLC:GW. The address includes the words "Favd by Mr Burr."

1. Matthias Ogden (1754–1791) and Aaron Burr (1756–1836) grew up together in the house of Burr's uncle in Elizabeth, New Jersey. Following the battles of Lexington and Concord, Burr, who was then studying law in Litchfield, Conn., wrote to Ogden at Elizabeth, proposing that they join the American army outside Boston. Ogden at first declined to go, but after the Battle of Bunker Hill, Burr went to Elizabeth and persuaded his friend to come with him. Both young men accompanied Arnold's march to Quebec in the fall of 1775 as unattached volunteers. Ogden was wounded at Quebec on 31 Dec. but joined the 1st New Jersey Regiment as a lieutenant colonel in March 1776. He was promoted to colonel on 1 Jan. 1777, and in October 1780 he was captured in a skirmish with the British at Elizabeth. Following his exchange the next spring, Ogden resumed his duties and remained in the army until April 1783. Burr returned from Quebec to New York City in the spring of 1776 and apparently served for a few weeks on GW's staff before becoming an aide to Maj. Gen. Israel Putnam on 22 June. On 4 Jan. 1777 Burr was made lieutenant colonel of Col. William Malcolm's additional regiment. He resigned from the army on 3 March 1779 on the grounds of ill health.

2. Congress took GW's letter to Hancock of 10–11 July 1775 under consideration on 19 July (*JCC*, 2:190). For Congress's actions, see Hancock to GW, 24 July 1775.

General Orders

Head Quarters, Cambridge, July 20th 1775.

Parole, Albany. Countersign, Ticonderoga.

Certain Drums in, and near Cambridge, very improperly beat the Revellie this morning before day; Although the Troops are ordered to be under Arms, half an hour before day light; it does not follow the drums are to beat at that time. The Reveille is to beat when a Centry can see clearly one thousand Yards around him, and not before.

All Aids-de-Camp, and Majors of Brigade, are to keep regularly entered in a book; all the General Orders of the army, as well as those of the Brigades they belong to: As the General in Chief, will not for the future, admit as an Excuse for the Breach of Orders; the plea of not knowing them.

Samuel Osgood and Joseph Ward Esqrs. being appointed Aids-de Camp, to Major General Ward, they are to be obeyed as such;[1] and all orders coming from Aids-de Camp, are to be consider'd, as the Orders of their respective Generals, and whether written or verbal, to be forthwith obeyed: It may be necessary once more to repeat to the Army, that every Aid-de-Camp and Major of Brigade, will be distinguished by a green ribband.[2]

Certain Corps, having been dilatory in delivering last Saturday, their weekly Returns, as positively directed by former orders;[3] The General is determin'd for the future, not to excuse any neglect in sending the Returns every Saturday, to the Adjutant General. As the Commanding Officers of Regiments, are to be answerable for the due observance of this Order, it is expected they are exact in obliging their respective Adjutants, to fullfill their duty.

Varick transcript, DLC:GW.

1. Samuel Osgood (1748–1813), a merchant in Andover, joined the American army after the Battle of Lexington as captain of a Massachusetts militia company. He served as an aide-de-camp to Artemas Ward until 23 April 1776, eventually achieving the rank of colonel. From 1781 to 1784 Osgood sat in the Continental Congress and was a member of the Board of Treasury. Joseph Ward (born c.1737), a Massachusetts schoolmaster, was an aide-de-camp to his second cousin Artemas Ward until 23 April 1776 and then his secretary until 20 Sept. 1776. On 10 April 1777 Joseph Ward became commissary general of musters for the Continental army with the rank of colonel, and three years later he was appointed commissary general of prisoners, which office he held until the end of the war.

2. This insignia was first prescribed in General Orders, 14 July 1775.

3. For GW's previous orders regarding returns, see General Orders, 12, 13, and 17 July 1775.

Letter not found: to Lund Washington, 20 July 1775. In a letter of 15 Oct. 1775 to GW, Lund Washington referred to GW's letter of "July . . . 20th."

To Samuel Washington

Camp at Cambridge about ⟨5⟩[1] Miles from Boston

Dear Brother, July 20. 1775.

Agreeable to your request I am now set down to write to you, although in the first place I have scarce time to indulge an Inclination of the kind, and in the next place do not know how or whether it may ever get to your hands.

I came to this place the 2d Instant & found a numerous army of Provencials under very little command, discipline, or order—I found our Enemy who had drove our People from Bunkers Hill strongly Intrenching, and from Accts had reason to expect before this, another attack from them; but, as we have been incessantly (Sundays not excepted) employed in throwing up Works of defence I rather begin to believe now, that they think it rather a dangerous experiment; and that we shall remain sometim⟨e⟩ watching the Motions of each other, at the distance of little more than a mile & in full vie⟨w⟩—from the best Accts we have been able t⟨o⟩ get, the number of the Enemy amounts to between 10 and 12,000 Men; part of which are in Boston, & part on Bunkers Hill just by—our numbers including Sick, absent &ca are between 16 & 18,000; but then, having great extent of Lines & many places to defend, & not knowing where the attack may be made (as they have the entire command of the Water & can draw their whole force to any one point in an hour or twos time without any person but the Commanding Officer who directs it having the least previous notice of it) our situatio⟨n⟩ is a little unfavourable. but not so bad but that I think we can give them a pretty warm reception if they think proper to make any advances towards us—their situation is such as to secure them from any attack of ours.

By what we can learn, they are sadly distressd for want of fresh Provisions—Beef (the Milch Cows in Boston) sells from One shilling to 18d. Sterg pr lb.—Mutton higher, & these only to be had for the Sick. the number of thos⟨e⟩ killed & wounded in the engagement on Bunker⟨s⟩ Hill could not fall short of 1100, ours did not exceed 450—a few more such Victories woul⟨d⟩ put an end to their army and the present contest.

The Village I am in, is situated in the midst of a very delightful Country, and is a very beautiful place itself, th⟨ou⟩gh small—a thousand pities that such a Country should become the theatre of War—A Month from this day will bring on some Capitol change I expect; for if the Enemy are not able to penetrate into the Country, they may as well, one would think, give up the point & return home; for if they stay at Boston & a⟨t⟩ Bu⟨n⟩kers Hill (which is another Peninsula lef⟨t⟩ unto it, & seperated by a small Ferry over to Charles Town which is part of the Nec⟨k⟩ I say if they stay at those places f⟨or⟩ ever, the end for which they were se⟨nt⟩ cannot be accomplished; & to compel them to remain there, is the principal object we have in view indeed the onl⟨y.⟩

We have seen nothing of the Rifle men yet, nor have we heard any thing certain of them. I have only time to add my love to my Sister & the Family & to assure you that I am with unfeigned regard & truth Dr Sir Yr Affecte Brother and frien⟨d⟩

Go: Washington

P.S. In the late Ingagemt of the 17th Ulto the Enemy by the best Accts we can get had 1043 Men killed & W⟨o⟩und⟨e⟩d Wh⟨ere⟩of 92 Were Officers—our loss amounted to 13⟨9⟩ killed 278 Wounded & 36 Missing[2]—pray rememb⟨er⟩ me kindly to Mr Warner Washington ⟨and Family⟩[3] when you see them.

ALS, PHi: Dreer Collection.

1. Most of this number has been torn away, but a comparison with the dateline of GW's letter of 27 July 1775 to John Augustine Washington indicates that it was a "5."

2. GW put the British losses at 1,057 in his letter to Lund Washington of 20 Aug. 1775. The number of Americans who were killed in the battle is given as 139 in GW to George William Fairfax, 25 July 1775 and 138 in GW to John Augustine Washington, 27 July 1775.

3. These words, which are illegible on the manuscript, are taken from John C. Fitzpatrick, ed., *The Writings of George Washington from the Original Manuscript Sources, 1745–1799*, 39 vols. (Washington, D.C., 1931–44), 37:512–13. GW's cousin Warner Washington, Sr. (1722–1790), lived in the Shenandoah Valley of Virginia several miles south of Samuel Washington's house.

General Orders

Head Quarters, Cambridge, July 21st 1775.

Parole, Maldin. Countersign Chelsea.

Varick transcript, DLC:GW.

To John Hancock

Sir Camp at Cambridge July 21. 1775

Since I did myself the Honour of addressing you the 14th Instt, I have received Advice from Govr Trumbull, that the Assembly of Connecticut had voted, & that they are now raising two Regiments of 700 Men each, in Consequence of an Application from the Provincial Congress of Massachusetts Bay. The Rhode Island Assembly has also made an Augmentation for this Purpose:[1] these Reinforcements, with the Riffle Men who are daily expected, & such Recruits as may come in, to fill up the Regiments here, will I apprehend compose an Army sufficiently strong, to oppose any Force which may be brought against us at present. I am very sensible, that the heavy Expence necessarily attendant upon this Campaign, will call for the utmost Frugality & Care, & would therefore if possible avoid inlisting one unnecessary Man—As this is the first certain Account of the Destination of these new raised Troops, I thought proper to communicate my Sentiments as early as possible; least the Congress should act upon my Letter of the 10th, and raise Troops in the Southern Colonies, which in my present Judgment may be dispens'd with.[2]

For these 8 Days past, there have been no Movements in either Camp of any Consequence. On our Side, we have continued the Works without any Intermission, & they are now so far advanced, as to leave us little to apprehend on that Score. On the Side of the Enemy, they have also been very industrious in finishing their Lines both on Bunkers Hill, & Roxbury Neck. In this Interval also their Transports have arrived from New York, and they have been employed in landing & stationing their Men. I have been able to collect no certain Account of the Numbers arrived, but the inclosed Letter wrote (tho. not signed) by Mr Sheriff Lee, & delivered me by Captn Darby (who went Express with an Account of the Lexington Battle) will enable us to form a pretty accurate Judgment.[3] The Increase of Tents & Men in the Town of Boston is very obvious, but all my Accounts from thence agree, that there is a great Mortality occasioned by the Want of Vegetables, & fresh Meat: & that their Loss in the late Battle at Charles Town (from the few Recoveries of their wounded) is greater than at first supposed. The Condition of the Inhabitants detained in Boston is very distressing, they are equally destitute of the Comfort of fresh Provisions, & many of them are so reduced in their Circumstances, as to be unable to supply themselves with salt: Such Fish as the Soldiery leave, is their principal Support. Added to all this, such Suspicion & Jealousy prevails, that they can scarcely speak, or even look, without exposing themselves to some Species of military Execution.

I have not been able from any Intelligence I have received, to form any certain Judgment of the future Operations of the Enemy. Some Times I have suspected an Intention of detaching a Part of their Army to some Part of the Coast, as they have been building a Number of flat bottom'd Boats capable of holding 200 Men each. But from their Works, & the Language held at Boston, there is Reason to think, they expect the Attack from us, & are principally engaged in preparing themselves against it. I have ordered all the Whale Boats along the Coast to be collected, & some of them are employed every Night to watch the Motions of the Enemy by Water, so as to guard as much as possible against any Surprize.[4]

Upon my Arrival & since, some Complaints have been preferr'd against Officers for Cowardice in the late Action on Bunkers Hill. Though there were several strong Circumstances & a very general Opinion against them, none have been condemn'd, except a Captn Callender of the Artillery, who was immediately cashier'd. I have been sorry to find it an uncontradicted Fact, that the principal Failure of Duty that Day was in the Officers, tho. many of them distinguish'd themselves by their gallant Behaviour. The Soldiers generally shew'd great Spirit and Resolution.[5]

Next to the more immediate & pressing Duties of putting our Lines in as secure a State as possible, attending to the Movements of the Enemy, & gaining Intelligence, my great Concern is to establish Order, Regularity & Discipline: without which, our Numbers would embarass us, & in Case of Action general Confusion must infallibly ensue—In order to this, I propose to divide the Army into three Divisions at the Head of each will be a General Officer—these Divisions to be again subdivided into Brigades, under their respective Brigadiers: but the Difficulty arising from the Arrangement of the General Officers, & waiting the farther Proceedings of the Congress on this Subject, has much retarded my Progress in this most necessary Work. I should be very happy to receive their final Commands, as any Determination would enable me to proceed in my Plan.[6]

General Spencer returned to the Camp two Days ago, & has consented to serve under Puttnam, rather than leave the Army intirely. I have heard nothing from General Pomroy, should he wholly retire, I apprehend it will be necessary to supply his Place as soon as possible.[7] General Folsom proposes also to retire. In Addition to the Officers mentioned in mine of the 10th Instt, I would humbly propose that some Provision should be made for a Judge Advocate, & Provost Marshal[.] the Necessity of the first Appointment was so great, that I was obliged to nominate a Mr Tudor who was well recommended to me, & now executes the Office, under an Expectation of receiving Captains Pay; an Allowance, in my Opinion, scarcely adequate to the Service in new raised Troops, where there are Court Martials every Day. However as that is the Proportion in the regular Army, and he is contented, there will be no Necessity of an Addition.[8]

I must also renew my Request as to Money, & the Appointment of a Paymaster: I have forbore urging Matters of this Nature from my Knowledge of the many important Concerns which engage the Attention of the Congress; but as I find my Difficulties thicken every Day, I make no Doubt suitable Regard will be paid to a Necessity of this Kind. The Inconvenience of borrowing such Sums as are constantly requisite must be too plain for me to enlarge upon, & is a Situation, from which I should be very happy to be relieved.[9]

Upon the Experience I have had, & the best Consideration of the Appointment of the several Offices of Commissary Genl, Muster master Genl, Quarter Master Genl, Paymaster Genl & Commissary of Artillery, I am clearly of Opinion that they not only conduce to Order, Dispatch & Discipline, but that it is a Measure of Oeconomy. The Delay, the Waste, & unpunishable Neglect of Duty arising from these Offices being in Commission, in several Hands, evidently shew that the publick Expence must be finally enhanced. I have experienced the Want of these Officers, in completing the Returns of Men, Ammunition, & Stores, the latter are yet imperfect, from the Number of Hands in which they are dispers'd. I have inclosed the last weekly Return which is more accurate than the former, & hope in a little Time we shall be perfectly regular in this, as well as several other necessary Branches of Duty.

I have made Inquiry into the Establishment of the Hospital, & find it in a very unsettled Condition. There is no principal

Director, or any Subordination among the Surgeons, of Consequence, Disputes & Contention have arisen, & must continue, untill it is reduced to some System. I could wish it was immediately taken into Consideration, as the Lives & Health of both Officers & Men, so much depend upon a due Regulation of this Department[10]—I have been particularly attentive to the least Symptoms of the small Pox and hitherto we have been so fortunate, as to have every Person removed so soon, as not only to prevent any Communication, but any Alarm or Apprehension it might give in the Camp. We shall continue the utmost Vigilance against this most dangerous Enemy.

In an Army properly organized, there are sundry Officers of an Inferiour kind, such as Waggon Master, Master Carpenter &c. but I doubt whether my Powers are sufficiently extensive for such Appointments: If it is thought proper to repose such a Trust in me, I shall be governed in the Discharge of it, by a strict Regard to Oeconomy, & the publick Interest.[11]

My Instructions from the Hone Congress direct that no Troops are to be disbanded without their express Direction, nor to be recruited to more than double the Number of the Enemy.[12] Upon this Subject, I beg Leave to represent, that unless the Regiments in this Province, are more successful in recruiting than I have Reason to expect, a Reduction of some of them, will be highly necessary; as the Publick is put to the whole Expence of an Establishment of Officers, while the real Strength of the Regiment, which consists in the Rank & file, is defective. In Case of such a Reduction doubtless some of the Privates, & all the Officers would return Home; but many of the former, would go into the remaining Regiments, & having had some Experience would fill them up with useful Men. I so plainly perceive the Expence of this Campaign, will exceed any Calculation hitherto made, that I am particularly anxious to strike off every unnecessary Charge. You will therefore, Sir, be pleased to favour me with explicit Directions from the Congress on the Mode of this Reduction, if it shall appear necessary, that no Time may be lost when such Necessity appears.[13]

Yesterday we had an Account that the Light House was on Fire—by whom, & under what Orders, I have not yet learned. But we have Reason to believe, it has been done by some of our Irregulars.[14]

You will please to present me to the Congress with the utmost Duty, & Respect & believe me to be Sir, Your most Obed. & very Hbble Servt

Go: Washington

P.S. Captn Darby's Stay in England was so short, that he brings no other Information than what the inclosed Letter, & the News Papers which will accompany this, contain—General Gage's Dispatches had not arrived & the Ministry affected to disbelieve the whole Account—treating it as a Fiction or at most an Affair of little Consequence. The Fall of Stocks was very inconsiderable.[15]

LS, in Joseph Reed's writing, DNA:PCC, item 152; LB, DLC:GW; copy, DNA:PCC, item 169; Varick transcript, DLC:GW. Both the letter-book copy and the Varick transcript are dated 20 July 1775. A note on the letter-book copy indicates that the letter was "Sent by Fessenden Express."

1. For a discussion of the new Connecticut regiments, see Jonathan Trumbull, Sr., to GW, 17 July 1775, n.1. The Rhode Island general assembly, sitting on 28 June, "resolved, that six companies, consisting of sixty men each, including officers, be immediately raised in this colony, in addition to those already ordered to be raised; . . . that two companies be added to each regiment now in the service of this colony, and encamped near Boston, that as soon as twenty men in a company shall be raised, they be sent forward, . . . and the whole as soon as possible" (John Russell Bartlett, ed., *Records of the Colony of Rhode Island and Providence Plantations in New England*, 10 vols. [Providence, 1856–65], 7:354).

2. Congress took no action to raise southern troops for the Continental army, other than the Virginia and Maryland riflemen, before it recessed on 2 August.

3. Capt. John Derby (1741–1812), a prosperous merchant in Salem and a member of the Massachusetts provincial congress, received orders from the provincial congress on 27 April 1775 to hasten to England with accounts of the battles of Lexington and Concord in order that the American version of those events might be publicized in the mother country before the official dispatches from Gen. Thomas Gage were received. Derby succeeded in his mission, reaching London on 28 May, several days before the arrival of the packet ship that brought Gage's dispatches. He returned to Salem on 18 July and that same day reported to GW at Cambridge. For his report, see postscript and note 15. William Lee (1739–1795), a younger brother of Richard Henry Lee, moved from Virginia to London in 1768 to become a partner in a business firm, and in 1773 he was elected sheriff of the city. The four British regiments which landed at Boston between 22 June and 19 July came from Ireland. Their transports anchored at the entrance to New York Harbor in late June to take on fresh water before continuing on to Boston. See Schuyler to GW, 1 July 1775, n.3.

4. Joseph Reed wrote to Brig. Gen. John Thomas on 18 July: "I am directed by his Excellency the General to acquaint you that he thinks it necessary to procure as many more Whale Boats as possible & send them over immediately" (letter owned [1981] by Ronald Von Klaussen). For GW's efforts to obtain men to handle the whaleboats, see General Orders, 15 July 1775. On 24 July British Vice Admiral Samuel Graves reported to Philip Stephens: "The Rebels have collected near three hundred Whale Boats in the different Creeks round this Harbour, and begin to make little Expeditions to the Islands. . . . From their Lightness and drawing little Water, they can not only outrow our Boats, but by getting into Shoal Water, and in Calms, they must constantly escape. . . . Various are the Conjectures about the Design of the Rebels in bringing so great a number of Whale boats here, Robbing the Islands and burning the Houses and Hay thereon most certainly distresses the Garrison by depriving them of fresh Meat, Vegetables, Milk, Fruit and many other Advantages; but it is generally believed they were principally intended to land a Body of Men in the Night at the most defenceless parts of the Town, when a general attack should be made on the Lines, hoping, with the assistance of disaffected people in the Town, to occasion great confusion and terror and finally defeat his Majesty's Troops. Others are of opinion that in a calm Night they mean to surprize one of the Frigates of the Squadron and carry her by suddenly pouring in great Numbers of People" (William Bell Clark et al., eds., *Naval Documents of the American Revolution* [Washington, D.C., 1964—], 1:961–62).

5. For a discussion of Capt. John Callender's case, see General Orders, 7 July 1775, n.1. For the shortcomings of the officer corps as a whole, see Joseph Hawley to GW, 5 July, GW to Lund Washington, 20 Aug., and GW to Richard Henry Lee, 29 Aug. 1775.

6. GW announced the new organization of the army in General Orders, 22 July 1775.

7. For the dispute over rank involving Joseph Spencer and Israel Putnam, see GW to Hancock, 10–11 July 1775, Document II. Letter Sent, n.20. For the one involving Seth Pomeroy, see James Warren and Joseph Hawley to GW, 4 July 1775, n.1.

8. GW chose William Tudor, whom John Adams earlier recommended to become his secretary, to be judge advocate general on 14 July, and on 29 July Congress made the appointment (*JCC*, 2:221). Tudor soon changed his mind about his pay. In his letter to GW of 23 Aug. 1775, he threatened to resign his office unless Congress increased his salary.

9. Although Congress authorized a paymaster general for the army on 16 June, the position was not filled until the delegates chose James Warren on 27 July (*JCC*, 2:94, 211). On 1 Aug., the day before Congress recessed, it resolved "that the sum of five hundred thousand dollars be immediately forwarded from the continental Treasury, to the paymaster general, to be applied to the use of the army in Massachusetts bay, in such manner, as General Washington . . . shall limit and appoint; and if the above sum shall be expended before the next meeting of the Congress, then that General Washing-

ton . . . be empowered to draw upon the continental Treasury, for the sum of two hundred thousand dollars, in favour of the paymaster general" (ibid., 235–36).

10. Congress established "an hospital for an army, consisting of 20,000 men," on 27 July (*JCC*, 2:209–11). See also Richard Henry Lee to GW, 29 June 1775, n.5.

11. On 29 July Congress resolved "that the appointment of provost Marshal, waggon master, and master carpenter, be left to the commander in chief of the army, who is to fix their pay, having regard to the pay such receive in the ministerial army, and the proportion that the pay of the Officers in said army bears to the pay of our Officers" (*JCC*, 2:221). For GW's appointment of a wagon master general, see General Orders, 9 Aug. 1775, and for his appointment of a provost marshal, see General Orders, 10 Jan. 1776.

12. See Instructions from the Continental Congress, 22 June 1775.

13. GW discussed the problem of understrength regiments in more detail in his letter of 4–5 Aug. 1775 to Hancock.

14. For the burning of the lighthouse in Boston Harbor, see GW's third letter of this date to Hancock, and William Heath to GW, this date.

15. "Capt. John Derby," it was reported in the *New-England Chronicle: or, the Essex Gazette* (Cambridge, Mass.) of 21 July 1775, "returned last Tuesday, and the same Day came to Head-Quarters in this Place. Very little Intelligence has yet transpired—we only learn, that the News of the Commencement of the American War threw the People in England, especially the City of London, into great Consternation, and occasioned a considerable Fall of the Stocks. . . . Capt. Derby brought a few London Papers, some as late as the first of June, but we have not been able to obtain a Sight of them. We are informed they contain very little News, and scarce any Remarks on American Affairs." Excerpts from those newspapers are printed in the *Massachusetts Spy or American Oracle of Liberty* (Worcester, Mass.), 26 July 1775. James Warren wrote to John Adams on 20 July that Derby stayed in England for eight days, and "He says Trade and the Stocks were Amazeingly Affected in that short time" (Taylor, *Papers of John Adams*, 3:82–85). GW had gotten the truth of the matter, however. Stock prices declined only slightly. See GW to Schuyler, 28 July 1775.

To John Hancock

Dear Sir Cambridge July 21. 1775.

I am particularly to acknowledge that Part of your Favour of the 10th Instt wherein you do me the Honour of determining to join the Army under my Command. I need certainly make no Professions of the Pleasure I shall have in seeing you—At the same Time I have to regret that so little is in my Power to offer equal to Col. Hancock['s] Merits[1] & worthy his Acceptance. I shall be happy in every Oppy to shew the Regard & Esteem with which I am Sir Your most Obed. & very Hbble Servt

LB, in Joseph Reed's writing, DLC:GW; Varick transcript, DLC:GW. The last two sentences were extensively revised in the letter-book copy. Before they were changed, they read: "At the same Time I have to regret that so little is in my Power to offer which Col. Hancock merits & is worthy of his Acceptance. Whatever is in my Power you will please freely to command & believe me with great Truth & Regard, Sir Your most Obed. & very Hbble Servt."

1. Although Hancock was commissioned colonel of an independent company of cadets in Boston on 1 April 1772, he had no practical military training or experience. His only service in the field during the Revolution came in 1778, when, as a major general of Massachusetts militia, he briefly commanded a body of militiamen in the operations around Newport.

To John Hancock

Sir Cambridge Camp July 21t 1775 5 oClock. P.M.

Since closing the Letters which accompany this I have received an Account of the Destruction of the Light House, a Copy of which I have the Honour to inclose[1] & of again assuring you that I am with great Respect, Sir Your most Obed. Hbble Serv.

Go: Washington

P.S. I have also received a more authentick Account of the Loss of the Enemy in the late Battle than any yet receivd. Doctr Winship[2] who lodg'd in the same House with an Officer of the Marines assures me they had exactly 1043 killed & wounded, of whom 300 fell on the Field or died within a few Hours. Many of the wounded are since dead.[3]

G. W——n

LS, in Joseph Reed's writing, DNA:PCC, item 152; LB, DLC:GW; copy, DNA:PCC, item 169; Varick transcript, DLC:GW. A note on the letter-book copy reads "Sent by Fessenden Express."

1. The enclosure was William Heath's letter of this date to GW.

2. Amos Windship (1745–1813), a Boston physician, escaped from the city about this time by disguising himself as a sailor. He served without commission in the Continental hospital until he was appointed a surgeon's mate at the beginning of 1776. In September 1776 he became surgeon on the brig-of-war *Massachusetts* and in January 1779 surgeon on the Continental frigate *Alliance*.

3. GW put British losses at 1,057 in his letter to Lund Washington of 20 Aug. 1775.

From Benjamin Harrison

Dr General. Philadelphia July *21st*[–24] 1775

I received your very acceptable favor of the 10th Instant by express,[1] your Fatigue and various kinds of trouble I dare say are great, but they are not more than I expected, knowing the People you have to deal with by the sample we have here, the Congress have taken the two Regiments now raising in Conecticut into service, which with Rifle Men and Recruits to your Regiments will I hope make up the number voted by your Council of War,[2] I wish with all my heart your Troops were better and your Stores more compleat, every thing that we can do here to put you in the best posture possible I think you may depend, will be done, I trust you will have a Supply soon of Ammunition, without an accident, you may depend on it[3]—The want of Engineers I fear is not to be supplied in America, some Folks here seemed much displeased at your Report on that head, they affirm there are two very good ones with you, a Colo. Gridley I think is one,[4] I took the liberty to say that they must be mistaken, they were certainly either not in Camp or could not have the Skill they were pleased to say they had, this in my soft way put a stop to any thing more on the Subject, indeed my Friend I do not know what to think of some of these Men, they seem to be exceeding hearty in the Cause, but still wish to keep every thing amongst themselves, Our President is quite of a different Cast, Noble disinterested and Generous to a very great Degree—The Congress have given you the appointment of three Brigade Majors, Mr Trumbull has the Office you proposed for him, the appointment of the Commissary of Artillery, Do of Musters and Quartermaster General are also left to your disposal,[5] nothing is yet done as to the Hospital, but I will bring it on very soon[6]—your Brothers in the Delegation have recommended it to our Convention to send some virginians to the Camp at the Expence of our Colony to learn the Military Art, and I hope you will see them soon—we have given the Commission of first Brigadier to Mr Thomas, as Putnams Commission was delivered, it would perhaps have offended the old Gentleman to have superceded him, the other I hope will still act, the Congress have from your account a high opinion of him, and I dare say will grant any thing in their Power that he may hereafter require[7]—your hint for a remove of the Congress to some place nearer to you will come on to Morrow, I think it will not answer your Expectations, if we should remove, you shall have the result in the close of this;[8] The Military Chest I hope will be Supply'd soon, they begin to Strike the Bills this Day, so that I hope some may be forwarded to you next Week, what has occasioned the delay in this article I know not without an imitation of the Congress in its slowness is become fashionable—I have had no further account from our Country about the Governor except that he is still at York Town with three Men of War, He, Montague, and Foye, went the other Day by Water to his Farm, and were within three or four Minutes of being all taken by Captain Meridith with 70 Men from Hanover, who are with about 150 from other Counties guarding Williamsburg, from any attempts that he may make with his Boil'd crabs, Meridith says his Intentions were to carry his Lordship to Williamsburg to put him into the Pals. and promise him Protection to convince him and the World that no Injury was intended him, however as he miss'd his stroke I dare say he will be charged with intendg to Murder him[9]—We think the Season too far Advanced to send you any more Men from the Southward, but it seems to be the General opinion to send some Thousands early in the Spring, should this be the case, if I have the Honor of being here you may depend on my care of Mr Johnston, we have an imperfect account of an attack on New York, by some of the over Lake Indians, I hope it is not true, Indeed (betwixt you and I) I give very little Credit to any thing from that Quarter, and wish I could say I had no reason to be Suspicious of those People[10]—We yesterday received dispatches from Georgia, they have come into the Union and have appointed Delegates to the Congress, they have even done more, they with the South Carolinians Armed a Vessel and have taken a Ship with 140 Barrels of Kings Powder which they have divided betwixt them.[11]

23d The Debate about our remove was taken up yesterday, and determined in the Negative, I proposed a Committee, but could not carry it, I think the last Method would have answered your purpose best, but the Gentlemen could not think of parting with the least Particle of their Power;[12] Pendleton left us

Yesterday, all Maryland are gone off this day, and we intend to follow them next Sunday, if nothing material happens betwixt this and then, our going I expect will break up the Congress, indeed I think it high time there was an end of it, we have been too long together.[13]

Edmund Randolph is here and has the greatest desire to be with you, he has beg'd of me to say something in his favor, and that if you can with propriety, you will keep one of the Places now in your Gift for him, he is not able to support himself or he would not ask this of you, you know him as well as I do, he is one of the Cleverest Young Men in America, and if Mr Read should leave you, his place of Secretary can't be better Supply'd, he will set off for New York in a few days and I beg it as a favor of you to write a line to him, to be left at the Post Office there, till call'd for, this deserving Young Man was in high repute in Virginia, and he fears his Fathers Conduct may tend to lessen him in the Esteem of his Countrymen, he has taken this Method without the advice of his Friends to raise him into Favor, as he is determined on the Thing; I am sure our good old Speaker will be much Obliged for any favor you shew him, applications of this sort I fear will be too frequent, I shall avoid them as much as possible, but I could not refuse it on this Occasion, well knowing that a most valuable Young Man, and one that I love, without some Step of this sort may from the Misconduct of his Parent, be lost to his Country, which now Stands much in need of Men of his Abilities[14]—We have a Report that Robert Mckenzie was killed at Bunkers Hill, is it true, I had a great Friendship for him formerly, but can't help saying I shall be glad to hear the News confirmed.[15]

24th Nothing New in Congress or from Virginia to Day, I should therefore have closed this without saying more had not an application been made to me to introduce to you Captain Thomas Price of a Company of Rifle Men from Maryland, he comes with a high Character from thence and is looked on as most firmly attached to the cause of America, he has a large Family which he has left merely to forward the Service, the Deputies from that Country are gone home, I have seen a Letter in his favor to Mr Flighman highly Commending him, and as he could not thro' that Channel get a Recommendation I have been prevailed on to Introduce him which Liberty I hope you will excuse.[16] I am My Dr Sir your most affect. Servant,

(Sign'd) Benja. Harrison

P:S: We expect to leave this Place next Sunday, I shall yet beg the favor of a line now and then, and shall leave orders with Bradford[17] to forward them, in return you shall be most Minutely informed of every thing going forward in Virginia.

Copy, enclosed in Thomas Gage to Earl of Dartmouth, 20 Aug. 1775, P.R.O., C.O.5/92, ff. 252–54; copy, enclosed in Thomas Gage to Earl of Dartmouth, 20 Aug. 1775, Dartmouth MSS, William Salt Library, Stafford, England; copy, enclosed in Samuel Graves to Philip Stephens, 17 Aug. 1775, P.R.O., C.O.5/122, ff. 80–83; copy, MiU-C: Thomas Gage Papers; copy, MiU-C: Miscellaneous Collection. This letter fell into British hands when a party from a British warship captured its bearer, Benjamin Hichborn, while he was crossing Narragansett Bay on his way to Cambridge. See GW to Hancock, 4–5 Aug. 1775, and James Warren to GW, 5 Aug. 1775. The letter was forwarded to Vice Admiral Samuel Graves at Boston, who gave a copy to Gen. Thomas Gage, and both Graves and Gage subsequently sent copies to England. Graves apparently kept the original letter which has not been found. On 17 Aug. 1775 the *Massachusetts Gazette: and the Boston Weekly News-Letter* printed a doctored version of the letter, in which the following spurious paragraph appears at the end of the section dated 21 July: "As I was in the pleasing Task of writing to you, a little Noise occasioned me to turn my Head round, and who should appear but pretty little Kate the Washer-woman's Daughter over the Way, clean, trim and rosey as the Morning; I snatch'd the golden glorious Opportunity, and but for that cursed Antidote to Love, Sukey, I had fitted her for my General against his Return. We were obliged to part, but not till we had contrived to meet again; if she keeps the Appointment I shall relish a Week's longer stay—I give you now and then some of these Adventures to amuse you, and unbend your Mind from the Cares of War." Nothing is known about the authorship of this paragraph which was clearly intended to create a scandal among the Patriots. The copy in the Public Record Office that Gage enclosed to the earl of Dartmouth does not contain the spurious paragraph, nor does the copy of that copy at the William Salt Library. The copy in the Public Record Office that Graves enclosed to Philip Stephens, secretary of the Admiralty, and the two copies at the Clements Library, University of Michigan, do contain the spurious paragraph. Many American and British newspapers reprinted the doctored letter from the *Massachusetts Gazette*, and there are numerous manuscript copies of it in various repositories in addition to the ones cited here. For an account of this document and the spurious paragraph, see Allen French, "The First George Washington Scandal," in Mass. Hist. Soc., *Proceedings*, 65 (1935), 460–74.

Benjamin Harrison (c.1726–1791) of Charles City County, Va., served with GW for many years in the Virginia House of Burgesses and was one of his fellow delegates in both the First and Second Continental Congresses. Harrison remained in Congress until October 1777, playing a prominent role in military affairs. On 30 Sept. 1775 he was appointed to the three-member camp committee that went to Cambridge to confer with GW about ways of supporting and regulating the army. Harrison was named to the marine committee in March 1776, to another camp conference committee in May 1776, and to the newly created Board of War in June 1776. After his return to Virginia in 1777, he served as speaker of the house of delegates from 1778 to 1781 and as governor from 1781 to 1784. Although the spurious paragraph that was added to Harrison's letter was regarded as genuine by John and Samuel Adams and Arthur Lee among others, its publication apparently did not injure Harrison's close working relationship with GW.

1. Letter not found.

2. Congress recommended to the Connecticut government on 19 July that its two new regiments join the Continental army outside Boston as soon as possible (*JCC*, 2:192).

3. Hancock was directed on 19 July to write as president of Congress to the powder committees or committees of safety in Philadelphia and New York and request them to send to the Continental army as much gunpowder as they could spare (*JCC*, 2:191).

4. Harrison is referring to the complaints that GW made in his letter to Hancock of 10–11 July 1775. The second engineer was William Burbeck. John Adams was provoked to write to William Tudor on 23 July: "I want to know if there are any Engineers in the Province and who they are. I have heard the Generals were much disappointed, in not finding Engineers, and Artillery as they expected. P[lease] let me know the Truth of this, if you can learn it, and how they come to expect a better Artillery than they found" (Taylor, *Papers of John Adams*, 3:85–86).

5. Congress approved all of these measures on 19 July (*JCC*, 2:190–91). The last one, however, did not please John Adams. "I can never Sufficiently regret, that this Congress have acted So much out of Character, as to leave the Appointment of the Quarter Master General, Commissary of Musters and Commissary of Artillery to the General," Adams wrote to James Warren on 26 July. "As these officers, are Checks upon the General, and he a Check upon them: there ought not to be too much Connection between them. They ought not to be under any dependance upon him, or So great Obligations of Gratitude as these of a Creature to the Creator" (Taylor, *Papers of John Adams*, 3:100–101).

6. A committee on the establishment of a military hospital was appointed on 19 July, and its report was approved on 27 July (*JCC*, 2:191, 209–11).

7. For a discussion of these various disputes over rank, see James Warren and Joseph Hawley to GW, 4 July 1775, n.1, and GW to Hancock, 10–11 July 1775, Document II. Letter Sent, n.20.

8. For GW's hint that it would be better for Congress to sit somewhere nearer to Cambridge, see his letter to Hancock of 10–11 July 1775. Almost from the beginning of the Second Continental Congress in May 1775, there was some talk among the delegates out of doors about moving from Phila-

delphia to Hartford or New Haven, and in June Thomas Lynch of South Carolina went so far as to ask Silas Deane of Connecticut to engage lodgings provisionally for him and his family near Hartford (Silas Deane to Elizabeth Deane, 16 June 1775, in Smith, *Letters of Delegates*, 1:493–95). The matter, however, did not come to the floor of Congress (see note 12).

9. John Murray, earl of Dunmore (1732–1809), who had been governor of Virginia since 1771, boarded the British warship *Fowey* at Yorktown on 8 June 1775 with his family and his private secretary, Capt. Edward Foy, ostensibly to protect his wife and children from attack by the Patriots. The *Fowey* was commanded by Capt. George Montagu (born c.1751), a young officer who was destined for a long and distinguished career in the Royal Navy. On 7 July Dunmore, accompanied by Montagu and Foy, went up the York River by barge and landed at Porto Bello, his farm about six miles from Williamsburg. After dinner there, Dunmore's party was alarmed by the appearance of a company of Hanover County volunteers commanded by Capt. Samuel Meredith (born c.1731), a brother-in-law of Patrick Henry. Forced to flee, Dunmore returned to the *Fowey* and remained aboard until 15 July, at which time the *Fowey*'s impending departure from Virginia obliged him to transfer to another warship. Dunmore stayed in the Chesapeake Bay until the summer of 1776, attempting to reestablish his authority in the colony with military force, but failed in all of his efforts. He returned to England and later became governor of the Bahamas.

10. On 20 July Congress received and read a letter of 15 July from Maj. Gen. Philip Schuyler which contained the same intelligence regarding an anticipated Indian attack in the Mohawk Valley of New York as did Schuyler's letter of that date to GW (*JCC*, 2:192).

11. "The Liberty Gentlemen," Gov. James Wright of Georgia wrote to the earl of Dartmouth on 8 July 1775, "have fitted out a Schooner some say with 8 & some with 10 Carriage Guns Many Swivels & 50 Men." Two days later Wright informed Dartmouth that, since his previous letter, the Patriots' schooner had seized the British ship *Phillipa*, laden with gunpowder from London, "about 4 Leagues from the Bar [at Savannah] Conductd her in & then took out all the Gun Powder on Board Amounting to about Six Tons as the Capt. [Richard Maitland] tells me and which is now in the Hands of the Liberty People here who Forcibly Hold it against the Owners" ("Letters from Sir James Wright," in Ga. Hist. Soc., *Collections*, 3 [1873], 191–92, 194–95). For the appointment of the Georgia delegates to the Continental Congress, see Hancock to GW, 24 July 1775, n.15.

12. The debate and decision on the suggested adjournment of Congress to Connecticut apparently occurred in a committee of the whole.

13. Congress recessed on Wednesday, 2 August.

14. Edmund Randolph (1753–1813), a young lawyer from Williamsburg, belonged to a prominent Virginia family which was divided by the Revolution. His father, John Randolph (c.1728–1784), who served as attorney general of the colony from 1766 to 1774, was an outspoken Loyalist, while his uncle, Peyton Randolph (1721–1775), a brother-in-law of Benjamin Harrison and speaker of the House of Burgesses for the past nine years, became a

Patriot leader, serving as president of the first three Virginia conventions and of First and Second Continental Congresses. Edmund Randolph sided with his uncle and remained in Virginia when his father departed for England in September 1774. On 15 Aug. 1775 GW appointed Edmund Randolph one of his aides-de-camp, a position Randolph held until 2 Nov. 1775, when Peyton Randolph's death obliged him to return to Virginia to attend to family affairs. Edmund Randolph became attorney general of Virginia in the spring of 1776 and was a member of Congress in 1779, 1781, and 1782.

15. Capt. Robert McKenzie of the British 43d Regiment of Foot served under GW in the Virginia Regiment during the French and Indian War and remained on friendly terms with him as late as March 1775 (McKenzie to GW, 14 Mar. 1775). Although the list of British officer casualties at Bunker Hill that GW enclosed in his letter to Hancock of 14 July 1775 reports McKenzie as killed, he was only wounded and survived to become paymaster general under Gen. William Howe in August 1776. He later accompanied Howe to London as his private secretary.

16. Thomas Price (1732–1795) of Frederick, Md., marched with his men from Frederick on 18 July 1775 and arrived at Cambridge about 11 August. He returned home the following November and in January 1776 became major of Col. William Smallwood's Maryland regiment. In December 1776 Price was promoted to colonel of the 2d Maryland Regiment, a position that he held until he resigned from the army in April 1780. The name "Flighman" appears as "Tilghman" in the copies of this letter in the Dartmouth Mss. at the William Salt Library, in P.R.O., C.O.5/122, ff. 80–83, and in the Clements Library. He was probably Matthew Tilghman (1718–1790) of Queen Anne County, Md., who served in Congress from September 1774 to December 1776.

17. William Bradford (1722–1791) and his son Thomas Bradford (1745–1838) published the *Pennsylvania Journal; and the Weekly Advertiser* in Philadelphia.

From Brigadier General William Heath

Sir Camp at Roxbury [Mass.] July 21st 1775

I have the Pleasure to inform your Excellency that Major Vose of my own Regiment; beside⟨s⟩ securing the Barley on Nantasket; yesterday morning Landed on the Light-House Island with Six or Seven Boats, the Light House was set on Fire and the wood work Burnt, the Party brought off Three Casks of Oyl, all the furniture of the Light house, about 50 wt of Gun Powder, a Quantity of Cordage &c. (an Inventory of which will be forwarded to your Excellency;)[1] Some of the Brave men who effected this with their Lives in their Hands, have just now applied to me to know whether it was to be consid⟨ered⟩ as Plunder, or otherwise; I was not able to detirmine this matter, but told them that I would Lay the matter before your Excellency; I would beg leave to add that these Brave men, were some of them at Grape Island, Deer Island & at Long Island when each of those Islands were Stripped of their Stock &c.[2] I have the Honor to be your Excellency's most obedient & very Humble Servt

W. Heath

Copy, DNA:PCC, item 157; copy, DNA:PCC, item 169. The copy in PCC, item 157, was enclosed in GW to Hancock, 21 July 1775 (third letter).

1. On the night of 18 July, Maj. Joseph Vose (1739–1816) of Milton, Mass., led a detachment of about four hundred soldiers and mowers onto the Nantasket peninsula on the south side of Boston Harbor, where they cut and removed 1,000 bushels of barley and a large quantity of hay, which it was feared that the British were about to take for their use. Vose's raid of 20 July on nearby Lighthouse Island was made by a company of soldiers in whaleboats. The burning of the lighthouse alarmed the British warships in the harbor, and after the raiding party returned to Nantasket, several barges, a cutter, and an armed schooner attacked the Americans, resulting in the wounding of two of Vose's men. The lighthouse was again attacked on the morning of 31 July. See General Orders, 1 Aug. 1775, n.1, and GW to Hancock, 4–5 Aug. 1775, n.14.

2. For an account of the American raid of 11 July 1775 on Long Island, see GW to Hancock, 14 July 1775, n.5. The livestock on Grape Island was removed and its hay burned on 21 May 1775 after a skirmish with a British foraging party. Deer Island was cleared of sheep and cattle by American raiders on the night of 2 June 1775.

To Jonathan Trumbull, Sr.

Sir Camp at Cambridge 21st July 1775

I am to Acknowlage your Favour of the 17th Inst. informing me of the Destination of the Troops raising in your Colony; As the season is now advanced & the Enemy considerably reinforced we have the utmost Reason to expect any Attack that may be made will not be much longer delayed—I should therefore think it hig[h]ly necessary the new raised Troops should join the Army with all possible Expedition.[1]

Upon Inquiry with Respect to the Flower we find our Necessaties are not such as to require an immediate Transportation during the Harvist, but As soon as it can be done with Convenience you will please to give Directions for that Purpos⟨e.⟩

Colo. Trumbull will advise you to what Place it is to be Addressed & to whose Care.

Agreeable to your Intimation I have ordered the Express to wait on you & shall do so in future.

We have had no Occurrence in the Camp of any material Consequence; On both Sides we are strengthening our Lines in full View of each other. I am Sir with much Respect & Regard Your most Obedient & very Humble Servant

Go. Washington

LB, Ct: Trumbull Papers; LB, DLC:GW; Varick transcript, DLC:GW. The letter-book copy in DLC:GW includes the notation "Sent by Fessenden the Express." Both it and the Varick transcript are dated "July [ ] 1775."

1. The Connecticut council advised Governor Trumbull on 24 July "to order the colonels of the 7th and 8th regiments, to march their regiments as soon as possible, in whole or part companies, to the camp near Boston, and be placed under the commander-in-chief of the continental army" (Hinman, *Historical Collection*, 327). For the arrival of these regiments, see General Orders, 9 Aug. 1775, and Trumbull to GW, 15 Sept. 1775.

General Orders

Head Quarters, Cambridge, July 22nd 1775

Parole Nantasket. Countersign Mississipi.

A Court of Enquiry to sit forthwith, President Doctor Foster, Doctor Warren, and Doctor Eustace, Members, to examine into a Complaint exhibited by Mr John Spalding, surgeon to General Putnams regiment against Mr Penuel Chiney—Surgeon's Mate of the said regiment: All Evidences to attend the Court.[1]

Capt. Israel Putnam and Lieut. Samuel Webb, being appointed Aids-de-Camp to Major General Putnam; they are to be obey'd as such.[2]

Regularity and due Subordination, being so essentially necessary, to the good Order and Government of an Army, and without it, the whole must soon become a Scene of disorder and confusion. The General finds it indispensibly necessary, without waiting any longer for dispatches from the General Continental Congress, immediately to form the Army into three Grand Divisions, and of dividing each of those Grand Divisions into two Brigades: He therefore orders that the following Regiments vizt

Genl Wards	Col. Cottons
Gen. Thomas's	Col. Danielsons
Col. Fellows	Col. Dad Brewer's

compose one Brigade, and be under the Command of Brigadier Genral Thomas; that

Genl Spencers.	Col. Walkers
Col. Parsons.	Col. J: Reads.
Col. Learneards.	Independents.[3]

compose another Brigade, to be commanded by Brigadier Genl Spencer: That these two Brigades compose the right wing or division of the army; and be under the command of Major General Ward, and remain at Roxbury, and its southern dependencies. That

Col. Starks	New Hampshire.	Col. Nixons.	Massachusetts.
Col. Poors		Col. Mansfield.	
Col. Reeds		Col. Doolittles.	

be formed into another Brigade under the Command of Brigadier General Sullivan, and posted on Winter-hill. That

Col. Varnums	Rhode Island.	Col. Whitecombes	Massachusetts.
Col. Hitchcocks		Col. Gardners	
Col. Churchs		Col. J. Brewers	
		Col. Littles.	

be formed into another Brigade, and commanded by Brigadier Genl Green, and posted upon Prospect Hill; and these two Brigades compose the left wing or second division of the army under the Command of Major Genl Lee.

[That General Heath's, Colonel Patterson's, Colonel Scammons's, Colonel Gerrish's, Colonel Phinney's, Colonel Prescott's, be formed into another brigade, and commanded by Brigadier-General Heath, and be posted between Cambridge River and Prospect Hill.][4] That

Genl Putnams	Col. Bridges
Col. Glovers	Col. Woodbridges
Col. Fryes.	Col. Serjeants.

be formed into another Brigade, under the Command of the Senior Officer therein, and until the pleasure of the Continental Congress be known:[5] These two Brigades to be under the Command of Major General Putnam, also a Corps-de-reserve, for the defence of the several posts, north of Roxbury, not already named.

The Arrangement now ordered to take place, is to be made as speedily as possible, and the Majors General are to see it done accordingly, some inconveniencies may arise to certain Individuals by this change, but as the good of the service requires it to be made an alert and ready compliance is expected.

All applications from henceforward, by Officers or Soldiers for leave of absence, are to be made to the Major General commanding each division, who is to judge of the propriety of the application and grant Furloughs where they see cause, without applying to the Commander in Chief, provided it be not contrary to General orders.

General Heaths Regiment is to take post at No. 2 in lieu of General Wards, Col. Patterson's remains at No. 3: Col. Scammons to occupy No. 1: and the Redoubt between that and No. 2:[6] Col. Prescotts regiment to take post at the redoubt upon Sewells point, Col. Gerrishes Regiment to furnish the Companies for Chelsea, Malden, and medford.

Varick transcript, DLC:GW.

1. Penuel Cheney (Cheeney), who became a surgeon's mate in the 3d Connecticut Regiment on 1 May 1775, was accused by John Spalding of making "fraudulent Draughts upon the Commissary's Store and other malpractices" (GW to Jonathan Trumbull, Sr., 29 Oct. 1775). Instead of being court-martialed, Cheney was allowed to leave the army (Cheney to GW, 4 Sept. 1775), but on 4 Oct. the Connecticut council appointed him surgeon of his old regiment. New charges were subsequently raised against Cheney, and he was cashiered on 21 Nov. 1775 (Jonathan Trumbull, Sr., to GW, 6 Nov. 1775; General Orders, 21 Nov. 1775). Spalding continued as a surgeon in the Continental army until 31 Dec. 1776. Isaac Foster (d. 1781), John Warren (1753–1815), and William Eustis (1753–1825) were all Massachusetts surgeons. Foster served as deputy director general of the hospital for the eastern department from 1777 to 1780, when he retired from the army. Warren, who was wounded at the Battle of Bunker Hill, and Eustis remained as surgeons until the end of the war.

2. Israel Putnam, Jr., a son of Maj. Gen. Israel Putnam, was commissioned a captain in the 3d Connecticut Regiment on 1 May 1775. He served his father as an aide-de-camp until 3 June 1783. Samuel Blachley Webb (1753–1807), of Wethersfield, Conn., was the stepson and private secretary of Silas Deane, who took credit for obtaining this appointment for him. Webb remained with General Putnam until 21 June 1776, when he was appointed aide-de-camp to GW with the rank of lieutenant colonel. Wounded at the Battle of Bunker Hill while leading a Wethersfield militia company, Webb was twice more wounded during his service with GW, first at the Battle of White Plains and later at the Battle of Trenton. In January 1777 Webb became colonel of one of the addi-

tional Continental regiments. He was captured during an attack on Long Island in December 1777 and was exchanged a year later. Resuming command of his regiment, he served until the end of the war.

3. These four independent infantry companies were from Massachusetts.

4. This paragraph, omitted in the Varick transcript, is taken from William Henshaw, "Orderly Book," in Mass. Hist. Soc., *Proceedings*, 1st ser., 15 (1876–77), 129.

5. Col. James Frye (1709–1776) of Andover, Mass., apparently commanded this Cambridge brigade as senior colonel until his death on 8 Jan. 1776. His cousin Brig. Gen. Joseph Frye was given command of the brigade on 17 Feb. 1776. See GW to Hancock, 31 Aug. 1775, and General Orders, 17 Feb. 1776.

6. The redoubts were between the Charles River and the foot of Prospect Hill to protect Cambridge from attacks coming from Boston. Redoubt number one stood near the Charles; number three was near Prospect Hill; and number two lay in the middle. William Heath's regiment, which was moved from Roxbury to Cambridge by these orders, replaced Artemas Ward's regiment at redoubt number two because Ward's regiment was transferred to Roxbury.

From Captain Joshua Davis

Cambridge July 22nd 1775

Pursuant to your Excellency's Orders I herein Render an Account of such necessarys as will be wanting to Compleat One hundred Whale Boats for the Service—As Also for keeping Said Boats in good repair.

Wanted for Manning the Boats, 601 Men exclusive of Officers

One Officer, as Commander in chief
One Capt. & Two Lieuts. to each 96 Men
One master Boat Builder—at Capts. pay
Twenty five boat Builders—at Serjts pay
One Boat Master to each boat at Serjts pay
Six Men, Exclusive of Officers, to each Boat

Necessarys for the Boats

20 Small Swivel Guns
20 Small Anchors, or Graplins
10 fathom of Whale-Wharp[1] to each of the 20 Boats
5 fathom of Cordage for Each of the other boats
600 Oars & 600 Paddles—very good
2 barrs. Pitch & 4 do of Tarr
25 Small Pitch Pots & 5 Ladles
25 Small Pitch Mops—½ lb. weight each
100 lb. weight of White Oakum

6d. 4d. & Clapper Nails: & 100 Yards old Canvass
1500 feet Cedar Clapboards, Sawed for Whale Boats
100 Short Wool'd Sheep Skins for Muffling the Oars

Josha Davis

N.B. A Clerk of Stores & Provissions will be necessary.

LS, DLC:GW.

Joshua Davis, a ship captain from Boston, actively assisted the Massachusetts committee of supplies throughout the spring and summer of 1775 in obtaining cargoes of flour and other provisions. He also purchased whaleboats and vessels of a similar nature for the use of the colony, and on 11 July the Massachusetts provincial congress consigned all of the assembled boats to Davis's care (*Mass. Prov. Congress Journals*, 487). Davis later commanded privateers, and in 1781 he was captured by the British and imprisoned for a time in England.

1. Whale warp is rope used with harpoons and to haul boats from place to place.

From Captain Richard Dodge

Sir Chelsea [Mass.] July the 22 1775

thes are the Remarcks tackin on Sd Day from four to 6 Saw noth[i]ng From 6 to 8 Saw tow Brigs Bound out and tow B[o]tes from the Casel[1] to Boston—from 8 to 10 Saw 10 Botes Loded wit⟨h⟩ armed men from Boston to Chals.—from 10 to 12 Saw 18 Botes Pasing and Repasing Loded—one transport Bound out—from 12 to 2 Saw 19 Botes from Boston to Chals. full of men—12 from Chalston to Boston ful of men—from 2 to 4 Saw one Schoner Coming in apeard to have a Nomber of men—9 Botes from Chaleston to Boston—from Boston to Chals. 23 Botes Loded with men and Horses—from 4 to 6 Saw 8 Botes from Boston to Chals. Loded with men one tranesport went and Sterd East—Sir I ame your Houmble Servent at command

Richd Dodge Capt.

ALS, DLC:GW.

Richard Dodge was commissioned a captain in Col. Samuel Gerrish's Massachusetts regiment on 19 May 1775 and served at least until the end of the year. Dodge's company was posted at Chelsea as early as 14 July 1775. See General Orders, 13 July 1775, n.2. Over the next few months Dodge or his superior officer, Lt. Col. Loammi Baldwin, sent GW almost daily reports on ship traffic in Boston Harbor. The subsequent reports, similar in content to this letter, are enclosures in Joseph Leach's writing.

1. The fortress Castle William stood on Castle Island in Boston Harbor a short distance east of Dorchester Neck.

Letter not found: from William Trent, 22 July 1775. On 4 Aug. GW wrote to Trent: "Your Letter of the 22d Ulto came to my hands a few days ago."

General Orders

Head Quarters, Cambridge, July 23rd 1775

Parole, Brunswick. Countersign, Princeton.

As the Continental Army have unfortunately no Uniforms, and consequently many inconveniencies must arise, from not being able always to distinguish the Commissioned Officers, from the non Commissioned, and the Non Commissioned from the private; it is desired that some Badges of Distinction may be immediately provided, for Instance, the Field Officers may have *red or pink* colour'd Cockades in their Hatts: the Captains *yellow or buff*; and the Subalterns *green*. They are to furnish themselves accordingly—The Serjeants may be distinguished by an Epaulette, or stripe of *red Cloth*, sewed upon the right shoulder; the Corporals by one of *green*.[1]

The people employed to make spears, are desired by the General to make four dozen of them immediately, thirteen feet in lenght, and the wood part a good deal more substantial than those already made, particularly in the New Hampshire Lines, are ridiculously short and light, and can answer no sort of purpose, no more are therefore to be made on the same model.

The Commanding Officers of the different works and posts, are once more enjoined, to furnish themselves with a sufficient Number of Gabions and Fascines, which are to stop up the Entrances of their respective Redoubts and Lines; and to repair their works which may either be damaged by the weather, or the Fire of the enemy; it is observed that several of the Entrances of the Redoubts, are still left open without any sort of defence; The Commanding Officers of each Redoubt, are therefore ordered to cut a wide deep ditch, at the entrances, and throw a bridge of strong plank across; this to be done without delay.[2]

John Davis of Capt. Fosters Company, in Col. Gridley's regiment of Artillery,[3] tried for "Desertion and suspicion of intending to go to the Enemy" is acquitted by the General Court Martial.

Ensign Trafton accused by Col. Scammons of "abusive Language, to the said Colonel Scammons while under Arrest," tried by a General Court Martial of which Col. Nixon was president[.] The Court are unanimously of opinion, that the prisoner is Not guilty and do therefore acquit him with honour.

Lieut. Trafton to be forthwith released from his arrest.[4]

Michael Bury, Capt. Parkers Company, and Col. Prescotts Regiment,[5] tried by the same General Court Martial for "refusing his duty and enlisting in another Company:" The Court condemn the prisoner, and order him to receive thirty-nine Lashes. The General orders the sentence to be put in execution, at the Head of the regiment the delinquent belongs to.

Varick transcript, DLC:GW.

1. For the insignia that was designated for general officers and aides-de-camp, see General Orders, 14 and 24 July 1775.

2. For GW's previous instructions regarding gabions and fascines, see General Orders, 18 July 1775.

3. Thomas Waite Foster of Massachusetts served as an artillery captain in the Continental army until the end of 1776.

4. Joshua Trafton of Massachusetts was tried in August for another altercation with Col. James Scammans and was found guilty (General Orders, 25 Aug. 1775). Trafton, nevertheless, continued to serve in Scammans's regiment until the end of the year and was promoted to lieutenant in Col. John Paterson's regiment on 1 Jan. 1776. In June 1777 Trafton became a captain in Col. Henry Sherburne's Additional Continental Regiment, where he remained until he resigned from the army in April 1780. For Scammans's arrest and court-martial, see General Orders, 12 and 18 July 1775.

5. Capt. Oliver Parker of Massachusetts was cashiered on 2 Aug. 1775 (General Orders, that date; GW to Hancock, 4–5 Aug. 1775).

To Brigadier General John Thomas

Sir

Cambridge July 23d 1775.

The Retirement of a general Officer, possessing the Confidence of his Country & the Army; at so critical a Period, appears to me to be big with fatal Consequences both to the Publick Cause, & his own Reputation. While it is unexecuted, I think it my Duty to make this last Effort to prevent it; & after suggesting those Reasons which occur to me against your Resignation, your own Virtue, & good Sense must decide upon it. In the usual Contests of Empire, & Ambition, the Conscience of a Soldier has so little Share, that he may very properly insist upon his Claims of Rank, & extend his Pretensions even to Punctilio: but in such a Cause as this, where the Object is neither Glory nor Extent of Territory, but a Defence of all that is dear & valuable in Life, surely every Post ought to be deem'd honourable in which a Man can serve his Country. What Matter of Triumph will it afford our Enemies, that in less than one Month, a Spirit of Discord should shew itself in the highest Ranks of the Army, not to be extinguished by any Thing less than a total Desertion of Duty? How little Reason shall we have to boast of American Union, & Patriotism if at such a Time, & in such a Cause, smaller & partial Considerations cannot give Way to the great & general Interest. These Remarks can only affect you as a Member of the great American Body; but as an Inhabitant of Massachusetts Bay, your own Province, & the other Colonies have a peculiar & unquestionable Claim to your Services ⟨a⟩nd in my Opinion you cannot refuse them, without relinquishing in some Degree, that Character for publick Virtue & Honour, which you have hitherto supported. If our Cause is just, it ought to be supported, but where shall it find Support, if Gentlemen of Merit & Experience unable to conquer the Prejudices of a Competition, withdraw themselves in an Hour of Danger: I admit, Sir, that your Claim & Services have not had due Respect—it is by no means a singular Case; worthy Men of all Nations & Countries have had Reason to make the same Complaint, but they did not for this abandon the publick Cause, they nobly stiffled the Dictates of Resentment, & made their Enemies ashamed of their Injustice. And can America shew no such Instances of Magnanimity? For the Sake of your bleeding Country, your devoted Province, your Charter Rights, & by the Memory of those brave Men who have already fell in this great Cause, I conjure you to banish from your Mind every Suggestion of Anger & Disappointment: your Country will do ample Justice to your Merits—they already do it, by the Sorrow & Regret expressed on the Occasion and the Sacrifice you are called to make, will in the

Judgment of every good Man, & Lover of his Country, do you more real Honour than the most distinguished Victory.

You possess the Confidence & Affection of the Troops of this Province particularly; many of them are not capable of judging the Propriety & Reasons of your Conduct: should they esteem themselves authorized by your Example to leave the Service, the Consequences may be fatal & irretrievable—there is Reaso⟨n⟩ to fear it, from the personal Attachments of the Men to their Officers, & the Obligations that are supposed to arise from those Attachments. But, Sir, the other Colonies have also their Claims upon you, not only as a Native of America, but an Inhabitant of this Province. They have made common Cause with it, they have sacrificed their Trade, loaded themselves with Taxes & are ready to spill their Blood in Vindication of the Rights of Massachusetts Bay, while all the Security, & Profit of a Neutrality has been offered them: But no Arts or Temptations could seduce them from your Side, & leave you a Prey to a cruel & perfidious Ministry. Sure these Reflections must have some Weight, with a Mind as generous & considerate as yours.

How will you be able to answer it to your Country & your own Conscience, if the Step you are about to take should lead to a Division of the Army or the Loss & Ruin of America be ascribed to Measures which your Councils & Conduct could have prevented? Before it is too late I intreat Sir, you would weigh well the greatness of the Stake, & upon how much smaller Circumstances the Fate of Empires has depended. Of your own Honour & Reputation you are the best & only Judge, but allow me to say, that a People contending for Life & Liberty are seldom disposed to look with a favourable Eye upon either Men or Measures whose Passions, Interests or Consequences will clash with those inestimable Objects. As to myself Sir, be assured, that I shall with Pleasure do all in my Power to make your Situation both easy, & honourable, & that the Sentiments here expressed, flow from a clear Opinion that your Duty to your Country, your Posterity, & yourself most explicitly require your Continuance in the Service—The Order & Rank of the Commissions is under the Consideration of the Continental Congress, whose Determination will be received in a few Days.[1] It may argue a Want of Respect to that August Body not to wait the Decision; But at all Events I shall flatter myself that these Reasons with others which your own good Judgment will suggest, will strengthen your Mind against those Impressions which are incident to Humanity & laudable to a certain Degree; and that the Result will be, your Resolution to assist your Country in this Day of Distress—That you may reap the full Reward of Honour, & publick Esteem which such a Conduct deserves is the sincere Wish of Sir, Your very Obed: & most Hbble Servt

Go: Washington

LS, in Joseph Reed's writing, MHi: John Thomas Papers; Df, NHi: Joseph Reed Papers.

For the background to this letter, see James Warren and Joseph Hawley to GW, 4 July 1775, n.1. James Warren wrote to Thomas on 22 July urging him not to resign, as did Maj. Gen. Charles Lee on 23 July (Mass. Hist. Soc., *Proceedings*, 2d ser., 18 [1903–4], 425–26).

1. Thomas's new commission as first brigadier general, which Congress approved on 19 July, arrived at Cambridge by 4 Aug. (*JCC*, 2:191; Hancock to GW, 24 July 1775; GW to Hancock, 4–5 Aug. 1775, n.2).

To James Warren

Sir Cambridge Camp July 23rd 1775

I have had an Application made to me this day by the Several Captains of Colo. Phinneys Regiment from Casco Bay. They represent that their Men Enlisted & have marched down upon a Promise that they should receive 40/ Advance & Billeting Money at 8d. ℔ Day—that under this Expectation they left their Familys destitute & have detaind the Teamsters to carry back their Money—They have met with some Disappointments arising from the Situation of the Assembly which has raised an unhappy Spirit in the Regiment & requires immediate Attention—You will therefore please to lay the Matter before the General Court with my Request that proper Steps may be taken to Satisfy them; as I have engaged that upon their passing Muster, they shall receive the usual & legal Allowance.[1] I have the Honor to be Sir Your very Humble Servt

LB, in Thomas Mifflin's writing, DLC:GW; Varick transcript, DLC:GW.

1. Col. Edmund Phinney raised his regiment in Cumberland County, District of Maine, and marched it to Cambridge sometime in July after failing to obtain permission to leave all or part of his men at home to guard the coast

against possible British raids. On 24 July the Massachusetts house of representatives resolved "that Major *Stephen Cross*, be appointed to Muster and Pay the advance Pay to the Non-Commission'd Officers and Soldiers of Col. *Phinney's* Regiment" (*A Journal of the Honorable House of Representatives of the Colony of the Massachusetts-Bay in New-England, Begun . . . the Nineteenth Day of July, Anno Domini, 1775* [Watertown, Mass., 1775], 10, Microfilm Collection of Early State Records). Phinney commanded the regiment until he retired from the army at the end of 1776. For subsequent efforts to complete the paying of advance money to all of the Massachusetts troops, see General Orders, 1 Aug. 1775, and Committee of the Massachusetts Council to GW, 11 Aug. 1775.

General Orders

Head Quarters, Cambridge, July 24th 1775.

Parole Salisbury. Countersign Cumberland.

It being thought proper to distinguish the Majors, from the Brigadiers General, by some particular Mark; for the future the Majors General will wear a broad purple ribband.[1]

Notwithstanding the General Orders, marking the distinctions of General Officers, Aids-de-Camp, &c.—the Generals are frequently stopp'd by the Centinels, which can only happen from the Captains having neglected to read the Orders to their respective Companies; If any General Officer, Aid-de-Camp, or Major of Brigade, is again stopped through the Ignorance of the Centinels; the Captains will be responsible.

As any attempt the Enemy from their late disappointments, may have the rashness, or the hardiness to make; will be violent and sudden: The General expects the Officers and Soldiers will be not only resolute but alert to defeat; and in a particular manner, he enforces his orders to every Field Officer upon no account (duty excepted) to lay out of Camp; but upon every occasion, to shew by their Examples, that activity and steady Courage, so necessary to defeat an enterprising enemy.[2]

Notwithstanding the orders of the 11th Instant, expressly forbiding all Officers and Soldiers, from quitting their Guard before they are regularly relieved and dismissed; The General is informed such unsoldierlike practices are still committed; He therefore admonishes all Officers and Non Commissioned Officers, not to suffer any Person to quit their Guard, upon any pretence, care to be taken, the Men are properly supplied with provisions, before they mount guard.

Report being this morning made to the General That the main Guard room is kept abominably filthy and dirty; for the future one Commanding Officer is not to relieve another, upon that Guard, until he is assured that the Officers and Mens apartments are clean and in decent order.

The Surgeon of every Regiment in the Lines, Redoubts, or in, or near Cambridge, to deliver to morrow at twelve at Noon, to the Adjutant General at Head Quarters, an exact return of the sick, in the regiments they respectively belong to. The Names, Rank and Disorders, of each Officer, Non Commission'd Officer and Soldier to be mentioned in the Return. The Returns of the Surgeons of the Corps; Station'd in and near Roxbury, to be made to the Commanding General at Roxbury, Tuesday noon, in the manner, and form directed by the above Order, and the General, Commanding at Roxbury, will transmit them to Head Quarters at Orderly time, Wednesday.[3]

Varick transcript, DLC:GW.

1. For the insignia to be worn by brigadier generals, see General Orders, 14 July 1775.

2. For GW's order forbidding officers and soldiers who were posted in the lines from sleeping outside their encampments, see General Orders, 7 July 1775. See also General Orders, 18 July 1775, regarding the need for alertness in the lines.

3. Maj. Gen. Artemas Ward took command at Roxbury under General Orders, 22 July 1775.

From John Hancock

Sir, Philada 24th July 1775

Your letter of the 10th inst. with the enclosed papers being duly received was laid before Congress and immediately taken into consideration.[1]

In answer to the several matters therein contained I am to inform you, that the Congress appointed a committee to enquire what quantity of light Sail Cloth, Sheeting and Oznabrigs[2] could be obtained in this town for the purpose of making Tents, and in this business the committee are now closely imployed.

It is agreed that tow cloth will be most proper for hunting shirts, & of this the Congress are informed a sufficient quantity may be obtained in Rhode island and Connecticut. It is expected you will give orders for purchasing there the quantity necessary.[3]

Agreeable to your recommendation they have appointed Joseph Trumbull Esqr. Commissary-General of stores and provisions for the army of the United Colonies.[4]

The appointment of a Quarter Master General, Commissary of Musters, and a Commissary of Artillery is left to you, the Congress not being sufficiently acquainted with persons properly qualified for these offices.[5]

They have ordered a company of Matrosses to be raised in this city and sent forward.[6]

General Thomas, they have appointed First Brigadier-General in the room of Mr Pomroy who did not act under the commission sent him and have ordered General Thomas's commission to bear date the same day Genl Pomroy's did.

They have empowered you, if you think fit, to appoint three Brigade Majors of such persons as you chuse to honor with that command and to commission them accordingly.[7]

They have appointed a Committee to consider and report on the establishing an Hospital and appointing a director.

As soon as they have brought in their report and the Congress have come to any resolution on that subject you will be made acquainted with it.[8]

Letters are sent with a recommendation to the colonies of New hampshire, Massachusetts bay, Rhode island and Connecticut to compleat the deficiences in the regiments belonging to their respective colonies, which you shall retain in the Continental Army. Inclos'd are the Letters to N. Hampshire & Rhode Island, wch please to order forwarded by Express, immediately.[9]

And it is earnestly recommended to Rhode island to send forward to you three hundred and sixty men lately voted by their General Assembly, and to Connecticut to send forward fourteen hundred men lately voted by the General Assembly of that colony.[10]

Upon intelligence that Mr Johnson is endeavouring to instigate the Indians to acts of hostility the Congress have impowered General Schuyler to ["]dispose of and employ all the troops in the New York department in such manner as he may think best for the protection and defence of these colonies, the tribes of Indians in friendship and amity with us and most effectually to promote the general interest, still pursuing, if in his power, the former orders of this Congress and subject to the future orders of the Commander in chief."[11]

As the Congress are not fully acquainted with the number of the enemy you have to oppose and the extent of your operations, they reposing confidence in your prudence have resolved; that "such a body of troops be kept in the Massachusetts-bay as you shall think necessary provid⟨ed⟩ they do not exceed twenty two thousand."[12]

In a letter from Lord Dartmouth to Govr Martin dated Whitehall May 3d 1775 after recommending him to embody such of the men in four counties (which Govr Martin had represented as favourable to the Views of administration) as are able to bear arms is the following paragraph "I confess to you, Sir, that this appears to me to be a matter of such importance that I cannot too earnestly recommend it to your attention, and that no time may be lost, in case of absolute Necessity I have received his Majesty's Commands to Write to Genl Gage to apprize him of this favourable circumstance and to instruct him that he do, upon application to you, send some able and discreet officer to you in order to concert means of carrying so essential a service into effect and if necessary to lead the people forth against any rebellious attempts to disturb the public peace."[13]

Whither the five Vessells, you mention to have sailed from Boston on the 11th instant, are gone on this service time must manifest.[14]

The Bills ordered to be struck by Congress are in great forwardness; as soon as a sufficient quantity worth sending is compleated, it will be sent to you.

I have the pleasure to inform you that the Congress have received a letter from the Provincial Convention of Georgia dated 8th instant, informing that all the Parrishes in that colony except two, which it is supposed do not contain a score of freeholders inhabitants, met by their delegates in Convention on the 4th inst.; that those Parrishes that upon former occasions seemed reluctant have manifested a laudable Zeal on this occasion; that several Gentlemen in Savanna, that have hitherto been neuter or declared against America, now speak of the proceedings of Parliament as illegal and oppressive, that the Convention had applied to the Governor to appoint a day of fasting and prayer with which request the Governor informed them he would comply; that they have chosen five delegates to represent their colony in this Congress viz: John Houston, Archd Bullock Esqr. The revd Doctor Zubly, Lyman Hall and Noble Wimberly Jones Esqrs.; and lastly that they have resolved strictly to adhere to the Continental Association and are heartily disposed zealously to enter into every measure that the Congress may deem necessary for the safety of America.[15]

Mr Thomas & Mr Trumbull's Commissn⟨s⟩ are Inclos'd in unseal'd Letters to them.

When any thing Occurrs respectg your Department you shall be made Acquaintd.[16] I have the honor to be with great Esteem, Sir Your most Obedt hume servt

John Hancock President

The Inclos'd for Mr Trist if any oppory please to send into Boston.[17]

I have Sent five Bundles of Commissions 284 the rest shall follow.[18]

LS, DLC:GW; copy, owned (1970) by Nathaniel Stein. The LS is in Timothy Matlack's writing, except for the dateline, closing, and five sentences noted below, which are in Hancock's writing. See notes 9, 16, 17, and 18. Hancock also signed his name. Matlack incorrectly addressed the cover to GW at "Waterbury." Joseph Reed docketed the LS "Answd by Fessenden the Express Aug. 5." See GW to Hancock, 4–5 Aug. 1775.

1. Hancock presented GW's letter to Congress on 19 July, and most of the resolutions reported below were passed that day (*JCC*, 2:190–92).

2. Osnaburg is a type of coarse linen.

3. GW requested the purchase of tow cloth in his letters of 4 Aug. 1775 to Nicholas Cooke and Jonathan Trumbull, Sr. Tow cloth is made of short broken fibres from flax, hemp, or jute.

4. GW announced Trumbull's appointment in General Orders, 31 July 1775.

5. For GW's choices for these offices, see General Orders, 11, 14, and 17 Aug. 1775. For John Adams's objections to this resolution, see Benjamin Harrison to GW, 21–24 July 1775, n.5.

6. Matrosses were artillerymen who assisted gunners in loading, firing, and sponging the guns.

7. GW filled these three new positions in General Orders, 15 Aug. 1775.

8. The committee reported on 27 July, and Congress proceeded to pass several resolutions relating to the establishment of a hospital for the army (*JCC*, 2:209–11). See also Richard Henry Lee to GW, 29 June 1775, n.5.

9. The last sentence in this paragraph is in Hancock's writing. The letter to

the New Hampshire provincial congress, dated 22 July 1775, is printed in Bouton, *N.H. Provincial Papers*, 7:566–67.

10. For discussions of these reinforcements, see Jonathan Trumbull, Jr., to GW, 17 July 1775, n.1, and GW to Hancock, 21 July 1775 (first letter), n.1.

11. A copy of this resolution of 20 July 1775, in Charles Thomson's writing, was enclosed with this letter and can be found in DLC:GW. See also *JCC*, 2:194. For the rumors about an imminent Indian attack on the Mohawk Valley of New York, see Schuyler to GW, 15 July 1775, n.1, and Benjamin Harrison to GW, 21–24 July 1775, n.10.

12. This resolution was passed on 21 July (*JCC*, 2:202).

13. Josiah Martin (1737–1786), who had been governor of North Carolina since 1771, reported to the earl of Dartmouth on 6 July 1775 that a packet of dispatches from London had been opened in Charleston, and on 28 August he acknowledged receipt of a "duplicate" of the letter here quoted by Hancock (Davies, *Documents of the American Revolution*, 10:26, 11:88–92). Forced by crowds of armed citizens to abandon his palace at New Bern on 31 May 1775, Martin fled to Fort Johnston near the mouth of the Cape Fear River. When the fort was burned by Patriots on 10 July, he retired to a British warship anchored in the river. Martin remained there until May 1776, at which time he joined the British fleet that unsuccessfully attacked Charleston in June. He later assisted Lord Cornwallis in his southern campaign, but poor health forced him to go to England in 1781.

14. These British vessels went to Maine and Nova Scotia. See GW to Hancock, 10–11 July 1775, Document II. Letter Sent, n.31.

15. Lyman Hall (1724–1790) had represented St. John's Parish, Ga., in Congress since 13 May 1775, taking part in the debates but not voting until his credentials from the provincial convention arrived in Philadelphia on 20 July. With them came John Houstoun (1744–1796), Archibald Bulloch (1730–1777), and John Joachim Zubly (1724–1781). The fifth elected delegate, Noble Wymberly Jones (1723–1805), remained in Georgia. The letter of 8 July 1775 from the Georgia provincial convention is printed in *JCC*, 2:193, n.1.

16. This and the previous sentence are in Hancock's writing. The enclosures for John Thomas and Joseph Trumbull have not been found.

17. This sentence appears in Hancock's writing to the left of his signature. Nicholas Trist, an ensign in the British 18th Regiment at Boston, was stationed until the fall of 1774 in Philadelphia where he married an American woman and shared lodgings with some of the delegates to the First Continental Congress. See Silas Deane to Elizabeth Deane, 10–11 Sept. 1774, in Smith, *Letters of Delegates*, 1:60–63.

18. This sentence appears in Hancock's writing in the left margin of the first page of the manuscript. Hancock sent GW 550 more commissions in September (Hancock to GW, 26 Sept. 1775).

General Orders

Head Quarters, Cambridge, July 25th 1775

Parole, Hallifax. Countersign York.

Continual Complaints being made that Soldiers of regiments and Companies, after inlisting in one Company and regiment, have gone and enlisted in another insomuch that it would engross the General's whole time to hear the disputes upon this subject: For the future, any Officers who have any dispute in regard to the men reinlisted, are to apply to the Brigadier commanding their brigade, who will order a Court martial of the Brigade, to hear and determine the matter.[1]

The General Court Martial, of which Col: Nixon was president, to be dissolved this evening, and another General Court Martial of the Line, to sit to morrow Morning at the usual time and place, to try such prisoners as shall be brought before them: All Evidences and persons concern'd, to attend the Court.

Varick transcript, DLC:GW.

1. For GW's previous order concerning disputes over conflicting enlistments, see General Orders, 7 July 1775.

From John Dickinson

Philadelphia, 25 July 1775. Recommends "Mr Moylan a friend of mine [who] informs me that he intends to enter into the American Army."[1]

Morven M. Jones, "Brevet Brigadier-General Stephen Moylan," in *Potter's American Monthly*, 6 (1876), 14. Although the letter is printed with the dateline "PHILADELPHIA, *July* 26th 1775," the endorsement, which is said to be in GW's writing, reads "From Jno. Dickinson Esqr. 25th July 1775," and in his reply to Dickinson of 30 Aug. 1775, GW acknowledges "Your favour of the 25th Ulto recommendatory of Mr Moylan." Martin I. J. Griffin reprints the letter in *Stephen Moylan* (Philadelphia, 1909), 8, with the dateline "Philadelphia, July 25, 1775."

1. Stephen Moylan (1737–1811) of Philadelphia was appointed Continental mustermaster general on 11 Aug. 1775 (General Orders, that date). An Irish Catholic by birth, Moylan was educated in Paris and spent three years in the shipping business at Lisbon before moving in 1768 to Philadelphia, where he became a prominent merchant. As mustermaster general, he kept the muster rolls for the Continental army and inspected the troops and their equipment. During the fall of 1775 he also assisted in outfitting several armed vessels for the Continental service. On 6 Mar. 1776 Moylan be-

came one of GW's aides-de-camp, and on 7 June of that year he was made Continental quartermaster general with the rank of colonel. Encountering many difficulties in the latter office, Moylan resigned in September 1776. For a few months thereafter, he acted as a volunteer aide to GW. In January 1777 Moylan was commissioned to raise a regiment of light horse, and he served as a cavalry officer for the remainder of the war.

From Captain Richard Dodge

Sir [25 July 1775]

I am in formed By Josep groves from Boston to Day that the Shiping gon out is Bound for Block Island fishers Island and Long Island in order to Cil and Destroy all that Comes in thair way with Six hundrud men[.][1] the man i will Send to you as Soun as may Be[.] I am your humble Servent

Richd Dodge Capt.

ALS, DLC:GW. The date is taken from the docket, which is in Joseph Reed's writing. Dodge did not date the letter.

1. For additional intelligence on the sailing of this British fleet, see John Thomas to GW, 25 July, GW to Nicholas Cooke, 26 July, and GW to Hancock, 27 July 1775. These vessels raided Fishers and Gardiners islands between 6 and 8 Aug. 1775. See Norwich Committee of Correspondence to GW, 7 Aug. 1775, and Jonathan Trumbull, Sr., to GW, 7 Aug. 1775, n.2.

To George William Fairfax

Camp at Cambridge about 5 Miles from Boston.

Dear Sir, July 25th 1775.

On the other side you will receive a Copy of my last, dated at Philadelphia the 31st of May, and to which I refer.

I shall say very little in this Letter, for two Reasons; first, because I have received no Letter from you since the one dated in June 1774,[1] and therefore (having wrote often) can have nothing to answer; but, principally, because I do not know whether it may ever get to your hands: If it should, the principal, indeed only, design is to cover the seconds of those Bills forwarded in my last.

You will, I presume, before this Letter gets to hand, hear of my appointment to the Command of the Continental Army. I arrived at this Camp the 2d Instant.

You must, no doubt, also have heard of the engagement on Bunker's Hill the 17th Ultimo; but as, I am persuaded, you will have a very erroneous account transmitted, of the loss sustained on the side of the Provincials, I do assure you, upon my Word, that our loss, as appears by the Returns made me since I came here, amounts to no more than 139 killed 36 missing and 278 Wounded; nor had we, if I can credit the most solemn assurances of the Officers that were in the action, above 1500 Men engaged on that day. The loss on the side of the Ministerial Troops, as I am informed from good authority, consisted of 1,043 killed and wounded, whereof 92 were Officers.[2]

Inclosed I send you a second Address from the Congress to the Inhabitants of Great Britain; as also a Declaration, setting forth the Causes and necessity of their taking up Arms.[3] My Affectionate & respectful compliments to Mrs Fairfax[4] concludes me, Dear Sir, Your mo. obt humble Servt

G. Washington

Varick transcript, DLC:GW.

George William Fairfax (1724–1787), a close friend since GW's youth and a relative of Thomas, Lord Fairfax, proprietor of the Northern Neck of Virginia, lived at Belvoir near Mount Vernon until the summer of 1773, at which time he made an extended visit to England in order to look after property that he had inherited there. GW agreed to oversee Fairfax's business affairs in Virginia during his absence and received his power of attorney on 8 July 1773. Fairfax never returned to Virginia, staying in England for the remainder of his life.

1. Letter not found.

2. GW says in his letter to John Augustine Washington of 27 July 1775 that 138 Americans were killed in the Battle of Bunker Hill, and he puts the total British losses at 1,057 in his letter to Lund Washington of 20 Aug. 1775.

3. Congress accepted the final draft of its declaration on taking arms on 6 July, and two days later it approved an address to the inhabitants of Great Britain (*JCC*, 2:127–57, 162–70). A copy of the latter document was enclosed in Hancock to GW, 10 July 1775.

4. Sarah ("Sally") Cary Fairfax (c.1730–1811) married George William Fairfax in December 1748.

From Brigadier General John Thomas

Sir Roxbury Camp [Mass.] July 25. 1775

There was Information forwarded to Head Quarters yesterday P.M. of the Sailing of 13 Ships from Boston, I Sent one

Capt. Davis Down the Harbour to watch their Motion, and he reports on his return that they put to Sea & Stood their Course about E.S.E. which appears as if they were bound to the Southward: that Course would Lead them out by Cape Cod, & to the Chops of the South Chanel[1]—I am Sir with great respect your most Obedit Hume servt

Jno. Thomas

ALS, DLC:GW.

1. For the destination of this fleet, see Richard Dodge to GW, 25 July 1775, n.1.

General Orders

Head Quarters, Cambridge, July 26th 1775

Parole, Amsterdam. Countersign, Amboy:

It is recommended to the Commanding Officers of Corps, that all coverings made of Boards, be built in the form of barracks and in the most advantageous manner, at the same time so contrived as to be warm and comfortable in cold weather.[1]

All Passes to be discontinued for the future, and no person to be admitted into the Lines, unless introduced by an Officer, who can vouch for him, or by Order of the Officer commanding in the Lines.

It being represented that the present Hospital, is not large enough to contain the sick, Lieut. Governor Oliver's house, is to be cleared for that purpose, and care to be taken that no injury is done to it.[2]

Notwithstanding the strict and repeated Orders, that have been given against firing small arms, it is hourly practised, All Officers commanding Guards, posts and detachments, to be alert in apprehending all future Trangressors.[3]

Capt. Clarke of General Putnam's Regiment confined in Arrest, for "neglect of duty when upon guard," tried by a late General Court Martial, is acquitted and is immediately to be released from his arrest.[4]

Levi Woods, Soldier in Capt. Nuttings Company, in Col. Prescott's Regiment[5] confin'd for "absenting himself without leave and refusing to take the Oath, & threatening to leave the army": The Court Martial upon the prisoners pleading guilty, and promising to behave obediently for the future, recommended him to the General's mercy, who is pleased to pardon the prisoner.

Varick transcript, DLC:GW.

1. This order was apparently prompted by news of British preparations in Boston for the coming winter. See GW to Hancock, 4–5 Aug. 1775.

2. Andrew Oliver (1706–1774), a Loyalist who in 1765 provoked the wrath of Massachusetts Patriots by accepting appointment as a stamp officer, served as lieutenant governor of Massachusetts from 1771 to 1774. Before his death on 3 Mar. 1774, Oliver lived at Elmwood about a mile west of Cambridge.

3. For GW's previous order prohibiting the firing of small arms without cause, see General Orders, 4 July 1775.

4. Capt. James Clark (1730–1826) of Lebanon, Conn., remained in the Continental army until 18 Dec. 1775.

5. Capt. John Nutting (1731–1816) of Massachusetts served under Col. William Prescott until the end of 1776.

From Colonel Donald Campbell

Sir New York 26 July 1775:

After congratulating You on your safe Arrival at Camp & remaining undisturbed by the Ministerial Army I embrace this Opportunity to Acquaint you that I have the Honor of being Unanimously Appointed by the Honorable Continental Congress to be Deputy Quarter Master General with the Rank of a Colonel in the Army of the United Colonies, and have been directed to Attend General Schuyler to the Northward at present. Yet my most sincear Wish to be with the Main Body & Your Excellency, where more favourable Opportunitys of exerting past Experience in service & Testifying my Zeal for the Cause in a higher Degree from the Want of Officers there, as is Said, that I flatter myself with the Hope, if it remains in your Breast to Honor & Gratify Me. I am the more imboldened to be this brief by being told by Messrs Hancock & Adams & Secretary Thomson, After I had been appointed *Deputy* Quarter Master Genl (which at first I understood to be Quarter Master General, to General Schuyler) I requested Rank as Brigadier General by reason of the Persons Appointed Colonels here (under whome Many of the Gentlemen of the Congress Acknowledged I ought not to Serve & Lamented that my Disposition for Service had not been known to them Earlier). They then Annexed the Rank of a Colonel in the Army, & that if your Excellencey or General Schuyler Approved of the Additional Rank They would have no Objection to it as *Deputy* from the Circumstance of remaining in the province with our Regiment.

And I was further informed that what was then Offered was inferior to what the Gentlemen of the Congress would gladly appoint me to had I sooner applyed to them (which arose from a Rispect for this Province & desire of Serving it & not from the want of an Early & Glowing Zeal to serve my Country) and that if the Gentleman proposed as Quarter Master General (to me unknown)[1] Should not meet with your full Approbation as he is not yet Commissioned the road was paved for me to Succeed to that & the Additional rank. this & Leading me to the Ambition of my Soul to serve under your Eye & Command, & my small Share of Service Since 1756 may not be unacceptable from the present Cituation of the Forces: Therefore Dear Sir If you think the Service of the Country Cannot be injured by your Friendly Recommendation to permitt me the Honor of being in the Above Station near your Person in the Day of real Service You will Lay me under the most Lasting ties of Obligation Gratitude & Love & bind me in the Same to the Honorable Members of the Congress in Addition to their friendly Attention in their Late Appointment and Kind Disposition for my further Promotion from a Conviction of the Base Treatment Sustained by my Family by the breach of the Public Faith of this Province which Ruined them.[2]

I shall on Friday next proceed to Albany where General Schuyler is & doubt not his Supporting my Sanguine Expectations from the Congress as well as General Lee to whome I also write.

I shall be happy if it may be Convenient to honor me with a Line & Believe me to be with much Sincearity & fervent Prayers for your happiness, & Long being in the highest Esteem of your Country with felicity Dear Sir Your Most Obedt & Most Humble Servt

Donald Campbell

ALS, DLC:GW.

Donald Campbell of New York served as a lieutenant and quartermaster in the Royal American Regiment during the French and Indian War and was put on half pay in 1763. A Patriot sympathizer with a long-standing grudge against the royal government of New York (see note 2), he gave up his half pay on 17 July 1775 to accept appointment by the Continental Congress as deputy quartermaster general for the New York department with the rank of colonel (*JCC*, 2:186). During the fall of 1775, he accompanied Brig. Gen. Richard Montgomery's expedition to Canada. When Montgomery was killed at Quebec on 31 Dec., Campbell temporarily assumed command of Montgomery's force and ordered a retreat. In the summer of 1776 Campbell was tried by a court-martial on charges brought against him by Brig. Gen. John Sullivan. The court-martial ordered him to be cashiered, but on 13 Feb. 1777 Congress decided that Campbell should continue as a colonel in the army (*JCC*, 7:114). Campbell did not return to duty, however, and spent the rest of the war disputing with Congress over the settlement of his quartermaster accounts.

1. Congress left the appointment of the quartermaster general to GW (Hancock to GW, 24 July 1775), and on 14 Aug. GW appointed Thomas Mifflin to that office (General Orders, that date).

2. Donald Campbell's father, Capt. Lauchlin Campbell, came to America from Scotland in 1738 in search of land and agreed with Gov. George Clarke of New York to bring settlers from Scotland at his own expense in return for grants of 1,000 acres for each family so transported. Between 1738 and 1740 Captain Campbell brought eighty-three families to New York, but the governor broke his promise, and Captain Campbell received no land for his efforts. In 1763 Donald Campbell petitioned the New York government for 100,000 acres of land in settlement of his father's claims but received only 10,000 acres (Campbell's memorial, May 1764, in E. B. O'Callaghan and E. Fernow, eds., *Documents Relative to the Colonial History of the State of New-York*, 15 vols. [Albany, 1853–87], 7:629–31).

To Nicholas Cooke

Sir Camp at Cambridge July. 26th 1775.

Yesterday I had an Account that three Men of War and Nine Transports had sailed out of Boston—and in the Evening I received a Note the Copy whereof is inclosed.[1] The great Distress they are in at Boston for fresh Provisions makes it extremely probable they may make some Depredations along the Coasts: I have therefore thought it proper to give you the earliest Notice that the Owners of those Islands and the Inhabitants along the Coasts may take the necessary Precautions for the Security of their Property. At the same Time I must add that the Conduct of this Groves in getting into Boston again immediately renders his Intelligence very suspicious as to their Destination[2] But their Sailing may be depended on—You will Please to make use of this Intelligence under all its Circumstances as you shall judge most conducive to the publick Good—And beleive me to be with great Truth & Regard Sir Your most Obedient very Humble Servt

Go: Washington

Copy, RHi: Cooke Papers; LB, DLC:GW; Varick transcript, DLC:GW. The copy in the Cooke Papers is docketed "Copy of a Letter from General Washington July 26th 1775 The original being sent to Philadelpa by the Committee for settling the Accts of the Colony with the Congress." Joseph Reed wrote a similar letter for GW to Brig. Gen. David Wooster on this date. See GW to Hancock, 27 July 1775, n.3.

1. This enclosure was probably a copy of Richard Dodge to GW, 25 July 1775. See also John Thomas to GW, 25 July 1775.

2. Joseph Groves's information was correct in part. This fleet raided Fishers Island on 6 Aug. 1775. See Norwich Committee of Correspondence to GW, 7 Aug. 1775.

To George William Fairfax

Dear Sir, Campridge July 26th 1775.

In my hurry, Yesterday, I forgot the principal thing I had in view, when I sat down to write to you, and that was, to inform you of the indispensable necessity you must now be under of appointing another Attorney. The nature of the business I am now engaged in (which alone is full sufficient to engross the time and attention of any one Man) and the distance I am removed from your business, as well as my own, puts it absolutely out of my power to be of any further service to you in Virginia: It is a duty incumbent on me, therefore, to inform you of this circumstance, that you may, without delay, appoint some other Attorney to manage your affairs; as it would be folly in the extreme, in me, to undertake to conduct your business at the distance of 600 Miles, when it is utterly out of my power (but by means of a third person) to Order and direct my own.[1]

When I left home, I put Syme's Protested Bill (with some business of my own) into the hands of Colonel Lewis, to negotiate; and since I came to this place, have been informed by him, that, unable to get the Money, he obtained a second draft from Colonel Nelson in discharge of the first, which, I dare say, will be paid. I have therefore wrote to Mr Lund Washington to get this Bill and remit it to you.[2] I am, with sincere Regard, &c.

G. Washington

Varick transcript, DLC:GW; ADfS, sold by Thomas Birch's Sons, April 1891, catalogue 663, item 141; ALS, sold by Goodspeed's, June 1941, item 41.

1. In a letter to GW of 3 Aug. 1778, Fairfax suggested that Robert Carter Nicholas or Fielding Lewis take over the power of attorney that Fairfax had given GW in 1773, but apparently neither man did so. By 1785 Battaile Muse was handling Fairfax's business affairs in Virginia (GW to George William Fairfax, 27 Feb. 1785).

2. John Syme (1728–1805) of Hanover County, Va., was a half brother of Patrick Henry; Fielding Lewis (1725–1782) of Fredericksburg, Va., was GW's brother-in-law. GW instructed Fielding Lewis on 30 April 1775: "The Bill you receivd from Colo. Syme, in June last for Colo. Fairfax, is come back—He promised at Richmond that he would endeavour to take it up this Meeting—please to remind him of it—the Bills are herewith sent" (CSmH). See also Ledger B, 117. Thomas Nelson (1738–1789) of Yorktown, Va., was elected to the Continental Congress in July 1775 and became governor of Virginia in 1781. No letters from Fielding Lewis to GW or from GW to Lund Washington have been found for June or July 1775.

From the Virginia Delegates

Philadelphia, 26 July 1775. "We recommend our Countryman Mr Edmund Randolph to your patronage and favor. . . . You will readily discern Sir, how important a consideration it is, that our Country should be furnished with the security and strength derived from our young Gentry being possessed of military knowledge, so necessary in these times of turbulence and danger."

LS, in Richard Henry Lee's writing, DLC:GW. The letter is signed by Lee, Patrick Henry, and Thomas Jefferson. Another Virginia delegate, Benjamin Harrison, recommended Edmund Randolph in his letter to GW of 21–24 July 1775. See note 14 to that document.

General Orders

Head Quarters, Cambridge, July 27th 1775.

Parole, Bedford. Countersign, Guilford.

John Trumbull Esqr. being appointed Aid: D. Camp to his Excellency the Commander in Chief; He is to be obeyed as such.[1]

A Court of enquiry to sit to morrow Morning at eight OClock, in the Tutor's Chamber (Mr Hall) to examine into a Complaint exhibited upon Oath, in the public newspapers against Mr Benjamin Whiting, now a prisoner in the College; All Evidences and Persons concern'd to attend the Court.[2]

For the future when any Deserters come to any of the out Guards, they are with the least delay to be sent by a Corporals Guard, to the next Guard in the Lines, who is immediately to escort them in the same manner to the Major General commanding that division of the Army, who as soon as he has examined them will fort[h]with send them under a proper Escort from his guard to the head quarters: Some Deserters being made drunk, who came last night from the Enemy, before they reached Head Quarters; It will be considered as a Breach of orders in any person, who gives Rum to Deserters, before they are examined by the General.

A Subaltern Officer's guard to be mounted to morrow morning, at eight OClock, at a certain distance from the small pox Hospital; the Officer to come this evening, at six OClock, to the Adjutant General for orders.

Varick transcript, DLC:GW.

1. John Trumbull, the youngest child of Gov. Jonathan Trumbull, Sr., of Connecticut, became adjutant and "a sort of aid-du-camp" to Brig. Gen. Joseph Spencer at Roxbury in May 1775. In his autobiography John Trumbull says that a few days after GW arrived at Cambridge, "I was told by my eldest brother [Joseph Trumbull], the commissary general, that the commander in chief was very desirous of obtaining a correct plan of the enemy's works, in front of our position on Boston neck; and he advised me (as I could draw) to attempt to execute a view and plan, as a mean of introducing myself (probably) to the favorable notice of the general." Trumbull did draw a map of the British fortifications at Roxbury and sent it to GW. "This," he says, "(probably) led to my future promotion; for, soon after, I was presented to the general, and appointed his second aid-du-camp" (Theodore Sizer, ed., *The Autobiography of Colonel John Trumbull* [1953; reprint, New York, 1970], 17, 21–22). For Trumbull's map of Roxbury and another that he made of the whole Boston area, see GW to Hancock, 4–5 Aug. 1775, n.23. Trumbull served as an aide-de-camp to GW until he was appointed Spencer's brigade major on 15 Aug. 1775 (General Orders, that date). In June 1776 Gen. Horatio Gates made him deputy adjutant general for the northern department with the rank of colonel, but the Continental Congress did not approve that appointment until the following September. Disappointed that Congress put a September rather than a June date on his commission, Trumbull resigned from the army in February 1777. After studying art for a year in Boston, he volunteered to serve as an aide-de-camp to Gen. John Sullivan during the Rhode Island campaign of 1778. In 1780 Trumbull went to London to become a pupil of the distinguished American artist Benjamin West.

2. Benjamin Whiting (d. 1779), sheriff of Hillsborough County, N.H., was accused of having Loyalist sympathies. The charges against him appeared in

two depositions printed in the *New-England Chronicle: or, the Essex Gazette* (Cambridge, Mass.), 21 July 1775. In the longer of the two, dated 6 July 1775, Thompson Maxwell asserted "that in or about the Month of March last past, as I was riding from Hollis to Amherst (in New-Hampshire Government) in Company with Benjamin Whiting, Esq; who asked me what I thought of Major [John] Sullivan's taking away the Powder and Guns from Castle William and Mary? I answered him, that I looked on it as a Piece of good Conduct. The said Whiting answered, that the said Sullivan was a damn'd pervert'd Villain for so doing, and a damn'd Rebel, and deserved to be hanged, and that this Spring the King's Standard would be set up in America, and Proclamation made that those that would come in and enter their Names, would have a Pardon, and those that would not, would be deemed Rebels and suffer Death justly, and that within three Months said Sullivan and John Hancock would be hanged." In the other deposition, dated 13 July 1775, Robert Fletcher declared "that some Time in April or the begining of May, 1774, at Dunstable, . . . Benjamin Whiting, Esq; . . . said that a Man in the Deponent's Place, that did not endeavour that the Acts of Parliament should be put in Execution, ought to be damned." The court of inquiry cleared Whiting of all charges (General Orders, 29 July 1775). Whiting fled from New Hampshire in April 1777 on being accused of passing counterfeit money and joined Gov. John Wentworth's Loyalist volunteers as a lieutenant. He was killed on Long Island in 1779. Stephen Hall (d. 1795), in whose chamber Whiting's court of inquiry was held, was a tutor at Harvard College from 1772 to 1778 and a fellow from 1777 to 1778.

Letter not found: from George Clinton, 27 July 1775. On 25 Aug. GW wrote to Clinton: "Mr White presented me with your favour of the 27th Ulto."

From Captain Joshua Davis

Cambreg July 27 1775

Persuant to your Exelencys orders I Make Return of all The Boats Taken for the Coleneys Servis in manner following, Viz.

Thirty five Whale boats in Cambreg bay & River[1]

Fifty five Do In Dogester [Dorchester] Creke Near the metting house

Six Do In the Several Companeys Statinod in Waymoth Brantory & Sgantam[2]

Two Long boats three Yalls Eight moses boats[3] & one Bay boat In the Cornell belo Cambreg Bridge[4]

Two Long boats one Yall three Moses boats & one Gundelo[5] In Menotteme River[6]

Whale boats	96
Long boats	4
Yalls	4
Moses boats	11
Bay boats	1
Gundlos	1
Sum total	117

Pr Joshua Davis

ALS, DLC:GW.

1. Cambridge is on the Charles River.

2. Davis apparently meant Weymouth, Braintree, and Squantum Neck.

3. A moses boat is a very broad flat-bottomed boat propelled by oars which was used in the eighteenth century to transport heavy cargo across shallow waters.

4. The "Cornell" is apparently the corner or sharp bend which occurs in the Charles River a short distance downstream from the bridge at Cambridge.

5. A gundalow (gundelo) is a river barge with a high bow and a large lateen sail set on a short stumpy mast.

6. The Menotomy River (now Alewife Brook), located northwest of Cambridge, is a tributary of the Mystic River.

To John Hancock

Sir Camp at Cambridge July 27. 1775.

Nothing material has occurr'd in either Camp since I had the Honour of addressing you on the 21st Instt by Express. But on Tuesday 3 Men of War & 9 Transports sailed out of Boston Harbour & stood a Course about E.S.E.[1]

One Groves who came out of Boston the same Evening informed the Officer at one of the Out Posts, that the Transports had on Board 600 Men & were bound to Block Island, Fishers Island & Long Island to plunder them & bring off what Cattle they may find. The Fellow returned again into Boston under such suspicious Circumstances that it has led me to doubt the Truth of his Intelligence.[2]

A Deserter who came in afterwards informs me that it was given out in their Camp, that they were either gone for Indians or fresh Provisions, and that each Transport had but 20 Men on board. Upon this Intelligence I immediately wrote to Govr Cook of Rhode Island, & to General Wooster[3] that they might

[take][4] proper Precautions for removing the Cattle of those Islands & the Coasts, and to prevent any Surprize. As we are confirmed by every Account in the Scarcity of fresh Provisions in the Enemy's Camp, and particularly by this Deserter who says, they have had none since the Battle of Lexington, it is very probable this Voyage may be only intended for a Supply. But as it may possibly be otherwise I thought it best to transmit the Intelligence to the Honr. Congress that they may forward it to the Southward or take such other Step as they may judge proper.

Since writing the above 3 more Deserters have come out which makes four in 24 Hours. Their Accounts correspond with those of the first who came out, & which I have related above. I have the Honour to be Sir Your most Obed. & very Hbble Servt

Go: Washington

LS, in Joseph Reed's writing, DNA:PCC, item 152; Df, NHi: Joseph Reed Papers; LB, DLC:GW; copy, DNA:PCC, item 169; Varick transcript, DLC:GW.

1. Both the draft and letter-book copies read "6 Transports."

2. For Joseph Groves's report, see Richard Dodge to GW, 25 July 1775. This fleet did raid Fishers Island on 6 Aug. (Norwich Committee of Correspondence to GW, 7 Aug. 1775; Jonathan Trumbull, Sr., to GW, 7 Aug. 1775, n.2).

3. GW's letter to Nicholas Cooke containing this intelligence is dated 26 July 1775. Joseph Reed wrote a similar letter for GW on that same date to Brig. Gen. David Wooster (ALS, N: New York Provincial Congress Papers; LB, DLC:GW).

4. This word appears in both the draft and letter-book copies.

To Major General Philip Schuyler

Sir Camp at Cambridge July 27th 1775.

Yesterday a Deputation from the Provincial Congress of New Hampshire attended me with a Request that three Companies raised in that province, and now posted on Connecticut River at and between the two Cohhess[1] commanded by Capts. Timothy Reedle,[2] James Osgood & John Parker might be continued for the Security of the Frontiers of that Province on the Continental Establishment. As it did not appear to me that this Request could be complied with, and as I apprehend you have more immediate Occasion for them than I have, I thought it proper to give you the earliest Notice where they are that if you think proper you may order them to join the Troops under your Command, in which Case you will please to write to Matthew Thor[n]ton Esqr. President of their Provincial Congress. Each Company consists of 65 Men including officers, and are reported to me as able bodied, stout, active Fellows, used to the Woods, capable of any Duty, and having an Acquaintance with Canada. But you will please to remember, that they must continue under their own officers, to whom they are attached, and subject only to superior Command[3]—We have had no Transaction of any Consequence since I wrote you last—Our army is in good Health & Spirits well supplied with Provisions of all Kinds—The Situation of the Enemy is directly the reverse in every Respect and we have Reason to think Desertions will be very great. Four have come out within the last 24 Hours. I am with much Regard, Sir Your most obed. & very humble Servt

Go. Washington

LB, in John Lansing's writing, NN: Schuyler Papers; LB, in Richard Varick's writing, NHi: George and Martha Washington Papers; Df, NHi: Joseph Reed Papers; LB, DLC:GW; copy, Nh; Varick transcript, DLC:GW.

1. The Coos country lay along the Connecticut River to the west and north of the White Mountains, including the area around Newbury, Vt., and much of present-day Coos County, New Hampshire. The "two Cohhess" were probably settlements in the upper and lower parts of the Coos country.

2. The letter-book copy at NHi reads "Capt. Timothy Beedle."

3. The New Hampshire provincial congress authorized on 3 June 1775 the raising of these three ranger companies for service on the colony's western frontier. Timothy Bedel (c.1740–1787), a member of the provincial congress from Bath and a veteran of the French and Indian War, recruited one of the companies and on 23 June assumed command of all three with the rank of colonel in the New Hampshire service. The colony's committee of safety ordered Bedel on 7 July to take his men to the Connecticut River and establish garrisons. Unwilling that New Hampshire alone should bear the cost of maintaining Bedel's force, the committee of safety informed Bedel on 7 Aug. that the committee "has waited on G. Washington to endeavor to get the Compys raised to guard the Western Frontiers received into the pay of the Continent, but he Informed us that he cannot consistent with his Instructions receive more than 2[2] Thousd men; But has at our request wrote to General Schuyler recommeng his receiving them. . . . As the expence of these Comps will be so great on this Colony, and no danger as we apprehend on the Frontiers, unless those Comps can be received as aforesd they must be disbanded without going into actual service. Therefore We desire you would without loss of time . . . repair to Genl Schuyler at Crown Point before he gets his army fill'd up,

and Endeavour to get those three Compy into that service, & if there is Room for a Regiment you can have opportunity to negotiate the matter with him, as it must be a Continl & not a Colony matter" (Bouton, *N.H. Provincial Papers*, 7:573). Bedel joined Schuyler's army at Ticonderoga with some of his men on 16 Sept., and the rest apparently arrived soon afterwards (Schuyler to GW, 20 Sept. 1775). Bedel served with distinction at the siege of St. Jean during the fall of 1775, and in January 1776 he was appointed colonel of a New Hampshire regiment. His role in the surrender of the Cedars in May 1776 led to his being cashiered a few months later, but he was not barred from future service. In the spring of 1778 Bedel raised another regiment in northern New Hampshire, which participated in the ensuing campaign. Matthew Thornton (c.1714–1803) of Londonderry, N.H., was both president of New Hampshire's provincial congress and chairman of its committee of safety.

To John Augustine Washington

Camp at Cambridge about 5 Miles from Boston;
Dear Brother July 27th 1775.

On the 2d Instt I arrived at this place after passing through a great deal of delightful Country, covered with grass (although the Season has been dry) in a very different manner to what our Lands in Virginia are. I found a mixed multitude of People here, under very little discipline, order, or Government—I found the Enemy in Possession of a place called Bunkers Hill, on Charles Town Neck, strongly Intrenched & Fortifying themselves: I found part of our Army on two Hills (called Winter & prospect Hills) about a Mile & quarter from the Enemy on Bunkers Hill, in a very insecure state—I found another part of the Army at this Village and a third part at Roxbury, guarding the Entrance in and out of Boston—My whole time since I came here has been Imployed in throwing up Lines of Defence at these three several places; to secure in the first Instance, our own Troops from any attempts of the Enemy, and in the next, to cut of all Communication between their Troops and the Country; For to do this, & to prevent them from penetrating into the Country with Fire and Sword, & to harrass them if they do, is all that is expected of me; and if effected, must totally overthrow the designs of Administration, as the whole Force of Great Britain in the Town and Harbour of Boston, can answer no other end than to sink her under the disgrace and weight of the expence—Their Force, including Marines Tories, &ca, are computed from the best Accts I can get, at abt 12,000 Men; ours including Sick, absent, &ca at about 16,000; but then we have a cemi Circle of Eight or nine Miles to guard; to every part of wch we are obliged to be equally attentive, whilst they, situated as it were in the Centre of that Cemicircle, can bend their whole Force (having the entire command of the Water) against any one part of it with equal facility; this renders our Situation not very agreeable, though necessary, however, by incessant labour (Sundays not excepted) we are in a much better posture of defence now than when I first came. The Inclosed, though rough, will give you some small Idea of the Situation of Boston, & Bay on this side; as also of the Post they have Taken in Charles Town Neck, Bunkers Hill, and our Posts.[1]

By very authentick Intelligence lately receivd out of Boston (from a Person who saw the returns) the number of Regulars (including I presume the Marines) the Morning of the action on Bunkers Hill amounted to 7533 Men—their killed & wounded on that ⟨occasi⟩on amounted to 1043, whereof 92 were Officers. our loss was 138 killed—36 Missing & 276 Wounded.[2] The Enemy are sickly, and scarce of Fresh provisions—Beef, ⟨which⟩ is chiefly got by Slaughtering their Milch Cows ⟨in⟩ Boston, sells from one Shilling to 18d. Sterg pr lb.; & that it may not get cheaper, or more plenty, I have drove all the Stock within a considerable distance of this place, back into the Country, out of the Way of the Men of War Boats; In short I have, & shall continue to do, every thing in my power to distress them. The Transports are all arrived & their whole Re-inforcement Landed, so that I can see no reason why they should not if they ever attempt it, come boldly out and put the matter to Issue at once—if they think themselves not strong enough to do this, they surely will carry their Arms (having Ships of War & Transports ready) to some other part of the Continent, or relinquish the dispute; the last of which the Ministry, unless compeld will never agree to do—Our works, & those of the Enemy, are so near & quite open between that we see every thing that each other is doing—I recollect nothing more worth mentioning—I shall therefore conclude with my best wishes, and love to my Sister and the Family & Compliments to any enquiring Friends Yr Most affecte Brother.

Go: Washington

ALS, DLC:GW.

1. GW's sketch map is reproduced on pp. 186–87.

2. For other casualty totals given by GW, see GW to George William Fairfax, 25 July 1775, and GW to Lund Washington, 20 Aug. 1775.

General Orders

Head Quarters, Cambridge, July 28th 1775.

Parole Cumberland. Countersign Brookline.

The Surgeons of Learnerds, Heath, Little, Phinney and Parsons Regiments, having neglected to deliver in the Returns of the sick of their respective Regiments, to the Adjutant General, these Returns to be delivered fort[h]with, and the Surgeons of those Corps, are to be more exact in their obedience to orders.[1]

Varick transcript, DLC:GW.

1. For GW's order requesting these returns, see General Orders, 24 July 1775.

From Lieutenant Colonel Loammi Baldwin

Chelsea [Mass.] July 28th 1775 half after 4 oClock

May it Please your Excellency

Agreable to your order I Send the following observation taken by the Centry posted upon Powder Horn Hill, from about 7 oClock A.M. to 2 oClk P.M. one Ship gone out, three Ships & two Tenders Coming in, about 12 Boats passd from Boston to Charlestown Light Loaded, or almost Em[p]ty, three Boats passd from Charlestown to Boston Very heavy Loaded with Men.

I would beg leave to ask your Excellency whether it was the intent & meaning of your Orders to Send an Express to Head Quarters Every day when there is nothing more Occurs than has for two days passd. These from your Excellency's most Obediant Servent

Loammi Baldwin Lieut. Coln.

ALS, DLC:GW.

Loammi Baldwin (1745–1807) of Woburn, Mass., was a member of the Middlesex County convention in August 1774, and in April 1775 he joined Col. Samuel Gerrish's regiment as major. He became lieutenant colonel of that regiment on 16 June, and when Gerrish resigned his commission in August, Baldwin succeeded him as regimental commander. Baldwin fought at

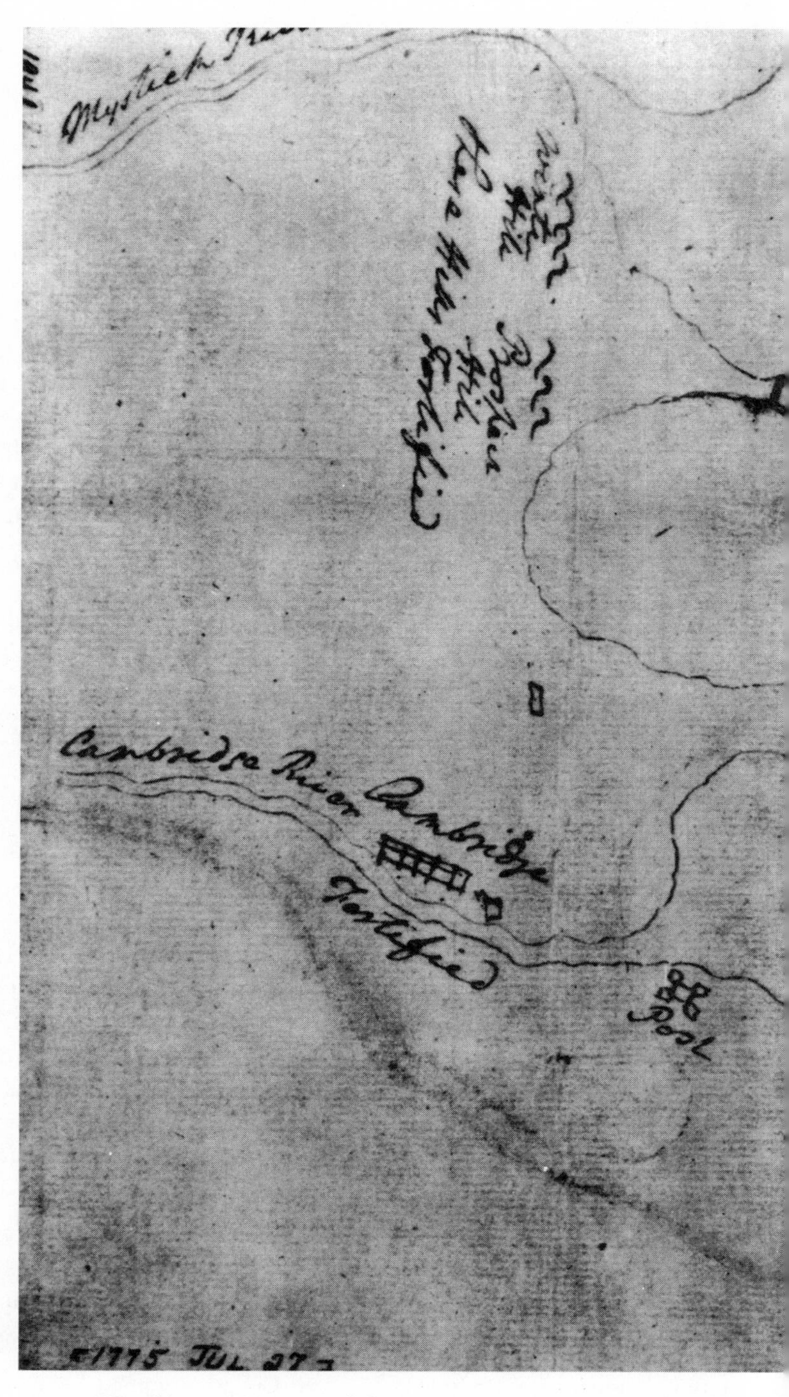

Washington's map of the Boston area (George Washington Papers, Library of Congress).

water

Water

water

Dorchester

Roxbury

the Battle of Trenton in December 1776, but ill health obliged him to retire from the army soon afterwards. An experienced surveyor and engineer, Baldwin undertook in June 1775 to survey some of the terrain between the lines at Boston. During the latter half of this year, he was the senior officer at Chelsea and oversaw the defense of that area and the important intelligence gathering activities that were conducted there. Except for about two weeks in late August when he was home sick, Baldwin wrote regularly to GW between this date and the middle of November, enclosing daily reports by Joseph Leach on ship traffic in Boston Harbor. Baldwin also relayed intelligence to GW from a spy in Boston and from the numerous refugees who came out of the city by way of Winnisimmet ferry. See Baldwin to GW, 29 July 1775, nn.1–3, and 31 July 1775, n.2.

To Major General Philip Schuyler

Dear Sir Camp at Cambridge July 28th 1775.

I wrote you Yesterday by way of New York, and in two Hours afterwards was favored with your's of the 15th & 18th Inst: with their respective Inclosures. I was extremely glad to find your first apprehensions of an Incursion by the Indians in some Degree removed by the later Advices: at the same Time I think it evident from the Tenor and Spirit of Col: Johnson's Letter, that no art or Influence will be left untried by him, to engage them in such an Enterprize.[1] Should he once prevail on them to dip their Hands in Blood, mutual Hostilities will most probably ensue, and they may be led to take a more decisive Part—All accounts I think agree, that the Canadians are very averse to engage in this unnatural Contest: But I am persuaded you will not abate in the least your vigilance to every Movement[2] in that Quarter notwithstanding their present pacifick Appearances.

I am much easier with Respect to the public Interests since your arrival at Ticonderoga, as I am persuaded those Abilities and that Zeal for the common Welfare which has led your Country to repose such Confidence in you will be fully exerted. From my own Experience I can easily judge of your Difficulties to introduce Order & Discipline into Troops who have from their Infancy imbibed Ideas of the most contrary Kind: It would be far beyond the Compass of a Letter for me to describe the Situation of Things here on my arrival, perhaps you will only be able to judge of it, from my assuring you that mine must be a portrait at full Length of what you have had in Miniature. Confusion and Discord reigned in every Department, which in a little Time must have ended either in the Seperation of the army or total Contests[3] with one another. The better Genius of america has prevailed and most happily the Ministerial Troops have not availed themselves of their advantages, till I trust the oppertunity is in a great Measure past over—The arrangement of the General Officers in Connecticutt & Massachusetts has been very unpopular, indeed I may say injudicious. It is returned to the Congress for farther Consideration and has much retarded my plan of Discipline—However we mend every Day and I flatter myself that in a little Time we shall work up these raw Materials into good Stuff. I must recommend to you, what I endeavor to practise myself, Patience and Perseverance. As to your Operations, my dear Sir, I can suggest Nothing which your own good Judgment will not either anticipate or controul, from your immediate View of Things and your Instructions from the Continental Congress.

The Express from hence to England with the account of the Commencement of Hostilities at Lexington has returned.[4] It was far from making the Impression generally [expected][5] here. Stocks fell but 1½ ℔ Cent, Genl Gage's accounts had not arrived & the Ministry affected to treat it as a Fiction. Parliament had been prorogued 2 Days, but it was reported, that it would be immediately recalled—our Enemy continues strongly posted about a Mile from us both at Bunker's Hill and Roxbury: But we are not able to get any Information of their future Intentions—Part of the Rifle Men are come in and the rest daily expected.

I did not expect your Returns would be very compleat at first: But I must beg your Attention to reforming them as soon as possible: and I beg Leave to add, that I would have you scrutinize with Exactness into the application of provisions & Stores —I have the utmost Reason to suspect Irregularities & Impositions here—You will be fortunate if the Contagion does not reach you—General Lee has removed about 4 Miles from me,[6] but I will take the first oppertunity to make your good Wishes known to him. Colonel Reed and Major Mifflin join me in the best Wishes for your Health & Success. I am Dr Sir Your affectionate & obed. Humble Servt

Go. Washington

Inclosed is a Copy of mine of Yesterday referred to in this.

LB, in John Lansing's writing, NN: Schuyler Papers; LB, in Richard Varick's writing, NHi: George and Martha Washington Papers; LB, DLC:GW; Varick transcript, DLC:GW.

1. Guy Johnson's letter of 8 July 1775 to the president of the New York provincial congress was enclosed in Schuyler to GW, 18 July 1775.

2. The letter-book copy in DLC:GW reads "your Vigilance to expidite every Movement."

3. The letter-book copy at NHi and the one in DLC:GW both read "fatal Contests."

4. For a discussion of John Derby's voyage to England, see GW to Hancock, 21 July 1775 (first letter), nn.3 and 15.

5. The word within the square brackets appears in both the letter-book copy at NHi and the one in DLC:GW.

6. "Our family," Joseph Reed wrote to his wife on 26 July 1775, "is much reduced by the departure of General Lee, who has taken the command of part of the army, and has his quarters four miles from us, at General Royal's" (William Bradford Reed, *Life and Correspondence of Joseph Reed*, 2 vols. [Philadelphia, 1847], 1:116). A Loyalist, Isaac Royall had abandoned his large house at Medford sometime during the past several months. Charles Lee whimsically dubbed the place Hobgoblin Hall. Lee was given command of the left wing of the army on Prospect and Winter hills in General Orders, 22 July 1775.

General Orders

Head Quarters, Cambridge, July 29th 1775.

Parole, Dartmouth. Countersign, Corke.

A Serjeant and six Men to parade at the Head quarters at eleven OClock, to escort certain prisoners and Deserters to Worcester, this party to be victualled for this day and to morrow: The Serjeant will receive his orders from the Adjutant Genl.[1]

Mr Benjamin Whiting tried by a Court of enquiry ordered in the General Orders of the 27th Instant, whereof Lieut. Col. James Brickatt was president;[2] The Court having maturely considered the Evidence, for and against the Prisoner, as well as what the Prisoner had to offer in his defence, are of opinion that the prisoner is Not guilty of the Crime laid to his charge, and do therefore acquit the prisoner: The General therefore orders the prisoner to be released.

James M'Daniel, tried by a General Court martial, whereof

Col. Glover was President for "forgeing an Order of General Putnams to obtain a quart of Rum, and for abusive Language to Col. Gridley" [is found guilty][3] and ordered to receive twenty Lashes. The General confirms the sentence, and orders it to be executed after prayer time to morrow.

James Foster of Capt. Butlers Company in Col. Nixon's regiment,[4] tried by the same General Court Martial for "robbing Dr Foster, Surgeon of the General Hospital" found Guilty of the Charge, is sentenced to receive thirty-nine Lashes, and suffer one Month's fatigue. The General approves the sentence, and orders it to be put in execution, at the Head of the Regiment, after prayer time to morrow morning.

William Winslow of Capt. Perkins's Company of Artillery[5] tried by the same Court Martial for "stealing a Cannon Cartridge of powder," is acquitted.

Varick transcript, DLC:GW.

1. Horatio Gates wrote to James Warren on 21 July 1775: "His Excellency General Washington has directed me to acquaint you, that there are several Prisoners now in Cambridge, whom it would be proper to confine in som Gaol, in one, or other of The Countys remote from Boston. and it is very probable, Prisoners taken from the Enemy, and those who may be proved Criminal of our own People, may shortly make it further necessary for The General to be acquainted where you think it most proper, & convenient to have them confin'd, so as to remove them out of the way of the Army, & at a distance from the Sea Coast; upon receiving The directions of The Assembly. I beg sir you will acquaint me, where they direct the prisoners now here, & those who may hereafter come hither, should be sent" (M-Ar: Revolution Letters). Gates's letter was referred to the Massachusetts council, and on 28 July 1775 Perez Morton, secretary pro tem of the council, informed Gates "that Gaols of Worcester, Springfield & Northampton, are the most suitable places for securing the Prisoners" (DLC:GW).

2. James Brickett (1737–1818), a physician from Haverhill, Mass., became lieutenant colonel of Col. James Frye's regiment on 20 May 1775 and was wounded at the Battle of Bunker Hill. He later served as a brigadier general of the Massachusetts militia.

3. The words within square brackets are taken from Artemas Ward's orderly book (MHi: Ward Papers).

4. Joseph Butler of Massachusetts served as a captain under Col. John Nixon until the end of 1776.

5. William Perkins (1742–1802) of Boston was a lieutenant in Capt. John Callender's artillery company at the Battle of Bunker Hill and became captain of that company after Callender was cashiered on 7 July 1775. Perkins served in the Continental artillery throughout the war, rising to the rank of major.

From Lieutenant Colonel Loammi Baldwin

Chelsea [Mass.] July 29th 1775 2 oClock P.M.

May it please your Excellency

About twelve oClock this day we wase all allarm'd by the approach of a Boat to Winnisimmit Ferry[1] & by a Signal Soon found them to be friends who Landed with their Houshold good: there ware Several of my Intimate acequa⟨in⟩tance[.] I have taken the names of all the Passeng⟨ers⟩ and Stopd the Letters which I now Send for y⟨our⟩ Inspection & Beg your Excellency would Send them Back to me again as soon as possable as the Bairers are Some of them in waighting and others are to call again tomorrow for theirs—Please to Keep the Inclosd Letters in there Respective covers.

I would Beg your Excelency would Send me Some Assistence as the Boats are to Continue passing (*That is if we can believe General Gage*) and Somthing may Escape for want of Proper assistenc that may turn to our disadvantag.[2]

Our officers are Very Sick here I have much upon my hands & mind, Scenc I Rec'd Mr Reed['s] Letter last Night.[3] Hope & Earnestly Expect Some assistence and your Excellencies Orders as Soon as the necessity of the mater Requires. I[n] great hast I am Sir your Excellences most Obediant Humbe Servnt

Loammi Baldwin Leut. Colo.

P.S: Should be much Obligd to your Excellency if you would Send down a few Sheets of Paper & wafers as I Cannot Procure any about here and am out—Pray Sir Excuse the Imperfections in this leter.

ALS, DLC:GW. Baldwin apparently enclosed with this letter "A Return of the Observations of the Day July the 29th," a detailed report on ship traffic in Boston Harbor written by Joseph Leach, similar in content to Richard Dodge's letter to GW of 22 July 1775. The report is in DLC:GW.

1. The Winnisimmet ferry landing was near the mouth of the Mystic River, about two miles southwest of Chelsea.

2. Gen. Thomas Gage agreed in late April 1775 to allow inhabitants of Boston to leave the city, provided that they took no arms or ammunition with them, but under pressure from Loyalists who wished to keep some Patriots in Boston to insure that the city would not be destroyed by the American army, Gage introduced new restrictions and delays that soon stopped all emigration from Boston. Gage unexpectedly reversed his policy on 28 July and had notices posted in the city, inviting "all persons, who inclined to go out, to leave

their names at a place appointed" ("Diary of Ezekiel Price, 1775–6," in Mass. Hist. Soc., *Proceedings*, 1st ser., 7 [1863–64], 200). The subsequent flow of refugees from Boston caused considerable administrative problems for American authorities during the next several weeks. See GW to James Warren, 29 July, GW to James Otis, 5 Aug., and GW to Hancock, 4–5 Aug. 1775, n.26.

3. Joseph Reed wrote to Baldwin on 28 July 1775: "In full Confidence of your Prudence & Secrecy as a Soldier a Man of Honour & a Friend to your Country the General has directed me to communicate to you a Scheme he is about to put into Execution to obtain constant & authentick Intelligence from Boston. The Plan is this. The inclosed Letter will be delivered by you to one Dewksbury who lives about five Miles from you towards Shirley Point. He will deliver it to a Waterman on whom he can depend who will convey it to John Carnes a Grocer in the South Part of Boston. The Answers and such Intelligence as he can procure will be forwarded to you thro. the same Channel: Which you are to transmit to His Excelly by Express immediately. As the Success of the Project & the Life of the Man in Boston may depend upon your Conduct, let it not escape you to the nearest Friend upon Earth, & for fear of Accident destroy this Letter as soon as you are sufficiently Master of its Contents. When you see Dewksbury give him the above Caution of Secrecy in the strongest Terms: And so to pass from him to the other. Your good Conduct & Discretion in this Matter will not fail to [be] duly noticed" (MHi: Miscellaneous Bound Collection). Baldwin sent GW on 16 Aug. a letter that apparently came from John Carnes. See Baldwin to GW, 15 and 16 Aug. 1775. Dewksbury was probably one of the several Tewksburys who lived east of Chelsea.

To James Warren

Sir, Cambridge July 29th 1775.

I have this Instt received a Letter from Chelsea, of which the Inclosed is an extract[1]—as the Inhabitants are coming out in a different manner than proposed by your Assembly to the Select men of the Town of Boston, I have not delayed a moments time in giving you the earliest Information of it; and request that you may take the matter into consideration, & determine what is proper to be done on the occasion—If you think it prudent to receive them in this manner, query, whether it may not be proper to appoint some person to attend the movement.[2] I am in haste, & with great respect Sir Yr Most Obedt Hble Servt

Go: Washington

ALS (photocopy), DNA: RG 93, Photographic Copies of State Records, c.1775–83; LB, DLC:GW; Varick transcript, DLC:GW.

1. The enclosed extract was apparently from Loammi Baldwin's letter to GW of this date. See also Baldwin to GW, 31 July 1775, n.2.

2. James Warren received this letter on the evening of 29 July. The next morning those members of the Massachusetts house of representatives who could be assembled (about fifty in number) met in an unusual Sunday session and decided that a joint committee of house and council members should go immediately to Chelsea "to inspect the State and Characters of such Inhabitants of *Boston,* as have, or may arrive there from thence; and that the said Committee be impowered and Ordered, to do and direct every Thing that they shall find absolutely necessary, for the Safety of the Country, and the immediate Relief of any helpless and indigent Persons." The council approved the same resolution that day. On 31 July the members of the committee reported to both houses that "on their Way to, and at *Chelsea,* [they] found sundry of the Inhabitants of *Boston,* who had been allowed to remove, and by them were informed, that the Small Pox had not lately prevailed in that Town, and that General *Gage* had directed that the Alms-House Poor should be sent to *Salem,* but finding that no Inhabitants were permitted to come out on the Day that they were there, and that from General *Gage's* past Failure in the Performance of his solemn Agreements with that Town, it was very uncertain whether others might come out agreeable to the just Expectations of the People; they impowered and directed the Selectmen and Committee of Correspondence of the Town of *Chelsea* . . . to make strict Enquiry into the State and Circumstances of all Persons who should arrive there from *Boston,* and take of and provide for the Indigent, and guard and secure the Country against the Small Pox" (*Mass. House of Rep. Journal,* July–Nov. 1775 sess., 25–26; "Records of the Great & General Court or Assembly for the Colony of the Massachusetts Bay in New England begun and held at Watertown in the County of Middlesex, on Wednesday the twenty sixth day of July 1775," 17–18, 20–22 [hereafter referred to as "Mass. Council Journal," July 1775–Feb. 1776 sess.], Microfilm Collection of Early State Records).

General Orders

Head Quarters, Cambridge, July 30th 1775.

Parole, Essex. Countersign Dublin.

William Tudor Esqr. being appointed Judge Advocate of the Continental Army, he is in all things relative to his Office, to be acknowledged and obey'd as such.[1] The Drummers & Fifers of the Regiment in, and about Cambridge, are to be order'd constantly to attend the Drum and Fife Major, at the usual hours for instruction.

Varick transcript, DLC:GW.

1. For Tudor's appointment, see GW to Hancock, 21 July 1775 (first letter), n.8.

To James Warren

Sir Camp at Cambridge July [30] 1775

I have Consider'd the Application made me yesterday, from the General Court, with all the Attention due to the Situation of the People in whose Behalf it is made, & the Respect due to such a Recommendation[1]—Upon refering to my Instructions & Consulting with those Members of Congress who are present as well as the General Officers, they all agree that it would not be consistent with my duty to detach any Part of the Army now here on any Particular Provincial Service. It has been debated in Congress and Settled that the Militia or other Internal Strength of each Province is to be applied for Defence against those Small and Particular Depredations which were to be expected, & to which they were Supposed to be competent.[2] This will appear the more Proper, when it is considerd that every Town & indeed every Part of our Sea Coast which is exposed to these Depredations would have an equal Claim upon this Army: It is the Misfortune of our Situation which exposes us to these Ravages, against which in my Judgment no such Temporary Relief would possibly secure us—The great Advantage the Enemy has of transporting Troops by being Masters of the Sea will enable them to harrass us by Diversions of this kind; & Should we be tempted to pursue them upon every Alarm, The Army must either be so weaken'd as to Expose it to Destruction or a great Part of the Coast be Still left unprotected: Nor indeed does it appear to me that such a Pursuit would be attended with the least Effect: The first Notice of Such an Incursion would be it's actual Exicutio⟨n⟩ & long before any Troops could reach the Scene of Action—the Enemy would have an Oppy to accomplish their Purpose & retire—It would give me great Pleasure to have it in my Power to extend Protection & Safety to every Individual, but the Wisdom of the General Court will anticipate me in the Necessity of Conducting our Operations on a General and impartial Scale, so as to exclude any first Cause of Complaint & Jealousy.

I beg Sir you will do me the Honour to Communicate these Sentiments to the General Court & to apologize for my involuntary Delay. As we were alarm'd this Morning by the Enemy & my Time taken up with giving the Necessary Directions.[3]

I shall be happy in every Oppy of Shewing my very great Respect & Regard for the General Court of Massachusetts Bay—And am Sir Your most Obedt & very hume Servt

G.W.

LB, in Thomas Mifflin's writing, DLC:GW; copy, DNA:PCC, item 152; copy, DNA:PCC, item 169; copy, NjMoNP; Varick transcript, DLC:GW. The copy in PCC, item 152, was enclosed in GW to Hancock, 4–5 Aug. 1775. Although all of the manuscript copies of this letter are dated 31 July 1775, internal evidence indicates that it was written on 30 July. The General Court's application of "yesterday" was that of 29 July (see note 1), and the alarm of "this Morning" was apparently that of 30 July (see note 3), although there was another alarm on 31 July.

1. A committee consisting of Benjamin Church, Benjamin Woodbridge, and Dummer Sewall from the house of representatives and James Otis and William Sever from the council called on GW on 29 July to "inform him of the distress'd Situation of the Inhabitants of the Eastern Parts of this Colony, and know of him, if he can, consistent with his Instructions, and the general Service, order a Detachment there, to prevent the Enemy from Ravaging the Country, and Plundering the Inhabitants of their Cattle, Sheep, Wood, &c. to supply themselves" (*Mass. House of Rep. Journal*, July–Nov. 1775 sess., 24). The committee reported verbally to the council later in the day that GW "gave them for answer that it was the expectation of the Congress that each Colony should defend their own Sea coast at their own proper expense" ("Mass. Council Journal," July 1775–Feb. 1776 sess., 16–17). GW's letter of this date was read in both houses of the General Court on 31 July.

2. In a resolution of 18 July Congress recommended forming both regular companies of militia and companies of minutemen for local defense and urged "that each colony, at their own expence, make such provision by armed vessels or otherwise, as their respective assemblies, conventions, or committees of safety shall judge expedient and suitable to their circumstances and situations, for the protection of their harbours and navigation on their sea coasts, against all unlawful invasions, attacks, and depredations, from cutters and ships of war" (*JCC*, 2:187–90).

3. Lt. Paul Lunt of Col. Moses Little's Massachusetts regiment wrote in his journal for 30 July, that "Last night, twelve o'clock, a party of General Washington's Riflemen crept within the Regulars' sentries, but being discovered were fired upon, which occasioned a skirmish between them and the Regulars' main guard. . . . Between the hours of twelve and one o'clock we had an alarm, and we were all paraded, and there was an immediate cry for volunteers to follow such officers as would head them, when all our company marched out to follow the officers wherever they went, and some part of every company in the regiment. We marched up into the fort, and were ordered [to] ground our arms and wait for orders: the alarm was occasioned by the Regulars intrenching upon Charlestown Common. The intent of the volunteers was to go down and beat them off, but upon further consideration

the generals thought it not prudent to proceed, they being under cover of their cannon upon Bunker's Hill and the floating batteries and the ships. The generals ordered us to return, and be ready at a moment's warning" ("Lunt's Book," 196). For a brief account of the night's events by GW, see GW to Hancock, 4–5 Aug. 1775.

General Orders

Head Quarters, Cambridge, July 31st 1775.

Parole, Falkland. Countersign Edenton.

The Continental Congress having been pleased to appoint Joseph Trumbull Esqr. to be Commissary General, to the army of the United Colonies:[1] All Commissaries heretofore appointed by any of the distinct Colony Congresses, or by particular Authority of any particular district or colony, are forthwith to make an exact Return of the provisions, and all the different Species of provisions, they have in, or near the Camps, at Cambridge and Roxbury; thereupon Commissary Genl Trumbull being assured by the report of his Clerk, assistant, or from his own examination, that such Return is just and true, is to give his Receipt for the quantity deliver'd into his hands, which receipt will be a good Voucher, in the passing the accompt of the different Colony Commissaries, heretofore appointed, and will be allowed as such.

The Commissaries, at present appointed by the several Colonies; are forthwith to make up their Accounts unto the third of August inclusive; ready to be laid before the Commander in Chief, and by him transmitted to the Continental Congress; or to be adjusted and finally settled by him, as the Continental Congress shall think proper to direct.

A Return signed by the Commanding Officers of regiments and Corps, to be delivered to the Adjutant General to morrow morning, at general orderly time, of the Names, Ranks & Dates of the Officer's Commissions, in their respective Regiments and Corps, mentioning also the Vacancies, and how occasioned.

A General Court Martial to sit immediately, to try Captain Christopher Gardner, of Col. Varnums Regiment for "Cowardice, abandoning his post and deserting his men." All Evidences and persons concern'd to attend the court.[2]

Varick transcript, DLC:GW.

1. Congress appointed Trumbull to this office on 19 July (*JCC*, 2:190).

2. Christopher Gardner, Jr., of Rhode Island became a captain in Col. James Mitchell Varnum's regiment on 3 May 1775. The incident for which Gardner was court-martialed occurred on the night of 30 July 1775. "The [British] regulars about 60 of them," James Warren wrote to John Adams the next day, "pushed out suddenly on Boston Neck, drove back a few of our Centinels, and by the Negligence of our Main Guard, and the Cowardice of the Captain [Gardner], Burnt the George Tavirn, and retired without loss. This is Esteemed the greatest disgrace we have suffered" (Taylor, *Papers of John Adams*, 3:108–12). Gardner was cashiered on 2 Aug. (General Orders, that date).

From Lieutenant Colonel Loammi Baldwin

Chelsea [Mass.] July 31th 1775

May it Please your Excelency

This covers the Observations of part of yesterday & today.[1]

Should be glad to know in what manner I am to procceed, with the People that come out of Boston, in order to pr[e]vent there going into Camp.[2]

two boats only have come with Passingers from Boston this Day, the first Brought Coln. Ingersoll[3] who Informed me that there was one Regular Officer & Several other person badly wounded brought to Boston Just as he come away which was about Eight or Nine oClock A.M. and that then went from Boston in the Night meaning Last night a large number of Granedears & Light Infantry in larg flat bottomd Boats for the Southward Shore it was Suposd.

I Should be glad to know your Excellencies Pleasure with regard to all the letters that come out of Boston whether my Inspection Shall be Sufficient to Let any pass that I Should think proper or whether you would chuse to see them all your Self.

There are People now waiting to know your Excelleny's Answer that want to proceed into the Country. Supose if they pass me as a number did before I had your Order to they may if they are So desposd go into the Camps and I am now obliged to let them go about among the neighbour for Suport as they Brought nothing of that nature with them.

I would Inform your Excelency that I was up and with my Men upon the Hills neighest our Enemy part of Last night &

this morning till the Sun 7 or 8 hours high and watchd them Very Critically but could not discover any thing Worth troubling your Excelency about. I am your Excellencys most obediant Servnt

Loammi Baldwin Leut. Col.

I Send the letters that I have stopd today hop I Shall Receive them by the hand of the Bairer with your directions.

ALS, DLC:GW.

1. Baldwin enclosed "A Return of the Observations of the Day July 31," which includes intelligence on the movement of British shipping in Boston Harbor from three o'clock on the afternoon of 30 July to two o'clock the next afternoon. The return in Joseph Leach's writing is in DLC:GW.

2. Horatio Gates wrote to Baldwin on 1 August: "The General has seen your letters, and reports, from Chealsea; and very much approves your Vigilance & attention to the Service. Yesterday in the Evening The General referrd your letter to The Council, and Assembly, in respect to preventing the inhabitants of Boston coming from your post to The Camps of Cambridge or Roxbury. They have promised to send this day a proper person for to Assist you in the disposal, & care of the poor people Sent to Chelsea from Boston" (Gregory and Dunnings, "Gates Papers"). For the actions of the Massachusetts General Court on this matter, see GW to James Warren, 29 July 1775, n.2.

3. Joseph Ingersoll (c.1725–1789) served as a colonel in the Massachusetts forces during the French and Indian War and from 1764 to 1775 operated the Bunch of Grapes Tavern in Boston.

From Nicholas Cooke

Sir Providence July 31st 1775

I am favoured with your Excellency's Letter of the 26th instant; having just before the Receipt of it had Accounts by a private Hand of the Sailing of a Number of Men of War and Transports from Boston; which I conjectured were designed to supply the Enemy with fresh Provisions. I immediately sent the Intelligence to Block-Island together with a Quantity of Powder Ball and Flints to enable them to defend their Property, and gave them Assurances of further Assistance if necessary.

We have no Accounts of this Fleet from any Part of our Coast; so that I think it probable they were destined to the Eastward.[1]

I desire your Excellency to oblige me with a Return of the Army; and when any Thing of Importance occurs I shall esteem an early Communication of it a Favour. I am with great Truth and Regard, Sir Your Excellency's Most humble and most obedient Servant

Nicho. Cooke

LS, DLC:GW.

1. These vessels bypassed Block Island to raid Fishers and Gardiners islands. See Norwich Committee of Correspondence to GW, 7 Aug. 1775, and Jonathan Trumbull, Sr., to GW, 7 Aug. 1775, n.2.

From Colonel Timothy Danielson

Roxbury Camp [Mass.] 31 July 1775. "General Thomas has made known to your Petitioner That he has your Excellencys Order, to turn out from Quarters Capt. Ball and Company belonging to your Petitioners Regiment . . . in Order to accommodate One Mr Waters with a convenient House of Entertainment. . . . That the said Ball should be ousted of his Tenement he agreed with The Landlord for, to gratify a Dram Seller, when Thire are a Redundancy in This Camp (and your Excellency will indulge Me to say, in general are The Pest of The Army) grieves your Petitioner to his Heart." He requests that the order be repealed.[1]

ADS, MHi: Artemas Ward Papers.

Timothy Danielson (1733–1791), a prosperous merchant from western Massachusetts, served for several years as chairman of the Hampshire County committee of correspondence and represented the town of Brimfield in all three Massachusetts provincial congresses. During the Lexington alarm he commanded eight militia companies, and in May 1775 he was commissioned colonel of a Massachusetts regiment. Danielson left the Continental army at the end of 1775 and subsequently served as a brigadier general in the Hampshire County militia and a member of the General Court.

1. Joseph Reed wrote on 15 July to Brig. Gen. John Thomas: "Collo. [Joseph] Trumbull applied to the General last Evening in Behalf of some Person who wants a House which some of your Soldiers occupy; to keep a Tavern—The General has directed me to let you know that he refers the Matter wholly to you—& if no Objections appear to you, it may be complied with. . . . Collo. Trumbull will furnish such Tents as may be necessary for the Men who remove in Consequence of any Directions you may give herein" (DLC:GW). Lebbeus Ball joined Danielson's regiment as a captain in May 1775. He was promoted to major in November 1777 and resigned from the army in October 1780.

From Colonel Timothy Danielson

Roxbury Camp [Mass.] 31 July 1775. "Should have deliverd The Substance of The enclosed Petition to you viva Voce, had it not been The Alarm in Camp[1] made it Necessary for Me to continue here. This I send by Major Leonard."[2]

ALS, MHi: Artemas Ward Papers.

1. Writing at Prospect Hill on this date, Lt. Paul Lunt described the previous night's events: "At ten o'clock another alarm; paraded immediately, marched up to the fort, but were ordered back. This was occasioned by a brisk fire at the lower sentries. The Regulars came out of their fort to drive in our sentries; but all was soon quieted, and [we] were ordered back. Turned in and got to sleep; at one o'clock were alarmed by the cry of 'Turn out,—for God's sake, turn out.' We paraded again and manned our lines, and there remained until after sunrise: the greatest part of the night the air was filled with the roaring of cannon and the cracking of small arms upon all sides. The Riflemen had engaged them upon Charlestown Common from two o'clock till after sunrise, killed a number, recovered five guns, and lost not a man. At the same time they were engaged at Roxbury with small arms. The Regulars set fire to a house and barn in Roxbury, and hove two bomb-shells" ("Lunt's Book," 196–97). It was the George Tavern that was burned in Roxbury. See General Orders, this date, n.2.

2. David Leonard served as major of Danielson's regiment from May to December 1775.

From Patrick Henry

Philadelphia, 31 July 1775. Recommends "the Bearer Mr Frazer,"[1] who "means to enter the American Camp, & there to gain that Experience, of which the general Cause may be avail'd. It is my earnest wish that many Virginians might see Service. It is not unlikely that in the Fluctuation of things our Country may have occasion for great military Exertions."

ALS, DLC:GW.

1. The bearer was apparently John Grizzage Frazer, a bankrupt Virginia merchant who owed money to GW. See GW to William Aylett, 6 Mar. 1775. Frazer became an assistant to the quartermaster general on 22 Sept. 1775 and served in that capacity on Prospect and Winter hills until the following spring.

From Major General Philip Schuyler

Dear General Tionderoga [N.Y.] July 31st[–2 Aug.] 1775

Since my last I have been most Assiduously employed in preparing Materials for building boats to Convey me across the Lake—the progress has hitherto been Slow as with few hands I had All the Timber to Cut, Mills to repair, to Saw the plank, and my draught Cattle extreamly weak for want of feed the drought haveing Scorched up Every kind of Herbage. I have now one boat in Stocks which I hope will carry near three hundred men, another is putting up to day, provisions of the Bread kind are scarce with me and therefore I have not dared to order up a thousand men that are at Albany least we should starve here.

I have had no Intelligence from Canada since my last to you, Major Brown has been gone nine days and I Expect him back If all is well by Saturday next.[1]

August 2d[.] I have not had a return from General Wooster Since my Arrival[.] I am therefore under the necessity of Makeing you a return of the troops here only.

Inclose your Excellency Copy of two Affidavids made by per[s]ons from Canada. I have transmitted other Copy's to the Congress.[2]

I am extreamly Anxious to hear from your part of the world, reports prevail that a body of troops have left Boston and are Gone to Canada. If so I fear we shall not be able to penetrate Into Canada or Even Attack St Johns with Success, tho. at all Events I am ordered to go there.[3] I am Your Excellencys Most Obedient & Most Hume Servt

Ph: Schuyler

I wish I could make you a regular return Even of the troops at this place and Crown point, but I have not yet got these people to be regular in any thing and therefore beg you to dispence with the following State—Fit for duty-–1 Colonel 3 Majors 9 Captain 1 Captain Lieutenant 21 subalterns 34 serjeants 18 Drums and fifes 933 Rank and file 1 Chaplain 2 Adjutants 1 Quarter Master 1 Surgeon & 2 Mat⟨es⟩—Sick—1 Lieutenant—4 serjeants 2 Drums 103 Rank and file.

ALS, DLC:GW; LB, NN: Schuyler Papers.

1. John Brown (1744–1780), a lawyer from Pittsfield, became a member of the Massachusetts provincial congress in October 1774 and the following March went to Montreal as an emissary from the Boston committee of correspondence to elicit support for the revolutionary cause from sympathetic Canadians. Although he found the Canadians unwilling to join the Continental association or to send delegates to the Continental Congress, he gathered much useful intelligence about Canada and Ticonderoga. On 6 July 1775 Brown was commissioned major of Col. James Easton's regiment, and on 24 July Schuyler sent him to reconnoiter the British forces in Canada. Brown returned on 10 Aug. to report that the British were building an armed schooner at St. Jean and that the Canadians would welcome an American advance. See Brown to Jonathan Trumbull, Sr., 14 Aug. 1775, in Trumbull to GW, 21 Aug. 1775, n.6. Brown participated in the ensuing Canadian campaign and became lieutenant colonel of Easton's regiment in July 1776. A quarrel with Benedict Arnold apparently caused Brown to resign from the Continental army in February 1777. He subsequently served as a Massachusetts militia colonel and was killed in an ambush in the Mohawk Valley on 19 Oct. 1780.

2. The affidavits, both dated 2 Aug. 1775, contain intelligence furnished by two men who had recently come to Ticonderoga from St. Jean: John Duguid, a cooper employed by the British commissary at St. Jean, and John Shatforth, a farm worker whose parents lived near the town. Both men describe in some detail the defensive works at St. Jean and at nearby Chambly, the troops and Indians at those posts, and the two armed schooners that were under construction at St. Jean. They also attest that provisions were in short supply in Canada and that the Canadians desired to remain neutral in the struggle between the colonies and the mother country. The copies of the two affidavits that Schuyler enclosed to GW are in DLC:GW. Schuyler also sent copies to John Hancock in a letter of 2 Aug. 1775 (DNA:PCC, item 153).

3. For Congress's resolutions of 27 June directing Schuyler to move into Canada, see Hancock to GW, 28 June 1775, n.1.

From Jonathan Trumbull, Sr.

Sir Lebanon [Conn.] 31st July 1775

By the Resolve in Congress of the 19th instant, it is recommended to the New England Colonies to compleat the Deficiences in the Regiments belonging to them respectively.[1]

I have not been informed of any Deficiency in the Number of Troops sent from Connecticut. It is recommended also to this Colony to compleat and send forward to the Camp before Boston as soon as possible the fourteen hundred men lately voted by our Assembly. The 25 instant I sent Orders to the Colonels of the last raised Regiments, to march forthwith to the Camp before Boston, by subdivisions if all were not in readiness. Expect many of the Companies will begin their March this Day—And that the whole will move forward very soon.[2]

The Honble President Hancock in his Favour of the 22nd instant informs, That you had recommended, and the Congress have appointed Mr Joseph Trumbull Commissary General of the American Army—I am also informed that you have taken Mr John Trumbull into your Service and Family—These instances of kindness shewn them justly claim my most grateful acknowledgements: A performance of their Duty answerable to your Expectation, will meet your approbation and continuance of Regard, and afford me peculiar satisfaction and Pleasure.

The Rose, Swan, and King Fisher ships of War, with a smal Tender the 25th instant came into the Harbour at New London, on the 27th some men landed near the Light House, broke off the Nutts and plugged up with old Files three or four Cannon—they sailed out again on Friday last. It is reported Mr Collector Stuart is packing up his effects, in Order to Leave that Port.[3] I am, with great Truth and Regard Your Excellency's most obedient and humble Servant

Jonth. Trumbull

ALS, DLC:GW; LB, Ct: Trumbull Papers. Joseph Reed docketed the ALS "Answd by Major Johnson." The bearer was Obadiah Johnson of Connecticut.

1. For this resolution, see *JCC*, 2:191.

2. For the arrival of the two new Connecticut regiments, see General Orders, 9 Aug. 1775, and Jonathan Trumbull, Sr., to GW, 15 Sept. 1775.

3. The British vessels left New London on Saturday, 29 July. The cannon that were spiked on 27 July lay on the western point of the harbor (*Connecticut Journal, and New-Haven Post-Boy*, 2 Aug. 1775). Duncan Stewart (d. 1793) was collector of customs at New London from 1764 to 1776. Though a royal official and a Loyalist sympathizer, Stewart remained undisturbed at New London until July 1777, when he left for New York. He later became collector of customs in Bermuda.

Letter not found: from Anthony White, 31 July 1775. On 25 Aug. GW wrote to White: "Your favours of the 31st Ulto and 1st Instt I have had the honour to receive."

From the Massachusetts General Court

[Watertown, Mass., July or August 1775]

This Court have had information from many respectable Persons, That intelligence is constantly conveyed to General Gage, Of all the operations pursued in this Colony for the restoration of our Liberty, by some bad men from the Province of New Hamshe, who are continually going to, and from, the Army under your Excellencys command, from thence it is carried on board the Scarboro Man of war now Laying in the Harbour of Piscataway and sent immediately to Boston by their Cutters—We beg leave to recommend this as a matter worthy, your Excellencys attention; and would suggest whether it might not be expedient to send some Forces into that Province to cut off all communication between the Inhabitants of sd Province, and the Ship of war now in said Harbour. If your Excellency does not approve of this method, We think at least their Provincial Congress may be informed of such transactions and that they be desired to use their utmost exertions for preventing such Villainous proceedings as the continuance thereof may be attended with important consequences.[1]

L, DLC:GW. This undated letter was written sometime between 26 July, when the new General Court was completed by the convening of the council, and 24 Aug., when the *Scarborough* left New Hampshire waters. See note 1.

1. The British warship *Scarborough*, commanded by Capt. Andrew Barkley, arrived in the Piscataqua River off Portsmouth, N.H., on 19 Dec. 1774 and remained there until 24 Aug. 1775, when it sailed for Boston with Gov. John Wentworth and his family aboard. On 13 Aug. the Portsmouth committee of safety, "finding it inconsistent with the peace and good order of the Town that any further communication should be kept up between the Ship Scarborough and the Town, . . . *Voted*, That henceforward no Boats pass or repass from said ship or the Town of New Castle, without a permit from this Committee, or the selectmen or Committee of New Castle" (Bouton, *N.H. Provincial Papers*, 7:389).

General Orders

Head Quarters, Cambridge, August 1st 1775.

Parole Gibralter. Countersign Fairfield.

The General thanks Major Tupper, and the Officers and Soldiers under his Command, for their gallant and soldierlike behaviour in possessing themselves of the enemy's post at the Light House, and for the Number of Prisoners they took there, and doubts not, but the Continental Army, will be as famous for their mercy as for their valour.[1]

Two Subs. two serjeants, one Drum and thirty Rank and File, to parade at Head Quarters at Noon; to escort the prisoners to Worcester. The Commanding Officer will receive his orders from the Adjutant General.[2]

For the satisfaction of all concerned; The General directs the following Resolution of the Legislature of this Colony to be inserted in General Orders. viz:

"In House of Representatives, Watertown 29th July 1775.

"Whereas sundry Complaints have been made, by some of the Soldiers raised by this Colony, that they have not received the allowance pay of Forty Shillings, agreeable to the Resolution of Provincial Congress,[3] therefore Resolved, that a Committee be appointed forthwith, to apply to the Colonels of the several Regiments, raised by the Colony, and to the Muster Masters and Pay Masters in the Camp, at Cambridge and Roxbury; and obtain of them a compleat List of the Non Commissioned Officers and Soldiers, in their respective regiments, distinguishing those that have been muster'd and paid; from those that have not, that such Methods may be pursued, as shall remove all just ground of Complaint—read and ordered, that Colonel Cushing and Mr Webster,[4] with such as the Honorable Board shall join, be a Committee for the purpose above mentioned.

"Sent up for concurrence.

James Warren, speaker.

"In Council, read and concurred, and Col. Lincoln[5] is join'd.

Albt P: Morton, secy."[6]

The Officers commanding Massachusetts Regiments, will pay all due Attention to the foregoing resolution.

One Man a Company, to be appointed a Camp Colour man, from every Company in every Regiment in the Army, whose particular duty it must be to attend the Quarter Master and Quarter Master serjeant, to sweep the Streets of their respective encampments, to fill up the old necessary Houses and dig new ones, to bury all Offal, Filth, and Nastiness, that may poison or infect the health of the Troops; and the Quarter Masters are to be answerable, to their Commanding Officers for a strict observance of this order, and by persevering in the constant and unremitted Execution thereof, remove that odious reputation, which (with but too much reason) has stigmatized the Character of American Troops. The Colonels and Commanding Officers of Regiments, are to be answerable to the General, for all due obedience to this order.

The General finding it is not uncustomary, for Officers to take the Liberty, of absenting themselves from Camp without leave, and going home; for the future, any Officer found guilty of so glaring an Offence, against all Order and Discipline, and setting so bad an Example to the Non Commissioned Officers and Soldiers, under their Command; such Officer or Officers so offending, may depend upon being punish'd with the utmost severity.

Least the late Successes against the Enemy, should occasion any relaxation in the Alertness of the Troops, the General recommends it in the strongest manner, to all the Officers and Soldiers of the Continental Army; to be the more vigilant in their duty, and watchful of the enemy; as they certainly will take every advantage of any supiness on our part.

Varick transcript, DLC:GW.

1. This attack on the Lighthouse Island in Boston Harbor occurred early on the morning of 31 July. After Maj. Joseph Vose's party burned the lighthouse on 20 July (see William Heath to GW, 21 July 1775), the British began rebuilding it, and by the night of 29 July their work was "in such forwardness as Actually to shew a Light" (James Warren to John Adams, 31 July–2 Aug. 1775, in Taylor, *Papers of John Adams*, 3:108–12). To destroy the new light and stop further construction, Maj. Benjamin Tupper set out with 300 men in whaleboats from Nantasket late on 30 July. They landed on Lighthouse Island about two o'clock the next morning, and after subduing the British marines stationed there, they burned all of the buildings on the island. For GW's and Tupper's accounts of the raid, see GW to Hancock, 4–5 Aug. 1775 and n.14. Benjamin Tupper (1738–1792), a resident of Chesterfield who served as an enlisted man during the French and Indian War, was appointed major of Col. John Fellows's Massachusetts regiment in April 1775. During July he participated in three raids: the one of this date on Lighthouse Island, one on Brown's house at Boston Neck on 8 July, and one on Long Island on 11 July. See GW to Hancock, 10–11 July 1775, Document II. Letter Sent, n.5, and 14 July 1775, n.5. In January 1776 Tupper became lieutenant colonel of the regiment commanded by Col. Jonathan Ward, and in July 1777 he was promoted to colonel. He commanded one or another of the Massachusetts regi-

ments until the end of the war, fighting at Saratoga and Monmouth among other places.

2. The prisoners captured on Lighthouse Island consisted of: 2 marine sergeants, 2 marine corporals, 20 marine privates, and 12 Loyalists. In his orders of this date to the officer commanding the guard detachment, Horatio Gates specified that the prisoners were to be delivered to the chairman of the Worcester committee of safety, who was then to order a detachment of the local militia to escort them to Springfield where they were "to be Secur'd, so as to be forthcoming whenever an Exchange of prisoners, or a happy reconciliation between Great Britain and her Colonies shall take place" (DLC:GW). The prisoners marched out of Cambridge about nine o'clock this morning and arrived in Worcester on 3 Aug. ("Stevens Journal," 53).

3. The Massachusetts provincial congress authorized this advance pay for the colony's noncommissioned officers and privates on 20 May 1775 (*Mass. Prov. Congress Journals*, 246).

4. Joseph Cushing (1732–1791), a lieutenant colonel in the militia, represented Hanover, and Jonathan Webster, Jr. (1747–1826), represented Haverhill in the provincial congress.

5. Benjamin Lincoln (1733–1810) of Hingham was a lieutenant colonel in the Suffolk County militia. He served in all three provincial congresses and was elected to the council on 21 July 1775. In February 1776 Lincoln became a brigadier general of the militia, and the following May he was promoted to major general. Lincoln's administrative abilities soon attracted GW's attention, and on his recommendation, Lincoln was commissioned a Continental major general in February 1777. He was wounded at Saratoga in the fall of 1777 and was captured at Charleston in the spring of 1780. After his exchange Lincoln participated in the Yorktown campaign, and from 1781 to 1783 he served as secretary at war.

6. Artemas Ward's orderly book reads "Attest. Perez Morton Secr'y" (MHi: Ward Papers). The resolution that appears here is nearly identical in wording to the version approved by the Massachusetts council on 29 July ("Mass. Council Journal," July 1775–Feb. 1776 sess., 15). The version that the house of representatives passed earlier on that date varies somewhat from the council's, but the differences are minor (*Mass. House of Rep. Journal*, July–Nov. 1775 sess., 22). For the General Court's further actions regarding advanced pay, see Committee of the Massachusetts Council to GW, 11 Aug. 1775, n.2. Perez Morton (1751–1837), a young attorney from Boston, was appointed temporary secretary of the council on 26 July 1775. When Samuel Adams was named permanent secretary on 10 Aug., Morton became his deputy, and because of Adams's long absences, he continued to perform most of the duties of the office until he resigned on 1 June 1776. During the Rhode Island campaign of 1778, Morton acted as an aide-de-camp to John Hancock.

From Richard Henry Lee

Dear Sir, Philadelphia 1st August 1775

After the fatigue of many days, and of this in particular, I should not sit down at eleven oClock at night to write to a Gentleman of whose goodness of heart I have less doubt than I have of yours. But well knowing that you will pardon what flows from good intentions, I venture to say that my hopes are, you will find from what the Congress has already done, and from what I hope they will do tomorrow,[1] that it has been a capital object with us to make your arduous business as easy to you as the nature of things will admit. The business immediately before us being finished, the approaching sickly season here, and the great importance of our presence in the Virga Convention,[2] have determined a recess of a Month, it standing now, that the Congress shall meet here again on the 5th of September. The capital object of powder we have attended to as far as we could by sending you the other day six Tons, and tomorrow we shall propose sending six or eight Tons more, which, with the supplies you may get from Connecticut, and such further ones from here, as future expected importations may furnish, will I hope enable you to do all that this powerful article can in good hands accomplish.[3] We understand here that Batteries may be constructed at the entrance of the Bay of Boston so as to prevent the egress & regress of any Ships whatever. If this be fact, would it not Sir be a signal stroke to secure the Fleet & Army in and before Boston so as to compel a surrender at discretion. While I write this, I assure you my heart is elated with the contemplation of so great an event. A decisive thing, that would at once end the War, and vindicate the injured liberties of America. But your judgment and that of your brave Associates, will best determine the practicability of this business.[4] I think we have taken the most effectual measures to secure the friendship of the Indians all along our extensive frontiers, and by what we learn of the Spirit of our Convention now sitting at Richmond, a Spirit prevails there very sufficient to secure us on that quarter—The particulars of their conduct I refer you to Mr Frazer for, who comes fresh from thence, & who goes to the Camp a Soldier of fortune—You know him better than I do, and I am sure you will provide for him as he deserves.

We are here as much in the dark about news from England as you are, the London Ships having been detained long beyond the time they were expected. The indistinct accounts we have, tell us of great confusion all over England, and a prodigious fall of the Stocks. I heartily wish it may be true, but if it is not so now, I have no doubt of its shortly being the case.

I will not detain you longer from more important affairs, than to beg the favor of you, when your leisure permits, to oblige me with a line by Post, to let us know how you go on.

There is nothing I wish so much as your success, happiness, and safe return to your family and Country, because I am with perfect sincerity dear Sir Your Affectionate friend and countryman

Richard Henry Lee

ALS, DLC:GW.

1. Although Congress's official journal indicates that the recess began on 1 Aug., the letters and diaries of several delegates confirm that Congress met and adjourned the following day (*JCC*, 2:239; Smith, *Letters of Delegates*, 1:694–95).

2. The third Virginia convention met from 17 July to 26 Aug. 1775.

3. On 25 July Congress, learning that about six and a half tons of gunpowder had arrived in Philadelphia, ordered the Pennsylvania delegates "to have it sent under a safe convoy with all possible despatch to Genl Washington at the Camp before Boston" (*JCC*, 2:204). The second shipment of gunpowder contained 5 tons. According to *JCC*, 2:238, Congress ordered that supply sent to GW on 1 Aug., but it probably happened the following day as Lee says here (see note 1). For another account of the sending of this gunpowder, see Jonathan Trumbull, Sr., to GW, 8 Aug. 1775, n.3.

4. The blockading of Boston Harbor was a favorite project of Josiah Quincy, Sr., who lived on the shore of the harbor near Squantum Neck. "Had we a sufficient Supply of Powder and battering Cannon," Quincy wrote to John Adams on 11 July 1775, "such is the Spirit and Intrepidity of our brave Countrymen, we should very soon, and with little or no Hazard, lock up the Harbor and make both Seamen and Soldiers our prisoners at Discretion" (Taylor, *Papers of John Adams*, 3:73–77). Adams replied to Quincy on 29 July: "I have a great opinion of your knowledge, and judgment, from long experience, concerning the channels and islands in Boston harbour; but I must confess your opinion that the harbour might be blocked up, and seamen and soldiers made prisoners, at discretion, was too bold and enterprising for me, who am not apt to startle at a daring proposal" (ibid., 104–6). Quincy made a more detailed suggestion for blockading the harbor in a letter to GW of

31 Oct. 1775, but GW did not think the scheme a practical one. See GW to Quincy, 4 Nov. 1775. For GW's rejection of a similar proposal by Joseph Palmer, see GW to Palmer, 22 Aug. 1775.

From the Massachusetts Committee of Supplies

Chamber of Supplies Water Town [Mass.] Augt 1. 1775

May It please your Excellency

Mr Cheever[1] has applyed this afternoon for 200,000 small Arm Cartridges in Consequence of An Application from the Adjutant General, to answer the Demand of Major General Lee.

Mr Cheever is able to furnish abt 36000 It being the Whole Quantity now made, & there remains but 36 barells in Store of the Quantity collected from the Towns in this Colony & recd from the others this ⟨si⟩de Maryland.

there are also about two Tons of Lead & not any Flints in Store, of which We think it necessary to give immediate Information.

We are in daily Expectation of some Powder from the West Indies, but cannot say what Success our plans will meet with; indeed We have exerted Ourselves to obtain It several Ways which may be communicated at a more convenient oppertunity, With respect to Lead & Flints Colo. porter was dispatched sixteen Days since for New york for 2 hhds Flints & 10 Tons Lead but We have heard nothing from him since[2]—We are ready to exert to the utmost to serve the Cause, provided the Commissary General desires it for the present—the powder shall be sent immediatel⟨y⟩ if ordered or be made into Cartridges as soon as maybe. We are sir respectfully your most ob. Sert

Elbridge Gerry ℔ Ord.[3]

LS, DLC:GW.

1. The Massachusetts provincial congress appointed Ezekiel Cheever to be storekeeper of ordnance on 27 June 1775, and on 17 Aug. GW made him Continental commissary of artillery stores (General Orders, that date). Later in the war Cheever served as commissary of military stores at Springfield, Mass., and he eventually became a deputy commissary general with the rank of colonel.

2. Elisha Porter (1742–1796), a lawyer from Hadley, served in the third Massachusetts provincial congress and was appointed to the committee of supplies on 22 June 1775. In January 1776 he became colonel of a Massachusetts regiment and subsequently participated in the Canadian campaign.

Porter left the Continental army in August 1776 on account of illness, but the following year he commanded a regiment of Hampshire County militia at Saratoga.

3. Elbridge Gerry (1744–1814), who represented Marblehead in all three Massachusetts provincial congresses, was appointed to the committee of supplies on 9 Feb. 1775. A merchant with many commercial connections in Spain, Portugal, and the West Indies as well as in New England, Gerry played a major role in obtaining supplies for the Continental army throughout 1775. In December of this year, the house of representatives, of which Gerry was also a member, chose him as one of the colony's delegates to the Continental Congress. Gerry attended Congress from 1776 to 1780 and from 1783 to 1785, serving during the early years on the Board of Treasury.

Letter not found: from Anthony White, 1 Aug. 1775. On 25 Aug. GW wrote to White: "Your favours of the 31st Ulto and 1st Instt I have had the honour to receive."

General Orders

Head Quarters, Cambridge, August 2nd 1775

Parole Hallifax. Countersign Geneva.

Capt. Oliver Parker of Col. Prescotts Regiment, tried by a General Court Martial whereof Col. Glover was President, for "defrauding his men of their advance pay, and by false Returns, imposing upon the Commissary, and drawing more Rations than he had men in his company, and for selling the provisions he by that means obtained" is by the Court found guilty of the whole charge against him and sentenced to be cashiered, mulcted of all his pay and rendered incapable of future service.

Capt. Christopher Gardner of Col. Varnums regiment, in the Rhode Island Brigade, tried by a General Court martial, whereof Col. Thomas Church[1] was president, for "deserting his post," is found guilty of the Crime, and unanimously sentenced to be cashiered, as incapable of serving his Country in any military capacity.

The General approves both the above sentences, and orders the Commanding Officers of the Regiments, to see the prisoners dismissed the army.

Varick transcript, DLC:GW.

1. Thomas Church (1727–1797) commanded the 3d Rhode Island Regiment until December 1775, at which time he returned home to Rhode Island.

From Lieutenant Colonel Loammi Baldwin

Chelsea [Mass.] Augt 2d 1775

May it Please your Excellency

Inclosd are the Observations taken by the Sentinal Posted upon Powder horn Hill and also two Letters in one cover Directed to Mr Nathl Noyes, Andover. which I thought Proper to Send for your Excellencies Perusal.[1]

Nothing Extraordinary has hapned Scince yesterday⟨.⟩[2] Two Boats only have come over with Passengers from Boston this day. I am your Excellencys most Obediant Humbe Servnt

Loammi Baldwin Liut. Colo.

ALS, DLC:GW.

1. "A Return of the observations of the Day august the 2d" in Joseph Leach's writing is in DLC:GW. Of the two letters to Nathaniel Noyes, one was apparently that of 1 Aug. 1775 from his father Belcher Noyes, a copy of which GW enclosed in his letter to Hancock of 4–5 Aug. 1775. See notes 25, 29, 30, and 36 to that document. Nathaniel Noyes (1743–1823), a Boston apothecary, left Boston for Andover in May 1775 and did not return until the British evacuated the city in the spring of 1776.

2. Baldwin's report of 1 Aug. was sent to Horatio Gates: "I am just informed that there was this forenoon about 1400 regulars paraded in Boston, and afterward marched down in order to go over to Charles Town Heights as they call Bunker hill. Suppose they are all over before this time—Another person told me there was not more than 1000 men, and that they were going to reinforce Bunker hill. I send the observations as usual—It gives me unspeakable satisfaction that my conduct is approved of by the General. Nothing that his in my power to perform shall be wanting to render his Excellency's command easy and life happy. . . . I trust you will give the enclosed to the General" (Sprague transcript, DLC:GW).

From the Massachusetts Committee of Supplies

Chamber of Supplies Water Town [Mass.] August 2d 1775

May it please your Excellency

Colo. porter is just arrived from New york & has so far succeeded in his Business that abt 80,000 Flints & eight Tons of Lead are expected here Saturday next; It arrived at Hartford Sunday & Monday last.

Colo. Campbell the Deputy Quarter Master informed Colo. porter at New york that fifteen hogsheads of powder had arrived there & that he should give your Excellency immediate Notice thereof.

I apprehend We can have half a Ton Lead cast into Ball a Day, being provided with Moulds sized from 16 to 32 Balls to the pound—perhaps twice that Quantity on Emergency.

Colo. Burbeck[1] recd 16 half barells powder this Morning, before the Committee were Apprized of it by the Agent of Supplies; but We have given Orders for stopping all the Ammunition unless expressly ordered by your Excellency.

Colo. porter is desired to wait on you this afternoon & We remain with great Respect sir your most obt sert

Elbridge Gerry ℘ Ord.

P.S. The Subject of the Letter last Evening was of such a Nature that Mr Cheever was not made acquainted therwith, which We mention to your Excellency that your Mind may be easy with respect to the Secrecy of it.

P.S. ord⟨ers⟩ are to go to the Town immediately for powder.

LS, DLC:GW.

1. The Massachusetts provincial congress appointed William Burbeck (1716–1785) an engineer in the colony's forces on 26 April 1775, and on 21 June it made him lieutenant colonel of Col. Richard Gridley's artillery regiment. Burbeck served with the Continental artillery until 25 May 1776, at which time the Continental Congress dismissed him from the army for refusing to serve outside of Massachusetts. He later became comptroller of the Massachusetts state munitions laboratory.

From Brigadier General John Sullivan

Winter Hill [Mass.] August 2d 1775

May it Please your Excellencey

I have Examined into the State of The Ammunition in my Department & find Remaining in the Magazine of the Powder Supplied from New Hampshire 19 Barrels of 100 wt Each, Scarcely any Balls & no flints Except what the Soldiers are possessd of: They are in General well Provided with amunition for one Ingagement we have 50 Rounds of Cartridges to Each Cannon That is mounted which is all the ammunition in the Brigade assigned To your Excellenceys most obedt Servt

Jno. Sullivan

ALS, DLC:GW.

General Orders

Head Quarters, Cambridge, August 3rd 1775.

Parole, Ireland. Countersign, Hartford.

When any plünder is taken from the Enemy (not excepted by the Continental Articles of war) such plunder must be all surrender'd to the Commanding Officer, and as soon as convenient after his arrival at Head Quarters, public Notice must be made, that an Auction will be held in the front of the Encampment for the sale thereof the next day at noon, and the money arising therefrom, is to be equally divided between the Officers and Men, that took it. This Order is not to be construed to extend, to permitting unlawfull and irregular plundering; as any Officer, or Soldier, who shall be found guilty thereof, will be punished with the greatest severity.[1]

All the Armourers, belonging to any of the regiments in the three Brigades, posted in the Lines, or in Cambridge, and those employed in the Artillery; to be at Head Quarters by eight OClock, to morrow morning, and none will be entitled to any pay hereafter, who does not attend at that time.

Varick transcript, DLC:GW.

1. The Continental articles of war stipulate in article 29 that "all public stores taken in the enemy's camp or magazines, whether of artillery, ammunition, cloathing, or provisions, shall be secured for the use of the United Colonies." Article 30 adds that "if any officer or soldier shall leave his post or colours, in time of an engagement, to go in search of plunder, he shall, upon being convicted thereof before a general court-martial, suffer such punishment as by the said court-martial shall be ordered" (*JCC*, 2:116).

Council of War

[Cambridge, 3 August 1775]

At a Council held at Cambridge Head Quarters August 3d 1775

Present his Excelly General Washington.

Major Gens. Ward—Lee & Puttnam

Brigader Gens.

Thomas	Sullivan
Heath	Green
Spencer	Gates

The General communicated sundry Letters respecting the State of the Ammunition which appears to be far short of the Return made some Time ago, & having explained in what Manner the Mistake had happened desires the Opinion & Advice of the Generals present on this Subject. Upon the Returns now made—the whole Stock of the Army at Roxbury & Cambridge & the adjacent Posts consists of 90 Bbbls or thereabouts.[1]

It was proposed to make an Attempt on the Magazine at Halifax where there is Reason to suppose there is a great Quantity of Powder—And upon the Question being severally put it was agreed to by a great Majority. & that the Detachment for this Enterprize consist of 300 Men. Also to endeavour to collect a Supply from the neighbouring Provinces of New Hampshire, Rhode Island & Connecticut.[2]

D, in Joseph Reed's writing, DLC:GW; Varick transcript, DLC:GW.

1. Horatio Gates wrote to Artemas Ward on 2 Aug. 1775: "His Excellency General Washington desires Yourself, with the Brigadiers General, Thomas, & Spencer, will be at Head Quarters at Cambridge by Nine O Clock tomorrow morning. he further requests you will bring an Exact state of all the Ammunition now in Store in all, & every Post, & Station, in your Department" (NjP: deCoppet Collection). For the return of ammunition in John Sullivan's brigade, see Sullivan to GW, 2 Aug. 1775. The letters laid before the council of war probably included also those of 1 and 2 Aug. 1775 to GW from the Massachusetts committee of supplies. For a more detailed account of the ammunition shortage, see GW to Hancock, 4–5 Aug. 1775.

2. See GW's letters of 4 Aug. 1775 to Nicholas Cooke, the New Hampshire committee of safety, and Jonathan Trumbull, Sr.

From Lieutenant Colonel Loammi Baldwin

Chelsea [Mass.] August: 3d 1775

May it Please your Excellency

This covers the observation of the day to this time.[1]

Two ferry Boats Came on Shore at the ferry ways[2] at 12 Last night with about 20 Passenger from Boston and the Signal upon Powder horn hill was Just Erected denoting more coming[.] am Just going down to the ferry.

Nothing Extraordinary Occurd Since I wrote Last I would beg leave to ask your Excellency whether I might attem[p]t to move the old wreck now on the ferry ways which greatly Obstructs the Passenger in bringing up their good at Low water. I am your Excellencys Most obediant Humb. Servnt

Loammi Baldwin Liu. Col.

ALS, DLC:GW.

1. "A Return of the observations of the Day august 3d" in Joseph Leach's writing is in DLC:GW.

2. Baldwin is referring to the Winnisimmet ferry near Chelsea.

From the New York Provincial Congress

Sir. In Provincial Congress New York Augt 3d 1775

We are informed in a Letter from the Continental Congress that the General would make out the Commissions for our Regiments to such Persons as this Congress should recommend;[1] but are at a loss to know whether You, or General Schuyler are to issue the Commissions.

We understand however that they have been transmitted to You. If this should be the Case, and the Commissions are to be filled up by General Schuyler, we beg you will send them to him or us without Delay. If they are to be filled up by Your Excellency, we submit it, whether, to prevent Delay, it would not be proper to send them in blank to General Schuyler, or to us; that the Names may be filled up agreable to the Arrangement made by this Congress. The Number of Commissions wanted will be about two hundred.[2] We are with the greatest Respect Your Excellency's Most Obedient humble servants

By Order.

P. V. B. Livingston President

LS, DLC:GW. Endorsed in Joseph Reed's writing "Recd 9th & answd the 10th." See GW to Peter Van Brugh Livingston, 10 Aug. 1775.

1. Hancock wrote similar letters, dated 27 June 1775, to the colonies of Rhode Island, Massachusetts, and New Hampshire (Smith, *Letters of Delegates*, 1:547).

2. GW instructed Schuyler in June to apply directly to the Continental Congress for the commissions needed for the New York department, but Congress had not yet responded to Schuyler's letter of 28 June on that subject. See Schuyler to GW, 1 July 1775, n.5, and GW to Schuyler, 10–11 July 1775.

From James Warren

Sir Watertown [Mass.] Augt 3. 1775

I Inclose Agreable to your Excellencys desire a List of Such Officers in the army as have received Commissions from the Congress of this Colony: and Also the Resolves of the Congress: which though Inaccurate may serve to Shew in what manner the Congress Intended to Rank the several Regiments raised in this Colony.[1] I am with the Greatest Respect Your Excellencys most obedt humbe Servt

Jas Warren

ALS, DLC:GW.

1. The resolutions to which Warren refers are probably those of 19 May 1775 in which it was provided that a committee should "bring in a resolve, settling the rank or number of the regiments, according to the rank or age of the counties from whence the majority of the regiments shall come" and "that the rank of the regiments, where there are more than one in each county, be according to the rank which those regiments (have) formerly sustained in the old arrangement from which they are taken, provided that can be ascertained, and where that cannot be determined, the rank to be determined by lot" (*Mass. Prov. Congress Journals*, 243). GW apparently wanted this information for use by a board of field officers that was to set the precedence of all regiments and officers in the Continental army. See General Orders, 5 Aug. 1775.

General Orders

Head Quarters, Cambridge, August 4th 1775

Parole, London. Countersign, Ireland.

It is with Indignation and Shame, the General observes, that notwithstanding the repeated Orders which have been given to prevent the firing of Guns, in and about Camp; that it is daily and hourly practised; that contrary to all Orders, straggling Soldiers do still pass the Guards, and fire at a Distance, where there is not the least probability of hurting the enemy, and where no other end is answer'd, but to waste Ammunition, expose themselves to the ridicule of the enemy, and keep their own Camps harrassed by frequent and continual alarms, to the hurt of every good Soldier, who is thereby disturbed of his natural rest, and will at lenght never be able to distinguish between a real, and a false alarm.[1]

For these reasons, it is in the most peremptory manner forbid, any person or persons whatsoever, under any pretence, to pass the out Guards, unless authorized by the Commanding Officer of that part of the lines; signified in writing, which must be shewn to the Officer of the guard as they pass. Any person offending in this particular, will be considered in no other light, than as a common Enemy, and the Guards will have orders to fire upon them as such. The Commanding Officer of every regiment is to direct, that every man in his regiment, is made acquainted with Orders to the end, that no one may plead Ignorance, and that all may be apprized of the consequence of disobedience. The Colonels of regiments and commanding Officers of Corps, to order the Rolls of every Company to be called twice a day, and every Man's Ammunition examined at evening Roll calling, and such as are found to be deficient to be confined.

The Guards are to apprehend all persons firing Guns near their posts, whether Townsmen or soldiers.

Varick transcript, DLC:GW.

1. For GW's previous orders regarding the unauthorized firing of guns, see General Orders, 26 July 1775. "The General," James Warren wrote to John Adams on 9 Aug. 1775, "has been obliged from Principles of frugality to restrain his rifle men. While they were permitted Liberty to fire on the Enemy, a great number of the Army would go and fire away great quantitys of Ammunition to no Purpose" (Taylor, *Papers of John Adams*, 3:114–16).

From Lieutenant Colonel Loammi Baldwin

Chelsea [Mass.] Augst 4th 1775 5 oClock P.M.

May it please your Excellency

This covers the Observations as Usual.[1]

Capt. Morton[2] who came out of Boston yesterday in the afternoon informs that a little before he came away the Generals went over the ferry to Bunker Hill to consult (as it was said) upon the propriety of taking possession of a considerable eminence in this Town a little West of Winnisimmit Ferry commonly known by the name of Greens Hill; and I am informd by some persons who left Boston this morning that the Soldiers told them as they was coming away that they ware Fools to go to Chelsea for tomorrow they (the Regulars) ware a going to take possession of that Place & burn & distroy all before them, and this it was said was to be done in consequence of the determination of the Council of War held yesterday on Bunker Hill.

This Intiligence is Just as I Received it & your Excellency will pay what attention to it you think Proper.[3]

I feal my Self under Indispensible Obligations to transmit to your Excellency all the Intiligence I can get from our Enimy and you will be pleased to Excuse it if I Should Sometimes trouble you with imperfect accounts & matters of Little consequence as I cannot tell what may or what may not prove true.

I am this moment Informd that a Man of War & one Schooner (the schooner commanded by Cap. Dawson) is Just Come in with two Sloops & one Schooner which I supose they have Piratically Seized and made Prizes of.

hope I Shall be able to give a more full account of this affair tomorrow.[4]

Nothing further Extraordinary I Subscribe myself your Excellencys most Obediand Servnt

Loammi Baldwin Lieut. Colo.

ALS, DLC:GW.

1. "A Return of the observations of the Day august the 4th" in Joseph Leach's writing is in DLC:GW.

2. Capt. Morton may be Thomas Morton, a Boston shipmaster.

3. John Trumbull replied to Baldwin on behalf of GW in a letter of this date: "His Excellency Receiv'd yours of this Day Informing the Intention of the Enemy to take Possession of Green's hill; he is very glad of every Information with regard to their Movements & thanks you for your Attention, but cannot think, that, if any such Affair was on foot the Soldiers would be allow'd to know any thing of it—& therefore concludes we need not be under any Apprehensions On that Score" (MH: Baldwin Papers). British troops did cross the Mystic River on 6 Aug. and burn a house at Penny ferry near Green Hill (Baldwin to GW, that date).

4. Lt. George Dawson commanded the British armed schooner *Hope*, which sailed from Boston for the Bay of Fundy between 19 and 21 July and did not return until 10 September. Baldwin's intelligence may be a delayed report of Dawson's earlier captures of two sloops and a schooner laden with firewood. See Samuel Graves's narrative, 1 July 1775, and Simeon Turner's statement, 20 July 1775, in Clark, *Naval Documents*, 1:796, 936–37.

To Nicholas Cooke

Sir

[Cambridge] August 4. 1775

I was yesterday favoured with yours of the 31st July—we have yet no certain Account of the Fleet which sailed out of Boston the 25th but if our Conjectures & Information are just we may expect to hear of it every Hour.[1]

I am now, Sir, in strict Confidence to acquaint you that our Necessities in the Articles of Powder & Lead are so great as to require an immediate Supply—I must earnestly intreat you will fall on some Measures to forward every Pound of each in the Colony which can possibly be spared—It is not within the Propriety & Safety of such a Correspondence to say what I might upon this Subject: It is sufficient that the Case loudly calls for the most strenuous Exertions of every Friend of his Country and does not admit the least Delay—No Quantity however small is beneath Notice, & should any arrive I beg it may be forwarded as soon as possible—But a Supply of this kind is so precarious not only from the Danger of the Enemy but the Oppy of purchasing that I have revolved in my Mind every other possible Chance & listned to every Proposition on this Subject which could give the smallest Hope—Among others I have had one made which has some Weight with me as well the General Officers to whom I have proposed it. One Harris is lately come from Bermuda, where there is a very considerable Magazine of Powder in a remote Part of the Island, & the Inhabitants well disposed not only to our Cause in General, but to assist in this Enterprize in particular:[2] We understand there are two armed Vessels in your Province commanded by Men of known Activity & Spirit:[3] One of which it is proposed to dispatch on this Errand with such other Assistance as may be requisite: Harris is to go along as the Conductor of the Enterprize & to avail ourselves of his Knowledge of the Island but without any Command: I am very sensible that at first View this Project may appear hazardous, & its Success must depend upon the Concurrence of many Circumstances but we are in a Situation which requires us to run all Risques—No Danger is to be considered when put in Competition with the Magnitude of the Cause & the absolute Necessity we are under of increasing our Stock—

Enterprizes which appear chimerical often prove successful for that very Circumstance[.] Common Sense & Prudence will suggest Vigilance & Care where the Danger is plain & obvious but where little Danger is apprehended the more the Enemy is found unprepard & consequently there is the fairer Prospect of Success. Mr Brown[4] has been mentioned to me as a very proper Person to consult upon this Occasion, you will judge of the Propriety of communicating it to him in Part or the whole: And as soon as possible favour me with your Sentiments & the Steps you may have taken to forward it. If no immediate & safe Oppy offers you will please to do it by Express. Should it be inconvenient to part with one of the armed Vessels perhaps some other might be fitted out or you could devise some other Mode of executing this Plan, so that in Case of a Disappointmt the Vessel might proceed to some other Island to purchase.

My last Letter from the Hon. Continental Congress recommends my procuring from the Colonies of Connecticut & Rhode Island a Quantity of Tow Cloth for the Purpose of making Indian Shirts for the Men many of whom are very destitute of Cloathing.[5] A Pattern will be sent you[6] & I must request you to give the necessary Directions throughout your Government that all the Cloth of the above kind may be bought up for this Use & suitable Persons set to Work to make it up. As soon as any Number is made worth the Conveyance you will please to direct them to be forwarded. It is designed as a Species of Uniform both cheap & convenient.

We have had no Transactions of any Consequence in either Camp since my last, but what are in the publick Papers & are related with tolerable Accuracy. The Enemy still continue strengthning their Lines & we have Reason to believe intend to bombard our Lines with the Hope of forcing us out of them. Our Poverty in Ammunition prevents our making a suitable Return.

Since writing the above Col: Porter has undertaken to assist in the Matter or to provide some suitable Person to accompany Harris to you who will communicate all Circumstances to you.[7]

Df, in Joseph Reed's writing, NHi: Joseph Reed Papers; LB, DLC:GW; Varick transcript, DLC:GW. The draft is endorsed "Sent by Col. Porter." The dateline of the letter-book copy in DLC:GW reads "Camp at Cambridge Aug. 4. 1775."

1. For the sailing of these British vessels which raided Fishers and Gar-

diners islands, see Richard Dodge to GW, and John Thomas to GW, both 25 July 1775.

2. There were 112 barrels of gunpowder in the royal magazine near the government house at St. George. Harris may be Capt. Benjamin Harris (Jones, "Cooke Correspondence," 262, n.1).

3. On 12 June 1775 the Rhode Island general assembly directed its committee of safety "to charter two suitable vessels, for the use of the colony, and fit out the same in the best manner, to protect the trade of this colony." Abraham Whipple (1733–1819) was named commodore of both vessels and commander of the larger one, the sloop *Katy*. The other vessel was commanded by John Grimes (Bartlett, *R.I. Records*, 7:346–47, 361).

4. Mr. Brown is probably one of the four brothers who were prominent merchants and manufacturers in Providence: Nicholas Brown (1729–1791), Joseph Brown (1733–1785), John Brown (1736–1803), or Moses Brown (1738–1836).

5. See Hancock to GW, 24 July 1775.

6. With his letter to Cooke of 14 Aug., GW sent a hunting shirt to be used as pattern.

7. Joseph Reed wrote to Elisha Porter earlier this day: "If you could spare Time to ride down to Head Quarters this Afternoon the General would be glad to confer with you on a Matter of some Importance which you mentioned to him on your Return from New York" (MHi: Elisha Porter Papers).

To John Hancock

Sir Camp at Cambridge August 4th[–5] 1775

I am to acknowledge the Receipt of your Favour of the 24th July accompanied by 284 Commissions, which are yet much short of the necessary Number.[1] I am much honoured by the Confidence reposed in me of appointing the several Officers recommended in mine of the 10th ult.; and shall endeavour to select such Persons, as are best qualified to fill those important Posts.

General Thomas has accepted his Commission, & I have heard nothing of his Retirement since, so that I suppose he is satisfied.[2]

In the Renewal of these Commissions some Difficulties occur, in which I should be glad to know the Pleasure of the honbe Congress. The General Officers of the Massachusetts, have Regiments, those of Connecticut, have both Regiments, & Companies, & the other Field Officers have Companies each.[3] From Rhode Island, the General Officer has no Regimt, but the Field Officers have Companies: But I do not find they have, or expect Pay under more than one Commission. Should the Commissions now to be delivered pursue these different Establishments, there will be a Distinction between General & Field Officers of the same Rank—In Order to put New Hampshire, Massachusetts & Rhode Island upon a Line with Connecticut, it would be necessary to dismiss a Number of Officers in Possession of Commissions, without any Fault of theirs; on the other Hand, to bring the Connecticut Generals, & Field Officers to the same Scale with the others, will add to the Number of Officers, & may be deemed inconsistent with the Terms on which they entered into the Service, altho. you add nothing to the Expence, except in the Article of Provisions. Upon the whole, it is a Case, which I would wish the Honbe Congress to consider & determine.[4]

Col: Gridley of this Province, who is at the Head of the Artillery has the Rank of Major Genl from the Provincial Congress. Will it be proper to renew his Commission here in the same Manner? It is proper here to remark, that in this Case he will take Rank of all the Brigadiers General, & even the Majors General, whose Commissions are subsequent in Date, & can answer no good Purpose, but may be productive of many bad Consequences.[5]

These are Matters of some Importance, but I am embarassed with a Difficulty of a superiour kind. The Estimate made in Congress, supposed all the Regiments to be formed upon one Establishment, but they are different in different Provinces; & even vary in the same Province, in some Particulars. In Massachusetts, some Regiments have Ten Companies, others Eleven; The Establishment of the former is 590 Men Officers included, of the latter 649. The Establishment of Rhode Island, & New Hampshire is 590 to a Regiment, Officers included. Connecticut has 1000 Men to a Regiment. Should the Massachusetts Regiments be completed; with the new Levies from Rhode Island & Connecticut and the Riffle Men, the Number will exceed 22,000. If they should not be completed, as each Regiment is fully officer'd, there will be a heavy Expence to the Publick without an adequate Service. The Reduction of some of them seems to be necessary & yet is a Matter of much Delicacy, as we are situated. I most earnestly request it may be taken into immediate Consideration, & the Time & Mode of doing it, pointed out by the Honbe Congress.[6] By an Estimate I have made, from the General Return, when the new Levies arrive, & the Regiments are completed there will be 24,450 Men on the Pay & Provision of the united Colonies. Some of the recruiting Officers who have been out on that Service, have returned with very little Success, so that we may safely conclude, the Number of 2064 now wanting to complete will rather increase than diminish[.][7] There are the Regiment of Artillery consisting of 493 Men, & one under Col: Sergeant who has not received any Commission; altho. he had Orders to raise a Regiment from the Provincial Congress here,[8] which are not included in the above Estimate. This last Regiment consists of 234 Men by the last Return, but a Company has since joined—By adverting to the General Return, which I have the Honour of inclosing (No. 1.) it will be seen what Regiments are most deficient.[9]

If the Congress does not chuse to point out the particular Regiments, but the Provinces in which the Reduction is to be made, the several Congresses & Assemblies may be the proper Channell to conduct this Business: which I should also conceive the most adviseable, from their better Acquaintance with the Merits, Terms, & Time of Service of the respective Officers—Reducing some Regiments, & with the Privates thereof, filling up others would certainly be the best Method of accomplishing this Work, if it were practicable; but the Experiment is dangerous, as the Massachusetts Men under the Priviledge of chusing their own Officers, do not conceive themselves bound if those Officers are disbanded.

As General Gage is making Preparations for Winter, by contracting for Quantities of Coal; it will suggest to us the Propriety of extending our Views to that Season. I have directed that such Huts as have been lately made of Boards, should be done in such a Manner, that if necessary they may serve for covering during the Winter. but I need not enlarge upon the Variety of Necessities such as Cloathing, Fuel &c.—both exceedingly scarce & difficult to be procured, which that Season must bring with it; if the Army, or any considerable Part of it is to remain embodied.[10] From the Inactivity of the Enemy since the Arrival of their whole Reinforcement, their continual Addition to their Lines, & many other Circumstances, I am inclined to think that finding us so well prepared to receive them, the Plan of Operations is varied; & they mean by regular Approaches to bombard us out of our present Line of Defence, or are waiting in Expectation that the Colonies must sink under the Weight of the Expence; or the Prospect of a Winters Campaign, so discourage the Troops as to break up our Army. If they have not some such Expectations, the Issue of which they are determined to wait; I cannot account for the Delay, when their Strength is lessened every Day by Sickness, Desertions, & little Skirmishes.

Of these last, we have had only two worthy of Notice: Having some Reason to suspect they were extending their Lines at Charles Town, I last Saturday Evening, ordered some of the Riffle Men down to make a Discovery, or bring off a Prisoner—They were accidentally discovered sooner than they expected; by the Guard coming to relieve, & obliged to fire upon them: We have Reason to believe they killed several. They brought in two Prisoners whose Acct confirmed by some other Circumstances removed my Suspicions in part:[11] Since that Time we have on each Side drawn in our Centries, & there have been scattering Fires along the Line. This Evening we have heard of three Captains who have been taken off by the Riffle Men & one killed by a Cannon Shot from Roxbury besides severall Privates; but as the Intelligence is not direct, I only mention it as a Report which deserves Credit.[12] The other happened at the Light House. A Number of Workmen having been sent down to repair it with a Guard of 22 Marines & a Subaltern,[13] Major Tupper last Monday Morning about 2 oClock landed there with about 300 Men, attack'd them killed the Officer, & 4 Privates, but being detained by the Tide, in his Return he was attack'd by several Boats, but he happily got through with the Loss of one Man killed & another wounded. The Remainder of the ministerial Troops, 3 of which are badly wounded, he brought off Prisoners, with 10 Tories all of whom are on their Way to Springfield Gaol.[14] The Riffle Men in these Skirmish lost one Man who we hear is a Prisoner in Boston Gaol—The Enemy in Return endeavoured to surprize our Guard at Roxbury, but they being apprized of it by a Deserter, had Time to prepare for it; but by some Negligence or Misconduct in the Officer of the Guard, they burnt the George Tavern on the Neck;[15] & have every Day since been cannonading us from their Lines both at Roxbury & Charlestown, but with no other Effect than the Loss of two

Men—On our Part except straggling Fires from the small Arms about the Lines which we endeavour to restrain, we have made little or no Return.[16] Our Situation in the Article of Powder is much more alarming than I had the most distant Idea of. Having desired a Return to be made out on my Arrival, of the Ammunition, I found 303½ Bbbl's of Powder mentioned as in the Store: But on ordering a new Supply of Cartridges yesterday, I was informed to my very great Astonishment, that there was no more than 36 Bbbls of the Massachusetts Store, which with the Stock of Rhode Island, New Hampshire & Connecticut makes 9937 lb.[17] not more than 9 Rounds a Man: As there had been no Consumption of Powder since, that could in any Degree account for such a Deficiency, I was very particular in my Inquiries, & found that the Committee of Supplies, not being sufficiently acquainted with the Nature of a Return, or misapprehending my Request, sent in an Account of all the Ammunition, which had been collected by the Province so that the Report included not only what was in Hand, but what had been spent.[18] Upon discovering this Mistake, I immediately went up to confer with the Speaker of the House of Representatives, upon some Measures to obtain a Supply from the neighbouring Townships, in such a Manner, as might prevent our Poverty being known as it is a Secret of too great Consequence to be divulged in the general Court, some Individual of which might perhaps indiscreetly suffer it to escape him, so as to find its Way to the Enemy the Consequences of which, are terrible even in Idea[19]—I shall also write to the Governours of Rhode Island, & Connecticut, & the Committee of Safety in New Hampshire on this Subject, urging in the most forcible Terms, the Necessity of an immediate Supply if in their Power.[20] I need not enlarge on our melancholy Situation; it is sufficient that the Existence of the Army, & the Salvation of the Country, depends upon something being done for our Relief both speedy and effectual, & that our Situation be kept a profound Secret.[21]

In the Inclosures (No. 2 & 3) I send the Allowance of Provisions &c., made by the Provinces of Connecticut & Massachusetts, the Mode & Quantity are different from what has fallen within my Experience, & I am confident must prove very wasteful, & expensive. If any Alteration can be safely made, (which I much doubt) there might be a great Saving to the publick.[22]

A Gentleman of my Family, assisted by a Deserter who has some Skill in Fortification, has by my Direction sketch'd out two Draughts of our respective Lines, at Charles Town & Roxbury, which with the Explanations will convey some Idea of our Situation, and I hope prove acceptable to the Members of the honourable Congress. They are the Inclosures (No. 4 & 5).[23]

Since I had the Honour of addressing you last, I have been applied to, by a Committee of the General Court for a Detachment of the Army, to protect the Inhabitants of the Eastern Parts of this Province, from some apprehended Depredations on their Coasts—I could have wish'd to have complied with their Request but after due Consideration, & consulting the General Officers, together with those Members of Congress, who are here, I thought it my Duty to excuse myself. The Application, & my Answer are the Inclosures No. 6 & 7 which I hope will be approved by the honourable Congress.[24]

Since I began this Letter, the Original of which the Inclosure No. 8 is a Copy, fell into my Hands; as the Writer is a Person of some Note in Boston, & it contains some Advices of Importance not mentioned by others, I thought proper to forward it as I received it. By comparing the Handwriting with another Letter, it appears the Writer is one Belcher Noyes, a Person probably known to some of the Gentlemen Delegates from this Province; who can determine from his Principles & Character what Credit is due to him.[25]

The Army is now formed into three grand Divisions, under the Command of the Generals Ward Lee & Puttnam. Each Division into two Brigades, consisting of about 6 Regiments each, commanded by Generals Thomas, & Spencer at Roxbury; Heath at Cambridge, Sullivan & Green at Winter Hill.[26] By this you will please to observe, there is a Deficiency of one Brigadier General, occasioned by Mr Pomroys not acting under his Commission, which I beg may be filled up as soon as possible.[27] I observe the Honbe Congress have also favoured me with the Appointment of three Brigade Majors; I presume they have, or intend to appoint the rest soon, as, they cannot be unacquainted that one is necessary to each Brigade, & in a new raised Army it will be an Office of great Duty & Service.[28]

General Gage has at length liberated the People of Boston, who land in Numbers at Chelsea every Day, the Terms on which the Passes are granted as to Money Effects & Provisions correspond with Mr Noyes's Letter.[29]

We have several Reports that General Gage is dismantling Castle William and bringing all the Cannon up to Town, but upon a very particular Inquiry, Accounts are so various that I cannot ascertain the Truth of it.[30]

I am sorry to be under a Necessity of making such frequent Examples among the Officers where a Sense of Honour, & the Interest of their Country might be expected to make Punishment unnecessary. Since my last, Capt. Parker of Massachusetts for Frauds both in Pay, & Provisions, & Capt. Gardiner of Rhode Island for Cowardice in running away from his Guard on an Alarm, have been broke.[31] As nothing can be more fatal to an Army, than Crimes of this kind; I am determined by every Motive of Reward & Punishment to prevent them in future.

On the first Instt a Chief of the Cagnewaga Tribe, who lives about 6 Miles from Montreal, came in here, accompanied by a Col: Bayley of Cohoss. His Accounts of the Temper & Disposition of the Indians, are very favourable. He says they have been strongly sollicited by Govr Carlton, to engage against us, but his Nation is totally averse: Threats, as well as Intreaties have been used without Effect. That the Canadians are well disposed to the English Colonies, and if any Expedition is meditated against Canada the Indians in that Quarter will give all their Assistance. I have endeavoured to cherish these favourable Dispositions, & have recommended to him to cultivate them on his Return. What I have said, I enforced with a Present which I understood would be agreeable to him, and as he is represented to be a Man of Weight, & Consequence in his own Tribe: I flatter myself his Visit will have a good Effect. His Accounts of Govr Carltons Force & Situation at St Johns correspond with what we have already had from that Quarter.[32]

The Accession of Georgia, to the Measures of the Congress is a happy Event & must give a sincere Pleasure to every Friend of America.

August 5th.

We have Accounts this Morning of two Explosions at the Castle, so that its Destruction may now be supposed certain.[33]

I have this Morning been alarmed with an Information that two Gentlemen from Philada [(]Mr Hitchbourn & Capt. White) with Letters for General Lee & my⟨se⟩lf have been taken by Capt. Ayscough at Rhode Island, the Letters intercepted & sent forward to Boston with the Bearers as Prisoners. That the Captain exulted much in the Discoveries he had made & my Informer who was also in the Boat but released understood them to be the Letters of Consequence.[34] I have therefore dispatch'd the Express immediately back, tho' I had before resolved to detain him till Fessendens Return.[35] I shall be anxious till I am relieved from the Suspence I am in as to the Contents of those Letters.

It is exceedingly unfortunate that Gentlemen should chuse to travel the only Road on which there is Danger. Let the Event of this be what it will I hope it will serve as a general Caution against trusting any Letters that Way in future.

Nothing of Consequence has occurr'd in the Camp these two Days. The Inhabitants of Boston continue coming out at Chelsea but under a new Restriction that no *Men* shall come out without special Licence which is refused to all Mechanicks since the Tory Labourers were taken at the Light House.[36] I have the Honou⟨r to⟩ be Sir, Your most Obed. obliged & very Hbble Servt

Go: Washington

LS, in Joseph Reed's writing, DNA:PCC, item 152; Df, NHi: Joseph Reed Papers; LB, DLC:GW; copy, DNA:PCC, item 169; copy, NjMoNP; Varick transcript, DLC:GW. The LS is endorsed "Read before Congress Septr 13th" (*JCC*, 2:246). The draft is endorsed "Sent by Alexander," and the letter-book copy includes the memorandum "Sent by Alexandr the Express."

1. Hancock sent GW 550 more blank commissions on 26 September.

2. For a discussion of the controversy surrounding John Thomas's commission as brigadier general, see James Warren and Joseph Hawley to GW, 4 July 1775, n.1. Thomas served as a brigade commander at Roxbury throughout the siege of Boston and led the troops that seized Dorchester Heights in March 1776. Promoted to major general on 6 Mar. 1776, Thomas took command of the American army at Quebec on 1 May and died of smallpox a month later at Sorel.

3. The draft here includes the sentence "In New Hampshire the General Officers have no Regiments, nor the Field Officers Companies." This sentence also appears in the letter-book copy and the Varick transcript.

4. Congress recommended in late September that no attempt be made to establish a uniform system of commissioning officers until the army was reorganized for the coming year (Hancock to GW, 26 Sept. 1775). Before receiv-

ing that answer, however, GW acted on his own authority to end the practice of holding multiple commissions. See GW to Hancock, 21 Sept. 1775.

5. Congress resolved on 20 Sept. that Richard Gridley be commissioned only as a colonel in the Continental army (*JCC*, 2:256; Hancock to GW, 26 Sept. 1775). On 17 Nov. Gridley was replaced as commander of the artillery regiment by Henry Knox (*JCC*, 3:358–59).

6. No changes were made in the regiments until the army was rearranged for the next year (Hancock to GW, 26 Sept. 1775).

7. GW took this number from the general return of the army for 22 July 1775, which reports as wanting to complete the army: 131 sergeants, 102 drummers and fifers, and 2,064 privates. The general return for 29 July, enclosed in this letter, shows 124 sergeants, 105 drummers and fifers and 2,079 privates needed to bring the regiments to their authorized strengths. Both returns are in DNA: RG 93, Revolutionary War Rolls, 1775–83.

8. The Massachusetts council formally approved Paul Dudley Sargent's commission as colonel on 3 Oct. 1775 (GW to the Massachusetts Council, 4 Sept. 1775; Massachusetts Council to GW, 3 Oct. 1775).

9. A copy of the enclosed return, dated 29 July 1775 and signed by Horatio Gates as adjutant general, is in DNA: RG 93, Revolutionary War Rolls, 1775–83. An abstract of the return is in DNA:PCC, item 169. The most deficient Massachusetts regiments listed are those commanded by Jonathan Brewer, Ephraim Doolittle, Benjamin Ruggles Woodbridge, and William Prescott. The Connecticut, New Hampshire, and Rhode Island contingents are not broken down into regiments in the return. The total force reported present and fit for duty in the army around Boston, including both officers and enlisted men, is 13,899. With the sick and furloughed soldiers added, the total strength is 16,898.

10. For GW's order regarding the preparing of barracks for winter, see General Orders, 26 July 1775. In September Congress directed GW to "Take the proper Steps to provide your Troops with necessary Cover and Fuel for the Winter" (Hancock to GW, 26 Sept. 1775).

11. "This Morning," Joseph Reed wrote to Artemas Ward at 9:00 A.M. on 30 July 1775, "a Detachmt of Riffle Men surprized the Enemies Guard . . . on Charles Town Neck—& brought off two Prisoners, but they give no particular Information but what we have had before: It is supposed that two of their Men were killed, not one on our Side was either killed or wounded" (MHi: Ward Papers). See also Thomas Mifflin to Artemas Ward, 30 July 1775, MHi: Ward Papers, and GW to James Warren, 30 July 1775, n.3.

12. "Four Captains and a Subaltern," James Warren wrote to John Adams on 9 Aug. 1775, "were killed the beginning of last week cheifly by the rifle men, and I am persuaded they will do great Execution" (Taylor, *Papers of John Adams*, 3:114–16).

13. Both the draft and letter-book copy read "32 Marines & a Subaltern." On 22 July 1775 Vice Admiral Samuel Graves "ordered an Officer of Marines and thirty Men from the *Preston* and *Boyne*" to protect the laborers on the Lighthouse Island. "With this Party," Graves wrote, "the Engineers were of

opinion the Light House might well be defended, until Succours arrived, against 1000 men, and the Admiral expected to have the Building soon repaired and a Light shewn as before" (Graves's narrative, 22 July 1775, in Clark, *Naval Documents*, 1:950).

14. For a discussion of Maj. Benjamin Tupper's attack on Lighthouse Island on 31 July, see General Orders, 1 Aug. 1775, n.1. Tupper reported the casualties to Horatio Gates on 3 Aug.: "I find by examination that we killed Six persons on the spot one of which was A Leiutt that we have 5 merines and one Torey in the Hospital that one Died of his wounds before he arrived to Roxbury that one women & a Lad is still at Dorchester, so that ading the 15, above mentioned to the 38 which General [Artemas] Ward sent over to Cambridge makes 53 killd & taken. Majr [John] Crane with his feildpeice which was planted on Nantasket Beach to cover our Retreat Sunk one of their Boats, and probably killd Sundry of their crews as the Enemy approchd within 200 yards. on our side we lost one man only, had two just graizd with Balls, we stove one of our Boats & was oblidgd to leave it, we lost Seven small arms part of which were lost in Landing as the rocks were very steep some of the party Slipt in & let go their guns to save themselves and we have 25 small arms and Accutriments brought off with us and concive there were more taken but have been secreted by some of the party" (DLC:GW).

15. The George Tavern was burned on the night of 30 July. The officer of the guard was Capt. Christopher Gardner, Jr., of Rhode Island. See General Orders, 31 July 1775, n.2.

16. See General Orders, this date.

17. The draft and letter-book copy read "9940 lb."

18. GW apparently is referring to the undated return in DLC:GW that begins "Agreeable [to] your Excellencys desire the Committee of Supplies for the Colony of the Massachusetts Bay—Offer the following as a general state of the Ordinance & Ordinance stores Provided by them for the use of the Forces raised by this Colony." There follows a detailed list of various artillery pieces, shells, musket balls, gunpowder, and other items of military equipment. The information that only thirty-six barrels of gunpowder remained in the Massachusetts supply is in the letter that the committee of supplies wrote to GW on 1 August.

19. On 4 Aug. the Massachusetts General Court appointed a committee of nine men to collect gunpowder from various towns in the eastern part of the colony, leaving each town only a small quantity for its use. The committee was also empowered to take gunpowder from any other towns where it was available and to purchase it from any private person who had any for sale ("Mass. Council Journal," July 1775–Feb. 1776 sess., 45–46; *Mass. House of Rep. Journal*, July–Nov. 1775 sess., 42–43).

20. See GW's letters of this date to Nicholas Cooke, Jonathan Trumbull, Sr., and the New Hampshire Committee of Safety.

21. On 18 Sept. Congress resolved "that a (secret) Committee be appointed to contract and agree for the importation and delivery of any quantities of gunpowder, not exceeding, in the whole five hundred tons" and "that in case such a quantity of gunpowder cannot be obtained, then to contract for the

importation of as much saltpetre with a proportionable quantity of sulphur, as with the powder they may procure will make up the quantity of five hundred tons" (*JCC*, 2:253).

22. The rations for Massachusetts troops are specified in a resolution of the Massachusetts provincial congress dated 10 June 1775 (enclosure number 2), and those for Connecticut troops in an order of the Connecticut general assembly dated May 1775 (enclosure number 3). Both documents are in DNA:PCC, item 152. See also *Mass. Prov. Congress Journals*, 317–18, and Hinman, *Historical Collection*, 173. The daily ration for each Massachusetts soldier consisted of 1 pound of bread, ½ pound each of beef and pork, 1 pint of milk or 1 gill of rice, 1 quart of spruce or malt beer, and 1 gill of peas or beans "or other Sauce equivalent." If pork was unavailable, the meat ration was to be 1¼ pounds of beef, and once every week 1¼ pounds of salt fish were to be substituted for the meat. In addition, each man was allowed 6 ounces of butter and ½ pint of vinegar each week. One pound of common soap a week was allotted to six men. The Connecticut daily ration for each man was ¾ of a pound of pork or 1 pound of beef, 1 pound of bread or flour, 3 pints of beer "or Spruce Sufficient," and 1 pint of milk. Fish was to be substituted for the daily meat ration three times a week. Each man was also to receive every week ½ pint of rice or 1 pint of meal, 6 ounces of butter, and 3 pints of peas or beans. Each company had a weekly allowance of 9 gallons of molasses, 3 pounds of candles, 24 pounds or 4 shillings worth of soap, 2 gallons of vinegar, 6 pounds of chocolate, and 3 pounds of sugar. A gill of rum was allowed for each man on fatigue days. For the Continental rations, see General Orders, 8 Aug. 1775.

23. John Trumbull, who became an aide-de-camp to GW on 27 July, drew these maps. Enclosure number 4 is a "Plan of Lines at Roxbury," and enclosure number 5 is a "General Sketch of the Lines at Charlestown, Prospect Hill & Roxbury." They are reproduced on pp. 234–37. Trumbull says in his autobiography that he scouted the British fortifications on Boston Neck "by creeping (under the concealment of high grass) so nigh that I could ascertain that the work consisted of a curtain crossing the entrance of the town, flanked by two bastions, one on the western and the other on the eastern side, and I had ascertained the number of guns mounted on the eastern, (their caliber was already known,) when my farther progress was rendered unnecessary by the desertion of one of the British artillerymen, who brought out with him a rude plan of the entire work" (Sizer, *Trumbull Autobiography*, 22).

24. Enclosure number 6 is a copy of the resolution on coastal defense that the Massachusetts General Court passed on 29 July. See GW to James Warren, 30 July 1775, n.2. Enclosure number 7 is a copy of GW's letter to James Warren of 30 July 1775, which is incorrectly dated 31 July. See GW to Warren, 30 July 1775, source note. Both enclosures are in DNA:PCC, item 152.

25. Belcher Noyes's letter, dated at Boston on 1 Aug. 1775, was addressed to his son Nathaniel Noyes at Andover. "Since the Battle at Charlestown," he wrote, "some conjecture the Destruction of this Town is intended, for what purpose can't determine. We are now got to the Beginning of August and nothing turns up in favor of America. The General Talk now is that the En-

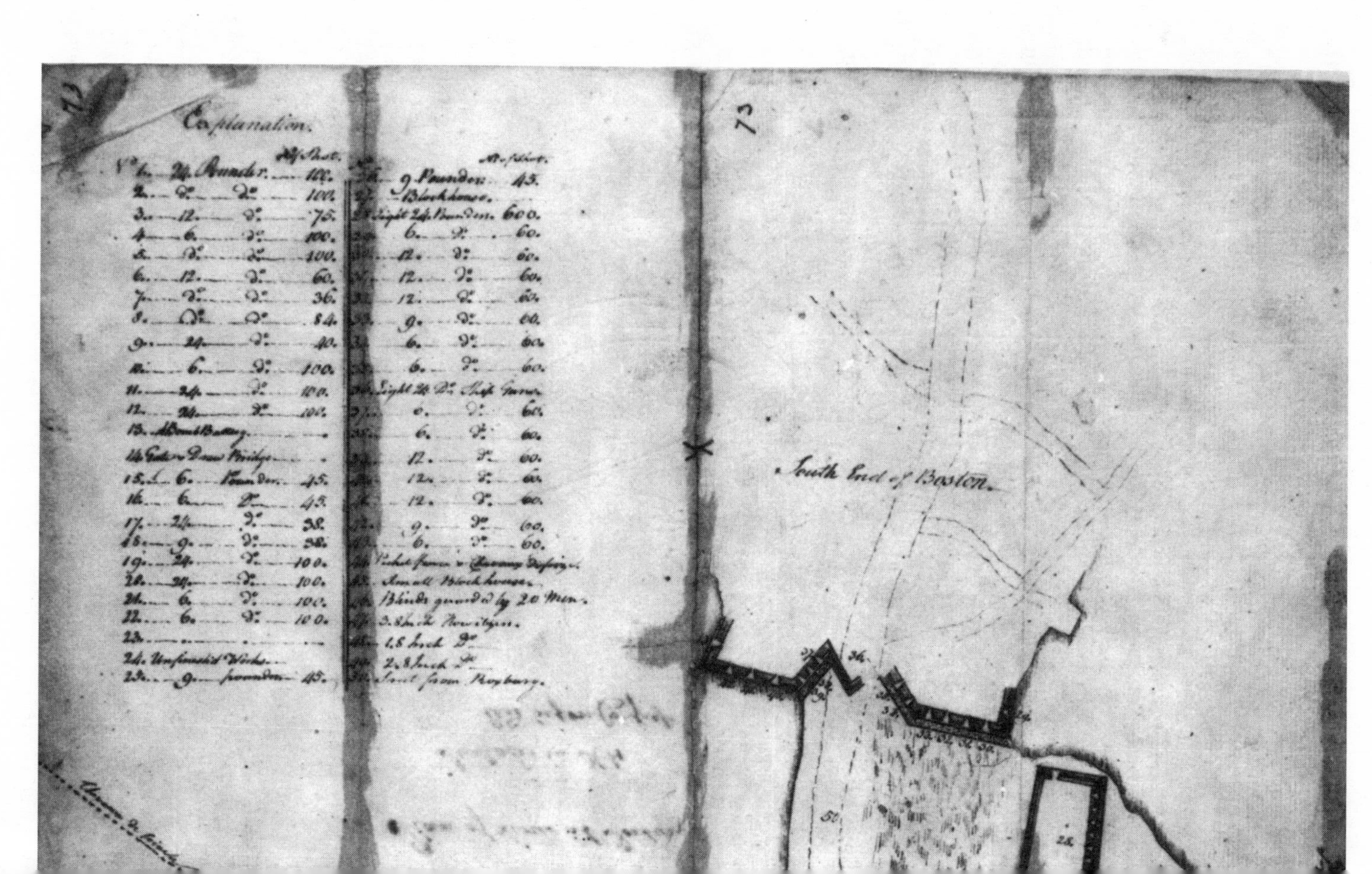
Explanation.
No. 1. 24 Pounder ... 100.
2. Do. Do. 100.
3. 12 Do. 75.
4. 6 Do. 100.
5. Do. Do. 100.
6. 12 Do. 60.
7. Do. Do. 36.
8. Do. Do. 84.
9. 24 Do. 40.
10. 6 Do. 100.
11. 24 Do. 100.
12. 24 Do. 100.
14. Gate & Draw Bridge
15. 6 Pounder 45.
16. 6 Do. 45.
17. 24 Do. 38.
18. 9 Do. 38.
19. 24 Do. 100.
20. 24 Do. 100.
21. 6 Do. 100.
22. 6 Do. 100.
23.
24. Unfinished Works.
25. 9 pounder 45.
9 Pounder 45.
Blockhouse.
Light 24 Pounders 600.
6 Do. 60.
12 Do. 60.
12 Do. 60.
12 Do. 60.
9 Do. 60.
6 Do. 60.
6 Do. 60.
6 Do. 60.
6 Do. 60.
12 Do. 60.
12 Do. 60.
12 Do. 60.
9 Do. 60.
6 Do. 60.
Small Blockhouse.
Blinds guarded by 20 Men.
Road from Roxbury.
73
South End of Boston.

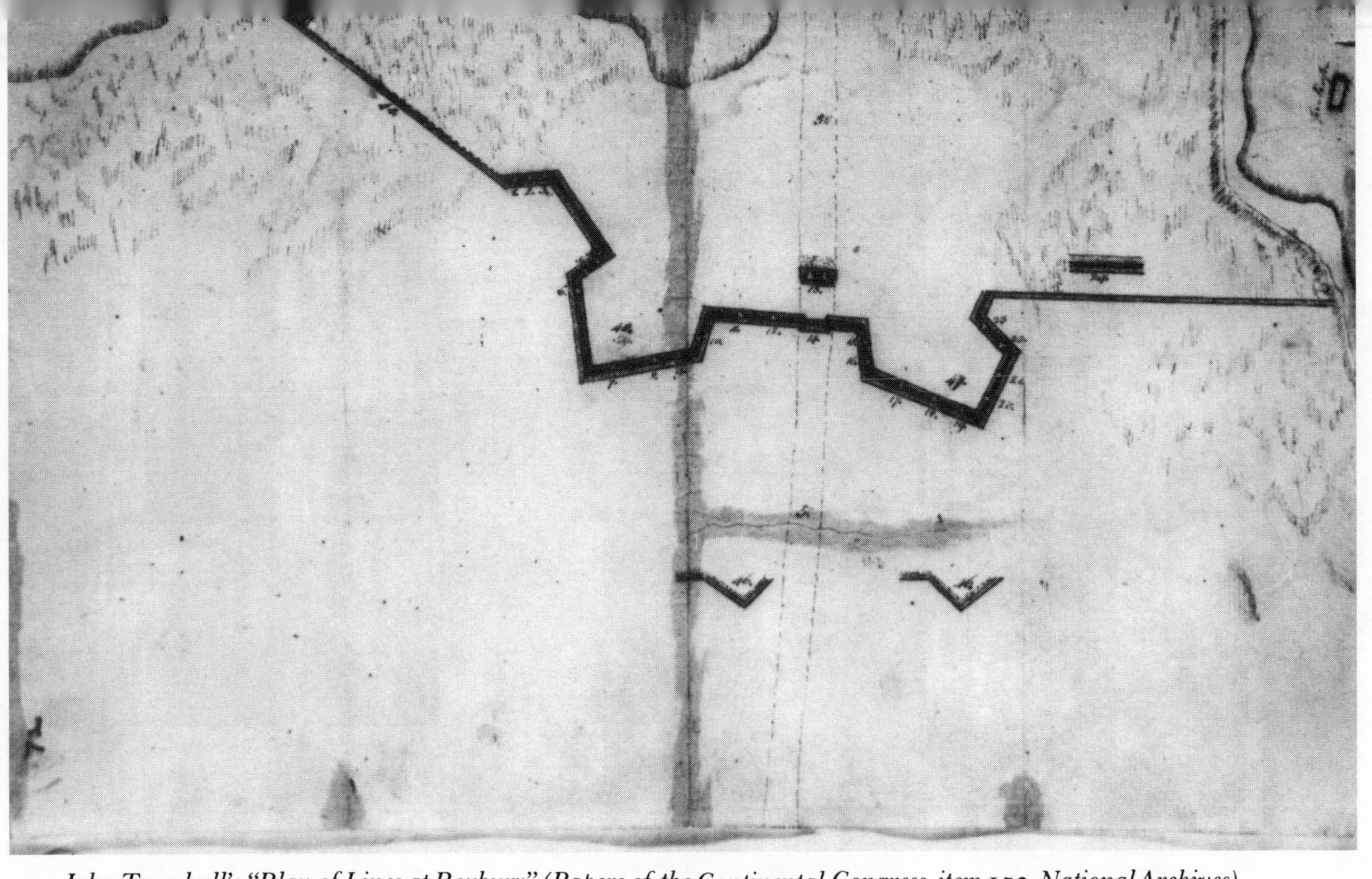

John Trumbull's "Plan of Lines at Roxbury" (Papers of the Continental Congress, item 152, National Archives).

74

Explanation.

No. 1. — Enemy's Lines on Bunker's Hill.
2. — Plowd Hill.
3. — Lines & Redoubt on Winter Hill.
4. — Lines & Redoubts on Prospect Hill.
5. — Redoubts on the Low Land.
6 & 7. — Redoubts towards the point.
8. — Town of Cambridge.
9. — Lechmere Point.
10. — Redoubt at Sewall's Point.
11. — Lines at Mill Creek Roxbury.
12. — Fort on Meetinghouse Hill.
13. — Redoubt on a Hill, Commanding the former
14. — Lines in the Swat leading to the Neck.
15. — Advanced Line nigh the George tavern.
16. — Lines & Redoubts at Dorchester Neck
17. — Enemies Advanced Lines on the Neck.
18. — Block house.
19. — Old fortification at the Entrance of the Town.
20. — Redoubt on Fox Hill.
21. — Beacon Hill strongly fortified.
22. — Battery on Cop's Hill.
23. — Ruins of Charlestown
24. — Small Transport Ship mounting 6 or 8 Guns.
25. — Large Ship in Charlestown ferry way.

John Trumbull's "General Sketch of the Lines at Charlestown, Prospect Hill & Roxbury" (Papers of the Continental Congress, item 152, National Archives).

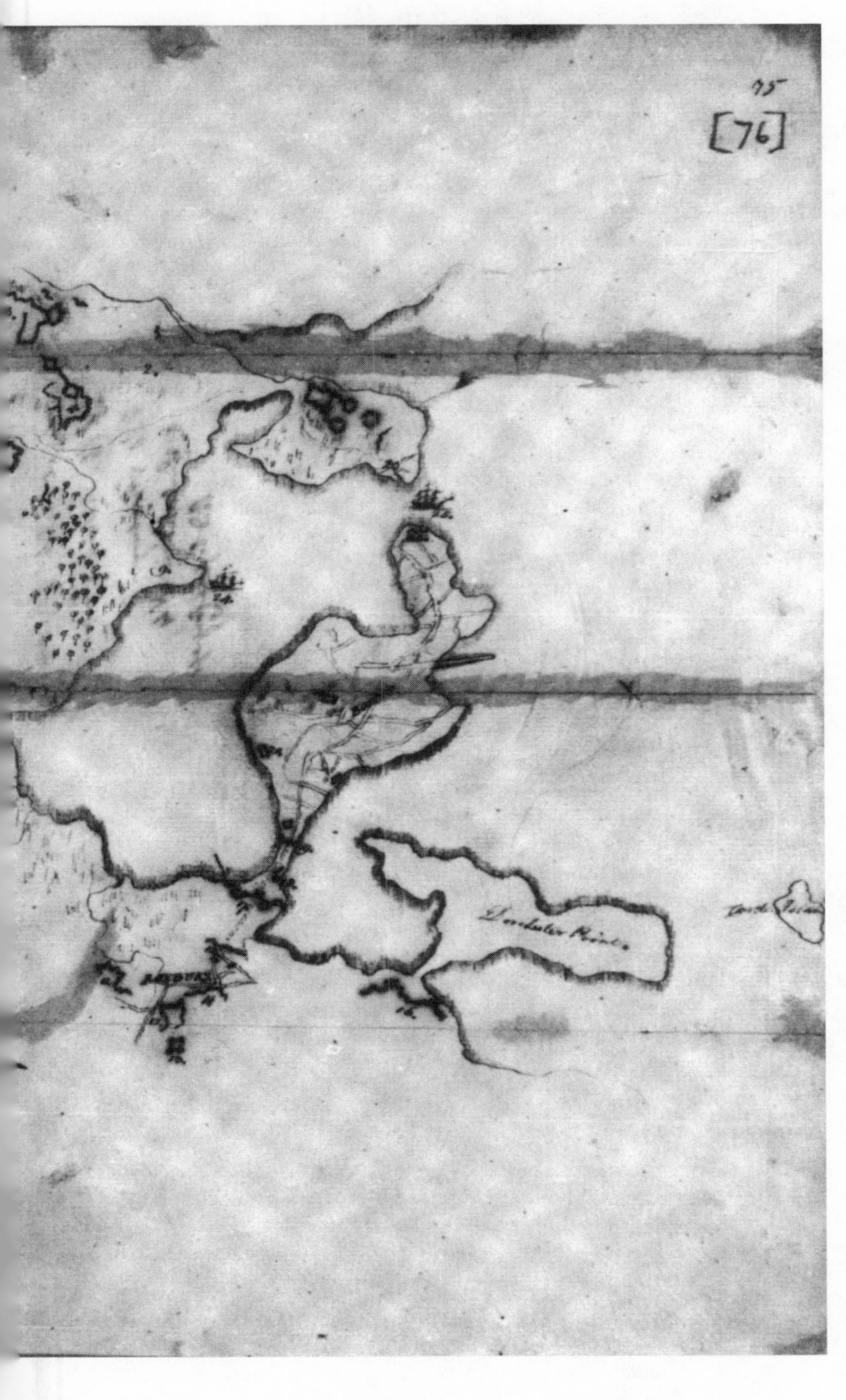
75
[76]
Dorchester Point

glish Troops are going to leave this Town, this seems evident from several things that are taking place; Vizt General Gage's family are going to England: Messrs [Robert] Auchmuty, [Jonathan] Sewall, &c., & others of that Stamp are going some to England and else where—I am pretty Confident the Army can't be Supported in this Town the ensuing Winter—Provisions Scarce and bad, no fuel, nor Money. People are jealous they will plunder and demolish the Town when they go off. . . . The Dysentery has prevail'd in this Town & been very mortal especially among Children also among the Soldiers of whom near 30 are buried in a Week as the Sextons say. . . . No Bells are permitted to toll for any Funerals on Account of the Sickness and Mortality among the Soldiers. . . . Since April 19. there have died of the Army including what were Slain in Battle June 17. near 2500, so that what Troops have arrived will not make good their Loss" (DNA:PCC, item 152). GW received the original of this letter from Loammi Baldwin (Baldwin to GW, 2 Aug. 1775). Belcher Noyes (c.1708–1785) operated an apothecary shop in Boston for many years.

26. For GW's reorganization of the Continental army around Boston, see General Orders, 22 July 1775.

27. For GW's recommendations for this brigadier general, see his letter to Hancock of 31 Aug. 1775. Joseph Frye was chosen for the position by Congress on 10 Jan. 1775 (*JCC*, 4:47).

28. For the appointments of the six brigade majors, see General Orders, 15, 17, and 30 Aug. 1775.

29. "Last Week," Belcher Noyes wrote in his letter of 1 Aug. to his son Nathaniel, "there was a Notification posted up, that all those who were desirous to leave the Town to give in their Names to James Urquhart Town Major, & in two days time upwards of 2000 entered their Names, & passes are now granted with this Adition to the former restriction—vizt No Plate of any kind, nor more money than £5—Sterling—The rout is by way of Winnisimmett" (DNA:PCC, item 152).

30. Belcher Noyes informed his son: "The Light House was burnt as it is Said by Order of the Continental Congress, and in Return for that Compliment they are dismounting Castle William, I beleive for want of Men to defend it" (Noyes to Nathaniel Noyes, 1 Aug. 1775, DNA:PCC, item 152). This and other reports of the destruction of the fort were false. See note 33.

31. For Capt. Oliver Parker's court-martial, see General Orders, 2 Aug. 1775. For the court-martial of Capt. Christopher Gardner, Jr., see General Orders, 31 July and 2 Aug. 1775.

32. The chief of the Caughnawaga tribe was Colonel Louis (Lewis), who was interviewed by a committee of the Massachusetts General Court on 3 Aug. (*Mass. House of Rep. Journal*, July–Nov. 1775 sess., 35–36). Several months after this visit to Cambridge, the Caughnawaga signed a peace treaty with Schuyler, promising to remain neutral in the struggle between the colonies and the mother country, but on 13 Jan. 1776 Colonel Louis and twelve other Caughnawaga arrived at Cambridge and expressed a desire to take up arms on behalf of the colonies. The Caughnawaga agreed to join the Continental army in Canada if called on by the Americans (GW to Schuyler,

27 Jan., 1 Feb. 1776). Although the Caughnawaga apparently were not asked to participate in the Canadian campaign, they remained on good terms with the Americans throughout the war. In 1779 GW referred to Colonel Louis as "my old friend . . . who I know is sensible, & beleive to be honest" (GW to Schuyler, 21 May 1779), and on one occasion during GW's Presidency, Colonel Louis dined with him in Philadelphia (Dorothy Twohig, ed., *The Journal of the Proceedings of the President, 1793–1797* [Charlottesville, 1981], 49). Jacob Bayley (1728–1815) lived at Newbury, Vt., in the area along the Connecticut River generally known as Coos (Cohos). He later became a brigadier general in the New Hampshire militia and a Continental deputy quartermaster general.

33. Castle William was not destroyed until the British evacuated Boston the following March (GW to Joseph Reed, 25 Mar. 1776).

34. Benjamin Hichborn (1746–1817), a young lawyer from Boston, was captured on 31 July when the packet boat on which he was crossing Narragansett Bay ran aground while being chased by the British sloop *Swan*, commanded by Capt. James Ayscough. During a visit to Philadelphia earlier in July, Hichborn begged several members of Congress, John Adams in particular, to give him letters to carry to Massachusetts as evidence of his patriotism. Having served some years before as a law clerk under Samuel Fitch, a well-known Loyalist, Hichborn was, he told Adams, "suspected and represented as a Tory, and this Reputation would be his ruin, if it could not [be] corrected, for nobody would employ him at the Bar" (Butterfield, *Adams Diary and Autobiography*, 3:319). Among the letters that Hichborn took with him was one of 21–24 July 1775 from Benjamin Harrison to GW (see source note for that document) and two of 24 July 1775 from John Adams, one to his wife Abigail and the other to James Warren. See Butterfield, *Adams Family Correspondence*, 1:255–58, and Taylor, *Papers of John Adams*, 3:89–93. Hichborn failed to destroy the letters when he had the opportunity immediately before and after his capture (Hichborn to Adams, 28 Oct. 1775, in Taylor, *Papers of John Adams*, 3:255–57). His captors soon discovered the letters and sent them and Hichborn to Vice Admiral Samuel Graves at Boston. Harrison's letter and Adams's two were printed in the *Massachusetts Gazette: and the Boston Weekly News-Letter* on 17 Aug. 1775. Hichborn remained prisoner on Graves's flagship, the *Preston*, until he escaped on the night of 18 Oct. 1775. While Adams and Warren forgave Hichborn for his blundering, GW apparently did not. See Hichborn to Adams, 28 Oct. and 25 Nov.–10 Dec. 1775, in Taylor, *Papers of John Adams*, 3:255–57, 320–27, and GW to James Warren, 6 Aug. 1775.

35. The express rider was Alexander. See source note.

36. Belcher Noyes wrote in a postscript to his letter of 1 Aug. to his son Nathaniel: "Since I finished this Letter, Passes are deny'd to *Men* without Special Leave" (DNA:PCC, item 152).

To a Committee of the Massachusetts Council

Gentn Camp at Cambridge Augt 4th 1775.

Inclosed you have an Extract of such parts of my Instruction's as I conceive you want to be informed in[1]—I did not know whether, as the proceedings of the Congress are not yet made publick, how far I was at liberty to communicate what I have—further I cannot go at present. I beg the favour of you to make a tender of my best respects to your honourable board & do me the justice to believe that I am Gentn Yr Most Obedt & Mo⟨st⟩ H. Ser.

Go: Washington

P.S. There are now at this place two or three Surgeons from Philadelphia, very powerfully recommended to me by some of the Delegates of the Continental Congress to be provided for; if you should want such, & will signify the same I will inform them thereof—they are strangers to me, but have the appearance of Gentlemen & strongly recommended as men of knowledge in their profession.[2] Yrs &ca

G. W——n

ALS (photocopy), DNA: RG 93, Photographic Copies of State Records, c.1775–83. The cover is addressed to "The Honble Mr Greenleaf, Mr Winthrop, & Mr Palmer [at] Watertown."

1. On 2 Aug. the Massachusetts council "ordered, that Mr [Benjamin] Greenleaf, Mr [John] Winthrop & Mr [Joseph] Palmer be a Committee, to wait on his Excellency, General Washington, and to request him to inform this Board of the Extent of the Powers delegated to him by the Honourable Continental Congress" (copy in Perez Morton's writing, DLC:GW). See Instructions from the Continental Congress, 22 June 1775.

2. These unidentified surgeons may have been protégés of Dr. William Shippen, Jr. See Richard Henry Lee to GW, 29 June 1775.

To Lewis Morris

Dr Sir, Camp at Cambridge Augt 4th 1775.

I have been favoured with your Letter of the 18th Ulto by Messrs Ogdan & Burr, & wish it was in my power to do that justice to the merits of those Gentlemen which you think them entitled to—whenever it is, I shall not be unmindful of your recommendations[1]—The two or three appointments with which I have been honour'd by the Congress were partly engaged before I receiv'd your Letter, & you will please to recollect, that the Ultimate appointment of all other Officers, is vested in the Governments in which the Regiments were originally raised; I can venture to pronounce therefore, that few Commissions in this army will be disposed of out of the four New England Governments; the good policy & justice of which, you may judge of as well as I can: As Volunteers from any other Colonies however deserving they may be of notice, or to be considered on acct of the Expenc⟨e⟩ which they are run to, will stand little chance whilst their is an application from any Person of the Government from whence the Regiment came. admitting this to be the case, & I believe hardly any one will doubt it, had not the Congress better reserve these appointments in their own hands? it will be putting the matter upon a much larger bottom, and giving merit a better chance; nor do I see any Inconvenience arising from it, as it is highly presumable that during the continuance of these disturbances the Congress will be chiefly sitting, or acting by a Committee, from whence Commissions might be as easily obtained as from a Provencial Assembly or Congress—I have taken the liberty of suggesting this matter, as I conceive the Service will be infinitely promoted thereby; as merit only, without a regard to Country, will entitle a Man to preferment when, & so often as vacancy's may happen—Having wrote fully to the Congress respecting the State of publick affairs I shall refer you to that Letter[2] & am with great regard Dr Sir Yr Most Obedt Hble Servt

Go: Washington

ALS, NjP: Aaron Burr Manuscripts from the C. P. G. Fuller Collection. The cover is addressed "To Colo. Lewis Morris of New York—now at Philadelphia."

Lewis Morris (1726–1798), a wealthy landowner who lived at Morrisania in Westchester County, N.Y., was a New York delegate in the Continental Congress from May 1775 to April 1777. On 27 May 1775 he was appointed with GW and others to the committee charged with supplying the colonies with ammunition and military stores, and during the New York campaign of 1776, he took a leave of absence from Congress to serve under GW as a brigadier general of the Westchester County militia.

1. Morris's letter of 18 July 1775 to GW has not been found. For John Hancock's recommendation of Aaron Burr and Matthias Ogden, see Hancock to GW, 19 July 1775.

2. See GW to Hancock, 4–5 Aug. 1775.

To the New Hampshire Committee of Safety

Gentlemen Camp at Cambridge August 4th 1775

Your publick Capacity, & the Hope that you will be both able & willing, to give us some Assistance, has led me to make this Application. The Situation of the Army, as to Ammunition, is by no Means what it ought to be. We have great Reason to suspect, the Enemy very soon intend to bombard our Lines; & our Stock of Powder is so small, as in a great Degree to make our heavy Artillery useless. I must therefore request you will exert yourselves to forward, whatever can be spared from your Province, as soon as possible. The Necessity is great, the Cause is of the last Importance; I am therefore perswaded, I need use no Arguments to quicken your Zeal. The smallest Quantities are not beneath Notice, as a considerable Stock may be formed from various Collections. Lead & Flints, are also very scarce, you will therefore furnish all you can spare—Next to making the Provision, its being seasonable is of great Importance, every Hour in our present Situation is critical.

Should there be any Arrivals in any Part of your Province, with this necessary Article I must request your forwarding all that can possibly be spared out of it. I am Gentlemen, very respectfully Your most obedt & very Hbble Servt

Go: Washington

LS, in Joseph Reed's writing, Nh-Ar; LB, DLC:GW; Varick transcript, DLC:GW.

To William Trent

Dr Sir, Camp at Cambridge Augt 4th 1775.

Your Letter of the 22d Ulto came to my hands a few days ago[1]—the hurry of business in which General Gates necessarily got Involved immediately upon his arrival at this Camp put your Memorandum out of his head; which was a matter of no consequence, as Colo. Mercer is already fully advertised of every circumstance relative to the Sale of his Estate.[2]

As I have none of the Papers with me, I cannot from Memory, recollect the particulars, or give answers to the sevl queries you have propounded; but, as I have before observed, a circumstantial acct was transmitted to the Colonel before I left Virginia in May. His Estate to the best of my recollection sold for upwards of £14,000 & was thought scarce sufficient to answer the Mortgages upon it in England & Virginia—it was sold at 12 Months Credit in November last, so that no Money will be due till next Novr; consequently none can be remitted sooner; & whether, in these times of publick distress & confusion, there can be any collection made I am unable to say. I am very glad to hear of the acquisition of Powder in So. Carolina[3]—& am Dr Sir Yr Most Obedt Hble Servt

Go: Washington

ALS, PHi: Etting Collection. The cover is addressed "To William Trent Esqr. at Trenton."

William Trent (1715–1787), an Indian trader and land speculator whom GW had known on the Pennsylvania frontier during the 1750s, was in London from the spring of 1769 to the spring of 1775, attempting to obtain royal confirmation of a large western land grant, first for the Indiana Company and later for the Grand Ohio or Vandalia Company. Those efforts failed, and on 21 April 1775 Trent sailed from London for Philadelphia. Formerly a resident of Lancaster and Carlisle, Pa., Trent made his home between 1768 and 1784 at Trenton, New Jersey. In 1776 the Indiana Company was reorganized, and Trent spent the remainder of the war years trying to make good the company's claim. He unsuccessfully petitioned the Virginia general assembly in 1779, and between 1779 and 1783 he presented several appeals to the Continental Congress, again without avail.

1. Trent's letter of 22 July 1775 to GW has not been found.

2. GW's friend and former comrade in arms George Mercer (1733–1784) now lived in England, where he had long been involved in various land speculation schemes. During the French and Indian War, Mercer served GW as both aide-de-camp and company commander. He became lieutenant colonel of Col. William Byrd's 2d Virginia Regiment in 1758 and participated in the Forbes campaign of that year. In 1763 Mercer went to London as agent for the Ohio Company, a position he held until 1770. He returned to Virginia in the fall of 1765 to be Stamp Act officer for the colony, but popular opposition to the act soon forced him to give up any hopes of carrying out his duties. Mercer subsequently decided to live in England and appointed GW trustee for his affairs in Virginia. In that capacity GW presided over the sale of Mercer's lands on Bull Run and in Frederick County during November 1774. See GW to George Mercer, 5 April 1775. Trent was interested in the sale of those lands, because he hoped that some of the proceeds would be used to repay the several hundred pounds that he loaned to Mercer earlier this year. That debt was never repaid. Mercer moved in August 1776 to Paris, where he lived at least until 1779. He died in London in April 1784.

3. South Carolina and Georgia Patriots captured a British vessel laden with gunpowder near Savannah between 8 and 10 July 1775. See Benjamin Harrison to GW, 21–24 July 1775, n.11.

To Jonathan Trumbull, Sr.

Sir Camp at Cambridge August 4th 1775

I am favoured [with][1] yours of the 31st July informing me that the new Levies were coming forward with all Expedition; As the Enemy has lain longer inactive than I expected I hope they will arrive in Time to give us their Assistance.[2]

My Last Letter from the Honble Continental Congress recommends my procuring from the Colonies of Rode Island & Connecticut a Quantity of Tow Cloth for the Purpose of making Indian or Hunting Shirts for the Men, many of whom are very destitute [of] Cloathing,[3] A Pattern is herewith sent you and I must request you[4] to give the necessary Directions throughout your Government that all the Cloath of the above kind may be bought up for this Use & suitable Persons set to work to make it up, As soon as any Number is made worth the Conveyance you will please to direct them to be forwarded, It is designed as a Species of Uniform—both cheap & convenient.

We have had no Transactions of any Consequence in the Camp since my last, but what are in the public Papers, & are related with tolerable Accuracy.

I am now sir, in strict Confidence to Acquaint you that our Necessaties in the Articles of Powder, Lead & Flints are so great as to require an immediate Supply—I must earnestly intreat you will fall upon some Measures to forward to us every Ounce in the Province that can possibly be spared, It is not within the Propriety or Safety of such a Correspondence to say what I might upon the Subject. It is sufficient that the Cause[5] loudly calls for the most strenuous Exertions[6] of every Friend to his Country and does not admit of the least Delay. No Quantity however small is beneath Notice & should any arrive I beg it may be forwarded to us as fast as possible.

This Express having left his horse at Hartford is under a Necessity of going that way. I am Sir, with much Regard Your Most Obedt Humble Servt

Go: Washington

LB, Ct: Trumbull Papers; Df, NHi: Joseph Reed Papers; LB, DLC:GW; Varick transcript, DLC:GW. The letter book in DLC:GW includes the notation "Sent ℔ Alexander the Express."

1. The word within the square brackets appears in both the draft and the letter-book copy in DLC:GW.

2. For the arrival of the two new Connecticut regiments, see General Orders, 9 Aug. 1775, and Trumbull to GW, 15 Sept. 1775.

3. See Hancock to GW, 24 July 1775. The word within the square brackets appears in both the draft and the letter-book copy in DLC:GW.

4. GW "sent a sample, with a cape ruffled" (Journal of the Connecticut council, 7 Aug. 1775, in Hinman, *Historical Collection*, 329).

5. Both the draft and the letter-book copy in DLC:GW read "the Case."

6. Both the draft and the letter-book copy in DLC:GW read "the warmest & most strenuous Exertions."

General Orders

Head Quarters, Cambridge, Augt 5th 1775

Parole, Westminster. Countersign Richmond

For the establishment of order, and to prevent disputes between Officers, as well for fixing a regular and proper distribution of the Commissions of the Continental Army, part of which are already arrived from the Congress and the rest hourly expected:[1] It is ordered, that a meeting of the Field Officers of each Brigade, be held to morrow Morning at Eight OClock,[2] as near as may be to the Center of the Encampment of each Brigade; who are to choose by Ballot, one out of their Body, to represent them in forming a Court, for the Adjustment and final settlement of First. The Rank of the Regiments of the Continental Army, and numbering of each Regiment accordingly; as all differences and distinctions are now to be laid aside; The Regiments of the several provinces that form the Continental Army, are to be considered no longer in a separate and distinct point of view, but as parts of the whole Army of the United provinces. Secondly. The Rank of all the Field Officers, of all the regiments forming the Continental Army. Thirdly. The Rank of all the Captains, Subalterns and Staff Officers; and as doubts may arise, which cannot be determin'd by the Six Field Officers so chosen by ballot; they are hereby directed, to choose by ballot, one Brigadier General, who will preside as Moderator of the Court, for finally settling the Rank of all the Corps, and all the Commission'd Officers, that compose the Army of the

United Colonies. This Court being duly constituted and appointed, are to sit on Monday Morning next, at Deacon Jones's, in Cambridge.[3]

The Church to be cleared to morrow, and the Rev'd Mr Doyles will perform Divine Service therein at ten OClock.[4]

Varick transcript, DLC:GW.

1. John Hancock sent GW an undetermined number of blank commissions with his letter of 28 June 1775, 284 with his letter of 24 July 1775, and 550 with his letter of 26 Sept. 1775.

2. Artemas Ward's orderly book reads "10 oClock" (MHi: Ward Papers).

3. Artemas Ward's orderly book reads "Deacon Jones's Tavern." The deacon may be Daniel Jones, who on 10 Aug. 1775 presented the Massachusetts house of representatives with an "Account for entertaining Captain *How's* Troop of Horse for the Reception of Generals *Washington* and *Lee*" (*Mass. House of Rep. Journal*, July–Nov. 1775 sess., 62). For the court's report, see General Orders, 20 Aug. 1775.

4. The church was apparently Cambridge's Christ Church which was used as a barracks by Connecticut troops during the siege of Boston.

From Jacob Duché

Sir Philadelphia, August 5th 1775

You will find by the inclosed, that I have taken the Liberty to inscribe to you a Sermon, which I lately preached to the First Battalion of our City commanded by Col. Dickinson; not doubting, but under the Sanction of your name, it will meet with the Public Candour.[1]

If the Manner in which I have treated the Subject should have the least good Influence upon the Hearts & Actions of the Military Freemen of America, or should add one more virtuous Motive to those, by which, I trust, they are already actuated, it will be the best Return I can receive from my Fellow-Citizens, for this little Labour of Love.

I have long been an Admirer of your amiable Character, and was glad of this Opportunity of paying you my little Tribute of Respect.

My Prayers are continually for you, and the brave Troops under your Command. O my dear General! Would to God a speedy and happy Reconciliation could be accomplished without the Effusion of one more Drop of valuable Blood[.] I know well, that your Humanity, and Christian Meekness, would ever prompt you to form the same benevolent Wish; and that the Love of Military Glory will in your Breast always give Way to the Love of Peace, when it can be virtuously and honourably obtained.

May Heaven crown all your truly Patriotic Undertakings with Success, cover your Head in the Day of Danger, and restore you unhurt to the Arms of your friends and your Country. I am, with the sincerest Esteem & Veneration Your Excellency's most obedient Humble Servant

Jacob Duché

ALS, DLC:GW.

Jacob Duché (1738–1798) of Philadelphia was rector of the united Anglican parishes of Christ Church and St. Peter's. One of the city's most popular preachers, he gave opening prayers for both the First and Second Continental Congresses, and on 9 July 1776 he was appointed chaplain to Congress. Duché resigned that office the following October, citing poor health and his parochial duties as his reasons. When the British occupied Philadelphia in 1777, they imprisoned Duché, but he promptly obtained his release by turning Loyalist. In a letter to GW of 8 Oct. 1777, he expressed strong misgivings about the Declaration of Independence and argued that the struggle against the British was both hopeless and needless. Duché sailed for England in December 1777 and became secretary and chaplain of an orphanage there. On 7 Aug. 1789 he wrote to GW begging permission to return to America. He arrived in Philadelphia in May 1792 and remained until his death a few years later.

1. This sermon, which Duché preached on 7 July 1775, was printed soon afterwards by James Humphreys, Jr., of Philadelphia under the title of *The Duty of Standing Fast in Our Spiritual and Temporal Liberties* (Philadelphia, 1775). Duché dedicated it to GW "as a Small Tribute of Respect for His Many Amiable Virtues as well in Private as in Public Life."

To James Otis, Sr.

Sir Head Quarters [Cambridge] Augt 5th 1775

The Bearer Colo. Baldwin has this Morning reported that among others out of Boston, the Barrack Master's Wife came Yesterday; and is now detain'd at Malden[1]—As there may be Inconveniences, from Persons being Suffer'd indescriminately to go thro. the Country, many of whom, are undoubtedly disaffected to the Publick Interest: I have caused a Court of Inquiry to set upon several, but the Business multiplies so fast, and we are so much Strangers to the Characters, and Conduct of many, that I would wish to put it on some more proper Footing: especially as it takes Several Field Officers every day from their Duty—You will please Sir, to lay this Matter before the General Court that they may either appoint some proper Persons more Competent to this Business, or take such other Steps as shall appear to them likely to remedy this Mischief.[2] Colo. Baldwin is refer'd to the General Court for Directions respecting Mrs Goldthwait—I have the Honor to be Sir Your most Obedt Humbe Sert

Go: Washington

Since writing the above Col: Baldwin being impatient to return to his Post—General Gates will be the Bearer of this.[3]

LS, in Thomas Mifflin's writing, M-Ar; LB, DLC:GW; Varick transcript, DLC:GW.

James Otis, Sr. (1702–1778), father of the prominent Patriot orator and pamphleteer James Otis, Jr. (1725–1783), was elected to the new Massachusetts council on 21 July and became president of the council soon afterwards. A prosperous merchant and self-trained lawyer from Barnstable, the elder Otis held several powerful political offices before the Revolution, including a seat on the governor's council, a colonelcy in the militia, and judgeships on the probate court and the court of common pleas. Although Otis remained a member of the governor's council until the beginning of hostilities, he supported the American cause in Barnstable, and upon hearing of the Battle of Lexington he ordered the Barnstable militia to march to the aid of the Patriots. During the fall of 1775 Otis's health apparently began to fail, and he did not attend the council after 11 November.

1. Hannah Brigham Goldthwait, wife of Major Joseph Goldthwait, barrack master of the king's troops in Boston, landed at Winnisimmet ferry with two other women about five o'clock on the afternoon of 4 August. Loammi Baldwin escorted them to Watertown for investigation by the General Court, which freed Mrs. Goldthwait's companions on 7 Aug., after finding them to be no threat to the liberties of America. That same day the General Court directed Mrs. Goldthwait "to go to *Stafford*, to endeavour the Recovery of her Health, by Use of the Waters there . . . and afterwards to remove to *Rehoboth* to reside with her Brother, Mr. *Joseph Brigham*, there to be under the Care of the Committee of Correspondence of said Town (without any Expence to the Public)." Later in the month the General Court gave her permission to take the waters at Newtown rather than at Stafford (*Mass. House of Rep. Journal*, July–Nov. 1775 sess., 49, 52, 97; also in "Mass. Council Journal," July 1775–Feb. 1776 sess., 50, 53, 149). Her husband was proscribed and banished in 1778.

2. GW's letter was referred on 6 Aug. to a committee of both houses of the General Court, and on the following day it was resolved "that Joseph Greenleaf Esqr., Capt. Edward Proctor and Mr John Peck be a Committee whose

duty it shall be to give constant attendance at the place where the People coming out of Boston to Chelsea shall land, and strictly examine into the characters and circumstances of all such persons as may arrive from Boston at the said Chelsea; and if upon enquiry any of the said persons shall appear to be enemies to this Country, then the said Committee are directed to keep in custody all such suspected persons untill a proper representation shall be made to this Court, and order given thereon" ("Mass. Council Journal," July 1775–Feb. 1776 sess., 51; also in *Mass. House of Rep. Journal,* July–Nov. 1775 sess., 49–50).

3. The postscript is in Joseph Reed's writing.

From James Warren

Sir Watertown [Mass.] Augt 5. 1775

I am Just Informed that Mr Benja. Hitchburne A Young Gentn from Philadelphia has been Intercepted by A Capt. of one of the Men of War at Newport. who took from him two Letters to your Excellency, & one to Me. what they Contained I cant say—they have sent him A Prisoner to Boston and the Bearer says he is now in Goal there.[1] I could Wish any Method could be devised for his Liberation. he is A Native of Boston. & by profession A Lawyer. I am Sir with the Greatest Respect Your Excellencys Most Obedt Humbe Servt

Jas Warren

ALS, DLC:GW.

1. For a discussion of Benjamin Hichborn's capture by Capt. James Ayscough of the British sloop *Swan,* see GW to Hancock, 4–5 Aug. 1775, n.34. Only one letter to GW is known to have been taken with Hichborn: that of 21–24 July 1775 from Benjamin Harrison. See the source note for that document. The letter to Warren that fell into British hands was the one that John Adams wrote to him on 24 July 1775. See Taylor, *Papers of John Adams,* 3:89–93.

General Orders

Head Quarters, Cambridge, August 6th 1775.

Parole, Manchester. Countersign Lancaster.

Varick transcript, DLC:GW.

Letter not found: from Lieutenant Colonel Loammi Baldwin, 6 Aug. 1775. On the night of 6 Aug., Baldwin informed GW: "I wrote you a Scroll from Malding this afternoon."

Letter not found: to Lieutenant Colonel Loammi Baldwin, 6 Aug. 1775. On 6 Aug. Baldwin wrote to GW: "I have Just Receivd your Excellencies Letter of this Evening."

From Lieutenant Colonel Loammi Baldwin

Chelsea [Mass.] Augt 6th 1775

May it Please your Excellency Sunday Night 12 oClock

I wrote you a Scroll from Malding this afternoon[.][1] The hurry I was in to return back to Chelsea again, the Inconveniances for writing I hope will Excuse me.

I think it my duty to give your Excellency a more full & Particular account of this affair[.][2] Between 4 & 5 Clock I heard the report of Cannon from the floating Battery's & Soon found they were upon the move[.] I emediatly ordered all the Companies to turn out & March down toward the ferry (Winisimit I mean) & I would ride forward and make what Discoveries I could, which I did, When I came to Greens Hill Point, I saw the Buildings at Penny ferry in flames, I was then within Larg Muskit Shot of Bunker Hill, & not but about 20 rods from Malding Point Sentry Box, the mouth of a Larg Crick between, & to go round was 4 Miles, I turnd Back and came to the Men (3 companes only the other was about 1½ miles off towards Chelsea Beach) ordred a detachment of an officer & 20 Men to Join the Main Guard then at the ferry Ways and go emediatly up to the top of Greens Hill & watch the Motions of the enimy and if they Should attempt to land to Salute them with Powder & Ball in the most Vigourous maner[.] the Main body was at a Certain Corner in the road near the Ferry with orders for part (in case of an ingagement) to go to there assistance while the remaining few was to Assend a Neighbouring Hill to the eastward & Guard their Retreat[.] These Orders being given with all possable dispatch, I proceeded to Malding as quick as possable found that Capt. Lindsey was gone home, & his Company dispersd, all but a few with the Lieut. was down at the House that was Burnt[.] I went to him and enquired into the matter who Informd me that the Capt. was gone Home & near one half the Company was fled & where they were gone he could not tell, I ordred him to Rally his Company & Guard his Post which he Seem'd willing & ready to preform as far as Lay in his Power.[3]

The Floating Batterys & Boats were by this time got over to the Enimys Shore and a considerable number of Men Paraded on the Bank & Beach near the Boats[.] I was anxious to Return to Chelsea had an oppertunity to Write which I did by Mr Chamberlin who was able to give some more full account than what I wrote in so great a hurry, I then went back to Chelsea & ordered a Guard of about 20 Men Including Office[r]s to go up to Malding Point & plant a Sufficient number of Sentrys to Guard the Place also ordred all the Guards (at Chelsea) doubled. we have no less than 4 Guards here in diferent Places also ordred all the Officers & men to turn out tomorrow morning Just before Day[.] I hope to be one with them.

I came up from the ferry about 10 oClock this Evening was informd thire, that the Large flat Bottomd Boat & Bearge (that went full of Men with the floating Batterys to burn the House) was Returnd to Boston on the Ships Just in the Grey of the Evening.

I have Just Receivd your Excellencis Letter of this Evening which Mentions 50 Regulars Landing.[4] I cannot tell the number nor Certainly how the Houses were fired as Som People Say they Saw them Landed others Say they did not Land, but they saw the Corcare Set them on fire, but its my oppinion at Present that they Landed & set them on fire[.] your Excellency desires me to Make a Strict Enquiry into the Conduct of that Company which I was determined to do tomorrow & Shall Report.[5]

If your Excellency Should have occasion to proceed with any of that company would Humbly Beg you would not Stile them Such or Such a one in Colonel Gerrishes Regiment as I think they never Properly belongd to sd Regiment and was Returned only as doing duty in Said Regiment.

Hoping Soon to give Your Excellency a more full account I Remain your Excellencys most Humbe And Obediant Servnt

Loammi Baldwin Lut. Col.

ALS, DLC:GW. Baldwin apparently enclosed with this letter Joseph Leach's observations for 6 Aug. and possibly his observations dated 5 Aug., which are both in DLC:GW.

1. This letter has not been found.

2. "In the afternoon," Lt. Paul Lunt wrote in his journal entry for 6 Aug., "the Regulars went from Bunker's Hill and set fire to a house at Penny Ferry; they fired a number of cannon from their floating batteries, but did no dam-

age; we returned the fire and silenced them" ("Lunt's Book," 197). Penny ferry was directly across the Mystic River from Bunker Hill and a short distance upstream from Winnisimmet ferry.

3. Capt. Eleazer Lindsey was arrested on 8 Aug. for being absent from his post, and on 16 Aug. he was cashiered (Baldwin to GW, 8 Aug. 1775; General Orders, 16 Aug. 1775).

4. No letter to Baldwin from GW or any of his staff officers has been found for this day.

5. Baldwin is referring to Capt. Eleazer Lindsey's company. See note 3, and Baldwin to GW, 8 Aug. 1775.

From Jonathan Boucher

The Lodge, Aug. 6th, 1775.

Dear Sir,—I thought it far from the least pleasing circumstance attending my removal hither that it placed me in your immediate neighbourhood. For having now been happy in your acquaintance several years, I could not help considering myself, nor indeed help hoping that I was considered by you, as an old friend; and of course I counted on our living together in the pleasing intercourse of giving and receiving the mutual good offices of neighbourhood and friendship.

That things have turned out much otherwise I need not inform you. Mortified and grieved as I confess myself to be at this disappointment, I am by no means prepared to say that you are wholly to be blamed for it; nor, as I would fain hope you in your turn will own, is it entirely owing to any fault of mine. I can easily suppose at least that we neither of us think ourselves to blame; and yet I cannot help thinking that had I been in your place I should, in this as well as in other things, have taken a different part from that which you have chosen. Permit me, sir, as one who was once your friend, and at any rate as one not likely to be soon troublesome to you again in the same way, once more as a friend freely to expostulate with you. If I am still in the wrong, I am about to suffer such punishment as might satisfy the malice of even the most vindictive enemy; and if you are wrong, as in some degree I think you are, it is my duty frankly to tell you so, and yours to listen to me with patience.

On the great points so long and so fruitlessly debated between us it is not my design now again to solicit your attention. We have now each of us taken and avowed our side, and with such ardour as becomes men who feel themselves to be in earnest in their convictions. That we should both be in the right is impossible, but that we both think we are we must in common candour allow. And this extreme difference of opinion between ourselves, where we have no grounds for charging each other with being influenced by any sinister or unworthy motives, should teach us no less candour in judging of and dealing by others in a similar predicament. There cannot be anything named of which I am more strongly convinced than I am that all those who with you are promoting the present apparently popular measures are the true enemies of their country. This persuasion, however, will by no means justify me, should I be so weak and wicked as to molest them while they do not molest me. I do not say this because I happen to be in what is called the minority, and therefore without any power of acting otherwise; it is the decision of truth and justice, and cannot be violated without doing violence to every system of ethics yet received in any civilized country. The true plan in such cases is for each party to defend his own side as well as he can by fair argument, and also, if possible, to convince his adversary: but everything that savours of, or but approaches to, coercion or compulsion is persecution and tyranny.

It is on this ground that I complain of you and those with whom you side. How large a proportion of the people in general think with you or think with me it is in none of our powers to ascertain. I believe, because I think I can prove it, that your party, to serve an obvious party purpose, exceedingly magnify the numbers of those whom they suppose to take part with you, and you tax us with doing the same. But there is this great, manifest, and undisputed difference between us. No Tory has yet in a single instance misused or injured a Whig merely for being a Whig. And whatever may be the boasted superiority of your party, it will not be denied that in some instances at least this has been in our power. With respect to Whigs, however, the case has been directly the reverse; a Tory at all in the power of a Whig never escapes ill treatment merely because of his being a Tory. How contrary all this is to all that liberty which Whigs are for ever so forward to profess need not be insisted on; it is so contrary to all justice and honour, that were there no other reasons to determine me against it, as there are thousands, I would not be a Whig, because their principles, at least as I see them exemplified in practice, lead so directly to all that is mean and unmanly.

It is a general fault in controversial writers to charge all the errors of a party on every individual of that party. I wish to avoid the disgrace of so indiscriminate a judgment; and therefore have a pleasure in acknowledging that I know many Whigs who are not tyrants. In this number it is but doing you common justice to place you. I wish I could go on, and with equal truth declare that, whilst you forbear yourself to persecute your fellow subjects on the score of their political creeds, you had been as careful to discourage such persecution in others. Scorning to flatter, as much as I scorn to tax you wrongfully, I am bold thus openly to tell you I think you have much to answer for in this way. It is not a little that you have to answer for with respect to myself.

You know, and have acknowledged, the sincerity and the purity of my principles; and have been so candid as to lament that you could not think on the great points that now agitate our common country as I do. Now, sir, it is impossible I should sometimes avow one kind of principles and sometimes another. I have at least the merit of consistency; and neither in any private or public conversation, in anything I have written, nor in anything I have delivered from the pulpit, have I ever asserted any other opinions or doctrines than you have repeatedly heard me assert both in my own house and yours. You cannot say that I deserved to be run down, vilified, and injured in the manner which you know has fallen to my lot, merely because I cannot bring myself to think on some political points just as you and your party would have me think. And yet you have borne to look on, at least as an unconcerned spectator, if not an abettor, whilst, like the poor frogs in the fable, I have in a manner been pelted to death.[1] I do not ask if such conduct in you was friendly: was it either just, manly, or generous? It was not: no, it was acting with all the base malignity of a virulent Whig. As such, sir, I resent it: and oppressed and overborne as I may seem to be by popular obloquy, I will not be so wanting in justice to myself as not to tell you, as I now do with honest boldness, that I despise the man who, for any motives, could be induced to act so mean a part. You are no longer worthy of my friendship: a man of honour can no longer without dishonour be connected with you. With your cause I renounce you; and now for the last time subscribe myself, sir,

Your humble servant,[2]
Jonathan Boucher.

Jonathan Boucher, "Reminiscences of an American Loyalist," *Notes and Queries*, 5th ser., 6 (July–Dec. 1876), 161–62.

Jonathan Boucher (1738–1804) was an Anglican clergyman who taught GW's stepson John Parke Custis between 1768 and 1773, first in Virginia, where Boucher was rector of St. Mary's Parish in Caroline County from 1764 to 1770, and later in Maryland, where he was rector of St. Anne's Parish in Annapolis from 1770 to 1771 and of Queen Anne's Parish in Prince Georges County from 1771 to 1775. During those years GW and Boucher were guests in one another's houses on many occasions, but after 1774, when Boucher moved to The Lodge on the Potomac River across from Alexandria, the two men parted paths politically. Boucher, who was born and raised in England, became an outspoken Loyalist, which made him highly unpopular in Queen Anne's Parish. "The Revd. Mr Boucher," Deputy Governor Robert Eden of Maryland reported to the earl of Dartmouth on 27 Aug. 1775, "is driven from his parish and possessions here and goes home in the *Choptank Frigate* from Patowmack in about ten days" (Davies, *Documents of the American Revolution*, 11:85–88). Boucher spent the remainer of his life in England, serving as vicar of Epsom from 1785 to 1804.

1. The allusion is to Aesop's fable of a boy stoning frogs for amusement.

2. Boucher again wrote to GW on 25 May 1784 and 8 Nov. 1797, and in the latter year he also dedicated a volume of his political sermons to GW. "I was once your neighbour and your friend," Boucher wrote to GW in his dedication, "the unhappy dispute, which terminated in the disunion of our respective countries, also broke off our personal connexion: but I never was more than your political enemy; and every sentiment even of political animosity has, on my part, long ago subsided" (Jonathan Boucher, *A View of the Causes and Consequences of the American Revolution* . . . [London, 1797]). GW replied to Boucher with a cordial letter of thanks on 15 Aug. 1798 but remarked that he had not read the book.

Letter not found: from Joseph Palmer, 6 Aug. 1775. On 7 Aug. GW wrote to Palmer: "Your favour of yesterday came duely to my hands."

From Major General Philip Schuyler

Tionderoga [N.Y.] August 6th 1775.

I thank You my Dear General for your very kind and polite Letter of the 28th ult., which I just had the Honor to receive.

Immediately on my Arrival here, I issued such Orders respecting the Provisions & Stores, (which I found had been most scandalously embezzled or misapplyed) as I hoped would effectually have brought Matters into a Right Train, but it is the Misfortune of the People here, that they do not know how to obey, altho' they should be willing.

I have therefore directed the Deputy Commissary General to send up a Person, (Whom I named and knew to be equal to the Buisiness) to examine the Commissaries at the several Posts on the Communication, and to give them such Directions as will I hope introduce Regularity in future. Mr John N. Bleecker is now employed in that essential Buisiness.[1]

With Respect to the Returns of the Army, You will see by the last Letter, I had the Honor to write You,[2] that I have had no Success in getting them properly made, Altho' I have drawn And given them Forms, Which I thought so clear, that no Possibility of mistaking remained.

I foresaw, my Dear Sir, that You would have an Herculean Labour, in Order to introduce that proper Spirit of Discipline & Subordination, which is the very Soul of an Army, and I felt for You with the utmost Sensibility, as I well knew the Variety of Difficulties, You would have to encounter, and which must necessarily be extreamly painfull & disgusting to You, accustomed to Order & Regularity, I can easily conceive, that my Difficulties are only a faint Semblance of Yours. Yes, my General⟨,⟩ I will strive to Copy your bright Example, & patiently & steadily, persevere in that Line, which only can promise the wished for Reformation.

Since my last, I have had a Verbal Confirmation by one of my Scouts of the Intelligence contained in the Affidavits which I sent You.[3] I am preparing with the utmost Diligence, to obey my Orders and move against the Enemy, unless Your Excellency or Congress should direct otherwise; in the Course of a few Days, I expect to receive the ultimate Determination; Whatever it may be, I shall try to execute It, in such a Manner as will best promote the just Cause in which we are engaged.[4]

Not a Man from this Colony has yet joined me, Except those I returned to You, and who were raised, and paid by the Committee of Albany—nor have I yet received those Necessary Supplies, which I begg'd the New York Provincial Congress to send me, As long ago as the third of last Month, and which the Continental Congress had desired them to do.[5]

The Troops here are destitute of Tents, they are crouded in vile Barracks, which with the Natural Inattention of the Soldiery to Cleanliness, has already been productive of Desease and Numbers are daily rendered Unfit for Duty.

I am so unfortunate as not to have one Carriage for Field Artillery, so that, If I am ordered to attack St Johns and am able to get down the Sorrel River,[6] I shall labour under vast Difficulty, to bring up the Cannon thro' a very swampy Country. They will be few indeed, as I shall have less than a Ton of Powder, when the Troops are compleated to twenty four Rounds a Man.

Congress has appointed Commissioners for Indian Affairs, as one of them, I have ordered Messengers to be sent into their Country, to invite them to a Conference at Albany. I have also requested the Canawaga's of Canada to meet me at this Place.[7] The whole Family of the late Sir William Johnston, have held a Line of Conduct, that Evinces the most Inimical Sentiments in them to the American Cause. Sir John Johnson has had four hundred Men partly Scotch Highlanders in Arms, to protect a Scoundrel Sheriff, who had repeatedly insulted the Good Inhabitants of that Country, which at Length they retaliated. The Inhabitants have however drove off the Sheriff And made the Knight promise he would interfere no farther. I should not have hesitated one Moment to have secured him and his Adherents, had I not been apprehensive of Evil Consequences from the Indians, I therefore thought it most prudent to advise Congress of the whole Matter.[8]

Altho' Sir, I am much in Want of Men and would wish to have the three New Hampshire Companies mentioned in the Copy of your Letter of the 27th Ult:, Yet they are so happily posted, either to awe the Mesisque & St Francois Indians, or to march to the Relief of the Inhabitants in this Colony, living to the Westward of where these Troops are now posted & on what are commonly called the New Hampshire Grants, That in Case of an Attack from the Savages I have mentioned, who, if any, are most our Enemies, I could wish them to remain under Orders there for that Purpose.[9]

I am extreamly happy to learn that You are so well supplyed

with Provisions. I have now a tolerable Stock of Flour, but very little Pork. Fat Cattle are however coming up, So that I do not apprehend we shall suffer in that Article.

My best wishes attend Colo. Read & Major Mifflin. I am most respectfully Your Excellency's Obedient & very Humble Servant

Ph: Schuyler

LS, DLC:GW; LB, NN: Schuyler Papers.

1. The deputy commissary general is Elisha Phelps. John N. Bleeker (1739–1825) of Albany was appointed by the New York provincial congress on 24 May 1775 to be one of the five agents charged with removing cannon and stores from Ticonderoga. In October 1775 he became a captain in the 1st New York militia regiment.

2. See Schuyler to GW, 31 July–2 Aug. 1775.

3. Schuyler is referring to the affidavits of John Duguid and John Shatforth, both dated 2 Aug. 1775, which were enclosed in his letter to GW of 31 July–2 Aug. 1775. See note 2 to that document.

4. The Continental Congress directed Schuyler on 27 June to march into Canada (*JCC*, 2:109–10). St. Jean was his immediate objective.

5. For Schuyler's letter of 3 July to the New York provincial congress requesting that a variety of military stores and provisions be sent to Albany, see *N.Y. Prov. Congress Journals*, 2:11. During July Schuyler sent repeated appeals to the provincial congress for those supplies and also asked that New York troops be sent to his army (ibid., 12–13).

6. The Richelieu River, also known in the eighteenth century as the Sorel or Chambly River, flows north from Lake Champlain past St. Jean and Chambly and into the St. Lawrence River at Sorel.

7. Congress appointed Schuyler one of the Indian commissioners for the northern department on 13 July (*JCC*, 2:183). For a discussion of Caughnawaga Indians and Schuyler's subsequent treaty with them, see GW to Hancock, 4–5 Aug. 1775, n.32.

8. Sir John Johnson (1742–1830), son of Sir William Johnson (1715–1774), inherited his father's title as baronet and most of his property in the Mohawk Valley, including Johnson Hall, but he did not immediately succeed Sir William as Indian superintendent for the northern department, that position going to Sir William's son-in-law, Guy Johnson. See GW to Schuyler, 25 June 1775, n.4. As a brigadier general in the New York militia, John Johnson used his position and influence in favor of the crown, corresponding with Gov. Tryon about the possibility of raising a force of Loyalists in the Mohawk Valley. When a band of Patriots tried to seize Sheriff Alexander White of Tryon County, an ardent Loyalist who had cut down a liberty pole and had jailed several Whigs, Johnson mustered his Scotch Highlander tenants to protect the sheriff. White was soon obliged to leave the country, but Johnson remained at Johnson Hall until May 1776, when he fled to Canada with about two hundred and fifty supporters. Commissioned a lieutenant colonel at

Montreal, Johnson raised a Loyalist regiment known as the Royal Greens. He participated in St. Leger's expedition in 1777, and during 1778 and 1780 he raided Tryon County. In 1782 Sir John succeeded Guy Johnson as Indian superintendent and was promoted to colonel in the British army.

9. The three New Hampshire companies under the command of Col. Timothy Bedel were posted in the Coos area on the Connecticut River. They joined Schuyler's army at Ticonderoga in September. See GW to Schuyler, 27 July 1775, n.3. Both the Missisauga and the St. Francis Indians lived in Canada: the Missisauga near Lake Huron and the St. Francis Indians on the St. Lawrence River between Montreal and Quebec. Representatives from the St. Francis Indians appeared at Cambridge on 13 Aug. 1775 and offered their services to GW (GW to Schuyler, 14 Aug. 1775). The New Hampshire Grants embraced the area that later became Vermont. Both New York and New Hampshire claimed the region at this time.

To James Warren

Sir Camp at Cambridge Head Quarters Augt 6. 1775.

I should be very glad to procure Mr Hitchbourns Release agreeable to your Favour of yesterday if I could think of any Mode in which it was practicable. To propose it on any other Footing than an Exchange would I fear expose the Application to Contempt. As I observe he is included in the Vote delivered me this Morning by a Committee from the General Court. I apprehend it had best be left on that Footing, & is the most likely to be successful.[1]

It is very surprizing if the Letters intercepted are of Consequence, that those Gentlemen should act so imprudent a Part—if their suffering only affected themselves I should not think it improper that they should feel a little for their Misconduct or Negligence.[2] I am with much Truth & Regard Sir Your most Obed: & very Hbble Servt

Go: Washington

LS, in Joseph Reed's writing, MHi; LB, DLC:GW; Varick transcript, DLC:GW.

1. On 5 Aug. the Massachusetts General Court resolved that two Loyalists who were being held in the Concord jail might be exchanged for several Patriots being held in Boston ("Mass. Council Journal," July 1775–Feb. 1776 sess., 49; *Mass. House of Rep. Journal*, July–Nov. 1775 sess., 47). Hichborn was specifically included in this resolution, but the proposed exchange did not occur. On the night of 18 Oct. 1775 Hichborn escaped from the British warship in Boston Harbor, where he was imprisoned, by lowering himself into a canoe

tied to the stern of the vessel and paddling ashore (Hichborn to John Adams, 25 Nov.–10 Dec. 1775, in Taylor, *Papers of John Adams*, 3:320–27). For a discussion of Hichborn's capture, see GW to Hancock, 4–5 Aug. 1775, n.34.

2. "General Washington does not yet appear altogether Satisfied with my Conduct," Hichborn wrote to John Adams on 28 Oct. 1775. "The only Satisfaction I have at present arises from the generous Reception I met with from Coll. Warren" (Taylor, *Papers of John Adams*, 3:255–57). A few weeks later in another letter to Adams, Hichborn reported that "a Gentleman called me aside and whispered that he had the day before been in a large Company, among whom were Collel. [James] Otis, Doct: [John] Winthrop and his Lady [Hannah Fayerweather Tollman Winthrop]. That Mrs. Winthrop censured my Conduct respecting the letters very highly; in which she was joined by her Husband and Col. Otis. One of the Company suggested that I had satisfied General Washington, but was answered by Colel. Otis, with a good deal of warmth, that *he knew* neither the General nor any of the Officers about him, were in any degree satisfied with my Conduct" (Hichborn to Adams, 25 Nov.–10 Dec. 1775, ibid., 320–27).

General Orders

Head Quarters, Cambridge, August 7th 1775.

Parole, Newcastle. Countersign, Maldin.

Captain Kilton of Col. Patterson's Regiment, tried by a General Court martial for "Neglect of duty" is found guilty of a Breach of the 49th Article of the Rules and Regulations for the Massachusetts Army; They therefore sentence him to receive a severe reprimand from the Commanding Officer at the head of the regiment.[1]

Application having been made for Sutlers to supply the different Regiments with Necessaries: The Commander in Chief has no Objection to each Colonel appointing one for his particular regiment, provided the public is not to be tax'd with any Expence by the Appointment, and provided also; that each Colonel doth become answerable for the Conduct of the Sutler so appointed, and taking care, that he conform strictly to all Orders given for the regulation of the Army, and that he does not in any Instance attempt to impose upon the Soldiers in the price of their goods. No Officer directly, or indirectly, is to become a Sutler.[2] It is in an especial manner recommended to the Commanding Officer of each regiment, to see that a store of shoes and shirts, are laid in for the Men, as those are at all times necessary. The General also recommends it to the Colonels, to provide Indian Boots, or Leggings, for their men, instead of stockings; as they are not only warmer, and wear longer, but (by getting them of a colour) contribute to uniformity in dress; especially, as the General has hopes of prevailing with the Continental Congress, to give each Man a hunting shirt.[3]

For the future, no Return is to be delivered to the Adjutant General, that is not signed by the Commanding Officer of the Regiment, or Corps, specified by the return; and it is expected, that the Commanding Officers of Regiments, do not receive any Return from their Adjutants, unless he at the same time, presents the said Commanding Officer, with a particular Return, signed by the respective Captains of Companys, in the regiment he commands.

Varick transcript, DLC:GW.

1. The reprimanded officer was apparently Samuel Kelson of Massachusetts. The 49th article of the Massachusetts regulations is a catchall: "All crimes not capital, and all disorders and neglects, which officers and soldiers may be guilty of, to the prejudice of good order and military discipline, though not mentioned in the articles of war, are to be taken cognizance of by a general or regimental court martial, according to the nature and degree of the offence, and be punished at their discretion" (*Mass. Prov. Congress Journals*, 128). Article 50 of the Continental articles of war is identical (*JCC*, 2:119).

2. Article 32 of the Continental articles of war stipulates that "all suttlers and retailers to a camp, and all persons whatsoever, serving with the continental army in the field, though not inlisted soldiers, are to be subject to the articles, rules, and regulations of the continental army." Article 65 requires the commanders of camps, forts, barracks, and garrisons "to see that the persons permitted to suttle shall supply the soldiers with good and wholesome provisions at a reasonable price," and article 66 forbids those commanders to "exact exorbitant prices for houses or stalls let out to suttlers" or to "be interested in the sale of such victuals, liquors, or other necessaries of life, which are brought into the camp, garrison, fort or barracks, for the use of the soldiers" (*JCC*, 2:116–17, 122).

3. For GW's efforts to obtain hunting shirts for the army, see GW to Hancock, 10–11 July 1775, Document II. Letter Sent, n.13, and Hancock to GW, 24 July 1775, n.3.

From the Norwich Committee of Correspondence

Norwich [Conn.] 7th Augt 1775

May it please your Excellency

We the Committe of Correspondence for the Town of Norwich Think it our indespensable Duty to Accquaint your Excellency of a Matter we think may possibly be of the utmost importance at this most Critical Juncture of affairs & hope the occasion of our Writing will Sufficiently apologize for the Liberty, we (tho. Strangers) have Taken—Yesterday Morning this Town was alarmed with an Acct of Eigh[t] Ships one Snow Two or three Brigs & Some other Vessels appearing of N. London Harbour three of Which Were Men of Warr—a Large Number of Men were Soon Collected under arms & Repaird to our Landing N. London Groton &C. when the Ships were Some time in the afternoon. Most of them Came too of the West End of Fishers island but So as to Cut off Communication between these & the Main—Duncan Stewart Esqr. Collector for the Port of N. London. by permission of the Committe of that Town Went over in a Boat to Gain Intelligence Last Evening. but was prevented Returning until this afternoon—When he Was brought back & he with the Boatman Who Carried him over informe[d] they had Taken of That Island about Two thousand Sheep & One hundred & fifty head of Cattle—indeed all the Cattle Sheep & hogs upon the Island Except a Number of Milch Cows—That they had also Taken a Sloop Outward bound from N. Haven with Thirty Six Head of Oxen all which will Probably be immediately forwarded to Boston[1]—We Can only Say we Wish Some Method might be devisd to Intercept them in Boston Bay before their Arival⟨.⟩ There is undoubtedly a Number of Schooners & Boats at Plymouth which might be improv'd for above purpose—The Bearer Capt. Samuel Wheat[2] Came from New London this afternoon he is a Gentlemen on Whose intelligence you may Rely & to whoom we Refer you for farther particulars Relative to this or any other Matter. he Goes on Purpose to accquaint your Excelleny of this matter—we are not without apprehensions they will Endeavour to Take off more Stock from the Neighbouring Island, Which We fear will not be in our power to prevent[3]—We have not been without Fears Something of this kind might happen & Last Week ordered the Commisary here to purchase all the fatt oxen & Sheep on Fishers island which was done & Brot of Last Friday viz. Fifteen Fatt Oxen & 100 Sheep we have only Time to add we are with Greatest Esteem Your Excellencys Mt Obed. Hbl. svts

Christr Leffingwell[4] } Comtee
Wm Hubbard }

LS, in Christopher Leffingwell's writing, DLC:GW. The cover includes the notation "Fav. ℘ Cap. Wheat Express." It is endorsed in Joseph Reed's writing "Answd Aug. 8. ℘ Major Johnson." The reply which Reed wrote on behalf of GW is dated 9 Aug. 1775: "I am directed by his Excelly Genl Washington to acknowledge the Receipt of your Favour last Evening ℘ Express & to thank you for your Zeal & Activity in forwarding the Intelligence. As very early Notice had been given of the Sailing of this Fleet & the very Island mentioned which it has plunder'd: the General cannot help being somewhat surprized, that effectual Measures had not been taken to remove the Stock: which would not only have sent them back with Shame & Disappointment, but have increased their Distress at Boston for fresh Provisions which was very great before this Supply. The Remedy proposed in your Letter would be extremely difficult in our helpless Condition at Sea[.] The Convoy & immediate Relief to be obtained from Boston would make it a very hazardous Enterprize" (LB, DLC:GW). The letter-book copy of Reed's letter is mistakenly addressed to the committee at New London, but a copy in the Nicholas Cooke Papers at the Rhode Island Historical Society is correctly addressed to the Norwich Committee.

1. For the sailing of this British fleet from Boston, see Richard Dodge to GW, and John Thomas to GW, both 25 July 1775. The warships included the *Rose* and the *Swan*, which joined the fleet off Newport on 5 August. On 10 Aug. an anonymous correspondent reported from New London: "Last Sunday morning [August 6] about six o'clock, we discovered nine sail of ships, one brig, one snow, one schooner, and two sloops, turning up to this harbour, with the wind at N.E. which alarmed the inhabitants of this town, but we soon found their design was to take the stock off Fisher's Island, which they accomplished on that day, consisting of 1130 sheep, 40 cattle, and 10 hogs" (*Dunlap's Pennsylvania Packet, or, the General Advertiser* [Philadelphia], 21 Aug. 1775, supplement). For another account of the raid on Fishers Island, see Jonathan Trumbull, Sr., to GW, 7 Aug. 1775, n.2.

2. Samuel Wheat of Norwich was captain of the 2d company in the 20th Connecticut militia regiment.

3. The British fleet raided Gardiners Island on 8 and 11 Aug. and returned to Boston on 15 August (Loammi Baldwin to GW, 16 Aug. 1775).

4. A man of considerable wealth, Christopher Leffingwell (1734–1810) of Norwich was involved in the manufacture of hosiery, paper, dye, flour, chocolate, and pottery. In a letter to GW of 15 July 1789, Leffingwell claimed that he was one of six men who in the spring of 1775 planned and funded the

Connecticut expedition against Ticonderoga and Crown Point. He was also a purchaser of supplies for Connecticut during the war and served in the Continental commissary department under Joseph Trumbull and in the Continental quartermaster department under Thomas Mifflin.

To James Otis, Sr.

Sir Head Quarters at Cambridge, Augt 7th 1775

By the General Return made me for last Week, I find there are great Number of Soldiers and non-commissd Officers, who absent themselves from Duty,[1] the greatest Part of which I have Reason to believe, are at their respective Homes, in different Parts of the Country; some employ'd by their Officers on their Farms, & others drawing Pay from the Publick, while they are working on their own Plantations, or for Hire. My utmost Exertions have not been able to prevent this base and pernicious Conduct; I must therefore beg the Assistance of the General Court, to cooperate with me, in such Measures, as may remedy this Mischief. I am of Opinion, it might be done, either wholly, or in Part, by the Committees in the Several Towns making Strict & impartial Inquiry of Such as are found Absent from the Army; upon what account they have left it, by whose Leave, & for what Time, to require such as have no Impediment of Sickness, or other good Reason, to return to their Duty immediately or in Case of Failure to Send an Accot of their Names, the Company, and Regiment to which they belong to me as soon as possible; that I may be able to make Examples of Such Delinquents.

I need not enlarge upon the ruinous Consequences of suffering such infamous Deserters and Defrauders of the Publick to go unnoticed, or unpunish'd, nor use any Arguments to induce the general Court to give it immediate Attention—The Necessity of the Case does not permit me to doubt the Continued Exertions of that Zeal which has distinguished the General Court upon less important Occasions.[2] I have the Honour to be Sir with much Respect and Regard Your Most Obedt hum. Servt

Go: Washington

The Inclosed respects a Prisoner Sent up from Prospect Hill, who is sent herewith under Gaurd for Examination of the Committee appointed for that Purpose.[3]

G. W——n

LS, in Thomas Mifflin's writing, M-Ar: Revolution Letters; LB, DLC:GW; copy, "Mass. Council Journal," July 1775–Feb. 1776 sess., 72; Varick transcript, DLC:GW. The LS includes, below the postscript on the second page of the manuscript, a copy in Perez Morton's writing of the minutes from the journals of the council and house of representatives respecting the appointment on 7 and 8 Aug. of a committee to consider GW's letter. See note 2.

1. The general return of 5 Aug. reports 750 men as sick and absent, 255 on furlough, and 1,011 on command (DNA: RG 93, Revolutionary War Rolls, 1775–83).

2. The council read GW's letter later this day and sent it down to the house of representatives, which appointed Dr. Benjamin Church, Col. Nathaniel Freeman, and Richard Devens to consider it. On 8 Aug. the council added Walter Spooner and John Winthrop to that committee. The committee's report closely followed GW's suggestions. On 13 Aug. both houses resolved that the committees of correspondence or selectmen in the towns "make careful and diligent enquiry from time to time, whether there be any non-commissioned Officers or Soldiers within their respective towns, belonging to the said army, and if any such shall be found that they bring them to a Strict and impartial examination upon what account they left the army, by whose leave, and for what time; and to require all such as have no furlough, or whose furloughs are out, and have no real impediment of sickness to return to their duty immediately; and in case they neglect it, that such Committees or Selectmen do without fail send an account of their names the Company & Regiment to which they belong, and the places where they are lurking, to his Excellency General Washington that so such infamous deserters, & defrauders of the Public may not go unpunished." The General Court also "strongly recommended to all the inhabitants . . . to be aiding & assisting to their said Committees and Selectmen in the execution of this Resolve, and they by no means countenance, harbour or conceal; but on the other hand give information of all such Delinquents to the said Committees or Selectmen" ("Mass. Council Journal," July 1775–Feb. 1776 sess., 72–73; also in *Mass. House of Rep. Journals*, July–Nov. 1775 sess., 51, 70. The General Court had the resolution printed in handbills for distribution in both the army and the towns (Massachusetts General Court to GW, 13 Aug. 1775). For GW's orders on this matter, see General Orders, 8 Aug. 1775.

3. The committee was probably the one that the General Court appointed on this date to examine people coming out of Boston. See GW to James Otis, Sr., 5 Aug. 1775, n.2.

To Joseph Palmer

Sir, Cambridge Augt 7th 1775.

Your favour of yesterday came duely to my hands—as I did not consider local appointments, as having any operation upon the general one, I had partly engaged (at least in my own mind) the Office of Quartermaster Genl before your favour was presented to me.[1] In truth Sir, I think it sound policy to bestow Offices indiscriminately among Gentleme⟨n⟩ of the different Governmts; for as all bear a proportionable part towards the expence of this War, if no Gentlemen out of these four Governments come in for any share of the appointments, it may be apt to create jealousies which will, in the end, give disgust; for this reason, I would earnestly recomd it to your Board to provide for some of the Volunteers who are come from Philadelphia, with very warm recommendation's, thô strangers to me.

In respect to the Boats &ca from Salem, I doubt, in the first place, whether they could be brought over by Land—in the Second, I am sure nothing could ever be executed here by Surprize; as I am well convinced that nothing is transacted in our Camp, or Lines, but what is known in Boston in less than 24 hours—indeed, Circumstanced as we are, it is scarce possible to be otherwise, unless we were to stop the Communication between the Country & our Camp & Lines; in which case, we shd render our Supplies of Milk, Vegetables &ca difficult & precarious. We are now building a kind of Floating Battery, when that is done, & the Utility of it discovered, I may possibly apply for Timber to build more, as circumstances shall require. I remain with great esteem Sir Yr Most Hble Servt

Go: Washington

ALS, PWCD. The cover is addressed "To Honble J. Palmer Esqr. at Watertown."

Joseph Palmer (1716–1788) of Braintree was a prominent member of all three Massachusetts provincial congresses and the committee of safety, and on 21 July 1775 he was elected to the colony's new council. Born in Devonshire, Palmer came to America in 1746 and was soon involved in the manufacture of glass, chocolate, candles, and salt at Germantown, near Braintree. He was present at the Battle of Lexington in April 1775, and on 7 Feb. 1776 he was commissioned a colonel in the militia. Promoted to brigadier general three months later, Palmer commanded two regiments of Massachusetts militia in the unsuccessful Newport expedition of 1777.

1. Palmer's letter of 6 Aug. has not been found, but in it Palmer apparently urged GW to appoint his son Joseph Pearse Palmer (1750–1797), the quartermaster general of the Massachusetts forces, to the new post of Continental quartermaster general. GW named Thomas Mifflin to that office on 14 Aug. 1775 (General Orders, that date).

From Jonathan Trumbull, Sr.

Sir Lebanon [Conn.] 7th August 1775.

Fessenden is not returned hither—Your Letter to Majr General Schuyler was forwarded ℔ Express the 1st instant[1]—enclosed is Copy of a Letter from Colo. Saltonstal received yesterday[2]—I Ordered him as Colo. of the third, Colo. Saml Coit of the 8th[3]—and Lt Colo. Saml Abbot of the 20th Regiment[4] in this Colony forthwith to raise so many Men of their Regiments as could speedily be got in readiness to march for our Defence and safety against any attacks or proceedings from that Fleet—I have Also Ordered Major Jonth. Latimer[5] & Capt. Edward Shipman[6] with their Companies of the seventh Regiment raised for our Special Defence, to rendezvous for the present at New London, notwithstanding the preceeding Orders given for their March to the Camp before Boston, not doubting it would meet your Approbation on the present Emergency. I am, with great Truth and Regard Sir Your Obedient humble Servant

Jonth. Trumbull

ALS, DLC:GW; LB, Ct: Trumbull Papers.

1. This letter must be either the one of 27 July or that of 28 July which GW wrote to Schuyler.

2. Gurdon Saltonstall (1708–1785) of New London was an officer in the Connecticut militia. He spent the fall of 1775 and the following winter in fortifying New London Harbor. On 16 Sept. 1776 he was appointed brigadier general over nine regiments of Connecticut militia which were ordered to march to GW's assistance in New York. Saltonstall left the army on account of illness in Feb. 1777 and resigned his commission soon afterwards. The enclosed letter from Saltonstall to Governor Trumbull concerned the British fleet off the Connecticut coast. Dated "New London Saboth Morning ½ past 9 Clo. Augst 6—1775," it reported that "This morning at sunrise apeared a Fleet of ten Sail at Anchor half way between Fishers Island West point & the Light house, Vizt 3 Men Ware, 5 other Ships a Briggantine & Schooner, they hove up Anchers about 6 Clo., & have been beating Eastward on first of the Ebb for Fishers Island sound; 3 of the Ships probably: the Men Warr, are got into sd sound & out of view, the remainder of sd Fleet still beating Eastward—their design is to cutt of all communication with the Main & sd Island, as is generaly concluded & then Rob the Island of the Stock—Yesterday Mr Mumford Commissary took off all the Fatt Cattle from thence 15 head—the drought has been so severe, that there was not a Fatt Sheep on the Island, (as I am told) Hence it appears that there remains a large Stock of Sheep & Cattle still on sd Island; which no doubt will be acceptable to the Kings Troops in

Boston—Notice through this County is gone East & West, to animate the people to hold themselves in readiness—The Companys of Foot in this Town Plot & neck are ordered to muster that they may this day receive Amunition" (DLC:GW). For other reports of the British raid on Fishers Island, see Norwich Committee of Correspondence to GW, 7 Aug. 1775, and Nathaniel Shaw, Jr., to Joseph Trumbull, 7 Aug. 1775, in Clark, *Naval Documents*, 1:1087–88.

3. Samuel Coit (1708–1792) of Preston (later Griswold) commanded his Connecticut militia regiment until September 1776, when the governor and council excused him from service on the expedition to New York on account of his age and infirmity. A member of the New London County committee of correspondence, Coit served also in the Connecticut general assembly and as a judge of the maritime court.

4. Samuel Abbot remained lieutenant colonel of the 20th regiment of the Connecticut militia at least until December 1776 and was subsequently promoted to colonel.

5. Jonathan Lattimer (1724–c.1790) of Montville became major of Col. Charles Webb's 7th Connecticut Regiment on 6 July 1775 and at the same time received command of the regiment's third company. Lattimer left the 7th Connecticut in December 1775 but returned to service in June 1776 as lieutenant colonel of Col. Samuel Selden's Connecticut state regiment, a position which he held until the following December. During the latter part of the war Lattimer was colonel of the 3d Connecticut militia regiment, which fought at Saratoga in 1777 and at New London in 1781.

6. Edward Shipman of Saybrook was a captain in the 7th Connecticut Regiment from 6 July to 19 Dec. 1775, and during the ensuing campaign he held the same rank in the 19th Continental Regiment. He later became a major in the Connecticut militia and state troops.

General Orders

Head Quarters, Cambridge, August 8th 1775

Parole Portsmouth. Countersign, Northumberland

As the number of absent Sick by the last returns, are astonishingly great;[1] it is ordered that the Names of each man (absent under that pretence) be given in by the Commanding Officer of each Regiment, and signed by him; setting forth the Town which each particular soldier is gone to, that the Committee thereof may be applied to, to inspect into the Nature of their Complaints, and make report of those, who are fit for duty.[2] It has been intimated to the General, that some Officers, under pretence of giving Furloughs to Men, recovering from Sickness, send them to work upon their Farms, for their own private Emolument, at the same time, that the public is taxed with their pay, if not with their provisions; These insinuations being but obliquely made, the General is unwilling to believe, that any Officer can be so lost to all Sense of honour as to defraud the public in so scandalous a Manner, and therefore does not at present pay any further Regard, to the Insinuation, than to declare, that he will shew no Favor to any Officer, who shall be found guilty of such iniquitous practices: But will do his utmost enedeavours, to bring them to exemplary punishment; & the disgrace due to such Mal-conduct.

The following is the Ration of Provisions allowed by the Continental Congress unto each Soldier. (viz:)[3]

One pound of fresh beef, or ¾ of a pound of Pork, or one pound of Salt Fish, pr diem.

One pound of Bread, or Flour pr diem.

Three pints of Peas, or Beans pr Week, or Vegetables equivalent; at 5/s. pr Bushel for Peas or Beans.[4]

One pint of milk pr Man, pr diem, when to be had.[5]

One half pint of Rice, or one pint of Indian meal pr Man, pr Week.

One quart of Spruce Beer per man, pr diem, or 9 Gallons of molasses pr Company of 100 Men.[6]

Three pounds of Candles to 100 Men pr Week, for Guards, &c.

Twenty-four pounds of soft, or eight pounds of hard Soap for 100 Men per week.

One Ration of Salt, one *ditto* fresh [meat],[7] and two *ditto* Bread, to be delivered Monday morning; Wednesday morning the same.

Friday morning the same, and one ditto salt Fish.

All weekly allowances delivered Wednesday morning; where the number of regiments are too many to serve the whole the same day, then the Number to be divided equally, and one part served Monday Morning, the other part Tuesday Morning, and so through the week.

Varick transcript, DLC:GW.

1. The general return of 29 July 1775 reported 690 men who were both sick and absent, and the one of 5 Aug. 1775 put the number at 750 (DNA: RG 93, Revolutionary War Rolls, 1775–83).

2. For the actions that the Massachusetts General Court took to assist GW in remedying this problem, see GW to James Otis, Sr., 7 Aug. 1775, n.2, and the Massachusetts General Court to GW, 13 Aug. 1775, n.1.

3. This schedule of rations was not officially approved by Congress until 4 Nov. 1775 (*JCC*, 3:322). For the rations previously allowed by Massachusetts and Connecticut, see GW to Hancock, 4–5 Aug. 1775, n.22.

4. Congress's resolution of 4 Nov. reads "at one dollar per bushel for pease or beans" (*JCC*, 3:322).

5. Congress specified "1 pint of milk per man per day, or at the rate of 1/72 of a dollar" (ibid.).

6. Congress approved "1 quart of spruce beer or cyder per man per day, or nine gallons of Molasses per company of 100 men per week" (ibid.).

7. The word within square brackets is taken from Artemas Ward's orderly book (MHi: Ward Papers).

From Lieutenant Colonel Loammi Baldwin

Chelsea [Mass.] Aug. 8 1775
5 oClock P.M.

May it Please your Excellency

This covers the Observation of yesterday & today[1]—I would Inform your Excellency that—A considerable number of the Kings Troops removed from Bunker Hill & pitched their Tents Towards the point near where the Battle was Fought at Charlestown and Cannon Hauld downe & Placed there, I have Seen a Large number of Men & Horses transported from Boston to Charlestown yesterday and to Day, am fully of the mind that they are determined upon taking Possession of Greens Hill. and Think very Soon. I am unhappy being in Such a situation as that it would be out of my Power to prevent it nothwithstanding every thing Should be done, possable for us to do, famous Character follow Success, & Infamous one Retreats Let the case and Circumstances be allmost what they will[.] I would Humbl[y] Beg your Excellency to consider our Situation & Suffer me to propos⟨e⟩ a Sufficiant number of men here to mount a Picket Gua⟨rd⟩ Just behind the Top of the Hill to consist of 80 or 100 men ready at a moments warning to repell or Impede them in there Landing but with Pleasure I submit it to your much Better Judgment, the Result of which I shall rest Content with, And your Excelleny may rest assured that what ever is in my power I shall preform towards the Distruction of our Enemis. This From your Excellencis most Humbl & obedient Servnt

Loammi Baldwin Lieut. Colo.

P.S. I was on my way to Head Quarters this forenoon to report the Conduct of Capt. Lindseys Company & Met General Lee on the road who Informed me that he had proceed[ed] to put the Capt. under arrest and also Confind two men that wore the most Culpable and that he did not Look upon it necessary for me to proceed as he Should go himself and acquaint your Excelleny with his Proceedure.[2]

ALS, DLC:GW.

1. Baldwin enclosed "A Return of the Observations of the Day august the 8th," which includes observations for both 7 and 8 Aug. 1775. The return in Joseph Leach's writing is in DLC:GW.

2. For the charges against Capt. Eleazer Lindsey, see Baldwin to GW, 6 Aug. 1775, and General Orders, 16 Aug. 1775.

From Nicholas Cooke

Sir Providence August 8th 1775

Last Evening Col. Porter delivered me your Letter of the 4th instant, to which I have paid all the Attention the Importance of it demands.

This Colony the last Fall, not confiding entirely in the precarious Supply of Powder that might be expected from the Merchants, imported a considerable Quantity, though not so large as was ordered. The supplying the Inhabitants, who were in a Manner utterly destitute, the Army near Boston, and our armed Vessels have so exhausted this Stock that the Powder now left which is all in this Place is greatly insufficient to resist even a short Attack upon it. Our Situation is the same with Respect to Lead. So that at present none of either Article can be spared from the Colony.

By a Vessel which arrived here on the 30th Ulto from Cape Francois we are informed that the Captain of the Vessel sent from this Port to the Cape for a Quantity of warlike Stores, in which the Committee of Safety for the Colony of the Massachusetts had interested themselves, had executed his Commission and was to sail with a large Quantity in a Day or Two, so that she may be hourly expected.[1] This Colony about Four Weeks ago dispatched a suitable Vessel with Money to purchase Fifteen Tons of Powder and other warlike Stores, which may also soon be expected. Of these Vessels we have the highest Reason to think the Enemy have gained Intelligence; the Ships of War upon this Station having for several Days past cruized continually off Block-Island, and from thence to Montauk-Point, and up the Sound. This hath made us think it absolutely necessary to send the smallest of our armed Sloops to cruize without the Ships of War and endeavour at all Hazards to speak with the Vessels expected with Powder, and order them to another Port. She will sail this Day. The other armed Sloop, by her being within the River, prevents the Cutters and Barges from committing Depredations; so that she cannot be spared: Nor indeed is a Vessel of her Force required for the Enterprize you mention.[2] We have in this Harbor a very fine sailing Pacquet that would answer the Purpose extremely well;[3] which might be equipped with Swivels, manned with about Twenty Men and be ready to sail in less than Two Days. But as I do not think it prudent that her sole Dependence should be upon getting Powder at Bermuda it will be necessary to send a Sum of Money to purchase a Quantity at some other Port in Case of a Disappointment at Bermuda. In the present State of the Colony I do not think it probable that a sufficient Sum can be procured here for that Purpose before the Sitting of the General Assembly; and therefore advise that Application be made to the General Court of the Massachusetts-Bay to advance Part of the Sum necessary.[4] I believe we may be able to supply One Half the Sum here. Col. Porter hath been at Bedford and along the Eastern Shore, but can hear nothing of Harris. He is now bound as far as New-London to endeavour to meet with him; but is greatly apprehensive that he is fallen into the Hands of the Enemy.

We have Information that several Ship of War and Transports were the Day before Yesterday at New-London; and that the Country round were all arming and mustering. We also hear that they have taken some Stock off the East-End of Long-Island.[5]

Sensible of the great Scarcity of Lead in the Country I some Time ago wrote to the Congress of the Massachusetts-Bay, and to our Delegates at the Continental Congress recommending that a Part of the large Quantity of Lead at Ticonderoga should be immediately brought down; and still think the Measure necessary.[6]

I shall immediately give Orders to the Committee of Safety to purchase for the Use of the Colony all the Tow-Cloth that can be had.

If the Powder supposed to be at Bermuda be private Property it must be immediately paid for. If not I imagine it will be settled with our other Disputes. This is a Matter that ought to be known and provided for. Upon further Consideration I am very doubtful whether a Vessel can be immediately provided with Men here; and therefore am of Opinion that Twenty five or Thirty Sailors had better be draughted from the Army & held in Readiness to embark immediately upon the Arrival of Harris.

This Letter waits upon you by my Son, whom I beg Leave to recommend to your favourable Notice.[7] I am with very great Esteem, Sir Your most obedient and most humble Servant

Nicho. Cooke

LS, DLC:GW; Df, MH: Cooke Papers; copy, M-Ar: Revolution Letters. GW referred this letter to the Massachusetts council. See Committee of the Massachusetts Council to GW, 11 Aug. 1775, and GW to Cooke, 14 Aug. 1775.

1. John Burroughs Hopkins commanded this vessel which was sent to Cap-Français (now Cap-Haïtien), Saint-Domingue, as a joint venture of the Massachusetts provincial congress and the Providence firm of Clark & Nightingale, each of which put up $4,000 to fund the trip. Hopkins's vessel landed at Norwich, Conn., on 28 Aug. with a cargo of gunpowder, lead, flints, and small arms (Cooke to GW, 30 Aug. 1775; Clark & Nightingale to GW, 2 Sept. 1775).

2. John Grimes commanded the smaller of Rhode Island's two armed sloops, and Abraham Whipple commanded the other one, the *Katy*.

3. The purpose was to seize the gunpowder in the royal magazine at Bermuda. See GW to Cooke, 4 Aug. 1775.

4. GW referred this letter to the Massachusetts council on 10 Aug. 1775, but a committee of the council, hearing that Bermudians themselves would send the gunpowder to the Continental Congress in return for the right to continue importing essential provisions from the mainland, dropped the idea of funding a voyage to the island (Committee of the Massachusetts Council to GW, 11 Aug. 1775; Cooke to GW, 11 Aug. 1775, n.2).

5. For accounts of the British raid on Fishers and Gardiners islands, see Norwich Committee of Correspondence to GW, 7 Aug. 1775, and Jonathan Trumbull, Sr., to GW, 7 Aug. 1775, n.2.

6. Cooke wrote to James Warren, president of the Massachusetts provincial congress, on 26 June 1775: "I would just hint to you, whether it would not be advisable to get down from Ticonderoga, as soon as possible, part of the musket balls there, as there is a great scarcity of lead in this country" ("Revolutionary Correspondence," in R.I. Hist. Society, *Collections*, 6 (1867), 107–8). GW instructed Gov. Jonathan Trumbull of Connecticut on 14 Aug. to bring part of the lead from Ticonderoga.

7. Of Cooke's twelve children, the most likely one to have carried this letter

is Nicholas Cooke, Jr., who in December 1775 was entrusted by his father with the task of escorting two prisoners to Hampshire County, Massachusetts (Nicholas Cooke, Sr., to Sheriff of Hampshire County, 13 Dec. 1775, ibid., 140).

To the New York Provincial Congress

⟨Gentlemen Camp at Cambridge Augt 8—1775⟩

It mus⟨t give great Concern to any⟩ considerate Mind that when ⟨this whole Continent at⟩ a vast Expence of Blood & Treasure ⟨is endeavouring to⟩ establish its Liberties on the most se⟨cure and Solid Founda⟩tions not only by a laudable Oppositi⟨on of Force to Force⟩ but denying itself the usual Advantages ⟨of Trade, there⟩ are Men among us so basely sordid as to ⟨Counteract⟩ all our Exertions for the Sake of a little Ga⟨in. You⟩ cannot but have heard that the Distresses ⟨of the Minis⟩terial Troops for fresh Provisions & many other ⟨Necessaries⟩ at Boston were very great: It is a Policy just⟨ifiable by⟩ all the Laws of War to endeavour to increase ⟨them,⟩ Desertions, Discouragement & a Dissatisfaction w⟨ith⟩ the Service, besides weakning their Strength are ⟨some⟩ of the natural Consequences of such a Situation⟨: And⟩ if continued might afford the fairest Hope of ⟨Success⟩ without farther Effusion of human Blood. ⟨A Vessell⟩ cleared lately out of New York for St Croix wit⟨h fresh⟩ Provisions & other Articles has just gone into ⟨Boston⟩ instead of pursuing her Voyage to the We⟨st Indies. I have⟩ endeavoured to discover the Name of ⟨the Captain or Owner but as yet without Success. The Owner (it is said) went to St Croix before the Vessel from which & her late Arrival I make no Doubt you⟩ will be able to disco⟨ver & expose the Villain⟩—And if you could fall upon som⟨e effectual Measure⟩s to prevent the like in future it would ⟨be doing⟩ a signal Service to our common Country.[1]

I have been endeavouring by every Means in ⟨my⟩ Power to discover the future Intentions of our Enemy here. I find a general Idea prevailing thro. the Army & in the Town of Boston that the Troops are soon to ⟨leave the Town & go to Some other Part of the Continent. New York is the Place generally mention'd as their⟩ Destination. I should think a Rumour or Suggestion of this kind worthy of very little Notice if it was not confirmed by some corresponding Circumstances⟨.⟩ But a four

Weeks total Inactivity with all their Reinforcements arrived & recruited, the daily Diminution by Desertions, Sickness & small Skirmishes, induce an Opinion that any Effort they propose to make will be directed elsewhere. I thought it proper ⟨jus⟩t to hint to you what is probably intended ⟨you will then consider what Regard is to be paid to it and what Steps will be proper for you to take if any.⟩[2] I am with grea⟨t Respect & Regard⟩ Gent. Your mos⟨t Obed:⟩ & v⟨ery hume Servt

G. W.⟩

L⟨S⟩, in Joseph Reed's writing, N: New York Provincial Congress, Revolutionary Papers; LB, DLC:GW; Varick transcript, DLC:GW. The L⟨S⟩ was badly damaged in the New York State Library fire of 1911. Missing portions of the text are supplied within angle brackets from the letter-book copy.

1. The New York provincial congress read GW's letter on 19 Aug. 1775 and referred the matter of the ship that was said to have sailed from New York to Boston to the New York City committee of safety for investigation. That same day the provincial congress resolved "that no cattle, sheep, poultry or live stock of any kind, except horses, be exported from this Colony, (save only such ship stores for which the chairman or deputy chairman of the committee at the port or place from whence any vessel may sail, shall give permission,) until it shall be otherways ordered by this or the Continental Congress" (*N.Y. Prov. Congress Journals*, 1:111).

2. For the steps taken by the provincial congress to obtain early warning of any British attack on New York, see GW to Peter Van Brugh Livingston, 10 Aug. 1775, n.3.

From James Otis, Sr.

Sir Council Chamber Watertown [Mass.] 8th Augst 1775.

The letter of August 7th which your Excellency was pleased to direct to me, has been Communicated to the General Court. they Intirely concur in opinion with your Excelly, that the Soldiers and Non-Commissioned officers, absenting themselves from their duty, must be of the most ruinous Consequences to the public, and are determined to exert all their powers to Compel such as have no impediment by Sickness, or other good Reason, to return to their duty immediately: and to prevent all others from absenting themselves without leave in writing under the hand of their Commanding Officer.[1]

With regard to the prisoner your Excelly sent hither, the Court desire your Excelly would be pleased to give orders to have the Witnesses of his conduct sent here to morrow morning at 9 oClock to attend a Committee appointed to examine that matter—I am with great respect Sir Your Most Obedt humbe Servt

James Otis

LS, DLC:GW. This letter was read in the Massachusetts house of representatives on the afternoon of 8 Aug. and then was forwarded to GW (*Mass. House of Rep. Journal,* July–Nov. 1775 sess., 55).

1. The General Court appointed a committee to study this problem on 7 and 8 Aug. 1775, and on 13 Aug. it passed a resolution requiring town authorities to investigate and report on noncommissioned officers and soldiers staying in their towns without leave from the army (GW to James Otis, Sr., 7 Aug. 1775, n.2; Massachusetts General Court to GW, 13 Aug. 1775).

From Jonathan Trumbull, Sr.

Sir Lebanon [Conn.] 8th Augt 1775

I received your favour of the 4th instant,—Observe the contents—The new Levies will come into camp in a short Space—save that on the present Emergency, so large a fleet appearing on our Coasts—I have Ordered Colo. Webb to leave one Captain with his Company at New-Haven for the present—In Addition to one quarter part of the Trained Soldiers of five of our Regiments lying on the Sea Coasts and Sound, to be officered, equip't and in readiness to march at a Minutes Warning.[1]

Yesterday letters were sent to our Commissaries to buy up all the Toe Cloath in this Government for the purpose you mention—The Pattern will be sent from one to another that sutable persons may be employed to make up the Same, to be forw⟨arde⟩d as is directed.

It gave me pain to read your next paragraph not having it in my power to afford further assistance although it is hoped for, & expected every Day.[2]

But I have now the relief and pleasu[r]e to congratulate you, on the supplies coming to you and going to Ty—— & Crown Point.[3] I am, with great Esteem and Regard Sir Your most Obedient humble Servant

Jonth. Trumbull

ALS, DLC:GW; LB, Ct: Trumbull Papers.

1. For accounts of the British fleet off the Connecticut coast, see Norwich Committee of Correspondence to GW, 7 Aug. 1775, and Trumbull to GW, 7 Aug. 1775, n.2. Part of Col. Jedediah Huntington's newly raised 8th Connecticut Regiment joined the Continental army outside Boston on 9 Aug. (General Orders, that date), but Col. Charles Webb's 7th Regiment and the last companies of Huntington's regiment apparently did not arrive until sometime during the latter part of September (Trumbull to GW, 15 Sept. 1775). The five regiments on the seacoast were militia units (Trumbull to GW, 7 Aug. 1775).

2. Trumbull is referring to GW's request for powder, lead, and flints. See GW to Trumbull, 4 Aug. 1775. On 7 Aug. Governor Trumbull and his council sent a letter to Col. Jabez Hamlin, asking him to inform them "of his progress in collecting and sending salt petre and sulphur, to New York, to be made into gun powder" (Hinman, *Historical Collection*, 329).

3. The Connecticut delegates at Philadelphia informed Trumbull in a letter of 28 July 1775 "that about Thirteen Tons of Powder has arrived in this City within a few Days which was sent for by this Congress since their arrival at this place about 6 Tons more is expected every day, the 13 Tons is forwarded to and partly on the way to our Army at Cambridge. We have also received Two Tons & a half from South Carolina which is forwarded directly to General Schuyler which will with what has been sent him before give him we believe about four or five Tons, further Supplies are expected in the several Provinces" (Smith, *Letters of Delegates*, 1:672–73). Congress voted on 25 July to send 6½ tons of gunpowder to GW and on 2 Aug. another 5 tons. See Richard Henry Lee to GW, 1 Aug. 1775, n.3. The first of this gunpowder arrived at Hartford on 11 Aug. (Trumbull to GW, 11, 12 Aug. 1775). The 2½ tons for Schuyler's army at Ticonderoga and Crown Point was approved on 28 July (Roger Sherman to William Williams, 28 July 1775, in Smith, *Letters of Delegates*, 1:674–76).

General Orders

Head Quarters, Cambridge, August 9th 1775.

Parole Rochester. Countersign, Plymouth.

The Commanding Officer of each Regiment, or Corps, is to send a Return at Orderly time, to morrow to the Adjutant General, of the number of Tents or boards, which are wanted to cover the men, that they may be provided as soon as possible. They are also to give in the Names of such of their men, who neither have received Blankets, or who lost them in the engagement, on Bunkers-hill.

As there are several Vacancies in the different Regiments, if there are any particular Gentlemen, who signalized themselves in the Action on Bunkers hill, by their spirited behaviour and good conduct, and of which, sufficient proof is adduced to the General; He will, in filling up the Commissions, use his endeavours to have them appointed (if not already Commission'd) to some Office, or promoted if they are; as it will give him infinite pleasure at all times to reward Merit, wherever it is to be found.[1]

Col. Learnerds Regiment to join General Thomas's Brigade, and Col. Huntington's to join General Spencer's brigade.[2]

Capt. Ballard of Col. Fryes Regiment tried by the late General Court Martial for "profane swearing and for beating, and abusing his men": The Court find the Prisoner guilty, in two Instances of profane swearing and of beating his men, and therefore sentence him to pay, a Fine of Four Shillings, for each Offence.[3]

Capt. Jesse Saunders of Col. Sargeants Regiment, tried by the late General Court Martial for "frequently drawing more Provisions, than he had men in his Company to consume; for forcing the Sentry, and taking away a Gun, the property of William Turner; and threatening the Life of Serjeant Connor, Cocking and presenting his Gun at him, when in the execution of his duty"—The Court are unanimously of Opinion, that the prisoner is *guilty* of the whole of the Charge, exhibited against him, and unanimously adjudge that he be forthwith cashiered. The General approves the above sentence, and orders them to be put in immediate execution.[4]

To morrow the Rules and Articles form'd by the Hon: the Continental Congress for the Government of the Troops of the Twelve United Colonies; will be delivered out, to be distributed through the several Corps of the Army—They are to be signed by the several Officers of each Regiment, beginning with the Colonels, and then by the Soldiers; in the blank Leaves left for that purpose; and after they are so subscribed, they are to be deposited with the Captain of each Company—If there are any Officers, or Soldiers, who refuse to sign them, their Names, the Company's & Regiments to which they respectively belong, are to be reported to the Commander in Chief without delay.[5]

Mr John Goddard is appointed by the Commander in Chief; Waggon Master General to the Army of the Twelve United Colonies, and is to be obeyed as such.[6]

Varick transcript, DLC:GW.

1. GW received recommendations of such persons in letters of 10 Aug. 1775 from the officers and men of Capt. Levi Spaulding's company, from Artemas Ward, and from Jonathan Ward.

2. Col. Ebenezer Learned's Massachusetts regiment, which was assigned to Brig. Gen. Joseph Spencer's brigade at Roxbury in General Orders, 22 July 1775, was transferred to Brig. Gen. John Thomas's brigade, which was also at Roxbury, in order to make room for Col. Jedediah Huntington's newly raised Connecticut regiment. Only part of Huntington's regiment apparently was at Roxbury at this time (Jonathan Trumbull, Sr., to GW, 15 Sept. 1775). Ebenezer Learned (1728–1801) of Oxford, Mass., served as a captain in a provincial regiment during the French and Indian War and represented his town in the provincial congress before being commissioned a colonel of a Massachusetts regiment on 20 May 1775. In March 1776 he acted as an intermediary between GW and Gen. William Howe during the British evacuation of Boston, and he is said to have personally opened the gates to the city. Although illness obliged Learned to leave the army in the spring of 1776, he returned a year later when the Continental Congress appointed him a brigadier general. Learned commanded a brigade during the Saratoga campaign but resigned his commission in March 1778 on account of recurrent ill health.

3. William Hudson Ballard (d. 1814) of Amesbury, Mass., continued to serve in the Continental army until 1 Jan. 1781. He was promoted to major of the 15th Massachusetts Regiment on 1 July 1779.

4. For GW's particular remarks on this case, see General Orders, 10 Aug. 1775.

5. Hancock sent printed copies of the Continental articles of war with his letter to GW of 5 July 1775. For a discussion of them, see Richard Henry Lee to GW, 29 June 1775, n.3. The first article required all present and future members of the Continental army to sign the Continental articles of war. "But," it went on to say, "if any of the officers or soldiers, now of the said army, do not subscribe these rules and regulations, then they may be retained in the said army, subject to the rules and regulations under which they entered into the service, or be discharged from the service, at the option of the Commander in chief" (*JCC*, 2 : 112). GW chose the first option when many officers and soldiers declined to sign for fear that this might obligate them to serve for a longer time than they had originally agreed. See General Orders, 24 Aug. 1775, and GW to Hancock, 21 Sept. 1775.

6. John Goddard (1730–1816) of Brookline served in the first Massachusetts provincial congress, and on 24 Feb. 1775 the committees of safety and supplies made him wagon master for the Massachusetts forces. Goddard remained Continental wagon master general until the spring of 1776, when he resigned rather than go to New York with the army. He served in the Massachusetts house of representatives from 1776 to 1777, from 1784 to 1789, and in 1792.

Instructions to John Goddard

[Cambridge c.9 August 1775]

1. The Army being in 3 Divisions, Roxbury, Cambridge & Prospect Hill under the Majors Genl Ward, Lee & Puttnam you are to have a sufficient Number of Teams for the Service of each Division.

2. When any Person applies to you for a Team he must produce an Order from the Commander in Chief, one of the Majors General for whose Division the Service is to be done, or the Commissary General otherwise you are not obliged to pay any Regard to it.

3. Once a Week on every Saturday you are to make a Return to the Commander in Chief of the Number of Teams in Service & what Work they have been employed the preceding Week—taking special Care not to put the publick to needless Charge by providing & keeping more Teams than are absolutely necessary.

4. As to the Manner in which the Teams are to be fed it will be best they should find themselves & be paid accordly. The Carts or Waggons may be numbered & the Number with the Words *Continental Army* on a Board put on some Part of the Cart or Waggon most easily seen.

Df, in Joseph Reed's writing, DLC:GW; Varick transcript, DLC:GW. The draft includes the heading "Instructions for the Waggon Master Genl." Neither the draft nor the Varick transcript has a dateline, but it is probable that these instructions were given to Goddard about the time of his appointment as wagon master general. See General Orders, this date.

To Jonathan Trumbull, Sr.

Sir Camp at Cambridge August 9th 1775

From some late Intelligence out of Boston & sundry corroborating Circumstances, there is great Reason to suspect, that the Ministerial Troop intend either to make a Diversion to the Southward, or wholly to remove—If they should do either, it is most probable New York is the Place of their Destination; I therefore think it most Adviseable, that the Troop of your Colony who have not yet march'd, or may easely be recalled, should wait further Orders—You will therefore Sir be pleased to give the necessary Directions for this Purpose As soon as possible.[1]

No Occurrence in the Camp of any Consequence since I had the Pleasure of addressing you last. I am with due Regard Your most Obedt humble Servant

Go. Washington

LB, Ct: Trumbull Papers; LB, DLC:GW; Varick transcript, DLC:GW. This letter was carried by Maj. Obadiah Johnson of the 3d Connecticut Regiment (Trumbull to GW, 11 Aug. 1775).

1. For Trumbull's orders regarding the disposition of Col. Charles Webb's and Col. Jedediah Huntington's regiments, see Trumbull to GW, 11 Aug. and 15 Sept. 1775.

General Orders

Head Quarters, Cambridge, August 10th 1775.
Parole Schuylkill. Countersign, Richmond.

It is a matter of exceeding great Concern to the General, to find, that at a time when the united efforts of America are exerting in defence of the common Rights and Liberties of mankind, that there should be in an Army constituted for so noble a purpose, such repeated Instances of Officers, who lost to every sense of honour and virtue, are seeking by dirty and base means, the promotion of their own dishonest Gain, to the eternal Disgrace of themselves, and Dishonour of their country—practices of this sort will never be overlooked, whenever an Accusation is lodged, but the Authors brought to the most exemplary punishment: It is therefore much to be wish'd, that the Example of Jesse Saunders, late Captain in Col. Sergeants regiment, will prove the last shameful Instance of such a groveling disposition, and that for the future, every Officer for his own Honour, and the sake of an injured Public, will make a point of detecting every iniquitous practice of this kind; using their utmost endeavours in their several Capacities, to lessen the Expence of the War, as much as possible, that the great Cause in which we are struggling may receive no Injury from the enormity of the expence.[1]

The several Pay Masters are immediately to ascertain, what pay was due to the different Regiments and Corps, on the first day of this Instant, that each Man may receive his respective due, as soon as the Money arrives to pay them. It is earnestly recommended that great Exactness be used in these settlements, First, that no man goes without his pay, and next, that not one farthing more be drawn than what is justly due; after this the pay may be drawn once a Month, or otherwise, as shall be found most convenient, in the mean while the Soldiers need be under no Apprehension of getting every Farthing that is justly their due: It is therefore expected that they do their duty with that cheerfulness and alacrity, becoming Men, who are contending for their Liberty, Property and every thing that is valuable to Freemen, and their posterity.[2]

Varick transcript, DLC:GW.

1. For the charges of which Saunders was convicted, see General Orders, 9 Aug. 1775.

2. For the settlement of pay accounts for the Massachusetts troops, see Committee of the Massachusetts Council to GW, 11 Aug.; GW to the Massachusetts General Court, 12 Aug.; Massachusetts General Court to GW, 18 Aug.; and General Orders, 24, 31 Aug., 5 Sept. 1775. For complaints about pay, see Officers of Col. Samuel Gerrish's Regiment to GW, this date.

From the Officers of Colonel Samuel Gerrish's Regiment

Camps at Chelsea, Malden, Medford, and Sewells Point [Mass.], the 10th Aug., 1775.

Your Excellencies' humble petitioners, We, the Subscribers, Officers of the Regiment, Commanded by Colonell Samuell Gerrish, Esqr.: formerly in the Massachusetts Colony Service, now in the Continental, humbly beg Leave to inform your Excellency, that the most, and even more than 2 thirds of us, have been here in actual Service, since the Beginning of the Campaign, and been to a vast Deal of Expense, and not receiv'd one farthing of our pay; we therefore humbly petition your Excellency would make just provision, that we might at least receive some part of our pay, it being impossible for us,—some being at a great Distance from home,—to subsist without it;[1] relying on your Excellency's kind Compliance, we think it an honour to subscribe ourselves, Your Excellency's Most humble, and most obedient Servants,

Thomas Mighill, Capt.
T. Baker, Jr., Capt.
Thos. Pike, Lieut.
Tho. Cumming, Lieut.
Mark Cresey, Lieut.
Caleb Robinson, Lieut.
Mica (?) Hoit, Lieut.
Jonas Johnson, Lieut.
all at Sewel's point.

Mellen Chamberlain, ed., *A Documentary History of Chelsea Including the Boston Precincts of Winnisimmet, Rumney Marsh, and Pullen Point, 1624–1824*, 2 vols. (Boston, 1908), 2:466–67.

Thomas Mighill (1722–1807), Thomas Pike (died c.1816), and Mark Cressey (1734–1816), all of Rowley, Mass., apparently served in the Continental army until sometime in 1776. Caleb Robinson (1746–1799) and Micah Hoit were New Hampshire residents, and both joined the 2d New Hampshire Regiment in November 1776. Robinson was made a captain in that regiment, and Hoit became a second lieutenant. Robinson was captured at the Battle of Hubbardton in July 1777 but was later released. He returned to the army to become a brigade inspector in July 1781 and a major in the 2d New Hampshire Regiment in October of that year. Robinson retired in March 1782. Hoit was promoted to first lieutenant in December 1777 and left the army in the spring of 1779. Lt. Jonas Johnson and Capt. T. Baker, Jr., have not been identified, although Capt. John Baker may have served in this regiment. See John Baker to GW, 14 Sept. 1775. Lieutenant Cumming may be Thomas Cummings (d. 1825), who served as a lieutenant in the 10th Massachusetts Regiment from November 1776 to October 1778.

1. For GW's efforts to pay the army, see General Orders, this date, and GW to the Massachusetts General Court, 12 Aug. 1775.

To Peter Van Brugh Livingston

⟨Sir Camp at Cambridge Augt 10: 1775⟩

Your Fa⟨vor of the 2d Inst. is⟩ duly received,[1] but it is out of ⟨my Power to Comply⟩ with the Request it contains, of f⟨orwarding Com⟩missions. All those I have yet rece⟨ived from the⟩ Honble Continental Congress, are far short ⟨of the Number⟩ required in this Army: for which Rea⟨son when⟩ at New York, & by Letter from this, I direct⟨ed Genl⟩ Schuyler to apply to the

Congress at Phila. ⟨for⟩ those of his Department, as the shortest & ea⟨siest⟩ Mode—To which I must also now refer y⟨ou.⟩[2]

We have had no Occurrence in the Camp for several Days worthy of Notice: But by some Advices from Boston, & several concurring Ci⟨rcum⟩stances; we have great Reason to suspect a P⟨art⟩ or the whole of the ministerial Troops are a⟨bout⟩ to remove: New York is the Place generally ⟨talkd⟩ of as their Destination: I give y⟨ou the In⟩telligence as it came to m⟨e, but do not vouch for it's Authenticity.[3] I a⟩m with the most re⟨spectful Regar⟩ds to yourself & the Body over wh⟨om you pres⟩ide Sir, Your most Obedt & very Hbble Servt

Go: Washington

LS, in Joseph Reed's writing, N: New York Provincial Congress, Revolutionary Papers; LB, DLC:GW; Varick transcript, DLC:GW. The LS was badly damaged in the New York State Library fire of 1911. Missing portions of the text are supplied within angle brackets from the letter-book copy at DLC:GW. This letter was read in the New York provincial congress on 17 Aug. 1775 (*N.Y. Prov. Congress Journals*, 1:109).

1. The letter from the provincial congress to which GW is responding is dated 3 Aug. 1775.

2. For GW's directions to Schuyler regarding commissions for the New York department, see Schuyler to GW, 1 July 1775, n.5, and GW to Schuyler, 10–11 July 1775. For the letter that the provincial congress wrote to Charles Thomson on 18 Aug. requesting 200 blank commissions, see Peter Van Brugh Livingston to GW, 21 Aug. 1775, n.2.

3. This intelligence prompted the provincial congress on 18 Aug. to order the sending of "two prime sailing boats . . . to the eastward, to observe if they can discover any fleet steering towards the westward" and "to give the speediest intelligence to this Congress of any fleet they may discover." That same day the provincial congress wrote to Brig. Gen. David Wooster asking him to return to his camp "at Harlem, with the utmost speed, to assist in the defence of this city and Province." It also requested the committees at Philadelphia and Elizabeth, N.J., to keep their militia "properly arrayed, to march at a moment's warning" to the assistance of New York (*N.Y. Prov. Congress Journals*, 1:110–11).

From the Marblehead Committee of Safety

Hond Sir Marblehead [Mass.] Augt 10th 1775

on the 8th Instant, Lambert Bromitt and Benjamin Silsby the Persons that accompany this Letter put in here from Boston, as they say on accot of the Weather, as they have been Conversing wth some of the Inhabitants of this place, we have Reason to Suspect they may carry some Inteligence wch might be determental to the cause of America, We have Examined them, & finding their Intention was to Return back, we have taken their Boat under our Care, and have sent them to Head Quarters, that there they may be treated as in your Wisdom shall be judged Necessary.[1] We are Hond Sir wth the greatest Respect your most Obedt & huble Servts the Committee of Safety of sd Marblehead.

℘ ordr
Edd Fettyplace Chairman[2]

LS, in Edward Fettyplace's writing, M-Ar: Revolution Letters. Perez Morton wrote on the second page of the manuscript "August 15th 1775 In Council read & ordered that Mr Sever Mr J. Taylor & Captn White be a Comee to take this Letter into Consideration & report."

1. The two men may be Lombard Brommett of Boston and Benjamin Silsbee (b. 1738) of Salem.

2. This is probably Edward Fettyplace (c.1721–1805) of Marblehead.

From Captain Levi Spaulding's Company

Winter Hill [Mass.] 10 August 1775. The subscribers commend "the conduct and undaunted courage of William Lee" at the Battle of Bunker Hill. "He not only fought well himself but give good advice to the men, to place themselves in right order and to stand their ground well, the said William Lee belonging to Capt. Spauldin's company in Colo. Reed's Regiment, and is the first or orderly sergeant of Capt. Spaulding's company and as their is a vacancie in the same company by a Lieut['s]. Death, it is desired for the Ensign to take his place, and sergeant Lee to take the Ensign's or second Lieut."[1]

Copy, MHi: John Sullivan Papers. The names of forty-one subscribers appear at the bottom of the document. They include three officers: Capt. Levi Spaulding, "Thomas Roffe. Ensign belonging to Capt. Spaulding," and "William Roby. Ensign belonging to Capt. [William] Walker." The copyist erred in the name of Spaulding's ensign. He was Thomas Buffe.

Levi Spaulding (1737–1825) was commissioned a captain in the 3d New Hampshire Regiment on 23 May 1775 and served to the end of 1776. He represented Lyndebourgh in the New Hampshire general assembly from 1780 to 1781.

1. William Lee was promoted to ensign at the end of 1775, and on 8 Nov. 1776 he became a second lieutenant in the 1st New Hampshire Regiment. Spaulding's lieutenant at the Battle of Bunker Hill was Joseph Bradford.

From Major General Artemas Ward

Camp at Roxbury [Mass.] 10 August 1775. "Capt. Baldwin, the Bearer hereof, has been for three Months past engaged as an Engineer in the Service of the united Colonies. he was upon Bunker's Hill, & behaved very well thro' the Engagment. . . . He has no Birth in the Army, If any Vacancy presents, & he can be advanced I doubt not he will do Honor to his Office."[1]

LS, DLC:GW.

1. Although Jeduthan Baldwin (1732–1788) of Brookfield, Mass., served with the American army as an assistant engineer throughout the siege of Boston, he received no rank until 26 April 1776, at which time Congress appointed him a lieutenant colonel (*JCC*, 4:312). As a provincial captain during the French and Indian War, Baldwin helped erect Fort William Henry on Lake George in 1755–56, participated in the siege of Ticonderoga in 1759, and late in the war oversaw the building of a new fort at Crown Point. In 1774 Baldwin represented Brookfield in the first Massachusetts provincial congress. He was involved in laying out the American defensive lines at Bunker Hill before the battle on 17 June 1775, and in the following months he worked on fortifications at Prospect Hill, Sewall's Point, Cobble Hill, and Dorchester Neck (Baldwin to John Adams, 21 Jan., 28 Mar. 1776, in Taylor, *Papers of John Adams*, 3:408–9, 4:93). Baldwin was assisting with the defense of New York City in April 1776, when he was appointed lieutenant colonel. He subsequently served the American army in the northern department as its chief engineer, and on 3 Sept. 1776 Congress promoted him to full colonel (*JCC*, 5:732). In July 1778 Baldwin became commander of the army's artificers, a position which he held until he resigned his commission in April 1782.

From Lieutenant Colonel Jonathan Ward

[c.10 August 1775]. "A Return of the Names of some of the Officers and Gentlemen in Genl Wards Regimt who Distinguish'd themselves by Valour and Courage in the Days of Engagement:" Capt. Seth Washburn, Capt. Samuel Wood, Lt. Loring Lincoln, and Lt. Joseph Livermore, all at Bunker Hill;[1] "Mr Thomas Davison a Volunteer in the Service, and Lieutenant in the Malitia," at Hog Island, Bunker Hill, and Light House Island. Ward requests that Davison "may have one of the Small Arms with the Accoutrements belonging to the same that was taken at the Light House Island."

ADS, DLC:GW.

1. These four officers apparently resigned from the army at the end of 1775. Capt. Seth Washburn (1723–1794) and his company distinguished

themselves at Bunker Hill by covering the retreat of other American units at the end of the battle. The other captain mentioned here was Samuel Hood, not Samuel Wood.

General Orders

Head Quarters, Cambridge, August 11th 1775

Parole Tunbridge. Countersign Squantum.

Complaints having been made by the Inhabitants to the East of Watertown, that their Gardens are robb'd, their Fields laid waste, and Fences destroyed; Any Person who shall for the future be detected in such flagitious, wicked practices, will be punished without mercy.

The Commander in Chief has been pleased to appoint Stephen Moylan Esqr. to be Muster Master General to the Army of the United Colonies; he is in all things touching his duty, as Muster, Master General, to be consider'd and obeyed as such.[1]

Varick transcript, DLC:GW.

1. This office was also called commissary general of musters (GW to John Dickinson, 30 Aug. 1775). For Moylan's duties as mustermaster general, see Dickinson to GW, 25 July 1775, n.1.

From Lieutenant Colonel Loammi Baldwin

Chelsea [Mass.] 11th August 1775

May it please your Excellency.

Your Excellency will excuse my not sending the Observations Yesterday, as the Docter[1] had one of the Express Horses to Cambridge for medicine for the Sick, which prevented it; for as there was nothing extraordinary in the Observations, I thought it of less consequence that they should not be sent to headquarters, than that we should be left without any Horse to go on Express in case any thing extraordinary should happen.

Inclos'd your Excellency will find the observations of the Day, as also of the 9th and 10th inst.[2] I am, with the utmost Respect, Your Excellency Most Obedient Humble Servant

Loammi Baldwin Commandg Officer at Chelsea

ALS, DLC:GW.

1. The surgeon of Samuel Gerrish's Massachusetts regiment was David Jones (d. 1822).

2. The returns of the observations for the days 9, 10, and 11 Aug. 1775, all in Joseph Leach's writing, are in DLC:GW.

From Nicholas Cooke

Sir Providence August 11th 1775.

Since my last to you Mr Ward One of the Delegates hath returned from the Congress.[1] He informs me that some of the Bermudians had been at Philadelphia soliciting for Liberty to import Provisions for the Use of the Island. They gave Information of the Powder mentioned in your Letter to me, and were of Opinion it might be easily obtained. They were told by the Delegates that every Vessel they should send to the Northward with Powder should be permitted to carry Provisions to the Island. Whether their Situation will not probably prevent them from bringing the Powder I submit to your Excellency.[2] Mr Porter, and Mr Harris are both here. To Mr Porter who can fully inform you in the Matter I refer you.

I have forwarded about 1300 lb. of Lead which is all that can be procured at present; that Article being extremely scarce among us. In my last to you I mentioned that I thought it might be brought from Ticonderoga with more Ease than it can be procured in any other Way; and am still of the same Opinion.

I have given Orders to the Committee of Safety to purchase all the Tow-Cloth that is to be bought in the Government; but am afraid the Quantity will be small; the Scarcity of course Linens in the Colony having occasioned a great Use of that Article in Families. I am with great Esteem, Sir Your Excellency's most obedient humble Servant

Nicho. Cooke

LS, DLC:GW; Df, MH: Cooke Papers. The addressed cover of the LS includes the notation "Favoured by Col. Porter." GW referred this letter to the Massachusetts General Court. See GW to Cooke, 14 Aug. 1775.

1. Samuel Ward (1725–1776), a prosperous merchant from Newport, served three terms as governor of Rhode Island during the 1760s. Elected a delegate to both the First and Second Continental Congresses, he represented his colony in Philadelphia until his death on 26 Mar. 1776 from small-

pox. His son Samuel Ward, Jr. (1756–1832), was an officer in the 1st Rhode Island Regiment.

2. Bermuda, having little agriculture of its own, relied heavily on shipments of provisions from the mainland colonies, and the islanders feared that they might starve when the Continental Congress's nonexportation program began on 10 Sept. 1775. To avert such a calamity, a delegation of Bermudians arrived in Philadelphia in early July to petition Congress for an exemption from some of the proposed nonexportation restrictions. Vulnerable to British retaliation, they were unwilling to support the American cause openly, but they were prepared to curtail their trade somewhat if allowed to continue importing basic foodstuff from American ports. About the middle of July it was privately agreed that Congress would grant the Bermudians their desired exemption if they supplied the Patriots with gunpowder. The Bermuda delegation returned home, and on 14 Aug. a group of islanders seized about one hundred barrels of gunpowder from the royal arsenal near St. George. That gunpowder was shipped to Philadelphia and Charleston, and in the fall Congress approved the exportation to Bermuda of specified amounts of corn, bread, flour, meat, peas, beans, and rice (*JCC*, 3:362–64).

To Lieutenant General Thomas Gage

Sir Cambridge August 11th 1775

I understand that the Officers engaged in the Cause of Liberty, and their Country, who by the Fortune of War, have fallen into your Hands have been thrown indiscriminately, into a common Gaol appropriated for Felons—That no Consideration has been had for those of the most respectable Rank, when languishing with Wounds and Sickness. That some have been even amputated, in this unworthy Situation.[1]

Let your Opinion, Sir, of the Principle which actuates them be what it may, they suppose they act from the noblest of all Principles, a Love of Freedom, and their Country. But political Opinions I conceive are foreign to this Point, the Obligations arising from the Rights of Humanity, & Claims of Rank, are universally binding and extensive, except in Case of Retaliation. These, I should have hoped, would have dictated a more tender Treatment of those Individuals, whom Chance or War had put in your Power—Nor can I forbear suggesting, its fatal Tendency to widen that unhappy Breach, which you, and those Ministers under whom you act, have repeatedly declared you wish'd to see forever closed.

My Duty now makes it necessary to apprize you, that for the future I shall regulate my Conduct towards those Gentlemen who are or may be in our Possession, exactly by the Rule which you shall observe, towards those of ours, who may be in your Custody. If Severity, & Hardship mark the Line of your Conduct, (painful as it may be to me) your Prisoners will feel its Effects: But if Kindness & Humanity are shewn to ours, I shall with Pleasure consider those in our Hands, only as unfortunate, and they shall receive the Treatment to which the unfortunate are ever intitled.

I beg to be favoured with an Answer as soon as possible. And am, Sir, Your most Obedt & very Hbble Servt

Go: Washington

LS, in Joseph Reed's writing, MiU-C: Gage Papers; copy, P.R.O., C.O.5/92, ff. 256–57; copy, DLC:GW; copy DNA:PCC, item 152; copy, DNA:PCC, item 169; copy, NjMoNP; Varick transcript, DLC:GW. The LS is endorsed "Recd Aug. 11th." The copy in the Public Record Office was enclosed in Gage's letter to the earl of Dartmouth of 20 Aug. 1775, and the copy in PCC, item 152, was enclosed in GW to Hancock, 31 Aug. 1775.

Thomas Gage (c.1719–1787), commander in chief of the British forces in North America from 1763 to 1775, became acquainted with GW on the Braddock expedition in 1755, and the two men remained friends until the beginning of the Revolution. A lieutenant colonel in Braddock's army, Gage rose to the rank of major general by the end of the French and Indian War and was named temporary commander in chief for North America in the fall of 1763. His appointment became permanent a year later, and in 1770 he was promoted to lieutenant general. When Gage went home to England on a leave of absence in the spring of 1773, GW attended the farewell dinner given him by the citizens of New York (*Diaries*, 3:182). During the year that Gage was gone from his post, events in America reached a crisis. Gage returned to America in May 1774 not only as commander in chief but also as royal governor of Massachusetts charged with implementing Parliament's punitive measures against that colony. He commanded the British army in Boston throughout the troubled months that followed. Receiving orders recalling him to England on 26 Sept. 1775, Gage turned his command over to Gen. William Howe on 10 Oct. and arrived in London on 14 November. He spent the remainder of his life in England in virtual retirement.

1. The prisoners held by the British in Boston included a number of American soldiers captured at the Battle of Bunker Hill, some of whom were severely wounded, and several civilians who were suspected of spying for the Patriots or otherwise assisting them. One of the jailed civilians, John Leach, wrote in his journal for 19 Aug. 1775: "The poor sick and Wounded prisoners fare very hard, are many days without the Comforts of Life. Doctor Brown Complained to Mr. [James] Lovell and me, that they had no Bread all that Day

and the day before. He spoke to the Provost, as he had the Charge of serving the Bread; he replied, they might eat the Nail Heads, and knaw the plank and be damn'd. The Comforts that are sent us by our Friends we are obliged to impart to these poor suffering Friends, and Fee the soldiers and others with Rum, to carry it [to] them by stealth, when we are Close Confined and cannot get to them. They have no Wood to burn many days together, to Warm their Drink, and dying men drink them cold. Some of the Limbs which have been taken off, it was said, were in a state of Putrifaction, not one survived amputation" ("A Journal Kept by John Leach during His Confinement by the British, in Boston Gaol, in 1775" in *New England Historical and Genealogical Register*, 19 [1865], 260).

From a Committee of the Massachusetts Council

In Council [Watertown, Mass.] August 11th 1775.

May it please your Excellency,

We have taken into consideration the Honble Govr Cooke's Lettr which your Excellency furnished us with; & by the Honble John Adam's Esqr. from the American Congress, we are informed, that the Powder mention'd, has been Sent for, & is, probably, now on the Water; & Provisions are allow'd to be exported, in Pay for that article.[1]

We have also considered your Excellency's message by Colo. Read; and acquaint your Excellency, that provision is made for finishing the Payment of the advanced Wages promised to the Troops; they have the liberty to take up of the Commissary, half their Wages; much has been taken up, & they have not had encouragement for any other payment 'till the end of the Campaign, & we apprehend, that they do not expect it: If they Shou'd be paid up to the first of August, it wou'd require a Settlement with 'em individually, which cannot now be attended to, without injuring the public Service.[2]

As to Vacancies of Commissions in the Army, we wou'd beg the favour of your Excellency to give us the earliest notice of Such as may happen in the Massachusetts Troops, & we will diligently attend to the matter, so that such Persons may be commissionated as will best promote the good of their particular Corps, & the general Service.

And as to the Prisoners, we wou'd recommend to your Excellency, that such of 'em as are of least importance, may be Secured in the Jails of Ipswich & Taunton; but there is a certain

Ichabod Jones, & some officers, which, we think, had better be Sent to Northampton Jail, or other inland place of Security: And we doubt not your Excellencys care to prevent such Prisoners being exchanged, as may be eminently serviceable to our Enemies.[3]

And as to the Contracts made by the Comtee of Supplies, we see not how, in honour, they can be vacated, without the consent of both parties; but if in this, or any thing else, we can assist your Exellency, to promote the general Service, you may be assured that we shall chearfully meet your warmest wishes.[4]

J. Palmer Chairman

LS, in Joseph Palmer's writing, DLC:GW; copy, M-Ar. The LS is prefaced with the statement "The Comtee appointed to take in consideration the Honble Govr Cooke's Letter of the 8th Inst., & his Excellency Genl Washington's Message of yesterday by Colo: Read, beg leave to Report by way of Letter to Genl Washington." At the end of the LS appear the words "August 11th 1775 In Council read & accepted Perez Morton Secry protem."

No record of this committee appears in the journals of either house of the General Court. Nicholas Cooke's letter of 8 Aug. is his of that date to GW, in which he proposes applying to the General Court for part of the money needed to send a ship to Bermuda for gunpowder. GW's message of 10 Aug. apparently was delivered orally by Joseph Reed. No letter or memorandum of that date from GW or Reed to the council has been found.

1. During the Continental Congress's late summer recess, John Adams attended some meetings of the Massachusetts council, to which he had been elected on 21 July by the house of representatives. He was present on 10 Aug. and apparently informed the committee of Congress's private agreement with a delegation from Bermuda to allow the Bermudians to continue to import foodstuffs from the mainland colonies in exchange for gunpowder. See Nicholas Cooke to GW, 11 Aug. 1775, n.2.

2. The General Court's resolution of 29 July, which established a committee to obtain a list of the men who had and had not received their advanced pay, appears in General Orders, 1 Aug. 1775. That committee reported on 9 Aug. that although it had applied to the colonels and paymasters of the Massachusetts regiments for the desired information, many of them had not yet responded, "which Delay causes great Uneasiness in those Regiments, at least where the Returns have been duly made, and will soon put it out of the Power of the Officers to quiet their Men, unless the Grounds of their Complaint are speedily removed." To correct the situation, the General Court resolved that same day to empower Richard Devens, a member of the house of representatives and the committee of safety, "to receive the Money out of the Treasury, and Pay the advance Wages to those Men who have not receiv'd it," as quickly as the committee was "able to ascertain to him the Numbers in each Regiment respectively" (*Mass. House of Rep. Journal*, July–Nov. 1775 sess., 56).

For GW's insistence on having all army pay accounts brought up to date, see General Orders, 10, 24, and 31 Aug. 1775, and GW to the Massachusetts General Court, 12 Aug. 1775. For the settlement of the Massachusetts accounts, see the Massachusetts General Court to GW, 18 Aug. 1775, and General Orders, 24, 31 Aug. and 5 Sept. 1775.

3. Horatio Gates wrote to James Otis on this date: "By Order of The Commander in Chief I send to wait your Orders, an Officers Party to Escort Seventeen Seamen taken Prisoners at Machias; and One Tory, Ichabud Jones; thirty Prisoners more taken at Cape Ann, will be at Watertown to day. I believe you will think it best to Detain this party at Watertown, until that [from] Cape Ann Arrives, when they may have your Orders to what Town they are to March to be confin'd. I have already sent a Number of Prisoners to Springfield & Torys to Worcester. perhaps you may approve of placing these at Northampton, as there are so many at present at Springfield" (M-Ar: Revolution Letters). Ichabod Jones, a merchant at Machias in the District of Maine, went to Boston in May 1775 and returned to Machias on 2 June with two sloops to obtain lumber for the British army. An armed schooner from the British navy accompanied him. On 11 and 12 June a body of Machias Patriots, led by Jeremiah O'Brien and Joseph Wheaton, attacked Jones and his British protectors, killing several of the party and capturing the rest. Jones was confined in Northampton, and his property at Machias was seized by the local committee of safety. The prisoners from Cape Ann were men from the British sloop *Falcon* who were captured on 8 Aug. when they attempted to seize an American merchant vessel in the harbor at Gloucester, Massachusetts. They included a British gunner, 15 British seamen, 7 British marines, a boy, and several Americans who had been pressed into service.

4. In a resolution passed by the house of representatives on 12 Aug. and approved by the council two days later, it was agreed "that as the *Massachusetts* Army, raised for the Defence of American Liberty, is now become Part of the Continental Army, that therefore all Contracts made by our Committee of Supplies, for Victualling said *Massachusetts* Army, are terminated; and the Commissary General of said Continental Army, is to be considered at Liberty to purchase Supplies for Victualling said Army, of such Persons, and in such Way and Manner as he shall see fit" (*Mass. House of Rep. Journal*, July–Nov. 1775 sess., 68; also in "Mass. Council Journal," July 1775–Feb. 1776 sess., 77).

From Jonathan Trumbull, Sr.

Sir Lebanon [Conn.] 11th Augt 1775

Yesterday 12 O'clo. received your Letter ℔ Majr Johnson.[1]

Immediately gave the necessary Directions, Some Companies I ordered to New London; others to New-Haven—Colo. Webb with the Companies that way if not marched to take his Station at Greenwich[2]—Same day at 11 O'clo. received a Letter from Brigr General Wooster, dated the 9th at the Oyster Ponds on

Long Island, he had with him 450 men besides Militia, designing to preserve the Stock at that Place—The Ships were then plundering Gardiner's Island—The People on the Island had left it—He applied to me for 300 lb. Powder[3]—before I had made my Answer and Order for the Powder—which I gave notwithstanding Our exhausted Condition—On receipt of your's inserted an Extract from it for his Observation.

I am informed a Quantity of Powder for the Camp is to be at Hartford this Evening, and more to follow Soon[4]—We have none lately arrived, which is daily expected—I request your Direction that of the Next quantity that comes to Hartford there may be lodged there so much as you shall judge Expedient—If what is expected do arrive in the mean Time Shall have no occasion to use your Allowance. I am, most respectfully Sir—Your most Obedient very humble Servant

Jonth. Trumbull

ALS, DLC:GW; LB, Ct: Trumbull Papers.

1. The letter was the one that GW wrote to Trumbull on 9 Aug. 1775. Obadiah Johnson served as major of the 3d Connecticut Regiment from 1 May to 16 Dec. 1775. He was lieutenant colonel of Col. Andrew Ward's Connecticut state regiment between May 1776 and May 1777 and later became a colonel in the Connecticut militia.

2. For a fuller account of Trumbull's stationing of various companies from Col. Charles Webb's and Col. Jedediah Huntington's regiments along the Connecticut coast to oppose any possible British landing there or at New York, see Trumbull to GW, 15 Sept. 1775.

3. "By the request of the Provincial Congress of New York," David Wooster wrote to Trumbull on 9 Aug. 1775, "I yesterday embarked from New York with four hundred and fifty men, and this afternoon arrived here [the Oyster Ponds], We find that the Inhabitants are in great need of powder—There is none in New York, I spared two Hundred weight from my own Stock which was forwarded from New York to this place for the use of the York Provincials who were stationed here, of consequence our Stock is reduced to about twenty rounds a man—The Regulars have taken the Cattle Sheep &c from Fishers Island & this day have employed themselves in the same business on Gardner's Island, when they have got through with that we may expect them upon this—I beg that your honour would with the greatest expedition possible forward to me, three hundred weight of powder, which I hope will be sufficient for the present exigency both for our own Troops and the Militia here" (Clark, *Naval Documents*, 1:1105). The Oyster Ponds were near Orient Point on the eastern end of Long Island.

4. This was the 6½ tons of gunpowder which the Continental Congress on 25 July ordered to be sent from Philadelphia to Cambridge. See Richard

Henry Lee to GW, 1 Aug. 1775, n.3, and Trumbull to GW, 8 Aug. 1775, n.3. For the arrival of the gunpowder at Cambridge, see GW to Schuyler, 14 Aug. 1775.

Letter not found: to Lund Washington, c.11 Aug. 1775. On 15 Oct. 1775 Lund Washington wrote to GW: "in the one [letter] of the 17th of Augst you speak of haveg wrote one abt the 11th."

General Orders

Head Quarters, Cambridge, Augt—12th 1775

Parole Ulster. Countersign Torrington

Varick transcript, DLC:GW.

To John Brown

Sir, Camp at Cambridge Augt 12th 1775.

I am exceedingly obliged to you for the Notice of your Ships Sailing for London—I have availd myself of the oppertunity of writing a Letter to a Gentn in England which I beg leave to recommend to your care.[1] Your Letter to Mr Loyd[2] shall be sent into Boston by the first Flag that goes with Letters & this happens every day almost. I have nothing further to give you the trouble of at present than to assure you that I am Sir Yr Most Obedt & Ob⟨liged⟩ Hble Servt

Go: Washington

ALS, PWCD.

John Brown (1736–1803) and his three brothers were leading merchants of Providence both before and after the Revolution. An outspoken opponent of the Stamp Act, John Brown strongly supported the nonimportation agreements of 1769 and 1775 and instigated the burning of the British revenue cutter *Gaspée* in 1772. Brown served the Continental army well by using his commercial connections to obtain gunpowder and other needed military stores. At the same time he did not hesitate to take advantage of the business opportunities offered by the Revolution, profiting handsomely from the manufacture of cannon at Hope Furnace and from numerous privateering ventures.

1. This letter has not been identified. It may have been written to George William Fairfax or George Mercer.

2. Henry Lloyd (1709–1795) of Boston was a close friend and business associate of the Brown family despite the fact that he was a Loyalist. He went to Halifax, Nova Scotia, in 1776 and died in London.

From Lieutenant Desambrager

Mon General cap[1] ce 12 aoust 1775

Monsieur Le Chevallier Derueville a Eu Lhonneur de vous Ecrire pour vous offrir Ses Services et ceux de trois de Ses camarades dont je Suis du nombre;[2] Lenvie que nous avons de nous distinguer nous fait desirer de Servir Sous vos ordres; nous Servons dans un regiment ou nous Sommes aimés et Estimes de nos Superieurs[.] Sy vous acceptez nos Services nous ferons notre possible pour meriter la même consideration. nous ne parlons pas Lenglois, Lenvie que nous avons de nous rendre util nous fait Esperer que nous ne Serions pas Longtemp Sans nous faire Entendre.

Nous attendons vos ordres. je Suis avec respec Votre tres humble et obeissant Serviteur

Desambrager Lieutenant en Second au regiment du cap

ALS, DLC:GW.

1. Cap-Français, Saint-Domingue.

2. This letter has not been found, nor has any record been discovered of these French officers serving in the Continental army.

To the Massachusetts General Court

Gentlemen Cambridge. Head Quarters. August. 12. 1775

I have considered the Papers you left with me yesterday: those of them, which relate to Jones, shew him to be a most malignant, & inveterate Enemy to his Country, & as such I trust he will meet with his Deserts: But I have such various, & important Matters requiring my constant Attention, that I must beg Leave to refer him, & all others under similar Circumstances to the Authority of the Province, both for safe Custody & Punishment.[1]

The Payment of the Troops is of such indispensable Necessity, that I must endeavour to use the Powers committed to me by the Honorable Congress so as to remove this Cause of Complaint. I propose to direct the new Paymaster[2] to commence his Payments from the 1st August, & hereafter continue them monthly. I have considered that there are few, if any Men, who have not served two Months; and tho. some have received their Advance twice, it cannot be supposed there are many who have had more: The two Months Service, will then be set against the double Advance, and if a strict Scrutiny is immediately made, which I would recommend; the Accounts may be settled to that Time, the Delinquents probably be detected, and in the End, Justice done both to the Province & the Men. If any Embezzlements have been made by the Officers, they will stand accountable to the Publick, but at all Events the Soldiers are intitled to, and must have their Pay, if any Service is expected from them.[3] The Shirts, Shoes, Stockings & Breeches provided by the Province can be taken on the continental Account; but I apprehend, there will not be the same Necessity to provide Coats, the Continental Congress having ordered Hunting Shirts as an outside Dress—under which, a warm Waistcoat will be cheaper, and more convenient.[4]

As to the Expedition proposed against Nova Scotia by the People of Machias; I cannot but applaud their Spirit & Zeal, but after considering the Reasons offered for it several Objections occur which seem to me unanswerable. I apprehend such an Enterprize inconsistent with the general Principle upon which the united Colonies have proceeded. It is true, that Province has not acceded to Measures of the Congress and they have therefore been excluded from all commercial ⟨Intercourse with the other Colonies; But they have⟩[5] not commenced Hostilities against them, nor are any to be apprehended: to attack them therefore is a Step of Conquest rather than Defence, & may be attended with very dangerous Consequences. It might perhaps be easy with the Force proposed to make an Incursion into the Province; to overawe those of the Inhabitants who are inimical to our Cause and for a short Time prevent their supplying the Enemy with Provisions, but the same Force must continue to produce any lasting Effects. As to the furnishing Vessels of any Force, you Gentlemen will anticipate me, in pointing out our Weakness, & the Enemy's Strength.[6] There would be great Danger, that with the best Preparation we could make, they would fall an easy Prey, either to the Man of War on that Station, or some who would be detached from Boston. I have been thus particular to satisfy any Gentlemen of the Court who incline to adopt the Measure: I could offer many other Reasons against it, some of which I doubt not will suggest themselves to the Honbe

Board: But it is unnecessary to enumerate them, when our Situation as to Ammunition absolutely forbids our sending a single Ounce out of the Camp at present.[7] I am with great Respect & Regard Gentlemen Your most Obedt and very Hbble Servt

Go: Washington

LS, in Joseph Reed's writing, MWA; Df, NHi: Joseph Reed Papers; LB, DLC:GW; Varick transcript, DLC:GW. The letter-book copy and the Varick transcript are dated 11 Aug. 1775, but the LS and draft are dated 12 Aug. 1775. Minutes in Perez Morton's writing on the LS indicate that the letter was read in the council on this date and referred to the house of representatives, which this same day appointed Col. Ebenezer Sayer (Sawyer), Col. Joseph Cushing, and Nathan or Seth Cushing to consider the letter and report on it. See also *Mass. House of Rep. Journal*, July–Nov. 1775 sess., 69. On 14 Aug., according to Morton's minutes, the council added John Whitcomb and Benjamin White to the committee. For the committee's report, see the Massachusetts General Court to GW, 18 Aug. 1775.

1. These papers have not been identified. For a discussion of Ichabod Jones's capture and imprisonment, see Committee of the Massachusetts Council to GW, 11 Aug. 1775, n.3.

2. James Warren, speaker of the Massachusetts house of representatives, was named Continental paymaster general by Congress on 27 July (*JCC*, 2:211). Warren held both offices concurrently.

3. For GW's determination to pay the army on a regular basis, see General Orders, 10 Aug. 1775. For the settlement of the Massachusetts pay accounts, see Committee of the Massachusetts Council to GW, 11 Aug., Massachusetts General Court to GW, 18 Aug., and General Orders, 24, 31 Aug., 5 Sept. 1775.

4. For the transfer of clothing from the Massachusetts to the Continental account, see GW to James Warren, 23 Aug. 1775.

5. The words within angle brackets, illegible on the LS, are taken from the draft.

6. The draft reads "Strength at Sea."

7. The Patriots at Machias in the District of Maine proposed to seize Windsor, Nova Scotia, with a force of one thousand men and a fleet consisting of four armed vessels and eight transports and then use the town as a rallying place for Patriot sympathizers in the province. A general uprising, they hoped, would ensue, enabling them to march on Halifax and take control of the provincial government. Although this expedition was not undertaken, a similar plan was put forward a few months later. See GW to Hancock, 30 Jan. 1776.

From Jonathan Trumbull, Sr.

Sir

Lebanon [Conn.] 12th August 1775

Since my Letter of Yesterday, desiring an Allowance to retain at Hartford such quantity of Powder as you shall judge expedient out of the next that comes; I have received a Letter from the Honble Henry Middleton, and Edward Rutledge dated Hartford August 11th 1775 informing that a Company of Rifflemen with eight Waggon Loads of Powder have come into that Town and the Article of which they have the Charge would be absolutely necessary at New-York in case an Attack should be made upon that Colony; Suggesting the Propriety of sending off an Express to you informing of their Situation and to Obtain An Order to Stay the Rifflemen and detain the Powder there, as most likely to be conducive to the public Safety.[1] All Circumstances considered, I have directed two Waggons of Powder to be detained, 'till your Excellency's Orders are received—The Rifflemen to proceed with the Other Six—You will soon have the pleasure to See those Two Gentlemen at Camp.[2] I am, with great Truth and Regard Sir Your most Obedient very humble Servant

Jonth. Trumbull

ALS, DLC:GW; LB, Ct: Trumbull Papers.

1. Henry Middleton (1717–1784) and Edward Rutledge (1749–1800), South Carolina delegates to the Continental Congress, took advantage of Congress's late summer recess to visit Cambridge. Middleton was president of the First Continental Congress for a time and attended the Second Continental Congress from May to November 1775. He subsequently became president of the South Carolina provincial congress and a leading member of the colony's council of safety. Although Middleton took an oath of allegiance to the crown in 1780 when the British invaded South Carolina, he was later forgiven by the Patriots and did not forfeit any of his extensive lands. Edward Rutledge, a young Charleston lawyer and Middleton's son-in-law, served in the First Continental Congress and remained in the Second Continental Congress until November 1776. He was a member of the committee that drafted GW's commission and instructions in June 1775, and in June 1776 he was named to the Board of War. As an officer in the Charleston artillery, Rutledge fought at Beaufort in 1779, and the following year he was captured at the siege of Charleston. For discussions of the gunpowder at Hartford, see Richard Henry Lee to GW, 1 Aug. 1775, n.3, and Trumbull to GW, 8 Aug. 1775, n.3.

2. The letter-book copy reads "By this Express shall expect your Direction—Those two Gentlemen Named are going onto your Camp."

General Orders

Head Quarters, Cambridge August 13th [17]75

Parole Williamsburgh. Countersign Torrington

A General Court Martial to sit to morrow morning to try Col. John Mansfield of the Massachusetts Forces, accused by three of his Officers of high Crimes and Misdemeanors:[1] One Brigadier General, and twelve Field Officers, to compose the Court.

President Brigdr Gen: Green

Col. James Ried	Col. Patterson
Col. James M: Varnum	Col. Woodbridge
Lt Col. [Isaac] Wyman	Lt Col. [Samuel] March
Lt Col. [Benjamin] Holdon	Lt Col. [William Turner] Miller
Major [Nathaniel] Cudworth	Major [Ephraim] Sawyer
Major [John] Butterick	Major [Israel] Angell

Members.

Varick transcript, DLC:GW.

1. John Mansfield (1721–1809), a well-to-do landowner from Lynn who served in the Massachusetts provincial congress before being commissioned colonel of one of the colony's regiments in May 1775, was accused of "remissness and backwardness" in reinforcing the American line during the Battle of Bunker Hill. The court-martial found him guilty and ordered him to be cashiered (General Orders, 17 Aug., 15 Sept. 1775).

From Lieutenant Colonel Loammi Baldwin

Chelsea [Mass.] Augt 13th 1775

May it please your Excellency

I herewith Send two men who deserted from The Lively Man of War this morning about 3 oClock and was taken up by our Guard at Chelsea Beach & conducted to me by a file of men.[1]

We have had a Small brush with the Enemy to day which began about 12 oClock and ended about ¼ of One occassioned by 2 Bearges & 2 Sail Boats going unto the floating Batterys that Lay near neck of Land Charlestown and bareing rather to near Malding Point[.] Supose Capt. Lindseys Company Suspected they had Som Evel designe, or a mind to Reveng passd Injuries gave them a prety Smart fire which made them return down the River and with there Swivel guns & Smal arms began a fire at our Chelsea Soldiers who returnd the fire Briskly haveing been alarmd by the first fireing at Malding[.] one of the Sail Boats Came round near to the old Wreck upon Winnessemet when we gave them the Best we had, and they Soon made of down among the Shiping & the fireing Ceased[.] we Sufferred no Damage by them[.] there was a great number of Balls Struck one of the Boats & belive wounded if not killed Some of the men, Some of our men declare they saw a number drop as if they were Shot dead whin a Volley was fired from our men its certain they nevr appeard much in Sight again.

nothing Extraordinary has appeard Since I Send the Observation as Usual.[2] I am with much Esteem Your Excellenys most Obediant Humbe Servnt

Loammi Baldwin Lieut. [Colonel] 1775

ALS, DLC:GW.

1. Baldwin is probably referring to the British warship *Fowey*, which had recently arrived at Boston from Virginia and was anchored at this time in the Mystic River near Charlestown. The *Lively*, which was normally stationed farther out in Boston Harbor in Nantasket Road, left on or before this date in search of the transports bringing livestock from Fishers and Gardiners islands and did not return to Boston until 15 Aug. (Samuel Graves to Thomas Gage, 13 Aug. 1775, Samuel Graves to Philip Stephens, 17 Aug. 1775, in Clark, *Naval Documents*, 1:1134, 1164–66). The two deserters may have been British soldiers from Bunker Hill, for Lt. Paul Lunt writes in his journal entry for 13 Aug. that "Two Regulars deserted from Bunker's Hill, swam over to Malden, and were carried to Royall's, General Washington's headquarters" ("Lunt's Book," 198). Isaac Royal's house at Medford was actually Maj. Gen. Charles Lee's headquarters.

2. Baldwin enclosed returns of observations for 12 and 13 Aug. 1775, both in Joseph Leach's writing (DLC:GW).

From Lieutenant General Thomas Gage

Sir Boston 13th August 1775.

To the Glory of Civilized Nations, humanity and War have been compatible; and Compassion to the subdued, is become almost a general system.

Britons, ever preeminent in Mercy, have outgone common examples, and overlooked the Criminal in the Captive. Upon these principles your Prisoners, whose Lives by the Laws of the

Land are destined to the Cord, have hitherto been treated with care and kindness, and more comfortably lodged then the King's Troops in the Hospitals, indiscriminately it is true, for I Acknowledge no Rank that is not derived from the King.

My intelligence from your Army would justify severe recrimination. I understand there are of the King's faithfull Subjects, taken sometime since by the Rebels, labouring like Negro Slaves, to gain their daily Subsistence, or reduced to the Wretched Alternative, to perish by famine, or take Arms against their King and Country. Those who have made the Treatment of the Prisoners in my hands, or of your other Friends in Boston, a pretence for such Measures, found Barbarity upon falsehood.

I would willingly hope Sir, that the Sentiments of liberality, which I have always believed you to possess, will be exerted to correct these misdoings. Be temperate in political disquisition, give free Operation to truth, and punish those who decieve and misrepresent, and not only the effects, but the Causes of this unhappy Conflict will be removed.

Should those under whose usurped Authority you Act, controul such a disposition, and dare to call severity retaliation, to God who knows all hearts be the appeal for the dreadfull consequences. I trust that British Soldiers Asserting the rights of the State, the Laws of the Land, the being of the Constitution, will meet all Events with becoming fortitude. They will court Victory with the Spirit their cause inspires, and from the same Motive will find the patience of Martyrs under misfortune.

Till I read your insinuations in regard to Ministers, I concieved that I had acted under the King: Whose wishes, it is true, as well as those of his Ministers, and of every honest Man have been to see this unhappy Breach forever closed, but unfortunately for both Countrys, those who long since projected the present Crisis, and influence the Councils of America, have views very distant from Accomodation. I am, Sir, Your most Obedient humble Servant

Thos Gage

LS, DLC:GW; copy, MiU-C: Gage Papers; copy, P.R.O., C.O.5/92, ff. 258–59; copy, DNA:PCC, item 152; copy, DNA:PCC, item 169; copy, NjMoNP. The copy in the Public Record Office was enclosed in Gage's letter to the earl of Dartmouth of 20 Aug. 1775, and the copy in PCC, item 169, was enclosed in GW to Hancock, 31 Aug. 1775.

From the Massachusetts General Court

Sir Watertown [Mass.] 13th of August 1775.

The enclosed hand bills will sufficiently serve to satisfy your Excellency, that the General Court fully concur with you in your opinion of the importance and necessity of the utmost exertions for the reformation of the infamous practices mentioned in your Letter of the 7th instant, directed to the President of the hon'ble Board, and also of the readyness of the General Court to cooperate with you in every measure tending to remedy the mischief therein complained of.[1]

Copy, "Mass. Council Journal," July 1775–Feb. 1776 sess., 74. The letter is also in *Mass. House of Rep. Journal,* July–Nov. 1775 sess., 70–71.

1. The General Court's resolution of this date concerning soldiers absent without leave from the army (see GW to James Otis, Sr., 7 Aug. 1775, n.2) was printed on handbills and sent not only to GW but also to the committees of correspondence or selectmen of the various towns throughout the colony. GW received fifty of these handbills which, according to another resolve of the General Court, he was to have "posted up in such Publick Places in the Camps as to him shall seem proper, that the Soldiery of the Army may be excited to take into their serious Consideration, the Baseness, Fraud and Villainy of the abovemention'd Practice, that they may thereby be made sensible, that every one who shall be guilty thereof, will greatly disparage himself, become justly contemptible and deserving of severe Punishment, and wholly forfeit the respectable Character of an American Volunteer" (*Mass. House of Rep. Journal,* July–Nov. 1775 sess., 70; also in "Mass. Council Journal," July 1775–Feb. 1776 sess., 73–74).

General Orders

Head Quarters, Cambridge August 14th 1775

Parole York. Countersign Yarmouth.

Major Thomas Mifflin, is appointed Quarter Master General, to the Army of the United Colonies: He is to be obeyed as such.

As the Troops are all to be mustered, as soon as possible, The Muster Master General, Stephen Moylan Esqr.; will deliver the Commanding Officer of each Regiment, thirty blank Muster Rolls upon Friday next, and directions for each Captain, how he is to fill up the blanks.

Varick transcript, DLC:GW.

To Nicholas Cooke

Sir Camp at Cambridge August. 14th 1775.

Your Favors of the 8. & 11th Instant are duly received the former I laid before the General Court of this Province, but one of the Delegates having communicated to them, what Mr Ward did to you of the Proceedings of the continental Congress touching this Powder; nothing was done towards providing Specie, that the Vessel might proceed to other Places, in Case of Disappointment at the first.[1] I am of Opinion, that the Collection of any considerable Sum here would be difficult in the Time proposed: And I think there is the less Necessity for it, as there are few Colonies who have not some Vessels out on this Errand, and will probably bring all that is at Markett. Having conversed with Collo. Porter and farther considered the Matter, I am of Opinion it ought to be prosecuted on the single Footing of procuring what is in the Magazine. The Voyage is short, our Necessity is great: The Expectation of being supplied by the Inhabitants of the Island under such Hazards as they must run, is slender: so that the only Chance of Success is by a Sudden Stroke. There is a great Difference between acquiescing in the Measure, and becoming Principals, the former we have great Reason to expect, the latter is doubtful. The Powder by all our Information is public Property, so that as you observe it may be settled with our other Accounts. The draughting Men from here would be very difficult, and endanger the Discovery of the Scheme. I am not clear that I have Power to send them off the Continent, and to engage them as Voluntiers, it would be necessary to make their Destination known. I should suppose the Captain who is to have the Direction of the Enterprize, would rather chuse to have Men whom he knew, and in whom he could confide in Preference to Strangers. From what Collo. Porter informs me, I do not see that Harris's Presence is absolutely necessary, and as his Terms would add considerably to the Expence, after obtaining from him all the Intelligence he could give, his Attendance might be dispens'd with. The Vessel lately sent out to cruize for the Powder, seems to me the properest for this Voyage, and as the Ten Days will soon expire if no Objection occurs to you, she might be dispatched.[2]

I have given Directions respecting the Lead at Ticonderoga,

which I am of Opinion with you is the Surest Mode of Supply in that Article.[3]

I have sent by this Opportunity a hunting Shirt as a Pattern[.] I should be glad you would inform me what Number you think I may expect.

I had flattered myself with the Hope, that the Vigilance of the Inhabitants on the Islands & Coasts, would have disappointed the Enemy in their late Expedition after live Stock.[4]

I hope nothing will be omitted by the several Committees, & other Officers to guard against any future Attempts, by removing all the Stock from those Places where their Shipping will protect them in Plundering. I do assure you Sir, it would be rendering a most essential Service to the Publick Interest. Their Distresses before were very great, and if renewed after the present Supply is exhausted must be productive of very great Advantages. I am Sir, with much Esteem Your most Obed. & very Humble Servant

Go: Washington

Copy, MH: Cooke Papers; Df, NHi: Joseph Reed Papers; LB, DLC:GW; Varick transcript, DLC:GW. The copy in the Cooke Papers is endorsed "Copy of a Lr from Genl Washington Augt 14th 1775. The original being sent to Philadelphia by the Com[mitte]e for settling the Accot of the Colony with the Congress."

1. The delegate was John Adams, and the information concerned the agreement which the Continental Congress had made with the Bermudians for gunpowder. See Committee of the Massachusetts Council to GW, 11 Aug. 1775, n.1.

2. This was the smaller of Rhode Island's two armed sloops, the one commanded by John Grimes. A committee of the Rhode Island general assembly agreed a few weeks later to GW's proposal for taking the gunpowder in Bermuda, but the larger of the colony's sloops, the *Katy*, commanded by Abraham Whipple, was sent on the voyage (Cooke to GW, 2 Sept. 1775).

3. See GW's letters of this date to Schuyler and Jonathan Trumbull, Sr.

4. GW is referring to the British raids on Fishers and Gardiners islands. See Norwich Committee of Correspondence to GW, 7 Aug. 1775, and Jonathan Trumbull, Sr., to GW, 7 Aug. 1775, n.2.

To Major General Philip Schuyler

Dear Sir Camp at Cambridge August 14th 1775:

I received your Favor of the 31st July informing me of your preparations to cross the Lake, and inclosing the Affidavits of

John Shatforth, and Deguid—Several Indians of the Tribe of St Francis, came in here Yesterday, and confirmed the former Accounts of the good Disposition of the Indian Nations and Canadians to the Interests of America. A most happy Event, on which I sincerely congratulate you.[1]

I am glad to relieve you from your Anxiety respecting Troops being sent from Boston to Quebec: those Reports I apprehend took their Rise from a Fleet being fitted out about 14 Days ago, to plunder the Islands in the Sound of their live Stock: An Expedition which they have executed with some Success and are just returning: but you may depend upon it, no Troops have been detached from Boston to Canada or elsewhere.[2]

Among our Wants (of which I find you have your proportion) we feel that of Lead most sensibly, and as we have no Expectation of a Supply from the Southward, I have concluded to draw upon the Stock found at Ticonderoga when it fell into our Hands. I am informed it is very considerable, and that a part of it may be spared without exposing you to any Inconveniency.[3]

In Consequence of this I have wrote to Governor Trumbull, to take the Direction of the Transportation of it, supposing the Conveyance thro' Connecticut the most safe and expeditious, I expect he will write you on the Subject by this Opportunity.[4]

I have Nothing new my dear Sir to acquaint you with—We are precisely in the same Situation as to the Enemy as when I wrote you last, nor can I gain any certain Intelligence of their future Intentions—The Troops from the Southward are come in very healthy and in good Order: To Morrow I expect a Supply of powder from philadelphia, which will be a most seasonable Relief in our present Necessity.[5]

God grant you Health and Success equal to your Merit and wishes. Favor me with Intelligence as often as you can and believe me with great Truth & Esteem Your most obedt & very humble Servant

Go. Washington

LB, NN: Schuyler Papers; Df, NHi: Joseph Reed Papers; LB, DLC:GW; Varick transcript, DLC:GW. The letter-book copy in DLC:GW and the Varick transcript are dated 15 Aug. 1775. The letter-book copy in the Schuyler Papers and the draft are dated 14 Aug. 1775.

1. On 14 Aug. Joseph Reed wrote to James Otis, Sr., president of the Massachusetts council: "The Bearer is accompanied by an Indian Chief of the

Tribe of St Frances in Canada who has come down upon a friendly Errand. In a Conference this Morning it has been concluded that he Should leave some of his Company in this Camp & Return with one of our Stockbridge Indians by Way of Ticonderoga, when he will have an Oppy of Seeing General Schuyler, & making the Tender of his Service, which we have not the same Occasion for—The Person at whose Instance His Visit is made can give a more Circumstantial Account of him and his Business than the Limits of a Letter will admit—As it might be agreeable to the Members of the Honble Court to know from themselves their Sentiments towards the Colonies—His Excellency approved of their waiting on them personally, & directed me to Communicate what has passed here" (DLC:GW). A joint committee of the General Court was appointed on 16 Aug. to confer with Swashan, the chief of the St. Francis Indians. He declared his readiness to take up the hatchet on behalf of the Americans. "As our Ancestors gave this Country to you," Swashan said, "we would not have you destroyed by *England*; but are ready to afford you our Assistance." Asked by the committee if he feared retaliation from Gov. Guy Carleton, Swashan replied, "We are not afraid of it—he has threatened us; but if he attacks us, we have Arms to defend ourselves" (*Mass. House of Rep. Journal*, July–Nov. 1775 sess., 75, 80–81). See also GW to Schuyler, 20 Aug. 1775.

2. For the British raids on Fishers and Gardiners islands, see Norwich Committee of Correspondence to GW, 7 Aug. 1775, and Jonathan Trumbull, Sr., to GW, 7 Aug. 1775, n.2. For the return of the transports to Boston, see Loammi Baldwin to GW, 16 Aug. 1775.

3. Samuel Freeman, clerk of the Massachusetts house of representatives, wrote to Joseph Reed on this date, informing him that about two tons of lead were at Crown Point (DNA: RG 93, Miscellaneous Numbered Records ["Manuscript File"]).

4. See GW to Jonathan Trumbull, Sr., this date.

5. The troops from the southward were the riflemen raised in Virginia, Maryland, and Pennsylvania. The gunpowder was the 6½ tons sent by the Continental Congress's order of 25 July 1775. See Richard Henry Lee to GW, 1 Aug. 1775, n.3, and Jonathan Trumbull, Sr., to GW, 8 Aug. 1775, n.3.

To Jonathan Trumbull, Sr.

Sir Camp at Cambridge August 14th 1775

Your Favours of the 7th 8th & 12 Instant are all duly received. The Destination[1] of the New Raised Levies has happily coincided with my Intentions respecting them—In the present Uncertainty I think it best they should continue where they are, and I hope the Officers will be assiduous in Discplining, & improving them in the use of Arms.[2]

Upon the Subject of Powder, I am at a Loss what to say, our

Necesseties are so great, and it [is][3] of such infinite Importance, that this Army should have a full Supply, that nothing but the most pressing Exigince, would make it proper to detain any on its way. I have been informed that 15 Hhds ware lately landed at New York, & that further supplies were daily Expected both there, and at Connecticut. Should there be any Arrivals, I beg no Time may be lost in forwarding this from Hartford & what can be spared from the necessary Colony Stock. Indeed at present I should chuse you to forward one of these Waggons, and the other may remain where it is untill we see how the Issue of our Expectations on this Head—The Removal from Boston, I consider as very precarious, by no Means desiring[4] to have so much Striss laid on it.[5] We begin to feel a Scarcity of Lead, and as I do not learn, that we are to expect any from the Southward, I have concluded that a Part of the Stock found at Ticonderoga should be brought down to this Camp, for this Purpose have wrote to Genl Schuyler.[6] I am not sufficiently Master of the Geography of the Country to know the easiest & Safest Conveyance: But from the Time in which Letters have come this way throug your Hands, I apprehend Connecticut must be the best & most expeditious. You will therefore, Sir be pleased to give us your Assistance, by taking this Matter into your hands to Direct, in which I have not the least Doubt, you will attend as well to the Expence, as other Circumstances conducive to the public Service. To this Effect, I have wrote General Schuyler, & referred him to you, for Information of the Manner of Conveyance, You will doubtless be cautious, how you suffer it to be water borne, where there is any Danger of the Enemy's Shipping—Nothing new in the Camp for several Days past. Five Deserters[7] have come in within these 48 hours but they bring no Intelligence of any Consequence—I am, with much Regard & Esteem Your most Obedt & very humble Servant

Go. Washington

P.S. Since writing the above, I have been Informed there is a Lead mine in your Colony, which may be work'd to Advantage[8]—Cut off from all foreign Supplies, every internal Resource is worthy of attention & I make no Doubt if my Information is just, some proper steps may be taken to turn this to the public Advantage.

Go. Washington

LB, Ct: Trumbull Papers; Df, NHi: Joseph Reed Papers; LB, in Joseph Reed's writing, DLC:GW; LB, in Thomas Mifflin's writing, DLC:GW; Varick transcript, DLC:GW.

1. The draft and both letter-book copies in DLC:GW read "Detention."

2. For the temporary retention in Connecticut of Col. Charles Webb's regiment and part of Col. Jedediah Huntington's regiment, see Trumbull to GW, 8 Aug. and 15 Sept. 1775.

3. The word "is" appears in the draft and the two letter-book copies in DLC:GW.

4. The draft and both letter-book copies in DLC:GW read "deserving."

5. For Trumbull's desire to keep two of the eight wagons of gunpowder which arrived at Hartford on 11 Aug., see Trumbull to GW, 12 Aug. 1775. In the draft Joseph Reed originally wrote in place of the preceding two sentences: "In the mean Time, as you best know the State of New York & your own Colony, if they are really in a destitute State I shall acquiesce in the 2 Loads remaining where they are for the present time only."

6. See GW to Schuyler, this date.

7. Both letter-book copies in DLC:GW read "Three Deserters." In the draft the "3" has been changed to "5."

8. GW is referring to the lead mine at Middletown. See Trumbull to GW, 21 Aug. 1775, n.4.

General Orders

Head Quarters, Cambridge, August 15th 1775

Parole Arlington. Countersign Bedford.

David Henly Esqr. is appointed Brigade Major to Genl Heath's brigade.[1]

John Trumbull Esqr. is appointed Brigade Major to Genl Spencers brigade.

Richard Carey Esqr. is appointed Brigade Major, to the Brigade commanded by the eldest Colonel.[2]

Thomas Chase,[3] Daniel Box,[4] and Alexander Scammell Esqrs. are appointed to continue to do the duty of Brigade Majors, to the Brigades they respectively belong.

Edmund Randolph and George Baylor Esqrs. are appointed Aids-de-Camp, to the Commander in Chief: All and every of the above named Gentlemen, to be obeyed in their respective capacitys.

The Quarter Master General is without delay to examine the Encampments and Coverings of different Regiments and Corps, to see that those which are not designed to remain in Houses, are provided as soon as possible, with Tents or Boards, sufficient for their Accomodation, at the same time, he is to take care to prevent any unnecessary waste of the latter; and to put a stop to the Officers, building such large houses, as some of them are doing; unless they are intended for the Accomodation of a Number sufficient to fill them, Or are to be built at their own expence; But no large house to be placed near any of the Redoubts, or Lines.

In addition to the Order of the 4th Instant; The Colonel or Commanding Officer of each Regiment and Corps, is to cause an exact Account to be taken (by his Captains) of the Number of Cartridges which each Man is possessed of; & at evening at Roll Callg have them examined, as directed in the said Order; when, if any are wanting, and cannot be accounted for, the delinquent, over and above the punishment due to his Offence, is to be charged with the deficiency and so much of his pay stopt accordingly.

Varick transcript, DLC:GW.

1. David Henley (1748–1823) of Charlestown, Mass., was William Heath's brigade major until March 1776 when he accompanied Heath to New York on special detached duty. See General Orders, 19 Mar. 1776. Henley was named adjutant general of Gen. Joseph Spencer's division on 6 Sept. 1776, and two months later he became lieutenant colonel of the 5th Massachusetts Regiment. He raised one of the additional Continental regiments in 1777 and commanded it as colonel until he retired from the army in April 1779.

2. Richard Cary of Charlestown, Md., who had recently arrived in Cambridge with three young gentlemen from Baltimore, served as a brigade major throughout the siege of Boston. He and David Henley distinguished themselves on 8 Jan. 1776 in a raid against Charlestown, Massachusetts. On 21 June 1776 Cary was named an aide-de-camp to GW, and in August 1778 he accompanied John Hancock as a volunteer aide on the abortive Rhode Island expedition. See John Adams to James Warren, 27 July 1775, and Adams to William Tudor, 28 July 1775, in Taylor, *Papers of John Adams,* 3:103–4; and *Pennsylvania Gazette* [Philadelphia], 30 Aug. 1775.

3. Thomas Chase (d. 1787), a distiller from Boston who had been active in the Sons of Liberty, was appointed brigade major of Brig. Gen. John Thomas's brigade by mistake. The position belonged to Samuel Brewer, whose appointment to it was announced in General Orders, 30 Aug. 1775. Chase later became deputy quartermaster general at Boston.

4. Daniel Box (born c.1735) of Rhode Island was a former British soldier who in the early months of 1775 assisted greatly in forming and training the Rhode Island troops. His close friend Nathanael Greene, to whose brigade he was appointed, considered Box a capable disciplinarian despite his chronic drinking. During the campaign of 1776 Box helped Greene fortify Long Is-

land and Fort Lee. His service in the Continental army was cut short by a fall from a horse in December 1776, which permanently deprived him of the use of his left arm.

From Lieutenant Colonel Loammi Baldwin

Chelsea [Mass.] Augt 15th 1775

May it Please your Excellency

Inclosd are the Observations as usual.[1]

I hope to be able tomorrow to forward to your Excellency a letter from the Mr J. C. the Grocer[.][2] I heard from him yesterday informing that he Expected to git further Information by tomorrow if it comes to hand Shall forward it with all Conveniant Speed. I am your Excellencys most Obediant Humbe Servt

Loammi Baldwin Leut. Col.

ALS, DLC:GW.

1. Baldwin enclosed returns of observations for 14 and 15 Aug. 1775, both in Joseph Leach's writing (DLC:GW).

2. The Boston grocer is John Carnes. See Joseph Reed to Baldwin, 28 July 1775, in Baldwin to GW, 29 July 1775, n.3.

From Major Christopher French

Sir

Philadelphia 15th August 1775

Upon my arrival in this Province in Company with Ensn Rotton of His Majesty's 47th Regiment, & Mr McDermot a Volunteer[1] in order to join our Regiments we were (unknowing of Hostilities having been commenc'd) made Prisoners of War of which I make no doubt you have been inform'd.

As we are naturaly desirous to give our Friends the earliest notice of our Scituation we have, by permission of the Committee of safety wrote to them, which Letters I take the Liberty to enclose to you, with one for Genl Gage & another to Major Campbell who commands the 22d Regiment,[2] to which I belong, open for your perusal, when I request they may be sent to General Gage in order to their being forwarded. I have the Honor to be Sir, your most obedient and most humble Servant

Chris. French

ALS, DLC:GW.

Christopher French was major of the 22d Regiment of Foot, which arrived at Boston before him in July 1775. For an account of French's capture on 12 Aug. at Gloucester, N.J., near Philadelphia, see Pennsylvania Committee of Safety to GW, 17 Aug. 1775, n.1. A long controversy ensued over the terms on which French and his companions were held as prisoners of war and about their exchange for American prisoners. French, who had been a captain in the 22d Regiment since 1756, was promoted to major in July 1772 but remained in a captain's slot in the regiment until a vacancy enabled him to move up to the major's position on 24 June 1775. See note 2.

1. John Rotten was commissioned an ensign in the 47th Regiment of Foot on 28 Jan. 1775. His regiment, which had been stationed at Boston since October 1774, fought at Bunker Hill on 17 June 1775, losing several officers. The volunteer cadet was Terrence McDermot.

2. Gen. Thomas Gage was colonel of the 22d Regiment, and John Campbell was its lieutenant colonel. Campbell served as major of the regiment from 21 April 1768 to 24 June 1775, when he was promoted to lieutenant colonel in place of James Abercromby who was killed at the Battle of Bunker Hill. Christopher French replaced Campbell as major of the regiment.

General Orders

Head Quarters. Cambridge, August 16th 1775

Parole Cumberland, Counter Sign Dunstable.

Capt. Eleazer Lindsey of Col. Gerrishes Regt tried by a General Court Martial, for "absenting himself from his post, which was attacked and abandoned to the enemy." The Court on consideration are of opinion that Capt. Lindsey be discharged [from] the service, as a person improper to sustain a Commission.[1]

John Parke Esqr. is appointed an Assistant to the Quarter Master Genl; he is to be obeyed as such.

Varick transcript, DLC:GW.

1. For background to the charges against Capt. Lindsey, see Loammi Baldwin to GW, 6 and 8 Aug. 1775.

From Lieutenant Colonel Loammi Baldwin

Chelsea [Mass.] Augst 16th 1775

May it Please your Excellency Wednesday Evening

I have Receivd a Letter which I Supose came From Mr J. C. by the Hand of the Gentlemen Expected, who says he is going to Head Quarters in the morning to see about the Sheep that were brought off from Puding Point which I have wrote to the adjutant General about.[1]

I am informed by a person that had it from the Pilots Mouth this day that the Ships that come in yesterday Brought 2000 Sheep and about 140 Head of Horn Cattle Hogs & Poultry in plenty[.] how true it is I cannot Say[.] I saw a Large number of Sheep & a few Cattle grazing upon Charlestown Heights this afternoon.[2]

I would Inform your Excellency that for three afternoons passd when the people were onloading the ferry Boat a Number of Men of war men come down upon Noddles Island over agains the Ferry ways & keep almost a Constant fire for 2 or 3 hours at a time[.][3] we have returnd the fire till I am Sattisfied that Small arms will Signify little or nothing altho. Several of ther Ball Struck within a yard or two of me[.] one of these balls Struck in a house I was at—with so much Force as to bury it Self in the Board.

Som of the Rifle men prehaps could Shoot with more exactness, as our Ball we could plainly See went far enough beyond them, there Language & Behaviour is Very Insulting[.] Should be glad to be revengd on them.

Inclosed is the observations,[4] I did not Send this afternoon, Expecting to have an Oppertunity to Send by a Faithfull Hand Early in the Morning the Horses not being in good Order.[5] This From Your Excellencys most Humbe & Obediant Servnt

Loammi Baldwin Lieut. Colo.

ALS, DLC:GW.

1. "Mr J. C." is John Carnes, the Boston grocer who was supplying intelligence for the Americans. See Joseph Reed to Baldwin, 28 July 1775, printed above in Baldwin to GW, 29 July 1775, n.3. For the removal of livestock from Pullen Point, see General Orders, 13 July 1775. Baldwin wrote in his letter of this date to Adj. Gen. Horatio Gates: "We . . . meet with some dificulty about the Sheep that were brought away from Pudding Point[.] Inclosd, is a Short Representation of the affair, which together with this I suppose will be delivered by one of the owners of the Sheep who will Inform you furthe[r] about the matter" (DLC:GW). The enclosure was apparently Baldwin's letter of this date which he addressed: "I know not to whoom this Should be directed Prehaps to the Commissary General." In that letter Baldwin explained: "The sheep that were lately Brought off from Pudding-Point are now in Pound[.] I have Just Sent desireing that they may be Enlarg'd Informing the Trespassed

that I would write to Head Quarters and if possable procure the General Pleasure with regard to them, they are become Very mischevious, The grazeing land to which it was preposed that they Should be confined too is so bare of feed that the Sheep are becom very poor and som have actuaally died there are Scarcely any among them that are in any measure fit to kill. I know not the conditions upon which they were brought from the Point, Neither who Superintends the affair, I Beg your Honour would direct this to him be it whoom it may. I hope I Shall Receive som directions Should think if the Sheep are taken for the Use of the Army that som of them had better be Sold to the Farmers as store Sheep so that the remainder might faire the Better" (DLC:GW).

2. These vessels had recently raided Gardiners and Fishers islands. See Norwich Committee of Safety to GW, 7 Aug. 1775, and Jonathan Trumbull, Sr., to GW, 7 Aug. 1775, n.2.

3. This action occurred near Winnisimmet ferry.

4. "A Return of the observations of the Day august 16th" in Joseph Leach's writing is in DLC:GW.

5. For an account of the difficulties with one of the express horses, see Richard Dodge to GW, 19 Aug. 1775.

From Andrew Hamilton

Sir Watertown [Mass.] 16th August 1775.

Your Excellencys known Character for Candor, & humanity, has encouraged me to take the liberty of troubling you with this letter, & as I am certain you must be much engaged at present, will be as Concise as possible. I was made an Ensign in the 16th Regt in—59, a Lieut. in—65 & sold out in—71,[1] since which time I have lived in Annapolis, N: Scotia, on a farm, which, with a small stock on it, has afforded me a Comfortable maintenance, but insufficient, let my inclination be ever so great, to spare either a bundle of a hay, or a peice of meat of it.

The last of June I had a letter from my Brother (who is a Lieutenant in 52d Regt)[2] & another from my friends in Ireland, from whom I had not heard for three years before, & some affairs which I was obliged to settle with my brother, made me embrace the opportunity of sailing for Boston, in a sloop that was bound there with Hay. The hands of the sloop took possession of her, & Carried her into Kinnebeck river. The Committee at Georgetown examined me. The letters I had with me & the hands of the vessel cleared me of being Concerned either in the cargoe, or any other particular as an enemy to America. As

I had been in the army, they suspected me & sent me to the General Court. I have been examined three different times & the only thing the Court suspects me of, is, my intentions, should I get into Boston, of entering into the regular service. They therefore have determined to detain me & send me to some interior part of the Country.[3] I must beg Your interposition in my favor. If I am not allowed to return to my farm, the servants I left on it, who are only hired for a few months, may destroy my interest there, & I shall then be worse than a beggar. The only chance I can have of returning this fa⟨vor⟩ is, by getting leave to go into Boston. If I can have that liberty, my Honor & oath (which is the only security I can offer at present) I will freely give that I had not any intention of applying for any Commission, nor will I accept of any under General Gage, but will sail in the first vessel that is bound to any part of N. Scotia. If I can not have this liberty, I will be much obliged to Your Excellency, if You will allow me to go with the gentlemen of the Navy, as I am acquainted with them, & their Society will make Captivity less irksome. I am with the greatest respect Your Excellency's most Obedt Humble Servant

Andw Hamilton

ALS,DLC:GW.

1. Andrew Hamilton's regiment came to America from Ireland in 1767 and was stationed at Pensacola when Hamilton sold his commission.

2. George Hamilton was commissioned an ensign in the 52d Regiment of Foot on 13 Feb. 1762 and a lieutenant on 26 Dec. 1770. The 52d Regiment moved to Boston from Quebec in October 1774 and fought at Bunker Hill on 17 June 1775.

3. On 8 Aug. the Massachusetts General Court appointed a committee to examine Hamilton, and three days later it reported that he "appears to be a crafty, designing Person, formerly held a Commission under the Crown, does not give any good Reason for his taking Passage for *Boston*, and has been very officious in prying into the Management of the public Affairs of this Colony." On the committee's recommendation, Hamilton was ordered on 12 Aug. to be sent to the Springfield jail, where he was "to have the Liberty of the Yard during his good Behaviour, otherwise to be put under close Confinement" (*Mass. House of Rep. Journal*, July–Nov. 1775 sess., 53, 67; also in "Mass. Council Journal," July 1775–Feb. 1776 sess., 71).

To James Otis, Sr.

Head-Quarters, Cambridge, August 16, 1775.

Sir: I am informed that Captain *Oldien*, or some other person, has stopped the baggage of the officers taken at *Machias*, as a compensation for some expense incurred, which the General Court did not think proper to allow him. A procedure of this kind would, in my opinion, much dishonour the *American* arms, and be attended with very disagreeable consequences. I trust therefore, Sir, that the General Court need only to be informed of the transaction to do what is proper; and, as the prisoners are entirely under their direction, will, before they remove them to the place of their destination, give such orders in the matter as to prevent any reasonable cause of complaint.[1] I am, very respectfully, Sir, your most obedient humble servant,

Go. Washington

Force, *American Archives*, 4th ser., 2 : 147.

1. The name appears as "Captain Obrien" in Fitzpatrick, *Writings*, 3 : 426–27. Jeremiah O'Brien (1744–1818) of Machias, District of Maine, was one of the American leaders in the fighting which occurred at the town on 11 and 12 June 1775. See Committee of the Massachusetts Council to GW, 11 Aug. 1775, n.3. O'Brien subsequently took command of a British sloop captured in that engagement, and on 16 July he, with the aid of another American vessel commanded by Benjamin Foster, seized the British schooner *Diligent* and her tender *Tatamagouch* off Machias. O'Brien and Foster escorted the officers and sailors captured on those two vessels to Cambridge, and on 12 Aug. O'Brien submitted a bill totaling £244 12s. to the Massachusetts General Court for the expenses incurred in conveying the prisoners from Machias. He also claimed £41 1s. for his own time and expense in guarding them (Andrew Magoun Sherman, *Life of Captain Jeremiah O'Brien, Machias, Maine* [Morristown, N.J., 1902], 94–96). The General Court resolved on this date to pay O'Brien "*One Hundred Pounds*, towards his Account . . . he giving Security for the same, with one Surety to this Colony Treasurer, until he brings proper Vouchers to support said Account" (*Mass. House of Rep. Journal*, July–Nov. 1775 sess., 75). The General Court also today authorized O'Brien to raise a company of fifty men and officers at Machias, and a week later it agreed to fund and supply two armed vessels under his command (ibid., 75, 96). During the next few years O'Brien made cruises with several different ships and succeeded in taking a number of prizes. He was captured by the British in 1780 and was confined in Mill Prison, England, from which he soon escaped. O'Brien returned to America and resumed his naval activities for the remainder of the war.

General Orders

Head Quarters, Cambridge August 17th 1775

Parole Exeter. Countersign, Faulkland

Thomas Chase Esqr. is to continue to do duty as Major of Brigade, to Brigadier General Thomas's Brigade.[1]

Mr Ezekiel Cheever is appointed Commissary of Artillery stores—The Qr Mr General, Commissary General and Commissary of Artillery; are to make exact Returns of all the Stores, Provisions and Necessaries of every kind, within their several departments: and they are to lose no time, in collecting the several Articles, which may be in the hands of Committees, or other persons, into their immediate care; and they are to be answerable for the disposal of them.

The Commanding Officer of Artillery is to see that all the Ordnance Stores, are faithfully collected, and put under the Care of the Commissary of the Artillery; and the Commissary of Artillery, is to see that all the Powder, Lead and Flints, are placed in the Magazine appointed to receive them.

The Muster Master General, Stephen Moylan Esqr. to proceed as expeditiously as possible, in the mustering the Troops and when he has delivered his Blank Rolls to the several Regiments and Corps, he is to fix the days for mustering each Brigade, with the Adjutant General, who will give directions accordingly.[2]

The Army being regularly brigaded, and a Major of Brigade appointed and fix'd to each Brigade: They are to keep an exact Roster of duty for the Officers, Non Commissioned Officers and Soldiers of their respective Brigades. The Adjutant General will assi[s]t them with the best form of a Roster and earnestly recommends the Use thereof. All duties of Honor, begin with the eldest Officer of each Rank, and duties of fatigue with the youngest. Each Major of brigade, will forthwith fix upon a proper spot, as near as can be to the Center of the brigade, for a General parade of the brigade; where all parties with, or without Arms, are to be regularly paraded, and marched off, in presence of the Major of Brigade, and the General expects, that the Majors of Brigades, are not only alert, but exact in the performance of this duty.

The Court Martial ordered for the Trial of Col. Mansfield, to sit to morrow Morning at eight OClock at the College Chapel &c. for the Trial of Col. Gerrish: All Evidences & persons concern'd to attend the Court.[3]

Varick transcript, DLC:GW.

1. This appointment was an erroneous one. See General Orders, 15 and 30 Aug. 1775.

2. The mustering was scheduled to begin with Brig. Gen. John Sullivan's brigade on 22 Aug., but various circumstances obliged GW to postpone it to 1 Sept. (General Orders, 21, 22, 26, 28 Aug. 1775).

3. For the charge against John Mansfield, see General Orders, 13 Aug. and 15 Sept. 1775. For the charge against Samuel Gerrish, see General Orders, 19 Aug. 1775.

From Lieutenant Colonel Loammi Baldwin

Chelsea [Mass.] Augst 17. 1775

May it Please your Excellency 5 oClock

The Men of wars men I mentioned in my letter of Last Night have come to Noddles Island again and are now throwing up a Small Brest work almost against the Ferry ways[.] Shoul be glad to anoy them if Possable But have not the Materials.[1]

Inclosd are the Observations.[2] I am your Excellencys most obediant Humbe Servnt

Loammi Baldwin Leut. Coln.

I must Inform your Excellency I am Very unwell Scercly able to Set up.

ALS, DLC:GW.

1. Baldwin is referring to Winnisimmet ferry. Men from Baldwin's regiment destroyed the breastwork at Noddles Island on 21 Aug. (Richard Dodge to GW, that date).

2. "A Return of the observations of the Day august 17" in Joseph Leach's writing is in DLC:GW.

From the Pennsylvania Committee of Safety

Sir Philadelphia August 17th 1775

The Committee of Safety for this City & Province, being informed on saturday last, that a Ship from Cork had come up to Gloucester with some passengers, Officers of the Ministerial

Army, and a quantity of Cloathing for that Army at Boston, immediately sent down Capt. Bradford with thirty Men to take those officers prisoners, and at the same time an Armed Boat, to bring up the Cloathing, both which orders were accordingly executed.[1] The Officers we have enlarged upon their written Parole, to render themselves at your Camp; and two Soldiers taken with them, being their Servants, on the Parole of Major French the Principal Officer, Copies of which Paroles are enclosed.[2] The Major requested when he signed the Parole that we would for his Justification give him a Certificate of his making a Claim in behalf of himself & the others, and that his Claim was not admitted. We gratified him in this, and a Copy of our Certificate is Also enclosed.[3] They were allowed to take with them their own Baggage, but the Baggage of some other Officers now in Boston, which he also requested, was refused, on account of the detention of the Effects of our Friends there by General Gage. So this Baggage with the Cloathing (an Invoice whereof is Also enclosed) which we understand is for two Regiments, is Stored, to remain for the Direction and disposition of the Congress.[4] The Officers & Soldiers are to set out for your Camp on Tuesday the 22nd inst. accompanied by two respectable Gentlemen of this City Capt. Willing and Capt. Wharton, whom we beg leave to recommend to your notice, who will protect the Officers on the Road & forward their Journey.[5]

No more Gun powder is yet arrived here. On the 10th Instant we sent 2200 Wt to General Schuyler, which was all we could possibly spare.[6] with great Esteem and Respect, we have the Honour to be, Sir, your most Obedient humble Serts

By Order
B. Franklin, Presidt

P.S. with this you will also receive a packet directed to an Officer of The Ministerial Army, which we have not open'd, but submit it to your discretion.

LS, DLC:GW.

The Pennsylvania general assembly created a committee of safety on 30 June 1775 to oversee all military measures necessary for the defense of the colony. The original twenty-five committee members included Benjamin Franklin, who was unanimously elected president of the committee at its first meeting on 3 July. Franklin also served as a delegate to the Continental Congress during this time.

1. The ship *Hope* from Cork, Ireland, commanded by George Curwin, was seized in the Delaware River near Gloucester, N.J., on 12 August. On board the vessel were 7,500 suits of clothing for the British army at Boston and three British gentlemen who were on their way to join regiments in that city: Maj. Christopher French, Ens. John Rotten, and Cadet Terrence McDermot. See Christopher French to GW, 15 Aug. 1775. William Bradford (1722–1791) was a prominent Philadelphia printer who joined a battalion of the city's military associators as a captain sometime during the spring of 1775. In July 1776 he was commissioned a major in the 2d battalion of Pennsylvania militia, and he eventually became a colonel. Bradford was severely wounded at the Battle of Trenton, but he recovered sufficiently to act as chairman of the Pennsylvania state navy board from 1777 to 1778. Ill health and financial difficulties forced his withdrawal from public affairs after 1779.

2. The particular copies of the paroles that were enclosed in this letter have not been found. The parole form that French, Rotten, and McDermot each signed on 12 Aug. appears in the minutes of the Philadelphia committee of safety, as does a copy of the parole that French signed four days later for the two private soldiers, William Goldthorp of the 22d Regiment and Alexander Allen of the 45th Regiment (*Colonial Records of Pennsylvania, 1683–1800*, 16 vols. [Philadelphia, 1852–53], 10:302–3, 306).

3. The committee's certificate of 12 Aug. reads: "Major Christopher French, having among other engagements, given his Parole to render himself with all convenient speed at the Camp of General Washington, and there to submit himself to the disposition of the said General, but requesting as a favour, that it may be Certified in his behalf, that he had previously claimed the being considered as no prisoner of war, he having come hither without any knowledge of the Hostilities between the Army and the People of America, and not being taken in Arms, We, in compliance with his request, do Certifiie that he did make the said claim, but after his being informed that Hostilities had been commenced in America, he declaring that if he joined his Corps he should act as his Superior Officers directed; his claim was overruled, and, thereupon, gave his parole as aforesaid" (ibid., 303).

4. The invoice of clothing and baggage enclosed in this letter is in DLC:GW. Dated 17 Aug., it indicates that the baggage belonging to the three prisoners was to be "sent by Stage . . . to New York, to be forwarded from thence to the Camp of General Washington." Christopher French asked the Pennsylvania committee of safety on 14 Aug. for permission to "take with him the Packages that came in Capt. Curwin, for the use of the 22nd & 40th Regiment, as well those directed to the different Officers in Boston," but the committee did not consent (minutes of the Pennsylvania Committee of Safety, *Pa. Col. Records*, 10:305).

5. On 15 Aug. Richard Willing and John Wharton volunteered to escort the prisoners to Cambridge "on Condition of their Expenses being paid," and the next day the committee gave the two captains a letter of instructions regarding their mission (ibid., 305–6). Richard Willing (1745–1798), whom GW visited in Philadelphia on 21 May 1775 (*Diaries*, 3:331), was a captain in

one of the battalions of Philadelphia associators. His companion may have been John Wharton (c.1732–1799), a Philadelphia shipbuilder who served on the Continental Navy Board from 1778 to 1780.

6. At the urging of Benjamin Franklin, the committee of safety resolved on 9 Aug. to send Schuyler the 2,244½ pounds of gunpowder that remained in the city's magazine (minutes of the Pennsylvania Committee of Safety, *Pa. Col. Records*, 10:300). In letters to Schuyler and the Albany committee of safety, written on 10 Aug., Franklin said that he was sending 2,400 pounds of gunpowder, "which," he told Schuyler, "actually empties our Magazine" (Leonard W. Labaree, William B. Willcox, et al., eds., *The Papers of Benjamin Franklin* [New Haven and London, 1959—], 22:160–61).

From Major General Artemas Ward

Sir, Camp at Cambridge 17 Augt 1775

I send you a prisoner who calls himself Terry Owen—he says he swam from Boston to Dorchester last night—His account of himself has been contradictory, and by Papers found with him which are sent by the Guards, it appears he has been engaged in the Service of the Enemy. From your Excellency's Obedient and very humble Servant

Artemas Ward

LS, M-Ar: Revolution Letters.

Letter not found: to Lund Washington, 17 Aug. 1775. In a letter of 15 Oct. 1775 to GW, Lund Washington referred to GW's letter of "Augst 17th."

General Orders

Head Quarters, Cambridge, August 18th 1775

Parole Gloucester. Countersign Hartford:

John Conner of Capt. Olivers Company,[1] Col. Doolittles Regiment, tried at a General Court Martial for "stealing a Cheese," the property of Richd Cornell; is found guilty of the Charge and adjudged to receive thirty-nine Lashes upon his bare back. The General approves the Sentence, and orders it to be executed at the relieving the main guard; at the head of the two Guards.

Joseph Matthews of Capt. Perkin's Company of Artillery,

tried by the same General Court Martial, for "selling his Gun, which the Select Men of his Town had given him, and drawing pay for a Blanket, furnish'd by said Select-men." The Court sentence the prisoner to receive Ten Lashes upon his bare back, and order Twelve Shillings to be stopped from his pay, to repay Capt. Perkins for the blanket.

The General approves the Sentence, and orders it to be executed, at the head of the Guards, where the Company, the Prisoner belongs to is posted.

Varick transcript, DLC:GW.

1. Robert Oliver (1738–1810) of Barre was a lieutenant in a company of minutemen that marched to Cambridge in April 1775, and on 12 June he became a captain in Col. Ephraim Doolittle's Massachusetts regiment. Oliver served to the end of the war, rising to the rank of major in November 1777. Considered a good disciplinarian, he was appointed a brigade inspector in August 1778, and four years later he was given the command of a battalion of light infantry.

Letter not found: to Lieutenant Colonel Loammi Baldwin, 18 Aug. 1775. On 18 Aug. Baldwin wrote to GW: "I receeved your Excellenies message of this morning."

From Lieutenant Colonel Loammi Baldwin

Chelsea [Mass.] Augt 18 1775

May it please your Excellency

I receeved your Excellenies message of this morning to wait on you at the Ferry, and should have complied therewith instantly, had not bodily Indisposition prevented[1]—I have been followed very hard with a Dysentry yesterday & today—must beg leave to ask your permition to go to my Family a few days till I can in some measure recover my health—I have but very poor accomodations here, there being several people now sick in this House.[2]

An Express is just arrived from Shirley Point with the enclosed information, & that the people residing there are under fearfull apprehentions of the Enemies landing there, as they are frequently firing on them from the Boats.[3] Your Excellency will be pleased to give such order in this affair as you in your wisdom shall think proper.

Enclosed are the Observations of the Day[4]—I have nothing else Material to Write, but beg leave to subscribe my self your Excellencies most Obedient & very Humbe Sert

Loammi Baldwin Lieut. Col.

ALS, DLC:GW. The addressed cover includes the notation "pr Favour Doctor Jones." David Jones was the surgeon for Col. Samuel Gerrish's regiment, to which Baldwin belonged.

1. No letter to Baldwin from GW or any of his staff has been found for this date. The ferry to which Baldwin refers is probably Winnisimmet ferry.

2. Baldwin apparently returned to duty at the end of August (Baldwin to GW, 1 Sept. 1775). In the meantime, Capt. Richard Dodge sent reports to GW from Chelsea.

3. Baldwin enclosed two letters, both of which are in DLC:GW. In one dated 18 Aug. 1775, Daniel Sigourney of Point Shirley informs Baldwin "that there Are . . . About thirty men Well Armed Now Reaping the Rie & the barley on Dear Island." The other letter is an erroneously dated copy in Baldwin's writing of one from Abijah Willard (Willant), commander of the British foraging party that raided Gardiners Island between 8 and 11 Aug. 1775, to Benjamin Miller, overseer on the island. The copy bears the date "Augt 17th 1775 12 oClock at Night," but the letter as printed in the *New-York Journal; or, the General Advertiser*, 17 Aug. 1775, is correctly dated "Aug. 11th, 1775, 12 o'Clock at Night." Willard informed Miller: "As we have got loaded all the Vessels I cant come to your house according to promise I send you Account of what I have got off your Island—Sheep 823—Fat Cattle 59 Cows 3 Calves 3, One of the Calves got away[.] The Cheese I will take Account of. Send me some pigs, fowls and Potatoes and Ducks and some bread, when you come to Boston I will secure your Interest to you if in my power, I am sorry it is not in my Power to come to your house but so good a wind we cant stay, the hay you must send an Account of by Capt. Lawrance" (DLC:GW). The letter, according to the *New-York Journal*, "gives Reason to suspect that the Expedition (as to Gardiner's Island) was preconcerted with the Proprietor, or Manager." The copy that Baldwin sent to GW includes the following statement at the bottom: "Mr Miller says this is all he got for the Cattle &c. he neither got money nor any thing else, except one half Guinea and a pistereen an Officer left for the Victuals they Eat."

4. "A Return of the Observations of the Day august 18" in Joseph Leach's writing is in DLC:GW.

From the Massachusetts General Court

[Watertown, Mass., 18 August 1775]

May it please yr Excellency

This Court have attentively consider'd your Letter of the 12th Inst. & acquiesce in the Method propos'd of paying of the

Troops from the 1st Augst & would inform your Excellency that this Court have taken [Measures][1] that the Province may not be defrauded & Justice done to the Men & likewise fulfill their Engagemts made the Troops.[2]

As to the Cloathing propos'd we apprehend there is an absolute Necessity of our providing Coats for the Men & this Govermt having engag'd the same to our Troops a Part of which are already provided by the several Towns in this Govermt in Consequence of.[3]

Df (incomplete), M-Ar: Revolution Letters. The document is endorsed "Draft of a letter to Gen. Washington as to paying troops Aug. 18, 1775 In Council read & accepted & ordered to be forwarded P. Morton, D. Secry." No record of these actions appears in the council's journal. The letter probably was not sent.

In the manuscript the letter is preceded by the statement "The Comte appointed to take into Consideration some Paragraphs in General Washington's Letter take Leave to report the following Draft of a Letter to his Excellency in answer thereto. John Whetcomb ℘ order." This committee was the one that the two houses of the General Court appointed on 12 and 14 Aug. to consider part of GW's letter of 12 August. See GW to the Massachusetts General Court, 12 Aug. 1775, source note. No report of this committee appears in the journal of either house. John Whitcomb (Whetcomb, c.1713–1783) of Bolton became a member of the council on 26 July 1775. A provincial colonel during the French and Indian War, Whitcomb was appointed a general by the provincial congress on 15 Feb. 1775 and first major general on 13 June. He received no rank from the Continental Congress, however, and exercised no command in the army after the end of June.

1. This word is struck out in the manuscript, and no substitute is supplied.

2. For the settlement of the pay accounts for the Massachusetts soldiers, see General Orders, 24, 31 Aug. and 5 Sept. 1775.

3. The provincial congress resolved on 5 July to supply the colony's forces with 13,000 coats "made of good plain cloth . . . in the common plain way, without lappels, short, and with small folds." Each town and district in the colony, except Boston and Charlestown, was to provide a certain number of these coats in proportion to its share of the last provincial tax. The coats were to be delivered to the committee of supplies on or before 1 Oct. with "a certificate . . . sewed to the inside of each coat, purporting from what town it came, and by whom the coat was made, and if the cloth was manufactured in this country, by whom it was manufactured" (*Mass. Prov. Congress Journals*, 456–57).

General Orders

Head Quarters Cambridge, August 19th 1775

Parole Jersey. Countersign Kendal.

Col. Samuel Gerrish of the Massachusetts Forces, tried by a General Court Martial of which Brigadier Genl Green was Presdt is unanimously found guilty of the Charge exhibited against him, *That he behaved unworthy an Officer*; that he is guilty of a Breach of the 49th Article of the Rules and Regulations of the Massachusetts Army. The Court therefore sentence and adjudge, the said Col. Gerrish, to be cashiered, and render'd incapable of any employment in the American Army—The General approves the sentence of the Court martial, and orders it to take place immediately.[1]

Varick transcript, DLC:GW.

1. Gerrish was court-martialed for failing to repel a recent attack on Sewall's Point by a British floating battery. "The rascals can do us no harm," Gerrish is reported to have said, "and it would be a mere waste of powder to fire at them with our four-pounders" (Richard Frothingham, *History of the Siege of Boston, and of the Battles of Lexington, Concord and Bunker Hill* [Boston, 1851], 179). Gerrish had previously been accused of acting in a cowardly manner at the Battle of Bunker Hill. During the latter stages of the fighting, he allegedly panicked his men by shouting, "Retreat! retreat! or you'l all be cutt off!" (Richard M. Ketchum, *The Battle for Bunker Hill* [Garden City, N.Y., 1962], 126). Gen. Artemas Ward, however, ignored complaints about Gerrish's behavior at Bunker Hill, excusing him "on account of the unorganized state of the army" (Frothingham, *Siege of Boston*, 179).

From Captain Richard Dodge

May it please the General. Chelsea [Mass.] August 19th 1775

I have inclosed the Discoveries of the Day.[1] I have no intelligence of importance. I would acquaint your Excellency that one of the Horses under our care for the use of the Province for want of Shewing is intirely unfit for Service he has been sent to Mr Munro the blacksmith who Shews the Province Horses but the Horse not being branded the Blacksmith refused to Shew him. I would beg of your Excellency to let me know what method I must pursue as to that matter. the other horse will soon be worn out if he is rode every Day.[2] I remain your Excellency's humble Servt

Richard Dodge Capt.

L, in Loammi Baldwin's writing, DLC:GW. Endorsed in Joseph Reed's writing "Col. Bald⟨win⟩ Aug. 19."

1. "A Return of the observations of the Day august 19" in Joseph Leach's writing is in DLC:GW.

2. Loammi Baldwin informed Horatio Gates of this problem on 16 Aug.: "One of the Express Horses we have here Suffers greatly for want of Shoeing I wrote and Order & Sent with the Horse to Mr Munrowes near Head Quarter in Cambridge, who refused to Shoe him because he was not Branded ⟨on⟩ the Hoof. Should be glad to be directed how I shall get him Shod" (DLC:GW).

To Lieutenant General Thomas Gage

Sir Head Quarters Cambridge Augt 19th 1775.

I address'd you on the 11th Instant in Terms which gave the fairest Scope, for the Exercise of that Humanity & Politeness, which were supposed to form a Part of your Character—I remonstrated with you, on the unworthy Treatment shewn to the Officers, and Citizens of America, whom the Fortune of War, Chance, or a mistaken Confidence had thrown into your Hands. Whether British, or American Mercy, Fortitude, & Patience are most preeminent; whether our virtuous Citizens whom the Hand of Tyranny has forced into Arms, to defend their Wives, their Children, & their Property; or the mercenary Instruments of lawless Domination, Avarice, and Revenge best deserve the Appellation of Rebels, and the Punishment of that Cord, which your affected Clemency has forborne to inflict; Whether the Authority under which I act is usurp'd, or founded on the genuine Principles of Liberty, were altogether foreign to my Subject. I purposely avoided all political Disquisition; nor shall I now avail myself of those Advantages, which the sacred Cause of my Country, of Liberty, and human Nature give me over you. Much less shall I stoop to Retort, & Invective. But the Intelligence, you say, you have received from our Army requires a Reply. I have taken Time, Sir, to make a strict Inquiry, and find it has not the least Foundation in Truth. Not only your Officers, and Soldiers have been treated with a Tenderness due to Fellow Citizens, & Brethren; but even those execrable Parricides, whose Counsels & Aid have deluged their Country with Blood, have been protected from the Fury of a justly enraged Poeple. Far from compelling, or even permitting their Assistance, I am embarassed with the Numbers who crowd to our Camp animated with the purest Principles of Virtue, & Love of their Country.

You advise me to give free Operation to Truth, to punish Misrepresentation & Falshood. If Experience stamps Value upon Counsel, yours must have a Weight which few can claim. You best can tell, how far the Convulsion which has brought such Ruin on both Countries, and shaken the mighty Empire of Brittain to its Foundation, may be traced to those malignant Causes.

You affect, Sir, to despise all Rank not derived from the same Source with your own. I cannot conceive any more honourable, than that which flows from the uncorrupted Choice of a brave and free Poeple—The purest Source & original Fountain of all Power. Far from making it a Plea for Cruelty, a Mind of true Magnanimity, & enlarged Ideas would comprehend & respect it.

What may have been the ministerial Views which precipitated the present Crisis, Lexington—Concord, & Charlestown can best declare—May that God to whom you then appealed, judge between America & you! Under his Providence, those who influence the Councils of America, and all the other Inhabitants of these united Colonies, at the Hazard of their Lives, are resolved to hand down to Posterity those just & invaluable Privileges which they received from their Ancestors.

I shall now, Sir, close my Correspondence with you, perhaps forever. If your Officers who are our Prisoners receive a Treatment from me, different from what I wish'd to shew them, they, & you, will remember the Occasion of it.[1] I am Sir, Your very Hbble Servant

Go: Washington

LS, in Joseph Reed's writing, MiU-C: Gage Papers; Df, DLC:GW; copy, NHi: Joseph Reed Papers; copy, DNA:PCC, item 152; copy, DNA:PCC, item 169; copy, NjMoNP; copy, NNebgGW; Varick transcript, DLC:GW. The draft and Varick transcript are dated 20 Aug. 1775, but the LS and various copies are dated 19 Aug. 1775. The copy in PCC, item 152, was enclosed in GW to Hancock, 31 Aug. 1775.

1. On 14 Aug. Joseph Reed wrote to James Otis, Sr., president of the Massachusetts council: "His Excelly being oblijed to attend some Business in the Lines has directed me to acquaint you & the Honle Court that he has received a Letter [of 13 Aug.] from Gen. Gage which has determined him to order the Officers now at Water Town together with those from Cape Ann to be confined in Northampton Gaol. General Gage is resolved to know no Distinction of Rank among our Prisoners in his Hands—which obliges Gen. Washington (very contrary to his Disposition) to observe the same Rule of Treatment to those Gentlemen, to whom it will be proper to explain the Reasons of a Conduct, which otherwise may appear harsh & cruel—The common Men, the General Court will order to such Places as they think proper" (M-Ar: Revolution Letters). GW relented the next day. "When Capt. [John] Knight & the other Gentlemen went from hence yesterday," Reed wrote to the Northampton committee of safety on 15 Aug., "it was intended they should have been put into the same Confinement with Prisoners of a common Rank: But some Circumstances since have changed this Intention. I now therefore by Direction of his Excelly Gen. Washington am to acquaint you that Capt. Knight and such of his Company for whom he will engage giving his & their Parole of Honour not to go out of the Limits you prescribe them are to be indulged with the Liberty of walking about this your Town—And the General farther requests that every other Indulgence & Civility consistent with their Security may be shown them as long as they demean themselves with Decency & good Manners—As they committed no Hostilities against the People of this Country they have a just Claim to mild Treatment and the General does not doubt that your Conduct towards them will be such as to compel their grateful Acknowledgment that Americans are equally merciful as brave" (DLC:GW). See also John Knight to GW, 10 Jan. 1776.

From Major General Artemas Ward

Camp at Roxbury [Mass.] 19 August 1775. Recommends for the command of a regiment "Colo. Wm Henshaw who before the Arrival of Genl Gates officiated as an Adjutant Genl being appointed to that Office by the provincial Congress."[1]

LS, DLC:GW.

1. William Henshaw (1735–1820) of Leicester marched to Cambridge with a regiment of Worcester County militiamen shortly after the Battle of Lexington, and on 27 June the Massachusetts provincial congress, on the recommendation of General Ward, appointed Henshaw adjutant general of the Massachusetts army. Henshaw acted as GW's adjutant until Horatio Gates replaced him on 9 July. "I rode three or four days around the camp, showing him [Gates] the regiments and the colonels, intending to return home,"

Henshaw wrote many years later. "He requested me to stay through the campaign, as he could not do without an assistant, and I should have the same pay and rations as a colonel. General Gates told me to write to the Continental Congress for my wages, and he would write them that he had employed me and promised me the same pay as a colonel. I never wrote them, and have never received any pay for my services" (Emory Washburn, "Memoir of Colonel William Henshaw," in Mass. Hist. Soc., *Proceedings*, 1st ser., 15 [1876–77], 70–71). On 1 Jan. 1776 Henshaw became lieutenant colonel of the Continental regiment commanded by Col. Moses Little and served in the New York and New Jersey campaigns of that year. Henshaw left the army in Feb. 1777.

Letter not found: from Major General Artemas Ward, 19 Aug. 1775. On 20 Aug. Horatio Gates wrote on behalf of GW to Ward: "The General has this moment received Your Letter of yesterday, he is surprized to hear that the men you Mention are posted in so insecure & defenceless a Scituation, & wishes you would repair to Squantum, & examine into all the Circumstances, & if you think it prudent, Order all the Stock, & Sheep, to be drove off the peninsula. . . . Inclosed I return you the representation of the Lt Col. & Officers at in Command at Squantum."[1]

1. MHi: Ward Papers.

General Orders

Head Quarters, Cambridge, Augt 20th 1775

Parole Lebanon. Countersign, Mansfield.

In Obedience to the Orders of the 5th Inst:, The Brigadier Genl and Field-Officers chosen by Ballot, have made a Report to his Excellency the Commander in Chief, of the final Settlement of the Rank, of all the Regiments and Officers, in the Army of the United Colonies. The General entirely approves of the proceedings of the Brigadier & the Field Officers; and thanks them in this public manner, for the great pains, and care, they have taken, in establishing a point, of so much importance to the army—His Excellency strictly commands all Officers and Soldiers, to pay all due Obedience, to the Regulations so established. The Adjutant General will deliver to each Major of Brigade, this day, at Orderly time, a Copy of the Rank of the Regiments, of the Field Officers, and of the Officers in every Regiment, in their respective Brigades.[1]

A Court of enquiry to sit this day, at three in the afternoon, to examine into the Reasons for a complaint exhibited against Col. Ebenezer Bridge.[2]

Brigadier General Heath President

Col. Prescott. Col. Woodbridge

Col. Sergeant Lt Col. Johonnot[3]

Members

Varick transcript, DLC:GW.

1. This ranking of the regiments is apparently that given in an undated document entitled "A List of the United Army encampd near Boston" (MHi: William Heath Papers). The document is endorsed "Officers on the old Establmt" and contains the names of the field officers in order of their precedence.

2. Ebenezer Bridge (1744–1814) of Billerica received severe sword cuts on his head and neck while commanding a Massachusetts regiment in the American front line at the Battle of Bunker Hill, but some of his subordinates accused him of cowering under the walls of the redoubt during the fighting. The court of inquiry determined that the charge warranted a general court-martial (undated report signed by William Heath, MHi: Heath Papers), and Bridge was subsequently tried and acquitted (General Orders, 11 Sept. 1775). A well-to-do merchant, Bridge served during 1774 as a member of the Billerica committee of correspondence, chairman of the Middlesex County convention, and Billerica's representative to the first Massachusetts provincial congress, and on 10 June 1775 he was commissioned a Massachusetts colonel. Bridge remained in the Continental army until the following December or January (General Orders, 10 Dec. 1775). He lived in Cambridge from 1776 to about 1781 and then moved to Chelmsford. From 1781 to 1786 Bridge was adjutant general of Massachusetts with the rank of brigadier general in the state militia.

3. Gabriel Johonnot (1748–1820), a Huguenot merchant from Boston who had been a member of the city's cadet company before the war, was lieutenant colonel of Col. John Glover's Massachusetts regiment from 21 May 1775 to December 1776. Samuel Holden Parsons described Johonnot in a letter of 15 Aug. 1776 to John Adams as "Very good a fine Soldier and an extensive Acquaintance," and three days later William Tudor told Adams that Johonnot "has Fire, Sense and Courage" (Taylor, *Papers of John Adams*, 4:462–65, 473–76). Apparently denied promotion, Johonnot resigned his commission at the end of 1776.

From Captain Richard Dodge

Sir [Chelsea, Mass., c.20 August 1775]

I Recd your Leter Last Evaning[1] and I moust acknoledg my Self Not Eapuil [equal] to the Trust Reposed in me But Senc your Exelencey, has intrusted me with So importinant Post I

Shall mack it my Stodey to youse the Best of my Pouers to Keep Close to your orders and im Prove the furst and every oppertunity to A-Noy the Enemy at Notles Island[2]—I have in Closed the miniets tackin By mr Leach.[3] I am your Exelencies most Humble Servent

Richard Dodge Capt.

ALS, DLC:GW. Internal evidence indicates that this letter was written from Chelsea about 20 August. See notes 2 and 3.

1. Letter not found.

2. Loammi Baldwin reported on 17 Aug. that the British were entrenching on Noddles Island (Baldwin to GW, that date), and on 21 Aug. Dodge informed GW that some of his men had destroyed that fortification (Dodge to GW, that date). Dodge temporarily assumed Baldwin's duties at Chelsea beginning 19 Aug. (Baldwin to GW, 18 Aug. 1775; Dodge to GW, 19 Aug. 1775).

3. "A Return of the observations of the Day august 20th," written and signed by Joseph Leach, is in DLC:GW.

Letter not found: to George Mason, 20 August 1775. On 14 Oct. 1775 Mason wrote to GW: "I have to acknowledge Your Favour of the 20th of Augt."

To Major General Philip Schuyler

Dr Sir Camp at Cambridge August 20th 1775

Since my last of the 15th Inst.[1] I have been favored with your's of the 6th, I am much concerned to find the Supplies ordered you have been so much delayed: By this Time I hope Colonel McDougall whose Zeal is unquestionable, has joined you with every Thing necessary for prosecuting your plan.[2] Several of the Delegates from Philadelphia, who have visited our Camp, assure me that powder is forwarded to you, and the daily arrivals of that article give us Reason to hope, we shall soon have a very ample Supply.[3]

Animated with the Goodness of our Cause, and the best Wishes of your Countrymen, I am sure you will not let Difficulties not insuperable damp your ardour. Perseverance and Spirit have done Wonders in all ages.

In my last (a Copy of which is inclosed) I sent you an Account of the arrival of several St Francis Indians in our Camp and of their friendly Dispositions. You have also a Copy of the Resolution of Congress, by which you will find it is their Intention only to seek a strict Neutrality of the Indian Nations, unless the Ministerial Agents should engage them in Hostilities, and enter into an offensive alliance with them.[4] I have therefore been embarrassed in giving them an answer when they have tendered their Services and assistance. As your Situation enables you best to know the Motions of the Governor of Canada or the agents I proposed to the Chief to go Home by way of Ticonderoga, referring him to you for an answer which you would give according to the Intelligence you have had and the Judgment you have formed of the Transactions among the Indians: but as he does not seem in Haste to leave our Camp, your answer by the Return of this Express may possibly reach me, before he returns and alter his Rout—Four of his Company still remain in our Camp and propose to stay some Time with us.[5]

The Design of this Express is to communicate to you a Plan of an Expedition, which has engrossed my Thoughts for several Days: It is to penetrate into Canada, by Way of Kennebeck River, and so to Quebec, by a Rout 90 Miles below Montreal—I can very well spare a Detachment of 1000 or 1200 Men, and the Land Carriage by the Rout proposed is too inconsiderable to make an Objection.[6] If you are resolved to proceed, (which I gather from your last Letter is your Intention) it would make a Diversion, that would distract Carlton and facilitate your Views. He must either break up and follow this party to Quebec, by which he will leave you a free passage or suffer that important Place to fall into our Hands: an Event which would have a decisive Effect and Influence on the public Interests.

There may be some Danger that such a sudden Incursion might alarm the Canadians and detach them from that Neutrality they have hitherto observed but I should hope that with suitable Precautions and a strict Discipline observed, any Jealousies and apprehensions might be quickly removed—The few whom I have consulted upon it, approve it much: but the final Determination is deferr'd until I hear from you. You will therefore by the Messenger[7] inform me of your ultimate Resolution. If you mean to proceed acquaint me as particularly as you can with the Time and Force—What late Accounts you have had from Canada—Your Opinion of the Temper of the Inhabitants as well as Indians upon a penetration into their Country? What Number of Troops are at Quebec, and whether any Men of

War and all other Circumstances which may be material in the Consideration of a Measure of such Importance.[8]

Not a Moment's Time is to be lost in the Preparation for this Enterprize, if the advices from you favor it. With the utmost Expedition the Season will be considerably advanced, so that you will dismiss the Express as soon as possible.

While the 3 New Hampshire Companies remain in their present Station, they will not be considered as composing a Part of the Continental army, but as a Militia under the Pay and Direction of the Colony, whose Inhabitants they are or for whose Defence they were stationed—So that it will not be proper for me to give any Orders respecting them.[9]

We still continue in the same Situation here as to the Enemy, as when I writ[10] you last: But we have had 6½ Tons of Powder from the Southward which is a very seasonable Supply—We are not be able[11] to learn any Thing farther of the Intentions of the Enemy; and they are too strongly posted for us to attempt any Thing upon them at present.

My best Wishes ever attend you: Believe me to be with great Truth and Regard. Dear Sir Your most obedt & very humble Servant.

Go. Washington

LB, NN: Schuyler Papers; Df, NHi: Joseph Reed Papers; LB, DLC:GW; Varick transcript, DLC:GW.

1. See the source note for GW's letter to Schuyler of 14 Aug. 1775.

2. Alexander McDougall (1732–1786), a Scotch immigrant who became a successful New York City merchant and a leading radical politician, was commissioned colonel of the 1st New York Regiment on 30 June 1775 by the colony's provincial congress, despite the fact that his previous military experience was limited to privateering during the French and Indian War. Finding the recruiting and equipping of his regiment going slowly, McDougall in early August sent his second in command, Lt. Col. Rudolphus Ritzema, north with the completed companies to join Schuyler, who was in great need of additional troops for his proposed invasion of Canada. Those companies were the first New York regulars to reach Schuyler. McDougall intended to follow Ritzema as soon as he finished raising his regiment, but he became convinced that he should remain in the provincial congress to oppose the conservatives who were pushing for reconciliation with Britain. The next spring McDougall raised a new regiment and joined GW's army in defending New York City. On 9 Aug. 1776 McDougall became a Continental brigadier general, and on 20 Oct. 1776 he was promoted to major general. Although he fought at the battles of Long Island, White Plains, and Germantown, most of his wartime

service was in the Hudson highlands. McDougall remained with the army until the end of the war except for the years 1781 and 1782 when he was a member of the Continental Congress.

3. For discussions of the gunpowder that the Continental Congress sent to the two armies, see Richard Henry Lee to GW, 1 Aug. 1775, n.3, and Jonathan Trumbull, Sr., to GW, 8 Aug. 1775, n.3.

4. For GW's account of the arrival of the St. Francis Indians, see GW to Schuyler, 14 Aug. 1775, n.1. The congressional resolution to which GW refers is that of 1 July 1775 (*JCC*, 2 : 123). See also Richard Henry Lee to GW, 29 June 1775, n.2.

5. Schuyler was willing to use any available Indians (Schuyler to GW, 27 Aug. 1775), and at GW's conference with a committee from the Continental Congress held between 18 and 24 Oct. 1775, it was agreed that the St. Francis Indians and others might "be called on in Case of real Necessity."

6. Under the command of Col. Benedict Arnold, this expedition began leaving Cambridge on 11 Sept. and reached Quebec on 19 Nov. The proposed route, which had been explored and mapped by the British army engineer Lt. John Montresor in 1761, went up the Kennebec and Dead rivers, across a height of land to Lake Megantic, and from thence down the Chaudière River to the St. Lawrence near Quebec. In the draft of this letter, Joseph Reed originally wrote "12, or 1500 Men," but GW changed the number to "a thousd or 1200 Men." The force was to be composed of volunteers and "active Woodsmen" (General Orders, 5 Sept. 1775).

7. Both the draft and the letter-book copy in DLC:GW read "by the Return of this Messenger."

8. For Schuyler's reply, see Schuyler to GW, 27 Aug. 1775.

9. The three New Hampshire companies commanded by Col. Timothy Bedel joined Schuyler's army in September. See GW to Schuyler, 27 July 1775, n.3, and Schuyler to GW, 20 Sept. 1775.

10. Both the draft and the letter-book copy in DLC:GW read "I wrote."

11. Both the draft and the letter-book copy in DLC:GW read "We are not able."

To Lund Washington

Dear Lund, Camp at Cambridge Augt 20th 1775.

Your Letter by Captn Prince came to my hands last Night[1]—I was glad to learn by it that all are well. the acct given of the behaviour of the Scotchmen at Port Tobacco & Piscataway surprizd & vexed me—Why did they Imbark in the cause? what do they say for themselves? what does other say of them? are they admitted into Company? or kicked out of it? what does their Countrymen urge in justification of them? they are fertile in invention, and will offer excuses where excuses can be made.

I cannot say but I am curious to learn the reasons why men, who had subscribed, & bound themselves to each other, & their Country, to stand forth in defence of it, should lay down their arms the first moment they were called upon.[2]

Although I never hear of the Mill under the direction of Simpson, without a degree of warmth & vexation at his extreame stupidity, yet, if you can spare money from other Purposes, I could wish to have it sent to him, that it may, if possible, be set agoing before the Works get ruined & spoilt, & my whole money perhaps totally lost.[3] If I am really to loose Barraud's debt to me, it will be a pretty severe stroke upon the back of Adams,[4] & the expence I am led into by that confounded fellow Simpson, and necessarily so in Seating my Lands under the Management of Cleveland.[5]

Spinning should go forward with all possible dispatch, as we shall have nothing else to depend upon if these disputes continue another year[6]—I can hardly think that Lord Dunmore can act so low, & unmanly a part, as to think of siezing Mrs Washington by way of revenge upon me; howevr as I suppose she is, before this time gone over to Mr Calverts, & will soon after retug, go down to New Kent, she will be out of his reach for 2 or 3 Months to come, in which time matters may, & probably will, take such a turn as to render her removal either absolutely necessary, or quite useless—I am nevertheless exceedingly thankful to the Gentlemen of Alexandria for their friendly attention to this point & desire you will if there is any sort of reason to suspect a thing of this kind provide a Kitchen for her in Alexandria, or some other place of safety elsewhere for her and my Papers.[7]

The People of this Government have obtaind a Character which they by no means deserved—their Officers generally speaking are the most indifferent kind of People I ever saw. I have already broke one Colo. and five Captain's for Cowardice, & for drawing more Pay & Provision's than they had Men in their Companies. there is two more Colos. now under arrest, & to be tried for the same Offences[8]—in short they are by no means such Troops, in any respect, as you are led to believe of them from the Accts which are published, but I need not make myself Enemies among them, by this declaration, although it is consistent with truth. I daresay the Men would fight very well (if properly Officered) although they are an exceeding dirty & nasty people. had they been properly conducted at Bunkers Hill (on the 17th of June) or those that were there properly supported, the Regulars would have met with a shameful defeat; & a much more considerable loss than they did, which is now known to be exactly 1057 Killed & Wounded[9]—it was for their behaviour on that occasion that the above Officers were broke, for I never spared one that was accused of Cowardice but brot 'em to immediate Tryal.

Our Lines of Defence are now compleated, as near so at least as can be—we now wish them to come out, as soon as they please, but they (that is the Enemy) discover no Inclination to quit their own Works of Defence; & as it is almost impossible for us to get to them, we do nothing but watch each other's motion's all day at the distance of about a Mile; every now and then picking of a stragler when we can catch them without their Intrenchments; in return, they often Attempt to Cannonade our Lines to no other purpose than the waste of a considerable quantity of Powder to themselves which we should be very glad to get.

What does Doctr Craik say to the behaviour of his Countrymen, & Townspeople? remember me kindly to him, & tell him that I should be very glad to see him here if there was any thing worth his acceptance; but the Massachusets People suffer nothing to go by them that they can lay hands upon.[10]

I wish the money could be had from Hill, & the Bills of Exchange (except Colo. Fairfax's, which ought to be sent to him immediately) turnd into Cash; you might then, I should think, be able to furnish Simpson with about £300;[11] but you are to recollect that I have got Cleveland & the hired People with him to pay also. I would not have you buy a single bushel of Wheat till you can see with some kind of certainty what Market the Flour is to go to—& if you cannot find sufficient Imployment in repairing the Mill works, & other things of this kind for Mr Roberts and Thomas Alferd, they must be closely Imployed in making Cask, or working at the Carpenters or other business otherwise they must be discharged, for it is not reasonable, as all Mill business will probably be at an end for a while, that I am to pay them £100 a year to be Idle. I should think Roberts himself must see, & be sensible of the reasonableness of this request, as I believe few Millers will find Imploymt if our Ports are shut up, & the Wheat kept in the Straw, or otherwise for greater Security.[12]

I will write to Mr Milnor to forward you a good Country Boulting Cloth for Simpson which endeavour to have contrived to him by the first safe conveyance.[13] I wish you would quicken Lanphire & Sears about the Dining Room Chimney Piece (to be executed as mentioned in one of my last Letters) as I could wish to have that end of the House compleatly finished before I return.[14] I wish you had done the end of the New Kitchen next the Garden as also the old Kitchen with rusticated Boards; however, as it is not, I would have the Corners done so in the manner of our New Church. (those two especially which Fronts the Quarter.[)][15] What have you done with the Well? is that walled up?[16] have you any accts of the Painter? how does he behave at Fredericksburg?[17]

I much approve of your Sowing Wheat in clean ground, although you should be late in doing it, & if for no other purpose than a tryal[18]—It is a growing I find, as well as a new practice, that of overseers keeping Horses, & for what purpose, unless it be to make fat Horses at my expence, I know not, as it is no saving of my own Horses—I do not like the custom, & wish you would break it—but do as you will, as I cannot pretend to interfere at this distance. Remember me kindly to all the Neighbours who enquire after Yr Affecte friend & Servt

Go: Washington

ALS, NN: Emmet Collection.

1. Lund Washington's letter has not been found. Although there was a Capt. Asa Prince in Col. John Mansfield's Massachusetts regiment on Winter Hill, the bearer was probably Capt. Thomas Price of Frederick, Maryland. He left Frederick with his rifle company on 18 July and arrived at Cambridge about 11 Aug., after a brief stopover in Philadelphia, where he may have been given Lund's letter. See Benjamin Harrison to GW, 21–24 July 1775, n.16.

2. The town of Piscataway on Piscataway Creek in Prince Georges County, Md., is a few miles east of Mount Vernon. Port Tobacco lies in Charles County, Md., about sixteen miles south of Piscataway. Dr. Robert Honyman, who visited Port Tobacco on 2 Mar. 1775, wrote in his journal that he "went out into a field by the town & saw a Company of about 60 Gentlemen learning the military Exercise" (Philip S. Padelford, ed., *Colonial Panorama, 1775: Dr. Robert Honyman's Journal for March and April* [San Marino, Calif., 1939], 2).

3. As manager of GW's property at Washington's Bottom, Pa., Gilbert Simpson, Jr., was supervising the construction of a large gristmill near the

mouth of Washington's Run, a tributary of the Youghiogheny River. Begun in early 1774, the work on the mill had been slow and costly, which GW attributed to Simpson's mismanagement (Gilbert Simpson to GW, 31 Aug., 1 Oct. 1773, 4 May, 20 Aug., 24 Sept., 9 Nov. 1774, 6 Feb., 3 April 1775). The mill ran for the first time in the spring of 1776, but it produced no profits during the war years to reimburse GW for the £1,000 to £1,200 that he spent in building it. When GW visited western Pennsylvania in September 1784, he found the mill on Washington's Run in a state of total disrepair (*Diaries*, 4:20–21).

4. GW never received the £1,748 17s. in Virginia currency that the Norfolk firm of Balfour & Barraud owed him for flour and ship biscuit (Ledger B, 136). The contract that GW signed with an agent of the company at Mount Vernon on 4 Jan. 1775 called for GW to deliver the flour and bread by 1 March and for the company to pay him half of his money at the April meeting of the general court in Williamsburg and the balance at the court's October meeting. The company's failure to meet its April obligation may have been due to James Balfour's death early that month at his home near Hampton. GW's absence from Virginia and the wartime disruption of the economy in tidewater Virginia effectively prevented his bringing the firm's surviving partner, Daniel Barraud, to account (Fielding Lewis to GW, 14 Nov. 1775, 6 Mar. 1776; GW to Neil Jamieson, 20 May 1786). GW did receive some compensation, however, for the debt of £106 6s. 6d. in Virginia currency that Daniel Jenifer Adams (b.1751) of Charles County, Md., still owed him for flour that Adams had sold for GW in the West Indies during 1772. In a letter to Adams on 8 Mar. 1775, GW agreed to take 552⅓ acres of land in Charles County and a Negro slave in settlement of the debt, although he would have much preferred cash (Ledger B, 57, 99). Adams deeded the land and slave to GW in December 1775 (Lund Washington to GW, 10 Dec. 1775).

5. For a discussion of James Cleveland's efforts to perfect GW's rights to his lands on the Kanawha and Ohio rivers, see Valentine Crawford to GW, 24 June 1775, n.1.

6. For Lund Washington's difficulties in obtaining spinning wheels, see his letters to GW of 29 Sept. and 5 Nov. 1775.

7. For Lund Washington's accounts of the rumor that Virginia's royal governor, Lord Dunmore, might sail up the Potomac River and attempt to capture Martha Washington, see Lund Washington to GW, 5 and 15 Oct. 1775. No British vessel seriously threatened Mount Vernon until the spring of 1781. See GW to Lund Washington, 30 April 1781. Martha Washington visited Benedict and Elizabeth Calvert, her daughter-in-law's parents, at Mount Airy in Prince Georges County, Md., during part of August and between 30 Sept. and 3 Oct. 1775 (Peyton Randolph to GW, 6 Sept. 1775; Lund Washington to GW, 29 Sept., 5 Oct. 1775). On 17 Oct. Mrs. Washington left Mount Vernon to see her relatives in New Kent County, Va. (Lund Washington to GW, 22 Oct., 5 Nov. 1775). For GW's proposal to build a kitchen next to his small townhouse in Alexandria, see GW to Martha Washington, 18 June 1775, n.3.

8. The cashiered officers were Col. Samuel Gerrish and captains John

Callender, Christopher Gardner, Oliver Parker, Jesse Saunders, and Eleazer Lindsey (General Orders, 7 July, 2, 9, 16, 19 Aug. 1775). The two colonels awaiting trial were Ebenezer Bridge, who was acquitted of the charges against him, and John Mansfield, who was cashiered (General Orders, 13, 17, 20, 21 Aug., 11, 15 Sept. 1775).

9. GW earlier put the British losses at 1,043 killed and wounded. See GW to Hancock, 21 July (third letter), GW to George William Fairfax, 25 July, and GW to John Augustine Washington, 27 July 1775.

10. GW's friend Dr. James Craik of Port Tobacco, Md., did not enter the Continental service until October 1780. See Valentine Crawford to GW, 24 June 1775, n.2.

11. As steward of the Custis estate from 1772 to 1778, James Hill of King William County, Va., managed John Parke Custis's plantations and those which GW held in King William and York counties by virtue of Martha Washington's dower rights. George William Fairfax's bill of exchange was the one from John Syme, about which GW wrote to Fairfax on 26 July 1775. For the sale of two of GW's bills of exchange, see Lund Washington to GW, 29 Sept. and 5 Oct. 1775. Lund Washington set aside £300 in Pennsylvania currency for Gilbert Simpson, but he had trouble getting the money to him (Lund Washington to GW, 29 Sept., 15, 29 Oct., 17 Dec. 1775).

12. William Roberts was the miller at Mount Vernon from 1770 to 1785. During the fall of 1775, Roberts and his apprentice, Thomas Alfred (Alford), were employed for several weeks in repairing the milldams and millrace, which were twice damaged by freshets (Lund Washington to GW, 5, 15, 22 Oct. 1775), but Lund Washington found little else for them to do because barrels that were made in advance usually had to be rebuilt before they could be used (Lund Washington to GW, 12 Nov. 1775, 25 Jan. 1776). During GW's absence from Mount Vernon, Roberts turned increasingly to alcohol, and GW was finally obliged to dismiss him in the spring of 1785 (GW to Robert Lewis & Sons, 6 Sept. 1783, 1 Feb. 1785). GW continued to have a high opinion of Roberts as a miller and millwright and in 1799 was willing to hire him again (GW to Roberts, 17 June, 8 July 1799).

13. William Milnor was a Quaker merchant in Philadelphia who rented a fishery at Mount Vernon during 1774. A strong supporter of the American cause, Milnor assisted GW during the winter and spring of 1775 in obtaining various military accoutrements both for his own use and for the Fairfax and Prince William independent companies. Milnor also supplied GW with household and plantation goods from Philadelphia, and in the fall of 1773 he sent GW two yards of good bolting cloth, presumably for the Mount Vernon mill (Milnor to GW, 19 Oct. 1773; GW to Milnor, 16 Dec. 1773). Although no letter has been found from GW to Milnor requesting a bolting cloth for the mill at Washington's Bottom, Milnor did receive the order, and sometime before 15 Oct. he wrote to Lund Washington assuring him that the bolting cloth would be sent (Lund Washington to GW, 15 Oct. 1775). On 8 Feb. 1776 Lund Washington wrote to GW that he still had not received it.

14. GW decided as early as the fall of 1773 to extend the Mount Vernon

mansion house on both ends by adding a downstairs library and an upstairs master bedroom on the south and a two-story banquet room on the north. Work on the southern addition was begun in April 1774 by Going Lanphier (1727–1813), a house carpenter who had done smaller jobs at Mount Vernon in 1759 and 1765. This addition was finished by the end of 1775, and in 1776 Lanphier began raising the northern addition. The interior of the second addition was still incomplete when GW returned to Mount Vernon at the end of 1783. The work on the chimneypiece in the dining room, which adjoined the southern addition, was apparently the responsibility of William Bernard Sears. He was sick and absent from Mount Vernon during much of October 1775, but he returned in late fall to finish the chimneypiece and to paint the dining room and the new rooms (Lund Washington to GW, 29 Sept., 5, 15, 22 Oct., 10 Dec. 1775).

15. The new kitchen, which stood near the south end of the mansion house, was apparently finished by the end of this year. The new church was the Pohick Church, located a few miles west of Mount Vernon. It was completed and turned over to the Truro Parish vestry in February 1774 (*Diaries*, 3:233).

16. GW wished to have the brick lining of the well replaced. The old lining was removed without great difficulty, but the tendency of the unsupported sides to fall in made the replacing of the lining a dangerous job which workmen were reluctant to undertake. The new lining, nevertheless, was in place by the end of February 1776 (Lund Washington to GW, 17, 25 Jan., 8, 29 Feb. 1776).

17. The painter was apparently an indentured servant who belonged to GW (Lund Washington to GW, 29 Sept. 1775, 17 Jan. 1776; Fielding Lewis to GW, 14 Nov. 1775).

18. Lund did not begin sowing wheat until the latter part of August, and then frequent rains made the ground too wet to plow for several weeks. The sowing was still not finished as of 22 Oct. (Lund Washington to GW, 29 Sept., 5, 15, 22 Oct., 23 Dec. 1775).

General Orders

Head Quarters, Cambridge, August 21st 1775.

Parole, Norfolk. Countersign Oporto.

The Court of enquiry ordered to sit Yesterday upon Col. Ebenezer Bridge, to sit this day at three O'Clock P.M.[1]

Michael Berry tried by a late General Court Martial for "stealing a Hat from Capt. Waterman"[2] is found guilty, and sentenced to receive Thirty Lashes, but in Consideration of his long Confinement; the General pardons the prisoner.

General Sullivan's Brigade to be mustered to morrow—The Muster Master General, to begin with the Regiment posted on the left of the lines, exactly at Six O'Clock, with the next Regiment on the left at seven, and so on untill the whole are mustered: The Field & Staff Officers of each Regiment, are to be mustered in the eldest Captains Company, and such as were draughted to the Regimt of Artillery, are to be mustered only to the day they were draughted. The Regiment of Artillery to muster them from that time.

A Serjeant, Corporal & nine Men, to mount Guard to morrow morning, at Mr Fainweathers House, lately converted into an Hospital.[3] The Serjt to receive his Orders from Dr Church, Director of the Hospital.[4]

Varick transcript, DLC:GW.

1. For a discussion of the charge against Bridge, see General Orders, 20 Aug. 1775, n.2.

2. Andrew Waterman of Smithfield, R.I., was a captain in Col. Daniel Hitchcock's regiment from 3 May 1775 to the end of the year, and during the early months of 1776, he served as a captain in the Rhode Island state regiment commanded by Col. Henry Babcock. Waterman represented Smithfield in several sessions of the Rhode Island general assembly between 1776 and 1789.

3. Artemas Ward's orderly book reads "Mr Fayerweather's House" (MHi: Ward Papers). Thomas Fayerweather's house stood a short distance west of Cambridge near Andrew Oliver's mansion, Elmwood, which also served the Continental army as a hospital (General Orders, 26 July 1775).

4. Benjamin Church (1734–c.1778), a member of a distinguished Boston family and one of the city's leading physicians, was appointed director and chief physician of the army's hospital by the Continental Congress on 27 July. Church received his medical training during the 1750s, first under a Boston doctor and then in London hospitals. Returning to Boston with an English wife in 1759, he soon established a reputation as a skillful surgeon and an expert on smallpox inoculation. He also became known as something of a literary figure and a radical Whig politician. By 1770 Church was devoting much of his time and talent to revolutionary politics. He played a leading role in the Boston committee of correspondence, the Massachusetts provincial congress, and the colony's committee of safety, and on 2 June 1775 he presented to the Continental Congress the letter from the Massachusetts provincial congress which proposed that the delegates in Philadelphia adopt the army outside Boston (*JCC*, 2:76–78). That appearance before Congress may have contributed to his appointment as hospital director. Unknown to the Patriot leaders, however, Church had for many months been acting as a British agent, writing anonymous articles for Boston's Tory newspaper, the *Censor*, and furnishing much valuable information about American plans and activities to Gen. Thomas Gage. Church's double-dealing was not discovered until late September of this year. See Council of War, 3–4 Oct. 1775. He was imprisoned by the American authorities until sometime in 1778, when he was allowed to leave the country apparently for the West Indies. The vessel on which Church sailed was never heard of again and was presumed lost at sea.

From Captain Richard Dodge

Sir Chelsea [Mass.] August the 21th 1775

I would in form your Exelencey that I have Nothing Remarkable to Right[.] I Have I[n] closed the minetes tacken By the Person a Pinted for that Purpos.[1] I am your Exelencies most Humble Servent

Richard Dodge Capt.

P.S. Senc I Be[g]an to Right I am in formed that Sum fue of our men have Bin over and Destroied that Litl intrinchment at Noltes Island[.][2] I have Bin Doun to Pottrin Pint[3] and have got a Vary good Scow or gondelow and fetched hur up Vary Near my Qu[a]rtes[.] I tack hur to Carey 10 or 12 tun wait.

ALS, DLC:GW.

1. "A Return of the observations of the Day august 21st," written and signed by Joseph Leach, is in DLC:GW.

2. For the British entrenchment on Noddles Island, see Loammi Baldwin to GW, 17 Aug. 1775, and Dodge to GW, c.20 Aug. 1775.

3. Dodge probably means Pullen Point.

From Peter Van Brugh Livingston

Sir New York 21st August 1775

Your favors of the 8th & 10th Instant I have recd and communicated to our Provincial Congress. Our City Committie are ordered strictly to enquire for the Owner of the Vessel you mention to be arrived at Boston, Said to be cleared here for St Croix, and make Report; all possible care will be taken to prevent Provisions being sent from hence to Boston.[1]

If the Fleet and army should move we hope to have the earliest Intelligence from you by Express—We have wrote to Mr Thompson Secretary to the Continental Congress for Blank Commissions.[2]

Perswaded of the propriety that you Should be furnished with every Intelligence I inclose the Examination of Mr Carter taken by our Congress,[3] and have the honor to be Sir Your most Obedt Servant

P. V. B. Livingston

ALS, DLC:GW.

1. The New York provincial congress read GW's letter of 8 Aug. on 19 Aug. and his letter of 10 Aug. to Livingston on 17 Aug. (*N.Y. Prov. Congress Journals*, 1:109, 111). For the action taken by the provincial congress on 19 Aug. respecting the exportation of provisions from the colony, see GW to the New York Provincial Congress, 8 Aug. 1775, n.1.

2. The provincial congress wrote to Charles Thomson on 18 Aug., requesting that he send Schuyler about two hundred blank commissions if none had been sent previously (ibid., 110). The letter which the Continental Congress received is in DNA:PCC, item 67, but it is erroneously dated 8 July. On 9 Sept. the colony's committee of safety asked Congress for 400 commissions (DNA:PCC, item 67), and five days later Congress instructed John Hancock to send that number to Schuyler (*JCC*, 2:249).

3. John Carter's intelligence, as recorded by the provincial congress's secretary John McKesson on 19 Aug., chiefly concerns the capture on 25 July of the merchant vessel *Charming Sally* by the British warship *Glasgow*. The *Charming Sally*, aboard which Carter was a passenger, was bound from Philadelphia to Lisbon with 2,200 barrels of flour when it encountered the *Glasgow*. The master of the *Charming Sally*, Capt. Thomas Doman, made no attempt to avoid capture, Carter charged, and the vessel was taken to Boston, where, Gen. Gage said, "Captain Doman would get a good price for his Cargo." Carter also reported the capture and arrival in Boston of another Philadelphia vessel loaded with flour, apparently the schooner *Woodbridge*. For more information on the taking of these two vessels and GW's suspicions that their captains conspired with the British, see GW to Livingston, 30 Aug. 1775. Following the capture of the *Charming Sally*, Carter spent some time in Boston, and during his stay he obtained several bits of information about the British garrison, which he included in his report to the provincial congress. GW must have read with particular interest Carter's statements "that the Army at Boston are not making any preparations for an Embarkation—That they are destroying Castle William, & carrying the Cannon and Stores into Boston, but no appearance of any Intention of the Troops leaving that place . . . That the Army talked of laying in a Stock for Winter, and are sending to Hallifax for Provisions & wood . . . That a Victualler Transport had lately arrived at Boston in Eight Weeks passage—That according to the accounts received by that Transport, they expected Six Sail of the Line and Twenty Transports from England—That the Army in general appears to be exasperated against the Americans, and say America cannot make a Resistance; and speak of their going through America when they receive their expected Reinforcements" (DLC:GW).

Letter not found: from Joseph Palmer, 21 Aug. 1775. In his letter of 22 Aug. to Palmer, GW referred to "your favour of yesterday."

From Jonathan Trumbull, Sr.

Sir Lebanon [Conn.] 21st Augt 1775

Your Esteemed Favour of the 14th instant is received, No Powder is stopped according to my request, hope that t[i]s for the best[1]—None is lately arrived to this Colony, altho' daily expected—We are greatly exhausted, your Order to leave a quantity out of the next parcell that passes this Colony will be agreable, if none arrive here before. Shall Take Care of the Lead ordered from Ticonderoga—to forward it in the best way to Camp[2]—Seven or Eight Tons of rich Lead ore is already raised at Middletown, and Furnace &c. erecting to Smelt it;[3] In Woodbury another Rich Lead Mine is discovered formerly it was begun to be worked, but some controversy about the property of it & contention among the people prevented its progress.

There is no doubt of beds of Sulphur to be found—Our People are busy in making Petre[4]—I have enclosed for your Observation the Intelligence received from Brig. Genl Wooster.[5]

Since writing above have received and enclosed for your Notice the Intelligence from Tyconderoga;[6] you'l receive this by hand of our Mutual good Friends Colo. Dyer and Colo. Elderkin who will be able to inform better than I can by writing.[7] I am, with great Truth & Sincerity Your Excellency's most Obedient and very Humble Servant

Jonth. Trumbull

ALS, DLC:GW; copy, in Trumbull's writing, CtHi: Trumbull Papers; LB, Ct: Trumbull Papers. The copy at the Connecticut Historical Society is endorsed "Sent ℔ Bennet."

1. For Trumbull's request to keep at Hartford two of the eight wagonloads of gunpowder that the Continental Congress sent to the army outside Boston, see Trumbull to GW, 12 Aug. 1775.

2. For GW's request for this lead, see GW to Schuyler and GW to Trumbull, both 14 Aug. 1775. Governor Trumbull wrote to Schuyler on 17 Aug. asking him to send the lead from Ticonderoga and Crown Point to Commissary Elisha Phelps at Albany, who was to forward it to GW "in the most safe and expeditious manner." Trumbull wrote to Phelps about the lead on 21 Aug. (Hinman, *Historical Collection*, 330–31). See also Phelps to GW, 8 Sept. 1775.

3. In May 1775 the Connecticut general assembly appointed a committee to take over the mine in Middletown from its private owners and work it for the benefit of the colony. The committee operated the mine until February

1778, when the general assembly, being advised that the manufacture of the ore at Middletown "was unprofitable to the State," ordered the committee "to discontinue any farther smelting of lead at said mine, after having finished the ore, then on hand" (ibid., 183, 217, 313).

4. The Connecticut general assembly in May 1775 authorized a bounty of £10 for every 50 pounds of saltpeter made from materials found in Connecticut and a bounty of £5 for every 100 pounds of sulfur manufactured within the colony (ibid., 174).

5. The enclosure is a copy Trumbull made of a letter to him from Brig. Gen. David Wooster, dated 14 Aug. 1775 at the Oyster Ponds on Long Island. Wooster's letter chiefly concerns a raid that a British sloop of war and two transports made on Plum Island off Orient Point on 11 Aug. and the arrest of a Tory clergyman, the Rev. James Lyon, on Long Island. Wooster also reported: "I expect by thursday [17 Aug.] to be able to embark for New York" (DLC:GW).

6. The "intelligence" consisted of copies of letters to Trumbull, dated 14 Aug. 1775, from Maj. John Brown at Crown Point, from Col. Benjamin Hinman at Ticonderoga, and from Philip Schuyler at Ticonderoga (DLC:GW). Major Brown's letter describes the scouting expedition that he led into Canada between 24 July and 10 Aug. on Schuyler's orders. "Now sir is the time to carry Canada," Brown wrote, "it may be done with great ease & Little Cost, & I have no doubt but the Canadians would Join us. . . . Should a large reinforcement arrive in Canada it will turn the Scale immediately the Canadians must then take up Arms or be ruined—it Seames that some evil Planit has reigned in this Quarter this Year for notwithstanding the Season far advanced & a fine opportunity presents of making ourselves masters of a Country with the greatest ease which I fear may cost us much Blood & Treasure if delayed—New York have acted a Drole part & are Determined to Defeat us if in their Power they have failed in Men & Supplies." Colonel Hinman, whose Connecticut regiment had been placed under Schuyler's command, was also critical of the New Yorkers in his letter. "The Province of New York abounds with Officers," he reported, "but I have not had my Curiosity gratified by the sight of one Private." He feared that New York would not supply the tents it had promised for his regiment, and he reported that many of his men were too ill to do duty. Hinman hoped, nevertheless, "soon to be employed in Action." Schuyler was clearly determined to gratify that desire. "I hope the Provincial Congress of this Colony will make no Delay in forwarding Col. Hinmans Tents," Schuyler wrote to Trumbull, "as I propose moving in a few days, altho. not so strong as I cod wish, & very indifferently appointed. Shod the Tents not arrive in Time, Col. Hinman's People will suffer much, & so will Col. [James] Easton's."

7. Both of these residents of Windham, Conn., were lawyers and leading members of the Susquehanna Company, and both served on the Connecticut council. Eliphalet Dyer (1721–1807) was well acquainted with GW from serving with him in the First and Second Continental Congresses. He had come home during Congress's August recess and apparently visited GW's camp be-

fore returning to Philadelphia for the reconvening of Congress in September. A Connecticut colonel during the French and Indian War, Dyer did not seek a commission in the Continental army but remained in Congress for much of the war, taking a particular interest in military matters. Jedediah Elderkin (1717–1793) was commissioned colonel of the 15th Regiment of Connecticut militia in May 1775, but it was as a procurer of munitions and other supplies for the army, not as a field commander, that he contributed most to the American cause. A silk producer as well as a lawyer before the war, Elderkin undertook a very different type of manufacturing in December 1775 when he joined Nathaniel Wales, Jr., in erecting a powder mill at Windham. In the spring of 1776 the Connecticut general assembly paid the two men £30 for 1,000 pounds of gunpowder which they had made. Elderkin was also involved in the manufacture of cannon in Connecticut, the building of a powder magazine for the colony, the purchase of military clothing and tents, the planning of fortifications at New London, and the care of prisoners of war.

General Orders

Head Quarters, Cambridge, August 22nd 1775

Parole Portsmouth. Countersign Quinsey.[1]

As the Muster Rolls cannot be properly prepared before Saturday next, The General defers the mustering of the Brigades upon the left of the Lines, until next Monday; when the mustering the whole will take place without interruption.[2]

Capt. Pearl, of Col. Woodbridges Regiment, tried by a General Court Martial for "defrauding his men of their pay"—The Court are unanimously of Opinion, that the Complaint is in no part supported and being vexatious and groundless, and acquit Capt. Pearl: The Court order the chief Complainant, Daniel Davids, to be confined.[3]

The General does not mean to discourage the practice of bathing, whilst the weather is warm enough to continue it; but he expressly forbids, any persons doing it, at or near the Bridge in Cambridge, where it has been observed and complained of, that many Men, lost to all sense of decency and common modesty, are running about naked upon the Bridge, whilst Passengers, and even Ladies of the first fashion in the neighbourhood, are passing over it, as if they meant to glory in their shame: The Guards and Centries at the Bridge, are to put a stop to this practice for the future.

The Director General of the Hospital having complained,

that the sick under his care, are not only incommoded by a promiscuous resort of Soldiers to the rooms; but greatly injured by having improper things carried to them to eat, at the same time, that many disorders, under which the Sick are suffering, may be by them contracted and spread in the Camp, by means of this Intercourse, it is therefore ordered, that this improper Visitation be put a Stop to for the future—No Non Commissioned Officer, or soldier to be admitted into the Hospital hereafter, without the leave of the Surgeon then in attendance, or by a written Licence from the Colonel, or Commanding Officer of the Regiment they belong to; in either of which Cases, the Friends to the sick, and all those who have any real business with them, will never be denied the privilege and satisfaction of visiting.

Representations being made to the Commander in Chief, that Officers are frequently seen in Cambridge and Watertown, and in the Towns and Villages round the Camp, without any leave of absence previously obtained, and contrary to all good discipline and Order; and as such irregularity at this time, may be productive of the worst of consequences: The General directs the Commanding Officers of Corps, to be particularly attentive to the Behaviour of all their Officers, and without Favor or Affection, confine any Officer, who is absent from the Camp or Lines, where he is posted or encamped, without Leave in writing first had and obtained from the General commanding the brigade. And the Commanding Officers[4] are strictly enjoined, to put in Arrest, any Officer, who shall for the future disobey this order; When Officers set good Examples, it may be expected that the Men will with zeal and alacrity follow them, but it would be a mere phenomenon in nature, to find a well disciplin'd Soldiery, where Officers are relax'd and tardy in their duty; nor can they with any kind of propriety, or good Conscience, set in Judgment upon a Soldier for disobeying an order, which they themselves are every day breaking; The General is exceeding sorry to find occasion, to give such repeated Orders on this head, but, as the safety of the Army and Salvation of the Country, may essentially depend upon a strictness of discipline, and close attention to Duty; he will give no Countenance, nor shew any Favor to delinquents.

Varick transcript, DLC:GW.

1. Artemas Ward's orderly book reads "Quincy" (MHi: Ward Papers).

2. The muster of Brig. Gen. John Sullivan's brigade was further postponed from Monday, 28 Aug., to Friday, 1 Sept. (General Orders, 26 and 28 Aug. 1775).

3. Stephen Pearl remained a captain in Col. Benjamin Ruggles Woodbridge's Massachusetts regiment until November of this year. He became adjutant of the 1st Massachusetts Regiment on 1 Jan. 1777 and resigned from the army on 8 Mar. 1778.

4. Artemas Ward's orderly book reads "the Commanding Officers of Regts" (MHi: Ward Papers).

From Lieutenant Colonel James Babcock

Rhode Island Camp on Prospect Hill [Mass.] 22 August 1775. Requests "a discharge from the Service, by reason of the indisposition that attends his bodily health."

L, in unidentified writing, DLC:GW. The person who wrote and signed this letter also wrote and signed the letters of this date that GW received from John Parke and John Randall. All three men served in Col. James Varnum's Rhode Island regiment, and one of them may have written the letters for the other two, or some fourth person may have acted as their clerk.

James Babcock of Westerly, R.I., became lieutenant colonel of Varnum's regiment on 3 May 1775. He was apparently allowed to retire from the army soon after this letter was sent to GW. In April 1777 the Rhode Island general assembly appointed Babcock to advance bounties to soldiers at Westerly, and in July 1780 he was appointed to receive recruits there. Babcock represented Westerly in the assembly during the spring of 1777.

From Captain Richard Dodge

Sr Chelsea [Mass.] August the 22th 1775

I Have Sent a gentelmen to your Exelency that was from Boston yesturday, I Furst Saw him a Bout five of the C[l]ock But the Barer was gon to Head Quarters with the hors and it Did not Lay in my Pouer to git a Hors for him and he Said he Co[u]ld not goue on foot—he a Peard to Be vary noing—I inpuierd [inquired] in to his Cariter By gentelmen men of Note wich in formed me he was a man that mite Be Depended uppon & that he Nue The Situation of the armey as wull as aney man.

Sir I am with Respect your Exeleny most humble Servent a[t] Command

Richd Dodge Capt.

ALS, DLC:GW. Dodge may have enclosed with this letter Joseph Leach's "A Return of the observations of the Day august 22d," which is in DLC:GW.

From Major General William Howe

Sir Charles:town Camp [Mass.] August 22d 1775

The Men under your command having repeatedly fired upon the Officers of His Majesty's Troops before they were returned to the out:works of this Camp from Parlies that have been brought on by your desire; I am to request all farther intercourse between the two Camps may be at an end; your own letters excepted, which will be received if you are pleased to send them by a Drummer. I am Sir Yr Most Obt Sert

W. Howe

ALS, DLC:GW. This letter is addressed "George Washington Esqr. Cambridge."

William Howe (1729–1814), who served as commander in chief of the British forces in North America from 10 Oct. 1775 to late May 1778, arrived at Boston on 25 May 1775 to assist Gen. Gage, and on 17 June he commanded the detachment which drove the Americans from Breed's and Bunker hills. After the battle Gage put Howe in charge of the British lines around Bunker Hill, and Howe established his headquarters at Charlestown.

To Joseph Palmer

Sir, Cambridge Augt 22d 1775.

In answer to your favour of yesterday[1] I must inform you, that I have often been told of the advantages of Point Alderton with respect to its command of the shipping going in and out of Boston Harbour; and that it has, before now, been the object of my particular enquiries—That I find the Accts differ, exceedingly, in regard to the distance of the ship Channel, & that, there is a passage on the other side of the light House Island for all Vessells except ships of the first Rate.[2]

My Knowledge of this matter would not have rested upon enquiries only, if I had found myself at any one time since I came to this place, in a condition to have taken such a Post—But it becomes my duty to consider, not only what place is advantageous, but what number of men are necessary to defend it—how they can be supported in case of an attack—how they may retreat if they cannot be supported—& what stock of Ammunition we are provide⟨d⟩ with for the purpose of self defence, or annoyance of the Enemy—In respect to the first; I conceive our defence must be proportioned to the attack of Genl Gage's whole force (leaving him just enough to man his Lines on Charles Town Neck & Roxbury) and with regard to the second, and most important object, we have only 184 Barrls of powder in all, which is not sufficient to give 30 Musket Cartridges a man, & scarce enough to serve the Artillery in any brisk action a single day.

Would it be prudent then in me, under these Circumstances, to take a Post 30 Miles distant from this place when we already have a Line of Circumvalation at least Ten Miles in extent, any part of which may be attacked (if the Enemy will keep their own Council) without our having one hours previous notice of it? Or is it prudent to attempt a Measure which necessarily would bring on a consumption of all the Ammunition we have; thereby leaving the Army at the Mercy of the Enemy, or to disperse; & the Country to be Ravaged, and laid waste at discretion? To you Sir who is a well wisher to the cause, and can reason upon the effects of such a Conduct, I may open myself with freedom, because no improper discoveries will be made of our Situation; but I cannot expose my weakness to the Enemy (tho' I believe they are pretty well informed of every thing that passes) by telling this, and that man who are daily pointing out this—that—and t'other place, of all the motives that govern my actions, notwithstanding I know what will be the consequence of not doing it—namely, that I shall be accused of inattention to the publick Service—& perhaps with want of Spirit to prosecute it—But this shall have no effect upon my Conduct, I will steadily (as far as my judgment will assist me) pursue such measures as I think most conducive to the Interest of the cause, & rest satisfied under any obloquy that shall be thrown conscious of having discharged my duty to the best of my abilities.[3]

I am much obliged to you however, as I shall be to every Gentleman, for pointing out any measure which is thought conducive to the publick good, and chearfully follow any advice which is not inconsistent with, but corrispondant to, the general Plan in view, & practicable under such particular circumstances as govern in cases of the like kind. In respect to point Alderton, I was no longer ago than Monday last,[4] talking to Genl Thomas on this head, & proposing to send Colo. Putnam down to take the distances &ca, but considered it could answer no end but to alarm, & make the Enemy more vigilant, unless we were in a condition to possess the Post to effect. I thought it as well to postpone the matter a while. I am Sir Yr Very Hble Servt

G. Washington

ALS, owned (1970) by Richard Maass. The cover is addressed "To The Honble J: Palmer Watertown."

1. Palmer's letter to GW of 21 Aug. has not been found. In it Palmer apparently suggested a scheme for blockading Boston Harbor similar to the one about which Richard Henry Lee wrote to GW on 1 Aug. 1775. See note 4 to that document.

2. Point Alderton, located at the end of Nantasket peninsula, overlooks Nantasket Roads, the main ship channel leading into Boston Harbor. Point Alderton lies on the south side of the channel, and Lighthouse Island is on the north side.

3. GW repeated these arguments in his letter to Richard Henry Lee of 29 Aug. 1775. For his rejection of another proposal for blockading Boston Harbor, see GW to Josiah Quincy, 4 Nov. 1775.

4. GW apparently is referring to Monday, 14 Aug., not to 21 Aug., which was also a Monday.

From Lieutenant John Parke

Camp on Prospect Hill [Mass.] 22 August 1775. Requests "a discharge from the Service, by reason of his having at home a Sister in Law (whose husband was slain in the Battle at Charlestown) with a numerous Family, an aged Father and no Person remaining to provide for, and support them—and he being the only surviving brother."

L, in unidentified writing, DLC:GW. For a discussion of the handwriting, see James Babcock to GW, this date, source note. Parke's letter includes a cover addressed to GW in the same writing.

John Parke may be Capt. John Parke of Charlestown, R.I., who served much of the Revolution in the town's militia.

From Captain John Randall

Camp on Prospect Hill [Mass.] 22 August 1775. "By reason of the indisposition of his body, is reduced to the necessity of asking a discharge from the Service."

L, in unidentified writing, DLC:GW. For a discussion of the handwriting, see James Babcock to GW, this date, source note. Randall's letter includes a cover addressed to GW in the same writing.

John Randall, who was commissioned a captain in Varnum's regiment on 3 May 1775, apparently left the Continental army about this time and did not again serve in a military capacity during the Revolution. He may be Capt. John Randall who died at Pawtuxet, R.I., in 1823 at the age of 73.

Letter not found: from Major General Artemas Ward, 22 Aug. 1775. On 25 Aug. Ward informed GW: "I wrote your Excy . . . the 22d Inst."

General Orders

Head Quarters, Cambridge, August 23rd 1775

Parole Rumney.[1] Countersign Somersett.

Varick transcript, DLC:GW.

1. Artemas Ward's orderly book reads "Parole Romney" (MHi: Ward Papers).

To Major General William Howe

Sir [Camp Cambridge] Aug. 23. 1775

I flatter myself you have been m[is]inform'd as to the Conduct of the Men under my Command complained of in yours of yesterday. It is what I should highly disapprove & condemn.

I have not the least Objection to put a Stop to the Intercourse between the two Camps either totally or partially. It obtained thro. the pressing Sollicitations of Persons cruelly separated from their Friends & Connections & I understood was mutually convenient. I am Sir Your most Obed. Hbbl. Servt

Df, in Joseph Reed's writing, DLC:GW; Varick transcript, DLC:GW. The draft is addressed "The Hon. W. Howe Esqr." The words "Camp Cambridge" in the dateline are taken from the Varick transcript.

From Major General Charles Lee

Sir Prospect Hill [Mass.] August the 23d [1775] 8 oClock

A Gentleman whose name is Banister (as silly a Gentleman perhaps as lives) is accusd by his Country men the People of Newport, of being a most violent Tory—I believe He is neither whig nor Tory, but an eater and drinker—it is in my opinion not worth troubling You with him—but I am oblig'd through complacency to the Corps herein, to refer him to your Excellency ⟨The⟩y will I suppose bring their charges against him.[1] I am, Sir, Your most obed.

C. Lee

ALS, owned (1985) by Mr. Richard Maass, White Plains, N.Y.

1. John Banister (1745–1807), a wealthy merchant from Newport, was visiting the camp at Prospect Hill when "he was seized as a Tory, at the Instance of Capt [John] Topham of Newport, who requested Gen. Lee to retain Mr Banister as a Hostage till Capt [James] Wallace of the Rose Man o' War should deliver up Capt Topham's Negro" (Franklin Bowditch Dexter, ed., *The Literary Diary of Ezra Stiles* . . ., 3 vols., [New York, 1901], 1:608). Although Banister had a brother who was a Loyalist, he was apparently able to prove that he was not one and soon returned home. In June 1776 the Rhode Island general assembly awarded Banister £80 for damage done to his house by the colony's troops quartered there. While the British occupied Newport from December 1776 to October 1779, they used both his house in Newport and his farm in nearby Middletown, and in 1781 Banister sailed to England to press a claim of £2,000 for damage to his property. The British rejected Banister's claim because of his "rebellious principles" (John L. Sibley and Clifford K. Shipton, *Biographical Sketches of Graduates of Harvard University* [Cambridge, Mass., 1873—], 16:13–14). In America many thought that Banister went to England as a Loyalist refugee, but he again placated the Patriots and returned to Newport to live for the rest of his life.

To Jonathan Trumbull, Sr.

Sir Camp at Cambridge August 23d 1775

Yesterday I received Advice from Boston that a Number of Transports, have sailed on a second Expidition for fresh Provisions: As they meet with such Success before, it is probable they may pursue the same Course only advancing further—We think Montague Point[1] on Long Island a very probable Place of their Landing: I have therefore thought it best to give you the earliest Intelligence; But I do not mean to confine you[r] Attention or Vigilence to that Place—you will please to extend your Views as far as the mischief may be probably extended.[2]

We have no Transaction of sufficient Consequence in the Camp to make a Part of a Letter. I am Sir: with much Respect & Esteem Your most Oblidged & Humble Servant

Go. Washington

P.S. You will please to Let me know in your next what Progress you make with the Hunting Shirts.

LB, Ct: Trumbull Papers; LB, DLC:GW; Varick transcript, DLC:GW. Trumbull forwarded a copy of at least the first paragraph of this letter to Brig. Gen. David Wooster on Long Island. See Wooster to GW, 29 Aug. 1775.

1. The letter-book copy in DLC:GW reads "Montauck Point." Montauk Point is at the easternmost end of Long Island.

2. This large convoy sailed to the Bay of Fundy. See Vice Admiral Samuel Graves's narrative, 22 Aug. 1775, in Clark, *Naval Documents*, 1:1205.

From William Tudor

May it please your Excellency August 23d 1775

At the Time I had the Honour of your Excellency's Appointing me to the Office of Judge Advocate to the army, my Unacquai[n]tedness with the Nature of the Department rendered me an incompetent Judge of it's Duties.[1] The Experience I have since had convinces me that I am engag'd in a Service, extensive, laborious & important. I must therefore beg, Sir, your Indulgence, while I mention some Particulars, which I presume will satisfy your Excellency that the Conclusion I may deduce from them is not unreasonable.

I have your Excellency's Orders (through the Medium of the Adjt Genl) to attend every General Court Martial, both those of the Line, & each Brigade throughout the army; And to see that there is a fair Copy of the intire Proceedings in each Case, made out to be reported to the Commander in chief. The Number of Offences made cognizable by a General Court Martial only: the large Army here, & the Extent of the Camp (10 Miles at least) in each Quarter of which my Duty demands my Attendance, unitedly render my Station arduous & difficult. The Number of

Trials which have been reported your Excellency within six Weeks past, will I believe justify this Assertion.

It is not only expected that I give the proper Orders for procuring the Evidences, & putting all Matters in such a Train, that the Court may having Nothing else to do than to hear the Witnesses & form a Judgement but that I also analyse the Evidence & state the Questions that are involv'd in it for the Opinion of the Court—But I mean not to detain your Excellency by a tedious Detail. It is sufficient to acquaint you that I am oblig'd to act as Advocate, Register & Clerk—for a Stipend of 20 Dollars a month, without the least Assistance, or a single Perquisite of Office.

In the British army General Courts Martial sit only in capital Cases, or for the Trials of commissioned Officers. The Judge Advocate there is allow'd 10/ sterlg P. Day, besides drawing Pay as an Officer. This Duty is easy, because the strict Discipline maintain'd among regular Troops, make General Courts Martial but rare.

Almost every Day since my appointment, a general Court Martial has sit in one or other Part of the Camp. A Court at Roxbury adjourn'd for six Days successively, because my Duty would not permit me to leave Cambridge. This must frequently be the Case, while I am without an assistant.

I will no longer trespass on your Excellency's Time—than to beg, that a Representation of this Office may be made from the Commander in Chief, to the honble Continental Congress who I am inform'd were intirely unacquainted with the Business of this Department, especially in an American Army—The Information they may receive from your Excellency on this Subject will doubtless prevail with them to affix a Salary something more adequate to the Service. Should they not I shall be under a Necessity of begging your Excellency's Permission to resign an Employment, The Duties of which leave me without an Hour to call my own, & the Pay of which will not afford a Maintenance.[2] I am with profound Respect Your Excellency's most obt hum. Servt

Wm Tudor

ALS, DNA:PCC, item 152; copy, DNA:PCC, item 169; copy, NjMoNP; copy, DLC: John Hancock Papers. The ALS was enclosed in GW to Hancock, 31 Aug. 1775.

1. For Tudor's initial willingness to serve with a captain's pay, see GW to Hancock, 21 July 1775 (first letter).

2. On 21 Sept. Congress agreed to pay Tudor $50 a month from the time of his appointment for himself and a clerk (*JCC*, 3:257).

To James Warren

Sir Camp at Cambridge Head Quarters August 23. 1775

In a late Conference with which I was honoured from the General Court, it was mentioned that a Quantity of Shirts, Breeches, Stockings & Shoes had been provided by Order of the Committee of Supplies: As there are Numbers in the Army very destitute of those Articles, I should be glad the General Court would direct all that are provided to be delivered to the Quarter Master General & such as are in Hand to be hastened; He has Orders to receive them on the Continental Account.[1] I am Sir, with due Respect & Regard Your most Obedt & very Hbble Servt

Go: Washington

LS, in Joseph Reed's writing, M-Ar: Revolution Letters; LB, DLC:GW; Varick transcript, DLC:GW.

1. The Massachusetts house of representatives read GW's letter on this date and referred it to a committee consisting of colonels Ebenezer Sayer, Jerathmiel Bowers, and Joseph Cushing. After the committee reported the next day, the General Court approved a resolution ordering the clothing to be delivered to the Continental quartermaster general (*Mass. House of Rep. Journal*, July–Nov. 1775 sess., 98, 100–101; also in "Mass. Council Journal," July 1775–Feb. 1776 sess., 147).

General Orders

Head Quarters, Cambridge, August 24th 1775

Parole Tunbridge: Countersign Ulster.

Lieut. William Ryan of Col. Nixons Regiment, tried by a General Court Martial of which Lieut. Col. Brickett was Presdt is found guilty of a breach of the 6th and 49th Articles of the Rules and Regulations for the Massachusetts Army and is unanimously adjudged to be cashiered. The General approves the Sentence and orders it to take place immediately.[1]

The Quarter Master General is to see that the different Brigades, or at least each Division of the Army, are provided with Armourers, sufficient to keep the Arms therein in proper repair—that they have proper places provided to work in, that they are properly attended to, to prevent impositions of any kind. He is also to employ Brickmakers under the Care of Capt. Francis of Col. Mansfield's Regiment; and sett them to make Bricks immediately: The necessary attendance is to be applied for by Capt. Francis to the Adjutant General.[2]

The Qr Mr General is also to receive from the General Court of the Massachusetts Government, or from such persons as they shall appoint, to deliver them; all the Shirts, Shoes, and Stockings, Breeches and Waistcoats, which have been provided by Order of their Committee of safety, for the Use of the Army; & settle for the same, and not deliver any from his Store, without an Order in writing from the Commander in Chief.[3]

An exact Return of the Company of Artificers, under the Care of Mr Ayres, to be given in—where they have been to work, and how employed.[4]

The General would be glad to have the Rules and Regulations of war (as established by the Continental Congress) returned to him signed, as he will thereupon proceed to distribute the Continental Commissions, agreeable to the Ranks lately settled.[5]

The late Pay Master of the Massachusetts Forces, is once more called upon, in a peremptory manner, to settle his Accounts with the different Regiments, that it may be known, what money is due to the men up to the first of this month (August)[.] The General is sorry, that any difficulty or delay, should have happened, in a matter so plain, and simple in its nature. He now assures the Regiments of Massachusetts, as they seem to be the only Complainants and Sufferers, that if they do not get paid by their own Colony pay Master, before the first day of September, that he will order James Warren Esqr. Continental pay Master General, to pay each of the Massachusetts Regiments, for the month of august, and that he will moreover, use his endeavours to have their pay up to the 1st of August settled for and adjusted, as soon as possible.[6]

Twenty Men from Col. Mansfields Regiment, & *ten* from Col. Gardiners, and *two* from each of the other Regiments in the Lines; and in Cambridge, to be sent, to join Capt. Francis, of Col. Mansfields regiment, to be forthwith employed in making of bricks none but Men who are acquainted with that service to be sent upon it.

Col. Prescott, with two Companies of his regiment; to march to Sewells point this day; The Col. will apply to the Quarter Master General, for the Tents that will be wanted for this detachment.

Varick transcript, DLC:GW.

1. Artemas Ward's orderly book gives this officer's name as "Lieut. Wm Rison" (MHi: Ward Papers). Article 6 of the Massachusetts articles of war provides that "any officer or soldier, who shall strike his superior officer, or draw, or offer to draw, [his sword,] or shall lift up any weapon, or offer any violence against him, being in the execution of his office, on any pretence whatever, or shall disobey any lawful commands of his superior officer, shall suffer such punishment, as shall, according to the nature of his offence, be ordered by the sentence of a general court martial" (*Mass. Prov. Congress Journals*, 122). Article 7 of the Continental articles of war is nearly identical in wording. For article 49 of the Massachusetts articles of war, see General Orders, 7 Aug. 1775, n.1.

2. Ebenezer Francis (1743–1777) of Beverly remained a captain in Col. John Mansfield's Massachusetts regiment until the end of this year. On 6 Nov. 1776 Francis became colonel of the 11th Massachusetts Regiment, and he was killed at the Battle of Hubbardton on 7 July 1777.

3. For the General Court's resolution ordering the delivery of this clothing, see GW to James Warren, 23 Aug. 1775, n.1. The clothing was provided by order of the committee of supplies, not the committee of safety.

4. Capt. Joseph Eayres of Dunstable, Mass., became major of Col. Benjamin Flower's regiment of artillery artificers in July 1776 and retired from the Continental service in August 1780.

5. For GW's previous orders regarding the signing of the Continental articles of war, see General Orders, 9 Aug. 1775.

6. The Massachusetts receiver general, Henry Gardner, apparently acted as paymaster of the colony's forces. For GW's earlier orders calling on all of the provincial paymasters to settle their accounts with their regiments, see General Orders, 10 Aug. 1775. For the payment of the Massachusetts troops by James Warren, see General Orders, 31 Aug. and 5 Sept. 1775.

From the Gloucester Committee of Safety

Glocester [Mass.] August 24, 1775

May it please your Excellency

The Committee of Safety for the town of Glocester beg leave to acquaint your Excellency—that James Grant who has a family in this town has for Several months last past been employed in Catching Fish for the Kings Navy and for the Inhabitants (as he says) at Boston and for his protection he had a Fishing pass from Admiral Graves.

also that Mr James Jordan of this town was Master of a Sloop loaded with Wood and Boards which was taken by the enimy and carried into Boston about 7 weeks ago and said Jordan has been there during that time till last Sunday, when he shipt to go and Fish with Grant and by that means make his escape,[1] but when the boat put in here we did not think it proper that Grant should go back to Boston with her till we had your Excellency orders. as Mr Jordan was so long in Boston and not confined there, he had an opportunity of observing the Situation of the enimy, we think it our duty to desire him to go and carry Grant with him to your Excellency for examination, and have desired Major Collins to present them.[2]

we pray your Excellency would please to order what shall be done with the Boat which Grant came in, as She is not his property. we are your Excellencys most Obedient Humble Servants

per order
John Stevens Chairman[3]

LS, DLC:GW.

1. James Jordan's sloop *Sally*, carrying wood from Georgia, was seized by the British while it was attempting to enter Gloucester Harbor. The British detained the vessel in Boston and distributed the cargo of wood among the ships of the British fleet.

2. James Collins (1724–c.1778) of Gloucester was major of Col. Moses Little's regiment until the end of 1776, when he left the army to command a privateer. Collins and his vessel were apparently lost at sea in 1778.

3. John Stevens (1707–1779) was a prominent Gloucester merchant and apparently a colonel in the militia.

From Lieutenant Colonel Jonathan Ward

Dorchester [Mass.] 24 August 1775. Requests that "Mr Willm Prentice a good Student & Young Practitioner," who enlisted in Colonel Doolittle's Regiment but has been assisting Dr. Flint, chief surgeon of General Ward's regiment, be transferred to General Ward's regiment, "as I can't do well without him."[1]

ALS, PHi: Gratz Collection; Sprague transcript, DLC:GW. Although this letter is signed "J. Ward Colonel," the references to the regiment as "General Ward's" indicate that Jonathan Ward was still a lieutenant colonel acting as colonel of Artemas Ward's regiment. See General Orders, 7 July 1775, n.7.

1. William Prentice got the job. He served as surgeon's mate of Ward's regiment throughout 1776.

General Orders

Head Quarters, Cambridge, August 25th [17]75

Parole Wilmington Countersign Yorkshire

If the Officers who were sent upon the recruiting service, are not all return'd to Camp; they are to be forthwith recalled, and no more men are to be enlisted, until further Orders.[1]

The Company late under the Command of Capt. Ebenezer Lindsey, is to join Col. Woodbridges Regiment, as that Regt has at present only nine Companies.[2]

As the Commander in Chief has heretofore approvd all the Sentences of the General Courts Martial, which have been laid before him, and thought himself happy in agreeing with them in opinion, so will he not now disapprove the Judgement, respecting Ensign Joshua Trofton, as the Court have intimated, that they were influenced by some favourable Circumstances; Disobedience of orders, is amongst the first and most atrocious of all military Crimes, he desires that the Conduct of Ensign Joshua Trofton, (however he may have been provoked) may never be drawn into a precedent; as there are certain Modes by which inferior Officers, may obtain redress of grievances, without proceeding to any unjustifiable Acts of violence.

Ensign Joshua Trofton of the 30th Regt of Foot, in the service of the United Colonies, Commanded by Col. Scammons, tried by a General Court Martial for "offering to strike his Colonel, and for disobedience of orders," is found guilty of a Breach of the 6th Article, of the Rules and Regulations of the Massachusetts Army; and sentenced, to be confined to his Tent for three days.[3]

A Return signed by the Commanding Officer of each regiment, of the Commission'd Officers vacant, distinguishing their names, rank, and by what means vacant; this must be delivered to the Adjutant Genl at orderly time to morrow.

Varick transcript, DLC:GW.

1. In General Orders, 10 July 1775, GW directed the colonels of the Massachusetts regiments to send out recruiting officers, but few recruits were obtained. See also GW to Hancock, 4–5 Aug. 1775.

2. This company was previously in Col. Samuel Gerrish's regiment. For the cashiering of Eleazer Lindsey, see General Orders, 16 Aug. 1775.

3. In July Colonel Scammans accused Lieutenant Trafton of using abusive language to him, but a court-martial cleared Trafton of that charge (General Orders, 23 July 1775).

To George Clinton

Dear Sir, Camp at Cambridge Augt 25th 1775.

Mr White presented me with your favour of the 27th Ulto[1]—you may rely upon it, that any Civilities which may be in my power to shew this young Gentleman shall not be wanting—if an acquaintance of mine, for whom I have wrote to Virginia (knowing his promptitude to business) should not come, as there is reason to doubt,[2] I propose to take Mr White into my Family as an Aid de Camp—the mode by which the Congress have left the ultimate appointment of Officers in this Army, confines all Offices (in its consequences at least) to the Governments in which the Regiments Originated; as, without the gift of Prophecy, I think it may be foretold, that no volunteers, not of those Governments to which the Regiments belong, will come in for a share; the propriety, & good policy of which, I leave you to judge of. I am with sincere esteem Dr Sir Yr most Obedt H: Servt

Go: Washington

P.S. I refer you to my Public Letters for the Occurrances of the Army &ca.

ALS, NN: Washington Collection. The cover is addressed in GW's writing "To George Clinton Esqr. of New-York—now at Philadelphia. Favour'd by Mr Barrell." Beneath the address an unidentified person wrote "now at New Windsor in New York." William Barrell (d. 1776), formerly of Portsmouth, N.H., was at this time the Philadelphia agent for the Boston mercantile firm of Amory & Taylor. Barrell also carried GW's letter of 29 Aug. to Richard Henry Lee and that of 30 Aug. to John Dickinson.

1. GW apparently is referring to the letter from Clinton which is printed above under the date of 4 July 1775.

2. In a letter of 28 Aug. 1775 to Lund Washington, which has not been found, GW apparently asked Lund to sound out Robert Hanson Harrison about becoming an aide-de-camp. The letter did not reach Mount Vernon until 3 or 4 Oct., and not until several days later was Lund able to see Harrison and obtain his consent (Lund Washington to GW, 5, 15 Oct. 1775). Harrison was appointed an aide-de-camp in General Orders, 6 Nov. 1775.

From Captain Richard Dodge

Chelsea [Mass.] August the 25 1775

I would in form your Exelencey that thare is one man from Boston that Runaway and has now Bisne to git a Liven and would Enter, with me in to the Servis and one that was Presed on Bord the Ship Glasco[1] that is of the Sam mind if your Exelencey will give Leave, thay have Now gounes.

I would in form your Exelencey that I maid in Quirey Respecting the Vissels you Wrote a Bout and the Sentres Say thay that thay all Came to a Anker at Nantasket Ro[a]d Excepte one.[2] I am your Exelencies most Humble Servnt

Richd Dodge Capt.

ALS, DLC:GW.

1. The British warship *Glasgow* was stationed in Rhode Island at this time.

2. Dodge apparently is referring to the large British convoy about which GW wrote to Jonathan Trumbull, Sr., on 23 August. It was sailing to the Bay of Fundy.

From Major General Artemas Ward

Sir. Camp at Roxbury [Mass.] Augt 25th 1775

The Relations of Several Persons last out of Boston all tending to confirm our Belief that our active & restless Enemy are making large Preparation for some important Step & having ocular Demonstration that they have stript Colo. Hancocks

Lime Trees as well as many other Trees in Boston which we are informed was done for the Purpose of making Facines[.] I beg Leave to suggest to your Excellency that Dorchester Hill would be a very important Post to them as it would inevitably deprive us of the Advantage of a very considerable Part of our Works & supply the Enemy with Forage for their Cattle which we may rationally Judge is no inconsiderable Object of their Wishes: As we ever ought to be watching a Powerful & sagacious Enemy & considering what Posts they might take which by Nature are rendered easily defensible & convenient to annoy us so also we ought carefully to consider what Steps may be taken consistent with Prudence & Safety should an Enemy in Part gain such an Ascendency—If Sir, the Object they have in View is to entrench upon Dorchester Hill (their Facines are Indicative of entrenching or throwing up a Breast Work somewhere) I beg your Excellency to give me some Instructions relative to my Duty in that Case: I need not inform you of the Situation of the Hill nor how narrow the Passage is from the main Land to the Hill. Whether an Attempt (should the Enemy move that Way) is to be made to dislodge them or whether they are to be permitted to go on unmolested in fortifying the Hill I shall be much obliged for particular Orders which I always shall endeavor faithfully to ex[e]cute.[1] I am with the greatest Respect your Excellencys most obedient Servant.

Copy, MHi: Ward Papers.

1. The strategically important Dorchester Heights, overlooking Boston Neck and the southern part of the city, were not occupied by either side until the Americans fortified the heights in early March 1776.

From Major General Artemas Ward

Sir, [Roxbury, Mass.] 25 Augt [17]75

Of the Ordnance, Implements, Ordnance Stores &c. which I wrote your Excy for the 22d Inst:[1] only the follg are sent Viz. two—12 Pounders—2 doz: Cannisters without powder, a proper complement of round Shot. Implements for the Cannon only 1 Sponge to each. also a Gin[2]—The cannon recd can be of no service witht powder. It appears a little mysterious that all the articles were not sent as I am informed that they were ordered by your Excy.

I have wrote yr Excy twice respectg Lt Stedson who has been confind a week to-day on a Complaint of Capt: Hamlen who charged him with maliciously aspersing his Character.[3]

I have now Sir to inform you that Lt Cadwell of Colo. Danielson's Regt is confin'd for encouraging mutiny[4] Would request of your Excy to give such directions respectg the above prisoners as that they may be bro't to a trial with all convenient Speed.

This Division of the Army is put to very great inconveniences for want of a Laboratory.

Chief, if not all the Vessels which came to an Anchor near the light House are put to Sea.[5] I am &c.

P.S. Am just informed by a young man from Boston that the wife of the Chief N. York Carpenter is come out of Boston, & that she has a number of Letters secreted about her.[6]

Copy, MHi: Ward Papers.

GW's aide-de-camp Edmund Randolph replied to this letter on this date: "Our Situation with Respect to Powder requires Oeconomy in the Destribution of it. Each Division of the Army must receive equal Supplies: but, as their respective Claims and Necessities for that Article must be first ascertained, Colo. Burbenk [William Burbeck] will wait on you for this Purpose in the Afternoon. He will then settle the Proportion you may expect, & conclude something as to the Laboratory. The Judge-Advocate has been so thoroughly engaged in Courts martial for some Time past, that till this day he has not had an opportunity of attending to Stedson's and Cadwell's Cases. By Command of his Excellency, A Gentleman is dispatched in quest of Mrs Hampton" (MHi: Ward Papers).

1. Ward's letter of 22 August has not been found.

2. A gin is a device, consisting essentially of a tripod and windlass, for lifting cannon on and off carriages.

3. Prince Stetson (b. 1741) of Hanover, Mass., and Eleazer Hamlin of Pembroke, Mass., were officers in Brig. Gen. John Thomas's regiment. Both men served at least part of the ensuing campaign in the regiment commanded by Col. John Bailey. Neither of Ward's letters to GW concerning Stetson has been found.

4. Daniel Caldwell was a second lieutenant in Col. Timothy Danielson's Massachusetts regiment.

5. Ward apparently is referring to the large British convoy about which GW wrote to Jonathan Trumbull, Sr., on 23 August.

6. The woman was apparently "Mrs Hampton," whom Edmund Randolph mentioned in his letter of this date to Ward. See source note. She was probably the wife of Jonathan Hampton, a New York carpenter, who, although said

to be bankrupt before the Revolution, made a fortune during the war as an employee in the British engineering department (Jones, *History of New York*, 1:336, n.1).

To Anthony White

Dear Sir, Camp at Cambridge Augt 25th 1775

Your favours of the 31st Ulto and 1st Instt I have had the honour to receive;[1] and you may believe me sincere, when I assure you, that it will give me pleasure to shew any kind of Civility in my power to your Son, whose modest deportment richly entitles him to it. I am under some kind of Ingagement to a very worthy Gentleman of my acquaintance in Virginia to appoint him one of my Aid de Camps; or more properly, I had wrote to him on this subject—his answer not received—should he decline the offer, as I know he is much engaged in other business, I shall, with pleasure, take your Son into my Family in that Capacity.[2] in the meanwhile, I shall be happy in making his time as agreeable as possible to him whilst he remains in the Camp.

In respect to Mr Dunham, I thought it but a piece of candour to inform him, that I saw but little prospect of his getting an Imployment in his profession here upon which I believe he has changed his Plan.[3] As I am almost always in a hurry, myself, and as I do not doubt but your Son will give you an Acct of every remarkable Occurrance which happens In this Camp, I shall only add my best respects to your good Lady & family, & that I am with great esteem Dr Sir Yr Most Obedt Sert

Go: Washington

ALS, CSmH.

1. Neither letter has been found, but Anthony White apparently solicited GW to find positions in the army for his son Anthony Walton White and Mr. Dunham. See note 3 and George Clinton to GW, 4 July 1775.

2. For a discussion of GW's offer to appoint Robert Hanson Harrison one of his aides-de-camp, see GW to George Clinton, 25 Aug. 1775, n.2.

3. This may be Stephen Dunham, who joined the 3d New Jersey Battalion as a first lieutenant on 7 February 1776. He resigned in July of that year and later served in the New Jersey militia.

General Orders

Head Quarters, Cambridge, August [26] 1775

Parole, Amboy. C. Sign Brookline.

Genl Sullivan's Brigade to be mustered upon Monday Morning next in the manner and form, directed by the General Orders of the 21st Inst.[1]

Varick transcript, DLC:GW. The manuscript is incorrectly dated 27 August. A comparison with Artemas Ward's orderly book shows that the date should be 26 Aug. (MHi: Ward Papers).

1. Sullivan's brigade was not mustered until Friday, 1 Sept. (General Orders, 21, 22, 28 Aug. 1775).

From Captain Richard Dodge

Sir Chelsea [Mass.] Augest the 26th 1775

I would in form your Exelencey tha[t] as Soun as I Could after I Recd your orders to Send a Partey of men to Dear Island I Proc[ee]ded and Sent Leut. Feirfeild[1] with a Bout 20 or 30 men and he Proceded and Reportes as folowth (VIZ.) the Sumer-Set lyes a gainest the Island and tow Tranes Portes and a Small Ship that is mr Hanckock.[2] when they furst got thare No Person on the Island tow Bearges Landed a Bout a: 11 of the Clock Stad a litle while and Returned Douing nothing He is in formed that thay have Cut and thrashed and Cared of the Litle grain that was on the Island. Further Saieth not I would in form your Exelency that the Reason of my Sending sow Lait is I wated for the a Bove Return wich came Sun a Bout on our hy I [am] your Exelencies most Humble Servent at Comand

Richd Dodge Capt.

ALS, DLC:GW.

1. Matthew Fairfield (b. 1745) of Wenham, Mass., joined Col. Samuel Gerrish's regiment as a first lieutenant on 19 May 1775. During 1776 Fairfield served in the regiment commanded by Col. John Greaton, and on 1 Jan. 1777 he was promoted to captain in the 13th Massachusetts Regiment. Fairfield resigned from the army in November 1777.

2. The British warship *Somerset* was ordered about this time to go to Halifax "to stop her leaks" (Disposition of H.M.'s Ships and Vessels in North America, 17 Aug. 1775, in Davies, *Documents of the American Revolution*, 11:75–76). The small ship apparently belonged to John Hancock.

General Orders

Head Quarters, Cambridge, August 27th 1775
Parole, Colchester. Countersign Dover.

Varick transcript, DLC:GW.

From Major General Philip Schuyler

Sunday Albany 27th August 1775.
6 oClock A:M:

Dear Sir

Your Excellency's favors of the 14th and 20th Inst: were delivered me last night.

I left Tionderoga on thursday the 17th Instant and hoped to have returned in four days, but on my arrival at Saratoga I received Information that a large body of Indians of the Six nations were to be here as on tuesday last, And that my presence was Indispensibly necessary. I therefore Attended and on Wednesday the Congratulatory Ceremony was performed, and On Friday the Treaty agreable to their request was opened by them, By giving an Answer to the Messages that had been sent them by the Committee of this place[.] In this speach they Anticipated part of what we had in charge to deliver them, being (as we concieved) Apprehensive that we should request them to take Arms in our Cause; they explicitly declared that as It was a family quarrel, they would not Interfere, but remain neuter and hoped we would not desire more of them; we have not got above half thro. what we are directed to say to them, and Altho. I hardly know how to leave them, yet such is the nature of the Intelligence Contained In the papers which I do myself the honor to Inclose your Excellency, that I consider myself und⟨er⟩ the necessity of leaving the Indian business to my Colleagues, and repairing Immediately to ⟨the⟩ Army.[1]

That Governor Carlton and his agent⟨s⟩ Are exerting themselves to procure the Savages to act against us I have reason to believe from the various accounts which I have received, but I do not believe he will have any Success with the Canada tribes, tho. I make no doubt but he is Joined by some of the more remote Indians who I believe will assist him, and who have already served him as Scouts from St Johns. I should therefore not hesitate one moment to Employ any Indians that might be willing to Join us.

I thank your Excellency for the honor you have done me in communicating me your plan for an Expedition Into Canada.[2] The Inclosed Information of Fèrè's which Corroborates not only the Information of Major Brown; that Contained in the two Affidavits of Duguid & Shatford;[3] but Every other we have had leaves not a trace of doubt on my mind as to the propriety of going into Canada And to Do It, has been my determined resolution (unless prevented by my Superiors) for some time, And I have Accordingly since my Arrival here, requested Gen: Montgomery[4] to get every thing in the best readiness he could, for that I would move Immediately, weak and Ill appointed as we were, and I learn with pleasure that he has since the receipt of Gerriffins Information[5] ordered the Canon to be Imbarked and he will probably be off from Tyconderoga so soon, that I shall only be able to Join him, at Crown point; Such being my Intentions and such the Ideas that I have form⟨ed⟩ of the necessity of penetrating Into Canada Without delay. Your Excellency will Easily Concieve that I felt happy to learn your Intentions, and only wished that the thought had Struck you sooner[.] The force I shall carry is far short of what I would wish[.] I believe It will not Exceed Seventeen Hundred men, and this will be a body Insufficient to Attempt Quebec with; after leaving the necessary Detatchments (at St Johns, Chamble, and Montreal should we Succeed and Carry those places,) which must be respectable to keep an open & free Communication with Crown point &ca. having now given your Excellency the time, force, and latest Intelligence I have had, together with my Opinion of the Sentiments of the Canadiens, I proceed to Inform you of the Enemys Strength as far as I have been able to learn It. 350 or 400 at St Johns 150 or 200 at Chamblé About 50 at Montreal, and one Company at Quebec, these are regular troops, besides between three and five hundred Indians, Scotchmen & some few Canadians with Colo: Johnson at La Chene,[6] Of this party the Indians that are at St Johns are a part. wether any Ships of war are at Quebec, I cannot say—as none have been mentioned to me I am rather Induced to believe there are none, Should the detachment of Your body penetrate Into

Canada and we meet with Success Quebec must Inevitably fall into our hands, should we meet with a repulse, which can only happen from foul play in the Canadiens I shall have An Opportunity to Inform your party of It, that they may Carry into Execution any orders you may give In case such an Unfortunate Event should arise.[7]

Your Excellency will be pleased to be particular in your orders to the Officer that may Command the detatchment that there may be no Clashing Should we Join.

I shall leave orders at Tionderoga to forward all the lead that Can be Spared.

Excuse these Scraps of paper, necessity obliges me to use them, having no other fit to write on.

Be pleased to make my Compliments to the Gentlemen of your Suit, Colo. Read will be so good as to Excuse my not Answering his letter as I really cannot find time. I am Dr Sir with the most respectful Sentiments Your Excellency's Obedient Hume Servt

Ph: Schuyler

ALS, DLC:GW; LB, NN: Schuyler Papers.

1. As one of the Indian commissioners appointed by the Continental Congress for the northern department, Schuyler was required to attend the conference with representatives of the Six Nations which began at Albany on Wednesday, 23 August. The other commissioners were Turbot Francis, Volckert P. Douw, and Oliver Wolcott. For the speech that the Continental Congress instructed the commissioners to deliver to the Six Nations, see *JCC*, 2:178–83. The commissioners concluded a treaty of neutrality with the Six Nations on 1 Sept., but Schuyler did not attend after the session of 26 Aug. (Proceedings of the Commissioners Appointed to Negotiate a Treaty with the Six Nations of Indians, 1775, DNA:PCC, item 134).

2. For Benedict Arnold's planned expedition against Quebec, see GW to Schuyler, 20 Aug. 1775, n.6.

3. In the enclosed affidavit, taken at Ticonderoga on 18 Aug., John Baptist Féné of Chambly said that a council of some of the town's inhabitants had sent him to Ticonderoga "to enquire whether the Army was coming down to Canada to relieve them or not." The Canadians, Féné reported, were anxious to release several persons imprisoned at Montreal for expressing views friendly to the Americans "& therefore wish the Army to come into that Country, That they may have a Pretext for taking up Arms & will upon Arrival of the Continental Army, summons the Town of Montreal for the Discharge of the Prisoners. . . . about 1500 Men can be raised by the Friends of America on the River of Chamblee in 24 Hours & double that Number in 48 Hours, but not all with Arms." The affidavit also includes intelligence about the strength

of the British at St. Jean and the intention of the Canadian Indians to remain neutral in the struggle between the mother country and the colonists (DLC:GW). John Duguid and John Shatforth's affidavits, both dated 2 Aug. 1775, were enclosed in Schuyler to GW, 31 July–2 Aug. 1775. See note 2 to that document. For Major John Brown's report on his recent reconnaissance into Canada, see Schuyler to GW, 31 July–2 Aug. 1775, n.1, and Jonathan Trumbull, Sr., to GW, 21 Aug. 1775, n.6.

4. Richard Montgomery (1738–1775) of New York was appointed a brigadier general by Congress on 22 June, and at this time he was Schuyler's second in command. A native of Ireland, Montgomery joined the British army in 1756 as an ensign in the 17th Regiment of Foot and served in Canada and the West Indies during the French and Indian War, rising to the rank of captain by 1762. He sold his commission ten years later and moved to New York, where he married Robert R. Livingston's daughter and settled on her estate near Rhinebeck. In the spring of 1775 Montgomery was elected to the New York provincial congress, which on 7 June recommended him to the Continental Congress as a brigadier general. Montgomery apparently received his commission from GW when GW stopped at New York on 25–26 June. With Schuyler ill throughout most of the fall of 1775, the command of the Canadian invasion devolved on Montgomery. He captured St. Jean, Chambly, and Montreal, but in an unsuccessful assault against Quebec on 31 Dec. he was killed.

5. The information that Peter Griffin, a soldier in Col. James Easton's Connecticut regiment, obtained on a scouting expedition into Canada between 12 and 24 Aug. is contained in an affidavit taken at Ticonderoga on 25 Aug., a copy of which Schuyler enclosed with this letter. Griffen saw the British fortifications at St. Jean on 21 Aug. and reported that the two vessels under construction there appeared to be nearly ready for launching. Like Féné, he gave a favorable account of the Canadians' readiness to assist the Americans. "The French & English Inhabitants along the Lake [Champlain]," Griffin said, "are very impatient to have the Army down the Lake, . . . they declared their Willingness to supply the Army to the Utmost with Greens & Sauce" (DLC:GW).

6. Lachine is near Montreal.

7. See the eighth paragraph in GW's Instructions to Benedict Arnold, 14 Sept. 1775.

General Orders

Head Quarters, Cambridge, August 28th 1775

Parole Essex. Countersign Falmouth.

As the extraordinary duty necessary for some days past, prevents the mustering Genl Sullivans Brigade this morning: The General appoints Friday morning next for that purpose, and orders that Brigade to be relieved from all but the ordinary Camp duty of their particular encampments Thursday morning that they mave [may] have that day to prepare for their mustering.[1]

As nothing is more pernicious to the health of Soldiers, nor more certainly productive of the bloody-flux; than drinking New Cyder: The General in the most possitive manner commands, the entire disuse of the same, and orders the Quarter Master General this day, to publish Advertisements, to acquaint the Inhabitants of the surrounding districts, that such of them, as are detected bringing new Cyder into the Camp, after Thursday, the last day of this month; may depend on having their casks stove.

Varick transcript, DLC:GW.

1. Sullivan's brigade was involved in the occupation of Plowed Hill on 26 August. See GW to Richard Henry Lee, 29 Aug. 1775, n.6. For GW's previous orders regarding the mustering of this brigade, see General Orders, 21, 22, and 26 Aug. 1775.

Letter not found: to Lund Washington, 28 Aug. 1775. In a letter of 15 Oct. 1775 to GW, Lund Washington mentions receiving "your letter . . . dated the 28th of Augst."

General Orders

Head Quarters, Cambridge, August 29th 1775

Parole Georgia. Countersign Harvard.

For the future, the several Guards mounted upon the General Hospitals, are to be reduced into one Guard, consisting of one Sub: three Serjts three Corporals, one fife, and thirty men; The Officer after seeing his Centries posted, is to receive his orders from Dr Church, Director of the General Hospital of the Army of the United Colonies.

The Quarter Master General and Commissary General, are to see strict regard paid to the 6th Article of the General Orders of the 7th of July last; as Complaints are continually making of the badness of the bread, served to the regiments.

Varick transcript, DLC:GW.

To Richard Henry Lee

Dear Sir, Camp at Cambridge Augt 29th 1775

Your favour of the first Inst. by Mr Randolph came safe to hand—the merits of this young Gentleman, added to your recommendation, & my own knowledge of his character, induced me to take him into my Family as an Aid de Camp in ⟨the room of⟩ Mr Mifflin who I have appointed Quarter Master Genel[1] from a thorough perswation of his Integrety—my own experience of his activity—and finaly, because he stands unconnected with either of these Governments; or with this, that, or t'other Man; for between you and I, there is more in this than you can easily immagine.

As we have now nearly compleated our Lines of Defence, we have nothing more, in ⟨my o⟩pinion, to fear from the Enemy provided we can keep our men to their duty and ma⟨ke⟩ them watchful & vigilant; but it is among the most difficult tasks I ever undertook in my life to induce these people to believe that there is, or can be, danger till the Bayonet is pushed at their Breasts; not that it proceeds from any uncommon prowess, but rather from an unaccountable kind of stupidity in the lower class of these people, which believe me prevails but too generally among the Officers of the Massachusets part of the Army, who are ne⟨ar⟩ly of the same Kidney with the Privates; and adds not a little to my difficulties; as there is no such thing as getting Officers of this stamp to exert themselves in carrying orders into execution—to curry favour with the men (by whom they were chosen, & on whose Smiles possibly they may think they may again rely) seems to be one of the principal objects of their attention.

I submit it therefore to your consideration whether there is, or is not, a propriety in that Resolution of the Congress, which leaves the ultimate appointment of all Offices below the Rank of Generals to the Governments wher⟨e⟩ the Regiments originated, now the Army is become Continental? To me it appears imp⟨ro⟩per in two points of view; first, it is giving that power and weight to an Individual Colony, which ought, of right, to belong ⟨only⟩ to the whole, and next it damps the spirit & ardour of Volunteers fro⟨m⟩ all but the four new England Governments as none but their people have the least chan⟨ce⟩ of getting into Office—Would it not be better therefore to have the Warrants which the Commander in Chief is authorizd to give Pro tempore, approved or disapproved, by the Continental Congress, or a Committee of their body, which I should suppose in any l⟨ong⟩ recess must always Sit? In this ca⟨se every⟩ Gentleman will stand an equal chance of being promoted, according to his merit; in the other, all offices will be confined to the Inhabitants of the 4 New England Governmts which in my opinion is impolitick to a deg⟨ree.⟩[2]

I have made a pretty good Slam among such kind of officers as the Massachusets Government ⟨a⟩bound in since I came to this Camp, having Broke one Colo. and two Captains for Cowardly beh⟨aviour in⟩ the action on Bunker's Hill—Two captains for drawing more provisions and pay than they had men in their Company—and one for being absent from his Post when the Enemy appeared there, and burnt a House just by it.[3] Besides these, I have at this time one Colo., one Major, one Captn, & two Subalterns under arrest for tryal[4]—In short I spare none & yet fear it will not all do, as these Peeple seem to be too inattentive to every thing but their Interest.

I have not been unmindful of that part of your Letter respecting point Alderton—before the receipt of it, it had become an object of my particular enquiry, but the Accts of its situation differ exceedingly in respect to the command it has of the Ship Chan⟨nel⟩ but my k⟨no⟩wledge of this matter would not have been confined to enquiries only if I had ever been in a condition, since my arrival here, to have taken possession of such a Post; but you well know my good Sir; that it becomes the duty of an Officer to consider some other matters, as well as a Situation. namely, what number of men are necessary to defend a place—how it can be supported—& how furnished with Ammuniton.

In respect to the first I conceive our defence of this place (point Alderton) m⟨ust⟩ be proportioned to the Attack of Genl Gage's whole force, leaving him just enough to man his Lines on Boston & Charles Town Necks—& with regard to the Second, and mos⟨t⟩ important, as well as alarming object, we have only 184. Barls of Powder in all (including the late supply from Philadelphia) wch is not sufficient to give 25. Musket Cartridges to each man, and scarcely to serve the Artillery in any brisk Action one single d⟨ay⟩—under these Circumstances I daresay you will agree with me, that it would not be ver⟨y⟩ eligable to take a post 30 Miles distant (by Land) from this place, when we have already a line of Circumvalation round Boston of at leas⟨t⟩ 10 Miles in extant to defend any part of which ma⟨y⟩ be attacked without our having (if the Enemy will keep their own Council) an hours previous notice of it; and that, it would not be prudent in me, to attempt a measure which would necessarily bring on a consumption of all the Ammunition we have, thereby leaving the Army at the Mercy of the Enemy, or to disperse; and the Country to be ravaged and lai⟨d⟩ waste at discretion—to you Sir I may acct for my conduct, but I cannot declare the motives of it to every one, notwithstanding I know by not doing of it, that I shall stand in a very unfavourable light in the opinion of those who expect much, & will find little done, without understanding, or perhaps giving themselves the trouble of enquiring into the caus⟨e⟩—such however is the fate of all those who are obliged to act the part I do, I must therefore submit to it, under a consciousness of having done my duty to the best of my Abilitie⟨s.⟩[5]

On Saturday night last we took ⟨possession⟩ of a Hill advanced of our own Lines & within point blank shot of the Enemy on Charles Town Neck—we worked incessantl⟨y⟩ the whole Night with 1200 Men, & before Mor⟨n⟩ing got an Intrenchment in such forwardness as to bid defiance to their Cannon; abou⟨t⟩ nine Oclock on Sunday they began a heavy Cannonade which continued through the day without any injury to our work, and with the loss of four Men only, two of which were killed through their ⟨own fo⟩lly—The Insult of the Cannonade however we were obliged to submit to with impunity, not daring to make use of Artillery on Acct of the consumption of powder, except with one Nine pounder placed on a point, with which we silenced, & indeed sunk, one of their Floating Ba⟨t⟩teries.

This move of ours, was made to prevent the Enemy from gaining this Hill, and we thought was giving them a fair Challeng⟨e⟩ to dispute it (as we had been told by various people who had just left Boston, that they were preparing to come out) but instead of accepting of it, we learn that it has thrown them into great consternation which mig⟨ht⟩ be improved ⟨if we had⟩ the means of doing it—Yesterday afternoon they began a Bombardment without any effect, as yet.[6]

There has been so many great, and capital errors, & abuses to rectify—so many examples to make—& so little Inclination in the Officers of inferior Rank to contribute their aid to accomplish this work, that my life has been nothing else (since I ⟨came here) b⟩ut one continued round of a⟨nnoyance⟩ & f⟨at⟩igue; in short no pecuniary r⟨ecompense⟩ could induce me to undergo what I ha⟨ve espe⟩cially as I expect, by shewing so little Co⟨unte⟩nance to irregularities & publick abus⟨es to⟩ render myself very obnoxious to a gre⟨ater⟩ part of these People. But as I have alrea⟨dy⟩ greatly exceeded the bounds of a Letter I will not trouble you with matters relative to my own feelings.

As I expect this Letter will meet you in Philadelphia[7] I must request the favour of you to present my Affecte & respectful Compliments to Doctr Shippen, his lady, and Family, my Brothers of the Deligation, and any other enquiring friends—& at the same time do me the justice to believe that I am with a sincere regard Yr Affecte friend & Obedt Servt

Go: Washington

ALS, NNPM. Mutilated words and letters are supplied within angle brackets from a typed transcript at Washington and Lee University made in 1888 by Joseph Packard, Jr., of Baltimore. Only about half of the addressed cover remains. According to an undated document in the Joseph Reed Papers at the New-York Historical Society, which compares portions of the manuscript with the incomplete printed version in Sparks, *Writings*, 3:68–72, the cover originally read "To Richard Henry Lee, Esqr. to be left at Doctr Shippen's in Philadelphia. Favour'd by Mr Barrell."

1. Mifflin was appointed quartermaster general on 14 Aug., and Randolph became an aide-de-camp the next day.

2. GW expressed similar sentiments to the Delaware delegates on 30 August. For GW's power to brevet officers up to the rank of colonel, see Instructions from the Continental Congress, 22 June 1775.

3. Capt. John Callender was the only officer to date who had been cashiered for his actions at the Battle of Bunker Hill (General Orders, 7 July 1775). Col. Samuel Gerrish was accused of misconduct at the battle, but he was court-martialed and cashiered for failing to repel an attack on Sewall's Point (General Orders, 17, 19 Aug. 1775). The two captains who were dismissed from the service for embezzling provisions were Oliver Parker and Jesse Saunders (General Orders, 2, 9, 10 Aug. 1775). Capt. Christopher Gardner was cashiered for abandoning his post on Boston Neck and allowing the George Tavern to be burned on the night of 30 July (General Orders,

31 July, 2 Aug. 1775). The fifth captain cashiered was Eleazer Lindsey, who was convicted of being absent from his post at Malden when the British attacked nearby on 6 Aug. (Loammi Baldwin to GW, 6, 8 Aug., 1775; General Orders, 16 Aug. 1775).

4. The officers awaiting trial were apparently Col. John Mansfield, Maj. Scarborough Gridley, Capt. Moses Hart, and ensigns Moses Howe and Levi Bowen (General Orders, 13, 17 Aug., 5, 8, 11, 15, 24 Sept. 1775).

5. GW made the same argument against establishing a post at Point Alderton in his letter to Joseph Palmer of 22 August.

6. Plowed Hill near the Mystic River was occupied on the night of 26 Aug. by a force of about twenty-five hundred men under the command of Brig. Gen. John Sullivan. "About one thousand had tools, the other was to cover them in case of an attack from the enemy," wrote Lt. Paul Lunt. "As soon in the morning as the enemy saw our works, they cannonaded it from Bunker Hill and their floating batteries, killed two of our men with their cannon shot, belonging [to] Rhode Island, one of them was adjutant of Colonel Varnum's regiment, and his name was [Isaac] Mumford; wounded one Rifleman in the leg so that he was obliged to have it cut off; killed one Indian; they kept almost a continual fire with cannon and small arms all day" ("Lunt's Book," 199). The *New-England Chronicle; or, the Essex Gazette*, 31 Aug., reports that "two of the Enemy's floating Batteries attempting to annoy our People at Work upon the Hill, were silenced in Mistick River, and one of them partly sunk, by some of our Cannon placed at Temple's Farm."

7. Lee went home to Virginia soon after Congress recessed on 2 Aug. and did not return to Philadelphia until 24 Sept. (Lee to GW, 26 Sept. 1775).

To the Massachusetts Council

Gentlemen [Cambridge] August 29. 1775

The Quarter Master General of the Army has represented to me that notwithstanding he has offered 2/ ℔ Foot for Fire Wood—2/1½ ℔ Bushel for Oats—3/4 ℔ Ct for Hay he cannot procure those Articles for the Use of the Army. From the Information I have received I have great Reason to believe that this is an artificial Scarcity partly created by some Persons who are monopolizing those Articles in order to advance the Price, & partly by the Possessors of them in the Neighbourhood of the Camp who keep them up in order to profit by our Distress. As such a Combination must be attended with fatal Consequences both to the Country & Army I cannot doubt the Interposition of your Honours to provide some speedy & effectual Remedy. That which is usual & customary in such Cases is to fix the Prices to the several Articles bearing a Proportion to what is the ordinary Rate, & if Persons will not comply with a reasonable Tariff but still refuse to furnish such Necessary Articles, the great Law of Self Preservation must authorize us to compel them. This or any other Regulations which your Knowledge of the People & Zeal for the Service shall induce you to make will I doubt not remove the Mischief at present, & prevent it in future. If you should at the same Time extend your Views to other Articles besides those I have enumerated I flatter myself it would have a very beneficial Effect.[1] I am &c.

Df, in Joseph Reed's writing, NHi: Reed Papers; LB, DLC:GW; Varick transcript, DLC:GW.

1. Because the General Court was in recess between 24 Aug. and 20 Sept., no action was taken on this matter until 6 Oct., when GW again wrote to the Council about it. The two houses read both of GW's letters on that date and appointed a joint committee to consider them.

Letter not found: from Major General Artemas Ward, 29 Aug. 1775. On 30 Aug. Horatio Gates wrote on behalf of GW to Ward: "In answer to your Favor of Yesterday, I am commanded by His Excellency to say, that He is intirely of your Opinion, that three Hundred proper Men and Officers, should be Selected for the Batteau Service but is not certain, wheather Captain Davis is the person who ought to be consider'd as the Commandant of that Body."[1]

1. MHi: Ward Papers.

From Brigadier General David Wooster

Sir, Oyster Ponds Suffolk County [N.Y.] Augt 29, 1775

I have with me at this place, four hundred and fifty of my Regiment: I should before this time have returned to my Station at Harlem, but General Scuyler having ordered the three Companies raised upon this End of Long Island for the Continental Service to join their Regiment at Ticonderoga; The County Committee requested me to remain here till the return of an express, which they sent to New York, to beg of their Congress, if possible to prevent the three Companies from being removed. The Express has now returned with liberty for the Companies to remain here ten days from last friday.[1] It is thought best that I keep my Station near New York though I shall not return there till I know the destination of the fleet, which I understand from your Excellency's information to Govr Trumbull have sailed out of Boston,[2] I hope and expect such measures will be pursued as will prevent their taking the Stock from this, or the adjacent Islands.

The Inhabitants here, think that had General Scuyler known their very exposed situation he would not have ordered the Companies away, The New York Congress suppose they have no right to counteract his Orders, they might indeed have sent to him, and receiv'd an answer in season, But they are so refined in their policy have so many private views to answer, and take such infinite pains to keep out of the plain path, conscious perhaps of their own superiour wisdom that they do nothing like other people. It is now too late to send to General Scuyler.

The Committee of Safety have therefore desired me to request your Excellency to continue their Troops upon this Station, I shall only say that I know of no place so much exposed to the Ravages of the Enemy, and if the companies raised here, who have, a great part of the good Arms in the County, should be removed, and their places not supplyed, I know of none so defenceless as this; It is my opinion after all the Soldiers are gone, that two hundred men might ravage the County notwithstanding all the Inhabitants could do to prevent it. From this representation I doubt not your Excellency will think proper to continue the Troops raised here upon this Station or order others in their Room. I am with great truth and regard your Excellency's most obedient Humble Servt

Davd Wooster

ALS, DLC:GW.

1. On 16 Aug. the New York provincial congress ordered the companies raised in Suffolk County to "proceed to Ticonderoga with all possible despatch to join the Continental army under the command of Major-Gen. Schuyler." Two days later, in consequence of GW's letter of 10 Aug. to Peter Van Brugh Livingston warning of a possible invasion of New York, the provincial congress requested Wooster to return to his camp at Harlem "with the utmost speed, to assist in the defence of this city and Province" (*N.Y. Prov. Congress Journal,* 1:108, 110). The Suffolk committee's letter of 22 Aug. protesting the removal of the local companies was read in the provincial congress on 24 August. "With the advice of Gen. Wooster," wrote the committee's chairman William Smith, "we have ventured to desire the captains not to march until we can send an express to you, to let us know whether we can have any hopes of relief" (ibid., 118). The provincial congress replied on 25 Aug., advising the county to form companies of minutemen from its mili-

tia to watch for British raiding parties and, if the enemy landed, to drive the livestock near the coast into the interior. "The repeated orders from Gen. Schuyler for the march of the troops raised in this Colony," the provincial congress explained, "makes it absolutely necessary that the companies raised in your county should immediately march. We will, however, venture to recommend their stay ten days from the date hereof at the most, to give you an opportunity, in the mean while, to complete the companies of minute men" (ibid., 120).

2. Jonathan Trumbull apparently sent Wooster a copy of at least the first paragraph of GW's letter of 23 Aug. regarding the sailing of a British convoy from Boston. Wooster quoted that paragraph verbatim in a letter of 27 Aug. to the New York provincial congress to justify his delay in returning to Harlem (ibid., 125).

General Orders

Head Quarters Cambridge, August 30th 1775

Parole, Ireland. Countersign Kingston.

One Field Officer, six Captains, twelve Subs. twelve serjts twelve Corporals, two Drums, two Fifes and three hundred Soldiers from Heaths Brigade, and the same from the Cambridge Brigade, to parade as soon as the weather is fair, to march to ploughd hill; one Surgeon & one mate from each Brigade to be provided with proper Instruments and Dressings, are to be ready to march with the above detachment.[1]

By the Orders of the 17th Instant, Thomas Chace Esqr. was, to the prejudice of Samuel Brewer Esqr., through mistake, appointed to be continued to do duty to Brigdr Genl Thomas's Brigade, as Major of Brigade: His Excellency orders that mistake to be rectified, and directs Samuel Brewer to be continued, to act as Major of Brigade, to Brigadier Genl Thomas—He is to be obeyed as such.

Varick transcript, DLC:GW.

1. This party was to relieve some of the troops who seized Plowed Hill on 26 August. See GW to Richard Henry Lee, 29 Aug. 1775, n.6.

From Burwell Bassett

Dear Sir M. Vernon 30 Augt 1775

The Convention broke up on Saterday last after a siting of six weeks, they have agreed to raise fourteen Hundred &

forty five Men & Appointed Patrick Henry to the Command of the first Regment & William Woodford to the second, Wm Christian & Charles Scoot are Lieut. Cols. & Frans Epps & Alexr Spotswood are Majr. Fore hundred of the Men are to be Stationd on the frontiars and the others about Wmsburg & Norfolk, They have laid the Country out in sixteen Districks each of which is to raise five hundred Men to be calld Minute Men they are to be ready to March on the shortest Notice, & are nearly under the same regulations as the Militia of England.[1]

The Convention have appointed a Committee of Safety of the following Gentlemen Edmond Pendleton, Geo: Mason John Page Cou[ncillo]r Thomas L. Lee Paul Carrington Richd Bland Dudley Diggs Wm Cabbell Carter Braxton James Mercer & John Tabb which are to have the Whole direction of the Army & so call out the Whole or any part of the Minute Men as they think best for the good of the Country,[2] Pendleton & Bland begd to be excuse[d] from going to the Congress & we have sent Wythe Thos Nelson & Frans Lee[3] & We have agreed to strike three hundred & fifty thousand pounds paper Currency to pay for the Indian War our part of the Continental Army & our own Army & Minute men.[4]

This is all the news that I can now send you, If you can spare a few Minutes from the great Hurry & fatigue that you must under go it would give me great Pleasure to hear that you are well.

Mrs Bassett & the Children join me in our best wishes for your Health & Happyness I am Dr Sr Yr Affnate Friend & Hble Servt

Burl Bassett

ALS, DLC:GW.

1. The third Virginia convention met in Richmond from 17 July to 26 August. For the act creating the various military forces for the defense of the colony, see 9 Hening 9–35. For the articles of war, see ibid., 35–48. William Woodford (1734–1780), a resident of Caroline County who served as a subaltern under GW during the French and Indian War, became a Continental brigadier general in February 1777 and was captured at the surrender of Charleston in 1780. William Christian (c.1743–1786) of Fincastle County, a veteran of Dunmore's War, commanded an expeditionary force against the Cherokees in 1776. Charles Scott (c.1737–1813) of Cumberland County, said to have been a noncommissioned officer in the Braddock campaign of 1755,

was commissioned colonel of a Virginia regiment in May 1776. Scott was promoted to brigadier general the following year and was taken prisoner with Woodford at Charleston in 1780. Both Francis Eppes (d. 1776) of Dinwiddie County and Alexander Spotswood (1751–1818) of Spotsylvania County became lieutenant colonels in the Continental service during the spring of 1776. Eppes was killed in the fighting on Long Island in August 1776. Spotswood was promoted to colonel in February 1777 and resigned his commission in October of that year. For the Virginia convention's selection of these officers, see William J. Van Schreeven, Robert L. Scribner, and Brent Tarter, eds., *Revolutionary Virginia: The Road to Independence*, 7 vols. (Charlottesville, 1973–83), 3:400–401, 457–59.

2. For the convention's act establishing the committee of safety, see 9 Hening 49–53. For the appointment of the members, see Van Schreeven, *Revolutionary Virginia*, 3:456–57. Edmund Pendleton became president of the committee of safety. The other members were George Mason (1725–1792) of Fairfax County, John Page (1743–1808) of Gloucester County, Thomas Ludwell Lee (1730–1778) of Stafford County, Paul Carrington (1733–1818) of Charlotte County, Richard Bland (1710–1776) of Prince George County, Dudley Digges (1718–1790) of York County, William Cabell (1730–1798) of Amherst County, Carter Braxton (1736–1797) of King William County, James Mercer (1736–1793) of Fredericksburg, and John Tabb (d. 1798) of Amelia County. Of this group only John Page had been a member of the governor's council before the Revolution.

3. The convention appointed George Wythe (1726–1806) of Williamsburg and Thomas Nelson, Jr. (1738–1789), of Yorktown to the colony's congressional delegation on 11 Aug., and four days later it added Francis Lightfoot Lee (1734–1797) of Richmond County. Peyton Randolph, Richard Henry Lee, Thomas Jefferson, and Benjamin Harrison continued to serve as delegates (ibid., 418–19, 446–47). Wythe, a prominent lawyer who had been clerk of the House of Burgesses for many years, attended Congress until the end of 1776. He became speaker of the Virginia house of delegates in 1777, was appointed to the new state court of chancery in 1778, and in December 1779 was named professor of law at the College of William and Mary. Nelson, a member of the governor's council from 1764 to 1775, served in Congress until the spring of 1777 and again in 1779. He was governor of Virginia during the latter half of 1781 and commanded the state militia at the siege of Yorktown. Francis Lightfoot Lee, a brother of Richard Henry Lee, had long been a member of the House of Burgesses and an active supporter of the American cause. He sat in Congress until June 1779 and later served several years in the state senate.

4. For the convention's act authorizing the issuance of these treasury notes, see 9 Hening 61–71. The Indian war was Dunmore's War of 1774.

From Nicholas Cooke

Sir Providence August 30th 1775

Your Excellency's Letter of the 14th instant is now before me; the Contents of which I have duly considered. When it came to Hand our small Sloop of War was out upon the Cruize which I mentioned to your Excellency in a former Letter. She hath since returned. The sending her on the Enterprize you propose could not be done without some new & further Powers from the General Assembly which sat here last Week; and the Nature of the Business was such that I did not think proper to lay it before so large a Body: I therefore procured a Committee to be appointed to transact all Business necessary for the common Safety during the Recess of the Assembly; particularly with Power to employ the Two Vessels of War in such Service as they should think necessary. The Committee is summoned to meet this Day before whom I shall lay your Letter. At present the Undertaking appears to me extremely difficult. The most suitable Man we have for the Purpose is confined to his Bed by Sickness.[1]

We have Accounts that a Number of Vessels have sailed lately from Boston, which we apprehend are designed to plunder the Stock along the Coast. The General Assembly have ordered it all to be removed from all the Islands in this Colony excepting Rhode Island. We have now about Three Hundred Men employed in that Business. I am requested by the General Assembly to apply to you to give Directions to the Commissary General that all the Stock taken from these Islands that are fit to kill be taken for the Use of the Army in Preference to any Stock which is secure in the Country. The Drought hath been so severe along the Sea Coast this Summer that there is no Possibility of providing for this Stock in any other Way.[2]

The Scarcity of coarse Linens hath caused such a Demand for Tow-Cloth for Family Use that upon Inquiry I find there is scarcely any of that Article to be had in the Government at any Rate.[3]

The Vessel our small Sloop was cruising for arrived on the 28th inst. at Norwich. She hath brought Powder, Lead, Flints & Small Arms—What Quantity of each I am not certain. They are now on their Way by Land.[4]

This letter waits upon your Excellency by Capt. Joseph Brown who is an eminent Merchant here, a true Friend to the Liberties of his Country, extremely well respected amongst us, and noted for his superior mechanical Genius. If he hath any Thing to propose for the Service of the common Cause I have no Doubt of your paying Attention to it and giving it the Weight it shall appear to you to deserve.[5] I am with very great Esteem and Regard Sir Your Excellency's Most obedient and most humble Servant

Nichols Cooke

LS, DLC:GW; Df, RHi: Cooke Papers.

1. The proposed enterprise was the scheme for seizing gunpowder in Bermuda. See GW to Cooke, 4 Aug. 1775. The committee that the Rhode Island general assembly appointed on 21 Aug. to act during its recess included Cooke as well as several members of the assembly (Bartlett, *R.I. Records*, 7:365). The ill man mentioned by Cooke is Abraham Whipple, commodore of the two Rhode Island vessels.

2. On 21 Aug. the general assembly appointed a committee to oversee and assist in removing livestock from the islands. If any owner refused to cooperate, the committee was empowered to have that person's livestock appraised and sent to the American army to be sold. The owner would be indemnified with the proceeds of the sale (ibid., 373). For the general assembly's request to GW that the commissary general take all of the evacuated livestock for the army, see ibid., 371. GW soon consented to receive the livestock. On 13 Sept. Horatio Gates wrote to Artemas Ward: "I am commanded by General Washington to Acquaint you, that all the Cattle, & Horses, in & about Roxbury Common, & on the Land unimproved by the Owners; are to be removed from thence; And the Cattle, and Sheep, Lately come from the Colony of Rhode Island, for the use of the Army, taken off the Islands out of The Enemy's reach, may be pastured there; You will please to give an Order for a proper Number of Centrys to take charge of them, until they be Killed for the Army" (MHi: Ward Papers).

3. The tow cloth was to have been used to make hunting shirts for the army (GW to Cooke, 4 Aug. 1775).

4. This vessel, commanded by John Burroughs Hopkins, was sent to Cap-Français as a joint venture of the Massachusetts provincial congress and the Providence firm of Clark & Nightingale. See Cooke to GW, 8 Aug. 1775, n.1. For the purchase of the military stores for the Continental army, see GW to Cooke, 31 Aug. 1775, and Clark & Nightingale to GW and Cooke to GW, both 2 Sept. 1775.

5. Joseph Brown (1733–1785), one of the four brothers who figured so prominently in the commercial life of Providence, was a skillful technician interested in architecture, electricity, steam engines, and other scientific and

technical subjects. Before the Revolution he ran the Browns' spermaceti candle factory, and during the war years he played an important role in converting the family's Hope Furnace to military uses.

To the Delaware Delegates

Gentn Camp at Cambridge Augt 30 1775

I endeavoured to pay the best attention in my power to your recommendation of Mr Parke, by making him an assistant to the Quarter Master General, an Office indispensably necessary in discharge of that Important, & troublesome business[1]—I wish it was in my power to provide for more of the young Gentlemen, who, at their own expence have travelled, & now continue here, from Pensylvania & elsewhere; but the Congress seems to have put it out of their own power to do this, leaving by their Instructions to me,[2] the ultimate appointment of all Officers as high as a Colonel to the Government in which the Regiments originated; the obvious consequence of which is, that, every Commission will be monopolized by these four New England Governments; the good policy, & justice of which, I submit to your better judgments; but should give it as my own opinion, that as the whole Troops are now taken into the pay of the United Colonies, the Congress (which I presume will either by themselves, or a Committee of their own Body always be sitting) ought to reserve the filling up of all vacancies themselves, in order that Volunteers from every Government may have an equal chance of preferment; instead of confineing all Offices to a few Governments to the total exclusion of the rest. I have dropt these thoughts by way of hint wch you may improve or reject as they shall appear to have, or want weight.[3]

For the Occurrances of the Camp—the State of the Army &ca I refer to my Publick Letters address'd to Mr Hancock & with great respect, & gratitude for the good wishes containd in your Letter I remain Gentn Yr Most Obedt Hble Servt

Go: Washington

ALS, DLC:GW.

1. GW appointed John Parke to this position on 16 Aug. (General Orders, that date). For the recommendation of Parke, see the Delaware Delegates to GW, 29 June 1775.

2. See Instructions from the Continental Congress to GW, 22 June 1775.

3. GW expressed these same opinions about the appointment of officers in his letter to Richard Henry Lee of 29 August.

To John Dickinson

Dear Sir Camp at Cambridge Augt 30th [17]75

Your favour of the 25th Ulto recommendatory of Mr Moylan, came duely to hand, & I have the pleasure to inform you that he is now appointed Commissary General of Musters—one of the Offices which the Congress was pleased to leave to my disposal[1]—I have no doubt, from your acct of this Gentleman, of his discharging the duty with honour and fidility.

For the occurrances of the Camp, I refer to my publick Letters, address'd to Mr Hancock, and am with sincere regard. Dr Sir Yr Most Obedt Hble Servt

Go: Washington

ALS, NNS. The addressed cover includes the notation "Favourd by Mr Barrell."

1. GW appointed Stephen Moylan to this position on 11 Aug. (General Orders, that date).

To Peter Van Brugh Livingston

⟨Si⟩r ⟨Camp at Cambridge—August 30th 1775.⟩

Your Favour ⟨of the 21st Instt is duly⟩ received, inclosing Mr Carter's In⟨formation of the⟩ Capture of the Charming Sally: whic⟨h from the circum⟩stances attending it, was undoubt⟨edly collusive.⟩ I have received Advice that another Ves⟨sel belonging⟩ to one White at Marblehead, whose os⟨tensible Voyage⟩ was to Casco Bay was carried in soon a⟨fter. Such⟩ Instances of Avarice, at such a Time, & in s⟨uch a cause,⟩ call for a severe Scrutiny, & exemplary Pun⟨ishment.⟩[1]

Mr Livingston & some other Gentlem⟨en from⟩ your City brought us the acceptable News of the ⟨safe⟩ Arrival of a large Quantity of Powder, & 500 Stand ⟨of⟩ Arms.[2] Our Situation is such as requires your immediate Assistance & Supply, in that Article. We have lately taken Possession of a Hill conside⟨rably⟩ advanced towards the Enemy, but our Poverty ⟨prevents⟩ our availing ourselves of any Advantage of Si⟨tuation.⟩[3] I must therefore most earnestly intreat that ⟨Measures⟩ may be taken to forward to this Camp in ⟨the most⟩ safe and Expeditious Manner whatev⟨er Ammu⟩nition can be spared from the immed⟨iate & necessary defence of the province. The value of whatever may be sent in Consequence of⟩ this Request, ⟨will be paid by Order⟩ from hence when delivered—or n⟨egociated with⟩ the Honbl. Continental Congress at Philad⟨a as ma⟩y be agreed with the Proprietors: I only req⟨uest th⟩at no Time may be lost thro. any such Difficu⟨lties⟩ as our Situation is so critical & the Exigence so great. The Mode of Conveyance I must leave with the Provincial Congress, or the Committee of the City: I doubt not they will take every Precaution to make it safe & expeditious.[4] I have the Honour to be Sir Your most Obedt & very Hbble Servt

Go: Washington

LS, in Joseph Reed's writing, N: New York Provincial Congress Revolutionary Papers; copy, DNA:PCC, item 152; LB, DLC:GW; Varick transcript, DLC:GW. The LS was extensively damaged in the New York State Library fire of 1911. The missing portions of the text are supplied within angle brackets from the copy in PCC, which the New York committee of safety enclosed in its letter of 9 Sept. 1775 to the Continental Congress.

1. For John Carter's intelligence regarding the capture of the *Charming Sally*, see Peter Van Brugh Livingston to GW, 21 Aug. 1775, n.3. The other vessel was the schooner *Woodbridge*, John Williamson, master. It was carrying a cargo of flour, bread, bran, and corn from Philadelphia to Newburyport when it was captured off Cape Ann on 31 July by the British sloop of war *Merlin*. The *Woodbridge* was subsequently condemned and sold at Boston.

2. This cargo of gunpowder and firearms belonged jointly to the Providence firm of Clark & Nightingale and the colony of Massachusetts, not to New York (GW to Nicholas Cooke, 31 Aug. 1775; New York Committee of Safety to GW, 9 Sept. 1775). "Mr Livingston" may be Peter Van Brugh Livingston's brother Philip Livingston (1716–1778) or his cousin Robert R. Livingston (1746–1813), both of whom were members of the Continental Congress.

3. For the occupation of Plowed Hill, see GW to Richard Henry Lee, 29 Aug. 1775, n.6.

4. Because the New York provincial congress was in recess from 2 Sept. to 2 Oct., this letter was referred to the colony's committee of safety, which on 9 Sept. wrote to the Continental Congress requesting that a supply of gunpowder from Philadelphia be sent to GW (New York Committee of Safety to GW, 9 Sept. 1775).

General Orders

Head Quarters, Cambridge, August 31st 1775

Parole London. Countersign Monmouth.

The Colonels or Officers commanding of each regiment of the Massachusetts Forces, are without delay to make out an exact abstract for the month of August of the pay due to the Commissioned, Non Commissioned Officers and private soldiers of each regiment, who were effective in the said Regiment during that Month, and who continue to be effective in the same: This Abstract must be signed by the Colonel, or Officer commanding each Regiment of the Massachusetts, and forthwith deliver'd by him to the Commander in Chief; to the end that each of those regiments, may immediately be paid one month's pay.[1]

Varick transcript, DLC:GW.

1. For GW's further orders on the payment of the Massachusetts soldiers, see General Orders, 5 Sept. 1775. Some of the Massachusetts regiments refused their pay warrants, declaring that they should be paid by the lunar month rather than the calendar month (GW to Hancock, 21 Sept. 1775).

To Clark & Nightingale

Gentlemen. Camp at Cambridge August 31st 1775

Hearing that you have imported a Quantity of Powder, Lead & Small Arms I have dispatchd Capt. Bayler, one of my Aids de Camp to treat with you for it. Whatever Engagement he shall enter into for the whole or any part I will confirm: And upon Delivery to him your Bills drawn on me for the Price agreed on shall be honor'd on the Shortest Notice.[1] I am Gent: Your very Humble Servt

G.W.

LB, in Thomas Mifflin's writing, DLC:GW; Varick transcript, DLC:GW.

John Clark and Joseph Nightingale (1748–1797) remained partners in this Providence trading firm throughout the Revolution.

1. The cargo, jointly owned by Clark & Nightingale and the Massachusetts government, arrived at Norwich on 28 Aug. (Nicholas Cooke to GW, 30 Aug. 1775). For George Baylor's purchase of most of these supplies, see Clark & Nightingale to GW and Nicholas Cooke to GW, both 2 Sept. 1775.

To Nicholas Cooke

Sir Camp at Cambridge August 31st 1775

Last Night I received Information that Messr Clarke & Nightingale of Providence had imported a Quantity of Gun Powder, Lead & 500 Stand of Arms:[1] Upon which I have dispatch'd Capt. Baylor one of my Aids de Camp to treat with those Gentlemen for the whole Importation if not otherwise dispos'd of. I have directed him to wait upon you immediately on his Arrival & must beg the Favor of your Advice & Assistance both in negociating the Purchase, & transporting it hither in the cheapest, Safest and most expeditious Manner. I flatter myself those Gentlemen will not take an under[2] Advantage of the Distresses of their Country so as to exact an unreasonable Price—& that a due Regard will be had to the very particular Necessities of this Army so as to prevent as far as possible any Part of this Supply being diverted to other uses. As I have the most perfect Confidence in your Attachment & Zeal for the Publick Interests, I am perswaded you will use your utmost Influence to give Effect to Capt. Baylor's Commission.[3] To him I must beg leave to refer you for the News of the Camp & am with much Respect & Esteem, Sir Your

In your next you will please to inform me what Progress you make with the hunting Shirts.[4]

LB, in Thomas Mifflin's writing, DLC:GW; Varick transcript, DLC:GW.

1. Cooke's letter of 30 Aug. informing GW of the arrival of these supplies had not yet reached Cambridge.

2. The Varick transcript reads "undue."

3. For Baylor's purchase of most of the supplies, see Clark & Nightingale to GW and Cooke to GW, both 2 Sept. 1775.

4. Cooke was unable to obtain tow cloth for the hunting shirts (Cooke to GW, 30 Aug., 2 Sept. 1775).

From Captain Richard Dodge

Sir [31 August 1775]

I am Vary Sorey that thare was aney Misunder Standing in the mesage that your Eadeyeon Braught me Respecting the Signal that I was to mack on Powder Horn Hill[.] I under Stood By him that when Aney movemen⟨t⟩ By See or Land By the

Regular trupes was mad that was Lickley that thay ware a Bout to Land I was to give the Signal on Said hill[.][1] I have in Closed the Remarckes.[2] I am your Exelencey most Humble Servent

Richd Dodge Capt.

ALS, DLC:GW. This document has no dateline, but it is endorsed in Thomas Mifflin's writing "From Capt. Dodge Augt 31. 1775."

1. On 28 Aug. Joseph Reed wrote to Dodge: "Before this reaches you the Generals Aid du Camp will have given you Directions about Signals. It is the Generals Intention that those Signals be continued if at any T⟨ime you⟩ observe any Motion of the Troops, or Preparation out of the ordinary Course" (MH: Loammi Baldwin Papers).

2. Dodge enclosed "A Return of the observations of the Day augt 31" and possibly those for 27, 28, and 29 August. All of these returns are in Joseph Leach's writing in DLC:GW.

To Major Christopher French

Sir Camp at Cambridge August 31 1775

I duly received your Letter of the 15th Inst. with the Inclosures which shall be forwarded into Boston agreeable to your Request.

I understand the Committee of Safety of Philadelphia have directed an Escort with you to this Camp.[1] The Accomodations, as well as many other Reasons, would make your Residence here extremely inconvenient, I have therefore directed that it be changed to Hartford—To this Effect I have wrote to the Committee there, who will take Care that Suitable Provission Shall be made for you and your Companions, & Shew you every Civility, consistent with their Duty, & the Interest of the publick[2]—Should Governour Trumbull think proper to make any Alteration of your Residence he is impower'd so to do, & I make no Doubt of your Acquiescence—I am Sir Your

LB, in Thomas Mifflin's writing, DLC:GW; Varick transcript, DLC:GW. A copy of this letter was enclosed in the letter of 3 Sept. 1775 that Joseph Reed wrote to French, but it has not been found. See French to GW, 3 Sept. 1775, n.1.

1. Richard Willing and John Wharton escorted French and his companions north toward Cambridge (Pennsylvania Committee of Safety to GW, 17 Aug. 1775).

2. On this date Joseph Reed wrote to Thomas Seymour, chairman of the Hartford committee: "I am directed by his Excellency, Genl Washington to inform you that he has given Orders that Majr French & some other Pris-

oners from Philadelphia should remain at Hartford instead of proceeding to this Camp as was proposed. Should there be any Doubt of their Parole of Honour given at Philadelphia being vacated by this Change of their Destination; you will require them to renew it before they are allowed the same Indulgences with the other Gentlemen, now under the Care of the Committee over which you preside. Should they have advanced beyond Hartford before this Letter reaches you, his Excelly requests you will immediately dispatch an Express for their Return; as their coming to this Place will be attended with many Inconveniences both to the Service & themselves" (DNA:PCC, item 78). Reed wrote a similar letter on this date to Capt. John Wharton (NjP: de Coppett Collection). French and his companions reached Framingham, Mass., before receiving GW's orders to return to Hartford (French to GW, 3 Sept. 1775).

To John Hancock

Sir [Camp at Cambridge August 31. 1775]

The inclosed Letter came under s⟨uch⟩ a Direction, & Circumstances as led me to supp⟨ose⟩ it contained some interesting Advices, either respecting a Supply of Powder; or the Cloathing lately taken at Philadelphia: I therefore took the Liberty of breaking the Seal; for which I hope the Service & my Motives will apoligize.[1]

As the filling up the Place of vacant Brigadier General, will probably be of the first Business of the Honourable Congress:[2] I flatter myself it will not be deemed assuming to mention the Names of two Gentlemen whose former Services, Rank, & Age may be thought worthy of Attention on this Occasion. Of the one I can speak from my own Knowledge, of the other only from Character. The former is Col. John Armstrong of Pennsylvania. He served during the last War in most of the Campaigns to the Southward, was honoured with the Command of the Pennsylvania Forces, and his general military Conduct, & Spirit much approved by all who served with him beside which, his Character was distinguished by an Enterprize against the Indians, which he plann'd with great Judgment, & executed with equal Courage, & Success. It was not till lately that I had Reason to beleive he would en⟨ter⟩ again on publick Service, & it is now wholly unsolicited & unknown on his Part.[3] The other Gentleman is Col. Fry of Massachusetts Bay. He entered into the Service as early as 1745, & rose thro' the different military

Ranks in the succeeding Wars, to that of Colonel, untill last June, when he was appointed a Major General by the Congress of this Province. From these Circumstances together with the favourable Report made to me of him I presume he sustained the Character of a good Officer—Tho' I do not find it distinguished by any peculiar Service.[4]

Either of these Gentlemen, or any other whom the Honourable Congress shall please to favour with this Appointment, will be received by me with the utmost Deference & Respect.

The late Adjournment having made it impractiable to know the Pleasure of the Congress as to the Appointment of Brigade Majors beyond the Number of three, which they were pleased to leave to me: And the Service not admitting of farther Delay, I have continued the other three, which I hope their Honours will not disapprove. These latter were recommended by the respective Corps to which they belong as the properest Persons for these Offices, untill farther Direction, & have discharged the Duty ever since. They are the Majors Box, Scammel & Samuel Brewer.[5]

Last Saturday Night, we took Possession of a Hill considerably advanced beyond our former Lines—which brought on a very heavy Cannonade from Bunkers Hill; & afterwards a Bombardment which has been since kept up with little Spirit on their Part, or Damage on ours. The Work having been continued ever since, is now so advanced, & the Men so well covered as leave us under no Apprehensions of much farther Loss. In this Affair we had killed one Adjutant, one Volunteer & 2 privates.[6] The Scarcity of Ammunition, does not admit of our availing ourselves of the Situation as we otherwise might do: But this Evil I hope will soon be remedied, as I have been informed of the Arrival of a large Quantity at New York; some at New London, & more hourly expected at different Places.[7] I need not add to what I have already said on this Subject; our late Supply was very seasonable, but far short of our Necessities.

The late Adjournment of the Hon: Congress having been made before my Letter of the 4th Instt was received, I must now beg Leave to recall their Attention to those Parts of it which respect the Provision for the Winter, the Reduction of the Troops, the double Commissions under different Establishments & Col. Gridlys Appointment of Major General. In all which I hope to be honoured with their Commands as soon as possible.[8]

The Advocate General has sent me a Memorial respecting his Service, which I have the Honour to inclose (No. 1).[9] And from the Variety & Multiplicity of Duty in a new Army as well as his regular Service, & Attendance I am induced to recommend him to the farther Notice of the Honorable Congress.

The Treatment of our Officers Prisoners at Boston induced me to write to General Gage on that Subject, his Answer, & my Reply I have the Honour to lay before the Congress in the Inclosures—No. 2. 3. 4.[10] Since which I have heard nothing from him. I remain with the greatest Respect & Regard, Sir, Your most obedt & very Hbble Servt

Go: Washington

LS, in Joseph Reed's writing, DNA:PCC, item 152; Df, NHi: Joseph Reed Papers; LB, DLC:GW; copy, DNA:PCC, item 169; copy, NjMoNP; Varick transcript, DLC:GW. The LS has no dateline, but the letter-book copy is dated "Camp at Cambridge August 31. 1775." The LS is endorsed "Read before congress 13. Septr" (*JCC*, 2:246). Parts of words in the mutilated portions of the LS are supplied within angle brackets from the draft.

1. This document has not been identified.

2. Seth Pomeroy's failure to accept his commission as a brigadier general from the Continental Congress left GW without a general officer to command one of the two brigades at Cambridge. See General Orders, 22 July 1775, n.5. Congress tried to fill the vacancy on 21 Sept., but the delegates became embroiled in a dispute over whether to appoint another New Englander, Joseph Frye, or John Armstrong of Pennsylvania. The two men tied in the voting, and the decision was postponed for some time (*JCC*, 3:257). Frye was finally commissioned a brigadier general on 10 Jan. 1776 (ibid., 4:47), and on 16 Feb. GW appointed him to command the vacant brigade at Cambridge (General Orders, 17 Feb. 1776).

3. John Armstrong (1717–1795) of Carlisle, Pa., first made a name for himself in 1756 by destroying the Indian town of Kittanning with a force of 300 Pennsylvanians. Two years later he commanded the colony's troops in the Forbes campaign, during which he and GW became well acquainted. Congress did not make Armstrong a brigadier general until 1 Mar. 1776 when he was sent to South Carolina. He participated in the siege of Charleston in June 1776, and during the following winter GW used him to rally militia and recruits in central Pennsylvania. Upon resigning his Continental commission in April 1777, Armstrong became a brigadier general in the Pennsylvania militia and fought throughout the ensuing campaign around Philadelphia. He was promoted to major general of militia in January 1778, and in November

of that year he was elected to the Continental Congress, where he served until 1780.

4. Joseph Frye (1712–1794) of Fryesburg, District of Maine, began his military career in 1745 as a Massachusetts ensign in the Louisburg expedition, and during the next two years he served with a provincial regiment on the colony's eastern frontier, rising to the rank of captain. In 1754 Frye was a major on the Kennebec expedition, and the following year he held the same rank on an expedition to Nova Scotia. Commissioned a colonel in 1756, Frye raised a Massachusetts regiment, and in August 1757 he and his men were among those who surrendered to the French at Fort William Henry. He escaped captivity, and from 1759 to 1760 he commanded a fort in Nova Scotia. The Massachusetts provincial congress made Frye a major general in the colony's forces on 21 June 1775 (*Mass. Prov. Congress Journals*, 370, 378). During the Continental Congress's long delay in appointing Frye a brigadier general in the Continental service (see note 2), the Massachusetts General Court named him commander of the colony's forces at Falmouth in the District of Maine (Samuel Freeman to GW, 17 Nov. 1775). Frye held that position from 11 Nov. 1775 to 16 Feb. 1776, when he was appointed a brigade commander by GW. Frye's Continental service lasted only a few weeks. Citing the infirm state of his health, he submitted his resignation from the army on 18 Mar., and on 23 April Congress accepted it. For GW's criticism of Frye's resignation, see GW to Joseph Reed, 7 Mar. and 1 April 1776.

5. For the appointments of the brigade majors, see General Orders, 15, 17, and 30 Aug. 1775.

6. Plowed Hill was occupied on the night of 26 August. See GW to Richard Henry Lee, 29 Aug. 1775, n.6.

7. The most recently arrived gunpowder was landed at Norwich, not New York or New London. See GW to Peter Van Brugh Livingston, 30 Aug.; Nicholas Cooke to GW, 31 Aug.; and the New York Committee of Safety to GW, 9 Sept. 1775.

8. Congress read GW's letters of 4 Aug. and this date on 13 Sept., the first official day of business after the recess (*JCC*, 2:246).

9. See William Tudor to GW, 23 Aug. 1775.

10. See GW to Thomas Gage, 11, 19 Aug. 1775, and Gage to GW, 13 Aug. 1775.

From Major General Philip Schuyler

Dear Sir Tionderoga [N.Y.] August 31st 1775

I arrived here last night and Immediately renewed my orders for Sending you the lead (my former ones having not come to hand) It will leave Crown point this Afternoon and be forwarded without Loss of Time to you.[1]

Gen: Montgomery leaves Crown point to day with twelve

hundred Men, and four twelve pounders, I follow him this Evening and have ordered the whole Strength I can Spare to Join me at Isle-au-noix with out delay. When they arrive there which I hope will be in five days, I Shall then be near two thousand Strong[2]—I am Still of opinion that the Canadiens and Indians will be friendly to us, unless the Imprudence of a Capt: Baker who without my Leave went upon a Scout and Contrary to the most pointed & Express orders Seeing some people in a boat that Belonged to us, Attempted to fire on them but his Gun missing he was Instantly Shot, thro. the head and Expired, his party Consisted of five men, and the other of an Equal number, one of which an Indian was only seen to paddle of,[3] I will neither detain Your Excellency nor waste my time (which is precious) in giving you a detail of the many wants I labour under, I hope they will Serve for an Evening Chat at some future day.

You would have Cause to blame me for not Sending a return of the forces under my Command, but I cannot get one that may in the least be depended upon, I know the reason, but so Critical is my Situation that I sacrifice every thing to the Grand Object. I have sent on only four twelve pounders[.] I expect to have no more than Six because, but I have promised not to Complain. Adieu My Dear General. I am with the most respectful Sentiments Your most Obedient Servant

Ph: Schuyler

My situation will apoligize for this blotted Scrawl. Since writing the above I have received the papers of which a Copy is inclosed.[4]

ALS, DLC:GW; LB, NN: Schuyler Papers.

1. For GW's request for lead, see GW to Schuyler and GW to Jonathan Trumbull, Sr., both 14 Aug. 1775.

2. Montgomery set out to invade Canada from Ticonderoga on 28 August. Sailing north on Lake Champlain with his troops aboard a fleet of galleys and small boats, he arrived the next day at Crown Point, where adverse winds prevented him from resuming his voyage until the morning of this day. Two days later Montgomery reached Isle La Motte near the north end of Lake Champlain, and on the morning of 4 Sept. Schuyler joined him there. Later that day the entire army landed at Ile aux Noix, a swampy island in the Richelieu River about twelve miles south of the British fortifications at St. Jean, the first objective of the American invasion.

3. Remember Baker (1737–1775), one of the leaders of the Green Mountain Boys, was killed on 22 Aug. on the Richelieu River near Ile aux Noix. The stolen boat was one that Baker and his companions had hidden while they

reconnoitered on foot. A Canadian scout and several Caughnawaga Indians discovered the boat and started down the river toward St. Jean with it. Encountering that party, Baker asked for the return of his boat and was refused. In the ensuing skirmish, not only was Baker killed but two of the Caughnawagas were wounded as well. Schuyler subsequently sent an apology to the Iroquois, who agreed to forget the incident.

4. The enclosure is an undated copy of a letter to Schuyler from James Livingston (1747–1832), an in-law of General Montgomery who lived near Chambly. "The Canadians have waited with the utmost Impatience your Coming & begin to despair of Seeing You," Livingston wrote, "Tho' I hope to revive their Spirits by sending Circular Letters to the Captains of the different Parishs of your Coming soon to relieve them . . . & shall endeavour to join (the Party You propose sending this Side the River) with what Men I can muster to block up the Communication from Montreal to St. John's &ca." The fort at St. Jean, Livingston went on to report, was well supplied with men, cannon, ammunition, and provisions, but "the Soldiers are much harrassed and would be Glad of Your Arrival & make no Doubt Numbers will desert upon the Sight of Your Army" (DLC:GW).

Letter not found: from Major General Artemas Ward, 31 Aug. 1775. On 31 Aug. Horatio Gates wrote on behalf of GW to Ward: "In Answer to your Favor of This Day to His Excellency General Washington, I have His Commands to say, that He approves of The Person being Appointed to the Command of the Boatmen being Declared in Publick Orders, before the Inlistment takes place."[1]

1. MHi: Ward Papers.

General Orders

Head Quarters, Cambridge, September 1st 1775

Parole, Newhaven. Countersign Ormond

Complaint has been made to the General, that the body of a Soldier of Col. Woodbridge's Regiment, has been taken from his grave by persons unknown; The General and the Friends of the deceased, are desirous of all the Information that can be given, of the perpetrators of this abominable Crime, that he, or they, may be made an example, to deter others from committing so wicked and shameful an offence.

The Magazine Guard in the Rear of Genl Sullivans brigade, to be relieved to morrow morning, by the brigade posted in, and near Cambridge.

Varick transcript, DLC:GW.

From Lieutenant Colonel Loammi Baldwin

Chelsea [Mass.] Sept: 1st 1775

May it Please your Excellecy

Yesterday morning I sent to the Select men of Chelsea desiring them to meet at my Quarters in the Evening of the Same day & they met accordingly I then laid before them the necessity of making some further provision for winter Quarters for the troops Stationed in this Town. They consulted freely with me and desired me to lay before your Excellency a brief account of the troops being Station'd in Chelsea & present accomodations for winter Quarters.

The exposed situation of the Town Induced the Committee of Safty in may last to give orders for a Company to be raised to keep a Guard which was accordingly raised under Capt: Sprague[1]—Some time after General Ward Sent a detachment to remove the Stock from some of the ajacent Islands which brought on Skirmishes which both destressed an[d] endangered the town upon which Genll Ward and Dr Warren upon viewing the Situation of things and Judging it of importance to defend the post ordered a detachment of three companies more to be Stationed at Chelsea which still remain here[.][2] The inhabitants of Chelsea Seem ready to do as far as their Abilities will possibly admit in their present impoverished Circumstances to accommodate Sd Companies in winter Quarters but are utterly unable to provide for them unless Somthing of the Barrack kind Should be erected for 70 or 80 Men[.] The Select men pray that your Excellency would direct that a Barrack be built Sufficient to contain the above Sd 70 or 80 Men & they will provide for the rest—There are about 36 houses in the town 7 of which are at the Ferry[3] and deserted by the Inhabitants which very much crouds the rest—They plead the Inhabitants are vastly destressed and impoverished by repeated difficulties, Such as Alarms removing their stocks &c.

Considering the Importance of the post for observation and other ways I would beg leave to give it as my opinion that a barrack had better be erected but your Excellencies pleasure Shall be punctually observed by your very humble Servant

Loammi Baldwin

ADfS, MH: Baldwin Papers.

1. The Massachusetts committee of safety resolved on 3 May "that two companies be raised in the towns of Malden and Chelsea, for the defence of the sea coast of said towns, the said companies to be joined to such regiments in future, as they may be ordered to, should there be occasion, or discharged from service as soon as the public good will admit of it" (*Mass. Prov. Congress Journals*, 533–34; also in Massachusetts General Court to GW, 26 Dec. 1775). Samuel Sprague (1712–1783) of Chelsea became captain of that town's company, and on 26 June the provincial congress added the company to Col. Samuel Gerrish's regiment. Sprague served at least until the spring of 1776.

2. On 27 May Col. John Stark led a party onto Noddles and Hog islands to remove livestock and destroy hay. While engaged in that business, Stark's force was attacked by several British warships and a detachment of marines, and there ensued a skirmish that lasted until the next day. The three companies sent to join Sprague's company at Chelsea were those commanded by captains Richard and Barnabus Dodge and William Rogers. All three belonged to Gerrish's regiment.

3. Baldwin is referring to Winnisimmet ferry.

General Orders

Head Quarters, Cambridge, Sept. 2nd 1775.

Parole Portugal. Countersign Quebec.

Capt. Edward Crafts of Col. Gridley's regiment of Artillery, tried yesterday by a General Court Martial, is acquitted of that part of the Charge against him, which relates to *defrauding of his men*," and the Court are also of opinion, that no part of the Charge against the prisoner is proved, except that of *using abusive expressions to Major Gridley*; which being a breach of the 49th Article of the Rules and Regulations for the Massachusetts Army; sentence the Prisoner to receive a severe reprimand from the Lt Col. of the Artillery in the presence of all the Officers of the regiment and that he at the said time, ask pardon of Major Gridley for the said abusive language.[1]

Lieut. Russell of Capt. Symonds Company, in the 21st Regt of foot, tried by the above Court Martial, for "disobedience of orders," is unanimously acquitted by the court.[2]

The General confirms the proceedings & Sentence of the above Court Martl.

Varick transcript, DLC:GW.

1. Edward Crafts of Worcester, Mass., continued to serve as a captain in the Continental artillery at least until the end of 1776. Scarborough Gridley,

one of Col. Richard Gridley's sons, was a major in his father's regiment, and William Burbeck was the regiment's lieutenant colonel. On 9 Aug. James Warren wrote to John Adams that Colonel Gridley "is grown old, is much governed by A Son of his, who vainly supposed he had a right to the second place in the Regiment that is before Burbank [Burbeck] and [David] Mason. The [Massachusetts] Congress thought Otherways. He was Sulkey. We had much Trouble with them, and I Understand the General has his Share yet" (Taylor, *Papers of John Adams*, 3:114–16). On 24 Sept. a court-martial ordered Scarborough Gridley to be dismissed from the army for misbehaving at the Battle of Bunker Hill (General Orders, that date).

2. William Russell was first lieutenant of Capt. Francis Symonds's company in Col. John Glover's Massachusetts regiment.

From Captain Abiathar Angel

Camp at Roxbury [Mass.] 2 September 1775. "Being in a Very Poor State of Health and Some Misunderstandings happening Between Me & Some of My Company, which I did Not Expect, which Renders it difficult for me to Serve With Pleasure—I therefor Move to Your Excelly for Leave to Resign My Command in Favor of Capt. Henry Work."

ALS, DLC:GW.

Abiathar Angel (1744–1830) of Lanesboro was a captain in Col. David Brewer's Massachusetts regiment. Angel rejoined the army in July 1776 as a captain in Col. Seth Warner's additional regiment and served at least until the following March.

Instructions to Captain Nicholson Broughton

[Cambridge, 2 September 1775]

1. You being appointed a Captain in the Army of the United Colonies of North America, are hereby direct⟨ed⟩ to take the Command of a Detachment of sd Army & proceed on Board the *Schooner Hannah* at Beverly lately fitted out & equipp'd with Arms Ammunition & Proviss. at the Continental Expence.

2. You are to proceed as Commander of sd *Schooner* immediately on a Cruize against such Vessels as may be found on the High Seas or elsewhere bound inwards or outwards to or from Boston in the Service of the ministerial Army & to take & seize all such Vessels laden with Soldiers, Arms, Ammuniton or Provisions for or from sd Army or which you shall have good Reason to suspect are in such Service.

3. If you should be so successful as to take any of sd Vessels

you are immediately to send them to the nearest & safest Port to this Camp under a careful Prize Master directing him to notify me by Express immediately of such Capture with all Particulars & there to wait my farther Direction.

4. You are to be very particular & diligent in your Search after all Letters or other Papers tending to discov⟨er⟩ the Designs of the Enemy or of any other Kind & to forward all such to me as soon as possible.

5. Whatever Prisoners you may take you are to treat with Kindness & Humanity as far as is consistent with your own Safety—their private Stock of Money, & Apparel to be given them after being duly search'd, and when they arrive at any Port you are to apply to the Committe⟨e⟩ or to any Officer of the continental Army Stationed at such Port for a Guard to bring them up to Head Quarters.

6. For your own Encouragement & that of the other Officers & Men to Activity & Courage in this Service, over & above your Pay in the continental Army you shall be entitled to one third Part of the Cargo of every Vessel by you taken & sent into Port (military & naval Stores only excepted, which with Vessels & apparel are reserved for the publick Service)—which sd third Part is to be divided among the Officers & Men in the followg Proportions.

Captain .... 6 Shares
1st Lieutt .... 5 Do
2d Lieutt .... 4 Do[1]
Ship's master .... 3 Do
Steward .... 2 Do
Mate 1½
Gunner 1½
Boatswain 1½
Gunner's Mate & Sergt 1½
Privates .... 1 Share each

7. You are particularly charged to avoid any Engagement with any armed Vessel of the Enemy tho' you may be equal in Strength, or may have some small Advantage; the Design of this Enterprize being to intercept the Supplies of the Enemy which will be defeated by your running into unnecessary Engagements.

8. As there may be other Vessels employed in the same Ser-

vice with yourselves you are to fix upon proper signals & your Stations being settled so as to take the greatest Range avoid cruizing on the same Ground—if you should happen to take Prizes in Sight of each other the Rules which take Place among private Ships of War are to be observed in the Distribution of the prize Money.

9. In Case of retaking the Vessel of any Friend to the American Cause I will recommend it to such Person to make a suitable Compensation to those who have done such a Service—but such Vessels are not to be deemed as coming within the Directions respecting other Vessels.

10. You are to be extremely careful & ⟨frugal of your⟩ Ammunition—by no Means to waste any of it in Salutes or for any Purpose but what is absolutely necessary.

Df, in Joseph Reed's writing, DLC:GW; copy, in Thomas Mifflin's writing, DNA:PCC, item 152; copy, DNA:PCC, item 169; copy, NjMoNP; Varick transcript, DLC:GW. Mifflin's copy was enclosed in GW to Hancock, 12 Oct. 1775. None of the manuscripts have datelines, but the version of this document printed in Force, *American Archives*, 4th ser., 3:633–34, closes: "Given under my hand, at Head-Quarters, *Cambridge*, this second day of *September*, 1775. GEORGE WASHINGTON." GW gave almost identical instructions to Sion Martindale on 8 Oct. 1775 (DS, in Thomas Mifflin's writing, P.R.O.: Adm 1/485) and to William Coit on 22 Oct. 1775 (DS [photocopy], in Thomas Mifflin's writing, DLC:GW).

Nicholson Broughton (1724–1798), an experienced shipmaster from Marblehead, became a captain in Col. John Glover's Massachusetts regiment on 19 May 1775. It was probably Glover, a fellow townsman and longtime business associate, who chose Broughton to command the *Hannah*, a 78–ton schooner formerly used in the West Indies trade which Glover leased to the Continental army on 24 Aug. for conversion into a warship. The first of several armed vessels that GW sent out to intercept British supply ships and troop transports, the *Hannah* sailed from Beverly on 5 Sept. and the next day recaptured an American merchant vessel (Broughton to GW, 7, 9 Sept. 1775). On 10 Oct. the *Hannah* ran aground while trying to evade a British warship, and although rescued, the *Hannah* was retired from military service soon afterward. Broughton took command of the armed schooner *Hancock* about 16 Oct. and a few days later sailed in company with the armed schooner *Franklin*, commanded by John Selman, to the mouth of the St. Lawrence River to intercept British powder ships (GW's instructions to Broughton, 16 Oct. 1775). The two captains missed the powder ships and subsequently displeased GW by seizing Canadian officials and property in violation of his orders to them (Phillip Callbeck and Thomas Wright to GW; GW to Hancock, both 7 Dec. 1775). Reprimanded by GW, Broughton and Selman resigned their Continental commissions in December. During 1776 Broughton participated in the New York campaign as major of Col. Timothy Pickering's Massachusetts militia regiment. He later served on a privateer that was captured by the British and spent some time in an English prison before securing his release and returning to America.

1. The Mifflin copy includes the ship's surgeon, who was also allowed four shares.

From Clark & Nightingale

Sir

Providence Septr 2d 1775

Agreeable to your request by Captn George Baylor your Excellency's Aid De Camp[1] we have deliver'd him all the Gun Powder & Lead with what arms his Honr Govr Cooke thought would be expedient to spare, the remainder of the Powder & Arms which are but few & not yet come to Town, he thinks will be best to continue here in order to supply the Inhabitants in case of an Attack upon these parts.

As our vessel is not arrived here, & we have not been able to obtain the Captns Accounts with respect to the voyage[2] we can not asscertain our proportion of these articles, The Provincial Congress of the Massachusets Bay being equally concerned with us in them, they having advanced four thousand Dollars to which we put the like sum to be invested in Military Stores if they could be procured, It will therefore be intirely out of our power to have this Matter adjusted till the Captns arrival; for which reason we must request your Excellency to inform Colo. Benj. Lincoln (to whom we wrote) as he was formerly one of the Committee of Supplies & now one of the Councel of the Massachussets Bay & the person with whom we contracted, that you have the Powder & Lead dld to you, & that the arms & five thousand flints will be sent by the first opportunity, for which your Excellency will please to settle with them, as soon as they know the amot which shall be, as immediately on the Captns arrival,[3] we are with due respect Your Excellency's Most Obedient & Most Obliged humble Servants

Clark & Nightingale

LS, DLC:GW.

1. See GW to Clark & Nightingale, 31 Aug. 1775.

2. The company's vessel, commanded by John Burroughs Hopkins (1742–1796), arrived at Norwich on 28 Aug., and most of the cargo was forwarded to Providence by land (Nicholas Cooke to GW, 30 Aug. 1775). Hopkins, a resi-

dent of Providence, served as a captain in the Continental navy from 22 Dec. 1775 to sometime in 1779, when, despite his success in taking several prizes, he was suspended from the Continental service for violating his instructions. During the following two years Hopkins commanded privateers.

3. In a letter to Benjamin Lincoln written on 7 Sept., Joseph Reed quotes the second paragraph of Clark & Nightingale's letter of this date and goes on to say: "I am now by the General's direction to acquaint you that 7298 lb. Nt Powder & 6 ct. 2 qt 3 lb. Lead have been received by the Commissary of Artillery of the Continental Army for which he will account with this Province whenever the Papers will enable him so to do" (DLC:GW). GW wrote Hancock on 7 Sept. that he had received 7,000 pounds of gunpowder from Clark & Nightingale and expected to receive 7 tons of lead and 500 firearms.

From Nicholas Cooke

Sir Providence September 2d 1775

I am favoured with your Excellency's Letter of the 31st of last Month by Captain Baylor; who hath purchased the warlike Stores imported by Messrs Clarke and Nightingale. The Prices appear to be very high; but considering the Cost, Expences, & Risque, I believe they are as low as can be reasonably expected.[1]

In the Letter I did myself the Honor to write you by Mr Brown I mentioned the extreme Scarcity of Tow Cloth in the Colony.[2] There is indeed none to be purchased.

The Committee appointed to act during the Recess of the General Assembly have given your Proposal, for taking the Powder from Bermuda, a full Consideration, and have come to a Resolution to make the Attempt. Capt. Abraham Whipple, the Commodore of the Two arrived Vessels in the Service of this Colony, who hath been very ill, but is now upon the Recovery, hath been consulted, and will undertake the Enterprize as soon as his Health will permit. He is deemed the most suitable Person to conduct it that we have.[3] He requests your Excellency to give him a Line under your Hand assuring the People of Bermuda that, in Case of their Assistance, you will recommend it to the Continental Congress to permit them to fetch Provisions for the Use of the Island. He does not purpose to make any Use of it unless he shall find it utterly impracticable to obtain the Powder without their Assistance.[4] I am, with much Esteem and Respect, Sir Your most obedient humble Servant

Nichols Cooke

LS, DLC:GW; copy, RHi: Cooke Papers.

1. See Clark & Nightingale to GW, this date.

2. See Cooke to GW, 30 Aug. 1775. The bearer was Joseph Brown.

3. Abraham Whipple (1733–1819) of Providence commanded a privateer during the French and Indian War, and in 1772 he led a party of Patriots who burned the British revenue cutter *Gaspée*. The Rhode Island general assembly on 12 June 1775 made Whipple commodore of the colony's two-vessel fleet. Whipple sailed for Sandy Hook on 12 Sept. to attempt to intercept a British packet ship and several days later proceeded to Bermuda. He returned to Providence on 20 Oct. (Cooke to GW, 9, 14, 15, 26, 29 Sept., 25 Oct. 1775). On 22 Dec. 1775 Congress appointed Whipple a captain in the Continental navy, and he subsequently made several cruises, taking a number of valuable prizes. Assuming command of the naval defenses of Charleston in late 1779, Whipple served throughout the siege of the city and was taken prisoner the following May when the American defenders surrendered to the British.

4. See Address to the Inhabitants of Bermuda, and GW to Cooke, both 6 Sept. 1775.

From the Pennsylvania Committee of Safety

Sir Philadelphia September 2nd 1775

We receiv'd last night Mr Reeds Letter of the 24th ult. respecting Major French & the Gentn made Prisoners with him & you will find by what we wrote by Capt. Willing & Capt. Wharton, those Prisoners were sent off for your Camp long before the receipt of this letter,[1] The Cloathing taken with them we had declared in a Certificate given Major French was detained untill the meeting of Congress on the 5th of this month to be disposed of as they may direct, consequently we cannot Consistantly send it forward without their order, but we will lay the matter before them the first day of their meeting and follow such directions as they think proper to give.[2] It is with great concern we learn your want of further supplys of Powder & altho. we are farr from being well provided for our own defence; Yet being extreamly anxious to promote your success, We dispatch herewith Two Tons of Powder which we hope will arrive safe & soon to your Command.[3] We are Sir Your Obedient humble Servts

Signed by order & on behalf of the Committee of Safety

Robt Morris, President pro tempore[4]

LS, DLC:GW.

1. Joseph Reed wrote the committee on 24 Aug.: "Several Letters from Philada having mentioned the Capture of Major French & some other Gentlemen & that you proposed to send them forward to this Camp: General Washington has directed me to request that you would order them to Hartford or some other Inland Town, as their coming hither would be attended with many Inconveniencies. If there have been any late Arrivals of Powder it is of the utmost Importance to forward as soon as possible all that can be spared from the necessary Defence of the Province—It is not within the Limits or Propriety of a Letter to enumerate our Difficulties in the Article of Ammunition. The late Supply was very seasonable but far short of our Necessities. It is also the Generals Opinion that the Cloathing lately intercepted should be secured & forwarded hither as soon as possible. The Army is in a very destitute Situation in this Respect & such a Supply would greatly relieve it" (DNA:PCC, item 169). The committee's letter to GW by captains Richard Willing and John Wharton was apparently the one of 17 August.

2. A list of the military clothing captured on the British ship *Hope* was appended to the committee's certificate of 12 Aug. (*Pa. Col. Records*, 10:303–4). See also Pennsylvania Committee of Safety to GW, 17 Aug. 1775, nn. 1 and 3. The committee resolved on 12 Aug. that the clothing "shall be stored 'till this Committee shall receive directions from the Continental Congress for the disposal of the same, unless it may be thought necessary by this Committee, before the meeting of the said Congress, to remove or otherwise dispose of them" (ibid., 304). On 14 Sept. Congress read Reed's letter to the Philadelphia committee of 24 Aug. and resolved "that the . . . cloathing be immediately forwarded, under a proper guard, by the delegates for Pensylvania, to Genl Washington, for the use of the American Army" (*JCC*, 2:248).

3. The committee resolved on 2 Sept. "that two tons of Gun Powder be immediately sent to his Excellency General Washington, and that William Jordan go with and take proper care of the Powder, until he has directions from the General" (*Pa. Col. Records*, 10:330).

4. Robert Morris (1734–1806), a partner in Willing, Morris & Co. of Philadelphia, was one of America's wealthiest merchants. Elected to the Pennsylvania committee of safety on 30 June 1775, he frequently presided at meetings in the absence of committee president Benjamin Franklin. Morris served in the Continental Congress from November 1775 to November 1778 and played a prominent role in supplying the army and managing the finances of the war. From May 1781 to September 1784 he was superintendent of finance. GW may have dined at Morris's mansion on the Schuylkill River in May 1773 and certainly did on 4 June 1775 (*Diaries*, 3:181, 334).

Instructions to Nathaniel Tracy

Head Quarters [Cambridge] Septr 2. 1775

You are hereby authorized & impowered to take up for the Service of the sd Colonies so many Vessels as shall be necessary for the transporting a Body of Troops to be detached from this Army on a secret Expedition:[1] Freight of such Vessels to be paid in such a Manner and at such a Rate as is indorsed hereon: And in Case of Loss or Damage to such Vessels or any of them such Loss or Damage to be compensated by the Publick according to an Estimation to be made before the sd Vessels proceed in the above Service.[2]

G. Washington

Df, in Joseph Reed's writing, DLC:GW; Varick transcript, DLC:GW.

Nathaniel Tracy (1751–1796) was a prominent merchant in Newburyport, Massachusetts. During the Revolution he outfitted a large number of privateers and for a time achieved considerable wealth. Tracy was bankrupt by 1786, however.

1. Benedict Arnold needed transports to take his expeditionary force to the Kennebec River, up which he planned to march toward Quebec. For Arnold's expedition, see GW to Schuyler, 20 Aug. 1775, n.6, and General Orders, 5 Sept. 1775. On 7 Sept. Joseph Reed wrote to Tracy: "Colo. [John] Glover has just informed the General that there are 5 Vessells at Beverly & two at Newbury which were fitted out for another Purpose, but will answer the Present equally well—as they are completely equipp'd with Platforms, Wood, Water &c.—It will be a saving both in Time & Expence to make Use of these, You will therefore be pleased in your Transaction of this Matter to consider these seven Vessells as a Part of the Transports, & only extend your Care to the Remainder. Whatever Expence may have accrued in preparing any Vessells which will not be necessary by this Arrangement must be carried to the General Account. But you will be careful not to add any Thing to it after this Comes to hand" (DLC:GW). Arnold's force sailed from Newburyport aboard eleven transports on 19 Sept. and landed at Gardiner, District of Maine, three days later.

2. On the reverse of this draft Joseph Reed wrote "To prevent any Disputes which may arise respecting the Freight of the within Vessels it is agreed that Col: [Azor] Orne of Marblehead with two other Persons to be nominated by him fix the Price which shall be binding on both Parties and that the sam Gentlemen do appraise the Vessels before they proceed. J. Reed Secy &c."

To Jonathan Trumbull, Sr.

Sir Camp at Cambridge, September 2d 1775

I am to acknowledge the Receipt of your Favour of the 21st Ult: with the Inclosures. By my last Letters from Ticonderoga, I expect a Quantity of Lead, will be forwarded soon to your Care from thence. In the mean Time, I am glad to hear there are such Prospects of a Supply of that Article, from the Mines in your Colony: I make no Doubt, they will receive such Encouragement both publick & private, as their Importance & Value demand.

By the Time you receive this Letter, you will be able to judge with some Certainty, whether the Fleet which last sailed from Boston, was destined for your Coasts, if it is not yet arrived, we may conclude it has sailed to the Eastward—if it has arrived, the Issue will be known immediately; so that in either Case, the Continuance of the new raised Levies along the Coast is unnecessary[.][1] You will therefore on the Receipt of this, be pleased to order them to march immediately to this Camp, directing the commanding Officer at the same Time to give me two or 3 Days Notice of the Time in which the Troops will arrive that suitable Accomodations may be prepared—Their Presence is the more necessary as I may in Confidence inform you that I am about to detach 1000 or 1200 Men on an Expedition into Canada by Way of Kennebeck River from which I have the greatest Reason to expect either that Quebeck will fall into our Hands a very easy Prey or such a Diversion made as will open a very easy Passage to General Schuyler.[2]

We are now so well secured in our late advanced Post on the Hill, that the Enemy have discontinued their Cannonade.[3] The Men continue in good Health & Spirits. I am with much Regard & Esteem Sir, Your very Obedt & most humble Servt

Go: Washington

LS, in Joseph Reed's writing, The American University of Beirut, Lebanon; LB, Ct: Trumbull Papers; Df, NHi: Joseph Reed Papers; LB, DLC:GW; Varick transcript, DLC:GW.

1. This fleet sailed to the Bay of Fundy. See GW to Trumbull, 23 Aug. 1775. The new Connecticut levies belonged to the regiments commanded by colonels Charles Webb and Jedediah Huntington. See Trumbull to GW, 17 July 1775, n.1.

2. For Benedict Arnold's expedition, see GW to Schuyler, 20 Aug. 1775, n.6, and General Orders, 5 Sept. 1775.

3. For an account of the occupation of Plowed Hill on 26 Aug., see GW to Richard Henry Lee, 29 Aug. 1775, n.6.

To Brigadier General David Wooster

Sir Camp at Cambridge September 2d 1775

I have just received your Favour of the 29th ult: by Express. I am very sensible that the Situation of the Inhabitants of Long Island, as well as of all those on the Coast, exposes them greatly to the Ravages of the Enemy; & it is to be wished General Protection could be extended to them, consistent with the Prosecution of those great Plans, which have been adopted for the common Safety. This was early foreseen, & the Danger provided for by a Resolution of Congress, that each Province should depend on its own internal Strength against these Incursions:[1] the Prejudice arising from them (even if successful) not being equal to that of separating the Army into a Number of small Detachments, who would be harassed in fruitless Marches, & Countermarches after an Enemy whose Conveyance, by Shipping is so advantageous, that they might keep the whole Coast in constant Alarm without our being able perhaps at any Time to give them vigorous Opposition. Upon this Principle I have invariably rejected every Application made me here, to keep any Detachments on the Coast for these Purposes.[2] I should therefore most probably have thought it my Duty to have ordered the three Companies mentioned in your Letter, to have joined your Army to act in the general Service, had they not been under Command from General Schuyler to join him: But as it is, I can by no Means interfere: He is engaged in a Service of the greatest Importance to the whole Continent, his Strength & Appointments far short of his Expectations, and to give any Counterorders may not only defeat his whole Plan, but must make me responsible to the Publick for the Failure. Instead therefore of their further Stay, I would have them march immediately, I fear, the Delay of the Ten Days may have very bad Effects as by my last Advices from Ticonderoga Genl Schuyler was to march in a few Days for Canada,[3] & it is highly probable, he may depend upon these Companies to occupy the Posts of Communication, which otherwise he must weaken his Army to do.

No Provincial Congress can with any Propriety interfere in the Disposition of Troops on the Continental Establishment, much less controul the Orders of any General Officer, so that in this Instance the Congress at New York have judged properly in declining to counteract General Schuylers Orders. I wish I could extend my Approbation equally to the whole Line of their Conduct.

Before you receive this Letter you will most probably be able to judge how far your Continuance on Long Island will be farther necessary.[4] If the Fleet which last sailed was destined for those Coasts, it must be arrived—if it is not, it is certainly gone to the Eastward, & your present Station is no longer necessary. The Importance of preserving the Communication of the North River,[5] & many other Reasons induce me to wish you were returned to your former Post. The late Transactions at New York, furnish additional Reasons for your being as near that City as is consistent with the Discipline & Convenience of your Troops. Your next therefore I flatter myself will inform me of your having resumed your former Station. I am, Sir, with much Regard & Esteem Your most Obedt & very Hbble Servt

Go: Washington

LS, in Joseph Reed's writing, CSmH; LB, DLC:GW; Varick transcript, DLC:GW.

1. For Congress's resolution, see GW to James Warren, 30 July 1775, n.2.

2. For the Massachusetts General Court's request for assistance in defending the coast, see ibid., n.1.

3. For a discussion of the march of Schuyler's army, see Schuyler to GW, 31 Aug. 1775, n.2.

4. For the sailing of this fleet, see GW to Jonathan Trumbull, Sr., 23 Aug. 1775. Wooster and his men returned to their camp at Harlem on 12 September.

5. The Hudson River is often referred to as the North River.

General Orders

Head Quarters, Cambridge, Sept. 3rd 1775

Parole, Roxbury. Countersign, Schenectady:

Benjamin Child Soldier in Col. Glovers Regiment, and in Capt. Broughton's Company, tried by a General Court Martial, upon an Appeal from a Regimental Court Martial: The Court were unanimously of opinion the proceedings of the regimental Court was irregular and therefore acquit the prisoner.

Varick transcript, DLC:GW.

Instructions to Reuben Colburn

[Cambridge, 3 September 1775]

You are to go with all Expedition to Gardnerstone upon the River Kenebeck, and without Delay proceed to The Constructing of Two Hundred Batteaus, to row with Four Oars each; Two Paddles and Two setting Poles to be also provided for each Batteau.

You are to Engage a Company of Twenty Men consisting of Artificers, Carpenters, and Guides to go under your Command to Assist in such Services as you, & they, may be called upon to Execute.

You are to Purchase Five Hundred Bushells of Indian Corn, to Provide the Workmen employ'd on Building The Batteaus.

You are to bespeak all The Pork, and Flour, you can from the Inhabitants upon the River Kennebeck, & a Commissary will be immediately sent from the Commissary General, to agree, and pay for the same; You will also acquaint The Inhabitants, that The Commissary will have Orders to Purchase Sixty Barrells of Salted Beef, of Two hundred & Twenty pounds each Barrell.

You are to receive Forty Shillings Lawfull Money for each Batteau, with the Oars, Paddles, and Setting Poles included, out of which, you are also to pay The Artificers, & for all the Provisions, Nails &ca they shall expend.[1] Given at Head Quarters at Cambridge this 3d day of September 1775

Go: Washington
By The Generals Command
Horatio Gates Adjt Genl

DS, in Horatio Gates's writing, DNA: RG 233, 22d Congress, folder 22A-G20.1. This document is entitled "Orders for Mr Rheuben Colbourn of Gardnerstone, upon the River Kennebeck in The Province of Massachusetts Bay."

Reuben Colburn of Gardiner (Gardinerston), District of Maine, arrived at Cambridge on 13 Aug. with Swashan, the chief of the St. Francis Indians, who offered his services to GW. See GW to Schuyler, 14 Aug. 1775, n.1. On 21 Aug. Benedict Arnold, who was then preparing for his expedition to Quebec, wrote to Colburn from Watertown: "His Excellency General Washington Desires you will Inform your self, how soon, there can be procured, or built, at Kenebec; Two hundred light Battoes Capable of Carrying Six or Seven Men each with their Provisions & Baggage, (say 100 wt to each man) the Boats to be furnished with four Oars two Paddles & two Setting Poles each, the expence of Building them & wheather a Sufficient quantity of Nails can be procured with you. you will Also inquire, what quantity of Fresh Beef can be procured at Kenebec, & the price. at Newbury you will Inquire the Size, & Strength of the two Armed Vessells, If Compleated, & wheather, bound on a Cruise or not. Also the Condition the Armed Vessells are in at Kenebec—you will Also get particular Information, from those People who have been at Quebec, of the Difuculty attending an Expedition that way, in particular the Number, & length, of the Carrying Places, wheather Over, Dry land, Hills, or Swamp. Also the Depth of Water in the River at this Season, wheather An easy Stream or Raised—Also, every other Intelligence which you Judge may be necessary to know, all which you will Commit to writing & Dispatch an express to his Excellency as soon as posable, who will Pay the Charge & expence you may be at in the Matter" (DNA: RG 233, 22d Congress, folder 22A-G20.1). Between 21 Aug. and 3 Sept. Colburn apparently went to Gardiner to obtain the information requested in Arnold's letter and returned to Cambridge to report to GW. After receiving GW's instructions of this date, Colburn again went to Gardiner. When Arnold arrived there on 21 Sept., he found the bateaux and provisions that he had requested ready for his expedition.

1. For Colburn's bills for these and other items, see Justin H. Smith, *Arnold's March from Cambridge to Quebec: A Critical Study Together with a Reprint of Arnold's Journal* (New York and London, 1903), 293–96.

From Major Christopher French

Sir Framingham [Mass.] 3d Sept. 1775

I am just now favor'd with a Letter from Mr Reed, enclosing me a Letter from you which informs me of your having been so kind as to forward the Letters I had the Honor to enclose you from Philadelphia, for which please to accept my Thanks.

In that from Mr Reed, who I presume is your Secretary, 'though not so sign'd, he tells me I am to return to Hartford with the Gentlemen who are Prisoners of War with me by your Order.[1] I chearfully submit, as do these Gentlemen, but must observe that when I gave my Parole it was conditionally, & that we might be sent to Cambridge in order to be the nearer for an Exchange whenever it might offer. These Sir were the Terms offer'd me by the Committee of safety & upon these Terms, & these only I consented rather than accept the alternative of remaining Prisoner at Philadelphia; I must farther offer to your Justice & knowledge of military Rules that before I would sign to my Parole, or let the two young Gentlemen (Novices in these matters) do it, I objected to our being by any means consider'd as Prisoners, first because we came to America unknowing of any Hostilities having been commenc'd, secondly that in case we had arriv'd, having heard of it at Sea, the Custom of War allots a certain Period for the departure of the ships & Subjects of the inimicable Nation; neither of these Reasons however had sufficient Weight with the Committee (though I must say I am of opinion they should) to prevent their considering us as Prisoners, under which Circumstance it was that we agreed to give our Paroles, which having been once given we are determin'd to preserve inviolably, & therefore I presume it will be unnecessary to renew them at Hartford,[2] and the more so as we flatter ourselves the cogency of the Reasons I have offer'd will incline you to have us return'd to our Regts without an Exchange being expected.[3] I have the Honor to be Sir your most obedient and most humble Servant

Chris. French

ALS, DLC:GW.

1. Joseph Reed wrote to French on this date: "By Direction of General Washington I herewith send you a Copy of a Letter he wrote you on Thursday last [31 Aug.] ℔ Post. General Gage has rejected in very indecent and illiberal Terms a Proposition made to him some Time ago respecting Officers who were Prisoners, so that your Hopes of being exchanged or even having an Interview with any of your Friends would not be answer'd by proceeding to this Place, as Genl Howe last Week desired all Intercourse between the Two Camps might be at an End—General Gage's Treatment of our Officers even of the most respectable Rank would justify a severe Retaliation—They have perished in a common Goal under the Hands of a Wretch who had never before been employ'd but in the Diseases of Horses. General Washington's Disposition will not allow him to follow so unworthy an Example. You and your Companions will be treated with Kindness, and upon renewing your Parole at Hartford you will have the Same Indulgence as other Gentlemen under the like Circumstances. Capt. [Samuel Blachley] Webb has Orders to accompany You to Hartford, & is particularly enjoined to shew you every Mark of Civility & Respect: It is not doubted but that you and the other Gentlemen will make his Duty easy" (DLC:GW). Reed's instructions to Webb of this date regarding French and his companions are in the Samuel Blachley Webb Papers, Webb Family Collection, Yale University. Reed also wrote on this date to Capt. John Wharton and to the Hartford committee of safety regarding the return of the prisoners to Hartford (DLC:GW). For GW's dispute with Gage over the treatment of prisoners, see GW to Gage, 11, 19 Aug. 1775, and Gage to GW, 13 Aug. 1775. For Howe's request for an end to communication between his camp and GW's, see Howe to GW, 22 Aug. 1775, and GW to Howe, 23 Aug. 1775.

2. For the parole that French and his companions, Ens. John Rotten and

Cadet Terrence McDermot, signed for the Pennsylvania committee of safety on 12 Aug., see Pennsylvania Committee of Safety to GW, 17 Aug. 1775, n.2. Joseph Reed enclosed a copy of that parole in his letter to the Hartford committee of safety of this date, observing that it was limited to the prisoners going to Cambridge. "As this may not now be deemed binding," Reed wrote, "it is the Gens. Intention they should renew it before they are admitted to the Same Liberty with the other Prisoners at Hartford—That being done General Washington requests they may be treated with Kindness & Civility" (DLC:GW).

3. Joseph Reed replied to French on 19 Sept.: "The General has directed me to acquaint you that on the fullest Consideration he is of Opinion that your Detention is both justifiable & proper. While the Appellation of Rebel is supposed to Sanctify every Species of Perfidy & Cruelty towards the Inhabitants of America, it would be a Strange Missapplication of Military Rules to enlarge Such Gentlemen as may think themselves bound by a mistaken Notion of Duty to become the Instruments of our Ruin" (DLC:GW).

Letter not found: from John Sullivan, 3 Sept. 1775. On 4 Sept. GW wrote to Sullivan: "I receivd your Letter of yesterday."

General Orders

Head Quarters, Cambridge, Sept. 4th 1775.

Parole Torrington. Countersign Urbanna

Varick transcript, DLC:GW.

From Penuel Cheney

Camp at Cambridge Septr 4th 1775

May it Please your Excellency.

as I was appointed by the Genl Assembly of the Colony of Connecticutt Surgeon's mate in Genl Putnams Regiment, and have faithfully served therein, 'til the late Appointment of Doctr Church, by the Continental Congress, Superintendant of the Hospital of the American Army, by which the sole Care of the sick and Wounded hath devolved on him, which hath rendered the Appointment of Regimental Doctors, or at least more than one, Useless and of no service: and as I am sure it was not for the sake of Interest that induced me to Join the Army: but for the Benefit of the Regiment the good of my Cuntry and the noble Cause in which this Army & Continent are now ingaged I would therefore humbly beseech your Excellency to discharge me from any future Attendence on said Regiment,[1] which is the Prayer of your Excellency's most Obedt Humble Servt

Penuel Cheney

ALS, DLC:GW. At the bottom of this letter Israel Putnam wrote "The above is consented to By me. Israel Putnam M.G."

1. Cheney's real reason for leaving the army was to avoid being court-martialed on charges of making illegal drafts on the commissary. See General Orders, 22 July 1775, n.1, and GW to Jonathan Trumbull, Sr., 29 Oct. 1775.

To the Massachusetts Council

Gentlemen Camp at Cambridge Septemr 4th 1775

Col. Sergeant has applied to me for his Commission in the Continental Army, & I have no Objection to comply with his Request but his not having received one under the Legislature of this Province. But as I do not mean to confine myself to Forms, if he has been considered by this Governmt as an Officer authorized to raise a Regiment, & would have received a Commission on the Provincial Establishment, and you will signify this to me for my Government & Security: I shall make no Difficulty to grant a Commission to him on the same Terms as are prescribed to other Officers.[1] I am Gentlemen most respectfully Your Obedt & very Hbble Servt

Go: Washington

LS, in Joseph Reed's writing, M-Ar: Revolution Letters; LB, DLC:GW; Varick transcript, DLC:GW. The LS is endorsed "In Council Septr 5th 1775 Read & Committed to Jno. Whetcomb Jedh Foster & Jabez Fisher Esqr. P. Morton Dpy Secry."

1. In its letter to GW of 3 Oct., the council authorized GW to give commissions to Paul Dudley Sargent and the other officers of his regiment. The council's response to GW's request was delayed because the General Court was in recess from 24 Aug. to 20 September.

To Brigadier General John Sullivan

Dr Sir, Camp at Cambridge Septr 4. 1775

I receivd your Letter of yesterday respecting Lieutt Sanborn, as also his application for a discharge—As it is not my wish to strain the Law to its full extent, but to exercise it in such a manner as to prevent irregularities, & for the support of due subordination, without which no army can long exist; & as Lieutt Sanborn stands fair in the opinion & esteem of both Officers and Soldiers, and seems by his application, to be thoroughly convinced of his error I shall have no objection to overlooking this (you say) first fault, provided Colo. Poor who confined him does not (as I think he has a right to do) insist upon his tryal—I must insist however before you do dismiss him, that you will give him a reprimand, and moreover, that you return my thanks to Colo. Poor for his vigilance & attention to the Service, shewed in this Instance; if all Officers would use their endeavours to enforce Orders, duty would go smoothly on, & we should soon be a very respectable Army.[1] I am with great esteem Dr Sir Yr Most Obedt Servt

Go: Washington

ALS, MAnP.

1. Neither Sullivan's letter of 3 Sept. nor Sanborn's application has been found. Lieutenant Sanborn was either Aaron Sanborn (born c.1743), a first lieutenant in Col. Enoch Poor's New Hampshire regiment, or Abraham Sanborn, a second lieutenant in that regiment. Both officers remained in the Continental army until the end of 1775. During the ensuing campaign Abraham Sanborn served as a first lieutenant in Col. Thomas Tash's regiment of New Hampshire militia.

Letter not found: to Lund Washington, 4 Sept. 1775. On 15 Oct. 1775 Lund Washington wrote to GW: "In your Letter of the 7th you mention haveg wrote one on the 4th."

General Orders

Head Quarters, Cambridge, Sept. 5th 1775

Parole, Waltham. Countersign, York.

The General Court Martial whereof Col. Experience Stors[1] was president is dissolved: Capt. Moses Hart of the 28th Regiment of foot, tried by the above mentioned Genl Court martial, is found guilty of "drawing for more provisions than he was entitled to, & for unjustly confining, and abusing his men"; he is unanimously sentenced to be cashiered—The General approves the sentence, and orders it to take place immediately.[2]

A Detachment consisting of two Lieut. Colonels, two Majors, ten Captains, thirty Subalterns, thirty Serjeants, thirty Corporals, four Drummers, two Fifers, and six hundred and seventy six privates; to parade to morrow morning at eleven O'Clock, upon the Common, in Cambridge, to go upon Command with Col: Arnold of Connecticut; one Company of Virginia Riflemen and two Companies from Col. Thompson's Pennsylvania Regiment of Rifle-men, to parade at the same time and place, to join the above Detachment:[3] Tents and Necessaries proper and convenient for the whole, will be supplied by the Quarter Master Genl immediately upon the Detachment being collected—As it is imagined the Officers and Men sent from the Regiments both here, and at Roxbury, will be such Volunteers, as are active Woodsmen, and well acquainted with batteaus; so it is recommended, that none but such will offer themselves for this service—Col. Arnold and the Adjutant General will attend upon the Common, in Cambridge, to morrow in the forenoon, to receive and parade the detachment—The Quarter Master General will be also there to supply tents &c.

The Colonels and commanding Officers of the Massachusetts regiments, who have deliver'd in their pay abstracts at Head Quarters, are immediately to apply to the General for his Warrant upon the Pay Master General, James Warren Esqr. for the pay for the month of August; agreeable to the General Order of the 31st of last month.

As great Complaints have heretofore been made, by the men in regard to their pay; The General expects the utmost exactness, and dispatch be made in this payment.

Varick transcript, DLC:GW.

1. Experience Storrs (1734–1801) of Mansfield, lieutenant colonel of the 3d Connecticut Regiment, served as regimental commander because the regiment's colonel, Israel Putnam, was a Continental major general. Storrs left the Continental army at the end of 1775 but commanded a Connecticut militia regiment in the New York campaign of 1776.

2. A captain in Col. Paul Dudley Sargent's Massachusetts regiment, Moses Hart of Lynn had not received a Continental commission prior to this time (GW to the Massachusetts Council, 4 Sept. 1775; Massachusetts Council to GW, 3 Oct. 1775).

3. Benedict Arnold's force left Cambridge between 11 and 13 September. For Arnold's expedition to Quebec, see GW to Schuyler, 20 Aug. 1775, n.6. The company of Virginia riflemen that marched with Arnold was commanded

by Capt. Daniel Morgan. Captains William Hendricks and Matthew Smith commanded the two Pennsylvania rifle companies. Col. William Thompson (1736–1781) of Carlisle served as a captain under John Armstrong on the Kittanning expedition in 1756, and on 25 June 1775 he was commissioned colonel of the rifle companies raised in Pennsylvania. By virtue of the early date of his commission in the French and Indian War, Thompson became senior colonel in the Continental army, and on 1 Mar. 1776 Congress promoted him to brigadier general. Thompson commanded the American troops at the defeat at Trois Rivières on 8 June 1776. Captured on the field by the British, he was soon paroled but was not exchanged until October 1780.

From Jonathan Trumbull, Sr.

Sir Lebanon [Conn.] 5th September 1775.

Your Excellency's favour of the 2nd instant was delivered to me last night; This afternoon received Genl Schuyler's of the 31st August—He has ordered the Lead to Albany with directions to forward it by the most direct route to your Camp.[1]

We are infested by Ministerial Ships and Transports—I gave your Commissary General a Narrative yesterday—beg leave to refer you to him, from the haste of this Express—Our Coasts are kept in continual Alarm, Three Ships of War with thirteen other Vessels of divers sorts were seen off Fisher's Island and in the Sound yesterday, they have gained no provisions from the Main—have heard nothing from Montaug or any part of Long-Island—New London is in great fears, and Stonington expect another Attack[2]—I have Ordered The new raised Levies to Guard and defend those two places, and the Coasts as far as Connecticut River—there are likewise four Companies of them beyond the river for Defence in those parts—This appears absolutely necessary for their Security at present—Hope this use of them 'till these dangers are over, will neither injure or hinder any of your Operations.[3]

Whether these are the same Ships your Excellency noticed us off remains uncertain—Yesterday Ordered the best intelligence to be gained to render that matter more certain.[4]

Lords day morning, constrained by the Weather, came into the Harbour at New London, a Schooner taken by the Rose, Capt. Wallace at Stonington four hands on board, One a White Man sent to Windham Goal, the Other Three Negroes, two belonging to Govr Cook, & one to Newport—Ordered to be returned to their Masters—And The Schooner to her Owner[5]—General Schuyler's Army is moved forward, a few days will determine the Event.[6]

I have Ordered our Commissaries in the Several Counties to send to your Camp all the Hunting Shirts they can procure.[7] I am, with great Esteem and Regard Sir Your very Obedient and most Humble Servant

Jonth. Trumbull

ALS, DLC:GW; LB, Ct: Trumbull Papers; copy, CtHi: Trumbull Papers. The copy at the Connecticut Historical Society is endorsed "Sent ℘ Bennet."

1. For Schuyler's orders regarding the lead at Crown Point, see Schuyler to GW, 31 Aug. 1775.

2. British warships attacked Stonington on 30 August. Hearing that the Rhode Island general assembly had ordered all livestock to be taken off Block Island, Capt. James Wallace of the British warship *Rose* set out on 29 Aug. with his ship and three armed tenders to stop the removal. Near Block Island that evening the tenders began chasing an American sloop and schooner and on the morning of 30 Aug. pursued them into Stonington Harbor. "The Tenders," Wallace later reported, "returned and acquainted me, the Town fired upon them. We stood in, the Tenders going ahead. One of the Tenders attempting to board a Vessel, a firing begun from the Town, the Tenders returned it, about this time we came to an Anchor off the South end of the Town—the Tender and the Town continuing the fire, About 10 Minutes after we were at an Anchor we received three or four Musket Shot from the Windmill, . . . upon which I ordered one of our Guns to be fired into the Town, and waited some time expecting that would put a stop to it—They took no Notice but continued firing from all parts of the Town—Then we began and fired about 120 Shot. . . . At the beginning of this Action there was about 300 Rebels in the Town, at the latter end more than 3,000 Skulking behind Hills and Rocks and fences. All the Country about came in" (Wallace to Samuel Graves, 9 Sept. 1775, in Clark, *Naval Documents*, 2:58–59). The inhabitants of Stonington claimed that the British attack was unprovoked. The *Boston-Gazette, and Country Journal*, 4 Sept. 1775, reported that when the American vessels entered the harbor on the morning of 30 Aug., a local pilot tried to help them and was told by one of the British tenders to desist. "He returned for Answer, he might do as he pleased: Immediately the Tender ran alongside of the Wharves, and fired a whole Broadside on the Town and People, which was returned by a Volley of Small Arms from the People." For a report of the sighting of the *Rose* and other vessels off Fisher's Island on 1 and 2 Sept., see *Connecticut Journal* (New Haven), 13 Sept. 1775.

3. The new levies were those belonging to the regiments commanded by colonels Charles Webb and Jedediah Huntington. See Trumbull to GW, 17 July 1775, n.1. On 4 Sept. Governor Trumbull and his council ordered two companies and a part of another one "to be stationed at or near Stonington harbor; and the other companies to remain at New London, under Maj.

[Jonathan] Lattimer; and the soldiers at both places were directed to make such intrenchments and works of defence as should be directed by the civil authority and field officers in those towns" (Hinman, *Historical Collection*, 332). For GW's overruling of these orders, see GW to Trumbull, 8 Sept. 1775.

4. Trumbull is referring to the British fleet that GW mentioned in his letter to Trumbull of 23 Aug. 1775. The fleet went to the Bay of Fundy.

5. Captain Wallace wrote Samuel Graves on 9 Sept. that he had seized five American vessels in Stonington Harbor: "a Schooner from Surinam loaded with Molasses and Sugar, a Schooner that was Employed carrying the Rebels over to Block Island to take the Stock, . . . a Schooner with Hay and two Sloops" (Clark, *Naval Documents*, 2:58–59). The recaptured schooner was driven into New London Harbor on 3 Sept. by a gale. The third black in the prize crew apparently belonged to John Collins of Newport (Hinman, *Historical Collection*, 332–33).

6. For a discussion of the beginning of Schuyler's invasion of Canada, see Schuyler to GW, 31 Aug. 1775, n.2.

7. For GW's request for hunting shirts for the Continental army, see GW to Trumbull, 4 Aug. 1775.

General Orders

Head Quarters, Cambridge, Sept. 6th 1775

Parole, Albany: Countersign Bolingbroke

Whereas a number of pretended Sutlers utterly disregarding the good of the service, sell Liquor to every one indiscriminately, to the utter subversion of all order and good Government; the Troops being continually debauched, which causes them to neglect their duty, and to be guilty of all those crimes which a vicious, ill habit naturally produces: To prevent such evils from spreading in the Camp: No Person is for the future to presume to sell any Stores, or Liquor to the troops, unless he be first appointed Sutler to some Regiment, by the Colonel or Officer commanding the same, who will immediately punish such Sutler for any Transgression of the Rules and Orders he is directed to observe; And if any Person, not regularly authorized and appointed, shall presume to sell Liquor, or Stores to the Troops in the Camp: It is recommended to the Brigadier General, to issue an order for securing their persons and effects—The Delinquent to be punished at the discretion of a General Court martial and his Effects to be applied for the refreshment of the Fatiguemen, and out Guards belonging to the brigade—This Order is not meant to extend to those Sutlers who are appointed by Government, and who are permitted to act as Sutlers to the regiments for which they were appointed; they being subject to all Rules and Regulations of the army, the same as if appointed by the Colonels.[1]

As the remoteness of some of the regiments from Head Quarters renders it difficult to send invitations to the Officers; The Commander in Chief requests, that for the future, The Field Officer of the day, the Officer of his own guard, and the Adjutant of the day; consider themselves invited to dine at Head Quarters, and this general invitation, they are desired to accept accordingly.

Varick transcript, DLC:GW.

1. For GW's previous orders regarding the sale of liquor and the licensing of sutlers, see General Orders, 11 July and 7 Aug. 1775.

Address to the Inhabitants of Bermuda

Gentlemen [Cambridge, 6 September 1775]

In the great Conflict which agitates this Continent I cannot doubt but the Assertors of Freedom & the Rights of the Constitution are possessed of your most favourable Regards & Wishes for Success. As the Descendants of Freemen & Heirs with us of the same glorious Inheritance we flatter ourselves that tho. divided by our Situation we are firmly united in Sentiment. The Cause of Virtue & Liberty is confined to no Continent or Climate it comprehends within its capacious Limits the wise & the good however dispersed & separated in Space or Distance. You need not be informed that the Violence & Rapacity of a tyrannick Ministry have forced the Citizens of America your Brother Colonists into Arms. We equally detest & lament the Prevalence of those Councils which have led to the Effusion of so much human Blood & left us no Alternative but a Civil War or a base Submission. The wise Disposer of all Events has hitherto smiled upon our virtuous Efforts, those mercenary Troops a few of whom lately boasted of subjugating this vast Continent, have been checked in their earliest Ravages, & are now actually encircled in a small Space their Arms disgraced & suffering all the Calamities of a Siege. The Virtue & Spirit & Union of the Provinces leave them nothing to fear but the Want of Ammunition:

The Applications of our Enemies to foreign States & their Vigilance upon our Coasts are the only Efforts they have made against us with Success. Under these Circumstances & with these Sentiments we have turned our Eyes to you Gentlemen for Relief. We are informed that there is a large Magazine in your Island under a very feeble Guard. We would not wish to involve you in an Opposition in which from your Situation we should be unable to support you, we know not therefore to what Extent to sollicit your Assistance in availing ourselves of this Supply: but if your Favour & Friendship to North America & its Liberties have not been misrepresented I perswade myself you may consistent with your own Safety promote & favour this Scheme so as to give it the fairest Prospect of Success. Be assured that in this Case the whole Power & Exertion of my Influence will be made with the Honourable Continental Congress that your Island may not only be supplied with Provisions but experience every other Mark of Affection & Friendship which the grateful Citizens of a free Country can bestow on its Brethren & Benefactors.[1]

Df, in Joseph Reed's writing, NHi: Reed Papers; LB, DLC:GW; copy, DLC:GW; two Varick transcripts, DLC:GW. The draft does not have a dateline, but it is endorsed "Letter to Inhabitants of Bermudas Sept. 6, 1775." The letter-book copy is dated "Camp at Cambridge 3 Miles from Boston Sept. 6. 1775."

This address was written at the request of Capt. Abraham Whipple, who was preparing to sail to Bermuda in quest of gunpowder for the Continental army (Nicholas Cooke to GW, 2 Sept. 1775). GW enclosed it in his letter of this date to Cooke. For a discussion of the scheme to import gunpowder from Bermuda, see GW to Cooke, 4 Aug. 1775.

1. For a discussion of the arrangement that Bermudians made with Congress, see GW to Cooke, 11 Aug. 1775.

To Nicholas Cooke

Sir Camp at Cambridge Septemr 6th 1775

Your Favours of the 30th August & 2d Instt are duly received. The Concurrence of the Committee in the Bermudas Voyage is very agreeable & I hope will prove a happy Earnest of its Success. Inclosed is a Letter to the Inhabitants of that Island of the Tenor you have suggested: but I shall depend upon

Captn Whipples not making Use of it except in Case of real Necessity.[1]

I am to acknowledge your kind Assistance to Captn Baylor in his late Errand, & must desire you to make known to Messr Clarke & Nightingale that I am very sensible of the patriotick & disinterested Part they have acted on this Occasion.[2]

As the Congress will depend on a Supply of Tow Cloth from your Colony unless they are apprized to the Contrary: I apprehend it will be proper through your Delegates to acquaint them of the State in which you have found this Article, in order to guard against a Disappointment.[3]

The Removal of the Stock from the Coast and Islands will I hope have its Effect in sending the ministerial Plunderers empty home: We have yet no Accounts of the last Fleet, except 6 who returned from Louisburgh with Coal a few Days ago.[4]

I need not mention to you the vast Importance of gaining Intelligence of the Enemy's Motions & Designs as early as possible: a great Saving to the Continent both of Blood & Money; a Detection of our secret & most dangerous Enemies, with innumerable other Advantages would result from the Interception of their Correspondence with England at this Juncture. I have therefore thought proper to propose to you the seizing the Mail by the next Packet: She is hourly expected from England—her Force of Men & Guns inconsiderable; none but Swivels & only mann'd with 18 Men. If the Vessel proposed to go to Bermudas should cruize for a few Days off Sandy Hook I have no Doubt she would fall in with her. In which Case she might with little or no Delay land the Mail in order to be forwarded & proceed on her Voyage: But if there are any material Objections to this Mode I am still so anxious upon the Subject that I would have it tried with another Vessel at the Continental Expence, and will for that End direct that any Charge which may accrue in this Service shall be paid by the Paymaster here upon being duly liquidated. It will be necessary that some Person well acquainted with the Packet should be on board our Vessel or the stopping inward bound Vessels indiscriminately will give the Alarm & she may be apprized of her Danger. The Choice of a proper Officer with the Care of providing a suitable Vessel &c. I must leave to you. Should it meet with the desired Success there can be no Doubt the Hon. Continental Congress will distinguish &

reward the Officers & Men who shall have done so essential a Service.[5] Nor shall I fail in making known to them how much the Publick Service is indebted to you for your Zeal & Activity on all Occasions—I am &c.

Df, in Joseph Reed's writing, NHi: Reed Papers; LB, DLC:GW; Varick transcript, DLC:GW. The letter-book copy includes the notation "℔ Mr Lux." The bearer was George Lux of Baltimore, who had recently come to Cambridge with some other young Marylanders apparently seeking positions in the army. Lux received no military appointment.

1. See Address to the Inhabitants of Bermuda, this date.

2. For George Baylor's purchase of gunpowder and lead from this Providence firm, see Clark & Nightingale to GW, and Cooke to GW, both 2 Sept. 1775.

3. Cooke informed GW in his letter to him of 30 Aug. that large quantities of tow cloth could not be purchased in Rhode Island.

4. GW is referring to the British fleet that he mentioned in his letter to Jonathan Trumbull, Sr., of 23 Aug. 1775.

5. Whipple was sent to intercept the packet but missed it (Cooke to GW, 9, 14, 26, 29 Sept. 1775).

From Lieutenant David Perry

[Cambridge, c.6 September 1775]. "Whereas God in his holy providence has frowned upon the Family of your petitioner, in that his Wife[1] is rendered incapable of taking care thereof, by reason of having both her Arms broke by a fall from an horse; and he has a Number of small & helpless Children, And no One to provide for them," he asks to be dismissed from the army.

ALS, DLC. This document has no dateline, but Perry is said to have resigned from the Continental army on 6 Sept. 1775 (Francis B. Heitman, *Historical Register of Officers of the Continental Army during the War of the Revolution, April, 1775, to December, 1783* [Washington, D.C., 1914], 437). Perry's regiment was stationed at Cambridge.

David Perry (1741–1826) of Killingly was a second lieutenant in Major General Israel Putnam's Connecticut regiment. He later served for a time as a first lieutenant in the Connecticut militia.

1. Perry married Anna Bliss in 1764.

From Peyton Randolph

Dear Sir Sepr 6th 1775

I have it in command to transmit to you the thanks of the Convention of Virginia for your faithfull discharge of the important trust reposed in you as one of their delegates to the Continental Congress. Your appointment to an office of so much consequence to America, and incompatible with your attendance on this duty, was the only reason that cou'd have induced them not to call you to the same service. Your Brother Delegates were unanimous in their acknowledgments, and you will believe it gives me the greatest satisfaction to convey to you the sentiments of your countrymen, and at the same time to give you every testimony of my approbation and esteem.[1]

The Convention appointed Mr Henry Colonel and commander in chief of the Army of Observation to be raised, which is to consist of 1000 men, to be divided into two regiments; Mr William Woodford commands the second; the Lieutenant Colonels are Christian and Scott. Besides these, the colony being divided into sixteen districts, each district is to raise 500 men, who are to be train'd and disciplin'd and are to be paid during the time of training, and whilst in actual Service. Mr Henry is excluded from the Congress, the Convention having resolved that no officer concern'd in the Military shall be a Member of the Congress, Convention or committee of Safety. Mr Pendleton and Bland both resigned, and in their room Colo. Nelson, Mr Wythe, and Colo. Frank Lee are appointed delegates to the Congress.[2]

I am much obliged to you for your letters; that relating to the motion of the men of War and transports did not come to hand 'till the account had been in Virginia some time.[3]

We heard upon the road that Mrs Washington was very well, she was in Maryland to Visit Mrs Custis, who has got a girl.[4]

I shall be much obliged to you to remember me to Edmund[5] from whom I expect to receive a letter next post. I am your most Obedient Servant

Peyton Randolph

ALS, PHi: Gratz Collection; Sprague transcript, DLC:GW.

1. The third Virginia Convention, over which Peyton Randolph presided, resolved on 11 Aug. "that the Thanks of this Convention are justly due, to George Washington Patrick Henry & Edmund Pendleton Esquires three of the worthy Deputies who represented this Colony in the late Continental Congress, for their faithful Discharge of that important Trust; and this Body are only induced to dispense with their future Services of the like Nature, by the Appointment of the two former to other Offices in the publick Service

incompatible with their Attendance in this, and the infirm state of Health of the latter" (Van Schreeven, *Revolutionary Virginia*, 3:418).

2. For another account of these actions, see Burwell Bassett to GW, 30 Aug. 1775. Richard Bland, who left Congress on 23 May 1775, was reelected by the convention on 11 Aug. but declined to serve, citing his advanced age and failing eyesight.

3. These letters have not been identified.

4. Martha Washington's firstborn grandchild unfortunately took ill and died during her infancy. Mrs. Washington visited her daughter-in-law, Eleanor (Nellie) Calvert Custis, at Mount Airy in Prince Georges County, Md., the home of Nellie's parents.

5. Peyton Randolph is referring to his nephew Edmund Randolph.

From Jonathan Trumbull, Sr.

Sir Lebanon [Conn.] 6th September 1775

I have received no further intelligence concerning the Ships which infest our Coasts—it is most probable they are not those your Excellency Notified to me.[1]

This afternoon received Intelligence from Mr Shaw of New London, That he had by Capt. Champlin who arrived and landed safe at New London last Evening about Three Tons of Powder for this Colony—I have Ordered it to Norwich, excepting a present supply for our two Armed Sloops.[2]

please to give me directions relative to such part thereof as may be thought fit to be spared for your Camp. I have the Honor to be most respectfully Sir Your most Obedient Humble Servant

Jonth. Trumbull

ALS, ViU: Gwathmey Autograph Collection microfilm; LB, Ct: Trumbull Papers.

1. See GW to Trumbull, 23 Aug. 1775, and Trumbull to GW, 5 Sept. 1775.

2. George Champlin (1738–1809) of Newport brought this cargo of gunpowder, later reported to be about four tons, from Môle-Saint-Nicholas, Saint-Domingue (Nathaniel Shaw, Jr., to Thomas & Isaac Wharton, 18 Sept. 1775, in Clark, *Naval Documents*, 2:135–36). Champlin's vessel, the brig *Nancy*, was owned by Nathaniel Shaw (1735–1782), a prominent merchant in New London who traded regularly with the West Indies before the Revolution. During the war Shaw operated a number of privateers and played a leading role in importing provisions and munitions for the Continental army. The Connecticut council on 10 July 1776 appointed him the colony's agent for naval supplies, and in 1778 the general assembly made him marine agent with power to oversee all of Connecticut's armed vessels. Shaw also

served as Continental prize agent for Connecticut beginning in April 1776. George Champlin was commissioned a lieutenant colonel in the Newport County militia in May 1775 by the Rhode Island general assembly. He nevertheless continued to sail to the West Indies for Shaw at least until 1777.

From Joseph Trumbull

Cambridge 6th Septr 1775

The Commissary General Proposes to Genl Washington the Expediency of purchasing, in Philadelphia, for the Use of the Continental Army 10 or 15,000 bbs. Flour—He supposes Flour may be purchased after the 10th Septr at Phila. at 13/ Currency ℔ Ct or under—that he can have it freighted to Newbury at 1/3 ℔ Ct he risking the Vessells, agst the Enemies Cruisers, only—& can have the whole Interest in Vessells & Flour covered in Phila. at 10 ℔ Ct which will not bring the flour, delivered at Newbury Port up to 13/ Lawful money of New England—whereas the lowest we get flour at from Connecticut is 13/ ℔ Ct there & 7/ ℔ Ct Carting—A saving worthwhile may be made[.] But as this mode is attended with a Risk, The Commissary, in this as in every other Case, thinks it his Duty to apply to your Excellency for direction, & likewise to hint to your Excellency, that it may occasion no material delay, if you Should lay the Matter before Congress for their Advice, as the Business must be transacted where that Body are now Convened.

The Commissary General also requests direction from your Excellency, as to procuring Pork, for Supplying the Army the Winter & Summer next Coming—The Season for killing Pork is approaching, when he can purchase that Article, in any Quantities in the Country, drive it in, & have it killed & Salted, at proper places, within 20 miles of Camp; & thereby save transportation—The Transportation of much the greatest part of the Pork Supplied to the Army the Summer past, has Cost 20/ & 21/ ℔ bb.—the Pork may be put up here as Cheap, as in Connecticut—& the whole Transportation saved—Salt, Barrels, &c. can be had here—& in a quantity sufficient for 20,000 Men one year more than £10,000 may be saved, & should the War be at an End the Pork will fetch it's first Costs, at Least, when the Trade Opens.

AL, DNA:PCC, item 152; two copies, DNA:PCC, item 169; copy, NjMoNP. GW enclosed this letter in his letter to Hancock of 7 Sept. 1775. Congress read GW's letter on 21 Sept., and Trumbull's proposals were referred that day to a committee of five members. The committee apparently did not approve the scheme for sending flour by water from Philadelphia to Newburyport, for fear that it would be captured by British warships, thereby depriving the Patriots of its use while increasing the British supply of provisions at Boston (*JCC*, 2:253, 3:257–58, 299; Eliphalet Dyer to Joseph Trumbull, 15 Sept. 1775, in Smith, *Letters of Delegates*, 2:14–15). Congress did accept Trumbull's plan for procuring pork, resolving on 3 Oct. "that the Commissary general contract for such quantities of beef and pork as may be thought proper by the General, and have the same salted up in convenient houses near the camp" (*JCC*, 3:273).

Letter not found: from Samuel Washington, 6 Sept. 1775. On 30 Sept. GW wrote to his brother Samuel: "Your favour of the 6th Instt . . . came safe to hand."

General Orders

Head Quarters, Cambridge, Sept. 7th 1775

Parole Cambridge. Countersign Dorchester

Repeated Complaints being made by the Regimental Surgeons, that they are not allowed proper Necessaries for the Use of the sick before they become fit Objects for the General Hospital: And the Director General of the hospital complains, that contrary to the Rule of every established army, these Regimental Hospitals are more expensive than can be conceived; which plainly indicates that there is either an unpardonable Abuse on one side, or an inexcusable neglect on the other—And Whereas the General is exceedingly desirous of having the utmost care taken of the sick (wherever placed and in every stage of their disorder) but at the same time is determin'd, not to suffer any impositions on the public; he requires and orders, that the Brigadiers General with the commanding Officers of each regiment in his brigade; do set as a Court of enquiry into the Causes of these Complaints, and that they summon the Director General of the hospital, and their several regimental Surgeons before them, and have the whole matter fully investigated and reported—This enquiry to begin on the left of the Line to morrow, at the hour of *ten* in Genl Sullivan's brigade.[1]

When a Soldier is so Sick that it is no longer safe, or proper for him to remain in Camp, he should be sent to the General Hospital—There is no need of regimental Hospitals without the Camp, when there is a general Hospital so near and so well appointed.

Col. Thompson's Regiment of Riflemen to be mustered to morrow morning at seven 'OClock—Genl Green's Brigade to be mustered, saturday morning at the same hour—These Corps are to be one day off duty, previous to their being mustered.

Varick transcript, DLC:GW.

1. On 9 Sept. the court of inquiry held in Sullivan's brigade reported: "After A full hearing of the Parties and their Evidences, it appears to the Court, That the Director General has never failed of supplying Necessaries for the sick, When properly Applied to, If the Articles were within his power, and that he has acquitted himself from the Charge with Honour. The Court further are of opinion that shifting the Channel of supplies for the Sick, from the Commissary to the Director General, has for want of being properly attended to, And understood by the Regimental Surgeons. Caused the Complaints against the Director General without any evil designs in them, or Neglect in him. As to the Extraordinary Expence incurred by Regimental Hospitals complained of By the Director General, he declares to the Court that he has no foundation of Complaint, against any of the Surgeons in this Brigade, Except Doctor Dole of Colo. Doolittle's Regiment. The Court after having fully heard and Examined the Evidence, laid Before them, Respecting him are of Opinion, that the Evidence offered falls Short of Proveing the Charge, therefore upon the evidence Produced He must Stand Acquitted" (DLC:GW). For the ordering of inquiries in the other five brigades, see General Orders, 14, 18, 24, 28, and 30 Sept. 1775.

From Ensign Levi Bowen

Roxbury Camp [Mass.] 7 September 1775. Admits being absent without leave from Col. David Brewer's regiment[1] because of "a Letter Recd from my Family, specifying that they where in a Poor state of Health, and knowing if that was the Case, that they Could not Do without my Assistance. . . . On my Return, my Collo. as was his Duty has Ordred me Under an Arrest, and am at Present Confined to my Tent." He asks to be released from arrest and dismissed from the army.

LS, DLC:GW.

A general court-martial convicted Levi Bowen of Rehobeth, Mass., of being absent without leave, and on 11 Sept. he was cashiered (General Orders, that date).

1. The Massachusetts provincial congress commissioned David Brewer of Kingston a colonel in the colony's forces on 17 June 1775. A court-martial

later found him guilty of fraudulent practices, and on 24 Oct. GW approved the court-martial's sentence dismissing Brewer from the army (General Orders, 23, 24 Oct. 1775).

From Captain Nicholson Broughton

Glocester [Mass.] September 7, 1775

May it please your Excellency

I beg leave to acquaint your Excellency that I sailed from Beverly last Tuesday at 10 oClock with a fair wind, proceeded on my Cruise; on the same day about 5 oClock Saw two ships of War, they gave me Chace, I made back towards Cape Ann but did not go in, next morning I saw a ship under my lee quarter she giveing me Chace I run into Cape Ann harbour,[1] I went out again that night about sun sett, and stood to the southward, next morning saw a ship under my lee quarter I perceived her to be a large ship, I tack'd & stood back for the land, soon after I put about & stood towards her again and found her a ship of no force, I came up with her hail'd & asked where she came from, was answer'd from Piscatuqua & bound to Boston, I told him he must bear away and go into Cape Ann, but being very loth I told him if he did not I should fire on him, on that he bore away and I have brought her safe into Cape Ann Harbour, and have deliver'd the ship and Prisoners into the hands & care of the Committee of Safety for this town of Glocester, and have desired them to send the Prisoners under proper guard to your Excellency for further orders.[2]

also have sent the Captain of the ship we took for your Excellencys examination,[3] and I shall proceed immediately in the further execution of your Excellencys orders and am your Excellencys most Obedient Humble Servent

Nicholasson Broughton

L, DLC:GW. This letter, including the signature, is in the writing of the unidentified person who wrote the Gloucester committee of safety's letter to GW of this date. Broughton signed his first name as "Nicholson." See Broughton to GW, 2 and 6 Nov. 1775.

1. The previous Tuesday was 5 September. Cape Ann Harbor is Gloucester Harbor.

2. The ship taken by Broughton was the *Unity*, a 260–ton American merchant vessel that on 5 Sept. sailed for the West Indies from Portsmouth, N.H., and on the same day was captured by the British warship *Lively*. A British

prize crew, consisting of a midshipman and six sailors, was taking the *Unity* to Boston when Broughton recaptured her. Owned by John Langdon, a prominent New Hampshire Patriot, the *Unity* and her cargo of lumber and provisions could not be condemned and sold for prize money under the rule governing recaptures that GW included in his instructions to Broughton on 2 September. Broughton attempted to get around the rule by arguing that the *Unity*'s destination from the start had been Boston and not the West Indies (Broughton to GW, 9 Sept. 1775). GW rejected that argument and ordered the *Unity* to be delivered to Langdon's agent (GW to Langdon, 21 Sept. 1775).

3. The *Unity*'s captain, John Flagg of Portsmouth, remained on his vessel after the British prize crew took over. Flagg's crew was taken off the *Unity* by her British captors.

From the Gloucester Committee of Safety

Glocester [Mass.] September 7, 1775

May it please your Excellency

We the Committee of Safety for the town of Glocester beg leave to acquaint your Excellency that Capt. Broughton of the armed schooner Hannah has this day brought into our harbour a ship he has retaken, and has committed the care of Vessel & Cargo & Prisioners to us according to the letter from him to your Excellency[1]—we beg leave further to say that as the Captain of the ship seems very desireous to go back to Portsmouth after his Vessels papers which he says the officers of the Kings ship Lively (who first took him) has taken from him Conserning the ships Clearance gives us a good deal of Jelousey that his proceedings has not been according to the good regulations of the united Counsels of the Colonies—and are afraid if he goes back he may give or that the Enemie by his means may have notice where his ship &c. is, and we in this town be very much expossed to some Violent attack from the Kings ships.

we now send your Excellency the Prisoners Capt. Broughton deliverd to us under the Conduct of Capt. John Lane.[2]

We wait your Excellencys further orders & are Your Excellencys Most Obedient Humble Servents

per order of the Committee
Winthrop Sargent Chairman[3]

P.S. we understand that Capt. Flag of the Captur'd Ship has purchased Some Quantity of Fish at Isle Shoales after his Vessel was clear'd unbeknown to the owner.[4]

LS, DLC:GW.

1. See Nicholson Broughton to GW, this date.

2. The seven members of the captured British prize crew arrived at Cambridge on 9 September. Capt. Lane may be John Lane of Massachusetts who became a captain in the 9th Continental Infantry on 1 Jan. 1776.

3. Winthrop Sargent (1727–1793), a merchant in Gloucester, served as a provincial officer on the Louisburg expedition in 1745 and was a member of the 1780 convention that drafted the Massachusetts constitution. His son Winthrop Sargent (1753–1820), who later became secretary of the Northwest Territory, was a volunteer in the Continental army at this time.

4. The Portsmouth, N.H., committee of safety announced to the public on 16 Sept. "that Capt. JOHN FLAG, lately sail'd for the West Indies, took on board a Quantity of FISH, at the Isle of Shoals, after he sail'd from this Port, contrary to a Resolve of the Provincial CONGRESS, and of this Committee, Therefore he is hereby deemed as an Enemy to his Country" (*New-Hampshire Gazette, and Historical Chronicle* [Portsmouth], 19 Sept. 1775). The Isles of Shoals are in the Atlantic a few miles off the New Hampshire coast. The owner of Flagg's vessel was John Langdon.

To John Hancock

Sir Camp at Cambridge Septemr 7th 1775.

I do myself the Honour of addressing you in Consequence of an Application from the Commissary General, who is by my Direction taking all proper Precautions on the Approach of Winter. I desired him to commit to writing such Proposals as his Experience & Knowledge of the Country might intitle him to make, which he has done in the Paper which I have the Honour to inclose.[1] The Difficulty of procuring a sufficient Quantity of Salt which I objected to him he has fully obviated by assuring me that there is so much now actually in Store in this and the Neighbouring Towns, as will remove all Possibility of a Disappointment.

I propose to do myself the Honour of writing in a few Days fully & particularly on several Heads, to which I must now refer.[2] In the mean Time I have only to inform the Honourable Congress that I have received a small Supply of 7000 lb. of Powder this Week from Rhode Island & in a few Days expect 7 Tons of Lead & 500 Stand of Arms a Part of the same Importation[3] and to request that more Money may be forwarded with all Expedition, the military Chest being nearly exhausted. I am with the greatest Respect Sir Your most Obedt & very Hbble Servt

Go: Washington

LS, in Joseph Reed's writing, DNA:PCC, item 152; LB, DLC:GW; copy, NHi: Joseph Reed Papers; two copies, DNA:PCC, item 169; copy, NjMoNP; Varick transcript, DLC:GW. The LS is endorsed "Read before Congress 21 Sept. A Committee appointed on the subject." See Joseph Trumbull to GW, 6 Sept. 1775, source note.

1. See Joseph Trumbull to GW, 6 Sept. 1775.

2. See GW to Hancock, 21 Sept. 1775.

3. George Baylor obtained these supplies from Clark & Nightingale of Providence (Clark & Nightingale to GW, 2 Sept. 1775).

From Major General Artemas Ward

Sir, Camp at Roxbury [Mass.] 7 Septr 1775

Last Evening a large Ship & a large Brig arrived at Boston, and this morning a Ship of War, a Transport Ship & a Topsail Schooner sailed from thence. From Your Excellency's most obedient humble Servant

Artemas Ward

LS, DLC:GW.

Letter not found: to Lund Washington, 7 Sept. 1775. On 15 Oct. 1775 Lund Washington wrote to GW: "I recieve'd on Sunday last two Letters . . . dated 7th & 11th of Septmbr."

Letter not found: from Samuel Washington, 7 Sept. 1775. On 30 Sept. GW wrote Samuel's wife, Anne Steptoe Washington: "The testimony of regard, which you were pleased to annex to my Brothers Letter of the 7th Instt filled me with grateful pleasure."

General Orders

Head Quarters, Cambridge, Sept. 8th 1775

Parole Edington[1] Countersign Falkland

Capt. Perry of Col. Walkers regiment, tried at a General Court Martial, whereof Col. Alden was president for "permitting persons to pass the Lines on Boston Neck," is found guilty of the Crimes laid to his charge; but from alleviating Circumstances, is sentenced only to be severely reprimanded at the head of his regiment—The General approves the sentence, and orders it to be put in execution accordingly.[2]

The Detachment going under the Command of Col. Arnold, to be forthwith taken off the Roll of duty, and to march this evening to Cambridge Common; where Tents, and every thing necessary, is provided for their reception—The rifle Company at Roxbury, and those from Prospect-hill, to march early to morrow Morning to join the above detachment:[3] Such Officers & men as are taken from Genl Green's brigade, for the above detachment, are to attend the Muster of their respective regiments to morrow morning at seven 'ÒClock, upon Prospect-hill, when the Muster is finished, they are forthwith to rejoin the Detachment at Cambridge.

Varick transcript, DLC:GW.

1. Artemas Ward's orderly book reads "Parole Edentown" (MHi: Ward Papers).

2. Capt. John Perry was probably a resident of Rehobeth, Mass., the town in which his regimental commander Col. Timothy Walker (1718–1796) lived. Walker represented Rehobeth in the first and second provincial congresses and became colonel of one of the colony's regiments in late May 1775. He remained in the Continental army until the end of this year. Ichabod Alden (1739–1778) of Duxbury was lieutenant colonel of Col. Theophilus Cotton's Massachusetts regiment at this time. In November 1776 Alden became colonel of the 7th Massachusetts Regiment, and he served in that position until his death two years later in the fighting at Cherry Valley.

3. Capt. Daniel Morgan's rifle company came from Roxbury. Captains William Hendricks and Matthew Smith were the commanders of the two rifle companies from Prospect Hill.

Circular to the General Officers

Gentn Cambridge Septr 8th 1775.

As I mean to call upon you in a day or two for your opinions upon a point of a very Interesting nature to the well being of the Continent in general, & this Colony in particular; I think it proper, indeed an incumbant duty upon me previous to this meeting, to intimate the end and design of it, that you may have time to consider the matter with that deliberation and attention which the Importance of it requires.

It is to know whether, in your judgments, we cannot make a successful attack upon the Troops in Boston, by means of Boats, co-operated by an attempt upon their Lines at Roxbury—The success of such an Enterprize depends, I well know, upon the allwise disposer of Events, & is not within the reach of human wisdom to foretell the Issue; but, if the prospect is fair, the undertaking is justifiable under the following, among other reasons which might be assigned.

The Season is now fast approaching when warm, and comfortable Barracks must be erected for the Security of the Troops, against the inclemency of the Winter—large & costly provision must be made in the article of wood, for the Supply of the Army—and after all that can be done in this way, it is but too probable that Fences, woods, orchards, and even Houses themselves, will fall Sacrifices to the want of Fuel, before the end of the winter—a very considerable difficulty, if not expence must accrue on acct of Cloathing for the Men now ingaged in the Service, and if they do not inlist again, this difficulty will be Increased to an almost insurmountable degree—Blankets I am inform'd are now much wanted, and not to be got, how then shall we be able to keep Soldiers to their duty, already impatient to get home, when they come to feel the Severity of winter without proper Covering? If this army should not Incline to engage for a longer term than the first of Jany what then is to be the consequence, but that, you must either be obliged to levy new Troops and thereby have two Setts (or partly so) in pay at the same time, or, by disbanding one set before you got the other, expose the Country to desolation, and the Cause perhaps to irretrievable Ruin. These things are not unknown to the Enemy, perhaps it is the very ground they are building on, if they are not waiting a reinforcement; and if they are waiting for succours, ought it not to give a Spur to the attempt? Our Powder (not much of which would be consumed in such an enterprize) without any certainty of Supply, is daily wasting: and to sum up the whole, in spite of every saving that can be made, the expence of supporting this army will so far exceed any Idea that was form'd in Congress of it, that I do not know what will be the consequences.

These among many other reason's which might be assigned, induce me to wish a speedy finish of the dispute; but, to avoid these evils we are not to loose sight of the difficulties—the hazard—and the loss that may accompany the attempt—nor, what will be the probable consequences of a failure.

That every circumstance for & against this measure may be

duely weighed—that there may be time for doing of it—and nothing of this Importance resolved on but after mature deliberation I give this previous notice of the Intention of calling you together on Monday next, at Nine oclock, at which time you are requested to attend at head Quarters.[1] It is unnecessary I am perswaded, to recommend Secrecy, as the Success of the Enterprize (if undertaken) must depend in a great measure upon the suddeness of the Stroke. I am with the greatest esteem Gentn Yr most Obedt Hble Servt

Go: Washington

ALS, MHi: Artemas Ward Papers; ADfS, RPJCB; LB, DLC:GW; copy, DLC:GW; copy, DNA:PCC, item 152; copy, DNA:PCC, item 169; copy, NjMoNP; Varick transcript, DLC:GW. The letter-book copy is addressed to major generals Ward, Lee, and Putnam and brigadier generals Thomas, Spencer, Heath, Sullivan, Green, and Gates. The ALS was sent to Artemas Ward. The copy in PCC, item 169, was enclosed in GW to Hancock, 21 Sept. 1775.

1. See Council of War, 11 Sept. 1775.

From Robert Carter Nicholas

Dear Sir. Williamsburg 8th Septr 1775.

Were I not apprehensive that I should appear rather late in doing it, I am sure none of your Countrymen could with greater Sincerity congratulate you on your Promotion to the very important & honourable Post you now fill.

You will no doubt have heard the distressful Situation this unhappy Country is now in. We have too much Reason to apprehend that our Enemies will exert every Effort to annoy us. A few Troops arrived some time ago & we hear that a Regiment is daily expected from the West Indies. If general Gage should remove his Troops from Boston, tho. we are told N. Yk will be the object of their Destination, I can't help suspecting that this Declaration is intended to amuse & lull us into a State of greater Security, being persuaded from Comparison of different Accounts, that his Visit is intended for Virginia. If Ld D——re[1] can get him here, I am confident he will. It might be of singular Service to us to receive the earliest Intelligence of any Movement this Way.

The young Gentleman, who waits upon you with this, goes

recommended from our Convention to your Patronage & Friendship. It rests with me to furnish his Pay from time to time, but I really do not know how to do it, *at so great a Distance*, without your kind Assistance. If you could by any means contrive to have him supplyed, I will honor your Drafts at Sight.[2]

That you may, my dear Sir, be shielded by the Lord of Hosts & protected from all our Enemies; & that you may long live to enjoy every Felicity this Life can afford is the ardent wish of yr very affte & mo. obt Servt

Ro. C. Nicholas

I shall be more certain of giving due honor to yr Drafts by Bills on London; if these can be made to suit, Specie grows very scarce here.

ALS, DLC:GW.

As treasurer of the colony of Virginia from 1766 to 1776, Robert Carter Nicholas (1728–1780) frequently dealt with GW on business matters and on several occasions entertained him in his Williamsburg house. A conservative Patriot, Nicholas opposed the declaring of independence but strongly defended colonial rights. He participated in all five Virginia conventions and the new house of delegates as a representative of James City County, and in 1779 he became a judge on the state court of chancery.

1. Nicholas is referring to Lord Dunmore.

2. The bearer was Francis Otway Byrd (1756–1800), a son of William Byrd III of Westover. On 26 Aug. 1775 the third Virginia convention resolved: "It appearing . . . that ⟨Francis⟩ *Otway Byrd*, esq; had, on account of his attachment to *American* liberty, resigned his provision and prospects in the *British* navy, and may be destitute of employment, . . . that the said *Otway Byrd*, esq; be strongly recommended to his excellency general ⟨George⟩ *Washington*, and the Conventions of our sister colonies to the eastward, for promotion in the army in that neighbourhood; and that until such promotion shall take place, or it be otherwise ordered by this Convention, that he be allowed ten shillings per day to support him as a cadet in the continental army, to commence the day he joins the said army, and that he be also allowed the sum of 50 *l.* to be paid immediately" (Van Schreeven, *Revolutionary Virginia*, 3:503). In quitting the Royal Navy, Otway Byrd sacrificed the monetary inheritance provided for him in his father's will contingent on his remaining in the navy until his mother's death. Byrd reached Cambridge about 2 Oct., and on 25 Oct. GW appointed him an aide-de-camp to Maj. Gen. Charles Lee (General Orders, that date). At the siege of Charleston in the spring of 1776, Byrd greatly impressed Lee with his courage and competence (Lee to GW, 1 July 1776). On 1 Jan. 1777 Byrd became lieutenant colonel of the 3d Continental Dragoons. He resigned his commission in July 1778.

From Elisha Phelps

Honor'd Sir Albany Septemr 8th 1775.

I received orders from His Honor the Governor of Connecticut, to forward the Lead according to your desire, which Lead I have forwarded immediately after it came to hand, which I trust you will receive as quick as possible by the bearer:[1] at the same time wishing your Honor Success with it, and those under your Command, & that you may with it gain a Compleat victory over our Enemys, & give our Land freedom to Latest Posterity, may God grant: I am with the Greatest Esteem your Honors very very Humble Servant at command.

Elisha Phelps

N.B., 19 full Boxes & one abot half full the wght not assurtd but about Ct 53.

ALS, DLC:GW.

Elisha Phelps (1737–1776) of Simsbury, Conn., served with Ethan Allen at Ticonderoga in May 1775. On 8 June 1775 Governor Trumbull, acting at the request of the Continental Congress, appointed Phelps commissary for the northern army, and Phelps subsequently took charge of the supplies at Albany.

1. For the sending of lead from Crown Point to Cambridge, see GW to Philip Schuyler and GW to Jonathan Trumbull, Sr., both 14 Aug. 1775, and Trumbull to GW, 21 Aug. 1775, n.2. Trumbull wrote to Phelps about the lead on 21 Aug. (Hinman, *Historical Collection*, 330–31).

To Major General Philip Schuyler

Dear Sir. Camp at Cambridge September 8th 1775

I have received your Favor of 31st august and am much engaged in sending off the Detachmt under Col: Arnold upon the Plan contained in mine of the 20th Ultimo: A Variety of Obstacles have retarded us since the Express returned with your's of the 27th August from Albany, but we are now in such Forwardness that I expect they will set out by Sunday next at farthest.[1] I shall take Care in my Instructions to Colonel Arnold, that in Case there should be a Junction of the Detachment with your army, you shall have no Difficulty in adjusting the Scale of Command.[2]

You seem so sensible of the absolute Necessity of preserving the Friendship of the Canadians, that I need say Nothing on that Subject; but that a strict Discipline & punctual Payment for all Necessaries brought to your Camp will be the most certain Means of obtaining so valuable and important an End. I shall inculcate the same principle most strongly on the Troops who go from hence, as that, on which their Safety, Success & Honour intirely depends.[3]

I am truly concerned that your Supplies and Appointments are so far short of your Expectations, but I trust you will have a feeble Enemy to contend with and a whole Province on your Side; two Circumstances of great Weight in the Scale.

Your Situation for some Time must be so critical and interesting that I hope you will not fail giving me constant Information of your Motions & Success. My best Wishes attend you. Believe me with much Truth and Regard Your most obed: & very humble Servt

Go. Washington

LB, NN: Schuyler Papers; LB, DLC:GW; copy, NHi: Joseph Reed Papers; Varick transcript, DLC:GW.

1. The first element of Benedict Arnold's detachment left Cambridge on Monday, 11 Sept., and the last element two days later.

2. See item number nine of Instructions to Arnold, 14 Sept. 1775.

3. See GW to Arnold, and Instructions to Arnold, both 14 Sept. 1775.

To Jonathan Trumbull, Sr.

Sir Camp at Cambridge September 8th 1775

Upon the Receipt of this you will please to give Directions that all the New raised Levies march Immediately for this Camp, By a Resolution of Congress the Troops on the Continental Establishment were not to be employed in the Defence of the Coasts or of any particular Province, the Militia being deemed competent for that Service: When I directed these Troops to remain in their own Province I had some Reason to suspect a remove from Boston to New York, on which Case they would have been able to have given them more speedy Opposition: But as that suspition now appears groundless, there will be an Impropriaty in continuing them where they now are consistant with the above Resolve.[1]

The Detachment which I mentioned in my last will march in 2 Days[2] & I shall have Occasion for the Troops from you to fill their Places, The Ministerial Expedition must I apprehend by this Time have come to Issue they either returned with Disappointment or have succeeded in their Errand,[3] In either Case the Men can be spared without Danger to the Country. But should not this be the Case and they are still hovering on the Coast it is to make no Difference in their March, so that I shall at all Events expect them here next Week for which you will please to give the Necessary Orders. I am with much Esteem & Respect Sir, Your most Obedient & very Humble Servant

Go: Washington

LB, Ct: Trumbull Papers; LB, DLC:GW; copy, NHi: Joseph Reed Papers; Varick transcript, DLC:GW. The document at the New-York Historical Society is endorsed "Draught to Gov. Trumbull," but no changes appear in the text.

1. The levies belonged to the regiments commanded by colonels Charles Webb and Jedediah Huntington. For GW's earlier letter permitting these troops to remain temporarily in Connecticut, see GW to Trumbull, 14 Aug. 1775. For Congress's resolution regarding local defense, see GW to James Warren, 30 July 1775, n.2.

2. GW wrote to Trumbull about Benedict Arnold's expedition on 2 September. Arnold's detachment began marching from Cambridge on 11 September.

3. GW apparently is referring to the British fleet that he mentioned in his letter to Trumbull of 23 Aug. 1775.

General Orders

Head Quarters, Cambridge, Sept. 9th 1775

Parole Geneva Countersign Hartford

The Major General commanding the division of the army, posted between Prospect-hill and Cambridge river,[1] is to be very exact in obliging the Colonels and Field Officers, to lay in the Encampments of their respective regiments; and particularly, the Colonel and Lieutenant Colonel of the 30th Regiment.[2]

Varick transcript, DLC:GW.

1. Maj. Gen. Israel Putnam commanded this division.

2. James Scammans was colonel of the 30th Regiment, and Johnson Moulton (d. 1793) of York, District of Maine, was its lieutenant colonel. A provincial captain during the French and Indian War, Moulton vied with

Scammans for command of the 30th Regiment while it was being formed during the spring of 1775. Moulton served as lieutenant colonel under Scammans until the end of the year, when he became lieutenant colonel of the 7th Continental Regiment. Moulton apparently left the army after the campaign of 1776. For GW's earlier orders requiring officers to sleep in their camps, see General Orders, 7 and 24 July 1775.

From Lieutenant Colonel Loammi Baldwin

Cheelsea [Mass.] Sept. 9th 1775

May it Please your Execellency

I Returnd to my post yesterday after Settleing cheaf of my affairs & found all Well. The Bearer of this will Conduct to your Excellency a Person who Says he was Servant to General How. he came on to Noddles Island from there, he waded as far into the water as he could toward our guard at Winnisimmitt ferry, & Calld to our Guard to Come & fetch him over which they did & conducted him to me & thought it my duty to Send him to your Excellency.

Inclosd are the Observations that have not been Sent before.[1] I am with all Respect your Excellencys most Obedent & Very Humble Servt

Loammi Baldwin Lt Colo.

ALS, DLC:GW.

1. The enclosures apparently included Joseph Leach's returns of observations for 2, 5, and 6 Sept., all of which are in DLC:GW.

From Lieutenant Colonel Loammi Baldwin

Chelsea [Mass.] Sept. 9 1775

May it Please your Excellency Saterday 4 oClock P.M.

Inclosed are the observations of this Day Nothing Remarkable.[1] This from your most obediant Humbe Servt

L. Baldwin Liet. Coln.

ALS, DLC:GW.

1. "A Return of the observations of the Day Sept. 9th" in Joseph Leach's writing is in DLC:GW.

From Captain Nicholson Broughton

Sir Glocester [Mass.] Sepr 9th 1775

As there is several Matters of Complaint turnd up (since my Capture of the Ship Unity) against the Capt. of sd Ship, I think proper to acquaint you of the Particulars, Viz. as follows—on my sending of an Officer on Board Sd Ship, his Treatment was such as I would rather have expected from a polite Enemy than a Friend to our Cause as Americans.

I would acquaint your Excellency in the next Place, that there is on Board sd Ship, a much greater Quantity of Naval Stores than is customary to import from our Ports.

There is likewise as I understand some considerable Quantity of Provisions, much more (in my Opinion) than is necssary for Ship's Crew. I would likewise inform your Excellency that the Capt. contrary to the Resolves of our General Assembly has taken on Board a Considerable Quantity of New Fish.[1] And from those, And many other Circumstances, I conclude that Capt. Flagg, was designd for the Port of Boston instead of any one of the West India Isles—from this Consideration Sir, I (with the greatest Deference to your own Judgement) should think it proper, that the Ship should be remov'd to Beverly, as a Place of much greater Security, than her present Port; the Lumber which she has on Board is considerable & might be much easier remov'd to Head Quarters, for Service, from thence, than the present Port—I shall leave the Ship with the Committee of Safety, 'till further Orders. With the greatest Respect, I am Sir, your most Obedient Humble Servant

Nicholasson Broughton

P.S. I would not neglect acquainting Your Excellency (in Excuse for my makeing a Short Stay Here,) that my first Lieuttenant Was accidentally wounded;[2] for the Particulars of which, or the Circumstances relative to my takeing the Ship, your Excellency will be pleas'd to inquire of the Bearer.

Nicholasson Broughton

L, DLC:GW. This letter was written and signed by the same person who wrote and signed Broughton's letter to GW of 7 Sept. 1775. See source note to that letter.

1. For the Portsmouth committee of safety's condemnation of Capt. John

Flagg for this action, see Gloucester Committee of Safety to GW, 7 Sept. 1775, n.4.

2. The first lieutenant of the *Hannah* was John Glover, Jr. (1755–1777), eldest son of Col. John Glover. John Glover, Jr., joined his father's regiment as a lieutenant in the spring of 1775. He served on the *Hannah* until October, when GW made him second in command aboard the armed schooner *Lee* with the rank of captain. By December 1775 John Glover, Jr., returned to his father's regiment to command a company, and the following year he fought with the regiment at the Battle of Trenton. He was lost at sea in August 1777, presumably aboard a privateer.

From Nicholas Cooke

Sir Providence Septemr 9th 1775.

I am to acknowledge the Receipt of your Excellency's Letter of the 6th instant, and to inform you that, Zealous to do every Thing in our Power to serve the common Cause of America, the Committee have determined, instead of the small armed Sloop, to send the large Vessel with Fifty Men upon the Bermuda Enterprize; with Orders to Capt. Whipple to cruize Ten Days off Sandy-Hook for the Packet expected from England; and if he is so fortunate as to meet her to put the Letters ashore at South-Hampton and send them by Express to your Excellency. She will sail Wind and Weather permitting the Beginning of the Week.[1]

There is in this Town a Mr Du Ville, a Frenchman, who hath made several Voyages from this Port during the last Four or Five Years, and is esteemed a Person every Way well qualified, and to be depended upon, for the Execution of the Plan he proposes. He was with Capt. Hopkins the last Voyage when he imported the Ammunition &c. lately purchased of Messrs Clarke & Nightingale for the Army; and hath brought with him a Set of Papers to qualify a Brig[an]t[ine] as a French Bottom. His Scheme is to proceed to Bayonne in France, where he is well acquainted, and there take in a Load of Powder, which he says can be effected in Three Days. This Dispatch will be so great that Intelligence of the Vessel cannot be sent to England timely enough for any Measures to be taken to intercept her upon her Return. I think the Plan practicable and likely to be attended with Success. We have here a Brigt., a fast Sailer, and otherwise a suitable Vessel for the Voyage, which will bring about Eighty Tons: And we will undertake to fit One Quarter of her, and to supply the Money to purchase One Quarter Part of that Quantity of Powder; which is the most we can do here.[2]

I have written to Governor Trumbull upon this Subject, and desired him, if the Plan meets with his Approbation, to dispatch a trusty Person to confer with you upon it, who can return through Providence and let me know the Result, so that we may immediately equip the Vessel for the Voyage.

I have communicated to Messrs Clarke & Nightingale that Part of your Letter which related to them. They desire me to present to you their respectful Thanks for the polite Notice you have taken of them. I have the Honor to be with much Esteem & Regard, Sir Your most obedient and most humble Servant

Nichols Cooke

LS, DLC:GW.

1. Capt. Abraham Whipple sailed on 12 Sept. in the armed sloop *Katy*. The committee mentioned by Cooke was appointed by the Rhode Island general assembly on 21 Aug. to act during its recess. See Cooke to GW, 30 Aug. 1775, n.1. For Cooke's instructions to Whipple, dated 11 Sept. 1775, see Clark, *Naval Documents*, 2:76–78.

2. This scheme was referred to Congress and was approved by the secret committee appointed on 18 Sept. to contract for the importation of gunpowder. See Cooke to GW, 14 Sept. 1775, n.2. Whether or not the voyage was ever made is uncertain.

From the New York Committee of Safety

In Committee of Safety for the Colony of New York

Sir: [New York City] Septr 9th 1775

In the Recess of the Provincial Congress it is the Duty of the Committee of Safety to answer Your favor of the 30th Ulto to our President[1]—We perfectly agree with You that the Instances of Collusion You mention are such Instances of Avarice at such a Time and in such a Cause as call for a severe Scrutiny and examplary Punishment.

Be assured, Sir, that we are vigilant for the Discovery of such Delinquents; and that those who may fall in our Way will not escape their just deserts.

The Gentlemen who informed You of the Arrival of a large

Quantity of Powder and five hundred stand of Arms, perhaps did not know that tho' they were landed on the East end of Long Island they were immediately transported to New London and did not belong to this Colony or any of its Inhabitants. We have had indeed about three thousand Six hundred Weight of Powder bro't in, and before its arrival we had not a Barrel in the Colony, except what was most sparingly distributed among individuals.

We deplore the Situation of the Army under Your Command; and were our Abilities equal to our Wishes, we should not fail to contribute to Your immediate Assistance and Supply. We are heartily sorry that your Poverty in the necessary Article in Question, prevents You from availing Yourself of the Advantage of Situation You have lately gained. But be assured, Sir, We have not Powder enough for the necessary Defence of this Colony; especially if any Disaster should happen to General Schuyler, which would render it requisite to give additional Strenght and Security to the Northern Parts of this Colony the Inhabitants of which at this juncture are most sparingly supplied with Arms and Ammunition.

We shall immediately forward a Copy of Your Letter to the Continental Congress and write to them on the Subject[2]—The quantity of Powder transported from Long Island to New London were Eight Tons as we have been informed. perhaps an Application to that Colony might prove successful. We are. Sir. most respectfully Your most Obedient humble servants

By Order.
Gilbert Livingston Chairman Pro. Temp.

LS, DLC:GW.

1. See GW to Peter Van Brugh Livingston, 30 Aug. 1775.

2. The committee wrote to Congress on this date: "We enclose you a Copy of a Letter which we have this day received from General Washington to which we beg Leave to refer you. As the General stands in need of a supply of Gunpowder, and as we are informed that a considerable Quantity has lately been received in Philadelphia, we doubt not you will forward as much as can be spared for this necessary Service. We have about Eight hundred weight in our Magazine, which we would willingly part with if our Citizens had a Supply. Be assured we shall be attentive to every requisition from the General. . . . Some time Since we forwarded to the Camp at Cambridge Nineteen hundred & fifty five pounds of Gunpowder: We Submit it to you whether it

would not be proper to replace us that Quantity from Philadelphia as we know not what demand may be for that article from General Schuyler" (DNA:PCC, item 67).

From John McKesson

Sir [New York] Sept. 9th 1775. 9 o'Clock P.M.

Since the Committee of Safety adjourned this afternoon, I am informed that one parcel of Powder landed at the East End of Long Island belonged at & was sent to New London but that a larger parcel was soon after landed at some small distance and forwarded to the owners in Rhode-Island—I could not be well informed of the Quantity in either parcel; but tho't it my Duty to give you this Information; and am most respectfully, your Excellency's most obedient & very humble Servant

John McKesson Secry to the Comme of Safety.

ALS, DLC:GW.

John McKesson (c.1735–1798), a prominent New York City lawyer and a political confidant of George Clinton, was at this time secretary to both the New York provincial congress and the colony's committee of safety. On 31 July 1776 the state convention appointed McKesson register of the court of admiralty, and in September 1777 he became clerk of the state assembly, a position that he held until 1794.

To Jonathan Trumbull, Sr.

Sir Camp at Cambridge September 9th 1775

Your Favour of the 6th Inst. is now before me, Our State of Ammunition disables us from availing ourselves of our present Stations as I would wish to do & requires every Assistance that can be given it: you will therefore on the Receipt of this be Pleased to forward Whatever can be spared from the Necessities of the Colony, And the more Expedition you can use the more acceptable it will be. Your most Obedt and humble Servant

G. Washington

LB, Ct: Trumbull Papers; Df, NHi: Joseph Reed Papers; LB, DLC:GW; Varick transcript, DLC:GW. In the draft the date was changed from 8 to 9 September.

General Orders

Head Quarters, Cambridge, Sept. 10th 1775

Parole Indostan. Countersign Kendall.

Varick transcript, DLC:GW.

From Brigadier General Nathanael Greene

8 oClock Prospect Hill [Mass.] Sept. 10. 1775

This moment reported me from the Whitehouse Guard that a deserter had made his escape into Bunker Hill—Two Centries fird at him but he made his escape I believe unhurt—As it is uncertain who it is or what he is I have thought proper to alter the Parole & Countersign for these Guards which if your Excellency Approves youl please to signify it at the return of the Sergeant—If this deserter has carried in the Countersign they may easily convey it over to Roxbury—it would [be] a pretty Advantage for a partisan frolick[.] The Rifflers seems very sulky and I am informd threatens to rescue their mates to night, but little is to be feard from them as the Regiment are all ready at a moments warning to turn out—and the Guards very Strong[.][1] I am with due defference your Excellencys most Obedient humble servant

N. Greene

Parole Coventry Countersign Germany

ALS, MHi: Artemas Ward Papers.

1. The trouble occurred among Col. William Thompson's Pennsylvania riflemen. "They had twice before broken open our guard-house and released their companions who were confined there for small crimes," Jesse Lukens wrote on 13 Sept., "and once when an offender was brought to the post to be whipped, it was with the utmost difficulty they were kept from rescuing him in the presence of all their officers. They openly damned them, and behaved with great insolence. However the colonel was pleased to pardon the man, and all remained quiet; but on Sunday last [10 Sept.] the adjutant [Lt. David Ziegler] having confined a sergeant for neglect of duty and murmuring, the men began again, and threatened to take him out. The adjutant being a man of spirit, seized the principal mutineer and put him in also, and coming to report the matter to the colonel where we were all sitting after dinner, were alarmed with a huzzaing, and, upon going out, found they had broken open the guard-house and taken the man out. The colonel and lieutenant-colonel

[Edward Hand], with several officers and friends, seized the fellow from amongst them, and ordered a guard to take him to Cambridge to the main guard, which was done without any violent opposition, but in about twenty minutes thirty-two of Capt. [James] Ross' company, with their loaded rifles, swore by God they would go to the main guard and release the man or lose their lives, and set off as hard as they could run. It was in vain to attempt stopping them. We stayed in camp and kept the others quiet. Sent word to Gen. Washington, who reinforced the guard to five hundred men with fixed bayonets and loaded pieces. Col. [Daniel] Hitchcock's regiment, (being the one next to us,) was ordered under arms, and some of Gen. Greene's brigade, (as the generals were determined to subdue by force the mutineers, and did not know how far it might spread in our battalion.) Genls. Washington, Lee, and Greene came immediately, and our thirty-two mutineers who had gone about a half a mile towards Cambridge and taken possession of a hill and woods, beginning to be frighted at their proceedings, were not so hardened, but upon the General's ordering them to ground their arms they did it immediately. The General then ordered another of our companies, Capt. [George] Nagel's, to surround them with their loaded guns, which was immediately done, and did the company great honor. However, to convince our people (as I suppose, mind,) that it did not altogether depend upon themselves, he ordered part of Col. Hitchcock's and Col. [Moses] Little's regiments to surround them with their bayonets fixed, and ordered two of the ringleaders to be bound. I was glad to find our men all true and ready to do their duty except these thirty-two rascals. Twenty-six were conveyed to the quarter-guard on Prospect Hill, and six of the principals to the main guard. You cannot conceive what disgrace we are all in, and how much the General is chagrined that only one regiment should come from the South, and that set so infamous an example" (*Pa. Archives*, 2d ser., 10:8–10). Lukens was a gentleman volunteer with the Pennsylvania riflemen. For the punishment of the mutineers, see General Orders, 11 and 13 Sept. 1775.

To James Warren

Sir Cambridge Sept. 10. 1775

Capt. Bayler waits upon you to receive the Specie prepared for Col. Arnold. You will at the same Time be pleased to pay him so much Continental Money as will make up the whole Sum £1000 lawful: A regular Warrt will be sent you in a Day or two which there are some Inconveniences in drawing at present.[1] I am Sir Your most Obed. Hble

LB, in Joseph Reed's writing, DLC:GW; Varick transcript, DLC:GW.

1. On 13 Sept. GW signed warrants of £1,000, £752 2s., and £2,590 16s. for Arnold (Military Warrant Book, 21 Aug. 1775–12 Aug. 1776, DLC:GW).

To John Augustine Washington

Dear Brother, Camp at Cambridge Septr 10th 1775.

So little has happend since the date of my last[1] that I should scarce have given you the trouble of reading this Letter, did I not immagine that it might be some satisfaction to you to know that we are well and in no fear or dread of the Enemy. Being, in our own opinion at least, very securely Intrenched, and wishing for nothing more than to see the Enemy out of their strong holds, that the dispute may come to an Issue. The inactive state we lye in is exceedingly disagreeable especially as we can see no end to it, having had no advices lately from Great Britain to form a judgment upon.

In taking possession about a fortnight ago of a Hill within point blank (Cannon) shott of the Enemy's Lines on Charles Town Neck we expected to bring on a general Action, especially as we had been threatned by reports from Boston several days before, that they (that is the Enemy) intended an Attack upon our Intrenchments nothing however followed but a severe Cannonade for a day or two, and a Bombardment afterwards for the like time; which, however, did us no other damage than to kill two or three men and wound as many more—Both are now at an end, as they found we disregarded their Fire and continued our Works till we had got them compleated.[2]

Unless the Ministerial Troops in Boston are waiting for reinforcements, I cannot devise what they are staying there after—and why (as they affect to despise the Americans) they do not come forth, & put an end to the contest at once. They suffer greatly for want of fresh Provisions notwithstanding they have pillaged several Islands of a good many Sheep and Cattle—They are also scarce of Fuel, unless (according to the acct of one of their Deserters) they mean to pull down Houses for Firing. In short they are from all accts suffering all the Inconveniencies of a Siege. It is true by having the entire Command of the Sea & a powerful Navy; & moreover, as they are now beginning to take all Vessells indiscriminately, we cannot stop their Supplies through that Channel; but their Succours in this way ⟨hath⟩ not been so powerful as to enable them to give the common Soldiers much fresh meat as yet. By an Acct from Boston of the

4th Instt the Cattle lately brought in there, sold at publick auction from Fifteen to £34.10 Sterg a piece & the Sheep from 30/ to 36/ each—& that Fowls and every other Species of Fresh Provisions went in proportion—The expence of this one would think must soon tire them were it not that they intend to fix all the Expence of this War upon the Colonies—if they can I suppose we shall add.

I am just sending off a Detachment of 1000 Men to Quebec by the way of Kennebec River, to co-operate with General Schuyler who by this is, I expect, at or near St Johns on the N. end of Lake Champlain; and may for ought ⟨I⟩ know have determined the Fate of his Army and that of Canada, as he left Crown point the 31st of last Month for the Isle-au-Noix (within 12 Miles of St Johns where Govr Carltons principal force lays)[3]—If he should succeed there, he will soon after be in Montreal without opposition and if the Detachment I am sending (though late in the Season) from hence should be able to get posession of Quebec the Ministry's Plan, in respect to that Government will turn out finely.

I have only to add my love to my Sister and the little ones, and that I am with the greatest truth Dr Sir Yr Most Affecte Bror

Go: Washington

ALS, DLC:GW.

1. See GW to John Augustine Washington, 27 July 1775.

2. For an account of the American occupation of Plowed Hill on the night of 26 Aug., see GW to Richard Henry Lee, 29 Aug. 1775, n.6.

3. See Philip Schuyler to GW, 31 Aug. 1775.

General Orders

Head Quarters, Cambridge, Sept. 11th 1775

Parole Lancaster. Countersign Middleton.

Col. Ebenezer Bridge of the 27th Regt of foot, in the service of the United Colonies; tried at a General Court martial, whereof Brigd. Genl Green was president, for "misbehaviour and neglect of duty, in the Action at Bunkers-hill, on the [1]7th of June last"; The Court are of opinion that Indisposition of body, render'd the prisoner incapable of action, and do therefore acquit him.[1]

Ensign Moses Howe of Col. David Brewers Regt tried by a General Court Martial, whereof Col. Alden was presdt—for "contempt of the service["]; The Court after due examination of the Evidence, acquit the prisoner.[2]

Ensign Levi Bowen—of the same Regiment, and tried by the same General Court Martial for "absenting from his regiment without leave"—The Court find the prisoner guilty of the Crime laid to his Charge, and do therefore sentence him to be *cashiered.*[3]

General Heath's Brigade to be mustered upon Thursday morning next, at eleven 'OClock, and Col. Fryes Brigade, upon Saturday morning at the same time.[4]

Col. Thompson's Battalion of Rifle-men posted upon Prospect-hill, to take their share of all duty of Guard and Fatigue, with the Brigade they encamp with.

A General Court Martial to sit as soon as possible to try the men of that Regiment, who are now prisoners in the main Guard, and at Prospect-hill, and accused of "*mutiny.*"

The Riflemen posted at Roxbury, and towards Letchmore's point, are to do duty with the brigade they are posted with.

The General Court Martial to meet to morrow morning at seven 'OClock; to consist of *three* Field Officers and *ten* Captains.[5]

Varick transcript, DLC:GW.

1. For a discussion of the charge against Bridge, see General Orders, 20 Aug. 1775, n.2.

2. Moses Howe of Belchertown, Mass., was a second lieutenant in the militia company that marched to Cambridge from Belchertown in April 1775. He served ten months in the army. David Brewer (1732–1799) became colonel of a Massachusetts regiment on 16 June 1775. A court-martial ordered him to be cashiered in October of this year for committing several frauds (General Orders, 15, 23 Oct. 1775).

3. For Bowen's admission of guilt and his efforts to avoid being court-martialed on this charge, see Bowen to GW, 7 Sept. 1775.

4. William Heath's brigade was to be mustered on 14 Sept. and James Frye's on 16 September. Artemas Ward's orderly book reads "7 oClock" (MHi: Ward Papers).

5. For a discussion of this mutiny, see Nathanael Greene to GW, 10 Sept. 1775, n.1. For the result of the court-martial, see General Orders, 13 Sept. 1775. The riflemen previously "were excused from all working parties, camp guards, camp duty," Jesse Lukens wrote on 13 September. "This indulgence, together with the remissness of discipline and care in our young officers, has rendered the men rather insolent for good soldiers. . . . in order that idleness

shall not be a further bane to us, the General's orders on Monday [11 Sept.], were 'that Col. Thompson's regiment shall be upon all parties of fatigue, (working parties,) and do all other camp duty with any other regiment'" (*Pa. Archives*, 2d ser., 10: 8–10).

Council of War

[Cambridge, 11 September 1775]

At a Council of War held at Head Quarters Cambridge Septr 11th 1775

Present

His Excelly General Washington
Major Genl Ward
Lee
Puttnam
Brig. Genl Thomas, Heath, Sullivan Spencer, Green.

His Excelly having communicated by Letter & verbally to the Generals for their Consideration a Proposition of making an Attack upon Boston, by Boats assisted by an Attempt on the Roxbury Lines[1]—assigned the following Reasons for such an Attempt.

First That the Winter was fast approaching when warm & comfortable Barracks must be erected for the Troops.

2d Large & costly Provision must be made in the Article of Wood (at 20/ ℔ Cord) & with the utmost Exertions Fences, Woods Orchards & even Houses will probably fall a Sacrifice to our Necessities in this Article, before the Expiration of Winter.

3. A considerable Difficulty & great Expence will accrue for Cloathing the Men now in the Service—& if they do not reinlist at the End of the present Term, it will be incr⟨eased⟩ to a great Degree—Blankets in particular are much wanted & not to be procured—the Soldiery grow impatient to get Home already—we shall find it a very hard Task to detain them when they feel the Severity of a Northern Winter without proper Covering.

4. If the present Army should not incline to engage for a longer Time than the 1st January—you must either levy new Troops & have two Armies (or partly so) in Pay at the same Time, or by disbanding one before the other is assembled expose the Country to Desolation & the Cause to Ruin.

5. Our Powder (not much of which would be consumed in such a Enterprize) is daily wasting & to sum up the whole with the utmost Oeconeomy the Expence of supporting this Army will so far exceed any Estimate yet formed that the Consequences may be very fatal.

On the other Hand the Hazard, the Loss of Men in the Attempt & the probable Consequences of Failure are to be considered.

After duly weighing the above Proposition, considering the State of the Enemies Lines, and the Expectation of soon receiving some important Advices from England it was unanimously agreed that it was not expedient to make the Attempt at present at least.

D, in Joseph Reed's writing, DLC:GW; Varick transcript, DLC:GW. An extract of this document, which omits GW's reasons for and against the proposed attack, was enclosed in GW's letter to Hancock of 21 Sept. (DNA:PCC, item 152). Copies of that extract are in DNA:PCC, item 169 and NjMoNP.

1. See Circular to the General Officers, 8 Sept. 1775.

From Captain Gideon Foster

11 September 1775. "Begs Leave to Resign his Command" of a company in Colonel John Mansfield's regiment, "being at this time in an ill State of Health & finds his disorder increasing on him, & . . . his intrest being in a different Situation from what he Expected when he Engaged in the Service whereby he is like to be a great sufferer in his Estate." He recommends Captain John Baker [1] as his successor.

ALS, DLC:GW.

Gideon Foster (1749–1845) of Danvers, Mass., led a company of minutemen on 19 April 1775 from Danvers to West Cambridge, where they attacked the British troops retreating from Concord. Foster left the army about the date of this letter and did not again serve with the Continental forces.

1. This Capt. John Baker was perhaps the one in Col. Samuel Gerrish's Massachusetts regiment who sent GW his resignation on 14 September. Another John Baker served as a captain in Col. Moses Little's Massachusetts regiment from May 1775 to the end of 1776, and there was a Capt. John Baker from Massachusetts in the 27th Continental Regiment throughout 1776.

From Major William Raymond Lee

Camp at Cambg. Sepr 11 1775

Return of the Officer of the Day.

Parole Lancaster. Countersign Middleton.

Went the Rounds, Visited Guards & Centries and found all Vigilent & Alert.

William Lee Officer of the Day

ALS, CtY: Miscellaneous Collections—Obadiah Johnson. Although no other returns from officers of the day directed to GW have been found for the siege of Boston, GW may have received such reports daily.

William Raymond Lee (1744–1824), a merchant from Marblehead, joined Col. John Glover's Massachusetts regiment as a captain on 19 May 1775 and a few weeks later became major of the regiment. Lee held that rank under Glover until January 1777, when Lee was promoted to colonel and was authorized to raise one of the additional Continental regiments. At the urging of Congress, GW offered Lee the position of Continental adjutant general in the spring of 1777, but Lee was obliged to decline in favor of GW's first choice for the job, Timothy Pickering, who, having earlier refused the office, changed his mind and accepted it. Lee recruited his regiment in Massachusetts, and in November 1777 it joined GW's army in Pennsylvania. Lee remained in Massachusetts, however, and on 24 Jan. 1778 he submitted his resignation, which Congress accepted five months later. For GW's favorable opinion of Lee's abilities as an officer, see GW to Richard Henry Lee, 18 Nov. 1777.

Letter not found: to Lund Washington, 11 Sept. 1775. On 15 Oct. 1775 Lund Washington wrote to GW: "I recieve'd on Sunday last two Letters . . . dated 7th & 11th of Septmbr."

General Orders

Head Quarters, Cambridge, Sept. 12th 1775

Parole, Newburry. Countersign, Ogdan.

Varick transcript, DLC:GW.

From Lieutenant Colonel Loammi Baldwin

Chelsea [Mass.] Sept. 12th 1775

May it please Your Excellency 4 oClock P.M.

Enclosed are the Observations of yesterday & to day.[1] I have observed that the Boat at Charlestown Ferry have passed more frequently than usual last Night & this Morning Those from Boston to Charlestown being deeply Loaded with Soldiers & those the Contrary way with none. Nothing Remarkable Since my Last. I am Your Excellencys Most Obediant & Very Humb. Servnt

L. Baldwin Lieut. Coll

ALS, DLC:GW.

1. Joseph Leach's returns of observations for 11 and 12 Sept. are in DLC:GW.

From Perez Morton

Sir, Council Chamber Watertown [Mass.] Septr 12th 1775

Agreable to your Request, I am directed by the Board to inform your Excellency, that in consequence of your Excellency's Letter to the Board, relative to the great Increase of Prisoners here,[1] they apprised the 3 other Colonies of New England, thereof by Letters to their several Assemblies[2]—In Consequence of Which they have received for answer, from Govr Cooke of Rhode Island, that their Assembly have resolved, & are accordingly ready to receive 15 Prisoners—whenever delivered from this Colony[3]—They have also received another Letter from his Honor Govr Trumbull inclosing a Resolve of Council of that Colony of Connecticut, purporting their readiness to receive their proportion of Prisoners, taken by the Continental Army, & pointing out the Counties of Hartford & Windham as the most eligible places for their Reception.[4]

Your Excellency will therefore, during the Recess of the Council[5] send all such Prisoners, as may fortunately fall into Your hands, into the Counties of Hartford & Windham, in the Colony of Connecticut, unless Your Excellency prefers the Colony of Rhode Island, where this Colony has a right to send only 15 in number—The Goals thro' out this Colony are crowded. I am with great respect Your Excellency's most Obedt humb. Servt

Perez Morton Dpy Secry

ALS, DLC:GW.

1. Morton may be referring to the letter that Horatio Gates wrote on behalf of GW to James Warren on 21 July asking for directions on where to send

current and future prisoners. Gates's letter was referred to the council. See General Orders, 29 July 1775, n.1.

2. On 18 Aug. James Otis, Sr., president of the Massachusetts council, wrote to Deputy Gov. Nicholas Cooke of Rhode Island: "In the frequent Encounters we have had with our Unnatural Enemies upon our Coasts, they have in almost every Instance been disappointed and defeated, and many of them have fallen into our hands. Yet this very circumstance has added to the Number of our difficulties. Most of the Goals in this Colony, are already so Crowded with them, that they can hardly contain them all. We therefore request of your Honor that we may send some of our prisoners into your Colony, and that you will be pleased to inform us what places you think proper to assign for the reception of them. As the Cause we are engaged in, is the Common cause of the Colonies, we Cannot entertain a doubt of your ready complyance with our request" (Jones, "Cooke Correspondence," 268–69). Similar letters were apparently sent to Governor Jonathan Trumbull, Sr., of Connecticut and Matthew Thornton, president of the New Hampshire provincial congress.

3. The Rhode Island general assembly resolved on 21 Aug. that Deputy Governor Cooke, "with the advice of the committee appointed to transact public matters during the recess of the Assembly, be requested to write an answer to the letter from the Council of the colony of Massachusetts Bay, dated August 18, 1775, to the Deputy Governor, and to take such orders respecting the prisoners therein referred to, as they shall think proper" (Bartlett, *R.I. Records*, 7:374).

4. Governor Trumbull laid Otis's letter of 18 Aug. before the Connecticut council on 4 Sept., and the council promptly acted: "Although our own prisons were much wanted for our prisoners from the northward, and tories at home; yet for the great affection for the common cause, the Governor and Council did not refuse to receive some of their prisoners, on condition that they should apply to Rhode Island and New Hampshire Assemblies for like favors, and send as sparingly to Connecticut as possible; and that such as they should send, should be sent to the gaols in Hartford and Windham" (Hinman, *Historical Collection*, 332).

5. The General Court recessed from 24 Aug. to 20 September.

Letter not found: from John Augustine Washington, 12 Sept. 1775. On 13 Oct. 1775 GW wrote to his brother John Augustine: "Your favour of the 12th Ulto came safe to hand."

General Orders

Head Quarters, Cambridge, Sept. 13th 1775

Parole Pembroke. Countersign Quebec

The thirty three Riflemen of Col. Thompsons Battalion, tried yesterday by a General Court Martial, whereof Col. Nixon was president, for "disobedient and mutinous Behaviour"; are each of them sentenced to pay the sum of Twenty Shillings, except John Leamon, who, over and above his fine, is to suffer six days imprisonment—The Pay Master of the regiment to stop the Fine from each man, out of their next Month's pay, which must be paid to Dr Church for the use of the General hospital.[1]

Varick transcript, DLC:GW.

1. For an account of the mutiny, see Nathanael Greene to GW, 10 Sept. 1775, n.1. Jesse Lukens wrote on 13 Sept. that the culprits received "too small a punishment for so base a crime. Mitigated, no doubt, on account of their having come so far to serve the cause and its being the first crime. The men are returned to their camp and seem exceedingly sorry for their misbehavior and promise amendment" (*Pa. Archives*, 2d ser., 10:8–10). John Leaman was a private in Capt. George Nagel's Pennsylvania rifle company.

General Orders

Head Quarters. Cambridge, Sept. 14th 1775

Parole Roxborough. Countersign Salem

In obedience to the General Order of the 7th Instant, the enquiry into the Conduct of Dr Church, the Director General of the Hospital, and the respective Regimental Surgeons, has been held in Genl Sullivan's Brigade; that being finish'd, the General orders the like to be held forthwith in Genl Green's brigade.

Varick transcript, DLC:GW.

To Colonel Benedict Arnold

Sir, Cambridge Head Quarters Septr 14. 1775

You are intrusted with a Command of the utmost Consequence to the Interest & Liberties of America: Upon your Conduct & Courage & that of the Officers and ⟨Soldiers⟩ detached on this Expedition, not only the Success of the present Enterprize & your own Honour, but the Safety and Welfare of the whole Continent may depend. I ⟨charge⟩ you therefore and the Officers & Soldiers ⟨under⟩ your Command as you value your own Safety and Honour, & the Favour and Esteem of your Country that you consider yourselves as marching not through an Enemies Country, but that of our Friends and Brethren, for such the Inhabitants of Canada & the Indian Nations have approved themselves in this unhappy Contest between Great Brittain & America.

That you check by every Motive of Duty, and Fear of Punishment every Attempt to Plunder or insult any of the Inhabitants of Canada. Should any ⟨American Soldier be so base⟩ and infamous as ⟨to injure⟩ any Canadian or Indian in his Person or Property, I do most earnestly enjoin you to bring him to such severe & exemplary Punishment as the Enormity of the Crime may require. Should it extend to Death itself, it will not be disproportionate to its Guilt at such a Time and in such a Cause. But I hope and trust that the brave Men who have voluntarily engaged in this Expedition will be govern'd by different Views that Order, Discipline, & Regularity of Behavi⟨our⟩ will be as conspicuous as their Courage & Valour. I also give it in Charge to you to avoid all Disrespect or Contempt of the Religion of the Country and its Ceremonies—Prudence, Policy and a true Christian Spirit will lead us to look with Compassion upon their Errors without insulting them—While we are Contending for our own Liberty, we should be very cautious of violating the Rights of Conscience in others; ever considering that God alone is the Judge of the Hearts of Men and to him only in this Case they are answerable.

Upon the whole, Sir, I beg you to inculcate upon the Officers,[1] the Necessity of preserving the Strictest Order during their March thro' Canada to represent to them ⟨the Shame & Disgrace⟩ and Ruin to themselves & Country if they should by their Conduct turn the Hearts of our Brethren in Canada against us. And on the other Hand the Honour and Rewards which await them, if by their Prudence, and good Behaviour they conciliate the Affections of the Canadians & Indians to the great Interests of America, & convert those favourable Dispositions they have shewn into a lasting Union and Affection.

Thus wishing you and the Officers and Soldiers under your Command all Honour, Safety and Success I ⟨remain⟩ Sir Your most Obedt Humble Servt

Go: Washington

LS, in Thomas Mifflin's writing, CLjJC; Df, DLC:GW; copy, NjMoNP; Varick transcript, DLC:GW. The LS is mutilated in several places. Illegible words and letters are supplied within angle brackets from the draft.

1. The draft reads "the Officers & Soldiers."

Instructions to Colonel Benedict Arnold

[Cambridge, 14 September 1775]

By his Excellency George Washington Esqr. Commander in Chief of the Army of the United Colonies of North America.

1. You are immediately on their March from Cambridge to take the Command of the Detachment from the Continental Army against Quebeck, & use all possible Expedition as the Winter Season is now Advancing, and the Success of this Enterprize (under God) depends wholly upon the Spirit with which it is pushed, & the favourable Disposition of the Canadians & Indians.[1]

2. When you come to Newbury Port you are to make all possible Inquiry what Men of War or Cruizers there may be on the Coast to which this Detachment may be exposed on their Voyage to Kennebeck River—and if you shall find that there is Danger of being intercepted you are not to proceed by Water, but by Land, taking Care on the one Hand not to be diverted by light, & vague Reports, & on the other not to expose the Troops rashly to a Danger which by many judicious Persons has been deemed very considerable.[2]

3. You are by every Means in your Power to Endeavour to discover the real Sentiments of the Canadians towards our Cause & particularly to this Expedition: Ever bearing in Mind that if they are averse to it, & will not Co-operate or at least willingly acquiesce it must fail of Success—In this Case you are by no means to prosecute the Attempt, the Expence of the Expedition & the Disappointment are not to be put in Competition with the dangerous Consequences which may ensue from irritating them against us, and detaching them from that Neutrality which they have adopted.

4. In order to cherish those favourable Sentiments to the America⟨n⟩ cause that they have manifested you are as soon as you arrive in their Country to disperse a Number of the Addresses you will have with you,[3] particularly in those Parts where your Rout shall lay, and observe the strictest Discipline & good Order, by no Means suffering any Inhabitant to be abused or in any Manner injured either in his Person or Property—punishing with examplary Severity every Person who shall trangress & making ample Compensation to the Party injured.

5. You are to endeavour on the other Hand to conciliate the Affections of those People & such Indians as you may meet with by every Means in your Power—convincing them that we Come at the Request of many of their Principal People, not as Robbers or to make War upon them but as the Friends & Supporters of their Liberties as well as ours: And to give Efficacy to these Sentiments you must carefully inculcate upon the Officers & Soldiers under your Command that not only the Good of their Country & their Honour, but their Safety depends upon the Treatment of this People.

6. Check every Idea; & crush in its earliest Stage every Attempt to plunder even those who are known to be Enemies to our Cause, it will create dreadful Apprehensions in our Friends, and when it is once begun none can tell where it will Stop, I therefore again most expressly order that it be discouraged & punished in every Instance without Distinction.

7. Whatever King's Stores you shall be so fortunate as to possess yourself of, are to be secured for the Continental Use agreeable to the Rules and Regulations of War published by the Honourable Congress.[4] The Officers and Men may be assur'd that any extraordinary Services performed by them will be Suitably rewarded.

8. Spare neither Pains or Expence to gain all possible Intelligence on your March, to prevent Surprizes & Accidents of every kind—& endeavour if possible to Correspond with General Schuyler so that you may act in Concert with him. This I think may be done by Means of the St Francois Indians.

9. In Case of an Union with General Schuyler, or if he should be in Canada upon your Arrival there, you are by no means to consider yourself as upon a Seperate & independant Command but are to put yourself under him & follow his Directions. Upon this Occasion & all others I recommend most earnestly to avoid all Contention about Rank—In such a Cause every Post is honourable in which a Man can serve his Country.

10. If Lord Chatham's Son should be in Canada, & in any Way fall in your Power you are enjoined to treat him with all possible Deference and Respect. You cannot err in paying too much Honour to the Son of so illustrious a Character & so true a Friend to America.[5] Any other Prisoners who may fall into your Hands you will treat with as much Humanity & Kindness as

may be consistent with your own Safety & the publick Interest. Be very particular in restraining not only your own Troops but the Indians from all Acts of Cruelty & Insult which will disgrace the American Arms—& irritate our Fellow Subjects against us.

11. You will be particularly careful to pay the full Value for all Provisions or other Accommodations which the Canadians may provide for you on your March. By no Means press them or any of their Cattle into your Service, but amply Compensate those who voluntarily assist you. For this Purpose you are provided with a Sum of Money in Specie, which you will use with much Frugality & Oeconomy as your Necessities & good Policy will admit—keeping as exact an Account as possible of your Disbursements.[6]

12. You are by every Opportunity to inform me of your Progress, your Prospects & Intelligence—& upon any important Occurrence to dispatch an Express.

13. As the Season is now far Advanced you are to make all possible Dispatch—but if unforeseen Difficulties should arise or if the Weather should become so severe as to render it hazardous to proceed in your own Judgment & that of your principal Officers (whom you are to Consult)—In that Case you are to return: giving me as early Notice as possible that I may give you such Assistance as may be necessary.

14. As the Contempt of the Religion of a Country by ridiculing any of its Ceremonies or affronting its Ministers or Votaries has ever been deeply resented—You are to be particularly careful to restrain every Officer & Soldier from such Imprudence & Folly & to punish every Instance of it—On the other Hand as far as lays in your Power you are to protect & support the free Exercise of the Religion of the Country & the undisturbed Enjoyment of the Rights of Conscience in religious Matters with your utmost Influence & Authority—Given under my Hand, at Head Quarters Cambridge, this 14th Day of September, One Thousand Seven hundred & Seventy five.

G. W.

Copy, in Thomas Mifflin's writing, DLC:GW; copy, DNA:PCC, item 152; copy, DNA:PCC, item 169; two copies, NjMoNP; Varick transcript, DLC:GW. The copy in PCC, item 152 was enclosed in GW to Hancock, 21 Sept. 1775.

1. Arnold's detachment left Cambridge between 11 and 13 September.

2. Arnold sailed with his men from Newburyport on 19 Sept. and reached Gardiner on the Kennebec River three days later.

3. See Address to the Inhabitants of Canada, c.14 Sept. 1775.

4. Article 29 of the Continental articles of war provides that "all public stores taken in the enemy's camp or magazines, whether of artillery, ammunition, cloathing, or provisions, shall be secured for the use of the United Colonies" (*JCC*, 2:116).

5. John Pitt (1756–1835), eldest son of William Pitt, first earl of Chatham (1708–1778), joined the 47th Regiment of Foot as an ensign in March 1774, and at this time he was in Canada acting as an aide-de-camp to the regiment's commander, Maj. Gen. Guy Carleton. "I hope," Thomas Jefferson wrote to John Page about 10 Dec. 1775, "Ld. Chatham may live till the fortune of war puts his son into our hands, and enables us by returning him safe to his father, to pay a debt of gratitude" (Julian P. Boyd et al., eds., *The Papers of Thomas Jefferson* [Princeton, 1950—], 1:270–71). Pitt and Carleton were nearly captured in September, and in October Carleton sent Pitt to England with dispatches. To avoid embarrassing his father, who strongly opposed the British government's American policy, Pitt resigned his commission in early 1776. At his father's death in 1778 Pitt became the second earl of Chatham, and that same year he rejoined the British army as a lieutenant. He was promoted to captain in 1779 and served at Gibraltar from 1779 to 1783.

6. See GW to James Warren, 10 Sept. 1775.

From Captain John Baker

Cambridge, 14 September 1775. "Whereas Some Deficulty has arose between him & Joseph Pettigill who Shall Command the tenth Company in the 38 Regiment Command[ed] By Colonel Baldwin," the matter was referred to "three officer[s] in Sd Regimt who brought in their award in favour of Sd Pettingall."[1] Baker asks to be discharged from the service.

LS, DLC:GW.

For a discussion of the various Capt. John Bakers in the Continental army during this period, see Gideon Foster to GW, 11 Sept. 1775, n.1.

1. The 38th Regiment, formerly commanded by Col. Samuel Gerrish, was now commanded by Lt. Col. Loammi Baldwin. Joseph Pettengill (Pettingill; 1741–1785) of Andover, Mass., served as an enlisted man on expeditions against Canada and Crown Point during the French and Indian War. He apparently joined Col. James Scammans's regiment as a second lieutenant in May 1775, and by 22 June he was a first lieutenant in Gerrish's regiment. Pettengill served as a captain under Baldwin until the end of 1776, when he transferred to the 9th Massachusetts Regiment. After some dispute about precedence with other Massachusetts captains, Pettengill was promoted to major in July 1779. A year later GW appointed him brigade inspector for a

Massachusetts brigade, and in Sept. 1781 Pettengill became major of the 1st Massachusetts Regiment. He served in that regiment until the end of the war.

Address to the Inhabitants of Canada

Friends and Brethren, [c.14 September 1775]

The unnatural Contest between the English Colonies and Great-Britain, has now risen to such a Heighth, that Arms alone must decide it. The Colonies, confiding in the Justice of their Cause, and the Purity of their Intentions, have reluctantly appealed to that Being, in whose Hands are all human Events. He has hitherto smiled upon their virtuous Efforts—The Hand of Tyranny has been arrested in its Ravages, and the British Arms which have shone with so much Splendor in every Part of the Globe, are now tarnished with Disgrace and Disappointment.—Generals of approved Experience, who boasted of subduing this great Continent, find themselves circumscribed within the Limits of a single City and its Suburbs, suffering all the Shame and Distress of a Siege. While the trueborn Sons of America, animated by the genuine Principles of Liberty and Love of their Country, with increasing Union, Firmness and Discipline repel every Attack, and despise every Danger.

Above all, we rejoice, that our Enemies have been deceived with Regard to you—They have perswaded themselves, they have even dared to say, that the Canadians were not capable of distinguishing between the Blessings of Liberty, and the Wretchedness of Slavery; that gratifying the Vanity of a little Circle of Nobility—would blind the Eyes of the People of Canada.—By such Artifices they hoped to bend you to their Views, but they have been deceived, instead of finding in you that Poverty of Soul, and Baseness of Spirit, they see with a Chagrin equal to our Joy, that you are enlightned, generous, and virtuous—that you will not renounce your own Rights, or serve as Instruments to deprive your Fellow Subjects of theirs.—Come then, my Brethren, unite with us in an indissoluble Union, let us run together to the same Goal.—We have taken up Arms in Defence of our Liberty, our Property, our Wives, and our Children, we are determined to preserve them, or die. We look forward with Pleasure to that Day not far remote (we hope) when the Inhabitants of America shall have one Sentiment, and the full Enjoyment of the Blessings of a free Government.

Incited by these Motives, and encouraged by the Advice of many Friends of Liberty among you, the Grand American Congress have sent an Army into your Province, under the Command of General Schuyler; not to plunder, but to protect you; to animate, and bring forth into Action those Sentiments of Freedom you have disclosed, and which the Tools of Despotism would extinguish through the whole Creation.—To co-operate with this Design, and to frustrate those cruel and perfidious Schemes, which would deluge our Frontiers with the Blood of Women and Children; I have detached Colonel Arnold into your Country, with a Part of the Army under my Command—I have enjoined upon him, and I am certain that he will consider himself, and act as in the Country of his Patrons, and best Friends. Necessaries and Accommodations of every Kind which you may furnish, he will thankfully receive, and render the full Value.—I invite you therefore as Friends and Brethren, to porvide him with such Supplies as your Country affords; and I pledge myself not only for your Safety and Security, but for ample Compensation. Let no Man desert his Habitation—Let no one flee as before an Enemy. The Cause of America, and of Liberty, is the Cause of every virtuous American Citizen; whatever may be his Religion or his Descent, the United Colonies know no Distinction but such as Slavery, Corruption and arbitrary Domination may create. Come then, ye generous Citizens, range yourselves under the Standard of general Liberty—against which all the Force and Artifice of Tyranny will never be able to prevail.

G. Washington.

Broadside, in English and French, DLC:GW; Df, in English, DLC:GW; copy, in French, DNA:PCC, item 35; copy, in English, DNA:PCC, item 169; copy, in English, NjMoNP; Varick transcript, in English, DLC:GW. None of the manuscript copies of this document are dated, but it must have been written about the same time as GW's letter and instructions to Benedict Arnold of 14 September. See item number 4 of Instructions to Arnold, this date. On 20 Sept. Joseph Reed sent Arnold a number of printed copies of the address to be distributed in Canada, apologizing for the delay in printing them (DLC:GW). Arnold received the printed addresses on 25 Sept. (Arnold to GW, that date). The French text of the broadside in DLC:GW is corrected grammatically in

Charles Lee's writing. The copy in PCC, item 169, is a copy of the copy that GW enclosed in his letter to Hancock of 21 Sept. 1775. The address was printed in many contemporary newspapers.

From Nicholas Cooke

Sir Providence Septemr 14th 1775.

I am favoured with a Letter from Govr Trumbull in Answer to mine proposing a Voyage to Bayonne, in which he informs me that the Council of the Colony of Connecticut are summoned to meet this Day to take the Scheme into Consideration.[1] This Sir is the Time to exert ourselves in sending to Europe for Powder, as the Vessels may perform their Voyages and return upon this Coast in the Winter, when the Enemy's Ships are unable to cruize. I have written to our Delegates strongly recommending it to them to use their Influence that Measures may be taken to procure sufficient Quantities of that necessary Article.[2] I have also advised them to move in Congress for opening some Lead Mines immediately, as the depending upon a precarious Supply by Sea when we have such Quantities in our own Country seems to me very preposterous. And I believe the Article in this Way will cost us less Money than it can be imported for.

Capt. Whipple sailed on Tuesday with Sixty-one Men on board; his Vessel being clean and every Way in good Order. I have given him Instructions to cruize Fourteen Days off Sandy-Hook for the Packet, and if he is so fortunate as to meet her to take her at all Events, to take out of her the Letters, Arms, Ammunition, and warlike Stores, and to land the Letters at South-Hampton and forward them immediately by Express. After the taking of the Packet or the Expiration of that Time he is immediately to proceed to Bermuda and, if possible, take the Powder into Possession without any Communication with the Inhabitants. I have given it to him strictly in Charge not to make any Use of your Address unless in Case of absolute Necessity.[3]

The noble Example set by the Lord Mayor, Aldermen and Livery of London in their late Address to the King, will, I hope have a good Effect in the other Parts of the Kingdom,[4] &, together with the Disaffection of the People of Ireland to the iniquitous Measures now pursuing against the Colonies, added to our own Efforts, compel the Ministry to depart from their favourite Plan of establishing arbitrary Power in America.

This Letter waits upon you by Joshua Babcock Esqr.—He is a Gentleman of a genteel Fortune, a Member of our General Assembly, and hath highly distinguished himself in the glorious Cause in which America is embarked.[5] I beg Leave to recommend him to your Excellency's Notice, and am with great Esteem and Regard, Sir Your most humble and most obedient Servant

Nichols Cooke

LS, DLC:GW. The addressed cover includes the notation "Favoured by J. Babcock Esqr."

1. The Connecticut council on this date answered Cooke "that the colony had expended their money so largely in the article of powder that their funds were nearly exhausted, and though they expected a supply, they refused the offer, but recommended to him to propose the measure to Gen. Washington" (Hinman, *Historical Collection*, 334).

2. Delegate Samuel Ward of Rhode Island laid Cooke's proposal before the members of Congress's secret committee on the importation of gunpowder. "I am instructed," Ward wrote to Cooke on 5 Oct. 1775, "to acquaint You That they approve of the Plan and in Behalf of the united Colonies agree to advance a sufficient Sum of continental Money to purchase sixty or eighty Tons of good Gun Powder as suits You best. . . . The Money shall be paid to your Order on Sight. . . . If the whole Quantity of Gun Powder cannot be got the Comee would have as much Salt Petre with a proportionate Quantity of Sulphur to manufacture with it purchased as will make up the proposed Quantity of Powder" (Smith, *Letters of Delegates*, 2:122–23). Whether or not this voyage was made is not known.

3. Abraham Whipple sailed in the armed sloop *Katy* on 12 September. For Cooke's instruction to Whipple, see Clark, *Naval Documents*, 2:76–78. The address was the one to the inhabitants of Bermuda, dated 6 Sept. 1775, printed above.

4. On 24 June 1775 the livery of the City of London approved an address petitioning the king to change his policy toward the American colonies: "We have seen, with equal dread and concern, a civil war commenced in America, by your Majesty's commander in chief: Will your Majesty be pleased to consider what must be the situation of your people here, who have nothing now to expect from America, but Gazettes of blood, and mutual lists of their slaughtered fellow-subjects. Every moment's prosecution of this fatal war may loosen irreparably the bonds of that connection, on which the glory and safety of the British empire depend. . . . Your petitioners therefore again pray and beseech your Majesty to dismiss your present Ministers and advisers from your person and councils for ever; to dissolve a Parliament, who, by

various acts of cruelty and injustice, have manifested a spirit of persecution against our brethren in America, and given their sanction to popery and arbitrary power; to put your future confidence in Ministers, whose known and unshaken attachment to the constitution, joined to your wisdom and integrity, may enable your Majesty to settle this alarming dispute upon the sure, honourable, and lasting foundations of general liberty" (*Pennsylvania Gazette* [Philadelphia], 13 Sept. 1775).

5. Joshua Babcock (1707–1783), a physician and merchant from Westerly who had studied medicine in England, became major general of the Rhode Island militia on 3 May 1776. He was a member of a committee of three members that the general assembly sent in Sept. 1776 to confer with GW about the defense of Rhode Island.

General Orders

Head Quarters, Cambridge, Sept. 15th 1775

Parole, Pittsburgh. Countersign, Ulster.

Col. John Mansfield of the 19th Regt of foot, tried at a General Court Martial, whereof Brigdr Genl Green was president, for "remissness and backwardness in the execution of his duty, at the late engagement on Bunkers-hill"; The Court found the Prisoner guilty of the Charge and of a breach of the 49th Article of the rules and regulations of the Massachusetts Army and therefore sentence him to be cashiered and render'd unfit to serve in the Continental Army. The General approves the sentence and directs it to take place immediately.[1]

Moses Pickett, Soldier in Capt. Merrits Company,[2] Col. Glovers regiment, tried at a General Court Martial for "Disobedience of orders, and damning his Officers," is found guilty, and sentenced to receive thirty Lashes upon his bare back, and afterwards drum'd out of the regiment—The General orders the punishment to be inflicted at the head of the regiment, to morrow morning at troop beating.

As Col. Frys Brigade is to be mustered to morrow Morning, Genl Heath's brigade will furnish the Guards in, and about Cambridge, for to morrow.

Varick transcript, DLC:GW.

1. For the appointment and sitting of Mansfield's court-martial, see General Orders, 13 and 17 Aug. 1775.

2. Capt. John Merritt of Marblehead commanded a company in Col. John Glover's Massachusetts regiment.

From Lieutenant Colonel Loammi Baldwin

Chelsea [Mass.] Sept. 15th 1775

May it please your Excellency Friday 2 oClock P.M.

I have Just Returnd to Chelsea am Informed that the Kings troops at Bunker Hill have thrown up a Short peice of Brest work with two Embrasures nearly oposite Greens Hill Point I have not Seen it my Selfe but prepose to go down directly & take a View of it, and if it appears formidable or Materially deferant from this account I shall Inform your Excellency by Express but the Bearer of this is now waiting.

Enclosd are the Observations up to this time that have not been Sent before.[1] I am your Excellencys m⟨ost⟩ obediant Humbe Servnt

Loammi Baldwin Lieut. Coll

P.S. The Said Brest work is about 30 yards from high water Mark & they were at work upon it yesterday.

ALS, DLC:GW.

1. Baldwin apparently enclosed the returns of observations for 13, 14, and 15 Sept., all in Joseph Leach's writing (DLC:GW).

From John Collins

Sir, Newport Sept. 15th 1775

Agreeable to a Vote of the Committee of Inspection for this Town, I inclose you a true Copy of an intercepted Letter from the late Govr Hutchinson to a Gentleman in this Colony, only omitting the Names of that Gentleman, and the Bearer of the Letter, both of whom are Friends to the Liberties of America.

The Letter was laid before the Committee the last Evening; and although it is of an old Date; yet as it contains a Paragraph which may respect your Excellency as Generalissimo of the Forces of the United Colonies of America, We thought it our Duty thus early to transmit you a Copy of it.[1] I am with the greatest Respect Your Excellency's most obedt Hble Servant

John Collins Chairn

LS, DLC:GW.

John Collins (1717–1795), a prominent merchant in Newport, was active on the town's committee of safety as early as January 1774. He served in the

Rhode Island general assembly from 1774 to 1778, and in Sept. 1776 he was a member of the committee that the assembly sent to confer with GW about defending the state. Elected to the Continental Congress in May 1778, Collins remained a delegate until 1783 except for a period of several months between the spring of 1781 and the fall of 1782.

1. Thomas Hutchinson (1711–1780), royal governor of Massachusetts from 1771 to 1774, had long been a leading antagonist of the radical Whigs in America. In June 1774 he sailed to England, expecting to return soon to his native Massachusetts, but the coming of the war obliged him to remain in exile for the remainder of his days. The copy of Hutchinson's letter that Collins enclosed to GW is dated 2 June 1775, St. James's Street, London. "I could not let —— go to America without a Line to my old Friend and Acquaintance," Hutchinson wrote. "I hope it will find you alive and in health, but looking forward towards the hopeful state of peace and quiet in a World to which you and I are hastening. If I had no Connexions with America, my Situation in England would be far from disagreeable, but I find my Attachment to my Native Country increased by my distance from it. I am distressed by the last News of Hostilities commenced between the King's Troops and the Inhabitants of Massachusetts Bay, and at present, see nothing but ruin and misery like to follow, the general Voice here being for greater force to be sent to America, but I am informed the Ministry wait for dispatches from General Gage which are not yet arrived. I think your State must be not unlike that of the Man who stands upon the Shore and sees the Ships, in the Storm, tossed with the Waves, and their Crews in danger of perishing every moment, and, though he feels pity and compassion for them, yet he blesses his Maker for preserving him in Security from the like Storms and Perils" (DLC:GW).

From Nicholas Cooke

Sir Providence Septemr 15th 1775

I observe that in the Cambridge Paper of Yesterday there is an Extract of a Letter from Bermuda to New York giving an Account that upwards of 100 Barrels of Powder had been taken out of the Magazine, supposed to have been done by a Vessel from Philadelphia and another from South-Carolina. This Intelligence appears to me to be true; and I beg to know your Excellency's Opinion of it as soon as possible, that if it be thought best to relinquish the Expedition I may recall Capt. Whipple as soon as his Cruize for the Packet is out.[1] His Station in this River is very necessary as Capt. Wallace hath equipped a Sloop with Six and a Schooner with Four Carriage Guns who may be very troublesome here.[2] I am with great Respect Sir Your most humble Servant

Nichols Cooke

LS, DLC:GW; Df, RHi: Cooke Papers.

1. The extract of this anonymous letter from Bermuda, dated 21 Aug. 1775, appears in the *New-England Chronicle: or, the Essex Gazette* (Cambridge, Mass.), 14 Sept. 1775: "Upwards of one hundred barrels of gun-powder has been taken out of our magazine: supposed by a sloop from Philadelphia, and a schooner from South Carolina: It was very easily accomplished, from the magazine being situated far distant from town, and no dwelling house near it." For an account of the raid on the magazine on 14 Aug. by a group of Bermudians, see Cooke to GW, 11 Aug. 1775, n.2. The sloop was the *Lady Catherine*, which the Pennsylvania committee of safety sent to Bermuda to obtain gunpowder, and the schooner was the *Charles Town and Savannah Packet*, dispatched on the same mission by the South Carolina committee of safety. The *Lady Catherine* arrived at Philadelphia on 26 Aug. with about eighteen hundred pounds of gunpowder, and the *Charles Town and Savannah Packet* apparently reached Charleston with its cargo about the same time. For Cooke's unsuccessful efforts to recall Abraham Whipple from his voyage to Bermuda, see Cooke to GW, 26, 29 Sept. and 25 Oct. 1775.

2. Vice Admiral Samuel Graves wrote on 1 Sept. 1775 that "it was by the Admirals allowing Captain [James] Wallace to keep on board the *Rose* a party of 37 Marines above his Complement, besides many supernumerary Seamen in his own and the other Ships and Vessels with him, that he was enabled to arm Vessels suited to the Navigation of the small Rivers and Creeks, and whenever occasion required to land a hundred men and upwards and ravage the coast" (Graves's narrative in Clark, *Naval Documents*, 1:1282–83).

From Jonathan Trumbull, Sr.

Sir Lebanon [Conn.] 15th September 1775

I have received your Excellency's Letter of the 8th instant ℘ Express who was detained by sickness, and did not deliver it 'till the 12th in the Evening, and my own bodily indisposition is some hindrance. Your peremptory requisition is fully complied with, all our new levies will be at your Camp, with all convenient Expedition.[1]

At the time they were by your direction to remain in the Colony on some reason to suspect a remove from Boston to New York, that they might be able to give them more speedy opposition[2]—I ordered Colo. Webb of our 7th Regiment, his men being raised in the Western part of the Colony, to take his station with three or four Companies at Greenwich the nearest Town of this Colony to New York, his Lt Colo. and Company at New Haven[3]—The Residue of his and Colo. Huntington's who were forward in their March, one Company to Norwich, and the rest to New London—last Week I sent Orders to Colo. Webb to march the Companies with him to New Haven, to be on his way so much nearer to your Camp.[4]

I am surprised that mine of the 5th instant was not received or not judged worthy of Notice, as no mention is made of it.

Stonington had been Attacked, and severely cannonaded and by divine Providence marvellously protected.

New London and Stonington are still menaced by the Ministerial Ships and Troops, that the militia cannot be thought sufficient for their security—That 'tis necessary to cast up some Entrenchments.[5]

We are oblidged actually to raise more Men for their Security and for the Towns of New Haven and Lyme[6]—I hoped some of the new Levies might have been left here 'till these dangers were Over, without injury to any of your Operations. I own that must be left to your Judgment—Yet it would have given me pleasure to have been acquainted that you did consider it.

I thank Divine Providence and you for this early warning to great care and watchfulness, that so the Union of the Colonies may be settled on a permanent and happy Basis.

I have before me your more acceptable Letter of the 9th instant—The Necessities of the Colony to supply our two armed Vessels, to furnish the men necessarily raised for Defence of our Sea Ports and Coasts, and to raise the Lead Ore, which appears very promising, prevents our being able to spare more than half a Ton—which is Ordered forward with Expedition—Before the Necessity of raising more Men appeared, We intended to send a Ton.[7]

You may depend on our utmost Exertions for the defence and security of the Constitutional Rights and Liberty of the Colonies, and of our own in particular—none have shewn greater forwardness and thereby rendered themselves more the Objects of Ministerial Vengeance. I am, with great Esteem and Regard for your personal Character Sir Your most Obedient and very humble Servant

Jonth. Trumbull

P.S. The Glascow and Rose Men of War are not at Newport, and threaten that on the Return of the Swan from Boston, probably with Men for the purpose they will attack New London and Stonington.[8]

All the Regiments in the Colony, at a great Expence have been extraordinarily disciplined, And one quarter of them on the Sea Coasts are selected, equiped and held in readiness as minute Men for every Emergency.[9]

ALS, DLC:GW; LB, Ct: Trumbull Papers.

1. GW's letter to Trumbull of 8 Sept. was laid before the Connecticut council on 14 September: "On this there was great consideration. The troops were much wanted in the colony at their stations in New Haven, New London, and Lyme, to throw up and build works of defence against the British ships that were hovering about the eastern coast of the colony. These but a short time before, had cannonaded Stonington, and threats repeatedly made after that attack, rendered it probable that some other places on the coast would soon be attacked by the British, and therefore that the removal of the troops to Boston would greatly endanger the towns on the coasts in the colony; but, fearing, that should they refuse to send said troops, advantage would be taken against the colony, and though they would not be as useful at the camp, as they would be in their employments at their stations, yet it was thought most prudent to comply with the demand; and they were immediately ordered to march to the camp near Boston" (Hinman, *Historical Collection*, 333–34).

2. In his letter to Trumbull of 14 Aug., GW permitted the recruits raised by colonels Charles Webb and Jedediah Huntington to remain in Connecticut as long as there was a threat that the main British army might move from Boston to New York.

3. On 1 July 1775 the Connecticut general assembly appointed Street Hall (1721–1809) of Wallingford lieutenant colonel and captain of the second company in Col. Charles Webb's regiment. A brother of Lyman Hall of Georgia, Street Hall served as a lieutenant colonel under Webb until the end of 1776.

4. At a meeting of the council on 8 Sept., "three companies, under Col. Webb, at Greenwich, were ordered to New Haven, to erect intrenchments at five mile point, or elsewhere, as Colonels Webb and Hall should advise; on condition that if the report in circulation, of the troops coming to New York, should appear to Col. Webb to be true, that he should remain at Greenwich until farther orders" (Hinman, *Historical Collection*, 333).

5. For an account of the British attack of 30 Aug. on Stonington and the council's defensive measures, see Trumbull to GW, 5 Sept. 1775, n.2.

6. On 14 Sept. the council directed Maj. Oliver Smith "to enlist 50 men . . . for the defence of Stonington, and for carrying on the works began there, until the 20th of October, 1775. And 70 men were ordered to be raised in the same manner and for the same purposes at New London, under Col. [Gurdon] Saltonstall; and 20 men to be raised at Lyme, to watch and guard at Black Point, Black Hall, &c., where the cattle and stock were the most exposed to be plundered, under Lee Lay, as ensign; also to raise 50 men at New Haven, to be employed there for defence, and to erect works of defence, if thought advisable by the people at New Haven,—to be under such officers as should

be nominated by Wm. Williams and Nath'l. Wales" (Hinman, *Historical Collection*, 334).

7. On 14 Sept. the council ordered ½ ton of gunpowder sent to GW. The arming of two vessels was authorized by the colony's general assembly on 1 July. For a discussion of the lead mine at Middletown, see Trumbull to GW, 21 Aug. 1775, n.3.

8. The British sloop of war *Swan* sailed for Boston with some transport vessels on 16 Oct. and returned to Newport on 26 November. "Altho' the *Swan* is not in a fit condition to be much longer on Service without being hove down," Vice Admiral Samuel Graves wrote to Capt. James Wallace of the *Rose* on 4 Nov., "yet her Captain being so well acquainted determines me to send her back to you again until I can relieve her with either a good Sloop or Frigate" (Clark, *Naval Documents*, 2:881–82). The British did not again attack Stonington during the war, and New London remained undisturbed until Benedict Arnold raided the town in 1781.

9. Trumbull is referring to the colony's militia regiments (Trumbull to GW, 8 Aug. 1775).

Index

Abatis, 129, 130
Abbot, Samuel: militia regiment, 267; id., 268
Abercromby, James: death, 312
Adams, Abigail: *letters from*: to John Adams, 117–18; *letters to*: from John Adams, 28, 239
Adams, Daniel Jenifer: debt to GW, 335; id., 338
Adams, John: and GW's appointment, 1–2, 8, 22; opinion of GW, 2, 2–3; makes recommendations, 12, 26; id., 26; and intercepted letters, 149, 239, 260; and Donald Campbell, 173; and scheme to blockade Boston Harbor, 210; attends Massachusetts council, 291, 292; and Bermuda expedition, 305; *letters from*: to Elbridge Gerry, 2–3, 20; to GW, 8–12; to James Warren, 10, 43, 45–46, 149, 239, 249; to William Tudor, 10, 12, 149; to Abigail Adams, 28, 239; to Josiah Quincy, Sr., 210; *letters to*: from James Warren, 62, 143, 198, 207, 219, 231, 398; from Abigail Adams, 117–18; from Josiah Quincy, Sr., 210; from Benjamin Hichborn, 260; from Samuel Holden Parsons, 330; from William Tudor, 330
Adams, Samuel, 45; and GW's appointment, 22; id., 26; makes recommendations, 26; and intercepted letters, 149; secretary to Massachusetts council, 208; *letters from*: to Elbridge Gerry, 26; to James Warren, 26
Adjutant general: appointed, 17, 18, 19, 78–79; and returns, 72, 107, 111, 122–23, 123, 134, 185, 197, 261, 277; and horses, 75; orders for guards, 178, 190, 206, 208; applies for ammunition, 211; and duty rosters, 317; orders for mustering, 317; William Henshaw acts as, 328, 328–29; and rank of regiments, 329; and brickmakers, 357; parades detachment, 415. *See also* Gates, Horatio; Henshaw, William
Adjutants: and general orders, 62–63, 123; and returns, 107, 111, 134; adjutant of the day, 419
Agriculture: corn crop, 30; wheat planting, 337, 340
Albany committee of safety: recruits troops, 256; *letters from*: to Continental Congress, 43, 91; to Philip Schuyler, 121; *letters to*: from Tryon County (N.Y.) committee of safety, 121
Alden, Ichabod: court-martial president, 431, 449; id., 432
Alexander, —— (express rider), 64, 84, 93, 96, 230, 239, 244, 245
Alexandria: GW's property in, 4, 5, 335
Alfred (Alford), Thomas, 336; id., 339
Alfred, William: reprimanded, 50
Allen, Alexander: captured, 320
Allen, Ethan: captures Ticonderoga, 40
Ammunition: for Virginia independent companies, 17, 77; shortage in New York, 35, 47, 121, 294, 299, 309, 443; for posts on Lake Champlain, 37; returns, 49, 54, 75–76, 139, 214, 216, 227, 232; committees of Continental Congress, 56, 241; artillery cartridges, 74, 191, 214, 363; for Massachusetts militia, 105; taken to religious service, 122; sent to Block Island, 199; conservation, 214, 218–19, 227, 310, 325, 364, 400; as plunder, 215, 460; for Connecticut militia, 268; shortage in Rhode Island, 271, 272, 273, 288; shortage in Connecticut, 294, 309, 344; magazine, 317; shortage in Pennsylvania, 321, 403;

Ammunition (*cont.*)
British supplies, 336, 395; laboratory, 364; for armed vessels, 398; orders to capture, 398, 400, 463
gunpowder: shortage in Continental army, 32, 35, 36, 85, 89, 211, 214, 216, 221, 227, 242, 244, 257, 277, 298, 304, 306, 307–8, 336, 350, 364, 373–74, 374, 385–86, 390, 391, 403, 404, 419, 433, 444, 451; sent to Continental army, 35, 36, 44–45, 45–46, 125, 126, 209, 210, 294, 294–95, 299, 307, 308, 309, 319, 321, 331, 333, 344, 373, 391, 401, 402, 403, 404, 424, 430, 443–44, 469, 471; collected in colonies, 36, 44–45, 45–46, 94, 145, 149, 211, 216, 221, 227, 242, 244, 277, 308, 385–86, 386, 444; manufacture, 36, 232–33, 277, 344, 345, 346, 464; purchases, 36, 272, 387, 388, 401, 464; British supplies, 99; captured from British, 146, 150, 151, 243, 244; importation, 209, 211, 213–14, 232, 271, 271–72, 273, 308, 382, 385, 386, 387, 388, 391, 393, 401, 424, 430, 442–43, 444, 468; Halifax expedition, 216; Bermuda expedition, 221–22, 272, 273, 288, 289, 291, 292, 304, 305, 382, 383, 402, 403, 420, 441, 463, 467, 468; sent to Long Island, N.Y., 294; Bayonne importation scheme, 441–42, 463, 464
lead: from New York, 211, 213; shortage in Continental army, 211, 214, 221, 242, 244, 306, 308; sent to Continental army, 213, 288, 401, 402, 430, 436; cast into ball, 214; collected in colonies, 221, 242, 244, 277; from Ticonderoga and Crown Point, 272, 273, 288, 304–5, 306, 307, 308, 344, 369, 393, 405, 416, 436; importation, 273, 382, 387, 388, 401, 430, 463; mines, 308, 309, 344, 344–45, 405–6, 463, 469; furnace, 344; purchases, 387, 388, 401

Angel, Abiathar: id., 398; *letters from*: to GW, 398

Angell, Israel: on court-martial, 300

Armorers: pay, 215; for brigades and divisions, 357

Arms: for riflemen, 24, 25, 94; firing restricted, 55, 172, 218–19, 227; for Virginia independent companies, 77; gunpowder for small arms, 89; captured from British, 93, 201, 232, 286; for Massachusetts militia, 105; pikes, 114; taken to religious service, 122; spears, 158; importation, 273, 382, 385, 386, 387, 388, 401, 430, 442–43; training, 307; illegal sale, 321–22; repair, 357; shortage among Canadians, 369; shortage in New York, 378, 443; purchases, 387, 388, 401; capture ordered, 398, 463; for armed vessels, 398; sent to Continental army, 402, 430
flints: from New York, 211, 213; shortage in Continental army, 211, 214, 242, 244; sent to Continental army, 213; collected in colonies, 242, 244, 277; importation, 273, 382

Armstrong, John: recommended, 390; appointment, 392; id., 392–93

Arnold, Benedict: at Ticonderoga, 40, 121; Quebec expedition, 332, 334, 368–69, 404–5, 406, 409–10, 415, 415–16, 432, 436, 437, 438, 448, 455–56, 457–59, 460; money for, 446; raids New London, 471; *letters from*: to Reuben Colburn, 409–10; *letters to*: from GW, 455–56, 457–60; from Joseph Reed, 462

Articles of war: drunkenness, 54–55; profanity, 54–55; religious services, 54–55; court-martial procedures, 83; plundering, 215, 458, 460; sutlers, 261, 418–19; assault on officers, 358
Continental articles: sent to GW, 7, 8, 64, 91, 279; adopted, 8,

Articles of war (*cont.*)
45, 46, 64, 85; compared with Massachusetts articles, 45, 46, 83; printed, 64; needed, 84, 91; distributed, 278; signing, 278, 279, 357; article 1, 279; article 2, 57; article 3, 57; article 7, 358; article 20, 57; article 29, 215, 460; article 30, 215; article 32, 261; article 50, 261; article 65, 261; article 66, 261
Massachusetts articles: compared with Continental articles, 45, 46, 83; article 1, 57; article 2, 57; article 6, 356–57, 358, 360–61; article 19, 57; article 49, 260, 261, 325, 356–57, 397, 465
Artificers: returns, 357; for Quebec expedition, 409; pay, 409
Artillery: floating batteries, 42, 43, 51, 86, 116, 117, 197, 250–51, 251–52, 266, 300, 325, 374, 376; in American lines, 51, 119, 363, 374; firing restricted, 55, 89, 242, 350, 373–74, 374; ammunition, 74, 75–76, 89, 191, 214, 242, 257, 317, 350, 363, 373–74, 374; returns, 75–76, 232; Continental regiment, 76, 224, 225, 231, 317, 341, 397, 398; in British lines, 86, 92, 99, 197, 229, 233, 343, 374, 376, 447; in raids, 93, 232; swivel guns, 156, 301, 421; matrosses, 165, 167; as plunder, 215, 460; in Canadian invasion, 257, 368, 394, 395; carriages, 257; ordnance stores, 317, 363. *See also* Commissary of artillery; Gridley, Richard
Asia (British warship), 33
Auchmuty, Robert: goes to England, 238
Austin, Jonathan Williams: recommended, 9; id., 12
Ayscough, James: intercepts letters, 230, 239, 249

Babcock, James: id., 348; *letters from*: to GW, 348
Babcock, Joshua: recommended, 464; id., 465
Baker, John, 283; id., 451; recommended, 451; *letters from*: to GW, 460–61
Baker, Remember: death, 394; id., 394–95
Baker, T., Jr.: petitions for pay, 282–83
Baldwin, Jeduthan: id., 286; recommended, 286
Baldwin, Loammi, 111, 157–58; id., 185–88; carries letter, 247; escorts refugees, 248; leave of absence, 323, 331; regiment, 460; *letters from*: to GW, 185–88, 192–93, 198–99, 213, 216–17, 219–20, 249, 250–52, 270–71, 287–88, 300–301, 311, 312–14, 318, 322–23, 396–97, 439, 452–53, 466; to Horatio Gates, 213, 313, 326; to Joseph Trumbull, 313–14; *letters to*: from Joseph Reed, 192, 193; from Horatio Gates, 199; from John Trumbull, 220; from GW, 250, 322; from Daniel Sigourney, 323
Balfour, James: death, 338
Balfour & Barraud: debt to GW, 338
Ball, Lebbeus: dispute over house, 200; id., 200
Ballard, William Hudson: fined, 278; id., 279
Banister, John: id., 353
Bant, William: recommended, 9; id., 11
Barkley, Andrew, 205
Barracks: cleanliness, 114, 257; construction, 172, 396, 433, 450. *See also* Huts; Tents
Barraud, Daniel: debt to GW, 335, 338
Barrell, William: carries letters, 362, 375, 385; id., 362
Bartlett, Samuel: court-martialed, 73
Bassett, Anna Maria Dandridge, 5, 13, 380; id., 14; visits Mount Vernon, 14
Bassett, Burwell: id., 14; visits Mount Vernon, 14; *letters from*: to GW, 379–81; *letters to*: from GW, 12–14

Batcheler, John: court-martialed, 67
Bayley, Jacob: and Indian affairs, 229; id., 239
Baylor, George: recommended, 109, 110; id., 110; appointment, 309; purchases military stores, 387, 388, 401, 402, 421, 431; carries money, 446
Baylor, John, 109, 110; id., 110
Bayonne: gunpowder importation scheme, 441–42, 463, 464
Bedel, Timothy: ranger companies, 181–82, 259; id., 182–83; joins Schuyler's army, 334; *letters to*: from New Hampshire committee of safety, 182
Belvoir, 171
Bennet, ——, 344, 417
Bermuda: gunpowder at, 221, 223, 272–73, 304, 402, 441, 463, 467, 468; negotiations with Continental Congress, 273, 288, 289, 291, 292, 305; GW's address to inhabitants, 419–20, 420–21, 463
Berry, Michael: pardoned, 340
Bixby, Samuel, 118
Black troops: in Continental army, 90
Bland, Richard: appointment, 380; resigns from Continental Congress, 380, 423; id., 381, 424
Blankets: for volunteers, 22; returns, 54, 76, 277; for Massachusetts troops, 67, 105; lost at Battle of Bunker Hill, 67, 277; shortage in Continental army, 67, 277, 433, 450; graft, 322
Bleeker, John N.: examines commissaries, 256; id., 258
Bliss, Anna: id., 422
Block Island: British threat to, 170, 180, 199, 200, 271–72; livestock removed, 417
Blue Hill. *See* Great Blue Hill
Boats: in Canada, 42, 43, 44, 203, 370; at Ticonderoga, 120, 202; flat-bottomed boats, 138, 198, 251; proposed attack on Boston, 142, 432, 450; carry British troops, 157, 185, 198, 251; bay boats, 179–80; gundalows, 179–80, 342; long boats, 179–80; moses boats, 179–80; returns, 179–80; yawls, 179–80; from Salem, Mass., 266; command of Continental boatmen, 377, 395; stolen by Indians, 394, 394–95
  bateaux: for Lake Champlain, 40; men for, 377, 415; construction, 409, 409–10
  whaleboats: in raids, 117–18, 119, 142, 152, 207, 232; men for, 118, 156; collected, 119, 138, 142, 157, 179–80; patrols, 119, 138; equipment, 156–57
Boston: conditions in, 117, 135, 137–38, 184, 233–38, 274, 447–48; map of area, 184, 186–87 (illus.), 236–37 (illus.); proposals to blockade harbor, 209, 349–51, 373–74; proposed attack on, 432–34, 450–51
Boston Neck, 92, 99; British defenses, 86, 137, 233; skirmish at, 198
Boucher, Jonathan: id., 255; sermons dedicated to GW, 255; *letters from*: to GW, 252–55; *letters to*: from GW, 255
Boudinot, Elias: *letters to*: from Joseph Reed, 57
Bowdoin, James: recommended, 9, 26; id., 11; *letters to*: from Thomas Cushing, 26
Bowen, David: id., 427
Bowen, Levi: court-martialed, 376; cashiered, 449; *letters from*: to GW, 427–28
Bowers, Jerathmiel: and clothing for army, 356
Box, Daniel: appointment, 309, 391; id., 310–11
Boyne (British warship), 231
Bradford, ——, 148
Bradford, Joseph: id., 285
Bradford, Thomas, 64; id., 151
Bradford, William, 64; id., 151, 320; captures British ship, 319
Bragdon, Daniel: and hospitals, 66
Braintree (Mass.), 179–80, 180
Brandt, Joseph, 121

Brattle, William, 56, 64; id., 58
Braxton, Carter: appointment, 380; id., 381
Brewer, David: regiment, 154, 427, 449; id., 427–28, 449
Brewer, Jonathan: regiment, 154, 231
Brewer, Samuel, 97; appointment, 379, 391
Brickett, James: court of inquiry president, 190; id., 191; court-martial president, 356
Brickmakers: drafted from army, 357, 358
Bridge, Ebenezer: regiment, 154; court of inquiry investigates, 330, 340; id., 330; court-martialed, 339, 448
Brigade majors, 91, 97, 329; appointed, 100, 145, 165, 178, 309, 317, 379, 391; duties, 133, 317; insignia, 134; authorized, 228
Brigham, Joseph, 248
Brigham, Timothy: court-martialed, 76; id., 77
British army: reinforcements, 13, 14, 17, 19, 35, 47, 48, 79, 81, 99, 125, 137, 141, 152, 184, 225, 238, 275, 433, 434, 447; strength in America, 21; casualties, 35–36, 44, 91, 93, 116, 117, 135, 136, 137, 144, 147, 151, 171, 184, 198, 201, 226, 231, 232, 238, 301, 336, 339; morale, 35–36, 87, 99, 117, 343, 395; strength at Battle of Bunker Hill, 36, 184; strength in Canada, 44, 129, 368, 369–70; rumored mutiny, 47; strength at Boston, 79–80, 81, 90, 115–16, 117, 135, 183–84, 226, 238; dispositions at Boston, 85–86, 99, 101–2, 135, 137, 138, 183–84, 196–97, 270, 466; superior firepower, 99, 336; command, 102, 290, 349; shortage of provisions, 116, 135, 137, 142, 175, 182, 184, 238, 263, 274, 305, 447; sickness, 117, 137, 182, 184, 226, 238, 275; troop movements in Boston, 157, 185, 198, 213, 251, 270, 452–53; rumored movements, 202, 274–75, 280, 284, 306, 308, 342, 343, 362–63, 434, 437, 468, 470; council of war, 219–20; preparations for winter, 225, 343; court-martial procedures, 355. *See also* Ammunition; Artillery; Deserters; Discipline; Forage; Fortifications; Fuel; Guards; Health; Horses; Intelligence; Prisoners; Provisions
British navy: transports at Sandy Hook, 47, 48, 141; sailors in British army, 79; transports arrive at Boston, 81, 137, 141, 184, 313, 343; convoys to Nova Scotia, 91–92, 97, 102, 117, 354, 362, 364, 379, 406, 408, 418, 421, 422, 438; rumored movements, 91–92, 102, 166, 170, 171–72, 175–76, 180–81, 199, 221, 306, 342, 353–54, 362, 377–78, 382, 406, 423, 424, 438, 469; builds battery on Copp's Hill, 92; attacks American raiders, 118, 152, 226, 232, 397, 400; coastal raids, 170, 176, 181, 200, 262, 263, 267, 272, 276, 293, 294, 305, 306, 314, 323, 345, 416, 417, 418, 421, 424, 447, 468, 469, 470, 471; advantages of sea power, 195, 407, 447; captures American vessels, 220, 262, 343, 359, 416–17, 418, 428–29, 447; ships captured by Americans, 293, 316, 318–19, 320; deserters, 300, 362; skirmish at Chelsea, 300–301; skirmish at Noddles Island, 313; captures slaves, 353, 416–17; impressment of sailors, 362; cruisers off coast, 425, 426, 457, 463; sailors captured, 428, 428–29, 430
warships: at New York, 33, 39; in Boston Harbor, 86, 117, 118, 142, 152, 157, 185, 220, 231, 239, 300, 301, 318, 366, 397, 431; in Rhode Island, 148, 239, 249, 263, 362, 467, 471; in Vir-

British navy (*cont.*)
ginia, 150; at New London, 204, 262, 263, 267, 272; at Piscataway, 205; off Block Island, 271–72; in Nova Scotia, 297; at Quebec, 368
see also Boats; Prisoners
Bromitt, Lambert, 284–85
Brommett, Lombard: id., 285
Brookfield (Mass.): GW at, 92
Brookline (Mass.), 93
Brookline fort, 76; GW inspects, 92
Brooks, Eleazer: confers with GW, 104–5
Broughton, Nicholson: id., 400–401; company, 408; recaptures ship, 428, 428–29, 429; *letters from*: to GW, 428–29, 440–41; *letters to*: from GW, 398–401
Brown, —— (capt.), 68, 68–69
Brown, —— (Dr.), 290–91
Brown, —— (Mr.), 222
Brown, John (1736–1803): id., 223, 295; *letters to*: from GW, 295
Brown, John (1744–1780): Canadian intelligence, 202, 203, 368; id., 203; *letters from*: to Jonathan Trumbull, Sr., 345
Brown, Joseph: id., 223, 383–84; recommended, 383; carries letter, 402
Brown, Moses: id., 223
Brown, Nicholas: id., 223
Brown's House: American attack on, 86, 92–93
Buffe, Thomas: makes recommendation, 285
Bulloch, Archibald: elected to Continental Congress, 167; id., 168
Bunker Hill: British defenses, 85–86, 99, 101–2, 137, 183, 189, 226–27, 466; description, 135; livestock at, 313
battle of: casualties, 10, 35–36, 44, 45, 57–58, 91, 96–97, 116, 117, 135, 136, 137, 144, 147, 151, 155, 171, 184, 238, 336, 339; accounts, 35–36, 44, 45, 74, 108, 117; blankets and clothing lost at, 66, 277; officer behavior, 74, 108, 138, 277–78, 285, 286, 286–87, 325, 330, 336, 373, 375, 398, 448, 465
Burbeck, William: engineering abilities, 94, 149; and gunpowder, 214, 364; id., 214, 398; reprimands officer, 397
Burke, Edmund: presents remonstrance, 49
Burr, Aaron: recommended, 132, 240; id., 133
Bury, Michael: punished, 159
Bushfield, 20
Butler, Joseph: company, 64, 191; id., 191
Butler, Walter, 121
Butterick, John: on court-martial, 300
Byrd, Francis Otway: recommended, 434–35; id., 435

Cabell, William: appointment, 380; id., 381
Caldwell, Daniel: arrested, 364; id., 364
Callender, John: cashiered, 71, 138, 338–39, 375; company, 73; id., 74
Calvert, Benedict, 335, 338
Calvert, Eleanor ("Nelly"). *See* Custis, Eleanor Calvert ("Nelly")
Calvert, Elizabeth, 338
Cambridge: GW arrives at, 50, 85, 92, 98, 135, 170, 183; GW's headquarters at, 50–51; troops at, 86, 87, 93; description, 135; bridge at, 179–80, 180
Campbell, Donald: id., 174–75; and gunpowder, 213–14; and Schuyler, 256; *letters from*: to GW, 173–75
Campbell, John: id., 312; *letters to*: from Christopher French, 311
Campbell, Lauchlin: id., 175
Canada: defenses, 42, 43, 44, 129, 203, 229, 332–33, 368, 369–70, 370, 395, 437, 448; invasion ordered, 42–43, 43, 45, 47, 202, 258; Schuyler invades, 202, 256, 257, 305, 331, 332, 345, 368, 368–69, 393–94, 394, 406, 407, 417, 437, 448, 458, 462; Quebec expedition, 332, 333, 334, 368, 368–69, 404–5, 405, 406, 409, 409–10, 415, 415–16, 432, 436,

Canada (*cont.*)
437, 438, 446, 448, 455–56, 457–59, 460, 461–62
Canadians: disposition, 42, 43, 44, 120, 129, 131, 188, 203, 229, 306, 332, 345, 368, 369, 370, 394, 395, 437, 455–56, 457, 458, 461–62; treatment, 332, 437, 455–56, 457, 458, 459, 462; GW's address to, 461–63
Cape Ann: British sailors captured at, 293, 328, 428, 428–29, 429, 430
Cap-Français, 273
Carleton, Guy: defense of Canada, 42, 43, 129, 332, 448; id., 43–44; recruits Indians, 43, 130, 229, 307, 367–68; aide-de-camp, 460
Carmiele, Daniel: punished, 115
Carnaghan, John, 31
Carnes, John: intelligence from, 193, 311, 312; id., 313
Carpenters: work on stables, 56; master carpenter for Continental army, 140, 143; chief carpenter at New York, 364, 364–65; for Quebec expedition, 409
Carrington, Paul: appointment, 380; id., 381
Carter, John: intelligence from, 342, 343, 385, 386
Cary, Richard: appointment, 309; id., 310
Cary, Robert. *See* Robert Cary & Co.
Castle William, 157, 158; rumors of dismantlement, 229, 238, 343; destruction, 239
Caughnawaga Indians: disposition, 43, 229; agreements with Americans, 238–39; confer with Schuyler, 257; and Remember Baker, 395
Cavet, James, 31
Chamberlin, —— (Mr.), 251
Chambly: British force at, 368
Chambly River, 258
Champlin, George: and gunpowder, 424; id., 424–25
Chaplains, 27. *See also* Religious services; Sermons
Charles Town and Savannah Packet (schooner), 468
Charlestown neck: skirmish at, 196–97, 201, 226, 231; map of, 228, 233, 236–37 (illus.)
Charming Sally (ship), 343, 385, 386
Chase, Thomas: appointment, 309, 317, 379; id., 310
Chauncy, Charles: recommended, 26; id., 27
Cheever, Ezekiel, 214; requests ammunition, 211; id., 211; appointment, 317
Chelsea: troops at, 111, 155, 396, 397; livestock removed, 118–19; refugees at, 192, 193, 194, 198, 199, 216, 228–29, 230, 248–49; skirmish at, 300–301; description, 396
Cheney (Cheeney), Penuel: court of inquiry, 153; id., 155; leaves army, 412–13; *letters from*: to GW, 412–13
Chester, John: company, 64
Chestnut Grove, 14
Chevaux-de-frise, 119, 127, 129
Child, Benjamin: court-martialed, 408
Choptank Frigate (ship), 255
Christ Church (Cambridge), 246
Christian, William: appointment, 380, 423; id., 380
Church, Benjamin: recommended, 9, 26; id., 10–11, 341; sends horses to GW, 68–69; escorts GW, 92; consults with GW, 196; and absent soldiers, 265; and hospital guard, 341, 371; appointed director of hospital, 412; inquiry into conduct, 426, 427, 455; receives fine, 455
Church, Thomas: regiment, 154; court-martial president, 212; id., 212
Clark, James: court-martialed, 172; id., 173
Clark, John: id., 387
Clark & Nightingale: import military stores, 273, 383, 386, 387, 388, 401, 402, 441; GW thanks, 421, 442; *letters from*: to GW, 401–2; *letters to*: from GW, 387

Clarke, George, 175

Cleveland, James: and seating of GW's western lands, 28–29, 30, 335, 336; id., 30; *letters from*: to Valentine Crawford, 28–29; to William Crawford, 28

Clinton, George: id., 59; *letters from*: to GW, 58–59, 179; *letters to*: from GW, 361–62

Clothing: for Martha Washington, 5, 6; for riflemen, 24; hunting shirts, 24, 88–89, 94, 164–65, 222, 244, 245, 261, 276, 297, 305, 354, 383, 388, 417; for Massachusetts troops, 67, 324; lost at Battle of Bunker Hill, 67; shortage in Continental army, 85, 88, 225, 356, 404; Indian dress, 94; tow cloth, 94, 164–65, 167, 222, 244, 272, 276, 382, 383, 388, 402, 421; as plunder, 215, 460; shirts, 260–61, 297, 356, 357; shoes, 260–61, 297, 356, 357; Indian leggings, 261; stockings, 261, 297, 356, 357; breeches, 297, 356, 357; coats, 297, 324; transferred to Continental account, 297, 356, 357, 358; waistcoats, 297, 357; captured from British, 319, 320, 390, 403, 404; needed for winter, 433, 450

Coit, Samuel: militia regiment, 267; id., 268

Coit, William: *letters to*: from GW, 400

Colburn, Reuben: id., 409–10; *letters to*: from Benedict Arnold, 409–10; from GW, 409–10

Cole, Gideon: court-martialed, 63; id., 64

Collins, James: escorts suspected persons, 359; id., 359

Collins, John: slave of, 418; id., 466–67; *letters from*: to GW, 466–67

Colonel Louis (Lewis; Indian): visits GW, 229; id., 238–39

Commissaries: purchase livestock, 119; and returns, 197; settlement of accounts, 197; deputy commissary for New York, 256, 258, 436; inspection of, 256; and tow cloth, 276; and provisions for Quebec expedition, 409; and hunting shirts, 417

Commissary general, 416; appointed, 12, 94, 113, 145, 165, 167, 197, 204; recommended, 12, 84, 88; needed, 84, 88, 139; of Connecticut forces, 88, 94; of Massachusetts forces, 111; purchases livestock, 111, 382, 383; and returns, 197, 317; and bread, 371; and provisions for Quebec expedition, 409; proposals for supplying army, 425, 426, 430; and medical supplies, 427. *See also* Pigeon, John; Trumbull, Joseph

Commissary of artillery: needed, 88, 139; authorized, 94, 145, 149, 165; appointed, 211, 317; and returns, 317. *See also* Cheever, Ezekiel

Connecticut: commissary general, 12, 88, 94; recruiting efforts, 80, 96, 124–25, 125–26, 136–37, 145, 152, 165, 203–4, 224, 267, 470–71; tow cloth, 164–65, 167, 222, 244, 276; gunpowder supply, 216, 227, 276, 277, 294, 299, 307–8, 309, 344, 424, 444, 469, 471; rations, 227, 233; lead mines, 308, 344, 344–45, 405–6, 469; armed vessels, 424, 469, 471; support of American cause, 469

troops: on Long Island, N.Y., 34, 293–94, 294, 377, 408; at New York City, 34, 47, 48, 280–81, 307, 408, 437, 470; on Prospect Hill, 86; at Roxbury, 86, 113, 116; well supplied, 88; at Cambridge, 113–14; casualties, 118; at Ticonderoga, 121, 345; sent to Continental army, 125, 126, 136–37, 145, 149, 152, 153, 165, 203–4, 224, 244, 276, 277, 406, 437, 438, 468, 470; dual commissions, 223–24; strength of regiments, 224; defend colony, 267, 268, 272, 276, 277, 293, 294, 406, 416, 417–18, 437, 438, 468–69, 470, 470–

Connecticut (*cont.*)
71; training, 470
see also Trumbull, Jonathan, Sr.
Connecticut council: and dispute over rank, 95; sends troops to Continental army, 153, 470; appoints agent for naval supplies, 424–25; accepts prisoners from Massachusetts, 453, 454; and Bayonne importation scheme, 464; defends colony, 470, 470–71; sends gunpowder to Continental army, 471
Connecticut delegates: make recommendation, 11; and dispute over rank, 95; *letters from*: to Jonathan Trumbull, Sr., 277
Connecticut general assembly: appoints officers, 94–95, 95, 113; raises new regiments, 96, 124–25, 136–37, 165, 203–4; sends gunpowder and money to Schuyler, 125, 126; specifies rations, 233; operates lead mine, 344–45; encourages gunpowder manufacture, 345, 346; appoints marine agent, 424–25; authorizes armed vessels, 471
Conner, —— (sgt.), 278
Conner, John: punished, 321
Connolly, John: arrested, 29, 32; Indian negotiations, 29, 31–32; id., 30, 31
Continental army: adopted by Continental Congress, 1, 2, 54; casualties, 10, 35, 44, 45, 57–58, 91, 96–97, 116, 118, 135, 136, 152, 171, 226, 226–27, 232, 374, 376, 391, 394, 395, 447, 451; authorized strength, 13, 14, 16, 17, 19, 21, 80, 140, 166; funding of, 13, 14, 16, 17, 19, 22, 88, 125, 126, 137, 139, 140, 142–43, 146, 166, 430, 433, 451; reinforcements, 20, 51, 70, 80, 81, 90, 96, 104–5, 115–16, 116–17, 124–25, 125–26, 136, 136–37, 141, 145, 146, 149, 152, 153, 165, 225, 244, 256, 257, 276, 277, 299, 306, 307, 406, 416, 417–18, 437, 438, 468–69, 470; reviewed by GW, 50; dispositions around Boston, 51–52, 86, 99, 102, 113–14, 135, 153–55, 183, 184; condition of troops, 52–53, 60, 87, 88, 90, 90–91, 93, 104, 107, 114, 120, 130, 135, 182, 183, 188–89, 206–7, 256, 257, 306, 335–36, 372; reorganization, 62, 88, 99–100, 111, 138, 139, 139–40, 140, 153–55, 223–24, 224–25, 228, 230–31, 231, 278, 279, 280, 360, 391; strength around Boston, 80, 81, 90, 99, 103–4, 135, 137, 224–25, 231, 265, 269; morale, 87, 88–89, 91, 99, 130, 138, 182, 282, 433, 445, 445–46, 449–50; strength in New York, 121–22; lacks uniforms, 158; rank of regiments, 218, 245–46, 329; preparations for winter, 225, 231, 277, 391, 396, 425, 430, 433, 450; strength of Arnold's force, 332, 334, 406, 415–16, 448; strength of Schuyler's force, 394; reenlistment, 433, 450. *See also* Ammunition; Arms; Artillery; Barracks; Clothing; Court-martials; Courts of inquiry; Deserters; Discharges; Discipline; Drummers and fifers; Equipment; Forage; Fortifications; Fuel; Furloughs; Graft; Guards; Health; Horses; Hospitals; Huts; Intelligence; Military stores; Money; Mutiny; Officers; Pay; Prisoners; Provisions; Punishments; Recruiting; Religious services; Returns; Riflemen; Rolls; Sutlers; Tents; Tools; Uniforms; Volunteers; Wagons
Continental Congress: adopts army, 1, 2, 54; appoints GW commander in chief, 1, 1–2, 2–3, 3–4, 6–7, 8, 12–13, 15, 16–17, 19, 21; GW's address to, 1–3; presidents, 1; appropriates pay, 2, 11, 355, 392; clerk, 7; instructions to GW, 7, 8, 21–22, 37, 85, 87, 195, 240, 384; secretary, 7, 8; adopts articles of war,

Continental Congress (*cont.*) 8, 45, 46, 64, 278, 458; appoints general officers, 13, 14, 17, 18–19, 19, 23, 54, 56, 61, 62, 89, 95, 96, 113, 132, 138, 145, 161, 162, 165, 167, 189, 223, 228, 390–91, 392, 393; authorizes currency, 13, 14, 16, 17, 19, 22, 166; sets size of army, 13, 14, 16, 17, 19, 21, 166; committee of the whole, 14; secrecy of proceedings, 14, 240; appoints adjutant general, 17, 18, 19, 23, 78–79; agrees to indemnify Charles Lee, 18; authorizes rifle companies, 20, 70, 110; policy on appointments, 21, 22–23, 149, 241, 361, 372–73, 384; considers queries from GW, 22; efforts to supply gunpowder, 36, 56, 94, 145, 149, 209, 210, 232–33, 241, 273, 277, 288, 289, 291, 292, 294–95, 304, 305, 307, 331, 442, 463, 464; and defense of New York, 37, 38, 38–39, 40; recommends arrest of dangerous persons, 39; Indian policy, 42, 45, 46, 165–66, 209, 257, 258, 331–32, 334, 369; orders invasion of Canada, 42–43, 43, 45, 47, 202, 203, 258, 462; establishes hospital department, 45, 46, 143, 145, 149, 165, 167, 341; and disputes over rank, 61, 61–62, 89–90, 95, 96, 113, 132, 138, 145–46, 161, 165, 189, 223, 224, 231, 392; treatment of Loyalists, 68; proposed move, 91, 146, 149–50, 150; appoints commissary general, 94, 145, 165, 167, 197, 204; approves hunting shirts, 94, 164–65, 261, 297; authorizes commissary of artillery, 94, 145, 165; authorizes mustermaster general, 94, 145, 165; authorizes quartermaster general, 94, 145, 165; and tow cloth, 94, 164–65, 421; and recruiting, 96, 165, 203; address to inhabitants of Great Britain, 97, 171; recess, 97, 146–47, 209, 210, 376, 391; authorizes hussars, 110; proclaims fast day, 112, 113, 122, 123; and southern reinforcements, 137, 141, 146; appoints paymaster general, 142; appropriates money for army, 142–43; authorizes master carpenter, 143; authorizes provost marshal, 143; authorizes wagon master general, 143; accepts new Connecticut regiments, 145, 149; authorizes brigade majors, 145, 165, 228, 391; slowness, 146; and tents, 164; authorizes matrosses, 165; declaration on taking arms, 171; appoints deputy quartermaster general for New York, 174–75, 175; policy on local defense, 195, 196, 228, 407, 437; settlement of accounts, 197, 386; and scheme for blockading Boston Harbor, 209; reorganization of army, 230; and winter preparations, 231; and supplies for Schuyler, 256–57; approves rations for army, 269, 270; negotiations with Bermudians, 273, 288, 289, 291, 292, 304, 305, 402, 420; and commissary general's proposals, 425, 426, 430; *letters from*: to New York provincial congress, 217; *letters to*: from GW, 32–34; from Massachusetts provincial congress, 34, 35–36, 36; from Albany committee of safety, 43, 91; from Philip Schuyler, 47, 48, 217; from New York committee of safety, 386, 443–44; from New York provincial congress, 386. *See also* Hancock, John

Continental naval activities: capture of British vessels, 146, 150, 243, 244, 293, 316, 398–400; Bermuda expedition, 221–22, 272, 304, 305, 382, 383, 402, 403, 420–21, 420, 441, 463, 467, 468; Rhode Island armed vessels, 221–22, 223, 271, 272, 273, 304, 305, 382, 383, 402, 403, 441, 442, 463, 464, 467;

Continental naval activities (*cont.*) American helplessness, 263; drafting of sailors, 273, 304; capture of British sailors, 293, 316, 428, 428–29, 429, 430; Massachusetts armed vessels, 316; GW's armed vessels, 398–400, 410, 428, 428–29, 429, 440; prize regulations, 398–400, 429, 440; recapture of American vessels, 400, 428, 429, 440; St. Lawrence expedition, 400; efforts to capture British packet ship, 403, 421–22, 441, 463, 467; transports for Quebec expedition, 404–5; Connecticut armed vessels, 424, 469, 471; casualties, 440, 441. *See also* Boats

Cooke, Nicholas: id., 109; and Bermuda expedition, 272–73, 304, 382, 402, 441; and military stores, 401, 402; slaves of, 416–17; *letters from*: to GW, 108–9, 199–200, 271–74, 288–89, 291, 292, 382–84, 402–3, 441–42, 463–65, 467–68; to James Warren, 273; to Jonathan Trumbull, Sr., 442; to Massachusetts council, 453, 454; *letters to*: from Nathanael Greene, 49, 81; from GW, 128–29, 175–76, 180–81, 221–23, 227, 304–5, 388, 420–22; from James Otis, Sr., 454; from Jonathan Trumbull, Sr., 463; from Samuel Ward, Sr., 464

Cooke, Nicholas, Jr.: id., 273–74

Cooper, Samuel: recommended, 26; id., 27

Coos (Cohos) country, 182, 239

Copp's Hill, 86, 92

Cornell, Richard, 321

Cotton, Theophilus: regiment, 154

Councils of war: Continental Congress's instructions, 22; minutes, 79–82, 215–16, 450–51; decisions, 80–81, 86–87, 90, 99, 104, 145, 216, 451; summoned, 90, 99, 104, 432, 434; British council of war, 219–20

Court-martials: of quartermaster, 56; of enlisted men, 63, 67, 73, 82, 115, 159, 172–73, 190–91, 191, 321, 321–22, 340, 408, 449, 454–55, 465; of officers, 71, 74, 76, 108, 123–24, 127, 159, 172, 175, 197, 198, 212, 260, 278, 300, 312, 318, 325, 330, 335–36, 346, 356–57, 360–61, 364, 373, 375–76, 397, 398, 414, 427–28, 427, 431, 448, 449, 465; attendance of witnesses, 82, 83; jurisdiction, 82, 83, 107, 119, 123, 169, 261, 358, 408, 418; times of convening, 83; dissolved, 106, 115, 169, 414; frequency, 139, 354–55; delayed, 355, 364; procedures in British army, 355; of surgeons mate, 413. *See also* Punishments

Courts of inquiry, 153, 155, 177, 190, 247, 330, 340, 426, 427, 455

Crafts, Edward: id., 397; reprimanded, 397

Craik, James, 336; western lands, 29; id., 30–31, 339

Crane, John: attacks Brown's house, 93; and raid on Lighthouse Island, 232

Crawford, Valentine: id., 30; *letters from*: to GW, 28–32; *letters to*: from James Cleveland, 28–29

Crawford, William, 31, 32; id., 30; *letters to*: from James Cleveland, 28

Cresap, Michael: recruits rifle company, 23, 24–25; id., 24

Cresap, Thomas, 23; id., 24

Cressey, Mark: petitions for pay, 282–83; id., 283

Cross, Stephen: pays troops, 163

Crostin, William: court-martialed, 67

Crown Point: American capture, 40; dispute over command, 121; lead from, 307, 344, 393, 436

Cudworth, Nathaniel: on court-martial, 300

Cummings, Thomas: petitions for pay, 282–83; id., 283

Curwin, George, 320
Cushing, Joseph: and soldiers' pay, 206, 298; id., 208; and clothing for army, 356
Cushing, Nathan: and soldiers' pay, 298
Cushing, Seth: and soldiers' pay, 298
Cushing, Thomas: and GW's appointment, 2; id., 26; makes recommendations, 26; *letters from*: to James Bowdoin, 26
Custis, Eleanor Calvert ("Nelly"), 15, 27; id., 16; birth of child, 423
Custis, John Parke ("Jack"), 27; assumes management of his estate, 15, 16; id., 16; education, 255; *letters to*: from GW, 15–16
Custis, Martha Parke ("Patsy"; 1756–1773): bank stock, 6
Custis, Martha Parke ("Patsy"; 1777–1854): finds letters, 5
Custis estate, 15, 16

Dandridge, Anna Maria. *See* Bassett, Anna Maria Dandridge
Dandridge, Frances Jones, 13; id., 14
Danielson, Timothy: regiment, 154, 364; dispute over house, 200; id., 200; *letters from*: to GW, 200, 201
Daniely, Thomas: court-martialed, 73
Dartmouth, William Legge, second earl of: corresponds with Joseph Reed, 56; *letters from*: to Josiah Martin, 166; *letters to*: from Guy Johnson, 39; from John Wentworth, 126–27; from James Wright, 150; from Josiah Martin, 168; from Robert Eden, 255
Davids, Daniel: arrested, 346
Davis, —— (capt.), 172
Davis, John: court-martialed, 159
Davis, Joshua, 377; id., 157; *letters from*: to GW, 156–57, 179–80
Davis, Thomas, 103, 125
Davison, Thomas: recommended, 286
Dawson, George: id., 220
Deane, Elizabeth Saltonstall: *letters to*: from Silas Deane, 94, 95
Deane, Silas, 150; makes recommendation, 11; and GW's appointment, 22; *letters from*: to Joseph Trumbull, 11; to Elizabeth Saltonstall Deane, 94, 95
Deer Island: American raid on, 152, 366; British raid on, 323
Delaware delegates: id., 44; *letters from*: to GW, 44; *letters to*: from GW, 384
Derby, John: intelligence from, 137, 141, 143, 189; id., 141
Derby, Richard, Jr.: id., 26–27; recommended, 26
Derueville, Chevalier: offers services, 296
Desambrager, —— (lt.): *letters from*: to GW, 296
Deserters: treatment of enemy deserters, 55; court-martialed, 67, 83, 159; enlisted in Continental army, 90; from British, 178, 180–81, 182, 226, 233, 275, 300, 301, 308, 321, 362, 395, 439; sent to jail, 190; intelligence from, 226, 228; from Continental army, 264, 265, 445
Devens, Richard: and absent soldiers, 265; and pay of troops, 292
Dewksbury, ——, 193
Dexter, Samuel: recommended, 9, 26; id., 11; and Massachusetts address to GW, 53
Dickinson, John: id., 70; makes recommendation, 70; military activities, 246; *letters from*: to GW, 169–70; *letters to*: from GW, 385
Digges, Dudley: appointment, 380; id., 381
Diligent (British warship), 316
Dill, John: recommended, 70
Discharges: dishonorable, 50, 71, 77, 138, 155, 175, 183, 198, 212, 252, 278, 312, 325, 335–36, 356–57, 373, 375–76, 398, 414, 427–28, 427, 449, 465; requested, 155, 348, 351, 352, 398, 412–13, 413–14, 422, 427, 451, 460
Discipline, 139, 207, 408, 418, 470; necessity of, 7, 17, 54, 77, 138,

Discipline (*cont.*)
307, 332, 347, 360, 414, 437, 456, 457; lacking in Continental army, 52, 60, 73, 90, 120, 129–30, 135, 183, 188, 189, 256, 449–50; at Port Tobacco, 337; in British army, 355
Dodge, Barnabus: company, 397
Dodge, Richard: commands at Chelsea, 111, 323, 331; return of livestock, 111; id., 157–58; company, 397; *letters from*: to GW, 157–58, 170, 325–26, 330–31, 342, 348–49, 362, 366, 388–89; *letters to*: from Joseph Reed, 389
Dole, —— (Dr.), 427
Doman, Thomas, 343
Doolittle, Ephraim: accuses officer, 124; id., 124; regiment, 124, 154, 231, 321, 360, 427
Dorchester, 51, 179–80; occupation of, 10, 80, 362–63
Doudel (Doudle, Dowdle), Michael: recommended, 70; id., 71
Douw, Volckert Pieterse, 369
Doyles, —— (Rev.), 246
Drummers and fifers, 50, 75, 349, 379, 415; salutes to general officers, 114–15; regulations, 133; instruction, 194
Drunkenness: forbidden, 54–55; triable by regimental court-martial, 83; problem in Continental army, 107; soldier convicted of, 115; among deserters, 178. *See also* Liquor
Duché, Jacob: id., 247; *letters from*: to GW, 246–47
Dueling: triable by general court-martial, 83
Duguid, John: id., 203; Canadian intelligence, 203, 258, 306, 368
Duncan, David: and indentured servants, 28–29; id., 30
Dunham, —— (Mr.): recommended to GW, 365
Dunham, Stephen: id., 365
Dunley, Edward: court-martialed, 67
Dunley, Thomas, 67
Dunmore, John Murray, fourth earl of, 30; seizes gunpowder, 18; and Indian negotiations, 31; escapes capture, 146, 150; id., 150; threat to Martha Washington, 335, 338; wants British army in Virginia, 434
Du Ville, —— (Mr.), 441
Dyer, Eliphalet: opinion of GW, 3; makes recommendation, 11; carries letter, 344; id., 345–46; *letters from*: to Joseph Trumbull, 3, 11, 18

Easton, James: regiment, 345
Eayres, Joseph: return of men, 357; id., 358
Eden, Robert: *letters from*: to earl of Dartmouth, 255
Elderkin, Jedediah: carries letter, 344; id., 346
Elizabeth (N.J.) committee of safety: *letters to*: from New York provincial congress, 284
Ellery, Benjamin: id., 124; introduced to GW, 124
Ellery, William (d. 1764): id., 124
Ellery, William (1727–1820): id., 124
Elmwood, 173, 341
Eltham, 14
Emerson, Phebe Bliss: *letters to*: from William Emerson, 93
Emerson, William: *letters from*: to Phebe Bliss Emerson, 93
Engineers: needed, 85, 86, 89, 94; and fortifications, 119; controversy over, 145, 149; repair Boston lighthouse, 231–32. *See also* Fortifications
Eppes, Francis: appointment, 380; id., 381
Equipment: furnished at Continental expense, 22; for riflemen, 24; returns, 54, 232; for Virginia independent companies, 339
Eustis, William: on court of inquiry, 153; id., 155
Express riders, 64, 75, 76, 84, 87, 91, 96, 98, 125, 130, 132, 141, 144, 145, 153, 167, 180, 185, 230, 244, 245, 263, 267, 299, 322, 332, 333, 342, 390, 407, 416, 436, 468

Fairfax, George William, 295; id., 171; power of attorney, 176, 177; bill of exchange, 336, 339; *letters to*: from GW, 170–71, 176–77

Fairfax, Sarah Cary ("Sally"): id., 171

Fairfax of Cameron, Thomas Fairfax, sixth Baron, 171

Fairfax County (Va.) independent company, 17, 339; *letters from*: to GW, 77–78

Fairfield, Matthew: id., 366; raids Deer Island, 366

Falcon (British warship), 293

Farley, Michael: and reinforcements, 105

Fascines, 127, 128, 158, 362–63

Fauquier County (Va.) independent company, 17

Fayerweather, Thomas: house of, 341

Fellows, John: regiment, 154

Féné, John Baptist: Canadian intelligence, 368, 369–70

Fenton, John: id., 68; *letters from*: to GW, 68

Ferry Farm: sale of, 4, 6

Fessenden, Josiah, 230, 267; carries dispatches, 64, 91, 125, 132, 141, 144, 153; id., 64

Fettyplace, Edward: id., 285

Fisher, Jabez: and commission, 413

Fishers Island, 416; British raid on, 170, 176, 180, 181, 200, 222–23, 262–63, 263, 267–68, 273, 294, 305, 314

Fitch, Samuel, 239

Flagg, John: sent to GW, 428; accusations against, 429, 430, 440; id., 429

Flags of truce: regulations, 107–8; frequency, 295; violations, 349, 352; halted, 411

Fletcher, Robert, 179

Flighman, —— (Mr.), 147

Flint, —— (Dr.), 360

Folsom, Nathaniel, 50; id., 51, 101; requests tools, 100; retires from army, 139; *letters from*: to New Hampshire committee of safety, 51

Forage: hay, 97, 116, 117, 118, 142, 152, 314, 376, 418; for British, 363; oats, 376

Forgery, 191

Fort Dunmore, 30, 31

Fort Fincastle, 31

Fort Ligonier, 31

Fort Pitt, 30, 31

Fortifications: in Hudson Highlands, 37, 38–39, 47, 48–49; at King's Bridge, N.Y., 39; in American lines at Boston, 51, 52, 76, 86, 89, 92, 102, 119, 127, 135, 137, 155, 156, 158, 183, 184, 336, 372, 447; in British lines at Boston, 85–86, 86, 99, 101–2, 137, 178, 183, 184, 233, 318, 331, 342, 363, 466; on Connecticut coast, 417–18, 470, 470–71. *See also* Engineers

Foster, Benjamin: captures British warships, 316

Foster, Gideon: id., 451; *letters from*: to GW, 451

Foster, Isaac, 191; on court of inquiry, 153; id., 155

Foster (Foshe), James: court-martialed, 63; id., 64; punished, 191

Foster, Jedediah: recommended, 26; id., 27; and commission, 413

Foster, Thomas Waite: company, 159; id., 159

Fowey (British warship), 150, 301

Fox, Joseph: and hospitals, 66

Foy, Edward: accompanies Dunmore, 146; id., 150

Francis, Ebenezer: and brickmaking, 357, 358; id., 358

Francis, Turbot, 369

Franklin, Benjamin: id., 319; and gunpowder, 321; *letters from*: to Philip Schuyler, 321

Franklin (American armed schooner), 400

Frazer, John Grizzage: id., 201; recommended, 201, 209–10

Freeman, Nathaniel: and absent soldiers, 265

Freeman, Samuel: id., 307; *letters from*: to Joseph Reed, 307

French, Christopher: captured by Americans, 311, 319, 320, 403; id., 312; sent to Hartford, 404,

French, Christopher (*cont.*) 410; *letters from*: to GW, 311–12, 410–12; to John Campbell, 311; to Thomas Gage, 311; *letters to*: from GW, 389–90; from Joseph Reed, 410, 411, 412
Fresh Pond, 58
Frye, James: regiment, 154, 278; id., 156; brigade, 309, 449, 465
Frye, Joseph: id., 156, 393; appointment, 238, 392; recommended, 390–91
Fuel: British supplies, 97, 117, 196, 225, 238, 343, 421, 447; needed for Continental army, 225, 376, 433, 450
Fundy, Bay of: British convoy to, 354, 362, 406, 418
Funerals: in Continental army, 55; in Boston, 117, 238; grave robbing, 395
Furloughs, 104; regulations, 55, 79, 155; violations, 105, 128, 172–73, 264, 265, 268–69, 275, 276, 303, 347, 427; number in Continental army, 231, 265

Gabions, 127, 128, 158
Gage, Thomas, 35, 65, 166, 205, 315, 343, 350, 373, 434; and Indian affairs, 39; dispatches to England, 141, 189, 467; and intercepted letters, 148; and refugees, 192, 192–93, 194, 228–29; prepares for winter, 225; and Castle William, 229; family goes to England, 238; treatment of prisoners, 289–90, 301–2, 319, 326–27, 328, 392, 411; id., 290; regiment, 312; *letters from*: to GW, 301–2, 392; *letters to*: from GW, 289–91, 326–28, 392; from Christopher French, 311
Gardiner (Gardinerston), Me., 409
Gardiner's Island: British raid on, 170, 200, 222–23, 263, 273, 294, 305, 314, 323
Gardner, Christopher, Jr., 232; court-martialed, 197; id., 198; cashiered, 212, 229, 338–39, 375–76
Gardner, Henry: id., 358
Gardner, Thomas: funeral, 55; id., 57–58; regiment, 76, 154, 358
Gaspée (revenue cutter), 295, 403
Gates, Horatio, 43, 109, 130, 242, 409; appointment, 17, 18, 19, 78–79, 328–29; id., 18, 24; carries letters, 45, 248; at councils of war, 79, 215; recruiting instructions, 83; arrives at Cambridge, 91; and prisoners of war, 208; and returns, 231; *letters from*: to GW, 23–25; to Massachusetts committee of supplies, 109; to James Warren, 191, 453–54; to Loammi Baldwin, 199; to Artemas Ward, 216, 329, 377, 383, 395; to James Otis, Sr., 293; *letters to*: from GW, 3, 432–34; from Samuel Washington, 25; from Perez Morton, 191; from Loammi Baldwin, 213, 313, 326; from Benjamin Tupper, 232
George Tavern, 118, 198, 201, 226, 232
Georgetown (Me.) committee of safety: examines prisoner, 314
Georgia: capture of gunpowder, 146, 150, 244; elects delegates to Continental Congress, 146, 167, 168; supports American cause, 146, 166–67, 229; fast day, 166–67
Germantown (Mass.), 117
Gerrish, Samuel: regiment, 76, 111, 154, 155, 251, 282, 312, 397, 460; id., 77, 325; court-martialed, 318; cashiered, 325, 338, 375; *letters to*: from Joseph Reed, 76
Gerry, Elbridge, 211, 214; recommended, 9, 26; id., 10–11, 212; confers with GW, 105; *letters from*: to GW, 79; *letters to*: from John Adams, 2–3, 20; from Samuel Adams, 26
Gibson, George, 31
Gill, Moses: escorts GW, 92
Gilpin, George: id., 78
Glasgow (British warship), 343, 362, 469
Gloucester (Mass.), 428; British sailors captured at, 293

Gloucester (Mass.) committee of safety: and prisoners, 428, 429; and recaptured vessel, 440; *letters from*: to GW, 359, 429–30
Glover, John: regiment, 50, 55, 76, 154, 398, 408, 465; id., 52; court-martial president, 190–91, 212; procures vessels, 400, 405
Glover, John, Jr.: wounded, 440; id., 441
Glover, Jonathan: and reinforcements, 105
Goddard, John: appointment, 278; id., 279; *letters to*: from GW, 280
Goldthorp, William: captured by Americans, 320
Goldthwait, Hannah Brigham: leaves Boston, 247; id., 248
Goldthwait, Joseph: id., 248
Goodwin, Ichabod: prepares letter to GW, 66
Graft, 397, 427–28, 449; provisions, 56, 120, 155, 189, 212, 229, 255–56, 278, 281, 335, 373, 375, 413, 414; military stores, 189; pay, 212, 229, 264, 268, 297, 322, 335, 346, 373; soldiers working for officers, 264, 268–69
Grant, James, 359
Grape Island: American raid on, 152
Graves, Samuel: and intercepted letters to GW, 148, 239; and defense of Lighthouse Island, 231–32; and fishing pass, 359; on naval tactics, 468; *letters from*: to Philip Stephens, 142; to James Wallace, 471; *letters to*: from James Wallace, 417, 418
Great Blue Hill, 81, 82
Great Britain: reconciliation with, 40, 41, 47–48, 49, 77, 97, 208, 246, 333, 343, 464–65; Parliament, 47–48, 49, 112, 189; intelligence from, 137, 141, 143, 189, 210, 447, 451, 466, 467
Greaton, John: raids Long Island, Mass., 118
Greene, Christopher: brevetted lieutenant colonel, 23
Greene, Nathanael: at councils of war, 79, 215, 450; id., 81; delivers letter, 128; brigade, 154, 228, 427, 432, 446, 455; court-martial president, 300, 325, 448, 465; and mutiny of riflemen, 445–46, 446; *letters from*: to Nicholas Cooke, 49, 81; to Massachusetts provincial congress, 107; to GW, 445–46; *letters to*: from Henry Ward, 49; from GW, 432–34
Greenleaf, Benjamin: id., 26; recommended to GW, 26; confers with GW, 240
Greenleaf, Jonathan: and Massachusetts address to GW, 53
Greenleaf, Joseph: and refugees, 248–49
Green's Hill, 250, 466; threat of attack on, 219–20, 220, 270
Greenwich (Conn.): troops at, 468
Gridley, Richard, 191; regiment, 64, 67, 73, 75–76, 82, 159, 225, 397; id., 76; engineering activities, 94, 119, 145; commission, 224, 231, 392; described, 398
Gridley, Samuel: company, 64
Gridley, Scarborough, 397; court-martialed, 376; id., 397–98
Griffin, Peter: Canadian intelligence, 368, 370; id., 370
Griffin, Samuel, 109, 130; appointment, 55; id., 58
Grimes, John, 305; id., 223, 273
Groves, Joseph: intelligence from, 170, 180; reliability, 175–76, 176
Guards, 128, 278, 321, 322, 419, 420, 445–46, 465; for hospitals, 56, 58, 178, 341, 371; for stores, 56, 67, 395; dereliction of duty, 63, 82, 83, 106, 129–30, 163, 172, 218, 226, 431; regulations, 72, 72–73, 75, 106, 107–8, 114–15, 133, 163, 164, 178, 219, 346; British, 86, 116, 119, 196, 226; for prisoners, 190, 206, 208, 264, 293, 399; at Prospect Hill, 201, 445; at Chelsea, 250, 300, 362, 439; at Malden Point, 250, 251; for Green's Hill,

Guards (*cont.*)
270; for livestock, 383; parole and countersign changed, 445; riflemen assigned as, 449, 449–50; inspection of, 452
Guy Park, 39

Haldimand, Frederick: goes to New York, 101; id., 102
Halifax, Nova Scotia: proposal to attack, 216
Hall, Lyman: elected to Continental Congress, 167; id., 168
Hall, Stephen, 177; id., 179
Hall, Street, 468; id., 470
Hamilton, Andrew: id., 314, 315; *letters from*: to GW, 314–15
Hamilton, George, 314; id., 315
Hamlin, Eleazer: accuses officer, 364; id., 364
Hamlin, Jabez: *letters to*: from Jonathan Trumbull, Sr., 277
Hampton, —— (Mrs.), 364–65
Hampton, Jonathan: id., 364–65
Hancock, John, 22, 45, 384, 385; and GW's appointment, 1, 7, 8, 22; id., 1, 11, 26, 97–98, 144; makes recommendations, 9, 26; desires to join army, 97, 143–44; praised, 145; and Donald Campbell, 173; denounced by Loyalist, 179; property of, 362–63, 366; *letters from*: to Joseph Warren, 8; to GW, 42–44, 64, 97–98, 132–33, 164–68; to Philip Schuyler, 43; to Jonathan Trumbull, Sr., 204; *letters to*: from GW, 34–36, 83–97, 115–18, 136–43, 143–44, 144, 180–81, 223–39, 390–93, 402, 430–31
Hancock (American armed schooner), 400
Hand, Edward: and mutiny of riflemen, 445–46
Hanna, Robert, 31
Hannah (American armed schooner), 398, 400, 429, 441
Harewood, 25
Harris, —— (Mr.), 272, 273; and Bermuda expedition, 221, 222, 304; at Providence, 288
Harris, Benjamin, 223
Harrison, Benjamin, 23; id., 24, 148–49; makes recommendations, 110–11, 177; reelected to Continental Congress, 381; *letters from*: to GW, 145–51, 239, 249; *letters to*: from GW, 98
Harrison, Robert Hanson: id., 17, 78; invited to be aide-de-camp to GW, 362, 365
Hart, Moses: court-martialed, 376; cashiered, 414; id., 415
Hartford: gunpowder at, 299; prisoners sent to, 389, 390, 404, 410, 453–54, 454
Hartford committee of safety: and prisoners, 389, 389–90; *letters to*: from Joseph Reed, 411, 412
Harvard College, 87, 93, 318
Hawley, Joseph: recommended, 9, 26; id., 11, 61; and Massachusetts address to GW, 53; *letters from*: to GW, 61–62, 65–66
Health, 87, 107, 468; of Continental army, 53, 55, 57, 104, 114, 164, 182, 192, 206–7, 257, 345, 371, 406; smallpox prevention, 55, 58, 140, 178, 194; care of sick and wounded, 66, 73–74, 346–47, 426–27; Continental sick returns, 164, 231, 265, 268, 269; of British army, 184, 226, 238, 275; dysentery, 238, 322; in Boston jail, 290–91; as reason for discharge, 348, 352, 398, 451; bloody flux, 371. *See also* Hospitals; Surgeons
Heath, William: dispute over rank, 61, 61–62, 90; id., 61–62; at councils of war, 79, 215, 450; account of Roxbury skirmish, 118; brigade, 154, 228, 309, 449, 465; regiment, 154, 155, 156, 185; court of inquiry president, 330; *letters from*: to GW, 151–52; *letters to*: from GW, 432–34
Hendricks, James: id., 78
Hendricks, William: on Quebec expedition, 416, 432
Henley, David: appointment, 309; id., 310

Henry, Patrick, 45; and GW's appointment, 2, 22; makes recommendations, 110–11, 177; id., 124; appointment, 380, 423; *letters from*: to GW, 124, 201
Henshaw, William: adjutant general, 50, 56; id., 75, 328–29; recommended, 328; *letters to*: from Joseph Reed, 63–64
Hichborn, Benjamin: captured by British, 148, 229–30, 239, 249; escapes, 239, 259–60; id., 239; prisoner exchange, 259; *letters from*: to John Adams, 260
Hill, James, 336; id., 339
Hinman, Benjamin: at Ticonderoga, 121, 129; id., 130; *letters from*: to Philip Schuyler, 130; to Jonathan Trumbull, Sr., 345
Hitchcock, Daniel: regiment, 154, 446
Hobart, Sloss: confers with GW, 33
Hobgoblin Hall, 190
Hoboken (N.J.): GW at, 33
Hodgkins, Joseph: *letters from*: to Sarah Perkins Hodgkins, 50
Hodgkins, Sarah Perkins: *letters to*: from Joseph Hodgkins, 50
Hog Island: American raid on, 286, 397
Hoit, Micah: petitions for pay, 282–83; id., 283
Holden, Benjamin: on court-martial, 300
Honyman, Robert, 337
Hood, Samuel, 287; company, 77
Hope (British warship), 220, 318–19, 320, 404
Hopkins, Daniel: and Massachusetts address to GW, 53
Hopkins, John Burroughs: importation of military stores, 271, 273, 383, 401, 441; id., 401–2
Horses, 411, 422; GW's horses, 13, 14, 56, 58, 68, 68–69, 82, 337; theft, 50; stables for, 56; captured, 63–64, 68; ownership disputed, 68–69; for outposts, 75, 81, 104, 105–6, 287, 313, 348; movement of British horses, 157, 270; exportation permitted, 275; teams for wagons, 280; unfit for service, 313, 325–26; blacksmiths, 325, 326; branding, 325, 326
Hospitals: department established, 45, 46, 139–40, 143, 145, 149, 165, 167; guards, 56, 58, 341, 371; smallpox, 58, 178; regulations, 66, 73–74, 346–47; house used for, 172, 341; prisoners in, 302; director of, 341, 346–47, 371, 412, 426, 427, 455; general hospital, 426–27; inquiry into, 426, 427, 455; regimental hospitals, 426–27; fines contributed to, 455. *See also* Church, Benjamin; Health; Surgeons
Hough's Neck, 117
Houstoun, John: elected to Continental Congress, 167; id., 168
Howe, Moses: court-martialed, 376, 449; id., 449
Howe, William, 411; commands at Bunker Hill, 86; assumes command of British forces, 290; id., 349; servant of, 439; *letters from*: to GW, 349; *letters to*: from GW, 352
Hubbard, William, 263
Hull, Robert: tavern, 33
Humphreys, Charles: id., 70; makes recommendation, 70
Humphreys, James, Jr., 247
Hunt, Shrimpton: in Boston jail, 117
Huntington, Jedediah: flour for army, 125; id., 126; regiment, 126, 277, 278, 279, 309, 406, 417, 438, 468–69, 470
Huntington, Samuel: *letters to*: from GW, xix
Hussars: authorized, 110
Hutchinson, Thomas: id., 467; *letters from*: to unknown, 466, 467
Huts: described, 93; construction, 225. *See also* Barracks; Tents

Ile aux Noix, 394, 448
Indians, 180–81, 390; Connolly's negotiations with, 29, 31–32; British efforts to recruit, 37, 39, 43, 130, 131, 165, 188, 229,

Indians (*cont.*)
307, 367–68, 368; disposition, 42, 43, 45, 46, 120, 129, 131, 229, 257, 306, 307, 331–32, 367, 370, 394, 455–56, 457, 458; American policy, 45, 46, 165–66, 209, 331–32, 334, 367, 368; threaten attacks on frontier, 121, 131, 146, 150, 188, 257; American negotiations with, 229, 238–39, 257, 258, 259, 306, 306–7, 331–32, 367, 369, 409; at Plowed Hill, 376; skirmish with, 394, 394–95; treatment, 455–56, 457, 458, 459
Ingersoll, Joseph: intelligence from, 198; id., 199
Intelligence, 304; sought by GW, 38, 55, 79, 91, 138, 306, 332–33, 399, 410, 421, 437, 458, 459; from Canada, 43, 120, 129, 130, 131, 188, 202, 203, 229, 256, 305–6, 332, 332–33, 367, 368, 369–70, 370, 394, 395, 410; from deserters and prisoners of war, 55, 180, 181, 226, 233, 308; from Roxbury, 79, 91, 431; communication of, 81, 91–92, 105–6, 199–200, 342; from Boston, 116–17, 137–38, 170, 175–76, 180–81, 184, 188, 219–20, 228, 229, 233–38, 238, 239, 280, 284, 306, 312, 342, 343, 348, 353, 359, 362–63, 364, 385, 447–48; from Mohawk Valley, 120, 121; from England, 137, 141, 143, 189, 210, 447, 451, 466, 467; from Chelsea, 157, 157–58, 185, 188, 192, 198–99, 199, 213, 216, 217, 219–20, 250–51, 270, 271, 287, 288, 300–301, 311, 312–13, 314, 318, 322, 323, 325, 331, 336, 342, 362, 366, 389, 439, 452–53, 466; spy in Boston, 188, 193, 311, 312, 313; British sources of, 205, 226, 266, 271, 284–85, 302, 326; from Connecticut, 262–63, 416, 424; from Long Island, N.Y., 344, 345; from Ticonderoga, 344, 345; attempted seizure of packet boat, 421–22, 441, 463, 467
Ipswich (Mass.): prisoners sent to, 291
Isle La Motte, 394
Isle of Shoals, 430

Jacobs Creek, 30
Jefferson, Thomas: makes recommendation, 177; reelected to Continental Congress, 381; *letters from*: to John Page, 460
Jewett, Abel: and reinforcements, 105
Jewett, Dummer: and reinforcements, 105
Johnson, Guy, 258, 259; conduct watched, 37, 121, 165, 188; id., 39; Indian negotiations, 131; at Lachine, 368; *letters from*: to earl of Dartmouth, 39; to Peter Van Brugh Livingston, 130, 131
Johnson, Sir John: Loyalist activities, 257; id., 258–59
Johnson, Jonas: petitions for pay, 282–83
Johnson, Obadiah: carries letters, 204, 263, 281, 293; id., 294
Johnson, Thomas: and GW's appointment, 2
Johnson, Sir William, 39, 257
Johnson Hall, 258
Johnston, —— (Mr.), 146
Johonnot, Gabriel: on court of inquiry, 330; id., 330
Jones, —— (deacon), 246
Jones, Daniel, 246
Jones, David, 287; id., 288, 323; carries letter, 323
Jones, Ichabod: imprisoned, 292; id., 293; GW's opinion of, 296
Jones, Noble Wymberly: elected to Continental Congress, 167; id., 168
Jones, Thomas, 33, 34, 48
Jordan, James, 359
Jordan, William: and gunpowder, 404
Judge advocate general: appointed, 12, 139, 142, 194; needed, 139; pay, 139, 142, 355, 356, 392; duties, 354–55, 364, 392. *See also* Tudor, William

Katy (armed sloop), 223, 272, 273, 305, 442, 464
Kelson, Samuel: id., 261
Kilton, —— (capt.): reprimanded, 260
Kingfisher (British warship), 204
King's Bridge (N.Y.): post proposed at, 39; GW at, 42
Knight, John, 328
Knox, Henry: appointment, 231

Lachine, 370; British force at, 368
Lady Catherine (sloop), 468
Lancaster County (Pa.): riflemen raised in, 110
Lane, John: escorts prisoners, 429; id., 430
Langdon, John: ship of, 429, 430
Langdon, Samuel: recommended, 26; id., 27; house of, 50–51
Lanphier, Going: construction at Mount Vernon, 337; id., 340
Lansing, John: id., 38
Lattimer, Jonathan: company, 267; id., 268; defends New London, 417–18
Lawrence, —— (capt.), 323
Leach, John: in Boston jail, 117, 290–91
Leach, Joseph: intelligence reports, 158, 188, 192, 199, 213, 220, 251, 271, 288, 301, 311, 314, 318, 323, 326, 331, 342, 349, 389, 439, 453, 466
Leaman, John: id., 455; punished, 455
Learned, Ebenezer: regiment, 154, 185, 278, 279; id., 279
Lechmere's Point, 50, 51, 51–52
Lee, Arthur: and intercepted letters, 149
Lee, Charles, 109, 130, 174, 211; appointment, 17, 18, 19, 54; id., 18; indemnified by Continental Congress, 18; accompanies GW to Cambridge, 27, 34, 42, 50, 53, 92; headquarters, 50–51, 189, 190, 301; aides-de-camp, 55, 122, 435; amends GW's addresses, 60, 462–63; at councils of war, 79, 215, 450; inspects American lines, 92; division, 154, 228, 280; letters intercepted, 230; arrests officer, 270–71; and mutiny of riflemen, 446; *letters from*: to Robert Morris, 94; to John Thomas, 162; to GW, 353; *letters to*: from GW, 432–34
Lee, Francis Lightfoot: elected to Continental Congress, 380, 423; id., 381
Lee, Richard Henry: and GW's appointment, 8, 22; id., 45; makes recommendations, 110–11, 177; proposes blockade of Boston Harbor, 209, 373–74; reelected to Continental Congress, 381; *letters from*: to GW, 44–46, 209–11; *letters to*: from GW, 98–100, 372–76
Lee, Thomas Ludwell: appointment, 380; id., 381
Lee, William (sgt.): id., 285; recommended, 285
Lee, William (1739–1795): intelligence from, 137; id., 141
Lee, William Raymond: id., 452; *letters from*: to GW, 452
Leffingwell, Christopher, 263; id., 263–64
Leonard, David: id., 201
Leonard, Noadiah: guard duty, 67; id., 67
Lewis, Fielding: and bill of exchange, 176, 177; id., 177; *letters to*: from GW, 177
Lexington: battle of, 189
Lighthouse Island, 349, 351; American raids on, 140, 144, 151, 152, 205–6, 207, 208, 226, 230, 232, 238, 286; defenses of, 231–32
Lightly, William, 103
Lincoln, Benjamin: and pay of soldiers, 206; id., 208; and importation of military stores, 401; *letters to*: from Joseph Reed, 402
Lincoln, Loring: recommended, 286
Lindsey, Ebenezer, 360
Lindsey, Eleazer, 361; absent from post, 250; id., 252; arrested, 270–71; company, 300–301; cashiered, 312, 338–39, 376

Liquor: sales regulated, 106, 107, 261, 418; rum given to deserters, 178; sold by innkeeper, 200. *See also* Drunkenness
Lispenard, Leonard: house of, 3[illegible]
Little, Moses: regiment, 123, 154, 185, 446; id., 124
Lively (British warship), 300, 301, 428, 429
Livermore, Joseph: recommended, 286
Livestock: removal, 111, 116, 117, 118–19, 152, 184, 263, 267, 305, 313, 313–14, 329, 382, 383, 396, 421; returns, 111; purchase, 119, 262–63, 382, 383, 425, 459; seized by British, 196, 262, 263, 272, 294, 305, 306, 313, 323, 378, 447, 447–48; export prohibited, 275; guarded, 470
Livingston, —— (Mr.), 385
Livingston, Gilbert, 443
Livingston, James: id., 395; *letters from*: to Philip Schuyler, 395
Livingston, Peter Van Brugh, 40, 217; id., 41; *letters from*: to GW, 342–43; *letters to*: from Philip Schuyler, 33; from Guy Johnson, 130; from Guy Carleton, 131; from GW, 283–84, 385–86, 442
Livingston, Philip: id., 386
Livingston, Robert R.: id., 386
Lloyd, Henry: id., 295
Lodge, The, 255
Long Island (Mass.): American raid on, 116, 117–18, 152; British threat to, 170
Long Island (N.Y.): British threat to, 180
Louisburg, 421
Lovell, James: in Boston jail, 117, 290
Low, Isaac: confers with GW, 40
Loyalists: on Pennsylvania frontier, 31–32; military activities, 32, 70, 79, 166, 257, 258–59, 302; in New York City, 32, 34, 37; in Massachusetts, 58, 69, 103, 117, 173, 190, 208, 230, 259, 296; property, 58, 172, 173, 190; arrest and capture, 68, 177, 208, 230, 345, 454; ask GW for assistance, 68, 69; in New Hampshire, 68, 178–79; in Virginia, 150–51; accused, 177, 178–79, 190, 353; viewpoint expressed, 252–55; treatment, 253–54, 302; in Maryland, 255; in Mohawk Valley, 257, 258–59; exchange, 259; in Connecticut, 454
Lukens, Jesse, 445–46, 449–50, 455; id., 446
Lunt, Paul, 50, 196–97, 201, 251–52, 301, 376
Lux, George: carries letter, 422; id., 422
Lyme (Conn.): troops at, 469, 470
Lynch, Thomas, 150
Lyon, James: arrested, 345

McCormick, James, 28; id., 30
McDaniel, James: punished, 190–91
McDermot, Terrence: captured by Americans, 311, 320; id., 312; paroled, 411–12
McDougall, Alexander, 331; id., 333–34
Machias (Me.): skirmish at, 293; inhabitants propose Nova Scotia expedition, 297, 298
McKean, Thomas: id., 44; makes recommendation, 44
McKenzie, Robert: rumored death, 147; id., 151
McKesson, John, 343; id., 444; *letters from*: to GW, 444
Maitland, Richard, 150
Malden (Mass.): troops at, 155, 397
Mansfield, John: regiment, 154, 357, 358, 451; court-martialed, 300, 318, 376; id., 300; cashiered, 339, 465
Maps: of British lines on Boston Neck, 178, 233, 234–35 (illus.); of Boston area, 184, 186–87 (illus.), 228, 233, 236–37 (illus.)
Marblehead (Mass.) committee of safety: *letters from*: to GW, 284–85
March, Samuel: on court-martial, 300

Markoe, Abraham: escorts GW, 28, 42
Marlborough (Mass.): GW at, 92
Martin, Josiah: id., 168; *letters from*: to earl of Dartmouth, 168; *letters to*: from earl of Dartmouth, 166
Martindale, Sion: *letters to*: from GW, 400
Maryland: riflemen, 19–20, 23, 147, 307; soldiers refuse to turn out, 335–36, 336; military exercises, 337; volunteers, 422
Maryland delegates: return home, 147
Mason, David, 398
Mason, George: appointment, 380; id., 381; *letters to*: from GW, 331
Massachusetts: gunpowder supply, 36, 212, 213, 214, 216, 227, 232; adjutant general, 75, 328; quartermaster general, 75, 266; recruiting efforts, 80, 81, 90, 103, 104, 116, 165, 224; militia reinforcements, 90, 105, 116, 116–17; commissary general, 111; rations, 227, 233; paymaster, 357, 358
  troops: clothing and blankets, 67, 88, 297, 324; strength, 81, 103, 224; at Cambridge, 86; at Roxbury, 86; poor quality, 90, 335–36, 372; pay, 105, 162, 206, 208, 282, 291, 292–93, 296–97, 323–24, 357, 358, 387, 415; on Prospect Hill, 154; on Winter Hill, 154; dual commissions, 223–24; choose own officers, 225; for coastal defense, 397
Massachusetts committee of safety, 8, 10, 26, 85, 106; and Bunker Hill, 35; chairman, 68; provides horses, 68–69; receives intelligence, 92; regulates liquor sales, 107; and clothing for army, 357, 358; raises troops, 397; *letters from*: to GW, 68–69; *letters to*: from Joseph Reed, 69
Massachusetts committee of supplies, 8, 10, 10–11, 26, 85, 106; provides clothing, 67, 356, 358; provides horses, 75, 105; and tents, 109; and gunpowder, 212, 213–14, 227, 232; contracts canceled, 292, 293; and importation of military stores, 401; *letters from*: to GW, 109, 211–12, 213–14; *letters to*: from Joseph Reed, 69; from Horatio Gates, 109
Massachusetts committee on state of the province, 8, 10, 11, 26
Massachusetts council, 401; elected, 10, 11, 26–27; president, 26, 248; and prisoners, 191, 285, 291–92, 293, 453, 454; secretary, 191, 208; appoints officers, 231, 291, 413; and volunteers, 266; and gunpowder, 291; and price-fixing, 376–77; recess, 453; *letters from*: to GW, 291–93; *letters to*: from GW, 240, 376–77, 413; from Jonathan Trumbull, Sr., 453; from Nicholas Cooke, 453, 454. *See also* Otis, James, Sr.
Massachusetts delegates: make recommendations, 8, 11–12, 12, 26; id., 26; bid farewell to GW, 28; *letters from*: to GW, 25–27
Massachusetts General Court: reestablished, 10; and pay of troops, 162, 206, 208, 291, 292–93, 296–97, 323–24; and refugees from Boston, 194, 199, 248, 248–49, 265; and coastal defense, 195, 196, 228, 233; and gunpowder, 232, 292; and prisoners, 259, 264, 275–76, 315, 316, 328; and absent soldiers, 264, 265, 275, 276, 303; praised by GW, 264; and Bermuda expedition, 272, 292, 304; cancels contracts, 293; and Loyalists, 296; and Nova Scotia expedition, 297–98; negotiations with Indians, 307; authorizes armed vessels, 316; settles accounts, 316; provides clothing, 324, 356, 357; recess, 377, 454; restricts purchase of fish, 440; *letters from*: to GW, 205, 303, 323–24; *letters to*: from GW, 296–98

Massachusetts house of representatives, 8, 25, 69; convenes, 10, 106; speaker, 10, 298; and gunpowder, 227. *See also* Warren, James
Massachusetts provincial congress, 8, 25; convenes, 10; presidents, 10, 11, 61; approves articles of war, 46; provides headquarters for GW, 50–51; address to GW, 52–53; address from GW, 59–60; appoints officers, 61–62, 76, 212, 214, 218, 224, 328, 391, 393, 427; vice president, 61; provides for sick and wounded, 66; provides clothing and blankets, 67; denies passes to Boston, 69; and horses, 69, 82, 104, 105; and disputes over rank, 75, 85, 89; praised by GW, 84, 88; provides escorts for GW, 92; arrests ship captain, 103; adjourns, 104, 106; and reinforcements, 104–5, 116–17, 124–25, 125–26, 136–37; regulates liquor sales, 106, 107; sets troop strength, 116; and whaleboats, 157; and pay of troops, 162, 208; and rank of regiments, 218; specifies rations, 233; raises troops, 397; and importation of military stores, 401; *letters from*: to Continental Congress, 34, 35–36, 36; to GW, 66; to Jonathan Trumbull, Sr., 103, 125–26; *letters to*: from Joseph Ward, 67. *See also* Warren, James
Matlack, Timothy: id., 7
Matson, James, 71
Matson, John: recommended, 70
Matthews, Joseph: punished, 321–22
Maxwell, Thompson, 179
Medford (Mass.), 51; troops at, 155
Menotomy River, 179–80
Mercer, George, 295; sale of his estate, 242–43; id., 243
Mercer, Hugh: purchase of Ferry Farm, 4, 6; id., 6
Mercer, James: appointment, 380; id., 381
Meredith, Samuel: attempts to capture Dunmore, 146; id., 150
Merlin (British warship), 386
Merritt, John: company, 465; id., 465
Middleton, Henry: id., 299; *letters from*: to Jonathan Trumbull, Sr., 299
Middletown (Conn.): lead mine, 309, 344, 344–45
Mifflin, Thomas, 109, 130, 189, 258; accompanies GW to Cambridge, 27, 42; appointments, 27–28, 54, 75, 175, 266, 303, 372, 375; id., 56–57
Mighill, Thomas: petitions for pay, 282–83; id., 283
Military stores, 40, 56, 241; returns, 21, 37–38, 54, 63, 75–76, 139, 317; removed from New York City, 37, 38; guards, 56, 67, 395; shortage of, 130, 145, 256–57; graft, 189, 255–56; importation, 271, 401; capture ordered, 463
Miller, Benjamin: *letters to*: from Abijah Willard (Willant), 323
Miller, Henry: recommended, 70; id., 71
Miller, William Turner: on court-martial, 300
Milnor, William: bolting cloth, 337; id., 339
Missisauga Indians, 257, 259
Môle-Saint-Nicholas, 424
Money, —— (capt.): company, 64
Money: Continental currency, 13, 14, 16, 17, 19, 22, 146, 166; shortage in Continental army, 84, 88, 120, 139, 282, 430; sent to Schuyler, 125, 126; appropriated for Continental army, 142–43; shortage in Boston, 238; for gunpowder and military stores, 304, 401, 442, 464; Virginia currency, 380, 381; for bateaux, 409; for Quebec expedition, 446, 459
Montagu, George: accompanies Dunmore, 146; id., 150
Montauk Point, 354, 416; British threat to, 353

Montgomery, Richard: confers with GW, 33; death, 175; invades Canada, 368, 393–94; id., 370
Montreal: British force at, 368
Montresor, John: id., 334
Moon Island, 118
Morgan, Charles, 28; id., 30
Morgan, Daniel: recruits rifle company, 23, 24–25; id., 24; on Quebec expedition, 415–16, 432
Morris, Gouverneur: confers with GW, 33, 40
Morris, Lewis: id., 241; *letters from*: to GW, 129; *letters to*: from GW, 240–41
Morris, Robert, 403; id., 404; *letters to*: from Charles Lee, 94
Morton, —— (capt.): intelligence from, 219
Morton, Perez: and minutes of Massachusetts General Court, 206, 265, 285, 292, 298, 324, 413; id., 208; *letters from*: to Horatio Gates, 191; to GW, 453–54
Morton, Thomas: id., 220
Moulton, Johnson, 438; id., 438–39
Mount Airy, 16, 338
Moylan, Stephen: id., 169–70; recommended, 169; appointment, 287, 385; musters troops, 303, 317
Mumford, Isaac: death, 376
Mumford, Thomas, 267
Munro (Munrowe), —— (blacksmith), 325, 326
Murray, Daniel: id., 69–70; *letters from*: to GW, 69–70
Murray, John, Jr.: id., 69
Murray, John, Sr.: id., 69
Murray, Robert: id., 69
Muse, Battaile, 177
Mustering: rolls for, 303, 317, 346; schedule, 317, 318, 340–41, 346, 348, 366, 370–71, 427, 432, 449, 465; regulations, 341
Mustermaster general: needed, 84, 88, 139; authorized, 94, 145, 149, 165; appointed, 287, 385; duties, 303, 317, 340–41. *See also* Moylan, Stephen
Mustermasters, 206
Mutiny: triable by general court-martial, 83; officer accused of, 124, 364; of riflemen, 445, 445–46, 449, 449–50, 454–55

Nagel, George: company, 446, 455
Nancy (brigantine), 103, 125, 424
Nantasket, 152, 351
Nelson, Thomas: bill of exchange, 176; id., 177
Nelson, Thomas, Jr.: elected to Continental Congress, 380, 423; id., 381
Newark (N.J.): GW at, 33
New Brunswick (N.J.): GW at, 33
New Hampshire: cannon sent to Continental army, 51; recruiting efforts, 165; gunpowder supply, 214, 216, 227, 242
  troops: sent to Continental army, 51; on Winter Hill, 51, 86, 154; protect frontier, 181, 182, 257, 259, 333; dual commissions, 224, 230; strength of regiments, 224; join Schuyler's army, 259, 334
New Hampshire committee of safety: and ranger companies, 182–83; chairman, 183; *letters from*: to Timothy Bedel, 182–83; *letters to*: from Nathaniel Folsom, 51; from GW, 227, 242. *See also* Thornton, Matthew
New Hampshire general assembly: and prisoners, 454
New Hampshire Grants, 259
New Hampshire provincial congress: condemns Loyalist, 68; and ranger companies, 181–82, 182; president, 183; stops communication with British warship, 205; restricts purchase of fish, 430. *See also* Thornton, Matthew
New Haven: GW at, 92; troops at, 468–69, 470
New London: British attack on, 204, 471; threatened, 416, 469; defense of, 417–18; troops at, 468–69, 470
Newmarket, 110
Newport committee of inspection: intelligence from, 466

New Rochelle (N.Y.): GW at, 34, 42
New York: militia escorts GW, 33, 34, 41–42; gunpowder supply, 35, 36, 47, 121, 213–14, 294, 299, 309, 385, 386, 442–43, 444; British threat to, 91, 274–75, 280–81, 284, 434; lead supply, 211, 213; recruiting efforts, 333
troops: for Schuyler's army, 256, 258, 333, 345, 377–78, 379, 407; on Long Island, 294, 377–78, 378–79, 407
New York City committee of safety: and trade with enemy, 275, 342
New York committee of safety: and trade with enemy, 442; sends gunpowder to Continental army, 443–44; adjourns, 444; secretary, 444; *letters from*: to Continental Congress, 386, 443–44; to GW, 442–44
New York delegates: and removal of military stores, 38
New York department: Schuyler assumes command, 36; deputy quartermaster general, 173, 175; deputy commissary, 256, 258, 436
New York general assembly: remonstrance to House of Commons, 47–48, 49
New York provincial congress: receives GW, 33, 34; purchases gunpowder, 36; and fortifications, 37, 38–39, 39, 47, 48–49; and removal of military stores, 38; address to GW, 40–41; address from GW, 41–42; president, 41; and commissions, 47, 217, 283–84, 342, 343; receives intelligence, 121, 284; and supplies for Schuyler, 256–57, 258, 345; and trade with enemy, 274, 275; and defense of colony, 275, 284, 294, 377–78, 378–79; secretary, 343, 444; and tents, 345; recess, 386, 442; GW's opinion of, 407–8; *letters from*: to GW, 217; to David Wooster, 284; to Elizabeth (N.J.) committee of safety, 284; to Philadelphia committee of safety, 284; to Charles Thomson, 342, 343; to Suffolk County (N.Y.) committee of safety, 378–79; to Continental Congress, 386; *letters to*: from Continental Congress, 217; from Philip Schuyler, 258; from GW, 274–75; from William Smith, 378; from David Wooster, 379. *See also* Livingston, Peter Van Brugh
Nicholas, Robert Carter: and George William Fairfax, 177; id., 435; *letters from*: to GW, 434–35
Nightingale, Joseph: id., 387
Nixon, John: regiment, 56, 64, 154, 191, 356; id., 58; court-martial president, 108, 123, 124, 127, 159, 169, 454–55
Noddles Island, 439; skirmishes at, 313, 318, 331, 342; American raid on, 397
North, Frederick, second earl of Guilford, 49
Northampton (Mass.): prisoners sent to, 191, 292, 293, 328
Northampton (Mass.) committee of safety: *letters to*: from Joseph Reed, 328
North Carolina: Loyalist activities, 166; royal governor flees, 168
North River, 408
Norwich (Conn.): troops at, 468
Norwich (Conn.) committee of correspondence: and seized vessel, 125; *letters from*: to GW, 262–64
Nova Scotia: proposed expedition against, 297–98, 298
Noyes, Belcher: id., 238; *letters from*: to Nathaniel Noyes, 213, 228, 229, 233–38, 238, 239
Noyes, Nathaniel: id., 213; *letters to*: from Belcher Noyes, 213, 228, 229, 233–38, 238, 239
Nutting, John: company, 172; id., 173

O'Brien, Jeremiah: and skirmish at Machias, 293; id., 316
Officers: appointments, 13, 17, 18–19, 54, 56, 61–62, 85, 89–90, 95, 96, 113, 132, 138, 145–46, 161, 162, 165, 167, 189, 223,

Officers (*cont.*)
228, 277–78, 285, 286, 291, 361, 380, 380–81, 390–91, 392, 393, 413, 423; disputes among, 18–19, 56, 61, 61–62, 85, 89–90, 94–95, 113–14, 120, 121, 132, 138–39, 145–46, 159–62, 174–75, 189, 245–46, 438–39, 458, 460; brevet commissions, 21, 23; appointment policy, 21, 22–23, 241, 384; commissions, 22, 43, 47, 48, 54, 64, 89, 95, 101, 145–46, 165, 167, 217, 218, 223, 224, 225, 230, 231, 241, 245–46, 277–78, 283–84, 291, 343, 357, 413; continued in rank and station, 54; duties, 55, 57, 60, 63, 65, 71–72, 72–73, 107, 114, 118, 123, 128, 163, 414; accused of cowardice, 65, 71–72, 74, 108, 127, 138, 197, 198, 212, 229, 330, 335–36, 373, 375; cashiered, 71, 74, 77, 138, 155, 175, 183, 198, 212, 229, 252, 278, 312, 325, 335–36, 338–39, 356–57, 373, 375–76, 398, 414, 427, 427–28, 449, 465; court-martialed, 71, 74, 76, 108, 123–24, 127, 159, 172, 175, 197, 198, 212, 260, 278, 300, 312, 318, 325, 330, 335–36, 346, 356–57, 360–61, 364, 373, 375–76, 397, 398, 414, 427–28, 427, 431, 448, 449, 465; precedence, 114–15, 317, 329; insignia, 115, 158, 163; accused of mutiny, 123–24, 364; retirement and resignation, 139, 159–62, 348, 351, 352, 398, 413–14, 422, 427, 451, 460; absent without leave, 207, 347, 427, 438, 449; dual commissions, 223–24, 230–31, 391–92; pay, 223–24, 282–83; chosen by enlisted men, 225; accused of graft, 229, 264, 268–69, 281, 297, 335, 373, 375, 397, 414, 427–28, 449; prohibited from being sutlers, 260, 261; reprimanded, 260, 414, 431; promotion, 277–78, 285, 286, 373; fined, 278; investigated by court of inquiry, 330, 340; accused of slander, 364; criticized, 372, 373, 375; arrested, 414, 427; invited to dinners, 419; officer of the day, 419, 452

Ogden, Matthias: recommended, 132, 240; id., 133

Oldien, —— (capt.), 316

Oliver, Andrew: house of, 172, 341; id., 173

Oliver, Robert: company, 321; id., 322

Orne, Azor: recommended, 26; id., 27; appraises vessels, 405

Osgood, James: ranger company, 181–82

Osgood, Samuel: appointment, 133; id., 134

Osnaburg cloth, 164, 167

Oswegatchie, 131

Otis, James, Jr.: id., 26, 248

Otis, James, Sr.: id., 26, 248; recommended, 26; consults with GW, 196; and Benjamin Hichborn, 260; *letters from*: to GW, 275–76; to Jonathan Trumbull, Sr., 454; to Matthew Thornton, 454; to Nicholas Cooke, 454; *letters to*: from GW, 247–49, 264–65, 316; from Horatio Gates, 293; from Joseph Reed, 306–7, 328

Owen, Terry, 321

Oyster Ponds, 293–95, 294

Page, John: appointment, 380; id., 381; *letters to*: from Thomas Jefferson, 460

Paine, Robert Treat: and GW's appointment, 2; makes recommendations, 9, 11, 26; id., 11, 26

Palfrey, William: appointment, 122; id., 123

Palmer, Joseph, 292; recommended, 9, 26; id., 10–11, 266; and reinforcements, 105; confers with GW, 240; proposal to blockade Boston Harbor, 349–51; *letters from*: to GW, 255, 343; *letters to*: from GW, 265–66, 349–51

Palmer, Joseph Pearse: id., 75, 266; recommended, 266

Pardons, 173, 340
Parke, John (lt.): id., 351; *letters from*: to GW, 351
Parke, John (1754–1789): id., 44; recommended, 44; appointment, 312, 384
Parker, John: ranger company, 181–82
Parker, Moses: death, 117
Parker, Oliver: company, 159; id., 159; cashiered, 212, 229, 338–39, 375
Parker, Timothy: and reinforcements, 105
Parsons, Samuel Holden: regiment, 154, 185; *letters from*: to John Adams, 330
Partridge, George: and Massachusetts address to GW, 53; prepares letter to GW, 66
Passes: requested, 69; discontinued, 172
Paterson, John: id., 115; regiment, 115, 154, 155, 260; on court-martial, 300
Patton (Patten, Pattin), William: court-martialed, 63, 73; id., 64; punished, 82
Pay: GW forgoes, 1, 2, 3, 375; for GW's secretary and aides, 3, 11; for Continental troops, 13, 81, 281–82, 296–97, 323–24, 433, 450; for Massachusetts troops, 105, 162, 206, 208, 291, 292–93, 296–97, 323–24, 357, 387, 415; for judge advocate general, 139, 142, 355, 356, 392; for provost marshal, wagon master, and master carpenter, 143; graft, 212, 229, 264, 268, 297, 322, 335, 346, 373; for armorers, 215; for dual commissions, 223–24; for New York troops, 256; officers petition for, 282–83; deductions from, 310, 455; for GW's miller, 336; for artificers, 409; for Virginia volunteer, 435
Paymaster general, 421; appointed, 10, 142; needed, 139; begins paying troops, 296; and pay of Massachusetts troops, 357, 415. *See also* James Warren
Paymasters: for Massachusetts troops, 206, 357, 358; settlement of accounts, 206, 281–82, 357; and fines, 455
Pearl, Stephen: court-martialed, 346; id., 348
Peck, John: and refugees, 248–49
Pendleton, Edmund: and GW's appointment, 2; drafts will for GW, 4; id., 5–6; makes recommendation, 110–11; leaves Continental Congress, 146–47; appointment, 380, 381; resigns from Continental Congress, 380, 423; *letters from*: to GW, 109–10
Pennsylvania: riflemen, 19–20, 70–71, 94, 110, 307, 415, 416; dispute with Virginia, 31, 32; Loyalists on frontier, 31–32; gunpowder supply, 35, 44–45, 45–46, 94, 149, 209, 210, 277, 294, 306, 319, 321, 373, 403, 404, 443–44; and gunpowder from Bermuda, 467, 468
Pennsylvania committee of safety: and prisoners, 311, 318–19, 320, 403, 404, 410, 411–12; and clothing, 319, 320, 403, 404; formation, 319; and gunpowder, 319, 321, 403, 404; president, 319, 404; *letters from*: to GW, 318–21, 403–4; *letters to*: from Joseph Reed, 403, 404
Pennsylvania delegates: id., 70; make recommendations, 70; recruit hussars, 110; *letters to*: from York County committee of correspondence, 70–71; *letters from*: to GW, 70–71
Pennsylvania general assembly: and riflemen, 70
Penny ferry: British attack on, 220, 250–51, 251–52
Perkins, Benjamin: court-martialed, 123–24; id., 124
Perkins, William: company, 191, 321–22; id., 191
Perry, David: id., 422; *letters from*: to GW, 422

Perry, John: reprimanded, 431; id., 432
Peter, Martha Parke ("Patsy") Custis. *See* Custis, Martha Parke ("Patsy"; 1777–1854)
Pettengill (Pettingill), Joseph: dispute over command, 460; id., 460–61
Phelps, Elisha: id., 258, 436; and lead for army, 344; *letters from*: to GW, 436; *letters to*: from Jonathan Trumbull, Sr., 344
Philadelphia: military associators, 57; militia battalions, 246
Philadelphia committee of safety: and gunpowder, 45; *letters to*: from New York provincial congress, 284
Philadelphia Light Horse: escorts GW, 28, 41–42
Phillipa (ship), 150
Phillips, Samuel, Jr.: and Massachusetts address to GW, 53; confers with GW, 105
Phinney, Edmund: regiment, 154, 162–63, 185; id., 162–63
Pickering, John, Jr.: and Massachusetts address to GW, 53; prepares letter to GW, 66
Pickett, Moses: drummed out, 465
Pigeon, John: id., 111
Pike, Thomas: petitions for pay, 282–83; id., 283
Piscataway, 334–35, 337
Pitt, John: treatment of, 458–59; id., 460
Pitt, William, first earl of Chatham, 458; id., 460
Pitts, James: recommended, 9, 26; id., 11
Pitts, John: recommended, 26; id., 27
Plowed Hill: American occupation of, 371, 374–75, 376, 379, 385–86, 391, 393, 406, 447
Plum Island: British raid on, 345
Plundering, 152; discouraged, 69; triable by general court-martial, 83; regulations, 215, 399, 458, 460; forbidden, 456, 458, 462
Pohick Church, 337, 340
Point Alderton, 349, 351, 373–74
Point Shirley, 111, 322
Pomeroy, Seth, 90; absence from army, 61, 89, 139; id., 62; commission revoked, 85, 96, 165, 228, 392
Poor, Enoch: regiment, 154; arrests officer, 414
Porter, Elisha, 272; confers with GW, 104–5, 214; and reinforcements, 105; id., 211–12; sends lead and flints, 211, 213; and Bermuda expedition, 222, 288, 304; carries letters, 222, 271, 288; *letters to*: from Joseph Reed, 223
Porto Bello, 150
Portsmouth committee of safety: restricts admittance to camp, 126; condemns ship captain, 430, 440–41
Port Tobacco, 334–35, 337
Posey, Amelia ("Milly"), 5; id., 6
Posey, John: id., 6
Powder Horn Hill, 111, 185, 213; signal on, 216, 388–89
Prentice, William: id., 360; transfer requested, 360
Prescott, William: regiment, 50, 154, 155, 159, 172, 212, 231, 358; id., 52; court-martial president, 82, 106; on court of inquiry, 330
Preston (British warship), 231, 239
Price, Thomas: id., 24, 151, 337; recruits rifle company, 24–25; introduced to GW, 147–48
Prices: women's suits, 5, 6; meat in Boston, 135, 184; firewood, 376, 450; forage, 376; proposal for price-fixing, 376–77; military stores, 388, 402; bateaux, 409; flour, 425; livestock, 448. *See also* Profiteering
Prince, —— (capt.), 334
Prince, Asa: id., 337
Prince William County (Va.) independent company, 17, 339
Prisoners, 21, 274; treatment, 55, 289–90, 301–2, 312, 316, 319, 320, 326–27, 328, 389, 389–90, 392, 399, 403, 404, 410–11, 411, 411–12, 412, 458–59; held in jails, 117, 190, 191, 206, 208, 226, 249, 289, 290–91,

Prisoners (*cont.*)
291–92, 293, 315, 328, 411, 416, 453, 453–54, 454; captured at Battle of Bunker Hill, 117; captured on Long Island, Mass., 117; guards for, 190, 206, 208, 264, 293, 399; captured on Lighthouse Island, 206, 208, 226, 230, 232; captured at Roxbury, 226; captured on Charlestown Neck, 226, 231; captured in Rhode Island, 229–30, 239, 249; escape, 239, 259–60, 445–46; exchange of, 259, 292, 312; examined by Massachusetts authorities, 264, 275–76; captured at Cape Ann, 293, 328, 428, 428–29, 429, 430; captured at Machias, 293, 316; captured on Delaware River, 311, 318–19, 320; appeal to GW, 311, 314–15, 410–11; captured at Dorchester, 321; at Montreal, 369

Proctor, Edward: and refugees, 248–49

Profanity: forbidden, 54–55, 57; officer court-martialed for, 278

Profiteering, 376–77, 388; prohibited, 260

Prospect Hill, 51, 99; troops at, 86, 154; GW inspects defenses, 92, 183; map of lines at, 233, 236–37 (illus.)

Provisions, 224, 268, 398; returns, 21, 37–38, 54, 63, 85, 197, 317; for posts on Lake Champlain, 37, 40; graft, 56, 120, 155, 189, 212, 229, 255–56, 278, 281, 335, 373, 375, 413, 414; bread, 72, 202, 233, 269, 371; for guards, 106; preparation of, 114; British shortage, 116, 135, 137, 142, 175, 181, 182, 184, 238, 263, 274, 305, 447; flour, 120, 125, 130, 152–53, 157, 258, 269, 343, 409, 425, 426; shortage at Ticonderoga, 120, 130, 202, 258; beef, 135, 184, 233, 269, 409, 410; sought by British, 175, 180–81, 199, 263, 323, 342, 343, 353, 416; Continental army's supplies, 182, 257–58, 266, 293; in Canada, 203, 370, 395, 459; rations, 212, 227, 233, 269, 270; as plunder, 215, 429, 440, 460; fish, 233, 269; pork, 233, 258, 269, 409, 425, 426; provided by sutlers, 261; for Bermuda, 288, 289, 291, 292, 402, 420; lack of in Boston jail, 291; corn purchased, 409; for Quebec expedition, 409, 410; salt supply, 430. *See also* Commissaries; Commissary general; Forage; Livestock

Provost marshal: needed, 139; authorized, 143

Pullen Point, 111; livestock removed from, 313, 313–14

Punishments: reprimands, 50, 260, 414, 431; cashiering, 71, 74, 77, 138, 155, 175, 183, 198, 212, 229, 252, 278, 312, 325, 335–36, 338–39, 356–57, 373, 375–76, 398, 414, 427, 427–28, 449, 465; wooden horse, 82, 83; whipping, 115, 159, 191, 321, 322, 340, 445, 465; fines, 278, 322, 455; hanging, 301–2, 326; imprisonment, 455; capital, 456; drumming out, 465. *See also* Court-martials

Putnam, Israel, 69, 191, 413; appointment, 17, 18, 19, 54, 89; id., 18, 95–96; regiment, 64, 153, 154, 172, 412, 415; at court-martial, 74; at councils of war, 79, 215, 450; and dispute over rank, 85, 89, 95, 113–14, 138–39, 145–46; and fortifications, 127; aides-de-camp, 153; division, 154, 228, 280, 438; surveying, 351; *letters to*: from GW, 432–34

Putnam, Israel, Jr.: appointment, 153; id., 155

Quartermaster general: assistants, 44, 201, 312, 384; appointed, 57, 75, 174, 265–66, 266, 303, 372, 375; and bread, 72, 371; of Massachusetts forces, 75, 266; needed, 84, 88, 139; authorized,

Quartermaster general (*cont.*) 94, 145, 149, 165; furnishes tents, 309–10, 358, 415; inspects housing, 309–10; and returns, 317; receives clothing, 356, 357; and armorers, 357; and brickmakers, 357; and new cider, 371; and firewood, 376; and forage, 376. *See also* Mifflin, Thomas
Quartermasters: graft, 56; care of pikes, 114; deputy quartermaster general for New York, 173, 175; and cleanliness of camp, 206–7
Quebec: British forces at, 306, 368
Quincy, Dorothy: marries John Hancock, 98
Quincy, Josiah, Sr.: proposes blockade of Boston Harbor, 210–11; *letters from*: to John Adams, 210; *letters to*: from John Adams, 210

Raids: on Brown's house, 86, 92–93, 207; on Long Island, Mass., 116, 117–18, 207; on Lighthouse Island, 140, 144, 151–52, 152, 205–6, 207, 208, 226, 230, 232, 238; British fear of, 142; on Deer Island, 152, 366; on Grape Island, 152; on New England coast, 196; on Fishers Island, 200, 262–63, 263, 294, 305, 307, 314; on Gardiners Island, 200, 294, 305, 307, 314, 323; on Plum Island, 345; on Stonington, Conn., 416, 417, 418, 469, 470. *See also* Skirmishes
Rand, Isaac, 56; id., 58
Randall, John: id., 352; *letters from*: to GW, 352
Randolph, Edmund, 423, 424; recommended to GW, 147, 177; id., 150–51; appointed aide-de-camp to GW, 309, 372, 375; *letters from*: to Artemas Ward, 364
Randolph, John, 147; id., 150–51
Randolph, Peyton, 147; id., 1, 150–51; reelected to Continental Congress, 381; *letters from*: to GW, 422–24
Read, George: id., 44
Read, Joseph: regiment, 154
Recruiting, 145; double enlistments, 73, 105, 115, 159, 169; recruiting officers, 80, 81, 82–83, 116, 225, 360; deficiencies, 90, 140, 165, 203, 225, 231; in Connecticut, 96, 124–25, 125–26, 152, 267, 470–71; in Rhode Island, 96, 141; in southern colonies, 137, 141, 379–80; halted, 360; reenlistment of army, 433, 450
Reed, Esther De Berdt: *letters to*: from Joseph Reed, 190
Reed, James: regiment, 154, 285; on court-martial, 300
Reed, Joseph, 130, 189, 258, 369; and preparation of GW's letters, xviii, 83–84; appointment, 12, 54; accompanies GW to Cambridge, 27–28, 42; id., 56–57; intends to leave GW, 147; message to Massachusetts council, 291, 292; *letters from*: to Elias Boudinot, 57; to William Henshaw, 63–64; to Massachusetts committee of safety, 69; to Massachusetts committee of supplies, 69; to Samuel Gerrish, 76; to James Warren, 105, 116–17; to John Thomas, 105–6, 142, 200; to David Wooster, 180–81; to Esther De Berdt Reed, 190; to Loammi Baldwin, 192, 193; to Elisha Porter, 223; to Artemas Ward, 231; to Norwich committee of correspondence, 263; to James Otis, Sr., 306–7, 328; to Northampton committee of safety, 328; to Richard Dodge, 389; to Thomas Seymour, 389–90; to John Wharton, 390, 411; to Benjamin Lincoln, 402; to Pennsylvania committee of safety, 403, 404; to Nathaniel Tracy, 405; to Christopher French, 410, 411, 412; to Hartford committee of safety, 411, 412; to Samuel Blachley Webb, 411; to Benedict Arnold, 462; *letters to*: from Samuel Freeman, 307

Refugees: arrive at Chelsea, 192, 193, 198, 213, 216, 228–29, 230, 313; permitted to leave Boston, 192–93, 238, 239; control of, 194, 198, 199, 247–48, 248, 248–49
Religious services, 127, 246; attendance required, 55, 57, 122; fast days, 112, 113, 122, 166–67; prayer time, 191; Roman Catholicism, 459. *See also* Chaplains; Sermons
Returns: of provisions, 21, 37–38, 54, 63, 85, 197, 317; requested, 21, 37–38, 49, 54, 63, 72, 75–76, 76, 111, 122–23, 127, 139, 164, 185, 189, 197, 199, 317; delayed, 47, 76, 84, 87, 98, 123, 134, 139, 185; of ammunition, 49, 54, 75–76, 139, 214, 216, 227, 232; of artillery, 75–76, 232; of Continental army, 80, 81, 90, 99, 103–4, 139, 225, 231, 264, 265, 269; forms, 87, 107, 111, 256, 261; mistakes, 98; of livestock, 111; from Schuyler, 120, 121–22, 130, 202, 256, 394; falsification, 212; of tents, 277; of wagon teams, 280; of military stores, 317; of artificers, 357
Rhode Island: recruiting efforts, 80, 81, 96, 137, 141, 165, 224; tents, 81; tow cloth, 164–65, 167, 222, 272, 288, 382, 421, 422; gunpowder supply, 216, 221, 227, 271, 382, 387, 388, 401; armed vessels, 221–22, 223, 272, 273, 304, 305, 382, 402, 403, 441, 442, 463, 464, 467; lead supply, 271, 272, 273, 288, 382, 387, 388, 401; arms supply, 382, 387, 388, 401
  troops: put under GW's command, 49; sent to Continental army, 81, 137, 141, 165, 224; at Sewall's farm, 86; on Winter Hill, 86; on Prospect Hill, 154; dual commissions, 223–24; strength of regiments, 224
  see also Cooke, Nicholas
Rhode Island committee of safety: and tow cloth, 272, 288
Rhode Island delegates, 421; and Bayonne gunpowder scheme, 463
Rhode Island general assembly, 464; puts troops under GW's command, 49; raises troops, 96, 137, 141, 165; supports American cause, 108–9; chooses new governor, 109; authorizes armed vessels, 223; and Bermuda expedition, 272, 305; committee to act during recess, 382, 383, 402, 454; and livestock, 382, 383; recess, 382, 383, 402, 454; appoints officers, 403, 425; accepts prisoners, 453, 454
Richelieu River, 258
Richmond, Ezra: and Massachusetts address to GW, 53
Richmond County (Va.) independent company, 17
Riflemen, 85, 147; arrival at camp, 20, 25, 136, 137, 145, 151, 189, 224, 299, 306; authorized, 20, 70, 110; described, 20, 24, 94, 313; recruited, 23, 24–25, 70, 110, 307; officers recommended, 70, 70–71; in skirmish at Charlestown Neck, 196, 201, 226, 231; firing restricted, 219; in skirmish at Roxbury, 226; on Quebec expedition, 415, 415–16, 432; mustered, 427; mutiny, 445, 445–46, 449, 454–55; guard and fatigue duty, 449, 449–50
Rison, William, 358
Ritzema, Rudolphus, 333
Robert Cary & Co.: GW's debt to, 5, 6
Roberts, William: employment of, 336–37; id., 339
Robinson, Caleb: petitions for pay, 282–83; id., 283
Roby, William: makes recommendation, 285
Rodney, Caesar: id., 44; makes recommendation, 44
Roffe, Thomas: makes recommendation, 285

Rogers, William: company, 397
Rolls: calling of, 63, 219, 310; for mustering, 303, 317, 346; duty rosters, 317, 432
Rose (British warship), 204, 263, 353, 416, 417, 468, 469
Roseboom, Gerrit: Canadian intelligence, 130, 131
Ross, George: id., 70; makes recommendation, 70
Ross, James: raises rifle company, 110; company mutinies, 446
Rotten, John: captured by Americans, 311, 320; id., 312; parole, 411–12
Roxbury, 51, 99; American defenses at, 86, 92, 183; troops at, 86, 154; tents for, 109; skirmish at, 116, 118, 201, 226; British defenses at, 189, 226–27; maps of, 228, 233, 234–35 (illus.), 236–37 (illus.); livestock at, 383
Roxbury Neck. *See* Boston Neck
Royall, Isaac: house of, 190, 301
Rush, Benjamin: and GW's appointment, 2
Russell, William: court-martialed, 397; id., 398
Rutledge, Edward: and GW's appointment, 8, 22; id., 299; *letters from*: to Jonathan Trumbull, Sr., 299
Rutledge, John: and GW's appointment, 22
Ryan, William: cashiered, 356–57

St. Clair, Arthur, 31
St. Francis Indians, 257, 259; confer with GW, 306, 306–7, 331–32; American use of, 334
St. George, Bermuda, 223
St. Jean (St. Johns), 44, 448; British defenses at, 129, 203, 229, 368, 395
Sally (sloop), 359
Saltonstall, Gurdon: id., 267; militia regiment, 267; defends New London, 470; *letters from*: to Jonathan Trumbull, Sr., 267–68
Sanborn, —— (lt.): discharged, 413–14
Sanborn, Aaron: id., 414
Sanborn, Abraham: id., 414
Sandy Hook: British ships at, 47, 48; Abraham Whipple patrols, 421, 441, 463
Saratoga: Schuyler's estate at, 121
Sargent, Paul Dudley: regiment, 72, 154, 225, 278, 281; id., 74; commission, 225, 231, 413; on court of inquiry, 330
Sargent, Winthrop (1727–1793), 429; id., 430
Sargent, Winthrop (1753–1820): id., 430
Saunders, Jesse: cashiered, 278, 281, 338–39, 375
Sawyer (Sayer), Ebenezer: and soldiers' pay, 298; and clothing for army, 356
Sawyer, Ephraim: on court-martial, 300
Scammans, James, 438; court-martialed, 108, 127; id., 108; regiment, 154, 155, 360; disputes with subordinate, 159, 361
Scammell, Alexander: id., 100–101; appointment, 309, 391; *letters from*: to GW, 100–101
Scarborough (British warship), 205
Schenectady committee of safety: *letters to*: from Tryon County (N.Y.) committee of safety, 121
Schuyler, Philip, 182–83, 267, 443; appointment, 17, 18, 19, 54; id., 18, 38, 121; accompanies GW to New York, 27, 34, 42; and William Tryon, 32, 37, 39, 47, 48; ordered to invade Canada, 42–43, 45, 202, 256, 258; and returns, 121–22, 202; gunpowder sent to, 125, 126, 277, 319, 321, 331, 444; money sent to, 125, 126; and Indian affairs, 165–66, 238, 257, 258, 307, 332, 334, 367–68, 395; and Donald Campbell, 173, 174; invades Canada, 202, 256, 257, 305, 331, 332, 345, 368, 368–69, 393–94, 394, 406, 407, 417, 437, 448, 458, 462; and commissions, 217, 283–84; and Suffolk County, N.Y., troops,

Schuyler, Philip (*cont.*)
377–78, 379, 407–8; *letters from*: to Peter Van Brugh Livingston, 33; to GW, 47–49, 120–22, 129–31, 202–3, 255–59, 367–70, 393–95; to Continental Congress, 48, 150, 217; to New York provincial congress, 258; to Jonathan Trumbull, Sr., 345, 416; *letters to*: from GW, 36–40, 101–2, 181–83, 188–90, 305–7, 308, 331–34, 436–37; from John Hancock, 43; from Albany committee of safety, 121; from Benjamin Hinman, 130; from Benjamin Franklin, 321; from Jonathan Trumbull, Sr., 344; from James Livingston, 395
Scott, Charles: appointment, 380, 423; id., 380–81
Scott, John: court-martialed, 63; id., 64
Scott, William: company, 72; id., 74
Sears, Isaac: and William Tryon, 39
Sears, William Bernard: construction at Mount Vernon, 337; id., 340
Selman, John: id., 400
Sermons, 255; dedicated to GW, 246, 247, 255
Sever (Seaver), William, 285; recommended, 9, 26; id., 11; consults with GW, 196
Sewall, Dummer: consults with GW, 196
Sewall, Jonathan: goes to England, 238
Sewall, Samuel: id., 93
Sewall's farm, 93; American defenses at, 86
Sewall's Point, 76, 92, 106, 283, 358; troops at, 155; British attack on, 325
Seymour (Semore, Semsy), John: court-martialed, 67
Seymour, Thomas: *letters to*: from Joseph Reed, 389–90
Shatforth, John: Canadian intelligence, 203, 258, 306, 368; id., 203
Shaw, Nathaniel: and gunpowder, 424; id., 424–25
Sherman, Roger: and GW's appointment, 2; makes recommendation, 11; *letters to*: from David Wooster, 95
Shewkirk, —— (pastor), 33
Shipman, Edward: company, 267; id., 268
Shippen, Alice Lee, 375
Shippen, William, Jr., 45, 100, 240, 375; id., 46
Signals, 388–89, 399–400
Sigourney, Daniel: *letters from*: to Loammi Baldwin, 323
Silsbee (Silsby), Benjamin, 284–85; id., 285
Simpson, Gilbert, Jr., 28; id., 30; and GW's mill, 335, 337, 337–38; money for, 336, 339
Six Nations: disposition, 45, 306; conference with Americans, 367, 369
Skirmishes, 275; at Roxbury, 116, 201, 226; on Charlestown Neck, 196, 196–97, 201, 226, 231; on Boston Neck, 198; at Penny ferry, 250–51, 251–52; at Machias, 293, 316; at Chelsea, 300–301; on Noddles Island, 313, 331, 342, 396, 397; at Sewall's Point, 325; on Plowed Hill, 374–75, 376, 391; with Indians, 394, 394–95; at Hog Island, 396, 397. *See also* Raids
Slaves, 302; captured by British, 416–17, 418
Smith, Devereaux, 29, 31
Smith, Matthew: raises rifle company, 110; on Quebec expedition, 416, 432
Smith, Oliver: recruits troops, 470
Smith, Thomas: confers with GW, 33
Smith, William, 34; *letters from*: to New York provincial congress, 378; *letters to*: from New York provincial congress, 378–79
Smith, William, Jr.: recommended, 9; id., 12
Somerset (British warship), 366
Sorel River, 258
South Carolina: and capture of gunpowder, 146, 150, 243, 244; gunpowder supply, 277; gun-

South Carolina (*cont.*)
powder from Bermuda, 467, 468
Spalding, John: accuses Penuel Cheney, 153; id., 155
Spaulding, Levi: id., 285; makes recommendation, 285
Spear, Joseph, 29, 31
Spencer, Joseph: dispute over rank, 85, 89–90, 95, 113–14, 138–39; id., 95–96; brigade, 154, 228, 278, 279, 309; regiment, 154; at councils of war, 215, 216, 450; *letters to*: from GW, 432–34
Spooner, Walter: and absent soldiers, 265
Spotswood, Alexander: appointment, 380; id., 381
Spotsylvania County (Va.) independent company, 17
Sprague, Samuel: raises company, 396; id., 397
Springfield (Mass.): GW at, 92; prisoners sent to, 191, 208, 293, 315
Squantum Neck, 118, 179–80, 180; livestock removed from, 329
Stark, John: regiment, 154; raids Noddles and Hog islands, 397
Stephen, Adam, 23; id., 25
Stephens, Philip: *letters to*: from Samuel Graves, 142
Stephenson, Hugh: recruits rifle company, 23, 24–25; id., 24
Stetson, Prince: arrested, 364; id., 364
Stevens, James, 50
Stevens, John: id., 359
Stewart, Duncan: id., 204; intelligence from, 262
Stewart's Crossing, 30
Stiles, Ezra, 353
Stiles, Jeremiah: company, 72; id., 74–75
Stockbridge Indians, 307; *letters from*: to Continental Congress, 46
Stone, Josiah: and reinforcements, 105
Stonington (Conn.), 471; threatened, 416, 469, 470; British attack on, 417, 469
Storrs, Experience: court-martial president, 414; id., 415
Suffolk County (N.Y.) committee of safety: and local defense, 377–78; *letters to*: from New York provincial congress, 378–79
Sullivan, John: arrives at Cambridge, 91; id., 96; brigade, 154, 228, 318, 340, 348, 366, 370–71, 395, 426, 455; denounced by Loyalist, 179; at councils of war, 215, 450; at Plowed Hill, 376; *letters from*: to GW, 214, 412; *letters to*: from GW, 413–14, 432–34
Surgeons, 191, 287, 288, 379; from Philadelphia, 45, 240; of hospitals, 58, 74; duties, 73–74; of regiments, 73–74, 412; disputes among, 139–40, 153, 155, 426, 427, 455; and returns, 164, 185; at Boston jail, 411. *See also* Health; Hospitals
Surgeon's mates, 360, 379, 412
Sutlers: regulations, 106, 260–61, 261, 418–19
Swan (British warship), 204, 239, 249, 263, 469, 471
Swashan (Indian): confers with GW, 306–7, 409; confers with Schuyler, 332
Syme, John: bill of exchange, 176, 339; id., 177
Symonds, Francis: company, 397, 398

Tabb, John: appointment, 380; id., 381
Tatamagouch (British warship), 316
Taunton (Mass.): prisoners sent to, 291
Taylor, John, 285; and Massachusetts address to GW, 53; and hospitals, 66; confers with GW, 104–5
Tents: requested, 81, 84, 85, 87, 109; in American camp, 93; in Boston, 137; provided for Continental army, 164, 200, 277, 309–10, 358; shortage in Schuyler's army, 257, 345; re-

Tents (*cont.*)
turns, 277; for Quebec expedition, 415, 432. *See also* Barracks; Huts
Tewksbury, ——, 193
Theft, 50, 63, 67, 73, 191, 321, 340
Thomas, John, 66, 200, 351; dispute over rank, 61, 61–62, 85, 89–90, 145–46, 159–62; id., 61–62, 230; commands at Roxbury, 79, 86, 97, 116; at councils of war, 79, 215, 216, 450; appointment, 96, 145, 162, 165, 167, 223; brigade, 154, 228, 278, 279, 317, 379; regiment, 154; *letters from*: to GW, 103, 171–72; *letters to*: from Joseph Reed, 105–6, 142, 200; from GW, 159–62, 432–34; from Charles Lee, 162; from James Warren, 162
Thomas, Nathaniel Ray, 116; id., 117
Thompson, William: regiment, 415, 427, 449, 450, 454–55; id., 416; and mutiny of riflemen, 445–46
Thomson, Charles, 22, 342; and GW's appointment, 7; id., 8; and Donald Campbell, 173; *letters to*: from New York provincial congress, 343
Thornton, Matthew, 182; id., 183; *letters to*: from James Otis, Sr., 454
Ticonderoga: American capture, 40; dispute over command, 120, 121; lead from, 272, 273, 288, 304–5, 306, 308, 344, 369, 405, 416
Tilghman, Matthew: id., 151
Tools: returns, 54, 127; needed, 86, 100; at Plowed Hill, 376
Topham, John, 353
Tracy, Nathaniel: id., 405; *letters to*: from GW, 404–5; from Joseph Reed, 405
Trafton, Joshua: court-martialed, 159; id., 159; punished, 360–61
Traveller's Rest, 24
Treason, 341; triable by general court-martial, 83
Trent, William: id., 243; *letters from*: to GW, 158; *letters to*: from GW, 242–44
Trist, Nicholas, 167; id., 168
Trumbull, John: id., 113, 178; appointment, 177, 204, 309; maps, 178, 228, 233, 234–35 (illus.), 236–37 (illus.); *letters from*: to Loammi Baldwin, 220
Trumbull, Jonathan, Jr.: id., 113
Trumbull, Jonathan, Sr., 11, 379; and dispute over rank, 95; id., 113; and prisoners of war, 389; and coastal defense, 417–18; and lead for army, 436; *letters from*: to GW, 112–13, 113–14, 124–26, 136–37, 203–4, 267–68, 276–77, 293–95, 299, 344–46, 416–18, 424–25, 444, 468–71; to Jabez Hamlin, 277; to Elisha Phelps, 344; to Philip Schuyler, 344; to Massachusetts council, 453; to Nicholas Cooke, 463; *letters to*: from Massachusetts provincial congress, 103, 125–26; from GW, 131, 132, 152–53, 227, 244–45, 280–81, 306, 307–9, 353–54, 405–6, 437–38, 470; from John Hancock, 204; from Gurdon Saltonstall, 267–68; from Connecticut delegates, 277; from David Wooster, 293–94, 294, 345; from Edward Rutledge, 299; from Henry Middleton, 299; from Benjamin Hinman, 345; from John Brown (1744–1780), 345; from Philip Schuyler, 345, 416; from Nicholas Cooke, 442; from James Otis, Sr., 454
Trumbull, Joseph, 152–53, 200; recommended, 9, 11; id., 11, 113; appointment, 12, 84, 88, 94, 145, 165, 167, 197, 204; provisioning proposals, 425–26, 430; *letters from*: to GW, 425–26; *letters to*: from Eliphalet Dyer, 3, 11, 18; from Silas Deane, 11; from Loammi Baldwin, 313–14
Tryon, William: arrives at New York, 32, 34; conduct watched, 32, 37, 39, 47, 48, 101; id., 34, 39

Tryon County (N.Y.) committee of safety: *letters from*: to Albany committee of safety, 121; to Schenectady committee of safety, 121
Tudor, William: recommended, 9, 11–12; id., 11–12; appointment, 12, 139, 142, 194; pay, 356, 392; *letters from*: to John Adams, 330; to GW, 354–56; *letters to*: from John Adams, 10, 12, 149
Tupper, Benjamin: attacks Brown's house, 93, 207; raids Long Island, Mass., 117, 207; raids Lighthouse Island, 205–6, 207, 226, 232; id., 207–8; *letters from*: to Horatio Gates, 232
Turner, William, 278
Turtle Bay (N.Y.), 38

Uniforms: hunting shirts, 88–89, 222, 244; insignia, 115, 158, 163; lacking in Continental army, 158; Indian leggings, 261
Unity (ship), 440; recapture of, 428, 428–29, 429
Urquhart, James: and refugees, 238

Van Dyke, Cornelius, 121
Varick, Richard: and transcripts of GW's papers, xix; id., 38
Varnum, James Mitchell: regiment, 154, 197, 212; on court-martial, 300
Vassal, John: house of, 51
Virginia: riflemen, 19–20, 23, 24–25, 307, 415, 415–16; dispute with Pennsylvania, 31, 32; attempt to seize royal governor, 146, 150; Loyalists, 150–51; threatened by Dunmore, 335, 338, 434; recruiting efforts, 379–80, 423; treasurer, 435
Virginia committee of safety, 423; appointed, 380, 381
Virginia convention: authorizes military forces, 18, 379–80, 423; and volunteers, 145; president, 151, 423; and frontier defense, 209; convenes, 210, 380; appoints committee of safety, 380, 381; appoints officers, 380, 380–81, 423; approves currency, 380, 381; elects delegates to Continental Congress, 380, 381, 423, 424; thanks GW, 422–23, 423–24; makes recommendations, 434–35, 435
Virginia delegates: make recommendations, 110, 145, 177; elected, 380, 381, 423, 424; thanked by Virginia convention, 423–24; *letters from*: to GW, 110–11, 177
Virginia House of Burgesses, 1, 147, 150
Virginia independent companies: arms and ammunition, 17, 77; training, 17, 77; formed, 18; equipment, 339; *letters to*: from GW, 16–19
Volunteers, 97, 446; rations, 21; equipment and blankets, 22; recommended, 44, 58–59, 132, 209–10, 240, 286, 434–35, 435; positions lacking, 241, 266, 361, 365, 372–73, 384; French officers, 296; for Bermuda expedition, 304; in British army, 311, 312; for Quebec expedition, 415; from Maryland, 422
Vose, Joseph: raids Lighthouse Island, 151, 207; id., 152

Wagon master general: needed, 140; authorized, 143; appointed, 278; GW's instructions to, 280. *See also* Goddard, John
Wagons: numbering, 280; carry gunpowder, 299, 308
Wales, Nathaniel, Jr., 346; nominates officers, 470–71
Walker, Timothy: regiment, 154, 431; id., 432
Walker, William: company, 285
Wallace, Hugh, 34
Wallace, James, 353, 416; attacks Stonington, 417; threatens Rhode Island, 467; tactics, 468; *letters from*: to Samuel Graves, 417, 418; *letters to*: from Samuel Graves, 471
Wanton, Joseph, 109
Ward, Artemas, 66; command of

Ward, Artemas (*cont.*)
New England army, 2, 57, 58, 87, 325, 396; appointment, 17, 18, 19, 54; id., 18; regiment, 77, 154, 155, 156, 286, 360; at councils of war, 79, 215, 216, 450; aides-de-camp, 133; division, 154, 228, 280; commands at Roxbury, 164; and prisoners of war, 232; *letters from*: to GW, 286, 321, 328–29, 329, 352, 362–63, 363–65, 377, 395, 431; *letters to*: from Horatio Gates, 216, 329, 377, 383, 395; from Joseph Reed, 231; from Edmund Randolph, 364; from GW, 432–34

Ward, Henry: id., 49; *letters from*: to GW, 49; to Nathanael Greene, 49

Ward, Jonathan, 73; id., 75; court-martial president, 106, 115; *letters from*: to GW, 286–87, 360

Ward, Joseph: appointment, 133; id., 134; *letters from*: to Massachusetts provincial congress, 67

Ward, Samuel, Jr.: id., 289

Ward, Samuel, Sr., 304; id., 288–89; returns from Continental Congress, 288; *letters from*: to Nicholas Cooke, 464

Warren, James, 65, 123, 206; recommended, 9, 26; id., 10–11, 61; and Massachusetts address to GW, 53; and reinforcements, 105; paymaster general, 142, 298, 357, 415; confers with GW, 227; and intercepted letters, 239, 249, 259, 260; *letters from*: to GW, 61–62, 79, 218, 249; to John Adams, 62, 143, 198, 207, 219, 231, 398; to John Thomas, 162; *letters to*: from John Adams, 10, 43, 45–46, 149, 239, 249; from Samuel Adams, 26; from GW, 103–6, 162–63, 193–94, 195–97, 259–60, 356, 446; from Joseph Reed, 105, 116–17; from Horatio Gates, 191, 453–54; from Nicholas Cooke, 273

Warren, John: on court of inquiry, 153; id., 155

Warren, Joseph, 396; recommended, 9, 26; death, 10, 35, 44, 45, 117; id., 10; *letters to*: from John Hancock, 8

Washburn, Seth: id., 286–87; recommended, 286

Washington, Anne Steptoe Allerton, 136, 431

Washington, George: aides-de-camp, xvii-xviii, xix, 3, 9, 11, 27–28, 54, 57, 110, 151, 169–70, 177, 178, 233, 361, 362, 365, 372; military secretary, xvii-xviii, xix, 3, 9, 11–12, 28, 54, 57, 147; papers, xvii-xxi, 5, 335; preparation of letters, xviii, 83–84; appointed commander in chief, 1, 1–2, 2–3, 3–4, 6–7, 8, 12–13, 15, 16–17, 19, 21, 49; expense account, 1, 2–3, 14; relations with Continental Congress, 1, 7, 12–13, 15, 16–17, 19, 21–22, 23, 36–37, 91, 98, 100, 240, 391, 391–92; concern for Martha Washington, 3–4, 13, 15, 20, 335; debts owed to, 4–5, 6, 335, 336, 338; makes will, 4–5; debts owed by, 5, 6, 336; purchases clothing, 5, 6; commission, 6–7, 8; horses, 13, 14, 56, 58, 68, 68–69, 82, 337; and Custis estate, 15, 16; and Virginia independent companies, 16–17, 18, 77; powers of appointment, 21, 22, 22–23, 48, 140, 143, 145, 149, 165, 225, 240–41, 265–66, 277–78, 336, 361, 372–73, 384, 385, 391, 413; indentured servants, 28–29, 30; and gunpowder shortage, 32, 35, 85, 89, 216, 218–19, 221, 227, 242, 244, 306, 307–8, 310, 331, 333, 336, 350, 364, 373–74, 385–86, 391, 400, 404, 419–20, 433, 444, 451; urges economy, 37, 137, 139, 140, 227, 281, 290, 433, 451, 459; and Hudson River defenses, 38–39, 408; congratulated on appointment, 40, 52–53, 77–78, 108–9, 112, 434; and drafting of articles of war,

Washington, George (*cont.*)
46; headquarters, 50–51; secures American lines, 50, 72–73, 75, 84, 86, 87, 102, 104, 106, 114, 119, 122, 127–28, 135, 137, 138, 158, 163, 183–84, 336, 372, 447; opposes provincial distinctions, 54, 88–89, 132, 241, 265–66, 361, 372–73, 384; urges cleanliness, 55, 114, 164, 206–7; promulgation of general orders, 62–63, 123, 133, 219; condemns destruction of property, 63, 122, 287; criticism of officers, 65, 71–72, 72–73, 107, 119, 123, 128, 134, 138, 163, 207, 229, 264, 268–69, 281, 335–36, 347, 360, 372, 373, 375, 438; evaluates British intentions, 65, 91, 99, 102, 116–17, 127–28, 135, 135–36, 138, 152, 163, 175, 180–81, 183–84, 188, 189, 207, 220, 221, 222, 225–26, 242, 244, 274–75, 280, 284, 306, 308, 333, 336, 353–54, 372, 374–75, 406, 408, 433, 438, 447–48; instructions on recruiting, 73, 82–83, 169, 360; critique of Boston lines, 84, 85, 85–87, 92, 99, 101–2, 104, 135, 183–84, 350, 374; reorganizes army, 84–85, 88, 99–100, 138, 139–40, 153–55, 223–25, 228, 245–46, 280, 317, 329; and coastal defense, 86, 195, 196, 228, 263, 406, 407–8, 421, 437–38; claims impartiality, 89, 132; and communication with enemy, 107–8, 119, 352; efforts to interdict British supplies, 116, 118–19, 175, 181, 274, 305, 398, 421, 447; and intercepted letters, 148, 229–30, 239, 249, 259, 260; preparations for winter, 172, 225, 433, 450; and George William Fairfax's affairs, 176, 336; map of Boston area, 184, 186–87 (illus.); and spies, 193, 311, 312–13; rejects blockade of Boston Harbor, 210–11, 349–51, 373–74; plans Bermuda expedition, 221–22, 304, 419–20, 420–21; Indian negotiations, 229, 238–39, 306, 306–7, 331–32; and Mercer estate, 242–43; sermons dedicated to, 246, 247, 255; criticized, 252–55; proposal to attack Boston, 266, 432–34, 450–51; and promotion of officers, 277–78, 390–91; necessity of paying soldiers, 281–82, 296–97, 357, 387, 415; treatment of prisoners, 289–90, 316, 326–27, 328, 389, 389–90, 392, 399, 404, 411, 412, 458–59; rejects Nova Scotia expedition, 297–98; plans Quebec expedition, 332–33, 404–5, 406, 409, 409–10, 415, 432, 436, 438, 446, 448, 455–56, 457–59, 461–62; treatment of Canadians, 332, 437, 455–56, 457–59, 462; gristmills, 335, 336–37, 337–38, 339; and spinning, 335; and remodeling of Mount Vernon, 337, 339–40; and wheat crop, 337, 340; condemns new cider, 371; proposes price fixing, 376–77; condemns grave robbing, 395; and armed vessels, 398–400; and sutlers, 418–19; invites officers to dine, 419; and British packet boat, 421–22; thanked for service in Continental Congress, 422–23, 423–24; and care of sick, 426; and reenlistment of army, 433, 450; and mutiny of riflemen, 446, 449, 449–50, 454–55

described: by John Adams, 2, 2–3; by Eliphalet Dyer, 3

land: Alexandria, 4, 5, 335; Ferry Farm, 4, 6; on Ohio and Kanawha rivers, 28–29, 30, 335; Washington's Bottom, 30, 335, 337–38

travels: leaves Philadelphia, 13, 14, 17, 18, 19, 20, 27, 27–28, 35; arrives at New York, 32, 33, 34; at Hoboken, N.J., 33; at Newark, N.J., 33; at New Brunswick, N.J., 33; at New Rochelle, N.Y., 34, 42; leaves New York,

Washington, George (*cont.*)
35, 36, 41–42; at King's Bridge, N.Y., 42; arrives at Cambridge, 50, 85, 92, 98, 135, 170, 183; at Brookfield, Mass., 92; at Marlborough, Mass., 92; at New Haven, 92; at Springfield, Mass., 92; at Wethersfield, Conn., 92; at Worcester, Mass., 123
views on: his military abilities, 1, 2, 3, 12–13, 15, 16–17, 19, 128; reputation, 1, 2, 4, 13, 19, 159–62, 350, 374; destiny, 4, 15; religion, 4, 13, 27, 55, 60, 131, 432–33, 456, 459, 461, 462; American cause, 13, 41, 54, 59–60, 63, 72, 128, 131, 132, 159–62, 221, 242, 244, 274, 281, 282, 289, 326–27, 334–35, 419–20, 455–56, 458, 461–62; discipline, 17, 54, 60, 73, 87, 90–91, 138, 139, 188–89, 207, 256, 307, 332, 347, 360, 372, 413–14, 437, 456, 457; seizing royal officials, 37; civil-military relations, 41; drunkenness, 54–55, 106, 178, 418; profanity, 54–55; plunder, 69, 215, 456, 458; cowardice, 71–72; militia, 90, 116; New England troops, 90–91, 104, 135, 183, 188–89, 335–36, 372; Battle of Bunker Hill, 135, 138, 171, 336; perseverance, 189, 331; profiteering, 274, 376–77, 388; indecent bathing, 346; impressment, 459
Washington, Hannah Bushrod, 448; id., 20
Washington, John Augustine: id., 20; *letters from*: to GW, 454; *letters to*: from GW, 19–20, 183–85, 447–48
Washington, Lund: and kitchen in Alexandria house, 4; id., 5; western land, 30, 32; and bills of exchange, 176; *letters to*: from GW, 78, 134, 295, 321, 334–40, 362, 371, 414, 431, 452
Washington, Martha: GW's concern for, 3–4, 13, 15, 20, 335; clothing for, 5, 6; destroys GW's letters to her, 5; goes to Cambridge, 5; goes to Eltham, 5, 14, 335, 338; goes to Mount Airy, 335, 338, 423; safety of, 335, 338; *letters to*: from GW, 3–6, 27–28
Washington, Mary Ball, 5
Washington, Samuel, 23; id., 25; *letters from*: to Horatio Gates, 25; to GW, 426, 431; *letters to*: from GW, 134–36
Washington, Warner, Sr.: id., 136
Washington's Bottom, 30; GW's mill, 335, 337–38
Waterman, Andrew, 340; id., 341
Waters, —— (Mr.), 200
Watertown (Mass.): prisoners at, 328
Webb, Charles: regiment, 126, 277, 309, 406, 417, 438, 470; defense of Connecticut, 276, 293, 468–69
Webb, Samuel Blachley: appointment, 153; id., 155–56; escorts prisoners, 411; *letters to*: from Joseph Reed, 411
Webster, Jonathan, Jr.: and pay of soldiers, 206; id., 208
Welch Mountains, 80, 81–82
Wells, David: court-martialed, 63, 82; id., 64
Wentworth, Hunking: id., 126–27; *letters from*: to GW, 126–27
Wentworth, John, 68; id., 127; goes to Boston, 205; *letters from*: to earl of Dartmouth, 126–27
West Augusta committee of safety, 29, 31–32
Westmoreland County (Pa.) committee of safety, 29, 31–32
West Point: posts proposed at, 39, 47
Wethersfield (Conn.): GW at, 92
Weymouth (Mass.), 179–80, 180
Wharton, John: escorts prisoners, 319, 320, 389; id., 321; carries letter, 403, 404; *letters to*: from Joseph Reed, 390, 411
Wheat, Samuel: intelligence from, 262; id., 263
Wheaton, Joseph: and skirmish at Machias, 293
Whipple, Abraham: id., 223, 273, 403; and Bermuda expedition, 305, 402, 420, 421, 441, 442,

Whipple, Abraham (*cont.*) 463, 464, 467; illness, 382, 383; and British packet boat, 422
Whitcomb, Asa: regiment, 154
Whitcomb (Whetcomb), John, 413; at court-martial, 108; and soldiers' pay, 298; id., 324; prepares letter to GW, 324
White, —— (capt.), 385; captured by British, 229–30
White, —— (Mrs.), 365
White, Alexander: Loyalist activities, 257; id., 258
White, Anthony, 58, 59; *letters from*: to GW, 204, 212; *letters to*: from GW, 365
White, Anthony Walton: recommended, 58–59; id., 59; proposed as aide-de-camp to GW, 361, 365
White, Benjamin, 285; and soldiers' pay, 298
White, John: court-martialed, 56; id., 58
Whiting, Benjamin: court of inquiry investigates, 177, 190; id., 178–79
Whiting, William: and Massachusetts address to GW, 53
Willard (Willant), Abijah: *letters from*: to Benjamin Miller, 323
Williams, William: nominates officers, 470–71
Williamson, John, 386
Willing, Richard: escorts prisoners, 319, 320, 389; id., 320–21; carries letter, 403, 404
Wilson, George, 29; id., 31
Wilson, James: id., 70; makes recommendation, 70
Windham (Conn.): prisoners sent to, 416, 453–54, 454
Windship, Amos: id., 144; intelligence from, 144
Winnisimmet ferry, 192, 439; old wreck at, 216–17, 301; skirmishes at, 313, 314, 318; described, 396
Winslow, —— (widow), 103
Winslow, Joshua, 103
Winslow, William: court-martialed, 191
Winter Hill, 51, 99; troops at, 86, 154; tools needed at, 100; American defenses at, 183
Winthrop, Hannah Fayerweather Tollman, 260
Winthrop, John, 260; recommended, 9, 26; id., 11; confers with GW, 240; and absent soldiers, 265
Wolcott, Oliver, 369
Wood, Samuel, 287; recommended, 286
Woodbridge (schooner), 343, 385, 386
Woodbridge, Benjamin: consults with GW, 196
Woodbridge, Benjamin Ruggles: regiment, 67, 154, 231, 346, 360, 395; on court-martial, 300; on court of inquiry, 330
Woodbury (Conn.): lead mine, 344
Woodford, William: appointment, 380, 423; id., 380
Woods, —— (capt.): company, 77
Woods (Wood), Henry, 49; id., 51
Woods, Levi: pardoned, 172–73
Wooster, David, 32; id., 33–34, 94–96; at New York, 47, 48; dispute over rank, 94–95, 113; and returns, 202; intelligence from, 344; ordered to Harlem, 378; *letters from*: to Roger Sherman, 95; to Jonathan Trumbull, Sr., 293–94, 294, 345; to GW, 377–79; to New York provincial congress, 379; *letters to*: from Joseph Reed, 180–81; from New York provincial congress, 284; from GW, 407–8
Worcester (Mass.): GW at, 123; prisoners sent to, 190, 191, 206, 208, 293
Work, Henry, 398
Wright, James: *letters from*: to earl of Dartmouth, 150
Wyman, Isaac: on court-martial, 300
Wythe, George: elected to Continental Congress, 380, 423; id., 381

Yale University, 92
Yates, Abraham, Jr., 121
Yates, Christopher P., 121

York County (Pa.) committee of correspondence: recommends officers, 70–71; *letters from*: to Pennsylvania delegates, 70–71

Ziegler, David, 445

Zubly, John Joachim: elected to Continental Congress, 167; id., 168